CHAIM SHAPIRO'S
WARTIME ODYSSEY

▶▶▶▶▶▶▶▶ The limit of the German advance, summer 1942
——— Borders (1939)

0   100   200   300   400   k m

khangelsk

orth Dvina

Ural Mountains

Nizhiny-Tagil

Sverdlovsk

Chelyabinsk

Magnitogorsk

S O V I E T   U N I O N

Gorkiy

COW

Booyan

Ryazan

Chapayevsk

Kuybishev

Volga

KAZAKHSTAN

Aralsk   Karmakhchi

Djusali   Kzyl
-Orda

Stalingrad

N E

Don

Gideon Dan

D1131137

JRKEY

Tehran

I shall not die, but live,
and declare the works of the Lord.

PSALMS 118:17

A young Jewish refugee's stor

GO, MY SON

of survival

by CHAIM SHAPIRO

FELDHEIM PUBLISHERS *Jerusalem □ New York*

First published 1989

Library of Congress Cataloging-in-Publication Data

Go, my son / by Chaim Shapiro.

ISBN 0-87306-500-X. — ISBN 0-87306-501-8 (pbk.)
1. Shapiro, Chaim.   2. Holocaust, Jewish (1939-
1945)—Poland—Lomza—Personal narratives, Jewish.   3. Lomza
(Poland)—Biography.   4. World War, 1939-1945—Personal narratives,
Jewish.
I. Title.
D804.3.S53 1989
940.53'18'094383—dc20   89-32595

FELDHEIM PUBLISHERS
POB 35002 / Jerusalem, Israel

200 Airport Executive Park
Nanuet, NY 10954

Printed in Israel

10 9 8 7 6 5 4 3

This book is dedicated to the six million Jews, including my entire family, who perished in the Holocaust; to the future generations, who include, thank God, my children, grandchildren, and great-grandchildren; and to all those Jews who return to our people and join the continuity of our faith, heritage, and destiny.

ACKNOWLEDGMENTS

I owe a great debt of gratitude
to my two excellent editors,
Mr. Joseph Paper and Mrs. M. L. Mashinsky.

PART ONE

1

OUR TRAIN was hurtling ahead at full speed, and the thick black smoke from the locomotive blew into my eyes through the open window. But it was not only the soot and cinders that made tears run from my eyes.

The clatter of the wheels on the rails and the roar of the warplanes overhead combined into a deafening crescendo. It was a race between the straining engine and the German planes. The German pilots tried again and again to bomb us, but missed every time. Each time we saw the planes diving towards us, we shrank into our corners as if that would somehow make us less vulnerable. Finally, mercifully, the train plunged into the thick forest and became invisible to the enemy.

The train's cargo was a human one, a multitude of people fleeing from war: stooped grandmothers wrapped in shawls, sturdy young peasant wives and elegant city matrons with their children, who were the families of Russian army men and government officials and were being evacuated from Poland to Russia before the invading Germans arrived. I was probably the only man on the crowded train among the frightened women and crying children, and I certainly wasn't a dependent of any Russian soldier!

I had found an empty corner on the floor and sat curled up in it. Soon the women and children were asleep. I sat listening to the train wheels bumping over the rails. They made a dull, rhythmic sound, and there was urgency in the words they seemed to say: "Go back home, go back home." How many words and phrases one can hear in the sound of speeding train wheels! I knew that these words were just my wishful thinking, though, for there was no way for me to go back home. To jump from the speeding train would mean instant death.

Without stopping, the train passed Stolpce, the last town before the old Polish-Soviet border. The next stop would be Minsk, located deep inside Russia.

I was terribly frightened. A young and sheltered rabbinical student, I was about to enter a country where religion was not only forbidden but despised and labeled the "opiate of the masses." In pre-war Poland, we had been able to lead a normal Jewish life, though not without difficulty. But now our once-secure world had been turned upside down, and who knew what tomorrow would bring!

Laboring through the dense forest, the wheels now changed their message: "Go, my son, go! Go, my son, go!" They seemed to be repeating my mother's last words to me, the words that had sent me on this terrifying journey.

It had all begun in the city of Lomza, in northeastern Poland. Lomza is a town spread out on a beautiful mountain top, and overlooking the Narew River which flows through its foothills. There I was born, the first of four sons.

My grandfather had been a wealthy landowner who had owned an entire village not far from Lomza. In Czarist days, when this part of Poland was under Russian control, the peasants had rebelled, intent on murdering and burning out the big landowners. My grandfather's devoted servants had warned him about the uprising, and he fled to Lomza with his family and fortune, where the police ensured his safety. He settled there, bought considerable property and established a hardware and building materials business. He was soon a prominent member of his new community.

Because of his wealth and position, he was able to marry his daughters to promising young Torah scholars. One of them was my father, learned in Talmud and a gentle, righteous Jew, a *ba'al musar* whose every action reflected his Torah learning.

My mother was a deeply religious woman. Her speech was gentle and pure and she treated everyone — Jew and gentile, scholar and servant — with kindness and courtesy. Our life was calm, comfortable and orderly. We lived in a spacious apartment above the hardware store that my father had inherited from my grandfather. We got up at the same time every morning, went to *shul* for morning prayers and then went to school. We came home at noon for a substantial meal, served by our Polish live-in maid, and Papa came home from work to join us.

Our life seemed as solid and permanent as the dark, heavy furniture in the living room and as predictable as the pendulum clock in the hall that ticked away the hours. It seemed to us that nothing would ever change. Papa's business was prospering, our days were comfortable and our household was run by Mama with skill and love.

We knew every street and alley of our native town and had a close acquaintance not only with our fellow Jews, but also with the gentile population surrounding us. Since Lomza was located near the East Prussian border, it had a substantial German community. Papa did business with the Germans, as had my grandfather before him.

One day when I came home from the yeshiva I attended in a nearby town, Mama, instead of greeting me happily, tried to ease me out of the house. She had also sent away our maid.

"What's the matter, Mama?" I asked. "Aren't you happy to see me home?" She replied that Mr. Hoffmann, a German acquaintance of my parents, would be coming for a visit at seven o'clock, and that she didn't want me to be there, since I always asked too many questions.

They hadn't seen Mr. Hoffmann lately, Mama said, because he was so ashamed of Germany, his native land, that he could not face his Jewish friends. I begged her to let me stay, and promised not to ask any questions. I added lightly that it would be interesting to observe a man who was guided by a guilty conscience.

Papa rebuked me from the next room: "The fact that he is a German, son, doesn't mean that he is responsible for the actions of the German nation. He is a Polish citizen, he lives in Poland, and he surely didn't help in any way to put Hitler in office."

Soon the doorbell rang, and we knew that Mr. Hoffmann, in his worn but well-pressed suit and polished high black shoes, had arrived with German punctuality. Over hot tea and cake, my parents and Mr. Hoffmann engaged in light conversation, inquiring about each other's health, family and business.

Suddenly Mr. Hoffmann fixed his gaze upon the photographs of World War I German army officers that hung on our walls. He said, "I'm surprised that you have not torn them down yet. Surely you must be aware of what they are doing to the Jews in Germany!"

A heavy stillness filled the room. Finally Mama sighed and broke the silence. "One really should not believe all that appears in the newspapers!

One might conceivably believe that illiterate Russian Cossacks could do such terrible things. But the civilized Germans? With their culture and their education? People from Frankfurt and Heidelberg universities?

"Impossible!" she declared. "I simply cannot believe that those German gentlemen, or their children, have suddenly become barbarians!"

Mr. Hoffmann lowered his head and in a solemn tone of voice he said, "My dear friends, I have just returned from a short visit with my brothers in Germany. What the newspapers are saying is true. Terrible things are being done, by the Germans, to the Jews in Germany!

"The Nazis are poisoning the minds of the entire people, especially the youth." He paused, and looked at my parents. "Just as my father was a friend of your family, and just as you and I are friends, I had hoped that our children would also be friends. But it is not to be. My Karl has become so affected by the Nazi lunacy that he refused to leave Germany and return home with me!"

Mr. Hoffmann then spoke of the fact that Czechoslovakia, which might have been able to deter the Nazi troops, had been taken by Hitler without even one shot fired in protest.

"Now there is no other army in eastern Europe capable of stopping Hitler, and I have no doubt that he will soon take the remainder," he said sadly. "My dear friends, I would surely emigrate from Poland if I were a Jew! What future is there for you and your sons? Who knows what is in store for any of us?"

The discussion with Mr. Hoffmann changed our lives, and emigration became the major topic of conversation in our house. We soon learned, however, that the entire world was closed to us. Europe was in the throes of war; the United States, with its restrictive quota system, had a long waiting list for Polish citizens. Palestine was blocked off by the British. It seemed there wasn't a safe place for a Jew in the whole world!

Only Papa had a chance to travel. Because he wrote a weekly column for a local newspaper, he could have qualified as a correspondent. But Papa said he would not consider going anywhere without the entire family; if we could not go with him, he would remain at home, come what may.

During the next few weeks, while Papa tried desperately but futilely to obtain visas for us all, Mama kept urging him to accept a correspondent's visa and leave Poland himself. Perhaps if he were on the other side of the "wall," she argued, he might discover a crack in it through which to get the rest of us out.

But Papa remained adamant. "It's all or none!" he insisted.

With resignation, Mama said to me, "A Jewish family is too closely knit. This has always been the strength of our people, but it is also our weakness."

Towards the end of August 1939, large red proclamations were posted in Lomza and in all Polish towns announcing a general mobilization. Reservists were instructed to report immediately to their army units. For a few days patriotic fervor was in the air, and the townspeople seemed almost enthusiastic about the coming struggle.

Disenchantment set in shortly. It began with the revelation that there was a vast shortage of uniforms. Worse than that, there was also a dearth of basic equipment, even rifles. But worst of all, there was a shortage of bullets! For each rifle, exactly ten bullets were issued; there was no more ammunition to be had! "Nine bullets for the enemy, and one for yourself," quipped the army officer who handed each reservist his ammunition.

Rumblings of dismay and criticism were heard. What had happened to the enormous sums of taxes which, for the last twenty years, had been confiscated from the people for the purpose of building a mighty army? How could Poland be defended without arms? The people, who had so trusted their leaders, were at first angry, and later frightened.

Lomza, the Polish city nearest the East Prussian border, was to be defended, but only three anti-aircraft guns were set up to protect the entire city. One was located about one hundred feet from our house, in front of the City Hall.

On Thursday morning, September 1, 1939, Germany invaded Poland. The air force base near Czervony-Bor, only twenty miles from Lomza, was so quiet that the Germans didn't bother to bomb it. Perhaps they knew that three days earlier an order had been received there to disassemble all of the airplanes for overhauling. Only five planes had not been disassembled yet, but there was no fuel for them!

Waves of German planes bombed Lomza without any interference. The crew of the anti-aircraft gun near our house fired exactly one shot, and then abandoned their post and fled in panic.

Bombs fell all around us, hitting the buildings next to our house. Flames and dense black smoke enveloped the neighborhood and within minutes the entire block was an inferno. We ran into the street, where we joined the growing crowd of frightened men, women and children fleeing from the fiery terror.

We rushed to the next block, heading for a building which we knew had an air-raid shelter in its basement. When we got there, we found that the shelter was already packed; there must have been a hundred people there, all standing pressed tightly against each other. Nevertheless, the six of us managed to squeeze in.

Bombs exploding nearby made the concrete floor shake. Papa expressed doubt about the wisdom of taking shelter in basements. "Suppose this five-story building should collapse on us." He had no sooner said this than two bombs hit the courtyard. Window glass, chimney bricks and building debris showered down. The heat from the explosions penetrated the walls, giving us a terrifying preview of what we might expect if we dared leave the cellar to try our luck outside.

At long last the explosions stopped. Many people were impatient to get out of the shelter, and we found ourselves being pushed towards the door by the crowd behind us. Perhaps they shared Papa's apprehension that the building might collapse and bury everyone in it.

Since we had been the last ones in, and nearest to the door, we were among the first ones out as the crowd began to surge towards the exit. My little brother Nosson, always energetic, ran ahead and was the first outside. At exactly that moment another bomb exploded and Nosson crumpled to the ground before our eyes.

Hearing the explosion, everyone stopped and froze in place — everyone except our family. We rushed out to little Nosson, who was bleeding profusely from a wound in his head.

At the sight of all the blood, my brother Shimon began to scream. Mama fell to her knees beside her bleeding son. From another wound, blood soaked Nosson's pants and shirt. His eyes stared skyward, as if pleading for help and mercy.

After the first moment of shock, Papa collected himself and tore off a piece of his shirt, crumpled it, and pressed it hard against the wound in Nosson's head, trying to stop the terrible bleeding.

Suddenly, in addition to the roar of airplanes above us, there came the rat-a-tat of machine guns. Bullets were flying all around us. The planes zoomed in so low that I could see the German pilots' faces. They were enjoying themselves greatly. There was no opposition, no danger to themselves, and plenty of terrified, scurrying people on whom to train their machine guns. They roared up and down Lomza's streets, spraying death everywhere.

Papa ignored the danger to himself, picked up Nosson and carried him into the nearest house. We followed, and Papa rushed out to find a doctor.

Little Nosson was conscious. Through his pain, he tried to comfort our weeping mother. "I'll be all right, Mama, you'll see," he told her in a weak voice. "Please don't cry anymore." This made Mama cry even harder, and she ran into another room, unable to control herself.

"Chaim, I feel so weak," Nosson said to me. "Tell me, am I going to die? Even before my _bar mitzvah?_"

"Oh, _Ribbono shel Olam_, save my brother! Don't let him...," I prayed desperately, over and over, gripping his hand as tightly as if I were holding on to life itself.

Bullets were still raining down on the street. Occasionally, one would find its way right into our room, through the shattered windows.

Papa returned. He had found one doctor, but the man had refused to go outside. The pharmacies, Papa reported, had all been bombed, burned and gutted. Shimon discovered two bullet holes in Papa's hat!

Nosson grew weaker and paler, and continued to bleed. Seeing his half-closed eyes and white face tore at our hearts. We all knew what was happening before our eyes, but no one dared bring the dreadful thought to his lips. Little Shimon offered to allow his vein to be cut in order to give Nosson a transfusion of his blood.

Nosson's complexion became ash gray. His breathing was almost imperceptible. We were completely helpless; we loved him so much, and there was nothing we could do to save him.

Then Nosson's eyes closed...forever.

We cried and cried. We cried for little Nosson and we cried for each other. Was this the beginning of the end of our world?

From the people passing by our window, we learned that the whole city was in flames and that there would probably be more bombings after dark. People were fleeing from the city, but my parents wouldn't consider leaving Nosson's body.

My uncle Yechiel, who had heard about our tragedy, found us. He urged Papa and Mama to escape from the burning city. When they adamantly refused, Uncle suddenly grabbed my two younger brothers, Shimon and Lazer.

"I am taking them with me, out of the city," he cried. "Choose whether to accompany your living sons or your dead one." He left the room, carrying a kicking, wailing boy under each arm.

"Wait!" Papa called. Uncle stopped and turned around. My brothers looked at Papa with pleading eyes. He helped Mama to her feet, and taking her by the arm, he led her to the door, weeping. I followed. They stopped and turned for a last look at their dead child and then we all walked out.

Outside in the street, the acrid smoke was so thick that we could hardly breathe. Many buildings had been destroyed, leaving only a single wall or the facade standing. Occasionally a teetering wall would collapse. To avoid the hazard of these crumbling walls, most of the people walked down the middle of the street. We couldn't always see the German planes through the dust and smoke, but we could hear them as they flew close over our heads, and we could see the splatter of their machine-gun bullets. At these times, we would all drop flat to the ground. After the planes were gone, we would get up and keep walking...but not always all of us....

Many who had taken shelter in basements were buried alive under the razed buildings. As the procession of refugees neared the outskirts of town, we occasionally heard shouts from beneath the heaps of debris — people had been buried alive and were pleading for help. One woman screamed, "I'll give a thousand American dollars to anyone who will dig me out!"

No one heeded her cry. Everyone was too anxious about his own and his family's safety to take the time to rescue others. With the police and fire departments abandoned and deserted, the heart-rending pleas went unanswered.

Towards evening we reached Rutki, a small town which was about fifteen miles from Lomza. We had no food with us, but this was a problem that could be postponed until tomorrow. Our immediate concern was to find some shelter for the night. The September nights were already cold and my brothers were shivering.

We searched barns, chicken coops and other out-buildings, but they were all crowded with refugees who had arrived before us. At last we found a barn which had room for us, even though there were already several other families inside. Darkness fell and everyone bedded down — some to sleep, some to lie awake in fear, and some to weep.

The next morning we arose and found that German soldiers were everywhere. Shortly before noon, they began rounding up all the men they could find, and they caught Papa too.

We climbed up to the barn loft, where there was a small window and we had a better view of what was going on. The men who had been rounded up did not seem to be unduly alarmed. They probably thought that some sort of work detail was being arranged. The women, however, and particularly Mama, were frightened and anxious. They were not so sure that this was just an innocuous work detail, and as it turned out, the women were right.

The men were marched off, out of sight of their wives and children. The soldiers forbade anyone to follow, but we, high up in the loft, could still see them. We saw the Germans march them to a field some distance away and order them to lie face down on the ground. Then the soldiers proceeded to set machine guns on mounts. We watched in horror. Were they going to shoot all those defenseless men? And Papa...?

In a few minutes they began to fire. Mama and the other women in the loft shrieked at the sound of the first shots. It was bedlam; a crescendo of screams arose from the women outside as well. They screamed, the children wailed and the German guards cursed them all loudly. Through it all we could hear the Germans shouting, "_Polnische Schweine! Dreckige Juden!_ — Polish Pigs! Filthy Jews!"

Finally the firing stopped. We were sure that all the men had been murdered, but from the loft we suddenly saw the men arise — all, that is, except three. A soldier walked over to where the three lay and kicked them over onto their backs. They were obviously dead. We watched, weeping and praying that Papa was not one of them; Mama was trembling with fear.

The assembled prisoners were marched back. Now, at the return of their menfolk from the grave, as it were, several of the lamenting women fainted. When Mama saw Papa alive, her tears became tears of thanksgiving, and we all wept.

The German soldiers were laughing uproariously, slapping their thighs and each other's backs in merriment. They appeared to be enjoying the greatest joke of their lives. Still, they did not yet permit the crowd to disperse; they had another display of savagery to exhibit.

The soldiers grabbed a tall, bearded man, the chief rabbi of Lomza, Reb Moishe Shatzkes, and tied him to a tree. An officer then stood a few feet from the tree, raised his sub-machine gun and aimed it at the rabbi. One of the Jews pleaded fervently with the officer to spare the rabbi's life, and the officer finally relented. Before he untied him, however, he grabbed a fistful of the rabbi's beard and, with a powerful yank, tore it right out of his face. I heard later that the man who had pleaded for the rabbi's life was a

German Jewish refugee who, during World War I, had been a captain in the German army and had been wounded defending the Fatherland.

This was our introduction to the Nazi savages; yet it was no more than a mild portent of things to come. I resisted the temptation to ask Mama if she still refused to believe that her German gentlemen had become barbarians!

For five days the Germans did not permit any refugees to return to Lomza. We subsisted by digging potatoes from the fields with our bare hands, trembling with fear lest the farmers catch us.

Finally, permission was granted to return to Lomza. As we entered our city we saw that the dead still lay where they had fallen. We rushed to the house where we had left Nosson's body. When we got there, Papa ordered us to remain outside while he went in. Soon Papa came out carrying Nosson; tears were streaming down his face and into his beard. Mama started sobbing too, and we suddenly let ourselves feel all the pain of the last six days. We wept with great sorrow and fear.

Papa carried Nosson's body to the Jewish cemetery and dug a grave. As we buried Nosson, Mama became so agitated that we had to restrain her from throwing herself into the grave next to him. Every shovelful of dirt we tossed into the grave was like a stone smiting our hearts. We walked home slowly, sobbing all the way.

Three-quarters of Lomza appeared to have been destroyed, including our house and our possessions. We were homeless and penniless; we had only the clothes on our backs. We faced two urgent problems: finding food and finding shelter. Fortunately, a friend whose house was on the outskirts of Lomza, and hadn't been bombed, invited us to use an old wooden shack on his property. We were overjoyed at our good fortune, for the sub-zero temperatures of winter were not far off.

Happiness and comfort are such relative things. Seven days ago, who would have believed that we would feel overjoyed at taking up residence in a shaky old wooden shack? The five of us were crowded into one small room, with no heat, no light, no water — but we were alive, and together!

"Man cannot live by bread alone," but needless to say, without food man cannot live at all. Thus, our most urgent problem was to get food somehow, and this continued to be a daily struggle; we were always hungry.

From conversations with friends, we learned how vicious and well-planned the German air attacks had been. For example, neither the three forts around the city nor the giant military barracks within the city had been damaged; the railroad stations and tracks had been left untouched. Yet the hospitals, although they had huge red crosses painted on their rooftops, were bombed mercilessly. Even though three-quarters of Lomza was destroyed, the German church was relatively undamaged. One had to acknowledge the German pilots' expert aim!

Having heard that the German church was not hit, we reasoned that the bakery across the street from it might also be standing. This bakery, which was in the basement of a two-story building, belonged to the father of a friend of mine.

Mama told me to go and see whether the bakery was still functioning. "If it is," she said, "ask your friend Zelig for some bread or some flour. You must tell him that we have no money and that he'll have to trust us."

On my way to the bakery I decided to avoid the center of Lomza because I did not want to see the blackened hulk of what was once our home. Besides, in that area there were many bombed-out buildings and precariously leaning walls, ready to crumble to the ground at the first gust of wind.

The route which I decided upon took me right past the Central Synagogue. This synagogue, a fine old building, had not been bombed by the Germans. This surprised us, but we soon learned that they had their own reason for not destroying it. When the German soldiers arrived in Lomza, one of their first pleasures was putting a torch to this synagogue. They sang and they danced in the light of the leaping flames; cheering, stamping and jumping, they rejoiced as they watched the flames devour our sacred building.

When I reached the site where the Central Synagogue had stood, I stopped and gazed at the heap of debris. Jutting out from a pile of rubble — as if someone had placed a gravestone there — stood the large marble tablet inscribed with the Ten Commandments, which had once decorated the majestic entrance to the synagogue. Only the top commandments in each of the two rows, the first and the sixth, were visible above the pile of rubble. The golden paint was burnt away, but the Hebrew letters etched in the stone could be seen clearly.

Reverently I read: "I am the Lord, thy God" and "Thou shalt not murder."

Several other Jews stopped and gazed at the heartbreaking sight with tears in their eyes. As soon as I return from the bakery, I thought, I'll bring the entire family to see this. Only a Moses could break the tablets, even though Hitler and his armies are certainly trying.

Deep in such thoughts, I continued walking to the bakery. Up ahead I could see the Gothic structure of the German church. Only a few more blocks, and then perhaps I'll smell the delicious aroma of Zelig's bread and rolls, I thought.

Suddenly I heard cries and shouts and I saw people running and scattering. German troops were blocking off both ends of the street I was on, interlacing their bayonet-tipped guns so that no one could get out.

"Halt! Halt!" the soldiers shouted. I was next to a wall, so I dashed behind it. At that instant a bullet zinged close to my head, and I realized that the shouts of "Halt! Halt!" were for me. I quickly emerged and raised my hands above my head. A German soldier grabbed me and brutally ran his huge hands all over me, searching for hidden arms. All the while he cursed me with the German soldiers' favorite expression: "*Polnische Schweine! Dreckiger Jude!*" Suddenly he swung me around and his boot landed hard on my lower back, knocking me down. Then he delivered a blow to my shoulder with his rifle butt. He ordered me to get up, poking me with his bayonet.

In another moment, I became part of a large group of men being herded together in the town square. The pressing question, whispered by the prisoners to each other, was "Where to?" To be shot? To forced labor? Our anxiety was considerably relieved when we found that we were being herded right into the German church. Surely not even the Germans would turn their own house of worship into a site for murder, or even a prison!

We were jammed inside, body to body. This was the first time in my life that I had ever been in a church; the high arched ceiling, the stained-glass windows and the soft gleam of gold everywhere were so striking that I removed my cap, overwhelmed. Several times I thought, well, they can't squeeze any more in; but a few minutes later the door would be opened again and another group of men would be forced in. We were packed like herring in a barrel. Finally the door stayed closed; evidently the round-up was completed. The pushing and the commotion ceased.

I found enough room to sit down on the stone floor. I was fortunately near a window, so I could at least have some fresh air.

For a while silence prevailed. Everyone seemed to be immersed in his own thoughts and apprehensions. Eventually conversations developed, at first hesitantly, then vociferously. The Poles spoke bitterly of their shameful government, and how it had deceived them into believing that they had an army and an air force which could protect them.

"An army? An eighteenth-century army of horses and sabers against tanks and planes — for that they took our money and our lives!" said a wizened old man with a veteran's ribbon in his buttonhole.

They spoke contemptuously of how their armed forces had collapsed like a house of cards, in only three days. They railed against their president, and claimed that he had carried his Swiss passport in his pocket for the past twenty years, and against the generals who had fled to neighboring Rumania, deserting their troops who were still fighting. They cursed the leaders who had betrayed them and they wept for their fate. They whimpered for their wives and mothers. After a while, a sullen silence fell in the stifling room.

Several hours passed, and it began to turn dark and cold. Hunger pangs were gripping my body, and the air in the room grew dense with the smell of sweat and of fear. No one was permitted to go outside, even to attend to physical functions; the men started to use the floor of the church as a latrine, and seemed quite pleased to do so.

How these Catholic Poles showed their contempt for the Protestant church! They used the foulest possible words to describe what they thought of it and what they would like to do with it, the mildest suggestion being to turn it into a stable. Thus for the first time in my life, I learned of the deep animosity between Catholics and Protestants.

I glanced at the dark statue of Jesus looming above us. It was strange how his facial features had been carved, for even though Jesus was a Jew, here he was portrayed as Nordic. His face was turned aside and looking downward. I thought to myself that he looked ashamed. Indeed, he had plenty to be ashamed of: the degradation and murder of Jews in his name for almost two thousand years. What a gulf there was between the theory and the practice of this religion of love and brotherhood! The cross had been twisted into a swastika by a Christian nation. My beloved little brother lay in a fresh grave in the Jewish cemetery and I was being held prisoner in a church.

The last rays of the sun left the long narrow windows, and then the blackness of night descended. Inside, the prisoners fell into an anxious silence. Outside, the German guards were marching back and forth, their hobnailed boots striking the sidewalk with a distinctive ring which seemed to symbolize their arrogance.

We dozed fitfully through the cold, miserable night. Several men attempted to escape through the windows, but the guards fired at them, and then shouted into the dark church, "Who's next? Step right up, *Polnische Schweine!*" The next morning we looked out of the windows and saw several corpses lying on the ground below.

By now, hunger and thirst were the main topics of conversation. We had been cooped up without any food or water for almost twenty-four hours. I had not eaten for some time, even before I was captured, and evidently there were many others here in the same state of extreme hunger.

When the front door opened at last, we hoped that food, or at least water, would be forthcoming. Instead, two German soldiers just stood there looking at us with sardonic grins on their faces.

One of them said to a Pole, "Take the shoes off that foul Jew there and I'll give you a piece of bread."

Without a moment's hesitation, like a dog obeying his master's command, the Pole leaped upon the startled Jew. They struggled, rolling over and over on the cold stone floor.

During the struggle, the Jew cried out at his attacker, "We're all in the same boat! Why are you helping the enemy?"

To this the Pole replied, "Whoever feeds me is my master."

With the aid of two other Poles, he finally succeeded in removing the shoes from the hapless Jew. He presented them proudly to the Germans, who in turn rewarded him with a slice of bread. Accepting it, the Pole bowed many times, thanking them obsequiously. Hundreds of eyes gravitated to that piece of bread and stared at it with envy.

The Pole backed away from us a few paces, and then shoved the piece of bread into his open mouth and began to devour it. All were silent. The German soldiers watched the Pole's frantic chewing and drooling and grinned contemptuously.

A few moments later the Pole, still chewing, again approached the Germans. He bowed deeply several times, and then cupped his hands and touched them to his mouth. Although he could understand the soldiers' German, he couldn't speak it himself. He was requesting a drink of water.

The Germans understood. One soldier said something to the other, who then left the church. In a moment he came back carrying a bucket full of water. Instinctively, all the prisoners inched forward, towards the tantalizing water. Suddenly the German soldier lifted the bucket and dumped the water all over the Pole, who immediately dropped to the floor and licked up as much as he could; others near him did the same. The German soldiers roared with laughter at the sight of men lapping water from the floor like animals.

Later, I heard raised voices outside. Some men were arguing heatedly in German, and I realized that one sounded exactly like our old friend Mr. Hoffmann. I looked outside and saw that it was indeed Mr. Hoffmann, as neat as ever, but looking smaller and frailer somehow.

I was overjoyed, certain that Papa had guessed I was imprisoned here and had asked Mr. Hoffmann to intercede on my behalf. However, Mr. Hoffmann appeared to be taking a great risk, for he was actually berating a German officer for having imprisoned us in such an uncivilized manner. "And in a church, yet!" I heard him exclaim.

I almost expected to hear a shot ring out; had he been a Pole, he certainly would have been killed on the spot.

With all the strength I could muster, I called out, "Here, Mr. Hoffmann, here I am! It's me, Chaim. I'm in the church!"

How good it was to hear him call back to me, in his dear familiar voice, "Chaim, go to the front door!"

As quickly as I could, I made my way through the mass of men, inadvertently stepping on an occasional hand or foot. Finally I got to the door and stood there a few moments, anxious and expectant. Then a soldier opened the door just enough for me to squeeze through and took me to Mr. Hoffmann, who was standing next to the minister of the church. They were arguing with the German officer. When Mr. Hoffmann saw me, he said, "Chaim, Chaim! Are you all right?"

"Mr. Hoffmann, please . . . some water, some bread. We haven't had a thing to eat or drink since yesterday," I pleaded. I found the strength to speak and told the minister about the dreadful mess inside the church, and then both men turned their eyes towards the German officer. I, too, looked at him, and was amazed to discover that I was looking at Mr. Hoffmann's son Karl, dressed in a black uniform and shiny tight boots. A death's head badge decorated his stiff cap.

I almost cried, "Hey, Karl! What are you doing here?" But the large swastika on his sleeve terrified me into silence. The words shriveled up and died in my mouth.

Karl Hoffmann was much shorter than his father. His friends used to tease him and call him Karlik, which means midget in Polish. So now Karlik himself had become someone to be feared, for he wore the uniform of a Nazi officer!

Mr. Hoffmann handed me half a loaf of bread. "Here, my friend, eat!" he said, and then repeated these words, this time louder, to be certain that all the German soldiers, and not only his son, heard him. I took a bite, but my mouth and tongue were so dry that I simply could not swallow. Mr. Hoffmann, discerning my distress, said, "I'll get you some water."

Karl stopped him. "I'll have some water brought for your Jew friend, father."

He nodded at a soldier. Within minutes the soldier handed Karl an army cup full of water. Karl brought the cup close to my mouth. I wanted to thank him, but I did not know how to address him, or indeed whether I should even try to speak to a German officer. I reached out to take the cup, but he insisted on holding it himself.

"Drink, Jew, drink. Let me serve you," he said with a tight smile.

As he touched the cup to my lips I sensed danger; it was unthinkable for a German officer to be serving a Jew! He tilted the cup and as its precious contents began to run down my chin, I instinctively parted my lips and drank. The sweet smell and taste of the water were irresistible and I swallowed again and again.

Suddenly Karl slammed the cup into my mouth with all his strength. Its metal rim cut into my gums and lips, and from the force of the blow I fell backwards. I remember Karl's voice screaming *"Du dreckiger Jude!"* and the soldiers' laughter ringing in my ears; then I fainted.

When I regained consciousness, I found myself in our shack. Mama was applying wet rags to my injured mouth, and I noticed that they were red with my blood. She smiled at me. This was the first time that I had seen her smile since the war began. And she was repeatedly murmuring her thanks to God and to Mr. Hoffmann for having saved me.

She told me that the men who had been imprisoned with me in the church had already been loaded aboard trucks and taken to an unknown destination, probably across the border into Germany.

As I regained my strength during the next few days, my parents argued over whether or not it was safe for Papa to visit Mr. Hoffmann and express his gratitude for saving my life. Papa wanted to go, because he felt that he had not thanked him properly, due to all the excitement of the moment. Mama argued that it was too dangerous for a Jew to visit a German whose son, a Nazi officer, was living in the same house.

As a matter of fact, it was dangerous just to be outside on the streets, for the trigger-happy German soldiers were now shooting Lomza's citizens with reckless abandon. We ourselves had heard about twenty-four innocent victims of such wanton shootings. One had been a close friend of ours, an old man in his late seventies who was totally deaf. He had been shuffling along the sidewalk with his cane, and did not hear the German soldier behind him who ordered him to halt. He was immediately shot in the back and killed.

Papa pointed out to Mama that if he could inform Mr. Hoffmann about all these atrocious street killings, perhaps Mr. Hoffmann could influence his son to put a stop to them. Mama finally acceded to Papa's arguments. He kissed us good-bye and left.

Two hours later he returned. After our initial relief at seeing him safe, we realized that he was very pale. He was so upset and in such a state of shock that for hours he rebuffed all our attempts at conversation.

Finally he began to calm down, color returned to his face and he was able to tell us what had happened. He had arrived at Mr. Hoffmann's house without incident and knocked on the door. It was opened by Mr. Hoffmann's daughter, who was as tall and sturdy as her brother was short and slight. For a moment she stood there, silent, as if confounded. Then suddenly she broke into a tirade, shouting abuse and insults at Papa. "Filthy Jew!" she screamed. "Have you forgotten that we are Germans? What are you doing at our house?"

Papa simply stood there, petrified. He wanted to flee, but his feet wouldn't budge. Even though Mr. Hoffmann had told him that the Nazis had poisoned his children's minds, and he had seen the evidence of Karl's behavior himself, Papa was unprepared for a reception such as this.

Suddenly, tiny Mrs. Hoffmann appeared in the doorway and, quick as a flash, slapped her daughter's face. "How dare you talk like that to your father's friend!" she exclaimed. With a venomous look at Papa, the daughter retreated to the back of the house.

Mrs. Hoffmann apologized profusely to Papa, and begged him to come in, to do her the honor for old friendship's sake. He entered the familiar parlor, which was decorated with the many awards Mr. Hoffmann had received as an exemplary soldier and citizen.

Mrs. Hoffmann then told Papa the dreadful news. Her husband had had a terrible argument with their son Karl about the Nazis' behavior. In the heat of the argument Mr. Hoffmann collapsed, and within an hour he was dead. He had been buried just the day before.

Then she asked Papa to do her a favor. Would he keep an eye on their house, water their flowers and tend her husband's grave while they were gone? "We will probably be leaving in a few days," she said.

Papa could hardly believe his ears and was struck by the incongruity. Our world was in turmoil, people were being shot in the streets, her own husband had been buried the day before, and yet what was on her mind? Her flowers!

Papa was curious about where they were going, but he didn't need to ask, for she volunteered the information. She had learned, she told him, that the Russians would be taking over parts of eastern Poland.

"However, it's not yet clear to us if Lomza will remain in German hands or will be turned over to the Russians," she continued. "If the Russians get Lomza, the Germans here will be evacuated to the Fatherland." She added that, in the meantime, the German army had been ordered to stop their brutality towards the local population "in order to leave behind a decent reputation."

After managing to express his sympathy for her loss, Papa hurried away from the Hoffmanns' house and came home shaken to the core.

In the days that followed, we indeed noticed a change for the better in the behavior of the German soldiers towards the citizens of Lomza. This was not the case, however, with the behavior of the Polish collaborators. This Polish auxiliary police force consisted of Poles who wore large white armbands decorated with swastikas. These lackeys persisted in their brutal behavior towards Jews in order to prove their fidelity to their German masters. The German soldiers themselves, however, restrained themselves from further acts of violence.

All of this, of course, served to substantiate Papa's fears that we might soon be under the Russian heel — out of the frying pan, into the fire! The older generation remembered only too well the Russian tyranny after the Revolution, when Lomza had been occupied.

Papa was especially worried, for he had written a weekly column for the local newspaper. Although most of his articles had been on philosophical subjects, occasionally he had written satirical sketches, many of them mocking Communism and its leaders. Although these had been published under a pseudonym, it was no secret that he was the author.

For every local collaborator who had eagerly offered his services to the Germans, there would be at least ten times as many who would do so for the Russians.

Papa also feared for the safety of his brother, who was the director of a bank in Bialystok and thus in a very dangerous position. Moreover, he had publicly made several anti-Communist speeches, not mincing words, and all this was on official record.

Several days passed. Then one morning the citizens of Lomza discovered to their amazement that there were no more German troops around. They had simply vanished, and no authority remained in this conquered city. That day and the following night were filled with uncertainty, dread and fear. People stayed inside, behind locked doors, apprehensive of what fate held in store.

At about four o'clock the next afternoon, we noticed an ominous rumbling noise, which steadily grew louder and louder. At last we were able to see what it was — a procession of large army tanks and trucks. As the long column passed, our shaky wooden shack shook so much that we feared it would surely collapse. The noise was deafening.

Finally the column stopped; its head must have reached the bombed-out City Hall in the center of town. One by one, the roaring engines were shut off, until at last there was silence.

People flocked out of their houses shouting, "The Russians have arrived! Our liberators are here! Bravo! Bravo!" They kissed the Soviet tanks and eagerly shook the hands of the Russian soldiers. After three weeks of occupation by the barbarian Germans, there was indeed a feeling of liberation in the air.

In the days of the Polish-Soviet War of 1920, the Russian soldiers who had occupied Lomza had not even had decent shoes or uniforms, and to this day were referred to by the older generation as *bosiaki* — barefooted. Thus we were surprised to see that now they appeared to be adequately dressed, well fed, and of course well armed, with ponderous tanks and formidable artillery.

There was a considerable contrast between the officers of this Red Army and the martinet officers of the now-defunct Polish Army. The corseted Polish officers had dressed in snug-fitting, doll-like uniforms; their demeanor had been snobbish and arrogant. The Soviet officers' uniforms, by contrast, were plain and baggy; there were no epaulets on their shoulders, and their insignia of rank were worn on their collars.

But the greatest surprise of all was that the enlisted men did not salute the officers! Officers and enlisted men, colonels and privates ate from the same pot, smoked together, sang together and fraternized freely with each other.

The official Russian title of their army was "the Red Army of Peasants and Workers." These troops personified just that. Their rough-textured uniforms reeked with a slept-in, peasant odor. They acted with friendliness towards the people, and the people responded in kind. Despite all this, some of the older people, remembering the Red Terror of 1920, retained a certain degree of reserve.

We listened to the official Russian announcement explaining the occupation of Poland, which was broadcast over Radio Moscow: "The Polish state has ceased to exist. Millions of our brethren, Ukrainians and White Russians, remain unprotected and we see it as our duty to protect them."

Yet in Lomza there were no Ukrainians or White Russians. In any event, this — the fourth partition of Poland — was a *fait accompli.*

ALTHOUGH the Communist Party was illegal in Poland, it nevertheless was very active and had many members. Rampant poverty, the usual breeding ground of Communism, was only one of many factors upon which it thrived. The contempt of the Polish government towards the minorities within its borders was responsible for driving members of these groups into the arms of the Party.

For example, there were three and a half million Poles who were Jews. Except for medical doctors, no Jew could be an officer in the Polish armed forces. No Jew could be a policeman. The government of Poland officially espoused an economic boycott against its Jewish citizens. Consequently many of them, especially the youth, gravitated to the Party, which proclaimed equality for all citizens.

Another nine million Poles were Ukrainians or White Russians. Actually, this group as a whole had no desire at all to be citizens of Poland. They resented their status, feeling that they had been victimized by the vagaries of politics in the November 1918 border delineations. The homes and farms which had been within the boundaries of their fatherlands — the Ukraine or White Russia — were suddenly declared to be part of a freshly-hatched, re-created Poland. Ever since that dismal November, they had wanted to disassociate themselves from this artificial creation. They did not want to be Poles; their most passionate aspiration was to be annexed to their respective "fatherlands."

The government of Poland, instead of making an effort to cultivate the good will of these people, with the long-range view of possibly assimilating their progeny, oppressed them outrageously. Ukrainians and White Russians of the older generation were, generally speaking, antagonistic towards the Soviet Union for religious and economic reasons. The youth, however, angered by the official oppression of the Polish government, thronged to the illegal Communist Party. In this area of Poland, the Party was particularly well-supplied with funds and propaganda from across the nearby Soviet border.

There were other minorities, such as the Germans, the Czechs and the Lithuanians, whose homesteads were also near the borders of their respective ethnic fatherlands. These groups too hoped to see the dissolution of Poland, and subsequent reunification with the lands of their origin. It was often said, "Only the Jews and the Poles want Poland to endure." The truth of this expression lay in the fact that, of all the minorities, only the Jews had no fatherland other than Poland.

The short-sighted government, however, seemed dedicated to an effort to alienate these minorities. The inevitable result of this oppressive policy was a further swelling of the Communist ranks. The jails were filled, bulging with Communist Party members. A special hard-labor camp for political prisoners was located in eastern Poland, near the Russian border.

Naturally, as soon as the Red Army arrived, their first accomplishment was to reverse the roles of the jailed and their jailers. Prisons everywhere were emptied of political offenders, and then quickly filled again — with judges, prosecutors, lawmakers, prison guards and policemen. This wave of mass arrests included capitalists, and that category comprised small shopkeepers and professionals, many of whom were Jews. It also included fascists, a broad and convenient category, and the leaders of any and all political parties, such as the National Democrats, the Polish socialists, the Jewish socialists (the Bund) and all the various Zionist parties.

The Communists explained the reason for the arrest of the socialists: "The so-called socialists are more dangerous to us proletarians than the fascists and capitalists. *They* are visible enemies, but the socialists are *hidden* enemies." The official Party spokesmen, spouting this declaration, attributed its authorship to the "best friend of all workers, our great and brilliant leader, Comrade Stalin."

Soon the people became annoyed by the incessant quotations attributed to Stalin, as if he were an infallible being. Worse yet, they were irritated by the phraseology used by Party members and propagandists whenever they made any reference to Stalin. It sounded as though the words had been plagiarized from the prayer books: "the great Stalin," "the mighty leader," "the sunshine of the world," "the wisdom of the human race," "the hope of the universe," "the teacher and leader of mankind."

Ironically, those Poles who, under the Polish regime, had been fascists, and under the Germans had worn the white armbands with the swastikas, suddenly switched loyalties once again. This time their arms were decorated with red bands, and their mouths were praising and deifying Stalin in Soviet style. But their collaboration did not protect them for very long. Since the local Communist Party members were well aware of the chameleon-like switch of loyalties of these opportunists, soon this group too was imprisoned.

The greatest shock of all, however, developed a few weeks later. Communists — genuine Communists — were arrested! Poles who had been dedicated Party members for many years, men and women who had devoted their lives to the cause, many of whom had spent years in Polish prisons for their Communist activities, were now arrested and imprisoned. How bitterly ironic it was for them to have rejoiced at the fall of the oppressive, semi-fascist Polish regime, and then to be themselves rounded up and jailed! They had been given just a taste of the power of "leading the people in the direction of true socialism"; now, suddenly, it was back to prison, or worse, for them.

They were charged with being "Trotskyites." Most Polish Communists had indeed followed the leadership of Leon Trotsky, who was a predecessor and opponent of Stalin — and a Jew! But it was not enough, it seemed, to dedicate one's life to the Communist cause: one's dedication had to be specifically to the Stalinist Communist cause. Supporting any brand of Communism other than Stalin's was a most serious offense.

There was another ironic twist as well. In the days of the reactionary Polish government, Communists at least had the right to be tried in a court of law, the right to have defense counsel and the right to appeal. Now, however, all suspected persons were rounded up and simply disappeared without a trace. Their close relatives and friends usually fled in fear to other cities, assuming false names. There were some families at first who did not try to escape, since they had great faith in Soviet justice. Most of them were never seen again.

Every episode of arrests increased Papa's anxiety, for he, too, was eligible for the dreaded knock on the door. After all, he was a former capitalist!

Suddenly, on October 10, 1939, one month after the Russians had arrived, there came the astonishing news of the Russian-Lithuanian treaty. For its own indiscernible purposes, the Russian government had seen fit not only to sign a treaty with the small country of Lithuania, but even to cede to Lithuania the city of Vilna and its environs. Vilna, formerly Lithuania's capital, had been forcibly annexed to Poland almost twenty years earlier by the Polish army and had now come under Russian control as part of conquered Poland.

Immediately, a stream of refugees began crossing the border from Russian-occupied Poland into free Lithuania. Many hoped to emigrate from Lithuania to various countries overseas. Among these refugees were the teachers and students of a number of yeshivas, including my own, the Kamenitzer Yeshiva.

Papa had decided that I should not flee along with my fellow students for, he reasoned, if he should be arrested, I would be the one upon whom Mama and my little brothers would have to depend. So — I remained at home.

One day it was announced that elections would soon be held. All citizens were obligated to attend political gatherings, and one's presence or absence was duly noted by Party delegates. Speakers appeared on every street corner, all fiercely proclaiming the same message: every citizen was to vote for annexation of Poland to the Soviet Union.

A typical harangue included the reading of a telegram which the spokesman had allegedly sent to the beloved Stalin. The message pleaded "for the sake of the people" that the glorious Stalin deign to "admit us into the happy family of nations, marching forward to true socialism, under the guidance of the sunshine of the human race, the father of all nations, the great and beloved Stalin." At the conclusion of a long and exhausting harangue, the speaker would invariably ask, "Who is against?"

An intimidated silence was the only reply.

"Then it is unanimous!" he would declare triumphantly.

Election day came, and a number of candidates were chosen. Our freedom of choice was limited, however, since all were members of the same political party — the Communists!

The newly-elected delegates of the northeastern portion of Poland unanimously asked to be annexed to the adjacent White Russian Republic. The delegates of the southeastern portion of Poland unanimously begged to be annexed to the adjacent Ukrainian Republic. In White Russia, the

Soviet parliament magnanimously granted the request, and the Ukrainian "Soviet" also approved the southeastern Poles' plea for annexation. The Supreme Soviet in Moscow promptly ratified these decisions. Thus the Iron Curtain was lowered upon us, and Lomza became part of the White Russian Republic.

The one outstanding benefit of Soviet citizenship was the Russian insistence upon universal education — there was to be free education for all. Until then in Poland, only seven grades of elementary school had been free. In the villages, the highest grade of free education was the fifth and sometimes only the fourth grade. High school and university were only for the rich. But being rich was not all that was necessary to get a higher education; one also needed to be socially, ethnically and politically acceptable. For example, the limitations and quotas placed upon Jewish applicants for the universities were extremely severe. Many Jewish students went to other countries to obtain a university education, if their parents could afford it.

For the lucky (or unlucky) Jewish students who were allowed to attend a university in Poland, conditions were harsh. They were relentlessly persecuted and harassed by the Christians, both faculty and students. In the classrooms, Jews were required to sit in segregated seats. As could be expected in such a condoned and official atmosphere of degradation, pugnacious rowdies constantly assaulted and humiliated the Jewish students. A Jewish boy or girl who wished to attend a university in Poland needed to be not only rich and lucky, but immensely brave as well.

Now, however, the prospects for more education for more of the people were vastly improved. Suddenly, one no longer needed to be rich to attend the university. One needed only to qualify academically. Stipends were provided by the new regime to support students through high school and university.

Ironically, it was this very feature — free education — which was the cause of my parents' anxiety, and was the motivation behind their ultimate decision to send me away! Papa had always contended that to a Jew, education was as vital as air to breathe, and that was why most Jews had been literate even while surrounded by an illiterate and superstitious people for over a thousand years. However, Papa and Mama wanted me to go to a yeshiva and not to a Soviet university. The "price" of attending a free Soviet university was simply out of the question. The price? A student must renounce God and his faith — and life itself was not worth that cost!

One particularly distressing example of the Soviets' efforts to eliminate any mention of God in the schools occurred with my own little brother, Shimon, in the central role. One day the principal of the local school entered Shimon's classroom, looking worried and anxious, accompanied by the Education Commissar, a stout Soviet official from Minsk.

The Commissar asked the trembling teacher, "Which student has the best marks?" The teacher called Shimon, who stepped forward. The Commissar presented Shimon with a prize — a freshly baked white roll. This was indeed a prize, for it was a delicacy which none of the children had even seen since the war began.

The Commissar invited Shimon to go ahead and eat it right then and there. So, naturally, Shimon pulled his cap out of his pocket, placed it on his head, and innocently began to recite the benediction over bread: "Blessed art Thou, O Lord our God, King of the Universe, who bringest forth bread from the earth." And half of the class answered "Amen"!

Comrade Commissar, recognizing a prayer when he heard one, began a furious tirade, directed at the principal, the teacher, poor little Shimon, and God. Yanking the white roll out of Shimon's hand, he screamed, "Have you ever seen God?"

"No, Comrade Commissar," stammered Shimon. Then, he somehow found the courage to add, "What kind of God would He be, though, if one could see Him and shake hands with Him?"

The principal and the teacher were aghast. After all, not only their present jobs, but their whole future, was dependent upon this angry Commissar. One word from him could send them to their doom!

Fortunately, his rage subsided somewhat, and he ordered Shimon to return to his desk. Then he proceeded to deliver an impassioned lecture to the children, castigating God and religion, using words like "opiate of the masses," "stupidity," "superstition," and "nonsense." He concluded by pointing to Stalin's picture on the wall and declaring, "Stalin, not God, is the one who gives you food, clothing, and shelter."

The principal and the teacher both apologized obsequiously to the Commissar. They nervously tried to assure him that they were making great progress in eradicating religious superstition from the children, and to prove their dedication, they ordered the children to sing "The Ballad to Stalin." The well-drilled voices rang out:

> Over the spacious, wonderful Fatherland,
> Hardened in battles and toil,

We composed a song full of joy,
About the Beloved Friend and Leader — Stalin!
Our Battle Glory, Stalin!
Our Youth and Bulwark, Stalin!
With songs in battle and victory,
Our people follow STALIN!

Little Shimon was subsequently removed from his post as editor of the class newspaper, "The Small Leninist." Papa pointed out that Stalin was apparently not very interested in the older generation: "It seems he is not in the 'soul-saving business.' He is really after the youth, the future generations."

Papa also pointed out that formerly, in Poland, a Jew could not get any government job, not even as janitor in a post office, except by converting to Catholicism. Yet, in spite of the tremendous poverty, there had been no takers! Now the whip had been moved from Rome to Moscow. Rome had proclaimed: "Christianity or everlasting damnation"; Moscow's choice: "Communism or Siberia." Rome had promised the Kingdom of Heaven after death, and Moscow offered free education and full employment here and now! Christians and Jews were now in the same boat, Papa noted, facing the challenge of Communism.

Papa was fairly certain now that he was not marked for arrest. The Reds had apparently either forgotten him, or else had decided not to bother about a broken-down ex-capitalist. He began to let himself get involved with the changes in our lives.

After the incident with little Shimon, Papa began to feel that something had to be done to save his children from succumbing to the influence of the atheists. During the following days, he sought out other men who felt the same concern and anxiety, and together they engaged in preparations to form a Jewish school. Such a school had to be cloaked in utmost secrecy, for teaching religion was forbidden by law in the Soviet Union, and the penalty was exile to Siberia for the entire family, or even execution!

As a front for their illegal school, the parents pretended to be forming a legitimate youth club. Recently, the Party Educational and Propaganda Department had been vigorously encouraging the formation of such groups as the Lenin Club, the Red Circle Club, the Leader Stalin Club and others. Thus, there was nothing suspicious about their plans.

The conspirators concluded that, for safety's sake, they dared not admit teenagers into the "club." Too many teenagers were already under the influence of the *Comsomol*, the Communist Youth. The *Comsomol* had been notoriously successful in inculcating Soviet patriotism: many boys and girls had even reported their own parents for being subversive. Teenagers took tremendous pride in their status as "Guardians Against the Enemies of the Socialist Fatherland." Younger children, however, still considered loyalty to the family more important than loyalty to the state.

A vacant room in an old building was found, only a few minutes' walk from our shack. We decorated the walls with pictures of Lenin and Stalin, framed in red, and left a few chess games and some propaganda magazines from the *Comsomol* prominently displayed. A little bell with a string was set up, and one child was constantly on watch outside. His instructions were to ring the bell on seeing the approach of any stranger, and then to run to our shack to call my mother, for a woman among a group of children would arouse less suspicion.

The school became reality, and in spite of the danger, the children and the parents loved it. Conspiracy is a fascinating game for children! They especially liked the drills, when they were supposed to hurriedly hide the books and start chess games on the boards which had been set up.

One day, though, it was no drill but a true emergency. Two uniformed men approached; the small guard rang the bell and rushed to call my mother. One of the men was a local policeman, the other a Russian lieutenant. When the two entered the "club," the children stopped their chess games and honored the visitors by spontaneously bursting out in song with the popular propaganda march, "Wide Is My Native Country":

> Wide is my native country,
> Many are her fields, forests and rivers.
> I don't know another country
> Where a man can breathe as bold and free.
>
> From Moscow to the very borders,
> From southern mountains to the northern seas,
> A man strolls like an owner
> In his unencompassable native land!
>
> Refrain: Wide is my native country....
>
> Everywhere, life is full and wide,
> Punctual and full the Volga flows,
> For our young there's an open road everywhere,
> For our old there is much esteem!

Our fields you cannot embrace with a glance,
You can't remember all our cities.
Our pride — the word "*TOVARISHCH*" — Comrade —
Dearer to us than all other titles!

With this word, we are everywhere at home,
With us there is no black, white or yellow,
This word is known to everyone...
With it we find relatives wherever we go.

Over the land a spring wind is blowing,
Life becomes happier with every passing day.
No one in the world knows better
Than we how to laugh and to love!

Before the children had finished singing, Mama entered the room, smiling. The sight of the strange Russian officer did not disturb her composure. However, when she saw the face of the Lomza policeman, she turned as white as a ghost. It was none other than Vladek, the janitor's son from our building in Lomza! Papa had owned the building, and I used to play with Vladek's little sisters when our family and theirs all lived there before the war.

Mama was frightened and confused. Should she turn around and walk out? That would certainly arouse suspicion. On the other hand, if she stayed, Vladek would certainly recognize her and also my little brother Shimon. Vladek knew Papa and Mama well enough to be sure that neither of them would be devoting his efforts to teaching children about Communism; reporting anti-Communist activity would be a feather in his cap.

Mama made her decision: she would turn around and walk out, and pray. And so she did...but then she heard Vladek hurrying out of the room after her.

Meanwhile, the Russian lieutenant complimented the children. He praised their spirited singing and their patriotic fervor. "When my own son arrives soon from Russia," he told them, "perhaps I will sign him up in your wonderful club." Becoming more effusive, he called out, "Would you like me to teach you an Army song?"

Of course, no one declined. He asked, "Who knows the song 'Yeslee Zavtra Voyna' — If Tomorrow There Is a War?" None of the children knew this one, so he proceeded to teach it to them, repeating the words over and over for them in his husky bass:

If tomorrow there is a war,
If tomorrow there is combat,
If a dark power attacks suddenly,
As one man, the entire Soviet nation
Will arise on Stalin's order!

On land, in the air and on the sea,
Our song is mighty and strong.
If tomorrow there is a war, if tomorrow there is combat,
Prepare for it TODAY!

While all this was going on inside, Vladek the policeman started talking to Mama outside.

Vladek's father, the janitor, used to beat him and his sister often. We would hear the whistle of his leather strap and the wailing of his children. Many a time, Mama had interceded, begging him, "Have pity, they're only little ones," and sometimes she succeeded in stopping the thrashing.

The whippings were usually brought on by their refusal to attend church. However, as they grew older and their father apparently had reconciled himself to the fact that they simply were not churchgoers, the beatings continued. Why? The reason was revealed one night when the Polish secret police burst into the janitor's apartment. There they searched for and discovered Communist propaganda, and the son and the daughter were arrested.

Mr. Zajewski later confided to Papa and Mama that he used to burn "that stuff," and whip them; but the whippings had no effect, and they continued bringing home more of "that stuff."

Then, to make matters even worse, Vladek's sister Zosha decided to marry a Party member. Both refused to be married in the church: this was a matter of principle with them. Consequently, when their baby was born, other parents would not permit their children to associate with the little fellow whose parents weren't married by a priest. Mama, however, had always made it a point to be friendly with Zosha and her husband. Papa and Mama instructed us to play with the baby whenever the opportunity arose.

The Polish police had attempted to arrest Zosha's husband for engaging in Communist activities. However, he escaped and went into hiding — no one knew where. Occasionally, Zosha received a letter from him through the underground.

Now, talking to Vladek outside the "club," Mama was relieved to learn that he had fond memories of her and that he felt good will towards us, even though he was a Communist policeman. Vladek was gracious enough not to ask Mama too many questions, and asked nothing at all about the "club" itself. He did not even ask her what she was doing there. In fact, he warned her: "Be careful with your Lenin Club!

"My sister Zosha is now a top official in the Bureau of Labor, and her husband is the Chief of Police in Lomza," Vladek went on to tell mother. "I know that everything of yours was destroyed, and you probably don't even have money for food. Why don't you stop in and see Zosha? I'm sure she can find jobs for you and your husband. I'll talk to her about it. You know, we talk about you quite often, but we didn't have the faintest idea where you were."

Mama accepted his invitation to see Zosha about a job, and then they parted: Mama headed back to our little shack, and Vladek headed back to the "club." When he entered the room, there was his companion, the Russian lieutenant, still lecturing the children. He was in the midst of an ecstatic description of the wonderful life in Russia, the "workers' paradise." He made it sound like a fairy tale, where candy grows on trees, and Stalin was the "good fairy."

The next day Mama went to the Bureau of Labor, and found Zosha's office. On the door there was a sign: "Comrade Zosha Wicek." Mama knocked, and a stern voice called, "Enter!" She walked into a spacious, well-furnished office with a secretary ready to take notes. And there, sitting behind a heavy, official-looking desk, was Zosha.

Quickly, even before the secretary could say anything, Zosha spoke.

"What is your name, citizen?" she asked in a formal tone, as if she had never seen Mama before.

"Mrs. Shapiro," replied Mama.

"State your business," said Zosha.

Mama stated her business: "I am looking for a job, and so is my husband."

"Be seated, Comrade. I will get to you in due time."

Mama took a seat, and for several hours she just sat there, while Zosha completely ignored her. The secretary watched Mama, watched Zosha, and scribbled busily in her notebook.

Mama watched Zosha. She was very active, very busy. It was obvious that she held a position of importance. Mama noticed, however, that all orders, even the most minor ones, had to go to the Party Committee for approval before they could be put into effect.

The general atmosphere seemed to be one of fear — the fear of being solely responsible for having made a decision. Apparently the policy was to spread the responsibility, to "collectivize" decisions. No one in the office ever seemed to say "yes" or "no." All applicants were given long forms to fill out, and were told to return in a month, or two, or three.

Finally, it was quitting time. The young secretary put on her coat and said, "Good night!" while staring at Mama curiously.

"Good night," Zosha replied evenly.

As soon as the door had closed behind the departing secretary, Zosha's businesslike face changed completely. A smile emerged — a genuine, affectionate, radiant smile. She hurried over to Mama and embraced her warmly.

"My dear friend, my dear friend," she exclaimed, "How happy I am to see you again!" Her voice was full of sincerity. They kissed. Zosha wiped tears from her eyes.

"Vladek told me last night that he found you, and that you said you would come to see me. Even though I expected you, when you walked in, something like an electric shock passed through my body. I suddenly remembered everything — the beatings, the whip, my father's brutality, and you! You have no idea how grateful we were to you! People said the most terrible things about us; they called me a tramp, and my child a rotten brat. Even my own parents did! You and your family were the only ones who didn't treat me and my baby like lepers. I've never forgotten it.

"Here I was in the vanguard of the labor movement, fighting for justice, for the proletariat. What did I get for thanks? They spat on me! I wanted to kill them all...except you! I knew I could trust you, and many times I almost confided in you. But our leader warned us never to trust a capitalist, and although I knew he was wrong in your case, I couldn't disobey."

Zosha put on her coat and helped Mama with hers; they went outside together.

On the sidewalk, Zosha continued. "I have two jobs for you. One is as a kindergarten teacher. We are organizing public kindergartens for working mothers, but I'm afraid the Party would disapprove of a former capitalist teaching future socialists. In fact, it might work against me, and possibly even against my husband. So I'll recommend the next best job. It's not as dignified, but it's safer. There'll be no problem about your past, and no danger to me for recommending you. The job is saleswoman in a bakery.

Your husband can be the night watchman in the same place. What do you say?"

Mama liked the idea of the watchman job for Papa. True, he'd have to work on the Sabbath, but the work of a night watchman is not one of the labors forbidden on Shabbos. It seemed to Mama as if a kind Providence had found this roundabout way of helping to feed her hungry family. Another thought — actually, a current popular expression — passed through Mama's mind: "In Soviet society, lucky's the one who can get bread without standing in line on his head."

"Zosha," Mama replied, "in a socialist society all labor is dignified, is it not? We're grateful for the jobs you're offering us. But tell me, Zosha, between you and me why do you seem so frightened? Surely now you have more freedom than you did under the Polish regime!"

Zosha must have thought that she detected some sarcasm in Mama's words. She replied, "Don't you feel bad, having to ask your ex-janitor's daughter for a job?"

"Not at all," Mama said. She realized that Zosha was upset, so she spoke carefully. "There's an old proverb: 'If you can't go over, you must go around.' I've never considered any job undignified. Your father was never made to feel embarrassed by any of us because he was a janitor — you know that. Besides, please remember that I came to see you only at Vladek's urging."

Comrade Zosha relaxed again, and smiled. "I'm sorry," she said. "I didn't mean to give you the usual treatment reserved for former capitalists." They walked along in silence for a few moments. Suddenly Zosha said, "What did you mean when you asked me why I'm afraid?"

"Well," replied Mama, "that's the impression I got from seeing you at work, and it's not only you. It's the impression I get whenever I see Party officials during the performance of their duties. Don't they trust you? After all, aren't all the officials Party members? And I don't mean those fakers who joined the Party just recently. I mean the Party members who spent years of their lives in Polish prisons, who sacrificed their lives for the Party, like your husband. Don't they trust him either? Why do they check and double-check each other all the time? What are they afraid of?"

It was a while before Zosha spoke. Finally, a deep sigh escaped her and she replied, "You're right, you know. We — all of us — live and work in constant fear. True, no one trusts anyone else. But remember, this is a revolution, not a carnival! The revolution needs blood to grease the wheels! The tempo of the times requires blood, and quickly, whether the victims are really guilty or not. Many revolutions have failed because of lack of bloodshed. Lenin and Stalin teach us that."

"But, my dear Zosha," Mama interrupted, "how can you revolutionaries be prosecutor, judge, jury, witness and executioner, all in one? I realize your husband suffered, and you suffered, when all Communists were persecuted. I can even understand if you want revenge, but still... many of you are riding high right now, but suppose 'the wheel turns again? Why is your husband so harsh with prisoners? Can't you tell him that with less blood, with slowing down the wheels of the revolution, you'll miss nothing, and might even gain from it?"

Zosha listened quietly. She offered her hand as they parted. "I want you to understand, my dear friend," she said, "that we are not free. We are in Soviet hands. They suffered terror in their own Revolution, or should I say they still live in permanent terror? Anyway, they are spreading it here. There is nothing my husband can do. He's Chief of Police, but he has no real power at all. We are in the game, and if we hold up the grinding of the wheels of revolution for one minute, we lose our own heads. It's as simple as that!

"Now, please come to see me on Monday. I'll give you and your husband all the necessary papers to start you on your new jobs."

When Mama told Papa that they both had jobs, he was certain that he was not on any roundup list. And so he came to the decision to release me from my responsibility as substitute head of the family, and to send me away, far from the temptation of free Soviet education.

It was Friday evening and Shabbos had been ushered in. Mama, Papa, my two brothers and I were seated around the table. Our Sabbath meals had always been festive occasions — ceremonious, full of song and spiritually uplifting. The food on Friday nights had been sumptuous. Mama had always shopped for the best foods, and she and our cook had spent hours chopping, kneading, cooking and baking. Now, however, those times were gone — gone forever!

It all seemed so strange, living here in a rickety, one-room shack, with the shaky old table covered with old newspapers instead of a white, starched tablecloth, and ordinary black bread instead of the delicious, crisp braided *challah*. Instead of gefilte fish there was a salted herring, and the golden chicken broth and crisp brown potato kugel were only memories. Gone were the lovely silver candelabra over whose glowing candles Mama had always recited the Sabbath blessing. Instead, there was one small candle, cut into halves, and set upon empty shoe polish cans. How our lives had changed! Instead of four sons around the table, there were three. Mama's gentle blue eyes now reflected only sorrow, and they were swollen from crying.

I looked at Papa, whose tall body was bent disconsolately. His dark hair had turned entirely white. His tired brown eyes were set deep within his face, but tonight they seemed to recede even more than usual — trying to hide his despondency, I thought.

All during the meal, Mama kept glancing at Papa, as if trying to communicate with him or urging him to do something. They looked like two conspirators, and I knew that it had something to do with me. I grew cold with apprehension. What was their secret? What were they planning?

Finally the meal was over, we sang hymns and recited the grace after meals. Mama sent my brothers to play outside even though it was dark. Papa, turning in his chair, looked away from me. He placed his hands over his face, and lowered his head until his elbows rested on his knees. Then, in a hoarse voice choked with emotion, he murmured, "Chaim." He faltered and could say no more.

Now Mama cried out, "Say it! Tell him, tell him!"

Papa took a deep breath and burst out: "Chaim, you must go! Your mother and I have agreed that you must go to Vilna!" He was still speaking through his fingers, turned away from me. Mama began crying and praying, both at the same time.

"To Vilna?" I asked, stunned. "To where my yeshiva escaped? But it's too late now, Papa, you know that! The border is closed, locked, sealed. They don't let anybody across now. I'll be arrested, and maybe even shot, trying to get across. If the Russian guards don't catch me, the Lithuanian guards on the other side will! Papa, Mama," I cried and turned to Mama, "you can't mean it. I won't do it! I won't go! I won't leave you!"

Papa had risen from his chair and was standing next to me. He placed his hand affectionately on my shoulder. Soothingly, haltingly, he spoke. "Chaimke," he said, "although you are seventeen, you are a small seventeen. If the border guards challenge you, surrender peaceably. Be extremely respectful to them. Bow and scrape. Tell them you are fifteen.

They'll believe you, I'm sure. They'll give you a stern warning, and they'll send you on your way — home to us again." Then I heard him whisper, "*Oy, Ribbono shel Olam* — Oh, Master of the Universe!"

Papa paused for a moment to pull himself together. I couldn't look at him; my eyes were full of tears.

"We're at fault," Papa continued, "for not letting you go with the yeshiva when they went to Lithuania, when it was still easy to cross the border. Now we realize that we should have let you go then. It was an unwise decision. And we're convinced that the longer you delay, the more tightly will the border be sealed. You *must* go, Chaim. You must go now — without delay. This Sunday — the day after tomorrow!"

I looked towards Mama. With my eyes, I begged her to say it wasn't so. But it was plain to see that, although Mama was crying and praying, these were not cries of dissent. Her tears were the tears of a broken-hearted mother, and her prayers were a supplication to the Almighty to grant her son a safe journey. No, Mama was not protesting; for, after all, wasn't she Papa's partner in this conspiracy?

I launched forth into desperate arguments in a last-ditch attempt to dissuade them from their decision. I pointed out how helpful I could be to them if I remained at home, and what dangers I might encounter on the way to Vilna.

After much argument and much shouting, Papa said in a voice firm and resolute with finality, "Chaim, you are a bright student. If you remain here, you'll have an excellent chance to become, say, a doctor or a lawyer or an engineer. But we want you to continue your Torah studies in a yeshiva, not to earn a degree in a Bolshevik university, God forbid."

Before I could protest, Papa continued. "It's not that we doubt your faith or your dedication, it's not that we don't trust you. It's just that your mother and I, being older, know their tricks. They're after the youth, and especially the bright youngsters. First they come with silk gloves and sugar-candy. Then — the whip!"

Although I realized that their verdict was irreversible, I appealed once more.

"Do you realize that we'll be cut off from each other, maybe forever? You won't even know if I made it across the border, or if I got killed." I fervently hoped that this would melt Mama's resistance.

Mama wiped her tears. "My child," she said, speaking with determination and with her eyes fixed sternly upon me, "it wasn't easy to come to this decision. We've gone through many sleepless nights, and we've thought of every argument that you can think of, and maybe some that you can't. But listen to me now. I gave birth to four sons. One God took back. The others I'm determined to return to Him as pure as they came. I don't want you to become an atheist. I want you to remain a good Jew and I'm prepared for the worst. There is only one thing that matters to me now — to know that you are a good Jew!"

What argument remained for me after such a declaration?

With sobs choking her voice, Mama whispered with love, "Go, my son, go!"

ALL THE NEXT day, I tried to reject the thought of what awaited me. I was sustained by the words of the Shabbos prayer: "May it be Your will, *Hashem*, that there be no distress, grief or lament on this day."

But after *havdalah* — for which we used two thin matches instead of the fat braided candle — I had to face it. I stayed up for hours, hoping that something would happen to make my parents change their minds. But not another word was said — Mama washed our few chipped plates and swept the floor, and Papa sat on a rickety bench, never once looking up from his little *musar* book. Finally, I went to my corner, murmured the *Shema* and tried to settle down for the night. Since there were not enough beds in the little shack, my bed was the earthen floor.

That night I just could not fall asleep. A strange feeling pervaded me. My fingers touched the floor gently, as if bidding good-bye to this ground, to this city in which I was born and which I loved, despite all that we had suffered here.

Recollections and memories passed through my mind. Out of the blackness of the night there emerged a vision of a white *tallis*. I recognized it — it was the one which Papa had wrapped around me when I was three years old and he had carried me to my first day of school, in accordance with orthodox tradition. The custom of covering the child with a prayer shawl symbolizes a fervent plea to God to keep this child sheltered from harm and hostile influences, and to bless him with success in his studies, so that he might grow up to be a credit to God and to his people.

Papa had always been a firm believer in "pushing" his children's education. Consequently, by the time I entered the first grade of *cheder*, elementary school, at the age of five, I already knew how to read. When I graduated from that school, I was two years younger than most of my classmates. Then, when I was 14, Papa and Mama enrolled me in Rabbi Elchonon Wasserman's yeshiva in Baranowitz, a city approximately 300 miles from Lomza.

Of course, Lomza was not without a similar school. But I had been sent to such a distant place because Papa believed that "a child cannot properly study while he remains under the solicitious eye of his mother." In Baranowitz, I became a devoted _talmid_ of Rabbi Elchonon Wasserman. Like a Heavenly mountain he towered over his _talmidim_, physically, mentally and spiritually. He spoke very little yet he influenced us deeply. During the _shiur_, the well-prepared Talmudic lecture, he would make a few remarks, seemingly out of context, yet when we dwelled on them later, his words overwhelmed us, and made a lasting impact. He left most of the talking to the _mashgiach_, Reb Yisroel Ya'akov Lubchanski. And when Reb Yisroel Ya'akov talked, the whole world listened! Reb Elchonon himself would sneak quietly in through the back door and take a seat among the boys on the next-to-last bench.

One _Pesach_ night, after I had been studying in Baranowitz for over two years and was home for the holiday, Papa declared that he had a special present for me. It was the custom, at the end of the _Seder_ ceremony, for Papa to award gifts to his children. To each of my three younger brothers — Lazer, Nosson and Shimon — Papa presented a toy or game. Now it was my turn. While Mama, who sat at our _Seder_ table like a queen, beamed approvingly, Papa said, "Chaim, the yeshiva of Kamenitz has accepted you!" Papa exuded pleasure as he said this, and a smile spread from his eyes all over his face, for he felt that he was giving me a priceless treasure.

The yeshiva at Kamenitz was world-renowned. Its scholastic standards were extremely high. The dean, Rabbi Reuven Grozovsky, had been Papa's classmate during their student days. No doubt this explained why I was accepted there at the unusually young age of seventeen.

Here a new world opened for me: my teachers included Reb Baruch Ber Leibowitz, _talmid_ of the great Rabbi Chaim Soloveitchik of Brest-Litovsk (Brisk), whose overwhelming love for Torah seemed to dominate his every thought, word and gesture; there was also his son-in-law, Reb Reuven Grozovsky, the _gaon_, the _ba'al musar_, who willingly carried the burden of the whole yeshiva upon his shoulders, and yet still found time to "talk in learning" with the boys, keeping his sharp eyes on everyone and everything. I loved the atmosphere of intense concentration on Torah learning; students had come from near and far to breathe in this spirit and to become part of it...and I was one of them, and had become part of it all...and now, I was being forced to go, alone, into the unknown.

My *rebbeim*, my parents, my dear little brothers, made even more precious by the loss of one...how could I leave them? I felt myself too young, too weak to manage alone. And there was also a nagging undercurrent of guilt — perhaps, by leaving now, I was really deserting them when they needed me. Wasn't I, as the oldest, responsible for them all?

The cold wind whistled mournfully through the cracks in the walls and windows of the wooden shack, as if it were joining my lamentations. Pain and sorrow overwhelmed me when I thought that tomorrow I would be leaving behind all those whom I loved and cherished. Would I ever see them again? I cried uncontrollably.

I finally slept, and when I awakened, it was nearly noon. Papa informed me that he had arranged for two other boys to cross the border with me — my friend Zelig, the baker's son, and my cousin Chaim, who had also been a student in the yeshiva which had fled to Vilna.

In a conspiracy, the fewer people who know, the better, particularly children. My two brothers, therefore, were told that I was going to visit our grandparents in nearby Tiktin. I could give them only a perfunctory hug and kiss. Then Papa sent them outside to play, and I stared out at them from the window, memorizing their faces.

Mama was leaning against the rough, splintered wall, shaking with sobs. I kissed her hand and embraced her. The thought of perhaps never seeing each other again was enough to reduce both of us to helpless tears.

In a quavering voice, she said, "Vilna isn't so far. And from there, you might get to *Eretz Yisrael* or even to America." Then she repeated, firmly, "Go, my son, go! And may God be with you!"

She placed her hands on my head and murmured a blessing. Then she gave me a package of food and returned to the pages of her little book of *Tehillim*, as I went out the door.

Walking down the rubble-strewn road, I thought I could feel her eyes fixed on me, but I didn't let myself turn around.

Only Papa accompanied me to the train station. As we walked, he suggested that wherever I go, I should locate the local rabbi since many were graduates of his alma mater, the yeshiva of Slobodka. By introducing myself as his son, I'd be taken care of.

"Colonel Samuel Snieg, the chief Jewish chaplain of the Lithuanian Army, is my dear friend and former roommate. Once you get into Lithuania, go to see him the first chance you get," Papa said. He then gave me a slip of paper with the name and address of another friend in the city of Lida, not far from the Lithuanian border. This man, Papa said, might be able to furnish information which would be helpful to me in crossing the border.

Zelig and Chaim were waiting for me at the train station. A slight nod was the only greeting which passed between us. Papa stepped up to the counter and purchased a one-way ticket to Lida. Presently the train pulled into the station.

To avoid attracting the notice of the Communist police and the ever-present secret agents, we only shook hands in a casual farewell. Knowing that it was imprudent to do so, I nevertheless leaned over and gave Papa a light kiss on his cheek. His eyes appeared to recede even more deeply than usual.

As the train pulled out of the station, I gazed back at my beloved city, wondering whether I'd ever see Lomza again.

Zelig, Chaim and I had an uneventful trip. We got off the train when it stopped in Lida, and we found our way to the address that Papa had given to me. When we arrived at the house and told Papa's friend why we were there, he refused to have anything to do with us. "I have five little children," he said, "and I can't get involved in something which might land me in Siberia and leave my children fatherless!"

"Please, can't you at least put us in contact with somebody who can give us, or sell us, some reliable advice about how to cross the border safely?" we implored. We promised that we would never reveal his name to the authorities, even if the alternative might be the firing squad.

Little by little, his attitude softened. He explained to us that there were two small towns nearby, Eishishki and Raduni, where the Chofetz Chaim had lived. Until the war, both these towns had been inside Poland. Now, however, the new border line ran directly between the two: Raduni was still on this side, but Eishishki was on the other side — in Lithuania. Because Raduni was situated almost on the border, it had been used extensively by people who were fleeing into Lithuania. Lately, however, this was no longer possible because the Russians had cracked down on any further border crossings. Raduni was full of soldiers, guards and secret agents; and since it was such a small town, a stranger would immediately be spotted and taken into custody for interrogation.

"So, by all means, you must avoid the town of Raduni," he warned us.

Eventually he gave us the name of a farmer who could be trusted to take us through the fields and across the border — for a price, of course. The farm was located on the far side of Raduni, and thus we'd be spared the jeopardy of passing through the town itself.

It was late in the afternoon when we finally arrived at the farm. The farmhouse was a log hut with a straw roof surrounded by a littered yard. Inside, the poverty, the smells and the filth were appalling. The farmer, a depressed-looking fellow with a suspicious squint, lay sick in bed. His "bed" consisted of a few boards and a little dirty straw; his "blanket" was a mangy sheepskin.

We told him that we had been sent to him by his friend in Lida, and that we wanted to cross the border into Lithuania. At first he feigned complete disinterest, and seemed to want to discuss only his illness with us. However, when we displayed money, he suddenly came to life, as if by magic, and asked us how much money we'd be willing to pay for a guide to take us across the border.

"One hundred rubles per head," was our offer.

Apparently this was more than enough, for he did not attempt to haggle for a higher price.

"I will send for my brother," he said, "and he will take you across."

While we anxiously awaited the arrival of his brother, the farmer began to tell us about his troubles.

"I'm a White Russian," he said. "A few years ago, the Polish government threw me off my farm and confiscated it. They claimed I hadn't paid my taxes, and right away they 'resettled' a Polish farmer on my farm."

By working hard, and scrimping and saving for a number of years, he eventually was able to buy back one hectare of his land.

"So now, after all that," he added, shaking his head disconsolately, "the Russians will drive us all into a collective farm anyway." He coughed, sighed, and turned his back to us.

Towards evening the brother arrived. He was a tall, husky peasant, profuse in swear-words and curses. He railed against everything, particularly "the cursed *kolkhoz* business" of the Russians, who, he was convinced, would soon be confiscating his farm. This man had a sharp, mean look about him, and did not strike us as trustworthy. However, we had no choice but to go along with him.

First he took us in a horse-and-wagon to his farmhouse, which was quite close by. There, he demanded the money in advance so that his wife could bury it in case we got caught. We gave him three hundred rubles.

Then we waited, and waited. He said that we'd set out after the border patrol had passed by on its rounds.

Finally, we began our trek across the border — at last we were on our way!

•

The night was black; neither moon nor stars were visible. It was difficult to follow our guide's footsteps in the snow. Crossing through one field, I happened to step aside from his tracks just a little bit, and suddenly I broke through ice, sinking to my knees in water. I choked back a scream, thinking that I might drown. The others pulled me out, and we continued on our way. Even though my pants, shoes and socks were freezing, I perspired from the exertion of keeping up with the huge steps of the farmer.

The fear of being caught, or shot at, kept our ears sharp and all our senses on edge.

Suddenly we heard footsteps in the darkness. We dashed for cover behind some bushes nearby. We were so scared that we barely breathed. After the sound of the footsteps faded in the distance, we asked the farmer if that had been another border patrol.

"No," he said, "that was probably another group of border crossers like you. Come on, let's go!"

We marched on behind him for a considerable distance, until we arrived at a frozen brook.

"This is the border line," he said. He pointed to some lights in the distance and said, "That is Eishishki. Cross this brook and you will be in the cursed Lietuva — Lithuania. Now I must be on my way back, before the cursed Russians catch me here."

In another moment he was gone from sight. For a few seconds, we heard his footsteps crunching through the snow; then the sound disappeared, and we were on our own.

Eagerly, we ran across the brook. The ice gave way beneath us, but the water was less than knee-deep. Once across the brook, we made a beeline across the frozen fields, heading towards the distant lights. Presently we found ourselves on a road. Walking was much easier now.

Suddenly, a number of headlights appeared from around a curve in the road up ahead. We jumped over to the ditch on the side of the road and threw ourselves into the deep snow. After the convoy passed, we arose and we all three said almost the same words: "Weren't those *Russian* trucks? What are Russian trucks doing here in Lithuania?"

As we continued on our way we discussed the Russian trucks, and we concluded that there must be a Soviet base stationed here on Lithuanian territory.

Suddenly, we heard a shout in the night: "*Stoy! Kto Idyot?* — Stop! Who is coming?"

Russian words! We were now thoroughly demoralized, for we knew that Lithuanian guards wouldn't be using Russian words.

Within minutes, we were encircled by a patrol of Russian soldiers, the bayonets on the ends of their rifles pointing at our throats. They marched us to a border patrol station. There we were stripped and every bit of our clothing was minutely examined. They were looking for money or documents or anything else which might have been sewn into our garments. Finding nothing, they gave us back our clothes.

Then they interrogated us, each one of us separately. We were well-prepared and we each told the same story: that our homes were in Vilna, that we had been visiting relatives in Brest-Litovsk, in Poland, just before the war broke out. We had been trapped in Poland, and now we were simply trying to return home, to Vilna. Our story had special merit, because it would not incriminate our parents in Lomza. And if the Russians believed that our parents lived in Vilna, then it was hardly likely that they would try to communicate with them there.

At the end of our interrogation, the Russian officer ordered, in a gruff voice, "Lock them up!" Immediately, the soldiers led us out of the little station house, and into a building next door. A peasant, apparently the former owner, still lived there, but it was also used as a lock-up.

Once inside, we were relieved to be able to lie down on the bare floor and rest our exhausted bodies. Another prisoner was snoring loudly in a corner of the room. We were too tired to talk, and quickly fell into an exhausted sleep.

The next morning, a Russian soldier brought in some bread and a can of water. He kicked us all awake: Zelig, Chaim, the stranger in the corner, and me. Soon, a desultory conversation developed among the four of us. The stranger seemed unusually curious about us, and we were equally interested in finding out about him. He asked us a number of questions about ourselves; we answered his questions with an equal number of lies. Then we asked him some questions and we had no doubt that his answers were lies too. After all, one never knows who might be an informer!

He told us that he had studied at the universities of Warsaw, Berlin, Paris, London and Berne. Perhaps some of this might have been true, for he showed us his Polish passport, and it did contain visas from Germany, France, England and Switzerland. He demonstrated his multilingual fluency by saying a few things in the various languages.

Several hours passed. Some of the time we spent in conversation; sometimes we were quiet, engaged in our own thoughts. We spent hours at the window, observing the passing scene. And always, always our thoughts were of those we had left behind.

Our fellow prisoner was staring out the window. Suddenly he turned around and exclaimed, "Hey, fellows, look — the guard is on the other side of the house now. All we have to do is open this window and slip out. We can disappear into those woods in one minute, and there we'll be safe from these Bolsheviks."

While the word "Bolshevik" is an honorable title in Russia, Poles use it among themselves as an insult. No one would dare use that word in its derisive connotation where he might be overheard by a Russian, for it might cost him ten years of hard labor in Siberia.

The spy had overplayed his hand!

Quickly, I replied, "Oh, no, thanks. We have no reason to be afraid, so why should we try to escape? We're minors; and besides, the Bolsheviks are treating us well. We have no complaints." And Zelig and Chaim added their agreement.

Later in the afternoon, we four and several more prisoners were marched to Raduni under guard, a walk of approximately five miles. During the march some conversation passed between the linguist "prisoner" and the Russian guards. We noticed that he spoke Russian with a perfect Muscovite accent.

Inside the Raduni police station, we were again interrogated, and we repeated our story, in somewhat different words, so that it would not sound too pat. To our great relief, the captain eventually barked at us, "You minors may leave, but don't let me catch you again!"

Encouraged by our success in winning our freedom, we pleaded with the captain to dispatch us across the border. "*Comrade Capitan*, we must

47

return home to our parents in Lithuania. Please, please, let us cross!"

Our pleas fell on unreceptive ears. "If you fools prefer a fascist, capitalist regime to our free socialist Soviet Union, then go," he growled, "but I can assure you you'll be shot at — if not by my men, then by the Lithuanian sentries."

It was clear to us that we'd better not press our luck any farther, so we humbly thanked the police captain and made a quick exit. Outside, we tried to plan our next step. We decided that we would return to the house of the sick farmer and confront him with his brother's treachery.

After a strenuous hike, we finally arrived at the farm. When we told the farmer about his brother's betrayal, he shrugged his shoulders indifferently and said, "So what do you want from me? It's him you did business with, not me."

Then Zelig said something which hit the mark: "You know, the Russians would happily put you and your brother out of business for a long, long time if someone were to tell them what your business is."

Instantly the farmer's indifference evaporated. "You'd better shut up," he sputtered, and after a few minutes added, "All right, I'll go with you myself. But only as far as no-man's land, not one step further! I just hate looking at those Lithuanian swine." He was already putting on his torn, dirty clothing, muttering to himself about the chances he was taking.

Again, we had to wait for darkness. Meanwhile, a wet snow mixed with rain began falling, and we sat on the floor, willing the night to fall and praying for the success of this attempt.

At last, several hours later, it was sufficiently dark and we started again on our trek. Somehow, this time it seemed less arduous than the journey of the night before. Perhaps it was because the elderly farmer's pace was not as vigorous as his tall brother's.

In less than half an hour, we reached a dirt road. Our guide stopped and said, "I swear to you, you are no longer on Soviet territory." With his right hand he drew the sign of the cross on his chest, to emphasize his sincerity.

"See that clump of lights, over there in the distance?" he said. "That is Eishishki. Walk quietly and cautiously, and keep your ears open for sentries. Maybe this rain and snow coming down will keep them inside, those cursed lazy Lithuanians!" He spit disdainfully.

We gave him some money, and advised him to collect our three hundred rubles from his treacherous brother. He thanked us for the money and bade us "Good luck!" In a moment he was gone.

We started walking towards the lights. Zelig walked in front, Chaim and I behind him. Zelig's every step, breaking through the ice-encrusted snow, made a crackling sound; so loud, I feared, that it could be heard half a mile away. Suddenly shots rang out. At first the shooting seemed to be coming from behind us, so we started running furiously forward, towards the lights. However, within a few moments we heard another volley of shots, and this seemed to be coming from up ahead.

Chaim yelled, "We're caught in cross-fire. Fall to the ground!" And we dropped down into the freezing snow.

The intensity of the firing increased from both directions. Bullets whistled over our heads. I wriggled into the snow as deeply as I could, wishing that I could squirm down even more deeply, down below the surface of the ground. After a while, that had seemed like an eternity, the shooting began to subside. Finally, it ceased altogether.

Lying there in the wet snow, thoroughly soaked, we conferred on our plight. Chaim said he had heard that border sentries sometimes shoot into the darkness "just for fun" and that this often caused the sentries on the other side of the border to start shooting too. At any rate, we concluded, one thing is certain: this surely must be no-man's land, with the Russian guns behind us and the Lithuanian guns ahead of us.

We decided that we must crawl on ahead and try to reach Eishishki before daybreak — or else!

As we crept through the wet snow I thought, "What a terrible thing it would be to be killed here, so close to freedom."

Further and further we crawled, and the lights of Eishishki drew closer and closer. Then suddenly we heard shouting in a strange language, and a moment later we were surrounded by soldiers. This time, however, we were relieved and delighted to be captured, for these were Lithuanian troops!

They took us to a nearby police station. The officer in charge, speaking Polish, accused us of being Communist agitators; we assured him that we were not. He accused us of being just plain spies; we assured him we were not that either. We explained that we were simply rabbinical students who were seeking asylum in the great free Lithuanian Republic in order to pursue our religious studies.

The officer told us, "We'll continue the interrogation in the morning. Now the sergeant will show you to a room. There are blankets there. You can get rid of your wet clothes and bed down on the floor for the night."

Inside the room, we removed our wet, freezing clothing, wrapped ourselves in blankets and lay down on the floor. Although we were physically exhausted, we were spiritually exhilarated, deeply grateful for having come safely across the border.

That cold stone floor in the Lithuanian police station felt like the most luxurious bed...and as I drifted off to sleep, I whispered over and over, *"Baruch Hashem! Baruch Hashem!"*

In the morning, we had an unexpected visitor — the local rabbi, the religious and civil leader of the Jewish community of Eishishki. He had come to determine for the authorities whether we really were rabbinical students. In a staccato Lithuanian Yiddish, the dignified rabbi asked us to name some of the faculty members of our respective yeshivas. He asked each of us several searching questions of an academic or theological nature, relating to the Bible, the Talmud and other sacred books. Our scholarly replies were convincing evidence that we were indeed yeshiva students. He assured the officer-in-charge that we were genuine rabbinical scholars.

The officer placed some documents on the desk, and the rabbi signed them, making himself responsible for our future actions. Then we were officially released.

The rabbi got three Jewish families to provide room and board for us temporarily. After three days of rest, each of us was presented with ten *lit*, Lithuanian currency, and a train ticket to Vilna, donated to us by the Jewish community of Eishishki.

4

FOR CENTURIES, the ancient city of Vilna was a source of conflict between Poland and Lithuania, who had once formed a mighty union. Both countries laid claim to the city, but to the Lithuanians it was more than just a city — it was their ancient capital, and they called it by its older name, Vilnius.

After the end of World War I in 1918, United States President Woodrow Wilson's foreign policy of self-determination brought both these countries back into existence. No sooner were they resurrected than Vilna again became a bone of contention between them. The League of Nations undertook the job of deciding whether the city should be assigned to Poland or to Lithuania. The Lithuanian delegation submitted as part of its evidence a very old Talmud, which contained this sentence: "Published in Vilna, capital of Lithuania." The League of Nations, after due deliberation, assigned the city to Lithuania.

Polish Marshal Juzef Pilsudski was born in a village near Vilna. He could not accept the decision of the League, nor could he openly defy the League. In 1920, Vilna was attacked with a small Polish army ostensibly against the wishes of the Polish government. The city was captured and swiftly annexed to Poland.

The Lithuanians consequently moved their capital temporarily to Kaunas (Kovno), but in their constitution, Vilnius remained the official capital. A state of war was declared between the two countries that lasted until the Second World War.

A few months earlier, in September 1939, the Russians, in the wake of their occupation of Poland, had occupied Vilna. Twelve days later the Soviet government invited the Lithuanian foreign minister to Moscow, offering to return Vilna to Lithuania; in return, Lithuania would grant Russia the right to establish military bases on Lithuanian soil.

It was inconceivable that any Lithuanian statesman would refuse the offer of Vilnius, the beloved ancient capital, regardless of the price involved. The President of Lithuania, Antonas Smetanas, was well aware of the danger of delivering Lithuania into the "paw of the Siberian Bear," but there was no alternative and he had to accept the deal. England and France were busy with their war against the Germans, and Germany had already seized one vital piece of Lithuania, the city of Memel, its only port.

Lithuania was helpless in the face of the giant powers surrounding her; she had to accede to a "protector" or face decimation. So, in October 1939, a "Friendship and Mutual Defense Treaty" was signed between Russia and Lithuania, a portion of which read: "Respecting the rights and feelings of the Lithuanian people, the Soviet government has decided to correct an historical injustice and return the city of Vilnius and its vicinity to Lithuania."

Soon thereafter, the other two Baltic states, Latvia and Estonia, were pressured by the Soviet Union into accepting similar treaties. Thus, by having military bases in all three Baltic republics, the Russians were vastly improving the defense of nearby Leningrad — despite the fact that the ink was hardly dry on "The Friendship Pact of 20 Years' Duration" between Soviet Russia and Nazi Germany. The first stage of the "Sovietization" of these three republics had been achieved.

As soon as the Soviet-Lithuanian treaty went into effect, the "mechanized divisions" of the Lithuanian army marched into Vilna. The first units of soldiers were mounted — on bicycles! Each soldier wore white gloves, and the rifle hanging from his shoulder faced barrel-down, as a sign of peace and goodwill. Behind the bicycle-mounted troops came seven miniature tanks, causing snickers of amusement from the spectators.

Those bystanders who were Lithuanians were in good spirits, since they were being "liberated" after enduring twenty years of Polish oppression. On the other hand, the Polish bystanders were very unhappy, for several reasons. First, Poland had lost a war in the shockingly brief period of only three days. Second, Poland was now occupied by the conquerors, Germans and Russians, and third, there was the additional humiliation of becoming subjects of tiny Lithuania! To lose a war against giants is one thing, but to be occupied by the troops of this contemptible little country was like rubbing salt into their open wounds.

And if this was not enough to destroy Polish delusions of grandeur, the *coup de grace* was not long in coming. Since the war had begun and ended so quickly, no one knew the fate of the northeastern Polish army which had been assigned to defend Vilna. Whatever had become of that formidable legion? There had been various rumors, but now we learned the truth — all those divisions had simply walked across the border, to Lithuania and safety. Lithuania, believing that it was being invaded by this Polish army, mobilized its own army to repel the enemy. The Poles, however, simply disarmed themselves and begged for asylum! This entire army had fired hardly one shot in defense of its country!

During the next few days, as these accumulated humiliations built up, they began to have an effect upon the Polish population of Vilna. Like a sudden explosion, the Poles "revolted." The looting of stores and homes was only the beginning; soon the revolt escalated to killing, to breaking into private homes and murdering all the occupants!

The first victims were, as usual, the Jews; and since the Lithuanian authorities didn't mind this pogrom, they didn't interfere. But then it got out of hand and the Poles began shooting at Lithuanian officials and killing Lithuanian policemen; the emboldened Poles were now beyond control. Suddenly, Russian tanks appeared in the streets. Like magic, the passion of the bloodthirsty Poles subsided. The sight of a Russian tank was enough to discourage even the most "courageous" Pole.

As a consequence of the riots, the Lithuanian government instituted a firm and rigid policy. It decreed that only the Lithuanian language be spoken in all public places; storekeepers, artisans and professionals were warned that they must learn the language within a specified time, or they would lose the license to do business. All public places were required to display prominently a picture of President Antonas Smetanas, and next to it, the national emblem — a Teutonic rider astride a horse rising on its hind legs.

The Poles reacted with insubordination, but it was silent this time since they did not want to be confronted with Russians again. They refused to learn Lithuanian. They joked about the national emblem: "Why doesn't the horse let down his front legs? Because he'll find himself across the border!"

The animosity between the Poles and the Lithuanians was most apparent in the churches. The Lithuanians insisted that only their language be used, but the clergy refused, and most of the clergymen in Vilna were

Polish. Two Lithuanian priests who had tried using that tongue in their churches were stabbed to death in the churchyard. In response, a Polish priest was killed the next day.

The Poles feared that the Vatican would replace the Polish clergy with Lithuanians. It was known that as soon as Hitler declared western Poland a part of Germany, the Vatican had replaced the Polish clergy with Germans; on the request of the Lithuanian government, the Vatican might do the same in Vilna. These killings were to warn Rome against such action, since the Poles felt that their churches were the last vestiges of Polish nationhood.

It was no surprise that the Poles and the Lithuanians put their respective national interests ahead of their common religion. For unlike the Jews, whose religion came first and nationality last, these peoples had nationhood long before they were forced to accept Christianity. To them, nationhood would always come first. However, while they were quarreling, the Kremlin was actively attempting to lure away their children, inviting both national and religious suicide!

It was in Vilna that the yeshiva of Kamenitz had re-established itself in one of the city's larger synagogues. When Zelig and I appeared there, the students and the faculty greeted us joyously, as long-lost sons. My cousin Chaim joined another yeshiva elsewhere in Vilna. I found that the yeshiva was pursuing its normal full course of education; although the site had changed, the curriculum had not.

Part of our financial support came from a committee in New York City which for years had been collecting donations for the support of the Kamenitzer Yeshiva. The balance of our requirements was supplied by the Joint Distribution Committee, the charitable arm of American Jewry.

Living in the shadow of "the Russian Bear," whose great paws might at any moment choke the freedom of Lithuania and our ability to pursue our studies, we felt an added urgency to study and to learn. Not a moment was wasted. The yeshiva routine, beginning with *Shacharis*, the morning prayers, at dawn, continued through the day, with well-attended lectures, and the sing-song repetition of the questions and answers of the Gemara. The day ended late, with a frugal meal and *Ma'ariv*, the evening prayers. It seemed as if the spirit of Kamenitz had been transferred, intact, to its new location.

Vilna contained the largest library of Judaica in Europe, the famous Strashun Library. Like thirsty travelers at a well, the students drank deeply of the knowledge in it, often tracking down rare volumes and studying them avidly. There was tremendous excitement when a student came upon a small book which seemed to us to prophesy the rise of Hitler, followed by the redemption of the Jewish people. As homeless refugees, we were especially excited and comforted by this prophecy.

Although many were apprehended by the Russians and sent to Siberia, thousands of refugees continued to pour across the border. All of them had one objective: to emigrate to anywhere in the free world. The Lithuanian authorities closed their eyes to this illegal immigration, for it meant more American dollars for their country. Besides, they may have felt that they themselves could easily become refugees as well, whenever the Bear would decide to close his paw. The Joint Distribution Committee established kitchens to feed the refugees, distributed clothing and furnished medical care.

•

The fact that mail from Russia arrived in Lithuania undisturbed made a lot of people nervous; they saw it as a sign that Moscow considered the Baltic states in its pocket. Thus, the feeling became stronger that it was imperative to try to get out. There was a rumor that President Roosevelt had promised five thousand visas for rabbinical students; but in order to get the American visa one needed a birth certificate. I wrote home, and soon received my birth certificate in Russian, plus a note from Papa.

"Lazer became very ill following his brother; but he is now well at home."

I interpreted this to mean that my 15-year-old brother Lazer had attempted to cross the border, and was arrested and sent home, perhaps because he was a minor. I grew more confused and frightened.

Because of the uncertainty of the times, many refugees had been patronizing a palm-reader, in a desperate effort to know what lay ahead for them. In Deuteronomy 18:10 and 11, the Torah prohibits Jews from resorting to occult powers. Palm-reading, however, is not considered witchcraft; it is merely reading, and describing what is seen, without claiming to know if the information concerns the present, future or past. I decided to try it as well.

When I arrived at the address I'd been given, I found a small apartment with a waiting room, like a doctor's office. People from every walk of life were waiting, and everyone seemed to be a little embarrassed about being there. It was interesting to observe the faces of those who came out of the "office" after their palms had been read. Some came out cheerful and smiling, and others looked grim.

Finally it was my turn. The palm-reader was a young man, who was holding a small book. The first thing he did was to caution me not to consider him a fortune teller.

"I merely read the lines on your palm. Skilled interpretation of the lines of life, wisdom and happiness have been tested over the centuries. What I will read will be a conglomeration of the past, present and future. I only read what I see, and I make no pretension of predicting anything."

He scrutinized the lines in my palm, and I began to feel foolish and embarrassed. After poring over several pages in his little book, he said, "I see blood. I don't know whether it's yours, or if it belongs to someone else in your family."

The smile on my face vanished, and my skepticism did too. He is talking about my little brother Nosson, I thought.

He continued, "I see a long life, happiness, children and wealth. I see a lot of travel from one place to another, and then a crossing of a large body of water — it must be a sea. You will be first in one country for a while, then another and another. Of course I don't know the order of these things, which come first and which second."

I emerged from his office encouraged and even happy, looking forward to my future. Looking back, a lot of those things did in fact come true!

•

Ten years in a Siberian work camp was the standard sentence for those caught attempting to cross the border. Although many were caught, and some were shot and killed in the process, border-crossers continued to arrive in Vilna. As a result, Vilna became so overcrowded that the Lithuanian government decided to disperse some of the refugees among other cities and towns throughout the country.

Since it was easier for the government to deal with one large group, like a yeshiva, than with many individual refugees, the day was not long in coming when our school was ordered to move to the city of Raseinai, north of Kaunas. It was a terrible blow to our emigration prospects; Vilna and Kaunas were the emigration nerve centers. There, one could be close to the sources of news and activities which were so vital to all of us. Moreover, we were all certain that it was only a matter of time until the Russians took over, and then there would be no more Republic of Lithuania and no possibility of emigration. Being shipped off to Raseinai, we would be cut off from contact with the emigration market.

And still the entire world continued to keep its doors closed to the stranded refugees.

Approximately three hundred of us boarded the train to Raseinai — students and faculty members with their wives and children. I obtained permission to leave the train at Kaunas because I wanted to deliver Papa's regards to his old friend Rabbi Samuel Snieg, who was now the chief Jewish chaplain of the Lithuanian army, with the rank of colonel.

When the train stopped at Kaunas I got off, and by asking directions of several people, I finally located Rabbi Snieg's office. He sat there behind a huge desk, stern and dignified in his Lithuanian army uniform.

"My name is Chaim," I said, timidly introducing myself, "and I'm the son of Alter Tiktiner."

Hearing this, the colonel looked at me and broke into a radiant smile. He opened his arms wide, embraced me and gave me a welcome kiss. Papa had predicted that he would greet me this way, and he had been right.

Rabbi Snieg and I had a lengthy conversation, during which I brought him up to date on my father and our family. Then he took me outside to see some of the sights of Kaunas. The colonel looked so handsome in his colorful officer's dress uniform that I was proud just to be walking next to him.

We arrived at the large, impressive Central Synagogue, a truly majestic-looking building.

"Right here on this street, Chaim," he told me, "your father and I used to stroll for hours on Shabbos, discussing every subject under the sun. Sometimes your father would fall silent and clasp his hands behind his back, and at these times I could tell that his mind was traveling far away. I soon learned that I must not disturb him at such times.

"He was brilliant," Rabbi Snieg continued. "On the one hand he was like any other young boy — full of jokes, life, and laughter — but at the same time, he wrote a brilliant, scholarly book on the subject of abstention. But I'm sure you must know all about your father's book, don't you, Chaim?"

"Oh, yes sir," I replied. "It's called _The Vow of a Nazirite_, and its about the laws and rules of becoming a _nazir_, and leading the life of one."

The colonel was pleased at my quick reply.

We were walking up a high, steep hill to the Central Synagogue which was situated at the top. We had almost reached the door when suddenly a strong gust of wind blew off the colonel's hat. I ran after it, caught it and returned it to him.

"There's a well-known story," he said, "that Napoleon passed by on this very hill on his march to Moscow, and the wind blew off *his* hat." Then he added pensively, "I wonder how many more army leaders will pass by here and lose their hats...and maybe even their heads."

Is he thinking of the Russians or of the Germans, I wondered.

Inside the synagogue we *davened Minchah*, the afternoon prayers. Then I said good-bye to my father's old friend and returned to the train station, taking the next train to Viduklis. From Viduklis it was a horse-and-wagon ride to the small town of Raseinai.

By Lithuanian standards it was considered a large town, and the Jews there welcomed us with brotherly love. The largest synagogue in town was assigned for the use of our yeshiva. We students were placed in private Jewish homes all over town.

The Jewish families considered it a privilege to offer succor to refugees, and they also felt it to be a singular honor to have yeshiva students in their homes. I was assigned to a childless, middle-aged couple, the Boracks, together with a student from Germany, Asher Katz (who presently lives in New York). These gentle and kind people treated us as if we were their own children. It was almost embarrassing to hear them say, as they often did, how honored they felt to have two yeshiva students living with them.

Within a few days, things settled down and the Kamenitzer Yeshiva was back in business again. During World War I, the yeshiva had been in flight from Kaunas and fled to Russia and then to Vilna. From Vilna it had gone to Kamenitz in Poland, and from there back to Vilna, in Lithuania. Now the yeshiva was again on the run, but still functioning, still teaching and still accomplishing wonderful things! And so we students again dedicated our days and nights to our studies.

Meanwhile, we had been supplied with the coveted Curaçao visas,* which had been obtained from Sweden by Rabbi Shlomo Wolbe (who presently lives in Jerusalem). In the event that no other country — including the United States — would issue us entry visas, at least we would be able to flee to Curaçao. But first and foremost, we needed passports; without them, we could not go anywhere, not even to Curaçao!

And so we waited — anxiously, prayerfully, helplessly — for our passports to arrive.

The international situation was deteriorating rapidly. On April 10, 1940,

---

* See Appendix.

Germany attacked Denmark and Norway, and swiftly conquered them. By May 10th, Belgium and Holland were conquered. The "Western Front" crumbled; England lost its continental army, managing to bring only a few survivors back to England in the Dunkirk evacuation. The French army collapsed and was utterly routed — all in an interval of only a few weeks.

Realizing that the Germans had now become the undisputed masters of Europe, the Russians began to reveal signs of anxiety. Despite their "Twenty-Year Treaty of Friendship" with Germany, they began to consolidate their position. This required, among other things, that the Lithuanian-German border be strengthened. However, the Lithuanian army could not be relied upon to repel a German invasion; Russia itself would have to man the line. The only practical way to bring this about was for Russia to swallow up the tiny Lithuanian Republic.

Russia chose to do this by politics, rather than by war. Towards the end of May, the prime minister of the Lithuanian Republic was invited to Moscow. With precision timing, a well-known Lithuanian Communist journalist, Justas Paleckis, and the country's poet laureate, Kreve Mickievicius, publicly appealed to Stalin to "help us, and liberate us from the capitalists and the fascists — the blood-suckers of the proletariat."

Suddenly, organized mass demonstrations of workers were held in the streets. On June 14, 1940, the Soviets presented an ultimatum to Lithuania, demanding that Lithuania (1) create a new pro-Soviet government and (2) permit the unrestricted entry of the Soviet army onto Lithuanian soil. Lithuanian President Smetanas abruptly flew to Germany, and it was alleged that he took with him the entire government treasury.

The Communist journalist Justas Paleckis was installed as the new prime minister, and then, by invitation, the Russian army moved in. On August 3, 1940, the government of the Independent Republic of Lithuania declared itself dissolved, and proclaimed Lithuania the "sixteenth sister republic of that happy family of nations, the Soviet Union, under the guidance of the great Yosipas Stalinas."

As the days went by, and some order began to replace chaos, we learned to our pleasant surprise that exit visas were still being issued to holders of passports. The Ministry of Internal and Security Affairs published a proclamation stating that all persons who wished to emigrate must register, which meant filling out a number of forms and furnishing three photographs. This we did, and thus we all became officially "registered."

Lithuania had always been a prosperous agricultural country. Its standard of living was considerably higher than that of neighboring Poland, and there was essentially no unemployment. Lithuanian agricultural products found a hungry market in Germany and Great Britain, and manufactured goods from Britain and Germany were always in bountiful supply in shops throughout Lithuania.

However, within a few days after the arrival of the Russian soldiers, the stocks in the stores and shops were depleted. With pockets full of rubles — with which there was virtually nothing to buy in Russia — they soon cleaned out the stores. Wide-eyed, the Russian troops learned for the first time that there were places in the world where people could buy anything they wanted — and without having to stand in line for hours! The Russian army wives were amazed and enchanted by what they considered the luxuriousness of the apartments of ordinary working people, and the Lithuanians now began to comprehend the incredible poverty which existed in Russia. These Russian women became the butt of jokes in every town. In their craze for silk (*sholk! sholk!*) the wives of the Russian officers dressed up in silk nightgowns and thus strolled off with their husbands to the parks and movies.

The average Russian soldier was understandably perplexed since, according to his daily ration of propaganda, he had been told that he was bringing "freedom and happiness to the starving workers of capitalist-ruled Lithuania." He was supposed to be liberating them, but he couldn't find anyone to liberate — except the storekeepers from their merchandise. The soldiers were chagrined at the lack of enthusiasm in the Lithuanians' reception of the "New Sunshine" streaming from the Kremlin.

As for us, the first sign of hindrance to our prospects for emigration came from *Intourist*, the Soviet agency which has exclusive rights over foreign tourists and transit passengers throughout the Soviet Union. Suddenly, *Intourist* refused to accept rubles, the Russian currency. It demanded, instead, American dollars.

The price for one fare from Kaunas to Russia's far-eastern port, Vladivostok, had now been doubled to the sum of three hundred and sixty American dollars — but the irony of it was that possession of foreign currency was illegal. If one was caught with even a single American dollar, or any other foreign currency, the penalty was ten years in prison or in Siberia. Yet here was *Intourist*, an official Soviet agency, demanding that one must bring to its office three hundred and sixty American dollars — and in cash!

Soon we found ourselves confronted with yet another obstacle. It was decreed that since Lithuania was now an integral part of the Soviet Union, one no longer needed a transit visa; instead, one needed a "permit to exit from Russia." This, on the face of it, sounded ominous. In any event, before even applying for such an exit permit, a visa from another country was needed on one's passport. And to further compound our troubles, all consulates and embassies in Kaunas had been closed by the Russian authorities. Henceforth, all consular activities would be conducted from Moscow.

We soon heard that the Japanese consul in Moscow was refusing to honor the Curaçao letters, as he had apparently discovered that they were not visas in the legal sense. This was a formidable blow to our hopes of emigration. The local forgery factories, able to forge almost any document or visa written in Latin letters, were at a total loss when it came to forging Japanese characters. Then it was discovered that there existed another Japanese consulate, this one in Chita, a city in far-eastern Russia. The chargé d'affaires there, we heard, _was_ granting visas on the basis of the Curaçao letters.

Finally the great day arrived and we all received Polish passports from the Polish embassy in Berne, Switzerland. Almost immediately, we left Raseinai, three hundred strong, and trekked to Kaunas to obtain the precious exit permits which would enable us to travel through the USSR to Japan.

When we arrived at the NKVD (Russian Secret Police) office in Kaunas, however, we were dismayed to discover that it was no longer in business! On the locked door there was a sign tacked up which announced: "By order of the Commissar for Internal and Security Affairs, the issuance of exit permits has been discontinued." We were dismayed; many of us cried. All dressed up, and nowhere to go! The passports were finally in our possession, with forty blank pages for visas, but now we could no longer leave!

Actually, this closing of the emigration doors had been expected, for we knew that emigration was contrary to the very nature and tradition of the Soviet Union. To paraphrase their propaganda: "One must be an imbecile or a subversive to want to leave the happy heaven of Communist Russia in exchange for enslavement under capitalism." We were miserable, not only because the emigration door had been shut, since we all knew that this would happen sooner or later, but rather because of the shock of the timing. All the time that the door had been open, we had had no passports; now we had passports, but the door had been slammed abruptly, right in our hopeful faces.

People whispered that the reason emigration had been allowed until now was in order to permit the Russians to send out spies along with the refugees; since that aim had been achieved, the door was closed. There was another rumor as well: the British in Palestine had discovered forged entry certificates, and had reported this to the Russian authorities. This was a great embarrassment to them, for under their very noses, a forgery factory was producing fake documents! Worse, they had issued exit visas and transit visas on the basis of these forged documents!

The Secret Service flew into a frenzy of action. They arrested a girl who was known to be active among Zionists. They tortured her until she died, but she did not reveal any information about the forgeries.

They did discover a small printing press which had been used for clandestinely printing a pocket-size Hebrew calendar, and had been operated by one of our own students. Fearing that, under the Russians, Jews might not be able to obtain Hebrew calendars and thus might be confused concerning the dates of the various holidays, he had published tiny three-year and ten-year calendars. For this he was sentenced to ten years in Siberia.

Facing dismal reality, I came to the conclusion that I ought to go back home to Lomza. I immediately mailed a letter home.

"The first-born's illness is worsening," I wrote. "Doctor says nothing can be done; the only remedy is mother's care." Papa replied in a letter which he mailed from another town, with a false name and a false return address:

"It is not that simple. The border is still guarded as before. From experience we presume that it won't be lifted until all capitalists and fascist elements are cleaned out of Lithuania. Besides, home town has been declared a border area and is off limits, even to Soviet citizens. The local population is furnished with special passes, with photographs attached, and these must be carried at all times by persons of sixteen years and over. It will take some time, and some doing, to get the same for first-born."

What an ironic twist of fate! As difficult as it had been for me reluctantly to escape from home, it now appeared that it would be just as difficult to get back home!

There was nothing I could do now but wait. Meanwhile, I spent my days studying at the yeshiva as usual, and my evenings in the home of that kind and generous couple, Mr. and Mrs. Borack.

5

THE GOVERNMENT placed six Soviet officers in the Boracks' house. Mr. and Mrs. Borack were required not only to house them, but also to serve them meals. I lost my room to them; I now slept on the sofa in the living room. These Russians were engineers, engaged in building an airfield near Raseinai. One of the six, I discovered, was Jewish. Another was a Bashkir from the Urals, a member of one of the many nationalities which make up the Soviet "melting pot."

The Jewish captain occasionally spoke Yiddish with me, and I learned some Russian words from him. However, I noticed that although he would speak Yiddish with me without hesitation in the presence of any of the other officers, he stopped abruptly whenever the Bashkir appeared. I soon realized that the Bashkir was not an engineer but an agent of the military secret service.

Prudence required me to arise early every morning and be out of the house by the time the Russian officers came down to have their breakfast. Usually I returned to the house at noon for a combination breakfast-lunch. One day, when I arrived for my meal, Mrs. Borack whispered to me that the Bashkir had been snooping around inside my battered suitcase.

Before I had finished eating, the Bashkir lieutenant came into the kitchen. Looking at me with cold, prying eyes, he exclaimed, "So, you are a Samurai!"

I didn't have the slightest idea what the word meant, but I could tell that it was not a compliment! His voice was stern and his manner was accusatory. My Russian was rudimentary, but Mrs. Borack knew Russian and she translated for me. "Samurai," she told me, "is a derogatory way of saying 'Japanese.'"

With the food still in my mouth, I burst out laughing. I realized at once that I shouldn't laugh — that it might enrage him — but I just couldn't restrain myself.

After a moment I calmed down. "What, me, a Japanese?" I asked the Bashkir, smiling.

His face remained dead serious. He pulled a postcard out of his pocket and triumphantly handed it to me. It was a card from my former roommate, Asher Katz, which I had received several days ago. It was indeed from Japan, from the port of Kobe. Asher had written that he had passed through Russia without serious incident and that he was now in Japan.

With the aid of Mrs. Borack, who acted as interpreter, I attempted to convince the angry lieutenant that, although the card was indeed from Japan, it was not from a Japanese; that it was written by a fellow student who only recently had been my roommate right here in this very house. Mrs. Borack even took him upstairs to his room and, pointing to the Bashkir's own bed, she emphasized that this was where the young man had slept until his departure only a few weeks ago. She assured him that neither Asher nor I was a *Samurai* spy.

This was my first face-to-face experience with a Soviet Intelligence officer. It was apparent that none of our explanations allayed his suspicions. He persevered: why was it that Asher Katz had left but I had remained here? Mrs. Borack replied, innocently enough, that Asher Katz, being a German citizen, had a passport and thus had been eligible to obtain a Russian transit visa and an exit permit. Unfortunately, her explanation only added fuel to the fire.

"Aha!" he raged. "A German, eh? The Germans and Japanese are allies. Their spies work together. The German spy has fled, but the *Samurai* spy remains!"

Mrs. Borack then translated this for me, and I replied, "So are Russia and Germany allies."

She suggested that it would be better if she did not translate this, so I contented myself by saying, "It is ridiculous to accuse a Jew of being a spy for Germany, or even for Japan. They are our worst enemies."

But the suspicion remained, and as a result of this episode, all the other officers — even the Jewish one — thereafter avoided me as if I were poison.

Only one week later the Bashkir reopened the case; this time he accused me of being an agent of the British Empire! He had been waiting for me at the door when I arrived home. Poor Mrs. Borack, standing behind him, was pale and nervous.

"What connections do you have with the British Empire?" he shouted in my face.

This time I did not laugh. I was very much aware of the fact that this was not a laughing matter, but rather a terrible danger to my future.

"The British Empire?" I asked. Meanwhile, my mind was racing furiously, trying to figure out the cause of this new accusation. I had been in correspondence with one cousin in Australia, and another cousin in Palestine. Both of them had tried their utmost to obtain an entry visa for me; both had been defeated by the iron walls of the immigration policies of their respective countries.

I said, "I suppose you have another letter for me?" I strove to appear calm, but in fact I was trembling with fear. After all, this man with the twisted mind could very well send me to Siberia if he took a notion to do so. In fact, with this spy charge he could even get me executed!

With a victorious smile on his face he reached into his pocket and pulled out an envelope.

"This letter," he exclaimed, "is from India!"

I began to ransack my memory: whom did I know who would be writing from India?

"From India!" he shouted at me. "Do you hear me?" His furious eyes were darting back and forth between me and Mrs. Borack.

I concluded that he must be bluffing, playing some kind of an "espionage" game with me. I felt confident that I had him licked when I replied, in an assured voice, "There must be some mistake. I don't know anyone in India. I've never written to anyone there."

Then he poked the envelope straight in my face and shouted, "This time you'd better tell me — what's your assignment? Who is your contact? Talk!"

I stared at the envelope in his hand. It was in fact addressed to me, and the postmark was "Bombay"! Now my knees began to shake. Slowly I reached for the envelope and looked at the sender's name. This was a letter from one of my favorite study partners, Shraga Plontchak (who presently lives in Israel).

Shraga's older brother had been fortunate, and had obtained a British certificate authorizing him and his family to enter Palestine from Lithuania. This required that they escape across the border into Lithuania. At about the same time that I had crossed over, Shraga and his older brother had also been crossing the border. Shraga, who was very short, posed as his brother's son, and the two headed for Palestine.

The envelope in my hand had already been torn open by someone. I pulled out the letter and hurriedly read it. Shraga wrote that when they had arrived in Moscow, the authorities had issued them a 24-hours-in-Moscow pass. They went immediately to the Turkish embassy, with the expectation of obtaining a transit visa through Turkey. To their horror, this was refused. It seems that the Turks were claiming neutrality: "Since all Polish citizens are subject to being drafted by the British army, Turkey cannot conscientiously violate its neutrality by increasing British might with two additional soldiers." The penalty for remaining in Moscow beyond the twenty-four hour limit would have been exile to Siberia, and the hours were ticking away fast. There was no Polish embassy, for Poland had severed relations with Russia when Russia had crossed its border. In a panic, Shraga and his brother fled to the British embassy. The British consul, sympathetic to their plight, had gotten them on a plane which took them to Bombay, India.

I decided to read the entire letter aloud to the Bashkir. Mrs. Borack translated each and every word. After we had finished, I said, "Britain and Japan are at war against each other. How can I be a spy for both of them?"

Although I feared that my explanations were falling on deaf ears — it seemed that his mind was impenetrable — he did not arrest me. However, from that day on I was constantly under his surveillance. After all, it wasn't every day that a Soviet security agent landed such a big fish: living under one roof with Soviet officers who were building top-secret airfields near the German border, there was a Japanese-British spy, posing as a 19-year-old rabbinical student!

I was not the only one under suspicion. My yeshiva, too, had by now become the object of surveillance by the NKVD. One day the Dean, Rabbi Naftali Leibovitz, was summoned to the NKVD office. It wasn't until the next morning that he returned home, limp and shaken. He had been interrogated throughout the entire night. They had demanded to know how the school existed: were we American or British or German spies?

Rabbi Leibovitz had explained that there were some devoted, compassionate Jews in America who sent money to the yeshiva. The Russians, however, insisted that we must have been repaying the Americans by furnishing them with certain services, such as spying. Besides, they said, it had been a considerable length of time since any funds had arrived from New York; "So how does the school exist?"

The rabbi dared not tell them that the Jews of the local community were also helping us, since this could have jeopardized all the Jews of Raseinai. Nevertheless, the Communists must have had some inkling of knowledge about this. Shortly before, a Mr. Caplan had organized a special clothing fund for making new suits for all the yeshiva students, since there were no ready-made suits. The committee had paid the tailors, and some of the tailors might have been Communists and reported the enterprise to the authorities. I, too, was now dressed in a new, custom-made, English wool suit.

Before another day had passed, the Dean was again summoned to the NKVD office for another night of incessant interrogation. He was constantly told by his interrogators that a man of his caliber should not lie. They demanded that he confess and admit that we were all spies and enemies of the Soviet Union. Of course he denied all these charges, and although they released him the following morning, it was obvious that they were not yet finished with him or with us. He told us that he feared gravely for the safety of the students and the faculty and their families.

"I can smell Siberia," he told us.

One Sunday morning we arose to hear dreadful rumors — all "wealthy" and all "politically unreliable" people had been arrested during the night, and the same had been taking place all over the country! The word "Siberia" and its euphemism, "White Bear," were fearfully whispered everywhere. Every man, woman and child was well aware of the horrors of this vast, frigid prison, where nine-month winters could produce temperatures of 20 to 30 degrees below zero. Siberia was the ultimate exile, for escape was impossible.

We yeshiva students had no illusions about our status. We realized that the Communist regime considered us "politically unreliable," and that our own arrest was only a matter of time. It may have been merely a technical problem, since the police could not round up all political unreliables in one night. When they were ready to arrest us, they would do it during the day, since that was when we were all together right here in the synagogue. What an easy prey we would be!

To observant Jews, as we were, the word "Siberia" evoked additional dread. To live an observant Jewish life under the existing atheistic regime, to avoid working on the Sabbath, to organize some sort of kosher food supply, to have a synagogue to pray in and to instruct our children secretly in the traditions of Judaism — in other words, to live even a minimal religious life — would be impossible if we were prisoners in Siberia.

When I returned to the house that afternoon, I was met by a weeping Mrs. Borack. I thought that she was crying because of the mass arrests of the previous night. Then I learned that there was a more immediate reason for her tears.

She whispered to me, "I overheard the Bashkir saying, 'Tonight it is the *Samurai*'s turn. And that whole gang of parasites.'"

She did not need to explain. I understood that the "*Samurai*" was me; and that all clergymen, which included all the faculty of our yeshiva, were "parasites" in the Soviet vocabulary.

I rushed back and sounded the alarm. Although it came as no real surprise to learn that we were all earmarked for arrest, this was still the first definite news of an exact date. Had a stranger been there observing our general reaction, he might have described it as lethargic or apathetic, but the truth was that we were engaging in the highest spiritual level of *bitachon* — faith in the Almighty.

There are three levels of *bitachon*. The lowest level is demonstrated by working frantically, as though fate depended only on one's own efforts, while of course hoping that God will help too. The next level consists of working moderately, and hoping that God will bring about factors to ensure success. The highest level is achieved when all human means are exhausted and there remains only the hope that it will be God's will to do all that needs to be done — through a miracle!

Our present predicament was very similar to that of the Jews of thousands of years ago. After their liberation and escape from slavery in Egypt, they were trapped between the great uninhabited desert — our Siberia — and the Red Sea — the Baltic — and were pursued by the relentless hordes of Pharaoh — Hitler.

At that time Moses had said to them, "Fear ye not. Stand still. You will see the salvation of the Lord, which He will work for you today. Be still; the Lord will fight for you" (Exodus 14:13 and 14).

This was *bitachon* at the highest level — but there was no Moses among us now, and therefore how could any of us be certain which level of *bitachon* was the correct one for this situation?

Our school body consisted mainly of two groups: those whose parents and homes were in western Poland, now under German occupation, and those whose parents and homes were in eastern Poland, under Russian occupation. Obviously, those whose homes had been seized by the Germans simply had nowhere to flee. On the other hand, those who, like myself, had a home in Poland should perhaps make an effort to escape from here, and try to get back. In other words, we should engage in a lower level of _bitachon_.

The mere thought of Mama losing another son — this time because of the Russians, after having already lost one son to the Germans — was unbearable. I began to feel an overwhelming compulsion to run back home. It was as though the force of a thousand magnets was drawing me home, home to my dear mother.

I had now made my decision and I told myself firmly, despite all the Lithuanian Communist police, and all the Russian sentries, and all the closely guarded borders, and all the hundreds of miles separating us, and Papa's grave warnings to me, with God's help I will make it home. I _must_ make it home!

I WENT to Rabbi Leibovitz and told him what I was contemplating. I asked for his permission to leave, and his blessing.

With tears streaming down his face and into his gray beard, he grasped my hand and said, "We have no right to hold anyone. Go in peace! Let us pray: 'Show us, God, Your Grace.'"

The old rabbi said no more. In his helplessness, he began to sob quietly.

I asked some of my friends who were comrades from Lomza or other towns in eastern Poland if they'd be willing to go with me. Everyone rejected the idea.

So as not to arouse the suspicion of the Bashkir, I didn't take any luggage with me. With my *tefillin* in one pocket and a tiny *Tanach* and a Hebrew calendar in the other, I said good-bye to the Boracks, who both cried and tucked a wad of rubles into my hand.

Slowly I set out on my journey, on foot, from Raseinai to Kaunas. After I was certain that I wasn't being followed, I quickened my pace. As I left the city limits, I met a peasant woman wearing *kloompas*, Lithuanian wooden shoes, and carrying two full buckets of water. This was supposed to presage good luck. Even to one who was not superstitious, any encouraging sign was welcome at a time like this! I was aiming for Slobodka, a suburb of Kaunas. There was a famous yeshiva there, where my father had studied. I hoped to find lodging, food and rest there while planning my next move — how to get across the border to Soviet-occupied Poland.

After walking all night, I arrived at the yeshiva at noontime. Across the street, there was a huge sign posted: "One Who Does Not Work Does Not Eat." This was a Marxist-Soviet warning to all clergymen, who are considered *darmoyedniki* — those who eat for nothing, who do not produce, since they do not work. In this case it was a direct insult and threat to the school's faculty and students.

Inside the building I was astonished to find everything littered and in disarray. I sat down on a bench to rest a bit, but just then a man poked his head in the doorway and whispered to me, "The police raided this place last night, and again this morning. They're arresting everyone. Run, young man, run!"

"Refugees," in Lithuania, were always people who had escaped from Communism to freedom; but now that Communism ruled Lithuania, a refugee automatically became "an enemy of the state," "an enemy of the Revolution." By its very nature, a yeshiva was considered a nest of enemies of the state, and I, whose photograph was in their hands, was here in this most dangerous place! I left promptly.

I began walking towards the city of Kaunas, and soon approached the bridge over the Nieman River. A number of Russian and Lithuanian sentries were patrolling it. If they would demand to see my documents, it would be the end of my journey home; instead, I'd be shipped to Siberia. But since I wanted to go home, I had to reach the railroad station, which meant that I had no choice but to cross this bridge and pass those sentries!

I tried to put on a confident expression, and strode onto the bridge. They looked me over but did not challenge me. My new suit and new hat, and my confident air, pulled me through this crisis. The fact that I had passed this test boosted my morale considerably.

At the station, visions of home filled my head, but they were premature. There was a cordon of police sentries at all the doors of the station. All persons entering and leaving were required to present their documents. If the students of my school had already been rounded up, they would know exactly who was still at large. The government was looking for me, and the police had my picture. I dared not stand there too long gazing at the inaccessible railroad station, for this might attract the attention of a policeman. But where could I go? Where could I rest, and think, and plan?

Suddenly I remembered the Central Synagogue, on the hill, where I had once *davened* with Rabbi Samuel Snieg! In such a large building there was surely a spot where I could hide and sleep overnight. But suppose the police were there? They might be lying in wait inside, waiting for refugees such as myself to wander into their trap. Having no alternative, I decided that I had to take that chance.

When I arrived at the synagogue I avoided using the main front or rear entrances. Instead, I went up the stairway to the ladies' balcony, tiptoeing as quietly as possible, keeping my ears open for any telltale noises. When I reached the top of the stairway, I opened a door which I hoped might lead to an attic. I had guessed right — behind this door there was a narrow stairway, leading to a dusty, low-ceilinged room. I closed the door behind me and sneaked up the steps.

It was dark up there; there were no windows. Thanks to a bit of daylight which came in under the cracked cornice, I was just barely able to make out an old bench. However, it was covered with a thick layer of dust, and it occurred to me that I should keep my new suit in immaculate condition, for its very newness kept me looking *not* like a refugee. I poked around a bit further and I found an old upholstered chair which seemed cleaner. With my handkerchief I disposed of as much dust as possible, and eased myself down into the chair. How good it felt to be resting!

Sitting there, I contemplated my predicament.

I realized that there was no longer any possibility of getting help from friends or through connections. Those who had not yet been arrested were living in imminent danger of being caught. All of us were hunted animals now! I sat in the gloom and lost myself in thoughts.

Suddenly, out of the dark, a shadow appeared. I was petrified! Then a second shadow, and a third — I was so frightened that I almost stopped breathing. Was I dreaming?

One of them came up very close to me, so close that I could feel his breath. He scrutinized my face for several moments, and then I heard him exclaim, "Chaim!"

I was stunned!

And then I recognized him — he was a young *chasid* from Lublin who had been a fellow-student in the yeshiva in Baranowitz. Two companions were with him.

The boys told me how they had escaped. The Russian and Lithuanian police had descended upon their school, in Ukmerge, and were rounding up everyone for arrest. During the first hectic moments, these three had jumped out of a window, unobserved by the police.

They had been hiding here in this attic for two days, with nothing to eat in all that time. They dared not show themselves on the street, for their clothes were shabby enough to label them as "refugees." Seeing these three terrorized, starving waifs made me realize all the more how much like hunted animals we were.

I asked, "Aren't there any Jews who come to the synagogue to pray? Couldn't they bring you food?"

"The Russians have confiscated this building," they replied. "It will be converted into a theater or a factory or something. Meanwhile, no one is permitted to come in here. Didn't you see the poster on the door?"

"No," I replied. "But what about the sexton? Surely he can come in."

"He refused to hand over the keys to them, so they arrested him," they answered.

Then I asked, "Are you all trying to get back to your homes?"

This evoked a melancholy look on their faces. After a moment, one replied, "We are from Lublin." He didn't need to say any more. The city of Lublin was now under German rule. There was no reason to go back there.

"Well," I said, changing the subject, "I have the clothes and the money, so I'll go out to a store and buy us some food."

Before I left I asked them whether anyone ever patrolled the building, and they said no. I walked down the stairs and slipped out of the building. It was only a block to the nearest grocery store.

During the next two days I made many trips to the vicinity of the railroad station. I was groping for a clue that would tell me how I could get past the police without being asked to show my documents. To avoid becoming conspicuous, I did not stop and stand around the square where the station was located. Instead, I continued walking right on through the square, and then around the block, while making mental notes of my observations.

As unobtrusively as possible I walked near the area of the railyards. I thought that perhaps I might be able to jump aboard one of the trains while it was leaving the station, before it picked up too much speed. I saw, however, that the railyards too were crawling with guards and railroad employees, and I concluded that there was no hope of jumping aboard a departing train.

Another thing I noticed was that the horse-and-buggy taxicabs were prohibited from unloading their passengers onto the sidewalk alongside the station. Instead, they had to unload passengers and baggage on the other side of the square. Then the passengers had to haul their baggage all the way across the square to reach the station. This way, they were confronted by police at the doors of the station who asked them to present their documents.

I also observed that the Russian soldiers going to the trains were loaded down with suitcases. Obviously, before going back to "Mother Russia" they had bought everything they could carry — for what was the good of taking any rubles back to Russia when there was nothing there to buy?

Walking back to my hideout, I conceived a daring plan. It was a wild idea, but if it worked, it would get me on one of the trains. And if it failed, I'd still get a train ride — to Siberia!

Near the synagogue I stopped at a grocery store and purchased a substantial quantity of food. I took it to our attic hideout and bid my companions farewell.

"This is the last batch of food, fellows. I'm leaving. I'm going to try to get aboard one of those trains. I have an idea — maybe it'll work, maybe it won't. Anyway, I'll have to take a chance and make my move.

"Friends," I continued, "hold on to this postcard. It's stamped and addressed to my family in Lomza. Wait three days, and then mail it. By then I'll either be home or on the way to Siberia."

On the postcard I had written to my parents: "Chaim is traveling. At this moment he is heading for home. Hope he gets there."

We bid each other good-bye and good luck, and I left.

When I reached the bottom of the stairs, I did not leave the building. Instead, I went into the synagogue for a last-minute plea to the Almighty, for I was greatly in need of courage.

All alone, surrounded by hundreds of empty pews, I found the solitude depressing. Again and again I reflected upon my situation and questioned my course of action.

Perhaps, I thought, I should have stayed with my yeshiva, after all. And if they are now on their way to Siberia, so what? God is there, too. Who am I to question the way He wants to run His world? Most likely I'll wind up in Siberia anyway, but instead of being with my devoted friends I'll probably be among thieves and murderers.

The last rays of the afternoon sun were streaming through the windows. They fell upon the tablets of the Ten Commandments and the two golden lions supporting them. No other sculpture is found in a synagogue except these traditional lions holding up the tablets. They symbolize the ancient proverb, "Be strong as a lion, to do the will of thy Father in Heaven."

How beautifully the golden letters of the tablets glowed in the sun's rays! "I am your God," beamed the first commandment.

Suddenly a strange thought occurred to me: since this building has been confiscated by the Communists and is to be converted into a movie theater or a factory, God forbid, then one might say that God Himself is also a refugee now! Both He and I are hunted and despised.

In that case, I am in excellent company indeed, I meditated; for to be close to God is the ultimate aim, the perpetual aspiration of a pious Jew. Still, to have arrived in God's company through the efforts of the atheists. . . . Well, I concluded, this must constitute an inferior level of religious attainment.

I looked up again at the Ten Commandments and this time my eyes were riveted to the fifth commandment: "Honor thy father and thy mother."

The very words "father and mother" evoked a throbbing pang of nostalgia. Suddenly, a realization overwhelmed me: it is because of Papa and Mama that I am a hounded refugee! It is _they_, not the atheists, who are responsible for my being "in God's company." Because of them I had deserted the ship, so to speak; and because of them, I would succeed in getting back home.

I ascended three steps onto the platform and walked several paces until I reached the Holy Ark, where the Torah scrolls are kept. I wanted to embrace a Torah scroll, and to pray, but when I opened the door I discovered that the scrolls were no longer there. It was good to know that the congregation had already removed the precious scrolls, preventing them from being desecrated at the hands of the enemy.

Across the top of the Holy Ark there was the traditional inscription in Hebrew, which stated, "Know before Whom you are standing." This inscription serves to remind one not to pray mechanically, by rote, or without emotion. I needed no such reminder. I put my head into the empty Holy Ark, and I prayed with such passion and feeling that I thought my heart would break. I cried like a helpless child — which is exactly what I was. For inside, I was terribly frightened, knowing that one wrong move meant I would never see my family again and I would be lost to them forever.

But how could I, young and inexperienced in life, expect to make no mistakes?

"If I succeed," I vowed to God, "the Torah will be my lifelong dedication and my way of life. For the sake of Papa and Mama who were willing to lose me forever for Your sake, and for Your sake only, please let my plan be successful.

"Watch over me — _Chaim ben Chava Ha-Kohen_ — and guide my

footsteps. Let me not falter or stumble, for the sake of Your Holy Name."

I felt refreshed and encouraged. Quietly I left the synagogue.

Outside, I marched off in the direction of the railroad station, with head held high and confidence in my stride. Meanwhile, I was reviewing my plan. It was daring, it was audacious — but now I was convinced that it would succeed!

Finally I arrived at the familiar square where the railroad station was located. I casually walked through the square and around the block several times. Then at last I spotted my quarry...a short, round Russian colonel. He had a heavy suitcase in each hand, and another bulging suitcase under each arm.

I dashed over to him.

"May I give you a hand, Comrade Colonel?" I asked. "I am going to the same train, empty-handed. I'll be happy to carry two of your suitcases."

This was a crucial moment. My heart almost stopped. He might become angry at my impudence. He might become suspicious and call over a policeman.

He opened a mouth full of straight, white teeth, and he said the crucial words: "Yes, thank you, Comrade." His face spread into a wide smile, forming deep dimples on his clean-shaven cheeks.

Instantly I grabbed two suitcases. "We'd better hurry," I said, "or we might be late for the train."

I kept so close to him that he stepped on my feet several times, but I felt no pain. He engaged in some small talk, but I refrained from replying because, by now, we were within earshot of the police and I certainly did not want the police to overhear my poor, accented Russian. Therefore, I merely nodded in reply, and smiled, and grunted now and then.

My plan was based on the premise that, since I was accompanying a Russian officer, the police would assume that I was either a secret agent or a foreign-service agent; for they were the only Soviet civilians who wore fine clothing. My new suit and hat, together with my companion — a Russian officer — should be sufficient to deter the police from inspecting my documents.

It seemed forever before we finally arrived at one of the station doors.

We walked right in! Apparently the police on the outside of the station were all Lithuanians, while the police on the inside were all Russians.

Well, we had passed through the Lithuanians; now to bluff my way through the Russians! Inside, the colonel asked directions of a Russian guard who pointed to the proper gate. Here there were two ticket controls. In order to go from the lobby of the railroad station to the platform alongside the tracks, one had to show his ticket to a gate officer outside. Later, aboard the train, one surrendered the ticket to the conductor.

Now we were approaching the gate officer, who was checking the tickets of all who passed through. I dashed ahead of the colonel. Just before we reached the gate officer I turned around and, pointedly addressing the colonel, I called, "*Pozdno! Pashli!* — It's late! Let's go!"

The Lithuanian guard didn't dare ask to inspect the tickets of a heavily burdened Russian officer and his important-looking companion.

Now we were past the gate officer. Just a short walk further, and we were next to the train. I headed for the carriage nearest us, but the colonel called, "No, not this one. Up ahead, that's where the first-class cars are."

In my haste I had forgotten. There was a choice of three classes of railroad cars, luxurious first, second, and shabby third, determined by the amount of the fare. True, we were supposed to be living in a classless society now, but colonels are colonels the world over, even Russian ones, and colonels ride first class.

We arrived alongside one of the first-class cars. The colonel opened the door of a compartment, and we shoved in the four heavy suitcases. We climbed in and he closed and locked the door behind us. Then we sank down upon the elegantly upholstered seats.

He was breathing heavily from the exertion. I struggled to avoid doing the same, fearing that if I breathed heavily I might attract someone's attention. I wanted to be as inconspicuous as possible. Not only had I stalked the bear's den, but now I had entered it!

I realized that at any moment now the colonel would start asking me friendly questions — what was my name, where was I going, what was I doing here?

Silently I begged God to put the right words in my mouth.

What could I answer if he questioned me?

I didn't even know the destination of this train! Was it Moscow? Leningrad? Riga? Vilna? Minsk?

Casually I looked out the aisle-window. What I saw on the next track almost made me faint. I saw a freight train, comprised of many cattle cars, constructed of boards with open spaces between the slats. Inside the cattle cars I saw masses of people — men, women and children so tightly packed that there was scarcely room to breathe.

The sight of this horror nauseated me. I mumbled something to the colonel and dashed out the door to the men's room, to vomit.

Once in the aisle I could actually hear the anguished cries of the captives in the train passing us.

Fortunately, the men's room wasn't locked.

I wondered whether I knew any of these hapless prisoners. Perhaps my own Kamenitzer Yeshiva was part of that Siberia-bound load!

While I was still in the lavatory, our train began moving out of the station. I washed my face and tried to collect my thoughts. I came to the conclusion that I must destroy my Polish passport. It was a dangerous document, for it practically announced: "Here is a Pole; worse, a Jewish refugee!" Also, the very fact that I was here in Lithuania was clear evidence that I had fled "Russian-liberated" Lomza.

I ripped apart my passport. Swiftly I tore each of the forty pages into little scraps, and flushed them down the toilet.

How my heart ached! If this passport had arrived just one month sooner, I might have been safely in Japan by now.

I decided to save the first page. It had my photograph on it and a Polish Embassy Seal affixed to it. Beneath the picture there was a physical description of me. The only other document which I now possessed was my birth certificate, in Russian, which Papa had mailed to me. I tucked them both into a slit in the waistband of my trousers. The belt kept them well-hidden and well-secured.

I returned to the compartment, bracing myself for the avalanche of questions I expected from the colonel; Russians have a notorious reputation for being inquisitive and suspicious. I wondered whether I might avert some questioning if I could keep him preoccupied. Then I remembered....

While I had been living together with the Russian officers in Mrs. Borack's house in Raseinai, I had noticed that Russians are avid chess players; in fact, chess is a national obsession. They concentrate deeply, play seriously, and remain almost silent during the game. Conversation, especially small talk, is definitely frowned upon. If I could engage the colonel in a game of chess, I might be spared some questioning. Also, the poor level of my Russian might remain undiscovered.

No sooner had I re-entered the compartment and closed the door behind me than I said, "I wish we had a chessboard. I assume you play, Colonel?"

His round face grew rounder as a big smile forced his fleshy cheeks out, almost covering his little eyes.

"I have a set right here," he replied, reaching for one of the suitcases. He pulled out a beautiful, brand-new chessboard. Snapping the suitcase shut, he commented, "Back home one cannot find a table made of such fine quality wood. Here they use it for chessboards!"

He set up the board and the chess pieces, but before we began to play he casually asked whether I'd like something to eat. Without waiting for my reply, he pulled out another suitcase; out of it came bread, salami and a bottle of vodka. True, I was certainly hungry. However, for me to eat non-kosher meat was unthinkable! Of course, I dared not explain why I could not accept his generous offer of salami, for this would surely bring up the subject of religion — and religion was the last subject in the world I wanted to discuss with the Russian colonel.

He insisted, most graciously, that I share his food with him; and I declined, graciously but firmly.

"But you won't refuse a taste of vodka, Comrade?" he asked.

I realized that many people considered it tantamount to an insult to be refused when they offered a drink. But I knew, too, that even the smell of alcohol would make me sick. Also, my dangerous situation demanded perfect sobriety; sickness or drunkenness would be disastrous. However, under the circumstances, I felt that I had no alternative but to accept a drink.

"For the sake of companionship, I will," I replied.

Even while I said this, the colonel was already pouring vodka into two tea glasses. One, half full, he handed to me; the other, three-quarters full, he retained.

"This is not *samogonka* — home-made, illegal brew," he said, "but the real stuff — delicious, genuine vodka!" Then, "To happiness!" he declared as he clinked his glass against mine.

In a moment he had gulped down all the liquor in his glass.

I pretended, as best I could, to be sipping mine. It must have been quite obvious to him, however, that I was a novice at this sort of thing, for he launched into a lecture on "how to drink and not become drunk." He demonstrated.

Dripping a few drops of the vodka onto a piece of bread, he handed it to me and said, "Here, smell it; the longer the better. Then eat the bread.

After that, you can drink and drink, and you'll never get drunk."

I sniffed and ate the vodka-saturated bread obediently, like a pupil obeying his teacher, but I postponed drinking the vodka.

We began to play chess. I did not play a good game, for my mind was distracted. For one thing, I was contemplating the problem of how to dodge the train conductor who would be coming around for our tickets soon. For another, there would be an inspection of documents as soon as we reached a border. I wondered, too, about the destination of this train; and I certainly couldn't ask the colonel!

He beat me with ease on the first game. I did better on the second game, but still he won.

By now it was dark outside. Fortunately, he had not asked me any questions so far. He poured himself another glass half-full of vodka, and gulped it down. Then he stretched and declared that it was time for bed, adding, "I have a busy day ahead tomorrow in Moscow. I hope they don't wake me up at the border with their silly controls!"

Now I knew that this was a Moscow-bound train.

I had already concluded that this was an express train, judging from the way we whizzed through a number of towns without stopping.

Well, let's see, I thought to myself. Even a Moscow-bound express train ought to be making a stop in Vilna. Maybe I should get off there, for it might not make another stop until it gets to Minsk, inside Russia.

The colonel had extracted two thick new blankets from one of his suitcases. He handed one to me, and said, "Here you are, Comrade; the nights are cold. By the way, how far are you traveling?"

"The first stop after Vilna," I replied, hesitantly.

"Aha, that must be Baranowitz," he said.

"*Pravilno!* — correct," I exclaimed.

Now I breathed more easily. Not only had I been able to answer his questions successfully, but I had also learned that this train would be stopping at Baranowitz. Baranowitz would be the perfect place for me to get off, for it was across the border, in Russian-occupied Poland. But that still left me with the problem of how to avoid the document inspection which invariably took place aboard all trains crossing all borders.

In fact, and more to the moment, how would I avoid the conductor, who would soon be coming around collecting tickets? I concluded that even if I should be lucky enough to hide from the conductor, I couldn't expect my luck to pull me through the document inspection as well.

Therefore, I concluded, I'd have to settle for getting off the train in Vilna, rather than taking a chance on crossing the Lithuanian border into what was formerly Poland.

The colonel's snoring might have been irritating to anyone else, but to me it was like music. After all, it was he who was affording me this opportunity to escape and reach my home. In fact, it was just as well that his snoring was keeping me awake, for I could not afford the luxury of sleep. I had to stay alert and prepare myself for the hazards which would confront me only too soon.

As the train rounded a curve, it brought the moon into view. Moonlight gleamed upon the three large stars on the epaulets of the colonel's over-coat, which was hanging near the window. Suddenly an idea struck me! I jumped up and pulled his coat off the hanger. Then I lay back down on the seat and, curling up, I covered myself with it. Now I, too, was a Russian colonel! No Lithuanian conductor would dare to awaken us colonels!

I congratulated myself for this brilliant idea.

Good, fast thinking, I said to myself; but another voice within me seemed to reply, Wait with your compliments until it is all over!

Eventually I heard the distant sound of the conductor's voice; he was calling out to the passengers to be ready with their tickets. Again, I directed a desperate supplication to God: "Do not forsake me, but protect me at this time of trial."

I could hear the conductor moving through the next compartment. In a few minutes I would know the verdict: success or failure. Suddenly I realized something: my civilian shoes were showing! My shoes would give me away! Moving as swiftly as lightning, I flung off my shoes, hid them under the seat, and inserted my feet into the colonel's big, knee-high army boots, which had been standing nearby. In another moment, I too was "snoring."

The conductor knocked on the door. Getting no response, he opened it with his passkey. My heart beat faster and louder. I started snoring even more heavily, to cover up the loudness of my heartbeats. I could sense the conductor's flashlight sweeping the compartment. Finally he mumbled one word to himself: _pulkonikas_ — colonels, in Lithuanian.

He closed and locked the door behind him!

Still stiff with fright, I whispered my thanks to God: for having sent me the colonel, for having given me the idea, and for having given me the courage which it had taken to accomplish it.

Now I began to feel a rising and inordinate self-confidence. Since this ruse had worked successfully on the conductor, why shouldn't it work on the Russian document inspectors, too? I glanced at the colonel; he was still snoring deeply. Moonbeams were playing on his face, and I thought I detected a slight smile. Did he know what had been going on? Or was it only that he was having a lovely dream?

Then a strange thought entered my mind. Perhaps he is not a Russian colonel at all! Could it be that he is Eliyahu *Ha-Navi* — Elijah the Prophet? According to the *Kabbalah*, Elijah appears, in all forms and shapes, in order to help people who are in distress. How else could the colonel's strange, un-Russian actions and attitude be explained? His mysterious smile, and even his snoring, suddenly became objects of reverence for me. I could hardly believe that I, Chaim, merited having as my traveling companion none other than Eliyahu *Ha-Navi*!

My reverie was broken by the voice of the conductor, who was calling out, "Vilnius! Vilnius!"

Soon the train came to a stop in the station. I could see that the place was swarming with policemen and, presumably, undercover agents. The sight of so many policemen convinced me that, despite the help of Eliyahu *Ha-Navi*, it might be safer to stay aboard and take my chances on somehow passing the document inspection at the border.

While the train was standing in the station, dreadful sounds of screaming and crying reached my ears. I peered out into the dark. What I saw and heard out there nearly sent me retching again. On a nearby track was another train-load of cattle cars packed with people, like the one I had seen earlier, and heavily guarded by Lithuanian and Russian soldiers. A Jewish girl, perhaps eighteen years old, was standing on the tracks, crying and begging the guards to let her get into a cattle car.

Apparently she had not been at home when her family was arrested. Now she had located them — they were inside this particular cattle car — and she was screaming hysterically at the soldiers to open the door and let her join her family. Several times the guards chased her away at bayonet point. Soon she would reappear, pleading with them to let her in — but to no avail.

I sat frozen in my seat, my face pressed against the window. I cried silently with her.

After an endless fifteen minutes our train started moving out of the station. It jerked several times, and I feared that the colonel would wake up. If he should awaken during the document inspection at the border, I wouldn't be able to use the same ruse as before; but fortunately, the bumping and the jerking of the train did not awaken "Eliyahu."

My premise that the inspection would take place as soon as we pulled out of Vilnius turned out to be correct. Very soon I heard a voice, in Russian, booming, "Prepare documents for inspection!"

Well, I was ready for them. Russian army boots were on my feet, ostentatiously poking out from under my Red Army overcoat; the three stars on my epaulets were distinctly visible. My face was almost hidden underneath the wide coat collar. I started snoring loudly, while silently pleading with the Father in Heaven to see me safely through this hazardous situation.

Then — a knock on the door! The inspectors are here!

They don't even wait for an answer; at once they unlock and open the door. Swiftly they step inside and switch on the lights. For what seems to me to be an eternity there is only silence. At last one of them speaks:

"You'd think two officers with a bottle would have invited somebody else to share it!"

To which the other one replies, "Nah, they're so drunk they must have finished it all themselves."

The first one apparently had picked up our bottle of vodka, for he exclaims, "Wow! These guys must be out cold. But look — they didn't even finish the bottle!"

He then invites his partner to take a swig, but the partner declines. "Not while we're on duty, old friend," he says.

They start out the door. "*Shchastlivye snee, Polkovniki!* — Happy dreams, colonels!" one says, and they lock the door behind them!

Drops of moisture rolled down my face. When they reached my lips I realized that they had a salty taste. They were tears — but tears of happiness, tears of thanks, to God and to Eliyahu *Ha-Navi*.

"Yes, I made it, I made it!" I whispered to myself under the colonel's thick coat. I was safely over the border! I couldn't believe it — imagine — just like that!

"Papa! Mama! I'm coming home!"

After a while the excitement within me subsided, and I returned to reality and began to make plans again. I had to be absolutely certain to get off this train at Baranowitz. This was crucial, since it was the last stop on this side of the Russian border. I knew the city of Baranowitz well, for I had studied there for three years, at the yeshiva of Rabbi Elchonon Wasserman.

I remembered an elderly man, a shoemaker, whose combination home-and-workshop was located not far from the railroad station. A very religious Jew, this old gentleman had always refused to accept money from the rabbinical students. When we would implore him at least to accept payment to cover the cost of the materials he had used, he refused, explaining that "a society of Jewish women repays me for the expense of the materials." I'm sure he was not telling us the truth, especially since I had once heard him say to a friend that he considered it to be "not only a *mitzvah*, but an honor to be making shoes for yeshiva students." I decided to seek refuge in the home of the shoemaker.

Soon the conductor could be heard announcing, "Baranowitz next, Baranowitz next!" Outside, the lights of the suburbs were beginning to appear. A few minutes later the train pulled into the station.

"Eliyahu" was still sleeping and snoring. I hung his coat up again and whispered to him, "I thank you. And my mother and father thank you, too."

But when I looked out the window and saw that no one else was getting off, and that this station too was crawling with police, I became frightened. I stayed aboard, growing increasingly panicky with every passing minute. At any moment now the train would begin to move. I was in a quandary.

Just then another train pulled into the station, and a number of passengers poured out. Heading from their train to the lobby of the station, they passed right by my door. I opened my compartment door, stepped down, closed the door behind me, and lost myself in the crowd.

7

"COME IN, come in!" the old shoe-maker called. Though he was only half-awake, he recognized me — at least, he claimed he did, and I entered. Inside, he pointed to the ceiling and, whispering, he told me that a Russian officer, and his wife and children, lived upstairs. He took me into the kitchen.

The old man's wife shuffled sleepily into the room and joined us. As soon as we had shaken hands, she immediately started preparing tea and something for me to eat. When I apologized for all the bother I was causing them, she replied, "Not every day do we have the honor of such a visitor!"

I explained my situation to them: that first, I had to write to Papa who would try to procure Soviet documents and mail them to me. Only after this, I explained, could I safely go home to Lomza.

The old folks assured me that I should consider this as my home as long as I needed it. As for the Russians upstairs, we agreed that I should be presented to them as a visiting nephew.

"How goes it with the yeshiva?" I inquired.

The old man grew misty-eyed as he told me what the Russians had done to the beautiful yeshiva building. It had of course been confiscated, and was now a cooperative shoe factory. Then, growing indignant, he said that they'd had the gall to assign him to work there, as a foreman and instructor.

"May my hands dry up and my eyes turn blind before I'll ever set foot in that desecrated holy building!"

The old couple furnished me with a blanket and I went to sleep on the sofa.

In the morning, the old lady sent off a telegram to Papa and Mama in Lomza. It read: "Cousin Chaim was very ill. Feels much better now. May have visitors."

I knew that this would bring Mama posthaste to Baranowitz. I was thrilled and excited, anticipating the reunion. I knew, too, that Papa would intensify his efforts to procure the necessary documents to enable me to come to Lomza. The old lady happened to make a comment, however, which cooled off some of my excitement.

"Well, today is Friday," she mused. "Let's hope your parents will get the telegram by Monday. This is what is known as Soviet efficiency."

To pass the time, I played with the children of the Russian lieutenant who lived upstairs, and the lieutenant and I played several games of chess. Meanwhile, I was constantly improving my ability to understand and speak Russian.

At about three or four o'clock on Sunday morning, we were awakened by the sound of terrible explosions. Quite close to our house, a huge building, a warehouse for drums of gasoline, was burning ferociously. Intermittent detonations rocked the area. Then we heard the drone of airplanes overhead and afterwards the sound of many more explosions. Somebody said that we were being bombed by the Germans. We turned on the radio, but there was only silence. The street was alive with excited, bewildered people.

With the light of dawn, we could see another wave of airplanes approaching. They were flying in formation, very high. Suddenly they dropped what looked to me like hundreds of sticks. Moments later these "sticks" — they were bombs — reached the ground and again there was explosion after explosion. Some of these were close enough to shake the house. We threw ourselves on the floor and automatically put our hands over our heads to protect ourselves from flying debris and bomb fragments.

Russian soldiers by the hundreds were rushing past the house, going in all directions. Some of them were still in their underwear or pajamas. Disorganization and confusion reigned; panic was growing. Women and children were in the street, wailing hysterically.

We still had electricity though, and at seven o'clock the radio station suddenly came to life. The announcer said, "Stand by." In a few minutes, we would hear the voice of Vyacheslav Molotov, who would be speaking to us from Moscow.

Presently, Molotov's voice came on the air. He informed the peoples of the Soviet Union that "conniving Germany, with whom the USSR had signed a treaty of friendship for the next twenty years, had attacked!" He proclaimed that we were now at war, and ended his brief speech with a declaration which was destined to become a very popular expression:

"Under the leadership of the great Stalin, the invincible Red Army will crush the enemy and push back the attacking beast, Germany, in order to destroy her on her own ground! To victory with Stalin!"

It was a momentous day — Sunday, June 22, 1941.

The German air force met with no resistance, and only light anti-aircraft fire. They bombed Baranowitz mercilessly.

At noontime, the lieutenant arrived with an army vehicle to collect his wife and children, and evacuate them from the city. He invited the old couple to go along, but they refused.

"We'd rather await death right here, where we've lived for over fifty years," said the old shoemaker. His wife expressed her agreement by nodding her head, but tears welled up in her eyes.

"But if you don't mind," she said, "I would be very grateful if you would take our young nephew with you. He still has a long life ahead of him."

"Certainly," said the lieutenant, and I climbed into the vehicle.

"We'll be back in a few days," the lieutenant assured the old couple as he climbed into the driver's seat. "Our Red Army will certainly succeed in pushing the enemy back in no time."

We had driven only about two blocks when an army patrol stopped us. They shouted something to the lieutenant. All around us we saw the devastation which had been wrought by the bombs. Rows of houses were now crumbled heaps of mortar and lumber. Pictures of bombed-out Lomza flooded my mind and I thought of the unfortunate victims who lay buried under the debris. But I did not have much time to dwell on the subject, for we had arrived at the railroad yard.

We drove right up to a large crowd assembled near a freight train which was attached to a puffing locomotive. The crowd consisted mainly of women and children, although there were some men too. Many of the women and children were sobbing, while Red Army men were instructing them to climb aboard.

The lieutenant hugged his wife and children, shook hands with me and told us to get aboard. "This train will take you out of the city, to safety," he assured us. He remained behind.

As soon as the crowd was aboard, the train began moving, at first slowly, then more and more rapidly. We passed through one town after another. When I saw the sign "Stolpce," the last station on this side of the old Polish border, a horrifying realization struck me. This train was heading in the direction of the Soviet border — we were going to Russia!

A wave of utter desolation engulfed me. All my desperate efforts to get home, all my tribulations, had been in vain. Now what? How long would I have to stay in Russia? Days? Weeks? Perhaps months, or even years.

The thought of being alone without family or friends in Godless Russia made me oblivious to everything around me. It even overshadowed the heartbreak of my failure to get home. My mind was absorbed with the trials awaiting me, of living in this atheistic land. Was I strong enough, spiritually, to face this test?

Throughout my school years I had been taught that life is a series of trials and temptations, and that everything which God has created has a purpose. The question is asked by our Sages: "What purpose did He have in creating this world?"

The answer: He created it for man, who is the crown and the glory of His creation. God, the source of all goodness, willed to give everlasting happiness to mankind. However, man must earn it. For this purpose, and only for this, is man brought into the world, into this testing ground so full of traps and temptations.

Captive within a body afflicted with yearnings and ambitions — although these are counterbalanced by the soul and mind, and laws and rules by which one may live a righteous life — man is assured of either reward or punishment at the end. A formidable dilemma indeed; but what is the short span of life on earth in comparison to everlasting happiness?

"Know What is above you: a seeing Eye and a hearing Ear; and all your deeds are written in a book."

"Rabbi Jacob said: This world is like a vestibule before the World-to-Come. Prepare yourself in the vestibule, that you may enter into the banquet hall."

These words, from *Ethics of the Fathers*, reverberated in my mind and heart. Oh, how I wished now that I had never left Raseinai! If only I had remained with the others at the yeshiva, it would have been much easier now to face these tests. For man is a social creature, and he is strongly influenced — for either good or evil — by his surroundings; and the society which I was about to face was in direct opposition to the values I had absorbed since my earliest childhood.

Words from a lecture which I had heard long ago came to my mind: "A person will not be condemned for failing to reach the spiritual heights of a

Moses; but he will be condemned for failing to reach the limit of his own individual potential."

Since I was now being thrust, alone, into this Godless testing ground, the Holy Creator surely considered that this too was within the limit of my capacities. Right then and there I vowed to do my best to live up to my training, so that if, and when, I ever returned home, I would be able to face Papa and Mama — and above all, God — with pride and self-respect.

The train stopped outside the city, and the locomotive refilled its boilers with water from the huge water tower next to the track. Then the train chugged on, and soon pulled into the station in Minsk, capital of the White Russian Soviet Republic. Here we were treated to bread and *kipyatok* — boiling water. I tried to get off here, for I had decided to try to catch a train going back towards Lomza; however, no one was permitted to get off.

"We cannot allow refugees to flood the city and add to our troubles," the guards said.

A woman argued that she was the wife of a Red Army captain, and that their home was right here in Minsk. Nevertheless, even she and her children were prohibited from leaving the train.

Minsk was in flames, and nearby we could hear the deafening roar of gunfire, anti-aircraft artillery which was shooting at German planes. While we watched, Russian air force planes suddenly appeared and engaged the German planes in battle. Before it ended, two German planes were knocked out of the sky and went down in flames. For the first time I was witnessing effective resistance to the Germans. Russia wouldn't be a pushover for the Germans, as Czechoslovakia and Poland had been, I thought.

Our train remained in the station only long enough for some more cars, packed with fleeing Russians, to be attached to it. Then we went on, riding all through the night.

After dawn the next morning we reached Smolensk. Again we were served bread and boiling water. During our break, we again saw German planes appear, dropping bombs upon the city. I shuddered when I realized just how many bombers Germany must have. The war was only two days old, yet many cities had already been devastated by German bombers — even cities deep inside Russia, like Smolensk.

This time I managed to leave the train. Resolved to get on the first train going west, I sat inside the station and waited. The tremendous surging crowd of travelers was bedraggled and tattered. At best, their clothes were shabby; many were in rags. My new suit stood out like a beacon, marking me as a foreigner (and, presumably, as a Western capitalist).

For the hundredth time I wondered if my parents had received my telegram from Baranowitz before the German attack. Suddenly two men grabbed me by my arms.

"*Pashli so mnoi* — come with me," one barked.

Keeping their grip on me, they led me out of the station and into a building next door. Entering, I saw a sign: *Narodny Komissaryat Vnutrenyikh Dyel*, Smolensk — NKVD — Peoples' Commissariat for Internal Affairs.

They took me straight to a captain, who immediately demanded to see my passport. Since I didn't have one, the only thing I could produce was my birth certificate, in Russian, which Papa had sent me.

The captain studied it, but became furious. "You mean to say that this is all you have to show? No passport, no photograph?"

In my broken Russian mixed with Polish, I explained that I had been living with relatives in Baranowitz when, early yesterday morning, the Germans had bombed the city. Hastily I had donned my good suit, never dreaming that I'd be leaving for a trip to Russia. A Russian officer had taken me to the railroad station together with his wife and children. We all assumed that the train was simply going to take us to safety outside the city, I explained, but instead it had brought us all the way here to Smolensk. In all the confusion and panic, who could remember to take along a passport? Even the Red Army officer's wife hadn't thought to bring her documents or the children's. It was only by pure luck, I added, that my birth certificate happened to have been in my pocket.

"So why did you get off the train here?" he demanded to know. "You were certainly told that you may not get off here!"

I replied, truthfully, that I got off because I wanted to take the first train going back.

"I am confident that the invincible Red Army will be pushing the enemy all the way back to Berlin in a few days," I said, and then hastily added, "under the leadership of the great Stalin."

I thought that this little speech of mine would help me. I was stunned, therefore, when he leaned over, close to me, and whispered, "Tell me, you're a spy, aren't you? What's your assignment here in Smolensk? Who is your contact?"

Now I began to grow really nervous. I stepped back a pace or two and replied, trembling, "Comrade Captain, I am a Jew. How could I possibly spy for the enemy of my people? That is ridiculous! Surely you know what the Germans are doing to the Jews?"

Again he closed in on me; he put his face so close to mine that I could smell his breath. This time, however, he didn't whisper, he shouted at me. "What do you take me for, a *durak* — a fool? Who says you are not a German? This lousy scrap of paper?"

He waved my birth certificate in my face. "Your hair is blond, your skin is fair. Come on now, make it easier on yourself; I can get it out of you, anyhow. So what's your assignment? Who's your contact here?"

Now I was panic-stricken. The NKVD had a reputation, even during peacetime, for torturing and killing suspects. Now, in wartime, who knew what they might do to me?

"Comrade Commandant," I protested, "if I were a spy, as you suspect, would I be conspicuously dressed up in a suit like this, attracting everyone's attention? Why don't you confront me with another Jew? Then I can convince you!"

That did it! He returned my birth certificate to me and ordered a policeman to escort me to the station next door, and to see to it that I was put on the first train going, not home to Lomza, but east.

"East, Comrade?" I objected. I was certain that he had simply made a little mistake.

"East!" he repeated, very deliberately.

The policeman took a couple of steps towards me and barked, "Get moving! Let's go!"

However, the commandant had some parting advice for me. "Comrade, in our glorious Soviet Union, no one makes decisions of this sort on his own. That would be anarchy! Here you obey orders, in time of peace and certainly in time of war! You'd better do as you are told or you'll find yourself in great trouble. Do you understand?"

I assured him that I understood. He handed me a loaf of bread and we proceeded to the station next door.

The next train that came along was also loaded with people heading east, to Moscow. The policeman put me aboard.

Eventually we arrived at a station just outside of Moscow. There we heard the familiar refrain: "The city prohibits more refugees from further inundating it." The engineer was ordered to transport us to Kuybishev, which is a city located on the Volga River, 530 miles southeast of Moscow.

Twenty-four hours and several *kipyatok*s later, we pulled into the station in Kuybishev. It was late at night. A long line of trucks was waiting, which transported us to a dock on the Volga. We clambered aboard the ship that met us at the dock.

I searched out a space with the fewest crying children and sat down on the wooden deck. It was quite chilly. I sat there, immersed in thought.... I thought about the strange coincidences which had brought me here to the Volga River, deep within Russia, far past Moscow. This was the place where the Siberian steppes begin.

An old man with a silver-gray beard asked if he might sit next to me. I was surprised, and impressed by his good manners.

"Certainly," I replied, and I moved over on the cold deck to make room for him.

He introduced himself as Professor Konstantin Ivanovich Rimanov. Before I could reply, he continued, "I can tell by your clothes that you are a Westerner. Welcome to our great Mother Russia!" I couldn't tell whether this was said with sincerity or sarcasm.

"I can see you are shivering, young man," he said, and offered me his coat. I thanked him for his gracious offer, but declined.

We started to talk, and I learned that he was a professor of languages, and that he was fluent in French, German and Polish. I was happy to find someone I could speak Polish with, for speaking Russian was still difficult for me.

The professor's last position had been at the University of Vilna. We discussed Vilna and Lithuania and Poland and the West in general. He was a man who knew the outside world, unlike the younger generation of Russians. In earlier years he had visited France and Germany. He commented that he found it much easier to discuss these things with a Westerner than with the Russian youth.

"Also, it's much safer," he added, winking an eye. "You have probably heard the joke about the Russian who looked into the mirror and said, 'One of us is an informer!'"

The professor and I found much to discuss, and I began to feel that we shared a mutual feeling of trust. And yet, when I asked, "Professor, what do you think about the war?" I still deemed it prudent to add the "insurance clause": "Of course, Professor, there's no question but that the invincible Red Army, under the brilliant leadership of the great Stalin, will beat the stuffing out of the Germans."

In the moonlight I thought I observed a smile through his silvery whiskers. His forehead creased like an accordion, and his clear eyes gazed into the distance. For a moment he remained silent, then he turned to me and said, "My dear young man, let me tell you a story. It's only a legend, but it makes the point.

"When Napoleon's army had reached the suburbs of Moscow, the great Napoleon himself arrived there one day, resplendent in his glittering coach.

"Every house or barn or shed had been burned to the ground — by the Russians themselves! This was General Kutuzov's famous scorched-earth policy, the idea being that the enemy should have absolutely no shelter from the fierce Russian winter.

"Well, Napoleon spied a Russian soldier off in the distance. He stopped his coach and sat there for a few minutes, observing him. The soldier was hungry, but all he had, apparently, was one piece of bread and it was frozen solid. The Russian tried but couldn't break off even one little bite from the bread. He then tried to smash the bread into pieces by hammering at it with a stone, but to no avail; the bread remained in one solid frozen piece. So finally — you must excuse the expression, but there is no other way to tell this legend — the Russian relieved himself on the bread. This softened it, and the soldier proceeded to eat it!

"When Napoleon saw this he turned to his aide-de-camp and declared, 'We are surely doomed to defeat. No Frenchman could do that. No soldier can endure like a Russian!'"

The professor rested for a moment, then continued. "A Russian soldier can live on frozen potatoes and still fight. This is what defeated Napoleon then, and this will defeat Hitler now!"

He looked around, checking to be certain that no one nearby was eavesdropping on us. Then he whispered, "If only they would stop beating the drums about the Socialist *Fatherland*! Instead, they should say that *Mother Russia* is in danger. Love of Mother Russia, not socialism, is what evokes the feelings of the masses and motivates them to make any sacrifice."

The professor seemed to enjoy having a good listener; the lecturer within him was rising to the surface. "Let me show you the heart of Mother Russia. You will almost be able to hear it beat."

He asked me whether I had ever heard of Stenka Razin and "The Volga Song."

"No," I replied.

He smoothed his long moustache a couple of times, as if to get it out of the way of his words: "Stepan Razin, whose nickname was Stenka, was a Cossack from the River Don. In the 17th century he organized an uprising against the tyrannical Czar and the big landowners; he escaped with his followers, and the Czar's police put a price on his head.

"One day, he and his group of warriors were floating down the Volga River on a barge. Stepan's comrades revealed to him that his girlfriend was a traitor — an agent of the Czar's secret police, the dreaded *Okhrana*. At first, he refused to believe the dreadful charge, but after much discussion his followers finally convinced him that it was true: his dearest companion and confidant was a spy!

"Stepan strode to the other end of the barge, and without a word grabbed his faithless companion and threw her into the raging waters of the Volga. Screaming, crying, pleading for mercy, protestations of innocence — nothing helped.

"Stenka just stood there, expressionless, watching until all struggles ceased. Then, with tears streaming from his eyes, he began to sing: '*Volga, Volga, mother of our country/ Volga, you Russian river/ Did you see the gift/ From a Cossack of the Don?'*"

The professor recited this poem with emotion. In Russian it rhymes beautifully.

"In time," he told me, "this poem became a song. Not just *a* song, but one that became ingrained into the very soul of the Russian people as a symbol of sacrifice. Want to see something?" he asked. "Watch all these sleeping Russians come to life!"

He started singing the song again, in a warm baritone. By the time he had finished one verse, several people nearby had joined him. Soon, many more joined in the choir, at first softly and then, like a wave, a powerful chorus rang out over the river. A soldier joined in with a harmonica, an old peasant with a balalaika. It was such a moving experience that I got goose pimples all over, and tears filled my eyes. Even the river seemed to respond to this inspiring chorus; the waves slapping against the side of our boat sounded like applause.

It was an unforgettable experience. For the first time, I was meeting the heart and the soul of the Russian people: oppressed, hungry, poor, a nation which had never had even a bit of freedom or democracy; and yet, a proud people determined that no invader would ever conquer them.

Eventually the singing and music subsided. The night grew quiet again, and there swept over me the memory of another sacrifice which had taken place in this same Volga River.

In 1825, Czar Nikolai decreed that Jewish children were to be rounded up and shipped off to serve a twenty-five year hitch in the army. This was only a new twist to the venerable tradition of trying to assimilate the Jews. Jewish children were kidnapped by the thousands and shipped across the continent. When they reached their destination, Christian clergymen were waiting for them, happy at the prospect of having so many Jewish souls to save. These children were known as _kantonisten_ — recruits.

No one will ever know how many thousands of such children were kidnapped, never to see their families again, but this incident is known and recorded: in 1825 over a thousand Jewish children were lined up along the banks of the Volga River, to be converted en masse. The ceremony began, and when the priests reached the appropriate part of the liturgy, the army officers instructed the children to wade into the water to be baptized.

The oldest children were 13 years old. As they marched into the river, some of the older boys declared that they would rather drown themselves than be converted to Christianity, and exhorted the younger children to do the same.

"For a Jew, even death is better than life as a Christian!"

These thousand children kept on going deeper and deeper into the river. The Czar's officers shouted orders to return to the shore, but the children continued to wade forward. Many were chanting "_Shema Yisrael_ — Hear, O Israel, the Lord our God, the Lord is One!"

The army officers cursed at the children's insubordination and the priests screamed about ingratitude and everlasting damnation, but the children — every one of them — ended their young lives in the depths of the Volga.

The sound of the water slapping against the side of the boat made me think of little hands applauding, praising such heroism. I wondered whether I would be capable of such an act of martyrdom. My parents were, of that I was certain. After all, they had sent me away, out of their lives, for the sake of the Almighty; certainly they would not hesitate to give their own lives for our faith. And my little brothers, and my fellow students from the yeshiva — what tests, what sacrifices were in store for them?

I remained absorbed in these thoughts for quite a while. Suddenly I realized that the professor was no longer beside me. I looked around, and saw him bent over the ship's rail. I walked over to him and discovered that the old man was crying, and I joined right in, crying with him.

The loneliness, the distance from home, the atmosphere of the night, the haunting Russian ballad and the thousand children's faces gazing up at me from the black water below all combined to open a fountain of tears within me. I wept and wept, and the professor wept together with me.

Suddenly we glimpsed bright lights, high up on the bank ahead. In a few minutes I was able to distinguish watchtowers, and soon we were so close that I could see the guards within the camp, and the clustered barracks and barbed wire fences. I turned to the professor and naively asked him if this was an army camp. The professor did not reply; instead, he turned away from me. At first I thought that this was out of embarrassment, because I had seen him weeping; but it was nothing of the sort. He placed his arm around my shoulders and said, "I was afraid you would ask me about that place. Of course, you'll find out about such things sooner or later, but I didn't want that to happen at the beginning of your acquaintance with our land. I wanted you to see only the good of our land, the beauty of our people, our roots and our strength; not our shame, our guilt, our wretchedness."

I didn't know what the professor was talking about.

"Normally," he continued, "I wouldn't dare tell a stranger what I am about to tell you; but I am convinced that you are trustworthy. I have seen you crying, and I know that only a good man, a man whose heart has compassion, is blessed with tears. So I will tell you this: In the Soviet Union there are three categories of people...."

"But Professor," I interrupted, "I thought that the Soviet Union is a classless society."

The old man smiled sadly. "I didn't say three *classes*; I said three *categories*. They are: one, the ones who were; two, the ones who are; and three, the ones who will be."

He paused a moment, to allow this complicated statement to register. Then he continued.

"Now, let me explain. I am speaking of that prison camp out there, which you thought was a military installation. Yes, son, to our everlasting shame, we have prison camps; plenty, too many, of them. And yet, believe it or not, it is almost a disgrace *not* to have been imprisoned in one at one time or another. The flower of our people — the scholars, the intelligentsia — one, they've been there; two, they are there; or three, they will be there.

"Nevertheless," he went on, "try not to belong to any of these categories. You are a foreigner; it would be just a waste of honor for you, too, to serve time in a prison camp. Keep your nose clean. Do I make myself clear, son?"

I nodded. I looked back at those powerful searchlights on the hill overlooking the river. They were probably anti-aircraft lights; their current assignment, however, was to light the ground and not the sky. Each watchtower had a machine gun aimed at the barracks.

"Professor," I asked, "to which of the three categories do you belong?"

Without a moment's hesitation he replied, "To the first, and I'm proud of it!"

He said this with such emotion that I realized I was touching a sensitive spot; I decided not to ask him any more questions about it. But he himself was not content to let it rest there, and continued.

"Especially when one is a teacher," he said, "sometimes just one word, even a wink of an eye, can get you into terrible trouble." He paused and heaved a sigh. "A professor who faces a class, and has to answer all kinds of questions — his danger is multiplied many times over. Sooner or later it is bound to happen, and eventually it happened to me. I was arrested. I had made a statement which, from the government's point of view, was counter-revolutionary."

He told me that after he was imprisoned, his wife died, broken-hearted. His son, a brilliant young teacher, vowed that he wouldn't rest until he obtained freedom for his father. He tried; and he tried so hard that one day he said something he shouldn't have, and he too was imprisoned. He was still there.

The professor, gazing back at the prison, said, "Who knows? My son might be inside that very prison camp!"

Turning to me again, he asked, "Would you like to know what it's like in those rehabilitation camps?"

"I would," I replied. "But did you say *rehabilitation?*"

"Yes," he said, "that's what they're called. Everybody knows that a house of correction does not correct, and a reformatory does not reform, and a penitentiary does not make penitents, so a brand new euphemism had to be created: rehabilitation camps."

He spat over the rail, into the river.

"And those places surely do rehabilitate, in a manner of speaking. They make thieves, liars and murderers of good decent people, because that's the only way a person can survive in those places!" After a brief pause, he said in a softer voice, "There is a famous expression about them:

> *Kto nye bill, tod budyet;*
> *A kto bill, nye zabudyet!*
>
> Who was not there, will be;
> And who was, will never forget!"

It was almost dawn when the boat tied up to a small dock, and all the passengers disembarked. Ashore, we were separated into various groups. The professor was put into a different group than I, and we bade each other a sad farewell. Trucks took the various groups to different destinations; to collective farms, we were told.

We traveled, mile after mile, over rutted dirt roads and at last we reached our assignment. The trucks unloaded us in a small town called Booyan, and I was assigned to *Kolkhoz Stalino*.

THERE ARE three kinds of farms in the Soviet Union. The first is the *soukhoz*, or state farm. This is a large, government-owned enterprise, on lands which once were owned by the wealthy and privileged, the nobility and the Church. The employees of a *soukhoz* are hired workers, just like factory workers, and are paid wages.

The second kind is the *kolkhoz*, or collective farm. On a *kolkhoz* the farmers themselves own the land collectively. Each assignment on the farm is worth a certain number of *trudo-dnee* — work-days. For instance, one day of digging potatoes is worth one work-day, but one day of working in the dairy barn is worth two, while the chairman of the *kolkhoz* earns five *trudo-dnee* per day. At the end of the year, after all taxes and other expenses have been paid (in produce, not in money), the balance of the harvest is divided among the farmers in accordance with the number of *trudo-dnee* earned by each farmer during the year.

The third, and disproportionately important, kind of farm is the private plot. Each family on a *soukhoz* or *kolkhoz* is allowed to cultivate its own little half-acre plot. In addition, each family may own one cow, which is allowed to graze on government-owned lands.

Providing these huge *soukhozi* and *kolkhozi* with the necessary tractors and other agricultural machinery is the job of the government-owned machine tractor stations. They are called, in abbreviated form, the MTS. Each *soukhoz* and *kolkhoz* pays the government in produce for the services of the MTS. The fees are, of course, set by the government.

One might imagine that the partner-owners of a *kolkhoz* would be more prosperous than the employees of a *soukhoz*. In fact, though, the opposite is usually the case. While the *soukhoz* employee is assured of his pay, the *kolkhoz* member often finds that he has worked all year for next to nothing, for taxes and the MTS fee have consumed nearly the entire harvest, leaving little, if any, profit. Fortunately, however, every farmer still has his half-acre plot and his cow and he hopes that this will provide him with minimal sustenance for his family.

When I arrived at the office of the *Kolkhoz Stalino*, the elderly foreman took one disgusted look at my hands and remarked, "*Rookee kak dyevushka* — Hands like a girl." He couldn't decide where to assign me, so he took me to the chairman. The chairman looked me over and declared, "*Karendashnik*" — slang for a pencil pusher, i.e., a white-collar man. He then gave me my assignment: "To the MTS!"

The personnel of the MTS, I learned, had been particularly hard hit by the draft. Since MTS men were proficient mechanics, they were especially in demand by the Army Tank Corps and the Air Force. Because the MTS manpower had been so severely depleted, there was no alternative but for every *kolkhoz* and *soukhoz* to send some of their own employees to the local MTS for a quick course in operating and servicing tractors, harvesters and threshers. The *kolkhozi* and *soukhozi*, themselves short of manpower, had been sending mostly girls to the MTS school. By sending me, the chairman could save himself a girl, probably calculating that she would be more useful on the farm than an inexperienced city boy like me.

I was worried, for without proper knowledge of the language, how could I possibly pass a course in mechanics? I was also completely ignorant about anything mechanical. In Poland I had never even seen a tractor, or if I had, I hadn't noticed! Here I'd be expected to learn how to operate and repair them.

The *Kolkhoz Stalino* had a quota of four to be sent to the MTS school. The other three, all girls, had already been chosen, but we wouldn't be sent until my papers were processed, which would take several days. (It appeared that I was "owned," for all legal and practical purposes, by the *Kolkhoz Stalino*. Various papers had to be prepared in order to transfer me to the jurisdiction of the MTS.) In the meantime, of course, there could be no loafing; so I was assigned to work in a field brigade.

The next morning our field brigade rode off in a horse-drawn wagon, the route taking us through the unpaved main street of Booyan. In front of one of the larger houses I noticed a line of waiting men, and in the back yard there were many women and children crying. I realized that this must be the draft board.

At last we arrived at the field. Our task was to thresh wheat which had been left over from last year's harvest. Wagons collected the bundles of wheat from the field and deposited them in front of the threshing machine. It was my job to feed the wheat stalks continuously into the hungry thresher, not allowing it to run empty.

I was the center of attention. First, there was the fact that I was wearing shoes; everyone else there was barefoot, including the foreman and the chairman! Then there was my fine English wool suit. I had taken the jacket off because it was hot, and several of the women were enjoying themselves by trying it on, modeling and posing in it for the amusement of their laughing friends.

After many hours of feeding the heavy bundles into the maw of the noisy thresher, I saw that the rough handle of the pitchfork was causing big blisters to develop on my hands. Soon the blisters opened and I saw that the handle was covered with my blood. This was the first day in my life that my hands had been occupied doing physical work all day.

The blizzard of chaff made it difficult for me to breathe, and my back, arms and legs hurt so much that I felt as if every bone in my body were broken. I stopped to wipe the sweat and chaff dust from my face and I noticed several of the women gazing at me queerly and crossing themselves. They told me that I looked like a ghost and urged me to rest; they were afraid I was not going to survive my first day. I swallowed my pride and accepted their advice, crumpling in a heap right where I stood. I felt much better when I remembered that my real assignment was to the MTS.

That night I couldn't sleep, not only because my bed was the hard floor of a barn, nor because every part of my body was aching. It was because I was engaged in a struggle with myself over a fateful decision: should I, or should I not, volunteer for the Red Army?

I acknowledged that I was not fit — at least, not now — for heavy farm work. Another thing: perhaps I would not even be able to pass the MTS training course, handicapped as I was with the language problem. And above everything else there was my hate for the Germans; desire for vengeance, retaliation and justice boiled within me. My youthful blood lusted to kill Germans.

Finally I came to a decision: I could accomplish more on the battlefield than on a farm. Tomorrow, I'd join the Red Army!

The next morning I was the first one in line at the draft board. The sign on the front door read "_Voyenny Commendant_ — Military Commander."

From the others waiting in line I learned that the commander himself was the entire draft board.

The sergeant in the front office handed me a form to fill out. When I told him that I could not write Russian, he looked me over from head to toe and then remarked, "*Aha, Zapadnik* — Aha, a Westerner!" He asked me my name and address and wrote them down on a blank piece of paper. Then he looked up at me and said contemptuously, "You may go back to the *kolkhoz* now. We'll know where to find you if and when we want you. At the moment our orders are not to accept Westerners." He winked at a clerk who was sitting at another table.

I was deeply offended. I was determined to know more about these alleged orders not to accept Westerners, so I said, "I insist upon seeing the *voyenkom* in person!"

The sergeant raised his eyebrows and replied coolly, "The *voyenkom* isn't here yet; come back later."

I stomped outside. After a while my anger subsided, and I realized that this was a perfect opportunity to stroll around Booyan and get a good look at the little town.

It was a dreary little town; there were no paved streets or sidewalks, only sand and mud everywhere. All the houses were constructed of logs, except for one very large brick building at the top of a hill. I found out that it was a factory which produced alcoholic beverages under the trade name of "Red Spirits."

For the first time in my life I saw oxen pulling wagons. I felt sorry for the poor animals, whose necks were rubbed raw by the crude wooden yokes. Some of the wagons were loaded with firewood, others with second-rate potatoes. Seemingly oblivious to the shouting and the whips of the drivers, the bony animals slowly plodded on, up the muddy hill towards the alcohol factory.

I passed a large wooden building which contained the school, a library and a post office. I learned that this little town was quite distinguished, as it was the regional center for a number of *kolkhozi* and *soukhozi* in the surrounding countryside, as well as for the MTS which serviced them all.

After a while I returned to the draft board, and the sergeant admitted me into the *voyenkom*'s office. The major was a heavy-set man. He offered me a chair and spoke to me in a friendly, fatherly manner. I was surprised at his civility; it was most unmilitary, I thought.

He asked me all sorts of questions, and I didn't mind telling him everything that he wanted to know. He said that he was pleased that I had asked to join the Red Army, "But what can I do?" he exclaimed. "Orders are orders, and my present orders are not to accept any Westerners."

He added some gratuitous advice. "But you know, before one can become eligible for the tough military discipline of the army, one must first prove his discipline in civilian tasks. We need bread to feed the army; so go on, young man, stick to the tractors, and supply the army with food. With the tractors, you are also doing your part to help beat the "Fritzes.""

He promised that he would induct me into the army as soon as the anti-Westerner order was rescinded. Then, with a friendly arm over my shoulder, he rose and began escorting me out of his office. Before we parted, I asked him for a favor.

"I have only one suit and one shirt," I told him. "I must get some work clothes."

With a broad, sympathetic smile he assured me, "That is the responsibility of the _profsoyuz_ — the union — at the MTS. You'll see, they'll certainly provide you with the necessary clothes."

Foolishly, as it turned out, I believed him... and went to the MTS in my good woollen suit.

The next day we were sent to the Machine Tractor Station, which was located not far from Booyan. The three girls from _Kolkhoz Stalino_ were in gay spirits, singing and joking. But I was morose, for the dread of failing here kept gnawing at me.

I was amazed by the large numbers of tractors and agricultural machinery on the MTS grounds. They were stored out in the open, while the repair garages and the administrative office were under a roof. We were informed that our classes would be held outdoors. In the meantime, until our first class would begin, we were invited to walk around and to get acquainted with the place and to meet the other students who were here from other _kolkhozi_ and _soukhozi_. Not all of my fellow students were Russians; there were also Mordvinians, Chuvash and Tatars. Even though each of these nationalities had its own autonomous republic, there were some ethnic villages here and there outside their own areas.

A ragged figure soaked with oil and grease crawled out from underneath a tractor. After he stood up, I realized to my amazement that "he" was a "she." Later, I saw other women engaged in all kinds of work which I had never dreamed possible for women: driving and greasing locomotives, loading coal, pushing heavy wheelbarrows, sweeping the streets, shoveling snow and so on.

Here, too, I was the center of attention because I was a Westerner. One of the students remarked, "I never realized there are people in the world who don't speak Russian!"

Then they were fascinated by my blond hair and city-white skin, and last but not least, there was my English wool suit. Although it was in dire need of a good cleaning and pressing, it nevertheless sufficed to make the right impression, or more likely, the *wrong* impression: "Capitalist!"

Our classes had begun. I was taught many new words, such as "radiator," "carburetor," "piston" and "battery"; it was a long time before I found out that these words were not really Russian. And to my great delight, I discovered that I was mechanically inclined after all. I was learning so much so quickly that I was quite proud of myself.

I had already done what the draft board major had advised me to do: speak to the *profsoyuz* — the union — about some work clothes. The union secretary was also the director for manpower at this MTS. He had asked me all kinds of questions about the unions in Poland. He especially wanted to hear about the Polish unions' "strikes against the bloodsuckers, the capitalists." I didn't know very much about such things, so I used my imagination to hide my lack of knowledge. As delicately as possible, I remarked that in Poland it was unthinkable for a "company man" to be a union official as well. He got the point, and launched into a didactic lecture on the subject of unionism in the Soviet Union.

"You see all those machines? All that farmland? Everything, absolutely everything, belongs to the people. To us! To all of us! We have no capitalists here to shear the poor, slaving sheep, like you have in Poland. So why should anybody here strike? The strike would be against himself! That's why we don't have any strikes here! And this is the greatness of Comrade Stalin. He has explained it so well that everybody can understand: it is no contradiction for a person to be a union official and a factory official and even a Party official, all at the same time. For a person really serves only one master: the people. Or the Party — which is one and the same thing, because the Party is the party of the people!"

I wanted to ask him, seriously, how the union sees its role and justifies its existence, but I decided against it. It would justify its existence, I meditated, if it would just get me a pair of work pants!

The gentleman assured me that after completing my training here at the MTS, I would be reassigned to a _kolkhoz_ or a _soukhoz_, and there I would be furnished with work clothes.

Foolishly, I believed him too.

One day during lunch a Mordvinian girl, who had seemed to be particularly curious about me, cornered me behind a harvester. Her freckled face was smiling, but also blushing. She asked me, "Is it true what you said, that you are a Jew?"

I was taken aback: in my pride at being a Jew, I was astonished at the way the question was put.

"_Konyechno!_ — Of course!" I exclaimed.

She told me that no one in the class believed it. "Everybody knows," she explained, "that Jews have horns."

Apparently these people had never seen a Jew, or rather, they were under the _impression_ that they had never seen a Jew. They had probably seen Jews but hadn't realized it, since their horns were missing! For a long time after that, whenever the villagers looked at me, I felt that they were checking — perhaps there were little horns hidden under my hair somewhere.

It was just about harvest time, so our training course had to be cut short. As soon as one became fairly proficient with a tractor, a harvester or a threshing machine, one "graduated." The graduates were assigned to various _kolkhozi_ or _soukhozi_. Wherever we were sent, there would be experienced MTS personnel there and therefore we could continue our training on the job. I "graduated" in less than two weeks, and was assigned to _Kolkhoz Karobka_.

Two experienced MTS men, old-timers, were due to leave here with a tractor and go to _Kolkhoz Karobka_, and I was assigned to go along with them. Fiodor, the older tractor man, was in charge. I asked him if I could drive.

"Not yet," he replied. "You might damage our socialist machine."

I studied his expression, expecting to see an indication that he was being sarcastic. But I looked in vain, for he revealed nothing of the sort. As time went by, I was to learn that it was standard practice to refer to valuable material as "our socialist" something-or-other, for, after all, it did belong to all of the people, not to a private owner.

Fiodor told Stepan to drive. I had met Stepan just yesterday, and we had had an interesting conversation. He told me that he hated tractor work, "but it keeps me from being drafted — and anything is better than going to the front!"

Stepan drove the tractor, Fiodor sat next to him and I sat on the back end. Mile after mile we made our slow and noisy way along a narrow, winding path; much of it cut through dense forest. There the path was overgrown with thick tree roots, which zig-zagged and intertwined, until they formed a heavy web over the path. At times we were riding on roots and not on the ground.

By late afternoon, we were within a mile of *Kolkhoz Karobka* when the radiator began to steam, so we stopped to let the water cool. We climbed down from the tractor to stretch our legs. While Fiodor poked around the engine looking for a possible water leak, I strolled into a thick grove of trees. The sudden cessation of the tractor's rumbling seemed to emphasize the vast silence.

The stillness was broken only by the sound of birds and crickets. The tranquillity was delightful. I inhaled the fresh aroma of the forest; I looked up to see the tops of the towering trees bending in the soft afternoon breeze. I ran my hands up and down some of the trunks to feel the differing textures of the bark. One tree trunk was so enormous that I could not resist trying to measure it. So with my arms stretched out wide I stepped right up to it and embraced it.

At that moment, someone behind me laughed uproariously, and a dog started to bark. Quickly I spun around. Standing close to me was an old man, as bony as a skeleton, and dressed in tatters from head to foot. The rags covering his body consisted of patches on top of old patches, in various colors; but despite all the patches, his scrawny elbows and knees poked out through big frayed holes. Just to look at him was frightening. In Poland, I thought to myself, a scarecrow would have been better-dressed!

His small, dried-up face peeked out from an overgrown bush of white hair. It was impossible to tell where the hair of his head ended and where his whiskers began. He continued laughing convulsively, revealing two lonely teeth; and all the while his dog circled and barked at me gruffly.

I ran back to the tractor, and the old man and his dog followed me. When Fiodor and Stepan saw him, they greeted him warmly, and introduced us. He was the shepherd of *Kolkhoz Karobka*. Although I had become accustomed to the local poverty, the appearance of this old man set new standards of destitution. How I wished for a camera! Without a picture, I thought, no one back home would ever believe me.

After a while, Fiodor decided that the engine had cooled off sufficiently, and it was time to go on. It was only a short distance, anyway, from here to our destination.

We started the engine and continued on through the dense forest. Suddenly, there was *Kolkhoz Karobka* before us: it was as though God had cleared out a tiny bit of the forest and installed there the little village of Karobka. The village consisted of perhaps thirty log cabins. In its center was a horse stable, a blacksmith shop and an administration office.

In front of the administration office, standing grandly, and waiting for us to turn off the engine, was a fine-looking old man. He must have been in his seventies, but he stood tall and erect. He had long, gray hair that hung down to his reddish-gray beard. His nose was flat and spread out wide, and his slanted Mongolian eyes seemed to reflect a kindly soul within. His most striking feature was a fiercely curled moustache that nearly reached his ears.

"Welcome, welcome, tractorists!" he called as we climbed off the tractor. He shook hands vigorously with Fiodor and Stepan. Then Fiodor introduced me to him.

"Comrade Anton Grigorovich, this is Chaim. He is a *Zapadnik* — a Westerner."

In Russian fashion, Comrade Anton Grigorovich stretched out his arms and embraced me, saying, "It's good to see a new face, especially a young one."

He was the chairman of *Kolkhoz Karobka*. Actually, his name was Anton Raskin, but according to Russian custom, when one speaks to a distinguished person, one addresses him by his first name and by his father's first name. Anton Grigorovich means "Anton, the son of Grigor." Children might address him as *Dedushka Anton* — Grandfather Anton.

A friendly, smiling crowd of villagers had gathered around us. From the way some of them stared at me, one would have thought I was a visitor from the moon. Their stares, and the giggles of the children, embarrassed me and I blushed deeply. The villagers in this isolated clearing in the vast Russian wilderness had obviously not seen many *Zapadnik*s, much less a Westerner wearing an English woollen suit!

Everyone, including the chairman, was barefoot.

Fiodor and Anton went into the administration office. Stepan headed for the well to get some water for the tractor. Now the smiling villagers encircled me, staring, but they turned away shyly when I looked at them.

Finally, one woman grew bold enough to reach out and touch my suit jacket. She stroked the English wool knowledgeably; then she made a face and nodded, indicating her approval of the quality of the goods! Everyone took turns feeling the wool and twisting the buttons of my jacket. Then the chairman came out of the office and rescued me. He chased the villagers away, ordering them to go back to work, and they dispersed, still chattering and giggling.

He took me by the arm and said, "Come, I will show you around our village."

He asked me where I had come from, and I told him that I was from Poland. He told me that during World War I he had been in the Russian army and had served in Poland, Rumania and Austria. In Austria he was captured and remained a prisoner-of-war there until the end of the war. Reminiscing about the "good old days," he said that the most difficult thing had been to get used to primitive village life again, after having seen sophisticated, gay Vienna.

He found an appreciative listener in me; I was eager to absorb the language and I was fascinated by the primitive and time-worn ways that the villagers followed here. A group of children followed us through the village, although they remained at a respectful distance.

"Don't mind them — they're just excited about seeing a stranger, especially a *Zapadnik*," he told me. Very few strangers ever came here, he went on to explain, because this village was very remote, even by rural Russian standards. As a result, there had been constant intermarriage between its inhabitants, so that by now all the villagers were practically one clan. These days, however, just about all of the males between 17 and 55 had been drafted and were far away; therefore, the village consisted mainly of women, children and old people. "And that's why we are all so happy to see a young man's face," he added, smiling.

Suddenly he stopped and looked me over, as if he were seeing me for the first time.

"Are these the only clothes you have?" he asked.

"Yes, Anton Grigorovich," I replied, "but I have been assured by the union secretary that *Kolkhoz Karobka* is well-supplied with work clothes."

The old fellow's eyes opened wide in astonishment. Then he burst out into a loud guffaw. "What, us?" he asked, incredulous. "Why, we ourselves don't even have enough clothes to wear! Everything that we wear, you know, we make with our bare hands."

At first I found it hard to believe; I thought he must be exaggerating. But I soon found out that what he had said was absolutely true. The villagers grew their own meager supply of cotton and raised their own wool, which they combed, spun and wove. Every house had a spinning wheel. The coarse fabric was sewn by hand into rough, baggy, ill-fitting clothing, which had to last for many seasons. The hides of sheep and wild animals were made into winter coats and boots.

Everyone went barefoot, except during the winter. However, on special holidays many of them wore _laptee_ — sandals. Anton showed me a pair of _laptee_, and explained how they were made. The bark of a tree was removed, leaving the inner skin of the trunk intact. This skin was stripped off and woven into sandals, which were then hung in the sun to dry and harden.

"Anyway, we just can't let you work on the tractor and ruin that beautiful suit," he declared. "Somehow, from somewhere, we'll get you some work clothes.

"But first," he continued, "we must find you a place to stay. Fiodor and Stepan have their own quarters from last year, but where shall we put you? Hmmm, let me think...." He mumbled some names of villagers, but apparently decided against them all. Finally he appeared to arrive at a decision which pleased him. He put his arm around my shoulders and said, "Young fellow, I like you. I feel we are going to be friends. You deserve the best quarters, the cleanest and the finest, and I've decided to take you to my daughter-in-law. My son, her husband, is away in the army, as are my two other sons, you know. And I'll go, too, if they want me — I'm a lieutenant in the reserves, you know."

We started off towards his daughter-in-law's cabin. Along the way, I asked him, "What's the latest news from the war?"

He prefaced his reply by stating that there was no radio or telephone in the village. "The village gets two newspapers every day, but they are about a week old by the time they arrive," he said. The newspapers were _Pravda_ — Truth, and _Izvestia_ — News. _Pravda_ is the organ of the Communist Party; _Izvestia_ is the organ of the Supreme Soviet. "But I really don't have time to read them," he told me.

I suspected that the reason he didn't have time to read them was probably ... that he couldn't read.

"But I trust Stalin to win the war," he added firmly.

I mused to myself: in the twentieth century, in the midst of a war which was utilizing the most modern and sophisticated implements of destruction, here was this place forgotten by time — no electricity, radio or telephone, hardly any link with the outside world.

We approached a low, thatch-roofed log cabin and he turned to me and said, "That's where she lives, my daughter-in-law. The *koornosaya* — turned-up nose — is out in the field now, but her mother is at home."

Without knocking, he opened the door and called out, "Hey, *starukha* — old woman — are you home? Where are you, *Babushka* — Granny?"

From a small barn behind the house a voice replied, "Here I am, Anton; I'm feeding the chickens."

We waited a few moments and soon a little old woman appeared. She wiped her face with a corner of her coarse apron, and gave us a toothless smile.

"*Babushka* Durova, this is Chaim, our new tractor driver. He will be staying here with you."

Then, to me, he added, "Make sure she gives you a good spot to sleep, and don't let them starve you. The *Kolkhoz* pays plenty *trudo-dnee* for your room and board, so you have a right to be comfortable and well-fed."

Then he leaned close to the old woman's ear and whispered, but loudly enough to be certain that I could hear, "Now your lamp won't be running out of kerosene anymore, and there'll be enough of it to wash all the hair of all the females in the house."

He was speaking with the solicitude of a grandfather looking out for the welfare of his family; at the same time he threw a wink at me. I understood the message — he'd be pleased if I'd pilfer enough fuel from our tractor for the ladies to wash their hair with. Kerosene kills lice, and was therefore a precious article to the bug-ridden villagers.

The old woman looked me over. Finally she said, "Welcome to you. It will be good to have a man around the house." She turned abruptly and went back to her chickens in the barn.

The chairman invited me to come to his home for supper later that evening. Then he, too, left and I was alone in the cabin. Outside the front door was a tiny porch with one step; I went outside and sat down on the step, waiting for the *babushka* to return.

The cabin was typical of rural Russia. It was built of logs, with the gaps between them sealed with a mixture of clay and grass. The roof was thatched with tightly pressed straw, and was steeply pitched so that the rain would run off quickly. Paint, apparently, was something which had never been heard of in this desolate spot.

The landscape was calm and beautiful. The sounds of croaking frogs came from a little brook nearby, and the air smelled pure and sweet. A soft breeze rustled through the treetops, and the late afternoon sun bathed everything in a golden light. I could almost feel the nearness of God, and the secrets of His creation.

I realized, as I sat there, how much I needed this rest, both physically and spiritually. I had been on the run for months, always hungry, always frightened.

Yet, even here, even now, I was faced with new problems. First of all, would I be able to find kosher food? The dietary laws, which constituted a vital part of my life as a Jew, might be hard for me to follow in this desolate spot. True, in the face of death these dietary laws are null and void, for the value of life transcends everything. But here there was no danger to my life, and I would have to make every effort to observe them.

I thought about it and realized that there must be plenty of dairy food available. Surely there were fresh vegetables, and the forest was full of berries and mushrooms, which were certainly permissible. So my problem really was: how could I explain my peculiar eating habits to these backward villagers?

A second problem gnawing at my mind was Sabbath observance. Never in all my life had I worked on the Sabbath. How could I avoid it now? I couldn't feign illness every seventh day, but what other way out was there?

A third problem was the matter of wearing my _tefillin_ during my daily morning prayers. Surely someone would notice. These atheists might tolerate an old man praying; they'd just consider him a silly old fool, a remnant of a superstitious and bygone world. But a _young_ man praying! This might border on heresy against the Party, against Stalin, against the Revolution. In these times of war, it might even be considered espionage or treason!

My thoughts were interrupted by the sudden appearance of the _babushka_. "Don't be bashful," she said. "Go on inside. I've got to go to the garden, but I'll be back soon." And off she went, carrying a large hand-woven willow basket.

Inside, the walls were exactly the same as they were outside: log upon log, with a grass mixture pressed between them. Running approximately the length of half the room was a wood-burning oven, built from clay. I soon learned that these stoves were called *pekelok*s, and that they were traditional throughout rural Russia. Meals are cooked and bread is baked in them, and during the winter they heat the house.

I peeked through a doorway in the middle of the long wall and saw two smaller rooms, one beginning at the door and ending at the front of the cabin and the other ending at the back wall. I realized that they must be bedrooms and that the large room I was in was a multi-purpose room. One of the little bedrooms boasted "modern interior decoration": the log wall was extensively papered with old *Pravda* and *Izvestia* newspapers.

The furniture was minimal. The beds were flat boards on legs, and on each board there was a straw-filled sack. There were no closets, or cabinets or bureaus. In the main room there was a small table and two benches. There was no other furniture in the house.

Presently *Babushka* returned, her basket filled with garden produce; with her were her daughter and her three grandchildren. The younger woman introduced herself:

"I am Anna Mikhailovna Raskin. You can call me Anna. This is my twelve-year-old son, Volodia, and my ten-year-old daughter, Zinna. And this is my eight-year-old, Lenka."

Anna appeared to be in her early thirties, intelligent, quite neat and clean. She was barefoot, like everyone else here, and her face bore the marks of a life of hard work and worry. Still, she seemed somewhat out of place in this crude peasants' dwelling.

"Where would you like to sleep?" she asked. "On the floor? On a bed? Or perhaps on the shelf near the ceiling, above the *pekelok*?"

There were only three beds in the house for these five people. I would not dream of displacing any of them, so this left me with a choice of either the floor or the shelf. The shelf, being above the stove and near the ceiling, would be ideal in winter; but this was summer, and it might get uncomfortably hot up there.

"The floor, thank you," I replied.

"My father-in-law said to tell you that you should eat supper here with us tonight, instead of at his house. He won't be at home; some kind of business has come up that he must attend to this evening.

While Anna and her mother busied themselves preparing supper, the children and I began to get acquainted. They told me that they were the envy of all the children in the village, because there was a *Zapadnik* in their home. They asked me all sorts of questions, some clever and some childish; and I replied in kind, sometimes seriously and sometimes in jest.

A pleasant aroma began to fill the room, coming from the two simmering earthenware pots in the *pekelok*. Finally *Babushka* removed one pot and placed it in the center of the bare table and called us all to come and sit down. Anna invited me to sit on the bench with Volodia and Zinna, while she sat across from us on the other bench with *Babushka* and Lenka. There were no dishes on the table — only the steaming pot in the center and six wooden spoons. These were large and deep, perhaps twice the size of a regular tablespoon. The boy, Volodia, grabbed a spoon and began to dig at the food in the pot. Instantly, Anna took another spoon and hit him on the head with it.

"Hey! Ouch!" he screamed.

His mother eyed him angrily and shouted, "*Molitsya* — Say grace — you little pig!"

They all made the sign of the cross, and then took their spoons and dug deeply into the pot; all, that is, except *Babushka*. She turned towards a corner of the room, whispered a prayer, bowed her head and then raised it, still gazing towards the corner. I looked too and suddenly noticed an ornate icon there; it looked out of place on the rough log wall.

I was afraid that there might be some meat in the pot. In that case, I could not eat anything, for it would all be *treif* — forbidden. Anna noticed my hesitation; she smiled and asked, "What's the matter? Aren't you hungry? Come on, eat, before there's nothing left. I can assure you my mother is the best cook in the world."

I did not want to offend these kind people, but I certainly could not eat food which was not kosher. Not knowing what to do, I came up with a bit of fiction: "In the West, where I come from, it is customary not to eat until one has been told what is in the pot."

This statement seemed to make quite an impression on them. They gazed at me, fascinated by the strange ways of the mysterious West, and I silently congratulated myself for having thought of this ruse.

Babushka said, "We call it *shchee*. It's made out of sauerkraut and all kinds of vegetables, mixed with some vegetable oil. We eat it almost every day. Don't be afraid — I'm sure you'll like it!"

Although this allayed my fears that it was not kosher, there still remained another deterrent: the hygiene factor. Six people eating from the same pot...quite enough to spoil one's appetite! What would Mama say? However, my hunger persuaded me to "do in Rome as the Romans do."

I picked up a wooden spoon and stuck it into the pot. Quick as a flash the other five spoons joined mine. Before I could extricate my spoon, loaded with the steaming soupy *shchee*, the other five spoons had been loaded, had traveled across the table to five mouths, and were already on the return trip to the pot.

How quick they are! I thought. I discovered that it was quite a trick to get that spoon to travel the long distance to one's mouth without spilling some of the soupy liquid, and it was a trick which I just could not learn. The children laughed at my clumsiness; Anna and *Babushka* smiled. No matter how hard I tried to avoid spilling drops of soup on the table, I failed. Soon there was a soupy path between me and the pot. It was exasperating: not a speck of liquid dropped from anyone else's spoon, only from mine. It took several weeks before I finally developed the ability.

When the pot of *shchee* was empty, Anna brought another clay pot from the *pekelok*. This one contained boiled potatoes, with their skins. However, instead of placing the pot on the table, she put it on the floor, underneath the table. Everyone reached down under the table, without looking, and brought up a steaming potato, dipped it into a wooden bowl of salt, and then proceeded to eat it.

I just couldn't restrain my curiosity — I had to have an explanation!

"There's room on the table, so why did you put the pot under the table?" I asked.

They looked at each other and burst out laughing.

Volodia, with a mouth full of potato, asked, "You mean to say, at your house they put the potato pot *on* the table?"

"Well, yes," I replied hesitantly, beginning to feel embarrassed at the queer way we did it at home.

Anna explained it to me. "If we put the pot *on* the table, out in the open, everyone would pick out the best potatoes. Then who would eat the rotten ones? This way, we eat what we take. We can't afford to waste even a little bit."

After this explanation, I joined them in reaching under the table, pulling out a steaming-hot potato, dipping it into the bowl of salt and eating it, skin and all. When the potato pot was empty, supper was over. There was not a speck of garbage to dispose of, no dishes to wash, and no tablecloth to shake out and fold; there were just the two pots and the six wooden spoons.

The children scampered outside to play. Anna, *Babushka* and I sat at the table together and Anna began to talk in a tired voice. "You might think that because we live on the land we have enough food, but that's not so. We eat whatever we can get, and we can't be picky about it. If Volodia keeps his hands under the table too long, feeling around for a better potato, he gets my spoon on his head, hard!"

We continued talking, and I learned something about the meat situation in relation to the local diet — or, rather, about the lack of meat in the local diet.

Under Soviet law, every family working on a collective farm was permitted to own one cow. Every calf born to the cow was to be sold at the age of one month, either to the collective or the government; but since the price established by the government was extremely low, most of the newborn calves were in fact slaughtered by the farmer who owned the cow. He would salt the meat thickly to prevent spoilage, and store it in the coolness of his cellar. Thus, the family had meat to eat.

"But since my husband went into the army, we haven't had a bit of meat in the house," Anna said sadly.

I sympathized with their plight, but I felt very relieved to learn about the absence of meat in this house, for it solved much of my *kashrus* problem.

Anna suggested that I go outside for some evening air. When they saw me, Volodia, Zinna and little Lenka started jumping up and down happily; they were so excited about their *Zapadnik*. They bombarded me with questions, all kinds of questions, but mostly about life in the West and about the tractor, which was a mechanical marvel in this village, where most work was still done by hand.

Innocently, Volodia mentioned that it was wonderful to have "a tractorist" in the house — because the tractorist always furnished plenty of kerosene to the family where he stayed; enough kerosene to kill all the lice on everyone's head, and enough to keep the lamp burning late into the night.

"Now we're going to have plenty of kerosene. We'll be able to stay up much later. Maybe we won't have to go to bed at all!" The children were excited and pleased at the prospect of staying up late at night.

They escorted me to the small shed which was their barn, and proudly showed me the family cow. "Her name is *Solodkaya* — Sweetie," they said. The girls, Zinna and Lenka, demonstrated their skill at milking *Solodkaya*.

Volodia explained that the cream is separated from the milk and beaten into butter, which is then given to the government as a tax. Of the remaining skimmed milk, a portion is used for making cheese, and the balance is used for drinking.

Volodia went on to tell me of another odd tax, this time on chickens; this one was paid by giving a quota of eggs to the government.

The children showed me the family's supply of hay and firewood. Proudly, Volodia boasted how he and his mother had cut down trees in the forest and then chopped them up to make these cords of firewood. The two girls, not to be outdone, bragged that they, together with their mother, had loaded all this hay into many wagonloads and had unloaded it here, all by themselves.

When I considered the proficiency of these children with such things as axes, pitchforks and scythes, contrasted with my own unfamiliarity with such things, I was overcome by a feeling of embarrassment and inadequacy. I'd have to learn these skills quickly or lose my present honored status!

"Come," they called. "See our *banya* — our bathhouse."

It was a tiny shed, located perhaps a hundred feet from the house. We stepped inside and Volodia explained the operation of the *banya*.

Approximately one third of the space inside the shed was taken up by a small clay stove, sort of a miniature *pekelok*, on which rested a metal pot and about a dozen rocks. From the public well, located about a hundred yards away, water was brought and the metal pot was filled; ten gallons were needed. A fire was built in the *pekelok*, which heated not only the water but also the rocks. Then a bucket of cold water was poured over the hot rocks. The rocks sizzled and a cloud of steam arose; soon the shed became filled with steam, making it warm and comfortable. Then one would bathe, using the water in the ten-gallon pot for both lathering up and rinsing off.

"This is where we keep the soap," said Zinna, pointing to an ancient wooden bucket, whose contents looked like white mud.

"This is soap?" I asked. "What's it made from?"

She smiled indulgently at my ignorance. "You take the ashes left over from the previous week, and you mix them with hot water."

Perhaps, I thought, it's because of the war that they cannot get real soap, so I asked, "Have you ever had any other kind of soap, the kind made in a soap factory?"

"Yes," Volodia replied. "Sometimes, when my uncle from the big city used to visit us, or when father went there, we got some city soap. But mother always used it all up doing the laundry. She said it kills lice on the clothes better."

"Anyway, we don't use this *banya* anymore," Zinna said. She explained that nowadays, since most of the men were away at war, two or three families got together and used one bath house, usually on Saturday nights.

Suddenly an idea popped into my head: this shed would be a perfect hideout for me to put on my *tefillin* each morning and recite *Shacharis*, the morning prayers.

Finally we went back to the house because it was getting dark. We talked some more, until it grew pitch black. Then we all went to bed, Volodia and I sharing a straw sack on the floor.

Rising early the next morning, I was sure that I was the first one up, but *Babushka* was already out in the barn, milking *Solodkaya*. I washed, using icy water that was in a bucket outside, and sneaked out to the *banya*. In utter privacy and with no fear of discovery, I put on my *tefillin* and recited *Shacharis*.

When I returned to the house, Anna and the children were outside washing. I pulled my toothbrush out of my pocket, moistened it with water (there was no toothpaste, of course) and started to brush my teeth. Anna and the children stared at me, fascinated.

"Haven't you ever seen anybody brush his teeth before?" I asked jokingly.

"No!" they replied in unison, amazed at this strange new Western custom.

Babushka called, "Breakfast is ready!"

We ate pancakes, holding the hot flat lumps in our hands. Then a bowl of brown kasha, buckwheat groats, was placed on the table. We used our wooden spoons to eat this, and again no one dropped a speck of food except me; there was the same embarrassing path of dropped food on the table, between me and the pot, as there had been the night before.

Suddenly we heard the loud peal of a bell. It was the chairman, clanging the bell outside his office door, announcing to the villagers that it was 6 A.M.

and time to go to work. In the entire village there was only one clock, the one in the chairman's office!

Anna and the children, who had no school in summer and helped in the fields, left the house to go to work. Only *Babushka* remained at home.

I found Fiodor, my tractor foreman, in front of the chairman's office. In another moment Stepan appeared. Then we trekked to the field where our machines awaited us.

Fiodor assigned Stepan to the harvester; the last seasons's wheat harvest was piled high, waiting to be gathered and threshed. It had been lying there in the field throughout the winter, and much of it had been spoiled by the rains and the snow. A large part of it had served to feed the field rats.

Fiodor told me to drive the tractor, while he and Stepan would man the harvester that was pulled by the tractor. I was very pleased with my skillful operation of the tractor: keeping the right wheel in the trenches, steering carefully to be sure that the harvester didn't miss any of the stacked wheat. As the day wore on, however, I occasionally veered off the straight-and-narrow a few inches. Each time this happened I was roundly cursed by Fiodor. His curses were awesome, revealing beauty of language and ugliness of thought. Some of them were remarkably lengthy, and he salted and peppered them with a four-letter flavor. Fiodor was extremely conscientious about the heavy responsibility of "protecting socialist property and wealth."

In general, Fiodor seemed pleased with my work on this, my first day, while I was absolutely delighted with myself. This was a day of achievement, a day to remember: I had worked a full day of hard labor driving a tractor! They'll never believe me back home, I thought. I felt so happy, but it was a bittersweet happiness: for how could I be so happy while my family back home might be in the most perilous circumstances?

A woman driving a horse and wagon delivered a barrel of water to us. Several times during the day we refilled the radiator of the tractor and of the harvester. We used the water for drinking, too. The same woman later brought us lunch — kasha and bread.

Late that afternoon Fiodor called a halt to the work. We went over our machines with screwdrivers and pliers, tightening nuts and bolts and screws, "to preserve socialist property and wealth," Fiodor reminded me as we crawled under and over the tractor.

It was nearly dusk when we ended our labor, and I was exhausted; still, I decided to take the long mud-path on my way back to the village. I had seen a one-room school there, where children were taught for the first five grades, and I planned to find the teacher tonight. I was eager to talk to an educated person.

9

"ZDRAVSTVOOYTYE — Hello! Welcome!" the schoolmaster greeted me when I introduced myself. "My name is Nikolai Yefimovich Goncharov. Please sit down."

He pointed to a bench in front of his cabin and we both sat down there. He was about forty years old, and apparently felt it necessary to explain to me, almost apologetically, why he was not in the army. He had repeatedly tried to enlist, he assured me, but was rejected on the grounds of being physically unfit, his disability being a result of an accident in his youth.

I asked him whether he might have an extra schoolbook, "a primer for beginners," I explained. "I would like to learn your language better."

"Of course," he replied. "Let's go inside."

Inside, it was very similar to the house in which I was boarding, except for one significant difference. There was no religious icon in the corner; instead, there was a shelf full of books. Just seeing all these books, even though I did not know how to read them, gave me a warm, glowing feeling inside. In fact, I must have been glowing on the outside, too, for suddenly the teacher exclaimed, "The People of the Book!"

Slightly bewildered by this remark, all I could say was, "What?"

"I said, 'The People of the Book!' It's so, isn't it? Look at you, gazing at those books here; you look like you've found a long-lost brother!"

While he was speaking, several thoughts raced through my mind. Obviously, he was making a reference to Jews, and it seemed to be complimentary. But it certainly would not surprise me if he, like most everyone else, were irrational on the subject. On the other hand, there was no icon on his wall; so I allowed myself the luxury of thinking that here was one man who had shaken off the Church's brainwashing.

"How did you know that I'm a Jew?" I asked quietly. "Are my horns showing?"

He laughed. "No," he replied, "your horns are very well hidden, and so is your tail. But everyone in Karobka knows you're a Jew; a stigma like that travels with you wherever you go, you know!"

Hopefully, I tried to believe he was being facetious.

"Everyone's talking about 'the *Zapadnik* Jew,'" he continued. "You're the hottest subject of conversation in the village, next to the war."

I relaxed. He doesn't hate Jews, at least not as much as the others, I decided. Then I picked up the conversation where we had left off.

"Yes, Nikolai Yefimovich, I love books. Nothing could please me more than to immerse myself in your library. But I don't know enough Russian. To carry on a conversation is one thing, but it is quite another to be able to read and understand Lermontov, Pushkin, Gorky and Tolstoy."

The teacher expressed delight in having a cultured man to talk to, in "this sea of ignorance and illiteracy." He said he would get me some beginners' books and assured me that I would be welcome to visit him often. Then he added, "Why don't you stay for supper with us?"

Before I could think of a reply he added, "Let's make it tomorrow night, instead, because tonight my wife is milking the *kolkhoz* cows and she'll be late getting home."

I hesitated. Suppose they had meat for supper? His sharp eye caught my hesitation, and he said, "There'll be no pork, I promise. I know Jews don't eat pig meat."

We agreed on a dairy meal.

In parting, I said, "I'll see you tomorrow night, as soon as the sun sets behind the trees on the second hill." Coming from my own mouth, this sounded so funny that I had to chuckle. I explained to him why I had laughed:

"I'm a city boy whose entire life has been regulated by clocks; and yet look how quickly I've learned to talk like a peasant!"

The next morning I woke up stiff. I didn't know whether it was due to the straw mattress or to the unaccustomed labor of the day before. I rushed to the *banya*, put on my *tefillin* and prayed. I thanked God for having delivered me to this peaceful oasis, and my tears began to flow as I begged Him to be merciful and to protect my family back home.

My morning devotions were suddenly interrupted by *Babushka's* voice calling me. I had to smile at the way she was calling both me and the chickens at one and the same time: "Chaim...Chaim...Tzippa... Tzippa!" Her voice wafted through the pure morning air, and echoed from the treetops. "Chaim...Chaim...Tzippa...Tzippa...Chaim...Tzippa!"

Almost every evening after supper, I went to the teacher's house. Before long, thanks to his kindness and patient help, I became quite proficient at reading and understanding his elementary school books. In fact, I followed a steady routine. Every evening, on my way to the teacher's house, I would read the latest newspaper to a group of elderly men who were illiterate.

The newspapers, *Pravda* and *Izvestia*, were vague about reporting the war; however, one could conjecture by reading between the lines. For example, *Sovinform*, the Soviet Information Bureau, might report that "Private Vladimir Ivanovich Gerasimov single-handedly knocked out three enemy tanks, killing forty-eight fascist beasts, thus contributing to the defense of the railroad station of Smolensk." From this, one could deduce that all of the territory as deep into Russia as Smolensk must be in enemy hands. Anyone having a knowledge of geography would realize that Russia was being conquered by the Germans. However, I could not tell whether or not my audience understood this: they never discussed the gravity of the losses and defeats, at least not in my presence.

Nor did I offer my comments on the war news. I followed along in the spirit of the newspapers, transforming defeats into victories "under the leadership of the greatest military genius who ever lived, the wise and beloved Stalin." This quotation was a refrain at the beginning, middle and end of every war story.

The entire coverage of the war took up half of the front page, and consisted of recounting individual soldiers' acts of heroism. There was not a word about any retreat.

The last page contained all the foreign news. Everything else was propaganda, extolling the virtues of Communism. Accounts of murder, thievery or accidents never appeared in these newspapers; perhaps this was because such things are not supposed to occur in a socialist society.

Frequently, of course, I would come upon a word whose meaning I did not know, and one of the men in my audience would explain it to me. Thus, the weeks passed and my proficiency in the Russian language grew and grew.

Russian has no "h" sound in its alphabet; instead, a "g" sound is used. Thus, "Hitler" is pronounced "Gitler," "Eisenhower" is pronounced

"Eisengower" and so on. However, when I read the newspapers to my audience I would pronounce these names as they should be pronounced, with an "h" sound, and not a "g" sound. In the beginning everyone thought this was very funny, but finally I convinced them that this was the correct way; this bit of knowledge earned me considerable admiration.

Reading the newspapers over a period of time benefited me in several ways; it helped to keep me abreast of world news and war news, it enriched my vocabulary and my diction and it accelerated my reading speed.

Soon, Goncharov and I became close friends. He began to converse more intimately with me than he dared to with anyone else, including his wife. He told me that he enjoyed talking with me because, first of all, I had not yet been "brainwashed by all the official propaganda." Also, I was not likely to become an informer, since I had no intention of remaining in Russia after the war ended. And last but not least, he told me, he enjoyed talking with me because he was in desperate need of a confidant for all the secret thoughts which had been pressing on his mind for years, unable to be voiced because there had been no safe outlet.

It was in the teacher's house that I witnessed just how pervasive is the suspicion which is engendered by the regime. Suspicion is ever-present; it even exists between husband and wife. One evening, in the course of our conversation, I happened to discuss my brief experience in the village of Karobka. I told them about my visit to the _Voyenkomat_, and how I had been turned down for the Red Army because I am a _Zapadnik_.

I complained to them, "Here am I, ready and willing to fight — in fact, dying to get into a uniform. Maybe not for the same reasons as the Russian citizens, for they are fighting for Russia, for Stalin and for the Soviet system, and it's true that these are not my reasons. But what difference does the reason make, as long as there is a mutual hatred of the same enemy? I'm a Jew and a Pole, and I am eager to pay back the Germans for what they are doing to us. Why am I forced to remain here, out of the war, while someone else is doing the fighting?"

The teacher grasped my arm and, with a wink, said, "Let's go outside and get some fresh air."

Outside, on the bench in front of his house, he spoke softly. "You may have confidence in me, just as I trust you; but in front of my wife watch your tongue. You see, she is a member of _Comsomol_, the Communist Youth Organization, and _Comsomols_ have such absolute faith in Stalin and the Party that they are unable to differentiate between a friendly complaint and counter-revolutionary activity. With them, any criticism is subversive — anti-Stalin, anti-Party, anti-Revolution."

He drew a deep breath, then continued. "You are a stranger here, perhaps even a spy. Now, common sense tells me you are not a spy; whatever could you be looking for in this hole in the woods? But *Comsomols* like my wife always manage to find something to nurture their suspicions. For instance, what do you do every morning inside the *banya*? Do you have radio equipment there? I don't think so, but the *Comsomols* wonder. I see you are surprised to learn that you are under surveillance!"

"Surprised" was an understatement; I was aghast!

Just then Yevgenia, his young wife, came outside, carrying the baby in her arms. She sat down next to me. I recoiled a little. She, a *Comsomol*, and I, a suspicious character...suddenly I was seized with terror.

Immediately the teacher changed the subject. "That was good, Chaim," he said. "You are making real progress in our language. Pretty soon you'll be a regular '*Chi Sammarra.*'"

"*Chi Sammarra?*" I asked. "What's that?"

Yevgenia replied to my question. "It's a colloquialism. Sammarra is the big city on the Volga which was renamed Kuybishev. The word '*Chi*' really has no meaning, and it's hard to explain. A person will say, '*Chi*, I've been waiting for you,' and another person will reply, '*Chi*, didn't I tell you not to wait?' So that's why the people living here, in the Sammarra area, are referred to as '*Chi Sammarra,*'" she said; then, with a smile, she added, "And now you're becoming one, Chaim — a regular '*Chi Sammarra.*'"

I thanked them for the compliment. After some more conversation she left us to visit a neighbor. The moment she was out of earshot, Goncharov picked up where he had left off when she interrupted us.

"Let it serve you as a rule," he said. "For every mistake, for any misfortune — from the smallest, like a dead chicken on a collective farm, to the biggest, like a disaster at the war front — there must always be a scapegoat! Someone must be made to pay! The war is going very, very badly. We have lost much land and whole armies. Someone has to pay for this misfortune; someone will be blamed for it; and the likeliest scapegoat, it seems to me, is some handy Westerner! So watch your step. Your chances of becoming a scapegoat are great. You are a stranger, with no family or friends or roots; you are a foreigner from a capitalistic country, and Poland was never our friend; and to top it all off, you're a Jew!"

What could I say? He was looking intently at me, to see whether I had grasped the gravity of his words. And indeed I had; I was speechless. This was a night of disillusionment, and I was overcome by a feeling of utter despair.

Leaving, I shook his hand, and mumbled that I was thankful to him for his friendship and advice.

That night I hardly slept. I was alarmed at knowing that I was considered a suspicious character. Perhaps, I thought, I ought to reveal what it is that I do every morning in the *banya*. Surely it must be less of a crime to be a religious Jew than to be a spy! Also, I decided, I'd better curb my curiosity and stop asking so many questions. This brought to my mind a vision of Mama. "Busybody," she used to call me, and how right she was!

The teacher's final words kept echoing in my ears: "and to top it all off, you're a Jew!" It was all so frustrating, since the one thing which should prove that I was not sympathetic to the enemy, Germany, was the fact that I was a Jew. Yet thanks to the legacy of Christianity, just being a Jew made me automatically suspect!

The next evening, after my daily newspaper-reading session, I went as usual to Goncharov's house. This time our conversation drifted to the subject of education.

"Is it true," I asked, "that the government gives *stipendia* — free tuition plus salary — to all students? Could I, for instance, attend college and receive a *stipendium*? After the war, of course!"

"I'll tell you the long and short of it," he replied sarcastically. "Those days are over! Neither you nor any of the children here in Karobka will ever get to a university! It's a simple matter of economics. True, education is free, but in order to get into a university one must first graduate from a high school. High schools are in the cities. No farmer can afford to send his child to a distant city, and pay for his food and clothing and a piece of floor to sleep on.

"There was a time, a few years ago, when Russia desperately needed to produce professionals, so there was a crash program. The government searched every nook and cranny in Russia to find promising students, and practically forced us to accept *stipendia* and go through high school and university. That's how I became a teacher, and that's how your *Babushka*'s son, Anna's brother, became an engineer. Do you know that he couldn't read or write when he was thirty years old? Somebody decided that he would make a good engineer, so the government started him in the first grade and subsidized his education all the way through to an engineering degree. Now he's a big shot in Leningrad; his wife, by the way, is a physician."

Goncharov was silent for several moments. Then he continued, "You can't imagine how backward this country was before the Revolution. More than ninety percent of the people couldn't read or write. The ignorance was unbelievable! For instance, when the first tractor reached this country — it came from America — the peasants fled from it in terror. They called it 'the Devil that Moves without Horses.'

"I'll tell you a funny story. It's about Marshal Voroshilov. He was a young lieutenant in the Red Army when it was fighting the White Army. The White Army, you know, was loyal to the Czar. Well, the story goes, Lieutenant Voroshilov was driving a steel-plated motor vehicle in hostile territory, when suddenly the engine conked out. Soon armed peasants, led by the local priests, who were of course loyal to the Czar, circled 'the Devil without Horses,' and they waited for the occupants to emerge from it. Voroshilov didn't dare come out. For hours everyone waited. Finally the peasants hitched a pair of oxen to the vehicle in order to pull it to their village. While they were pulling it, Voroshilov put the machine into gear, released the clutch and suddenly the engine coughed back to life. Frightened by the roar of the engine, the oxen broke loose and ran off, the terrified peasants and priests ran for their lives in all directions, and Lieutenant Voroshilov was on his way once again!"

I laughed at this tale, and Goncharov joined me, laughing uproariously. He liked to tell stories, and always laughed heartily at his own jokes.

"That reminds me," he went on, "of another episode about Marshal Govorov, who is today the Marshal of Artillery of the Red Army. During the Revolution, he was the commander of a division, and one day at a general staff meeting Lenin asked him to show him on the map where his division was located. Govorov placed his entire hand on the map and said, 'Right here.' Actually, his hand was covering almost all of Russia: his little finger was at Vladivostok in the far east and his middle finger lay on the Polish border. General Govorov couldn't read! Later he was packed off to school.

"Eventually, all who needed it got educated. But today there is no longer a shortage of professionals or intellectuals. And although city people can still manage to obtain a higher education, the villager or the farmer can't. *Stipendia* are very scarce now."

"I can hardly believe this," I replied. "I've heard so often that education in the Soviet Union is free and equal for everyone. But from what you're telling me, it sounds like the so-called classless society of Russia has degenerated into just another caste system — the son of a general will be a general, while the son of a peasant will be a peasant! Right?"

Goncharov nodded, and looking down at the ground in embarrassment, he said, "Yes, my friend, you've summed it up pretty well. And above everything else, a Party card is indispensable for opening the doors of opportunity; but the possession of a Party card is restricted to a privileged few."

He placed his arm around my shoulder and whispered, "Remember, Chaim, we must trust each other. I have never talked so confidentially to anyone. I really don't know why I trust you so much; maybe I've been yearning for someone like you for a long time, someone with whom I could speak honestly and without fear. But remember, not a word to anyone. Never!"

We shook hands affectionately. We were such an unlikely pair: a young Jewish boy from Poland, and a middle-aged Russian intellectual. I smiled as I said to him, "After all, we are both in the same boat."

Suddenly he kissed me on the cheek. "It's an old Russian custom, you know," he said. "It's our way of showing closeness."

"Before I leave, Comrade Goncharov," I said, "I want to confide in you about a problem."

"Please do," he said. "If I can help you...."

"Well," I said, "it's a rather delicate matter. Usually, by the time I arrive home from work, everyone else in the house has already eaten. So Anna serves me the *shchee* or kasha or sweet potatoes, but — and this is my problem — it is never enough. I am always hungry. All my earnings go to her, yet she simply does not give me enough to eat! And the strangest thing is, the other day I overheard *Babushka* telling Anna that I must be sick. 'Chaim eats practically nothing,' she was saying. How can I eat more when she doesn't give it to me? They never ask me: 'Chaim, would you like some more?' Perhaps I ought to move out, but what excuse could I give? I don't want to upset anybody."

In the bright moonlight I could see his forehead wrinkle as he pondered over my problem. He muttered, "I would never have imagined that the Raskins were that kind of people, taking advantage of you like that. There must be some reason...."

Goncharov advised me to say nothing about this matter to anyone; in the meanwhile he would give it much thought. He went inside, and I started walking home. I was almost there when I heard him calling me at the top of his voice, "Chaim...Chaim...Chaim...!"

I raced back to his house in a panic. What in the world could be wrong? When I arrived at his house, though, I found the teacher and his wife standing out in front and laughing.

"As soon as you left," he said, "my wife came home. A woman usually has a better approach to delicate situations like these, so I told her about your problem. Well, she hit on the solution instantly. It's so simple that it's funny! That's why we're laughing."

Yevgenia spoke. "Tell me, Chaim, after you finish eating the *shchee*, what do you do with your spoon?"

Were they both crazy? "What do you mean, what do I do with my spoon? I put it on the table, of course. Doesn't everyone?"

"All right," she continued. "Now, exactly how do you place the spoon — with the bowl of the spoon facing up, or facing down?"

I began to lose my patience. "What's the difference?" I snapped. "I don't know. I simply put it on the table. What am I supposed to do with it, eat it or something?"

My irritability only increased their mirth.

She giggled, "Oh, but it does make a difference, a big difference! You see, in our part of the country if a person places his spoon facing down, it means he doesn't want any more; if you place the spoon with the bowl facing up, it means you'd like some more to eat. Tomorrow, Chaim, place your spoon with the open end up, and see what happens."

Now I joined them in their laughter.

It was wonderful to be silly and light-hearted again; it had been such a long time since I'd enjoyed a hearty laugh — even if it was only for the moment.

10

It WOULD not be long until we tractor drivers — Fiodor, Stepan and I — would be finished with our work here at *Kolkhoz Karobka*. We were nearly finished with the threshing of last year's crops; then we would be moving on to another *kolkhoz*, and repeating the process. So far, I had managed to avoid working on Shabbos by feigning illness. Fiodor could have demanded a physician's statement, but he never did, since that would have meant sending me to Booyan on foot, which would have wasted the day anyhow. I used that excuse for several weeks, in constant fear that Goncharov would find out. Since he knew that Jews do not eat pork, he might also know that Jews do not work on Saturday! So far Fiodor had accepted my excuses, but that could not last forever. Sooner or later he'd discover that my illness arrived regularly, the same day every week.

Rosh Hashanah and *Yom Kippur*, the Jewish High Holidays, were approaching. I shuddered at the prospect of having to work on these holy days. Then I had an idea; perhaps I could avoid desecrating the holy days if I were working at a job which was not "work" in the usual sense. Perhaps I could be a helper in the horses' stable, feeding and watering the animals, for example.

I went to see the chairman, Comrade Anton Grigorovich, and told him that I'd like to remain here in Karobka rather than move on with the tractors. Naturally, he asked me why. I replied that I had grown fond of the people here in Karobka, and felt at home.

He explained certain facts of Soviet life to me. "No one," he said, "can legally change his job, or quit his job, at his own whim. Especially these days, with the country at war, there is a terrible shortage of working men and this law is very strictly enforced. Every worker is, in effect, 'owned.' Each chairman, or manager, or director who 'owns' workers holds on to them very tightly. But still," he added, "I have an idea as to how I might swing a deal with your 'owner,' the Machine Tractor Station."

Later, I told my friend Goncharov about my conversation with the chairman, and Goncharov said that he too would do whatever he could to help me get a transfer and thus stay in the village.

The next day the chairman went to see the director of the Machine Tractor Station and asked if they would release me, offering in return to give the station a sixteen-year-old Karobka boy named Ilya. Young Ilya loved the tractors; neglecting his own work in the stable, he constantly hung around them, wishing that he could become a tractorist.

Ilya's stepfather, a cross-eyed, hook-nosed man named Yefim, was in charge of the stable. More than once I had heard that Yefim hated his stepson with such a passion that he had often expressed his wish that Ilya would "hurry up and be drafted into the army, and get killed right away!"

Yefim was one of the men who daily congregated around me while I read the newspaper aloud. True, he looked mean, but he had always been civil towards me. Now, however, since the chairman had begun negotiating to get Ilya into tractor work, Yefim began to grow more and more hostile towards me. Goncharov explained:

"Tractorists, you see, are pretty much exempt from being drafted into the army because their services are so essential. Therefore, if Ilya is accepted into tractor work, it's less likely that he'll be drafted. And if he's not drafted then it's unlikely that he'll be killed. And that's why Yefim has become so nasty towards you — you're interfering with his plans for his stepson."

I would not have believed this ghastly explanation from anyone else, but I could not doubt the truthfulness of my friend Goncharov.

The next day after work, as I sat in front of the horse stable reading the newspaper as usual, Yefim suddenly shouted, "*Chi*, Chaim, did you hear of the hunter who went to buy a rifle in a Jew's store, and noticed that the barrel was bent? The Jew told him it was made that way, to shoot around corners."

Everyone laughed, and so did I; I did not want to give Yefim the satisfaction of knowing that I was offended.

"As a matter of fact," I said, "armaments engineers are working on developing exactly that — a rifle for shooting around corners."

I continued reading the newspaper. Yefim interrupted again. "Hey!" he exploded. "How come you're not out there fighting, instead of hiding here?"

Before I could say anything, he continued. "*Chi*, you are like the Jew who said to the draft official, 'Why should I go to the front lines to kill one or two of the enemy? *Chi*, I can kill five hundred of them if you'll just bring them here!'"

I replied calmly that I was registered for the draft. "I volunteered for the army even before I arrived at Karobka, but the commandant did not accept me."

I returned to reading the newspaper, and there were no more interruptions. When I'd finished reading, the paper was, as usual, divided among all present. The newspaper was used by the men for making cigarettes. Into a small square of paper they put a bit of "tobacco" which they made by crushing dried leaves from one of the local trees. Then they rolled up the cigarette, and licked the paper to make it stick. I used my share for other purposes... something which amazed and irritated the brutish Yefim; paper was for cigarettes, and I was robbing the valiant Russians of their fair share.

"Fancy fellow! Thinks he's better than the rest of us!" Yefim yelled, glaring at me.

When I left, the chairman caught up with me and put his hand on my shoulder. "Don't be afraid of that cockeyed imbecile," he assured me. "If he so much as touches you, I promise I'll beat the stuffing out of him."

I was very moved. I thanked him, and said, "Maybe we should drop the idea of getting permission for me to stay here. I don't want to be the cause of hard feelings."

"But you're wrong, son," he replied. "Everybody wants to see you remain here. Look, I'll prove it to you. Let's go back there, and you'll see for yourself."

I said that I'd rather not. "Chances are, Yefim will be there, and I don't want any more trouble with him today."

The chairman, however, insisted. "I'm the chairman here, and I order you to return with me!" That settled the matter. We turned around and began walking back.

"While we're at it, Chaim," the chairman added, "I want to take you into the stable. There's a new young mare in there and I want you to try her out!"

"But, *Dedushka* Anton," I pleaded, "have mercy! I'm a city boy. I've never been on a horse, and I'm scared of them!"

The old man was adamant. "In a *kolkhoz*," he said, "a man must be able to do everything!"

The usual crowd was still there in the yard in front of the stable. "You're my boy, Chaim!" one of them said, and another growled: "Good Comrade!"

As far as I could see, they all appeared well disposed towards me. The chairman had been telling me the truth when he said they wanted me to stay!

After a few pleasantries, I followed the chairman into the stable. I was relieved to find that Yefim was not there. The chairman stopped in front of one of the stalls.

He said, "Chaim, I want you to meet *Byeloye-Brukho* — White Belly." The horse was brown, but sure enough, the belly was white.

"He's a nice-looking mare," I commented politely.

With the palm of his hand the chairman slapped his forehead. "A mare is a female! *She's* a nice-looking mare! Oh, Chaim! Do you have a lot to learn about horses!"

I grinned, embarrassed, and said, "Well, I told you!"

In an effort to redeem myself, I boldly leaned over the stall-gate to pat her, but she turned her head and kicked at me. Fortunately, a piece of two-by-four received the kick instead.

"You've just had a demonstration of rule number one," the chairman said. "Before you try to lay a hand on a horse, first be sure it sees you. We have an expression: 'Do not approach a horse from the rear, do not approach a billy goat from the front, and do not approach a mean fellow from any direction.' Come to think of it, you've had several lessons today. First, with a mean man, and now with a horse.

"But don't let it scare you. A horse is man's best friend," he said. "You wouldn't like it, either, if somebody sneaked up on you from the rear. Let me show you what a good girl *Byeloye-Brukho* is."

Having first made sure that she saw him, the chairman proceeded to pat her. I stood next to him, and reached over and patted her too.

"I'm sure you two will end up good friends," he said.

The next day, shortly after lunch, the tractor broke down. It needed a new part, and such things could only be obtained from the tractor station at Booyan.

I accompanied Fiodor to the stable, where he took a horse and left for Booyan. I started walking towards my cabin when I heard someone call me. It was the chairman, sitting on a horse.

"Wait right there for me," he said. He rode his horse into the stable. Presently he emerged, leading White Belly towards me.

"Here you are, Chaim. Ride her around and get acquainted."

I tried to get out of it; I said that I was still afraid of horses, even if I did pat White Belly yesterday. The chairman remained unmoved.

"Well," I said, "at least let me have an older horse. White Belly is too rambunctious."

"Sorry," he replied. "All the other horses are out in the fields, doing their work. The only horse in the stable is the one I just took in there, and he's tired. Besides," he continued, "the horse that kicks is the one to be licked. You'll end up loving her the most, just you wait and see."

I patted White Belly on the neck, trembling and scared to death at the prospect of riding her.

"Talk to her! Let her get used to the sound of your voice," the chairman said.

I started talking to her. My voice was a little shaky, and I hoped White Belly wouldn't notice it.

"Let me have your left foot," the chairman demanded; so I raised my left foot.

In an instant I was being flipped up. I threw my right foot over the horse, and suddenly, there I was, sitting on White Belly's bare back. Immediately I began feeling authoritative. I took the reins in my hands. Now I was confident that I could handle the animal. In fact, I felt as if I could command men, too. Now I knew how kings and generals feel when they ride horseback on parade!

Slowly the horse began to move. Nothing to it, I thought to myself. I was enjoying it immensely, but I decided I'd better not push my luck; I steered her towards the stable, where I intended to dismount.

I was just about to get off when, suddenly, I heard a loud slap. White Belly reared up on her hind legs, and I grabbed her around the neck, so I wouldn't be thrown off. In another moment, she was racing at tremendous speed, with me hanging on to her neck for dear life.

White Belly ran like crazy. My face was next to her ear and I desperately spoke to her. "Shhh, Shhh, Shhh...," I said over and over; this is the Russian way of saying, "Whoa, stop." Then I tried it the Polish way: "Prrr,

Prrr, Prrr...," but still no luck — if anything, White Belly was racing even faster. I felt her hide growing warm and sweaty.

I even tried speaking to White Belly in Hebrew. It didn't convince her to stop, but it reminded me to pray, and I began to do so. Suddenly I was reminded of Absalom, King David's son, who was killed while on a run-away horse; his hair was caught in the branches of a tree. Instinctively I lowered my head, all the time pressing close against the mare. I was drenched with perspiration.

I prayed, "Dear God in Heaven. If I must die, at least let me die in battle. Let me kill some Germans before I die. Why here? Why like this?" Droplets running down my face reached my parched lips. They tasted salty, but not of sweat, rather of tears...gasping for breath, I prayed, "Save me, save me, Almighty! Please save me!"

Suddenly I made out the sound of another horse galloping, coming closer and closer. Cautiously I turned my head. To my amazement I saw a horse's head almost alongside mine. A hand reached over, grabbed the bridle rope and brought both horses' heads close together. In another moment, White Belly began to slow down, and soon both horses stopped!

I straightened my aching back, and wiped the sweat off my face. I looked at the rider of the other horse and was astonished to see that it was a girl. And there was something odd about her — her skin was yellow! She must have malaria, I thought, having heard that the medicine for curing malaria makes one turn yellow.

She was laughing now. I said, "Thanks for saving my life."

"My pleasure," she replied. "I love to chase runaway horses. My name is Suleika. What's yours?"

I wondered about her; I had never seen anyone whose skin was not white. Was she still sick? And if so, was it contagious?

"Well," she said, "have you forgotten your name? It certainly takes you a long time to speak up!" There was a note of teasing in her voice.

"My name is Chaim. Tell me, is Suleika a common name here? True, I haven't been in Russia very long, but this is the first time I've ever heard the name Suleika.

She smiled at me, then jumped lightly off her horse. Holding the horse's bridle with one hand, and shielding her eyes from the sun with the other, she said, "Come down; let your horse rest awhile."

I hesitated for a moment, but then I confessed. "To tell you the truth," I said, "I don't know exactly how to get off. And even if I got off, I'm afraid I wouldn't be able to get back on again. You see, this is my first time on a horse."

Her laughter rang out. Probably, I thought, she has never met anyone like me before: a *shlemiel* who doesn't know how to get off a horse, and is stupid enough to admit it!

Suddenly she jumped back up on her horse. "Watch me now," she said. "You get off like this." She brought her foot over the horse's back and then slowly slid down to the ground.

"Come on," she urged. "Get off. Your horse needs a rest. I'll show you how to get back on again, don't worry!"

Copying her actions, I slid down from the mare. How good it felt to be standing on solid earth again!

I saw a brook nearby, so I said, "I think I'll take White Belly to the water there. She must be awfully thirsty, after all that running."

Suleika rose, walked over to White Belly and patted her hide. Then she held up her hand, palm towards me, and said, "Look! That's her sweat you see here on my hand. If you give water to a horse in this condition, she'll be dead in a few hours. Never — now listen, city boy — *never* give water to a sweating horse. You know, if you do a stupid thing like that, and you kill a horse, you'll be imprisoned for destroying socialist property!"

I was subdued. She walked back to a spot of grass, and for a while we both sat there in silence.

Finally she spoke. "You asked if my name is unusual in Russia. I'm not a Russian. *Sovietsky*, yes; but not a Russian. I'm a Tatar."

A Tatar! Shades of Genghis Khan! I remembered that he was the leader of the Mongols who had conquered most of this part of the world, even as far west as Poland. There, the word "Tatar" was a euphemism for murderer, and was used to frighten little children.

As though she sensed what I was thinking, she said, "You're surprised? You probably don't even know that we have our own autonomous republic, the Tatar Autonomous Soviet Socialist Republic, which borders the Kuybishev region. Our capital is Kazan, and the Tatar University there is one of the best in the whole Soviet Union."

How things change, I thought. Nowadays a descendant of the cruel Tatars boasts of a university!

"And where are you from?" she asked.

"I'm from Poland," I replied, and then added, "I'm a Jew."

"A *what*!" Her eyes widened in disbelief. "A *Jew*?"

"Yes!" I enjoyed observing her shock. After a few moments, however, she jumped to her feet and proceeded to walk around me, eyeing me all the while. Suddenly she was down on her knees, closely inspecting my head. Then she broke into loud laughter.

"Forgive me," she said, "I never really believed it, but I had to prove it to myself."

"Prove what?" I asked.

"About Jews having horns," she replied. "Three years ago there was a lecture in my village, and the commissar told us that the fascist spy Trotsky had horns because he was a Jew, and that all Jews have horns."

With eyes averted she said, "I must have seemed awfully stupid to you! The way I acted, I mean. Imagine — believing such nonsense!"

She was so embarrassed and contrite that I was disconcerted. Finally I said, "Now that you're convinced about my horns, how about showing me the way back to Karobka?"

I got up and walked over to White Belly. Suleika did not move, nor did she say anything.

"You promised to help me get on the horse, remember?" I said. "But please don't pull me up by my horns."

"Forgive me," she said. "It was stupid of me, I know; but I beg you, please forgive me."

Suddenly she brightened and said, "I won't help you get on your horse if you don't forgive me, and it's a good six kilometers to your village! I'll tell you what, though. If you'll forgive me, I'll take you to see my village. I'll bet you've never seen a real Tatar village, have you?"

"All right," I replied, "I forgive you."

"Comrade?" she asked.

"Comrade," I replied.

Standing next to the mare, she clasped her fingers together and stooped slightly. "Now then," she ordered, "place your left foot in my hands and jump up. But don't grab her by her mane, you hear?"

I followed her instructions, and I jumped up and landed, more or less, atop White Belly. I crawled a little until I was in her middle; then I sat up straight.

"See?" she teased. "Nothing to it!" Then she walked over to her horse and, in one lightning move, she was gracefully seated.

"This way," she called as she turned her horse and started moving. White Belly followed her. The path through the woods was only wide enough for one, and I was glad that she was in front because I was afraid that otherwise White Belly might run wild again, and I'd had enough of that.

Turning around slightly, she asked, "Did you know that White Belly was born in my village?"

"Really?" I was surprised. "Then how did _Kolkhoz Karobka_ get him?" I asked.

"Her!" she reminded me.

"Her!" I repeated. "So how did Karobka get her?"

"Because we sold her to Karobka, that's how," she replied. "And do you know, I myself trained her. I spent so much time with her she probably thinks I'm her sister. By the way, her name, when she was in my village, was 'Brown Devil.'"

"Brown Devil? Well, is it customary here to change a horse's name when he — she — is sold?"

"No," she replied. "But Russians are scared of the word 'devil.' And so they changed Brown Devil's name to White Belly. Tell me, what happened to make her run like that?"

I told her, "Someone slapped her on the hind legs."

Just then she stopped and pointed. "There's my village," she said.

Up ahead — I could barely see it through the forest — was a red-roofed building. A tall, slender spire rose above the roof.

"What's that?" I asked, "Is it a church?"

"No, silly," she replied. "Churches are for Christians, and we Tatars are Moslems. That's a mosque. Rather, we _used_ to be Moslems, and that building _used_ to be a mosque. Now it's our warehouse. The old people still believe in all that nonsense, but not the young ones; we don't need any silly old mosques!"

As we approached the village I saw that all the other buildings had roofs of thatched straw, just like in Karobka. However, there was one big difference between this Tatar village and all of the Russian villages I'd seen. Here the houses were set much farther apart from each other, with perhaps five times as much space between neighbors as there was in Karobka. When I commented on this, she said, "Yes, I've noticed that the Russians don't mind living almost on top of each other. I couldn't stand that. I like my neighbors to be far enough away that it takes a horseback ride, and not a short walk, to visit one another."

Now I remembered something from the history books.

"Do you know who Genghis Khan was?" I asked her.

"Of course, silly!" she replied.

"Did you know that, although he burned to the ground all the cities he conquered, he didn't burn down the small villages?"

"Well," she said, "everybody knows about those cities, but I hadn't known that he left the small villages. Why?"

"Most historians agree that it was because Genghis Khan and his warriors detested cities. They believed that it's a horrible fate to live there, and so they probably felt that they were doing a good deed when they burned down a city."

"That's fascinating," she commented. "And you know what? He was right. It *is* a horrible fate to have to live in a city." I couldn't tell whether she was serious, or merely mocking me.

"It's getting late; I have to go now," she said. "It's time to get the cow and take her home. Well, *dosvidanya* — good-bye!"

"*Dosvidanya*," I replied. "And thank you!"

Suleika rode into her village, and I turned my mare around and rode the opposite way, back towards Karobka.

11

I HAD NOT gone far when I saw a man on horseback racing towards me, waving frantically. Finally, I recognized him: it was my schoolteacher friend, Goncharov.

He pulled up and said, "We've been searching all over for you! We were afraid something terrible had happened to you!"

"On the contrary," I said, and I told Goncharov all about my afternoon's experiences, while we rode back towards Karobka.

"I know Suleika. She's a very special girl," he commented.

I was surprised. "You know her? How? And what's so special about her?"

"I've substituted many times in the school there. She's got a good brain."

"She can't be that smart," I said, "if she actually believed that Jews have horns! Only after she inspected my head did she finally decide it's not true!" Then I told him about the Mordvinian girl at the Machine Tractor Station who also believed that Jews have horns. Goncharov laughed, but I was upset.

"Tell me, Nikolai Yefimovich Goncharov!" I exclaimed. "Where do these people get such crazy ideas?"

"Don't you know?" he asked, genuinely surprised. "They get it from the Bible. Haven't you ever seen the well-known picture of Moses? It shows him with horns."

"Oh, you're talking about Michelangelo's statue of Moses! That's right — he put horns on Moses. *Chi*, Comrade Goncharov," I said, "how would you like to learn something that most people don't know?"

"About religion?" he replied. "Not particularly, thank you!"

I had to laugh. "I'll tell you, anyway," I said. "The Bible was written in Hebrew, and it reads, 'The face of Moses *shone* when he spoke with the Lord.' The Hebrew words *'karan or'* mean 'sent forth rays of light,' or 'shone.' The Latin translation of the Bible reads 'horns of light,' for the Hebrew word *'keren'* can mean either 'horn' or 'ray.' Thus the medieval artists, including Michelangelo, were misled into representing Moses with horns protruding from his forehead!

"But," I added, "you haven't answered my question, Goncharov. Let's say, for the sake of the argument, that Moses *did* have horns. But he was only one Jew; who gave these people the idea that all Jews have horns?"

Goncharov gave me a knowing look. "Who do you think?" he said. "The Church, of course!"

But then I remembered something. "Just a minute, Goncharov," I said. "You forgot something. Neither Suleika nor that Mordvinian girl has ever been exposed to the Christian Church! They couldn't have learned it there!"

"It's like this, Chaim," he replied. "The regime has taught us that everything we have been told about God, Heaven, devils and angels is pure nonsense. But the regime has not seen fit to apprise us of the fact that everything we have been told about Jews is also nonsense. In other words, we have freed ourselves from some of that superstitious nonsense, but not all of it."

There was nothing more to say. We continued silently on our way to the village.

At last Goncharov spoke again. "You must have figured out that it was Yefim who whipped your horse and made her run wild," he said. "The chairman told him he'll be punished for it. And speaking of the chairman, you'll be happy to hear that in a few days he's going to have a talk with the director himself, Comrade Sonnenberg, about your transfer from the MTS!"

"Sonnenberg?" I asked, surprised. "Is he a Jew?"

"A *Jew*? Are you kidding?" he replied. "Of course not! He's a German."

I was even more surprised. "A *German*?"

"Yes, a German!" he replied. "There are lots of them in the Soviet Union. Haven't you *ever* heard about the two million Volga Germans?"

"No. Who are they?"

"They once had their own republic on the Volga, near Saratov, not far from here. But not any more! Some German spies parachuted down there and no one reported them to the authorities! Well, they found out anyway, and the entire area was cleared out. The women and children were shipped off to various parts of Asia, and the men to Siberia and the Urals. The German Autonomous Republic is as empty as a desert now. Maybe the government will resettle it with refugees," he added.

I was astonished. "But Goncharov, surely not all two million of those Germans were disloyal. What about the Communist Party members? Weren't they considered trustworthy?"

"Look," he replied, "if a local Party apparatus couldn't succeed, in twenty years, in educating their people to loyalty and patriotism, then that apparatus isn't worth anything! And certainly now, with the German army choking us, who's got time to try to figure out who's a traitor and who isn't?"

"So how is it that Sonnenberg is still director of the Machine Tractor Station?" I asked.

"Sonnenberg is just lucky," Goncharov said. "Lucky he was here, and not there in the German republic, when the big round-up took place! Luckier yet, he won't be drafted. The army doesn't want Germans, so he was kept here in his post. But you can be sure that lots of eyes are keeping a close watch on his every move."

At last we arrived back at Karobka and put our horses back in the stable. I noticed that Yefim was nowhere to be seen.

The next day at work, Fiodor said to me, "That German, Sonnenberg, is some tough inspector. We'd better take care of a few things before he gets here. You crawl under the tractor and see what you can do about stopping that oil leak. I'll take this lousy carburetor apart and clean it."

With a pair of pliers and a wrench in my hands, I slid under the tractor. Fiodor removed the carburetor and proceeded to dismantle it. Underneath, everything was oily and greasy. It was impossible to tell where the worst oil leak was, so I tightened every possible nut and bolt. Fiodor cleaned out the carburetor and put it back onto the engine. The moment he had finished replacing it, a two-wheel buggy pulled up next to our tractor. I peeked out and saw a man in his early fifties, with broad shoulders and graying blond hair, step out. There was a big smile on his face as he shook hands with Fiodor. I remained where I was, under the tractor, filled with wonder at the sight of a Soviet high official on an inspection tour acting in such a friendly manner.

Fiodor told him that he had just finished "repairing" the carburetor. "May I start the engine, Comrade Director? We'll see what kind of a job I did."

"By all means, Fiodor," Sonnenberg replied. "Start her up." Fiodor didn't even bother warning me as he started up the engine. I heard a sudden roar and I hastily crawled out from underneath; Fiodor turned off the engine at the same time. When I got to my feet I found myself facing a scene of disaster; the director was soaked with water, and Fiodor, whose face was white with horror, was extracting a screwdriver from the radiator. The screwdriver had pierced through the core of the radiator, apparently having been flung there by the fan blades. Sonnenberg was ranting, cursing Fiodor's forebears as far back as his great-grandmother, in an awesome display of German-Russian passion.

As I listened I became aware of the fact that Sonnenberg was cursing not only Fiodor, but also me. "Some help you've got," he shouted at Fiodor. Then, turning to me, Sonnenberg yelled, "You! Foreigner! Clumsy dog! Is this how you help win the war? By sabotaging the harvest? You low down....*Chi*, don't you know how vital this machine is to our war effort? Or is it because you *do* know that you sabotaged it?"

I was stunned and frightened. Should I defend myself, or should I wait until Sonnenberg's anger cooled off? I noticed that Fiodor didn't open his mouth in my defense. There was no one else around, no witnesses. Then it occurred to me that since Sonnenberg was a German, and I was a Jew, what could be more logical than for him to try to dispose of me? I had to do something, and fast!

"I was underneath the tractor, repairing an oil leak," I said quietly, trying to keep my voice restrained and respectful. "I wasn't working on top of the engine, so I couldn't possibly have left the screwdriver up there near the fan blades."

"You could have left it up there if you wanted to sabotage this machine!" he yelled.

Then I tried to cover up for both of us. "Comrade Director," I said, speaking softly and calmly, "while I was under the tractor I noticed some women standing nearby. They may have fooled around with some of the tools while Fiodor was up there assembling the carburetor."

Fiodor winked at me, as though to say "Good work." Sonnenberg's face relaxed a bit and I saw that this was the way out of this predicament; with returning confidence, I added one more sentence: "Comrade Director, that is the truth!" But for some inexplicable reason I said it in German. What a terrible blunder!

"You idiot! If you can't speak Russian, just shut up! What kind of rotten language is that, anyway? Speak so we can all understand, you stupid foreigner! Get into my carriage — there's been sabotage here, and I, Sonnenberg, will find the traitor!"

Terrified, I climbed into his two-passenger buggy. Sonnenberg ordered Fiodor to remove the radiator and to put it in the buggy. As we drove off, he said to Fiodor, "I hope to have it fixed and back to you by tomorrow."

I was in great anxiety; I might be accused of sabotage, and my accuser was a high Party member! I was just an unimportant foreigner, a Westerner; worse yet, a Jew! Would anybody believe me? And suppose I'd be asked to identify the women who allegedly had been standing around the tractor? Actually, there'd been several women near there an hour before the accident, but how could I accuse them and get them into trouble?

By now we were deep in the forest, and still no words had been exchanged between us. I decided to take the initiative.

"Comrade Director, I apologize for speaking German. I have some difficulty expressing myself in Russian. I still think in my native tongue, and then, in my mind, I translate into Russian. But when I was accused of something for which I was not to blame, I was so upset that it just came out in German."

Sonnenberg did not reply and there were several more minutes of silence. Finally he said, "So you are from Germany, eh?"

"No, Comrade Director," I replied, relieved that the ice had been broken. "I'm from Poland, from Lomza. It's only sixty kilometers from the German border, though, and there are many Germans there; some of them are good friends of ours."

He then started to speak to me in German. Sometimes, when he couldn't remember a word or a phrase, he would throw in some Russian. In this strange Russianized German, he said, "That was really stupid of you, speaking German in front of a Russian! After all, we're at war with Germany. Neither one of us is considered trustworthy; otherwise we would have both been in the army by now! I'm actually a captain in the reserves, but because I'm a German the army doesn't trust me. And in fact I feel more Russian than German; my wife is Russian; my two children are Russian."

We fell silent. I was thinking that across the front lines, the Germans were killing Jews, but here this German and I were in the same boat — strangers, outsiders, not trustworthy. My Poland had been liquidated, and his German republic had been wiped out too.

The director broke the silence. "Tell me, young man, what kind of people are these Germans? Are they really so cruel? Do they actually do the terrible things we hear about?"

Were these questions sincere or merely typical Russian "insurance"? I glanced at Sonnenberg, who was looking squarely at me; he paid no attention to the horse, which obviously knew its way home.

"Well," I began hesitantly, "the Germans I knew were not bad people, but to describe the general feeling about Germans, I'll quote from a famous novelist, a German himself. He described them as bricks in a wall; the brick knows that the one placed above him has to press him down, and he in turn has to press down the one below him. Actually it's an army saying, but it's applicable to German civilians as well. And Churchill described the Germans this way: 'If they are not at your feet, they are at your throat! For the sake of world security, we should keep them at our feet.'"

Sonnenberg was silent again. After a while, he began to question me about farming, unions, and the standard of living in Poland and in other countries. But he always came back to the subject of Germany. I remembered my father saying, "A German, no matter where he is — his heart is in Berlin." How his eyes glowed when I said something good about the Germans! And how his face darkened when I described their wickedness and cruelty!

Suddenly he asked, "When did you meet Summatov?" and before I could explain that I had never met him, he continued, "It's amazing! In the short time you've been here you've managed to make so many friends that everybody is asking me to let you stay in the village — the teacher, the chairman, and even Summatov the Tatar, the chairman of the council of villages."

I realized then that Summatov must be Suleika's father, and that he was supporting the Karobka chairman's plea for swapping me for Ilya the stable boy.

Sonnenberg added, "If you weren't Jewish and I weren't German you'd wind up in prison for that radiator! It's not important where you were at the time of the accident. By law and custom," he said with a cynical smile, "here is a damaged radiator, and a tractor that cannot produce for at least twenty-four hours. You are a refugee from fascist Poland and that's enough to get you five years; but in this case I'll call you a clumsy worker not fit to be around tractors, and gladly swap you for that boy."

I waited around for the rest of the day while the radiator was being repaired, and then walked home, carrying it on my shoulders. It was heavy, but my heart was light, for I also carried my release papers, signed by the director himself, Friedrich Gansovich Sonnenberg. Now I'd be able to stay in this village where I had no worries about _kashrus_ or Shabbos, and where the people accepted me as one of their own.

I was often invited to the _ulitzu_; literally, the word means "street," but since these villages did not have any streets, the word was used to mean "the meeting place." Since there were few eligible boys in Karobka, and the same situation prevailed in all the neighboring villages, the youth of several villages in the surrounding countryside would get together in one convenient village, mostly on Saturday or Sunday nights, for dancing and singing.

Although the villagers worked seven days a week, the young people still found the energy, after a hard day's work, to march off to the _ulitzu_ and dance. I had declined invitations a number of times, for I preferred to spend my free time reading the poems of Lermontov. Although I didn't understand all of the words, I had progressed in Russian enough to enjoy the beautiful poetry. This book, of Lermontov's poetry, which I'd borrowed from the teacher, was large enough for me to hide my little _Tanach_ in it. I was thus able to read it often, and with much yearning.

Eventually Anna, my well-meaning landlady, began to push me into accepting the invitations to the _ulitzu_. "What kind of a boy are you," she asked me, "if all you're interested in is books and more books? What about having a little fun?"

Finally I gave in, and one Sunday evening I took Anna's three children and, together with the Karobka gang, we started off towards the _ulitzu_. To preserve my shoes, which were quite dilapidated, I walked barefoot like everyone else. I could hardly keep up with them, though, for my feet were delicate and uncalloused, and hurt every time I stepped on a twig or stone;

but everyone else marched along without any trouble. After walking almost five miles, we reached the village where the *ulitzu* was being held.

The place was already full of teenagers. The girls outnumbered the boys by about ten to one. Barefoot, and wearing their shabby, stained working clothes, they were singing and dancing to the tunes of a screeching *garmoshka* — a primitive accordion. My feet were sore from the march, so I had an excellent excuse not to take part in the dancing.

I sat on a tree stump and listened to the *chastushki* — the folk songs. These were not sophisticated popular songs written by professional composers in Moscow, but true folk songs, coming from the very depths of the heart. What they lacked in poetry and perfection of lyrics was compensated for by the lovely melodies which seemed to emanate from the soul of the people. The songs told of friendship and betrayal, of Mother Russia, family, war and death. Usually, one person would begin singing and others would join in; then the *garmoshka* would pick it up and suddenly the entire crowd would be singing as one; and the plaintive melody would ring out all over the forest.

There was nothing to eat or drink, but there was no shortage of dancing and singing. The main attraction that evening was a girl from the big city, who created a lot of jealousy among the others. Here, where there were neither radios nor record players, songs traveled from mouth to mouth. People learned them by heart and sang constantly. This girl had brought some new songs from the city, and the young men in the crowd vied for her attention. Soon the tension was palpable, there were shouts and yells, and shiny blades flashed in the bright moonlight. I quickly rounded up my Karobka gang and we set out for home, determined to remove ourselves from the fight and the possibility of bloodshed. On the way, we sang a familiar yearning melody:

> Beloved village, may you sleep in peace,
> Familiar house,
> Green garden.
> Pleasant view!
> When battle's done, I'll return to you!

The frequent fights became my habitual excuse for refusing to attend another *ulitzu*.

In my new job in the stables, one of my duties was to bring water and sometimes lunch to the workers in the fields. Occasionally Suleika accompanied me on her horse. Goncharov began to tease me about her, pointing out the advantages of marrying the only child of Summatov, the Party boss of the district.

"But be careful — those Tatar girls are strong and tough!"

"In that case," I answered jokingly, "since my family is not here to protect me, the wedding is off!"

Goncharov replied seriously, his voice full of emotion, "Chaim, we are your family! All of Karobka is your family. Let them try to hurt you, and we'll happily cut every damned Tatar throat in their village!" There was a wild look in his eyes.

I couldn't explain to him how completely unthinkable it was for me to marry a girl who was not Jewish; I felt that I had to hide, even from him, my religious training and my attachment to the faith of my fathers.

I thought often of my own family — Papa, who had cried when we said good-bye to each other; Mama, so good, so loving, so devoted. Oh, what I would give to be able to hear her gentle voice again!

How different, and how far away, seemed the years of my youth, the safe, steady passage of days in Lomza. Which was real, and which was the dream — those bygone days, or the present? The past seemed to fade as I spent day after day, working and sweating with the peasants, driving the tractor, the smell of hay, earth and mold always in my nostrils.

Frequently, on the way to or from the fields, the workers would break into song. Traditionally, one singer — the _zapyevala_ — begins a song and then the audience joins in. The leader's voice, though not exceptional, was loud, powerful and apparently tireless; even after a hard day's work, the young people were still ready to sing and dance. Their vivacity cheered the others and brought them back to life after their day's exhausting labor.

Soon they discovered that I knew their songs. One day the wife of the chairman had walked into the stables while I was watering the horses. Unaware of her presence, I was singing some Yiddish and Hebrew songs; then I switched to Russian. I was startled to hear her voice: "Poor boy, you must be very lonely and longing for home; because only then does a person sing with such feeling!"

Once the word spread that I knew their songs, the workers prevailed upon me to become the _zapyevala_. I led them in their beloved Russian songs; they were full of sorrow and longing, poignantly reflecting the lives of the Russian peasants. One of the most popular was a military song about a girl and a pilot; it was demanded on every occasion:

The apple and pear trees blossomed,
Clouds and fog spread over the river.
Out for a walk on the bank was Katyusha,
On the steep, sharp bank of the river.
Softly, softly she walked along.
And remembering, she burst into song
About the blue-colored eagle, so brave and so strong.
About the one she is waiting for,
About the one whose letters she reads again and again.
Eagle, remember the simple girl,
Pilot, remember your promise so true.
Guard and defend the native soil
And Katyusha will be faithful to you!

The women often cried at the end; whether for themselves or for the devoted Katyusha I could never tell, but I felt very sorry for them. Their lives were hard, so hard; and with the men away, they took on the most difficult labors, willingly. Anything to keep alive, to feed their children.

Occasionally, all the manure of the stables had to be removed to the fields. Since it was the only fertilizer available, it was a most precious commodity and we spread it over the fields very carefully. This was a difficult task since the manure was heavy, and so two women were always assigned to help. Although it was one of the most strenuous jobs, it always amazed me to see how enthusiastically they volunteered, and even argued with each other, to get this assignment. On the way from the stable to the fields, they always invited me to stop at the house for a glass of milk and *piroshki* — filled pastry. I innocently accepted these invitations until one day, when I was inside a house drinking skimmed milk, I happened to look out the window. Then I realized that, while one woman plied me with food and drink and kept up a constant stream of talk with me, the other stole manure for her own private garden plot!

Thus the devotion to private enterprise quietly prevailed, even in this little commune. I closed my eyes to it — *laissez-faire* was my own economic preference.

IT HAD BEEN a tiring day for me. I had worked in the blacksmith shop with Goncharov, who became a blacksmith during the summer when school was not in session. We had finished an emergency job for the tractor, and despite the hard work, it had been pleasant, helping the teacher while he sang, recited poetry and told stories. He was particularly fond of Lermontov.

"A soul speaks to a soul," he quoted Lermontov, and then added, "That's me and you. Ah, will I be sorry if you leave!"

I was becoming a pretty good hand in the blacksmith shop, striking with the heavy hammer in exactly the right spot. With each blow I could feel my muscles hardening. Goncharov, keeping time with the rhythmic beat of the hammer, sang out the ballad of the Volga boatmen, the old famous "*Hey Ukhnyem.*"

That evening, reading the most recent newspaper to my attentive audience, I came across a news item on the last page, where all the foreign news was printed. The short sentence aroused tremendous excitement in me: "The government of the USSR has recognized the Polish government-in-exile, headed by Prime Minister Wladyslaw Sikorski in London."

To my listeners this meant nothing, but to me it was everything! I was so excited that I couldn't sleep that night. Again and again I touched the two pages which were all that remained of my Polish passport. I was so happy that I had kept them; one contained the seal of the Polish embassy in Berne, Switzerland, stamped on my photograph. Soon there would be a Polish embassy in Moscow. Just think of it, I told myself, my own embassy!

The next day another small item appeared: "Comrade Maiski, the Soviet ambassador in London, was accredited to the Polish government of General Sikorski." The renewing of diplomatic relations puzzled me,

although technically the two countries were not at war. The Polish government had been so preoccupied, scurrying for safety in 1939, that they never
got around to declaring war on the USSR. The day the Red Army crossed
the Polish border, the Polish ambassador merely left Moscow. At that
time, Russia's Molotov declared publicly, "Poland has forever ceased to
exist." Stalin had incorporated the eastern provinces of Poland into the
Ukrainian and White Russian Soviet Republics. And now Stalin and
Molotov were sending an ambassador to the Polish government-in-exile!

Poland, which had from time immemorial regarded the Russians as
Enemy Number Two — Number One being the Germans — would now
send an ambassador to Moscow! War does indeed make strange bedfel-
lows! And what about the lost territories? And my home town? Would it
remain a part of Russia? If so, then am I, God forbid, considered a Soviet
citizen? All these questions went through my mind. Those few short lines
in *Pravda* were tantalizing, but also frustrating. I couldn't wait to see if
there were new developments, and almost every day something new did
appear, adding to my excitement.

A Polish military mission, headed by Major General Bohusz Szyszko,
was being established in Moscow.

A Polish-Soviet military agreement had been signed.

A Polish army was being organized in the Soviet Union, which would
"fight shoulder to shoulder with the glorious Red Army against the common enemy of all Slavic nations, Germany!"

Then another item: General Wladyslaw Anders had been appointed by
General Sikorski to be commander-in-chief of the new Polish army in the
USSR.

At once I mailed a letter, addressed to "The Polish Embassy, Moscow,"
volunteering for the new Polish army. While I was anxiously awaiting a
reply from the embassy, all news on the subject of Poland ceased to appear
in the papers.

When no reply came from the embassy, I attributed it to the inefficiency of the Soviet mail delivery. Or perhaps, I thought, the letter was
lost, because of the war. So I wrote again, telling the embassy of my
yearning to fight the enemy "under the banner of our Polish White Eagle."

Days passed, and still no reply from the embassy! Now I blamed the
embassy for being disorganized; perhaps it was not yet established properly. Then I thought of the woman who picked up the mail in Karobka;
suppose she delivered the letter not to the district post office but to the

NKVD instead! Seeing a letter to a foreign embassy for the first time in her life, she may have decided to fulfill her "duties to Stalin and the Fatherland," since most officials, even minor ones, were secret agents of the NKVD.

So I wrote a third letter, in which I included the number of my passport, and asked for instructions on how to enlist in the Polish army of General Anders. That night I smuggled out my favorite mare and galloped off to Booyan, ten miles away. There I dropped the letter directly into the post office mailbox, and returned to Karobka.

Again I waited and waited day after day; no reply ever came. And still not a word in the newspapers!

Now I began to wonder about the reliability of post offices in rural Russia. They probably weren't used to letters addressed to foreign embassies, and assuming any contact with foreign countries to be espionage, they might have delivered my letter to the NKVD! And the police, not being able to read Polish, had probably destroyed the letter, or sent it off to Moscow for a translation. All these thoughts ran through my mind endlessly, especially at night.

I concluded that the only way I could get a letter to the embassy safely was by personally dropping it into a Moscow-bound mail car. However, the nearest railroad was in Chapayevsk, almost fifty miles away! Day after day I dwelt on the problem: how could I get to Chapayevsk?

One evening, a tall, yellow-faced rider on a beautiful white-gray stallion appeared at the newspaper-reading session. Although he was a stranger to me, I could tell he was no stranger to the others. In fact, by their deference towards him, I could sense that he was someone of importance. He had Tatar features, and they called him Comrade Summatov. He must be Suleika's father, I decided; there was certainly a family resemblance.

After a few minutes of banter, I was requested to continue with the reading. I had hardly begun when suddenly Comrade Summatov interrupted: "Comrade Chaim, _chi_, what do you propose we do with that rotten Gitler after we catch him?"

Out of the cloud of cigarette smoke there came many heated mutterings.

"Kill the rat!" an old farmer growled.

"Cut him up in little pieces, together with his gang!"

"_Chi_, whatever glorious Comrade Stalin will say will be done with him," said a crippled veteran, amidst general approval.

I was astonished at the question. The latest news from the front was very bad; the Nazis were pushing towards Moscow. Yet here were these Russians, wondering what to do with Hitler! Were they that ignorant, or just stupid? And the Tatar — surely he could grasp the situation? Perhaps this was a propaganda trick, and our loyalty was being tested by this Party official. Or it might simply be the natural instinct of the people to believe in victory. Besides, old *Dedushka Moroz* — Grandpa Frost — or, as he was sometimes called, "General Winter," was approaching, with temperatures of thirty degrees below zero.

Finally I declared, "In my opinion, killing Hitler would be making it too easy for him. *Chi*, I would (of course, subject to the approval of our great Comrade Stalin) put him in a cage, place him in the zoo of the Kremlin, and let the people come and spit in his face and stick needles into him."

"An excellent idea," said the Tatar, visibly pleased. Then he added, "I am Suleika's father."

I shook his hand and said, "I am Chaim."

"Yes, I know," he replied with a friendly smile. Then he left and I returned to my reading of the newspaper.

Apparently the Tatar hadn't come just for a friendly visit; soon after he left, two large posters appeared in front of the office. One read: "Food for the Heroic Defenders of Our Socialist Fatherland." The other called for "Grain for Embattled Leningrad!" The message spread through the village in an instant — grain deliveries had to be doubled! Normally, deliveries were made to the nearest town, Booyan, which was only ten miles away. But this time, because of the emergency, the grain would have to be taken straight to the railroad station in Chapayevsk, which was fifty miles away.

This was my chance! I'd be able to put my letter to the embassy directly into a mail car!

The regular delivery man was Victor Alexeyevich Zakharov. He was generally disliked by the villagers, but no one would tell me the reason for his unpopularity. When there was one wagon to deliver, he would take it to the road all by himself; if there were two, his fifteen-year-old son would drive the second. Now, with the increase "for embattled Leningrad," three wagons would have to be loaded. This is my chance, I thought, my only chance to get my letter on a train!

I hurried to the chairman, *Dedushka* Anton, and volunteered to drive the third wagon. His reply startled me.

"That's up to Vitia Zakharov," he snapped. So I hastened to find Vitia, and asked him if I could drive the third wagon.

His answer was short and sharp. "It's me and my two boys who'll drive the wagons!"

"But Victor Alexeyevich," I replied, using his full name as a sign of respect, "your younger son is too young to unload a wagon full of wheat. Semyon is fifteen, but Vladimir is only twelve!"

Vitia was obstinate. "I do the unloading. The boys only drive."

I returned to the chairman's office and told him about my disappointment. With a shrug of his shoulders, he said, "My dear Chaim, there's nothing I can do. The Party has placed him in absolute charge of deliveries."

I was mystified. Vitia could barely read and write, so he couldn't be a Party member. Then why had he been given such an important monopoly? I felt that this trip to Chapayevsk was a matter of life and death for me. I _had_ to deliver my letter to the embassy, for this was my only chance to get to fight the Germans; and in a Polish uniform, not a Russian one.

I returned to Zakharov's house, and again tried to persuade him to let me drive the extra wagon. "Why do you want to go along so badly?" he wanted to know.

I invented all kinds of reasons: "I've never been to Chapayevsk. Before I get drafted, I want to see the sights — a big town, a market, a Russian city."

"When you get drafted you'll see it all," he answered laconically.

Finally I "confessed." "The real reason is that I want to trade on the black market — some flour for a few _katyushas_," I confided. _Katyusha_ is actually a common female name, and so popular that any gadget, from a fancy little toy to the latest piece of artillery, was called _katyusha_.

The _katyusha_ I was referring to was a cigarette lighter. In a country where ordinary matches are considered a treasure, necessity, being the mother of invention, had produced the _katyusha_. It consisted of a piece of steel about the size of a domino. One would place a piece of cotton wool on the steel, and then strike the steel with the sharp edge of a stone. This would produce a spark, which would set fire to the cotton. This was easier said than done, however, for one had to strike the _katyusha_ many times until the sparks were sufficient to set the cotton aflame. Sometimes people called it a _godovshchina_, which means "anniversary," because it could take as many as twenty-five or even fifty blows before it would work!

On my first day at the MTS, a mechanic had offered to sell me a *katyusha*. However, at that time I was ignorant of its tremendous value, so I had declined his offer. Now I needed one badly, for in my present job in the stable, I had to light a fire in the blacksmith shop every morning. The other villagers were quite handy in "splitting" matches; they took one large wooden match and split it into four. Because of my clumsiness, however, every time I tried to split a match, even only in two, the sulfur would crack off, thus ruining a precious match! My favorite excuse for not making a fire on Shabbos was, "I ruined my match!" And I never did light a fire or work in the shop on Shabbos or *Yom Tov.*

I explained to Vitia that I intended to trade some flour for a few *katyusha*s to hand out as presents to my friends. He offered to take my flour to Chapayevsk and to bring back *katyusha*s in trade for it.

I lost my patience and blurted out, "Victor Alexeyevich, there must be some reason why you refuse to let me go with you, and I shall find out what it is!"

Actually I had not meant anything serious in my outburst, but from the instant change on his face I realized that I had touched a raw nerve. Suddenly his wife came in from the next room and said to him, "Vitia, he won't be in your way. While you're busy at the grain bins, he'll browse around the *tolchock* — the market. He might even buy you a *katyusha.*"

At last he agreed to let me be the third driver. I could have kissed his stubbly face, I was so happy and excited.

We looked like a caravan, with Vitia in the front wagon, followed by his son Semyon, and with me and White Belly at the end. Hour after hour we bumped slowly along. One could sleep all the time, except when the road went downhill. Then Vitia would yell, "Brakes!" Then we had to jump off our wagons and stick a piece of wood into the rear wheel, thus "braking" the wagons.

All through the night our caravan slowly lumbered along.

In the morning, by the bright sunlight, I began to write my letter to the embassy. I put my innermost feelings into it — my hate for the Germans, my patriotism for Poland, the details of my passport.

"Honorable Sir Mr. Ambassador," I wrote. "It is often said by historians that Poland lost all its wars, and won all its uprisings. We Poles, of course, know better; but even those historians will have to admit that this time, by a combination of an uprising from within and a fighting force from without under the glorious White Eagle, our beloved country shall win at last!" Then, as an insurance policy in the event that the letter might fall into Russian hands, I added: "Together with the glorious Red Army under Stalin, we shall destroy the enemy forever!"

Knowing the Polish sensitivity about Communism, I added that I was a rabbinical student, in the best of health, and that I could handle horses very well; and if the new army should be mechanized, that I was an experienced tractorist, too. "Please send the draft note, or any paper with instructions, either directly to me or to the Soviet military commandant in Booyan," I concluded.

To make doubly sure, I wrote out another copy of the letter, so I could drop them into two different mail trains. I was a little worried about how I'd manage to get to the trains, for I had heard that no one was permitted to step onto the platform without a *commanderovka* — a travel order — and tickets. I couldn't ask Vitia about it since, as far as he knew, my major objective was to buy *katyushas* on the black market.

Eventually, the path became straighter and smoother. Vitia climbed down from his wagon and ordered his son to take over the leading horse. While the horses continued along, without a break in pace, he climbed up next to me. He wanted to give me some advice, he said in a confidential tone, "in case you get arrested."

"Arrested? For what?" I asked, astonished.

"For speculation, *ponyatno* — you understand?"

He explained to me that normally everything that was produced or manufactured was distributed by the government. From the government it reached the population. And the government established the price for each product — both the price at which it was bought and the price at which it was sold. The same price was set for the entire enormous country, regardless of the local conditions and climate. There could be no middle-men, no speculators. The government made a concession, though, to the peasants of the collectives; it permitted them to sell in the open market — the *black* market — the products they raised on their own private lots.

"But you are not a farmer, you don't own a lot, you don't even look like a *kolkhoznik*, so the police might easily arrest you as a speculator if you're seen selling flour! And speculation in our country is as bad as sabotage," he declared, looking straight at me with his probing, bulging eyes.

"So what can I do? Can I depend on you to testify that I am a *kolkhoznik* and not a speculator?" I asked him anxiously.

"That's impossible," he replied. "I'll be busy at the delivery and no one can get in there because of the armed guard. And the police will not bother to look for me, or to send an inquiry to Karobka. And even if they did, by the time their reply reached the police, you'd already be condemned to five years and sent off to Siberia."

"In that case, maybe I'd better not go to the market alone, or even go at all — or are you simply trying to scare me so I'll be able to go and help you unload the wagons?" I asked.

He rolled a cigarette, and in a tone of authority, like an experienced attorney, he said, "No, you can go to the market alone; but when you're arrested, tell the police you stole the flour. They'll confiscate the flour, but they'll let you go free!"

I jumped up as if bitten by a snake. "You mean to tell me that I should confess to something I didn't do? To say I'm a thief, when I've never stolen anything in my life?" I shouted, suddenly whipping White Belly as though my distress were the poor mare's fault. I couldn't tell Vitia that I'd never risk arrest, since that could spoil my only chance of being admitted to the army — my only chance of fighting the Germans!

Vitia sat there, calmly smoking his terrible tree leaves, from time to time coughing out huge amounts of smoke mixed with laughter. Patiently he began again to instruct me, just like a lawyer explaining things to a client.

"You see, it's like this — in the Soviet Union we figure that if somebody steals something, he must need it badly, or he wouldn't have taken it. The one he took it from probably doesn't need it too badly; otherwise he would have watched over it much better, right? So why should the police waste their time with it? But speculation! This could lead to the ruination of our Soviet system! A speculator-parasite can undermine the whole economy! That's why the police and the courts are so hard on speculators. So I'm telling you, if the police nab you, just do as I told you — forget your conscience, tell them you're a thief, and then you'll be all right!"

He jumped off my wagon and returned to his own. I was thinking about the aim of the Soviet system, the Communist utopia — "From each according to his abilities, to each according to his needs." Though they were very far away from their goal, at the moment this creed was applied by thieves and sanctioned by the police, and with good reason — all confiscated items would remain in their possession!

We stopped a few times to give the horses a rest and to feed them. Freed from the harness, they enjoyed the fresh grass of the meadow, while we, too, had a bite of black farm bread and fresh cucumbers, washed down with water.

As we continued along the way, the sun began to disappear behind the trees. Soon total darkness enveloped us, and I was amazed that Victor could see the road. When a full bright moon emerged from behind the clouds, I calculated that we must be halfway towards our destination, for the sack of feed for the horses, measured for one way, was more than half empty. To my surprise, Victor Zakharov advised me to lie down in the wagon and go to sleep. He assured me that he would not be needing me to "brake" the wagon, for the way ahead was smooth and level. His extraordinary friendliness surprised me. I quietly recited the evening prayers, and lay down in the wagon.

Soon I started daydreaming. I imagined myself in a uniform, arriving home on a horse; or perhaps, even, in a tank! How proud my parents and family would be when I'd tell them how I'd paid back the Germans! I thought of poor little Nosson and what the Germans had done to him. I'd try to rise from the ranks. Perhaps I'd become an officer, with a chest full of medals, and lead a Jewish battalion against the enemy!

But it was hard to imagine this, in view of the discrimination against Jews in the Officers' Corps. In Poland there was a law that any high school or college graduate was automatically assigned to an officer training school upon entering the army. However, the Polish army did not wish to be contaminated by having Jewish officers, so it circumvented the law by not accepting any graduate who was a Jew, with the exception of medical doctors. Old Jewish officers were forced into the reserves. Thus, when the war broke out, most of the Jewish intelligentsia were without any military training. But now, I thought, they've learned their lesson; surely there is no reason why I couldn't come home as a multi-medaled, commissioned officer of the Polish army!

I fell asleep. I don't know how long I slept, but when the wagon stopped rocking, the stillness awakened me. I opened my eyes and saw two figures, Victor and his son, stealthily pulling a sack of grain from the wagon. I was afraid to move. While I watched, they pulled another sack down, from the second wagon. They carried the two sacks of grain to the field and hid them under the dense bushes. Then they dragged the horses' feedbags to another bush, gathered a number of rocks, and stuffed them into the feedbags. They returned to their wagons with the rock-filled feedbags and put them in their usual spot, under the driver's seat.

Now I began to understand why Victor had been so adamant in his refusal to let me come along. He didn't want to run the risk of anyone discovering his racket! But how could he get away with it? Just prior to our departure from Karobka, each bag of grain had been carefully weighed, and the weights were duly recorded on the document which was in Victor's pocket.

After concealing the rock-filled feedbags under the driver's seat, they continued the drive. Still pretending to be asleep, I lay there thinking about Victor, how poor and hungry he must be, to risk his life by stealing from military deliveries during wartime! Come to think of it, the Party had appointed him for this particular task, so they must have been under the impression that he was the most loyal and trustworthy person in Karobka. And how strange it was that no one in Karobka would talk to him, or about him. In fact, he was an outcast.

Finally the first streaks of color appeared on the black horizon. After the welcome sounds of roosters crowing and dogs barking, the sun came out in all her radiant splendor...first yellow, then white, then burning red. I was totally engrossed and transfixed by the miracle of creation I was witnessing and felt sorry for the city people who were deprived of seeing the glory of such a sunrise!

Victor's voice brought me back to reality.

"Wake up! Wake up!" he called. I got up and took the reins.

"The traffic will increase now," he told me. "We'll soon be there." He pointed to a high tower in the distance, the railroad's water tower. The market was in front of the station.

"We'll be going right past it, so you can get off and do your shopping. After you've bought your *katyushas*, follow the wagon tracks and you'll find the delivery station, where I'll be." Then he added, "Take your time, because you won't be able to get in there anyhow. The guards at the gate don't let anyone in unless he's on a wagon with a load to deliver."

Chapayevsk, like most small towns in Russia, had streets of sand and mud, and no sidewalks. There were a few brick buildings, probably government offices. All the other buildings were made of logs, and had never been painted.

The market was bustling with _kolkhoz_ women displaying their home-grown produce for sale. As I climbed down from the wagon, Victor said, "Maybe you'd better wait here for us. We'll pick you up on the way back."

I was disappointed, for I had wanted to see how he'd pull off his weight trick.

At the railroad station I was told that no one was allowed on the platform without a ticket. However, this restriction applied only when local trains were due; it did not apply when express trains came through, for they merely slowed down as they passed through the station. Usually, these express trains picked up a sack of mail while passing through.

At ten o'clock, a Kuybishev-bound express chugged through the station, slowly enough for me to reach the mail car and deposit one letter. I waited around, and at noontime a Moscow-bound express passed through, and I managed to throw in my second letter to the embassy. Now I was sure that at least one letter would reach its destination, and that I would soon be wearing a Polish uniform, and fighting the Germans!

In the crowded market, it didn't take me long to spot a man in oily, dirty clothes, typical of mechanics of the local MTS. He was happy to sell me six _katyusha_s. I left the market in a hurry, hoping that Victor and our three wagonloads of grain had not yet been processed through the weight-scales. I was eager to see how Victor would fare with the scale operator.

I arrived just in time. Although the armed woman guard at the gate refused to let me enter, she didn't mind my standing there and watching through the iron fence. I could clearly see Victor leading the first wagon onto a huge platform scale. After the driver guided the horse by his cheekpiece across the scale, he stopped, and only the loaded wagon remained on the scale. Then the operator wrote down the weight of the wagon and its contents (which included the bags of rocks). After the weight was recorded, the horse was guided to a warehouse where the wagon was unloaded. On the way out, the same procedure was repeated, the driver leading the horse over the scale-platform. Only the empty wagon remained on the scale; its weight was subtracted from the previous weight, and the difference was credited to the collective. Suddenly Victor's trick became quite clear to me: while the empty wagon was being weighed, I noticed the feedbag hanging from the horse's neck! He had simply taken the feedbag from the wagon and given it to the horse, thus receiving credit for rocks!

Victor was surprised to see me at the gate, but he was in a good mood, and full of smiles. I, too, was in a happy mood for I had succeeded in mailing my letters. I suggested that we let the horses have a rest and meanwhile see the town. He refused, explaining that the horses would rest better outside of town, grazing on the fresh grass. I knew he was in a hurry to get rid of the rocks. At the edge of town he stopped and went into a hut. When he came out he had a bottle of *samogon*, a raw, homemade whiskey, tucked inside his shirt. Once we were outside the city limits, he began to celebrate, downing big gulps of the malodorous liquid.

"Now where's my *katyusha*?" he demanded. "Didn't you promise me one?" I gave him one, but he asked Semyon to keep it for him, because he was afraid to light it near his bottle of whiskey. Time and again he urged me, "C'mon, have a drink." For a while I managed to resist his hospitality, but soon he began to insist. "You're insulting me," he growled.

Then it dawned on me that the reason he was so insistent was that he wanted me to fall asleep! We were nearing the place in the woods where his sacks of stolen grain were hidden. Once I understood, I happily pretended to drink and, after a while, claimed that I was sleepy. He graciously gave me permission to lie down in the wagon and take a nap. When we approached his "exchange station," Victor and his son looked back to make sure I was asleep. Convinced, they began their operation: taking the rocks out of the feedbags and placing them back under the bushes, ready for the next trip, and stowing the sacks of grain, which had been left there in the bushes, under the seats where they could not be seen.

We rode on for some time. In the meantime, I "woke up," and for effect I stretched and yawned. Zakharov was in a good mood, singing one song after another. Soon the forest on both sides of the road disappeared behind us, and a fresh green meadow spread out before us as far as the eye could see. Victor decided to give the horses a rest here, so they could feed on the grass and drink from the nearby brook. Our little caravan stopped at a specially lush spot.

Victor quickly freed his horse from the harness, and then he came to help me remove the harness from my mare. Curiosity had been gnawing at me all this time; now that he was in such a friendly, happy mood, I was seized by an overpowering impulse. Without thinking about the implications, I said, "Comrade Victor, you told me yesterday that if one fellow steals from another the police won't even bother to search. How about if someone steals from the collective? Or from the government?"

Victor spat scornfully, and replied, "From the government or the collective? Ha! This is not stealing; this is considered sabotage, counter-revolution, undermining the economy! For stealing five kilograms of potatoes you can get five years!"

Suddenly his face turned white and his little eyes seemed to bulge out of their sockets. I realized I shouldn't have asked, but it was too late now! As I bent over to put down the harness, he jumped me from behind, and before I knew it I was flat on my back, and he was on top of me with a knife in his hand. I could smell his whiskey breath, and the sour odor of his body. He pressed the blade against my throat. Through his thin lips he hissed: "Do you...want to see...your Pa and Ma again...? Hah?"

I could barely get a sound out of my mouth, because of the pressure of his body, and of the blade bruising my throat. But I _had_ to talk to save my life! I finally managed to squeak, "Sure, but what did I do?"

"It's not what you did; it's what you know! You know too much! I didn't want you coming on the delivery in the first place. Too bad! You'll never see them again!"

"But...but...," I sputtered. "Vitia, I don't know what you're talking about! I didn't see anything, I don't know anything! Aren't we friends?"

"Friends?" he exploded. "Friends! Ha, ha! Yes, I'll bury you right here in the forest, my friend!"

I pleaded for my life, trying to talk him out of his madness. Meanwhile, I noticed that White Belly's forefoot was only inches away from me. If a fly should bite her leg, she'd stamp her hoof right into my stomach. "Go on, White Belly, go on!" I squeezed the words out of my mouth. The horse obeyed at once and moved away.

Victor began to mutter again. "I'll bury you right here in the forest! No one will ever know where your grave is. I'll tell them you ran away!"

His eyes had a wild, queer look; I imagined this must be how a murderer looks at his victim. With all my strength, I grasped his thick wrist, trying to keep the blade away from my throat, but I was powerless against him. His arm broke loose and he raised his hand with the knife in it, for the final plunge. With my eyes fixed on the sharp blade I whispered, "_Shema_...."

Victor's son suddenly threw himself on his father. He grabbed the hand holding the knife, and screamed, "Pa, I'll tell the police! I'll tell everybody in the village! I won't let you do it! He's my friend! Let him go!"

With hope renewed, I also tried to grab Victor's hand. But both of us together were still no match for his strength.

He turned a face full of hatred towards his son and said, "Semyon, you wouldn't tell on your own father, would you?"

"I sure would!" was the reply. "You'll have to kill me too, Pa!" the boy cried out, tears rolling down his face.

"But I can't let that louse stay alive," whined Victor. "If he talks, it means ten years in prison for me, son." The old man began to plead for his son's permission to kill me.

"No!" Semyon cried, realizing his power now. "Chaim won't talk; Chaim is a friend of ours; he wouldn't tell on you, Pa."

His own son had turned against him, and this must have made a tremendous impression on Victor, for I could feel him weakening. With renewed strength, I gave a mighty heave and pushed him off me. I jumped up, and in an instant I was astride my mare, pressing my legs into her flanks. White Belly had put a good distance between Vitia and me, when I heard Semyon calling. I looked back and saw him galloping towards me. I stopped, and he pulled up.

"Chaim, Chaim, come back," he pleaded. "If you don't, he'll report you running away with the horse, and you know it belongs to the collective."

"What! *He'll* report me?" I burst out. "But he just tried to kill me! And you know why!"

"But who'll believe you, Chaim?" Semyon said, lowering his eyes. "Do you expect me to testify against my own father?"

I suddenly realized that he was right: who would believe me? Victor would laugh at my charges and say, "If I wanted to kill him, he'd be as dead as a doornail!" And how could I prove the business with the rocks? Anyway, he had the trust of the Party, and who was I?

"You don't expect me to go back now and give him another chance to kill me, do you?" I asked wearily, realizing I'd have to do just that.

"Here's the knife." Semyon stretched his hand out and handed it to me. The knife was still warm, but a cold chill passed through me. That sharp blade could have ended my life! Just like Victor said: I could have been buried right here in the forest, never to see my dear family again, and no one would know where my grave was!

While these thoughts were passing through my mind, Semyon turned the horses around and we began moving towards the wagons. I didn't resist.

"You don't know my father," Semyon reassured me. "He's crying like a baby right now. Sometimes he does terrible things and then he's sorry. He beats Ma and me and my brothers all the time; afterwards, he's sorry and cries. The whiskey makes him mean."

I put my hand on his shoulder. "Thank you, Semyon, for saving my life," I said.

He pressed my arm for a moment. "You know something, Chaim? Many times I've heard my father threatening to kill people, but he's never actually killed anyone — yet," he whispered. "*Chi*, he *did* try to kill you for sure! I'm glad he didn't, though."

"So am I," I said.

Victor was seated on his wagon, holding his bottle of whiskey in one hand and wiping his tears with the other. Between sobs he spoke to me. "Forgive me, *golubchik*, my little pigeon, I'm so sorry...I really am...I wouldn't have hurt you...not with my son around anyway...."

I ignored him. Without another word, the boy and I harnessed all three horses to the wagons, and started for home. An hour later Victor jumped off his wagon and climbed up on mine. I put my hand around the knife; I wasn't taking any chances. But I was soon convinced that his intentions were peaceful, for he began to plead again for forgiveness.

"You see, my dear boy, in our country everyone steals; everyone, that is, except Stalin. He doesn't need to steal; he owns it all, the entire country." He placed his arm on my shoulder and continued in a plaintive voice. "We all have to steal; otherwise we couldn't live. Look at me, for instance — I have eight children. Two sons are married and in the army fighting a war. So their two wives, those big-city tramps, came down from the big city and deposited their four brats with me. Now I have to feed them! Imagine, four additional mouths to feed! They claimed that people are starving in the big city, especially the children. I don't believe them for a minute, Chaim; I'm sure they just want to run around! So how can I possibly feed us all? Do you assume that because we live on the land we have enough to eat? Yes, I also thought that in the beginning — that we'd have plenty of food. That's what Stalin promised us, after all. He said, 'Why should a farmer have to work all day, and then come home and wash clothes and cook and feed the animals? It can be done so easily if you just divide the work among everybody, and live in a collective, and work only eight hours a day, and enjoy life!'

"And I was the first stupid fool here to believe him! I was the first one to join the *kolkhoz*. I even helped to get rid of those who opposed it, since I had nothing to lose. I never had anything; I was a sharecropper and laborer all my life. Well, twelve long years have passed since then, and the villagers still won't forgive me! Oh no, they won't come right out and say it; they're afraid of me because the Party is behind me!

"But I can read their minds. They'd rather be living like they did back in the old days. Even *panshchizna* — serfdom — is better than the collective. They all had their little plot of land then, and they worked for the noblemen, and they were happy. But why am I bothering you with all this? Listen, *golubchik*, one doesn't get punished for stealing, since everyone does it: the prosecutor, the judge, and the police. One gets punished for being caught! Understand? And tell me, what do they say in your country on your birthday?"

He suddenly stopped, as if a faucet had been turned off. I didn't understand his question. Even though he was still quite drunk, everything he'd said up to now had made sense; but what was this about birthdays?

"Well, *golubchik*," Vitia said again, "what do you wish someone on his birthday? Hah?"

"Many more years to come!" I finally replied.

"Not here!" he said. "Here we wish them only health; *years* Stalin will give. He's got plenty to give: five years, ten, fifteen, twenty — in Siberia! Now, would it make you happy, dear boy, if Stalin sent me away to Siberia for twenty years just because I stole a few kilograms of grain to feed all my hungry kids? Would it?"

Tears rolled down his pocked face. Suddenly tears filled my eyes too, and I was overcome with compassion, almost affection, for this man who had tried to kill me only a little while ago!

"Look, Vitia," I said, "I didn't see anything, and I don't know anything. So forget about everything."

He kissed me again and again, and offered me another drink from the half-empty bottle. I declined politely. How accurately Goncharov had described the nature of a Russian: "If he loves you, he'll kiss you; but if he hates you, watch out for a knife in the back!"

At last we were approaching Karobka. Here we parted: Victor and his son drove down a side path leading to their house, and I continued straight ahead to the village.

The place was deserted, with no one in sight. I drove directly to the stable, and fed and watered White Belly. When I left the stable and started to walk home, I saw, in the distance, a solemn procession of people moving across the valley. When it came nearer I could hear women crying. Could it be a funeral? But there was no wagon, no corpse. Piotr, the stooped, limping fellow in charge of the dairy cows, appeared to be leading the procession, with his three children hanging on to him, trailed by his wife and the entire population of the village.

As I got closer, I could hear his wife pleading with him, "Don't forget the children I raised for you," after which all the women broke out in loud crying. Like a choirmaster, Piotr's wife beseeched him with tearful pleas, and each was followed by a chorus of wails from the women behind her.

"Remember, I washed your feet, and made good meals, and baked _piroshki_ for you!"

"Oh, don't forget her and the children!"

"Come back to me — I'll wash your feet like always, and I won't even mind your beatings!"

"Come back even if you're crippled; she'll be glad to serve you."

"Even without hands or feet, I'll be happy to have you back again."

"Remember her and the children always, drunk or sober!"

The wife's shrill cries rose above the others, who responded with low sobbing.

The man was going off to war and this was the way the village said its good-byes. I realized how bad things must be if they were mobilizing men of Piotr's age. He was well over fifty, and I thought I could read an accusation in the villagers' eyes when they looked at me. Here was an old man leaving a wife and children and going off to war, while I was in the prime of life and was not drafted!

My heart broke every time the sorrowful woman pleaded with her husband not to forget her and the children, and to come home in any condition — just to come home again! The rest of the women, wailing in chorus, were mourning their own men at the front while weeping for her, and with her.

What could I do to convince these people that I was not hiding out in their village and avoiding the draft? They must have heard that I had volunteered to fight the Germans, the murderers of my people! But because I was a Westerner, and a Jew, Stalin and his War Commissar Marshal Timoshenko considered me untrustworthy and not fit to serve in their army.

When the procession arrived at the end of the village, everyone bid Piotr a final farewell. Like all the other remaining men, I too hugged the draftee and shook his hand.

"Piotr Pavlovich," I said, loudly enough for all to hear, "how I wish I were in your place! I have volunteered many times, but the *Voyenkomat* refuses to take me. I'll personally see to it that your family has firewood, and hay for the cow, as long as I'm here."

Piotr was visibly moved and I sensed that I had made an impression on the people. He kissed me, and said, "I've hardly ever left this village, and I've never met any Jews except you, but they must be good and kind people. After all, they are God's Chosen People! Thank you, my friend, and please see to it that they keep warm and have hay in the barn." Then Piotr and his wife climbed into the wagon, and the driver started on the trip to the *Voyenkomat*.

After the wagon disappeared in the forest, the crowd silently dispersed. Walking homeward, they seemed preoccupied with painful memories of not so long ago, when they had sent off their own sons and husbands. I walked Anna home. She wiped her tears and tried to suppress the sobs that shook her occasionally.

The woman's cry, "I'll wash your feet and I won't even mind your beatings!" was still ringing in my ears.

"Anna, tell me," I asked. "What did she mean about washing his feet? Can't he wash them himself? And about his beatings? Does he really beat her? And isn't she ashamed to say so in public?"

"What's there to be ashamed of? A good wife does everything for her husband, and if he yells at her and beats her, that just shows how much he loves her. Oh, how I wish my husband was here — I'd happily wash his feet and get a beating too!"

That night, I had the subject clarified by my friend the teacher. "Like I said before," Goncharov explained, "revolution can change things outside the home, but inside, evolution must make the change. Cruelty to wives has a long history behind it, going back to *panshchizna* — serfdom. The land and the peasants all belonged to the big landowner; he could tell the serf whom he should marry, and the bride had no choice about it either. The lord of the village could even kill his serfs. The husbands were the lords of their wives; they could abuse them without being punished. In 1861 the Czar freed the serfs, but the old slogan remains: 'We belong to the masters, but our wives belong to us.' The poor wife was practically the only object over which a serf could exercise his authority. And now, collectivization has again made the wife the only object of 'ownership,' for everything else belongs to the state."

Then he added, "There's another slogan from way back, which is still used frequently: 'We belong to the masters, but the earth — the holy Russian earth — belongs to us.' They used to say it against the masters, but they use it in connection with collective farming and government land-ownership. But don't you dare let anybody hear you say it! These are dangerous words!"

SINCE there were no young men left in the village, Nikolai the stableman began to teach me how to use a scythe proficiently. Scything is the hardest job on the farm, demanding much physical strength and stamina. One must swing the scythe from right to left as far as the arms can reach, cutting a perfect half-circle of hay. The hardest thing about it is working in a group of five or more men, each one cutting his swath to the side and slightly behind the man on his right. One can't stop, or even slow down, for the scythe of the man behind might cut one's feet off! It was like a parade-ground drill; all scythes began simultaneously, far to the right, and all bodies swung together to the left.

For a while, I practiced alone in the forest; later I was kept at the end of the five-man group for reasons of safety; and finally I was allowed to scythe in any position. Some days I was tempted to quit, but then I would think: what if the others laugh and mock the Jewish city boy as being soft? I felt a need to prove that I was the equal of any farmer, even though I realized that the safest place for me was at the end, for if my hands ever slowed down I might lose a foot!

After scything, the next step was to let the sun and the wind dry the hay for a day or two. Then it was raked together and forked into the wagon, loaded as high as a two-story house. Here, too, skill was needed in order to prevent the hay from sliding off, and to prevent the wagon from turning over on the wretched forest paths, full of holes and tree roots.

Thus the hay had to be loaded carefully and according to plan. Each forkload had to be placed in such a way that it would prevent the previous forkload from sliding off. At the same time, the entire wagon had to be kept balanced. Not just once, but many times, a wagon that was carefully loaded was later driven by me and turned over; this made me the laughing-stock of the village. And so it became a matter of pride to me to show them that a Jewish city boy was just as good as any Russian farmer.

I also had to learn how to chop down trees for firewood. Little Volka was happy to teach me; here, ten-year-old children were expert woodchoppers.

After the hay or firewood was ready to be brought home in the wagon, the usual problem was getting a horse. Since no farmer was permitted to own a horse, the peasants had to beg the stableman for one, and Nikolai was inclined to exercise his authority.

"I'm sorry, the horses have to rest. Come back tomorrow," was his usual reply.

So the people began to watch for his absences from the stables and turned to me. I never refused anyone; I even helped them load the wagons. It gave me peace of mind, for after all, their men were fighting "my" war.

Part of my job had been to help Goncharov in his capacity as temporary blacksmith. Suddenly my help was no longer needed, for a new, professional blacksmith was imported and he needed no assistant. The previous blacksmith had died of asthma just before I arrived and, while the chairman had been looking for a replacement, Goncharov was black-smithing. It seems that teachers are underpaid everywhere, even in the Soviet Union, and although his wife worked permanently in the dairy stables, milking cows by hand, he still had to make some extra money during the summer to make ends meet.

The new man, Boris, was brought to Karobka from the nearby Autonomous Republic of Mordovia. Besides being a blacksmith, he knew another very important trade: wheel-making. Throughout rural Russia, wagon wheels were made of bare wood, and were not covered with an iron or steel strap; thus their life expectancy was short. And quite an art it was, making wooden wheels!

I watched Boris in the forest, picking out the right type and quality of tree, cutting and trimming it to size. Then he softened the wood by soaking it and heating it to the right degree; then he smoked it, so it would not crack or break while it was being bent into a circle. Thus a wheel was made.

I spent so much time with him that I even learned some of his Mordo-vian language. The Revolution had done a lot for his people. Before, although they spoke their own language, they had no alphabet; they could speak but not read or write. After the Revolution, an autonomous republic was established, and a group of linguists from Moscow created an alphabet — the Russian Cyrillic, of course — and grammar books were published. Schools and colleges were opened, and children were forced to attend school.

Because of this newly arrived blacksmith, I was no longer needed in the blacksmith shop. This made me eligible for a new assignment; now I was to represent Karobka in the alcohol factory.

The spirit factory in Booyan that produced antifreeze was short on everything except the rotten potatoes and rotten grain used to produce the alcohol. All villages had tons of spoiled agricultural produce, and by order of the district Communist Party, the rotten produce was delivered to the factory. There was great urgency as the winter of 1941 was approaching, and antifreeze was needed on the northern and central fronts by the Red Army.

Since labor and firewood were in such short supply, the district ordered each collective to send one person for one month to the spirit factory "to save the freezing tanks defending Leningrad." The slogans became: "Fill up the radiators of the Red Army" and "Let's drown the Fritzes in antifreeze."

Apologetically, old *Dedushka* Anton, the chairman of Karobka, informed me that I had been chosen to represent the village for one month. The factory would pay the *kolkhoz* and Karobka would credit me with labor days. My food would be supplied by *Kolkhoz Karobka*.

The news upset me. Although the Polish embassy had not replied to my letter and the newspapers remained silent on the subject of Poland, my heart refused to give up hope, and I waited daily for an answer. Now I might be away in Booyan when the embassy letter arrived! Besides, my main reason for wanting to stay in this village was to be able to observe the Sabbath as much as possible; now I'd have to cut trees on Shabbos! But how could I decline? No one dared to refuse an order, and this was defense work essential to the army, which made it doubly hard to evade.

Now a different problem arose, this one of a very practical nature. I had no pants. The suit I was wearing when I arrived was practically in shreds and the old pants that I had been wearing, which belonged to Anna's husband, now had more patches than original material. The poor peasants, with all their good will towards me, could not or would not spare a pair of old pants, for they knew that they would never be returned; no clothing could possibly survive a month of tree-cutting and branch-trimming. Furthermore, as one of the farmers said, "It's for the *kolkhoz*, isn't it? It's for the army, isn't it? Well, let *them* supply clothes!"

Finally, the Tatar Summatov appeared with *koofika* — a pair of pants and a jacket made of layers of thick quilted cotton, and very warm. The only problem with these quilted garments was that they were a haven for lice. Once they got in, they would never leave unless the garment was burnt in its entirety.

To the villagers, this action of the Tatar indicated the great importance of the assignment. As Anna put it, "It looks like military business for you. You can be sure you won't be drafted for at least another month!" I myself suspected that Suleika might be behind it all, and had induced her father to provide the clothes.

At the factory office in Booyan, the men and women were divided into groups and brigades, each foreman assigning two people to a handsaw. My partner was an elderly Chuvash. The Chuvashy, like other backward peoples in the Soviet Union, had their own autonomous republic, whose capital was Cheboksary; but many of their people could be found throughout Russia. The Revolution had done wonders for them, giving them a written language, schools and higher education. But these were only for the younger generation: the old people had been taught to sign their names, and nothing else.

I liked the man from the minute I saw him. His name was Buraksan. Since he had a red nose (most likely from the homemade whiskey known as *samogon* — moonshine) and since in Russian, red beets are called *buraky*, I called him *Dedushka* Burak. He liked the name, laughing with his toothless mouth, which was like a dark hole among the gray hairs covering his face and head. His little eyes were hardly visible between the bushy black-and-gray brows, and the hair sticking out of his ears gave him a wild look. He smoked constantly, and the smell of his clothes was evidence that he hadn't bathed in years, if ever. But he was goodness itself, hard-working and strong.

After getting all our final instructions, the brigades were put on ox-carts and driven to the forest. Once at work, I tried hard to keep up with my partner, but he pulled the saw too fast for me. The Chuvash quickly realized that I was no match for him, so he did more than his share. He also always made the notch on the tree trunk which determined which way the tree would fall. Slowly I learned to be a woodcutter.

When we trimmed the trees, I always tried to choose a spot far away from my partner, away from the awful smell. The old man liked to talk about his house and his family and, above all, about how he made his whiskey. He would always say, "Can't you start on the tree next to me so I can talk with you?"

But I explained that, for safety's sake, I had to work at the other end. I was constantly worrying about how to avoid working on the Sabbath. It was only five days away....Could I feign sickness? There were a doctor and a hospital in town, and if I had no temperature I would really be in trouble for faking illness! Perhaps if I stayed closer to the old man, I thought, I would become sick from his horrible smell!

During the next rest period I forced myself to stand next to him. He scratched himself constantly and even asked me to help out with "a good scratch," but I declined, pretending to be too busy scratching myself. Soon he confided to me how he made his whiskey so strong and tasty.

"I'll let you in on my secret. After the potatoes boil for about two hours, I mix in some horse manure. Now I'm not going to tell you how much, that's my secret, but that's what makes it strong. Then, if you can get hold of some horse milk, that'll give it both taste and strength. If I get home next week, I'll bring you some. Maybe you can talk the foreman into letting me go home for just one day?"

I moved away a few feet, for I couldn't stand the smell any longer, and said, "The only way you'll be allowed to go home is to get sick. For that you need to have a fever; do you know how to get your temperature to go up?"

"I know how to get fever," said the old man.

I braced myself and moved closer, so as to miss nothing. "How?" I asked.

Old Burak rolled himself a smoke, pulled out a piece of cotton from his pants to catch the spark from his *katyusha* and while hitting it he said, "It seems that you Poles don't know anything! How do you get by in this world? Here everyone knows every trick, or you can't exist! You must tell me some day how people live in other countries.... Now, as for getting a fever, the main thing is not to get caught or you'll be in real trouble. The simplest way is when the nurse or doctor puts the thermometer under your arm: rub its tip when they're not looking. That makes the heat go up, but you've got to be very careful! I know a fellow who rubbed so much that the doctor later testified in court that it is impossible for a human being to live with a temperature that high. He got five years! Then there's another way. You hold your breath as long as you can, don't let yourself breathe; that'll raise the temperature, but the nurse will be on the lookout and keep talking to you on purpose, so watch out."

I spent a sleepless night. All kinds of ideas and plans to avoid working on the Sabbath went through my mind, but nothing seemed practical. The pain in my heart and the tears in my eyes finally put me to sleep.

I began to notice how cautiously and slowly the woodcutters worked. If one tree fell onto another and was suspended by it, instead of falling to the ground, hours were wasted planning just how to get both trees down. I realized that the workers felt no need to hurry. After all, why should they? The payments went to the collective, not to them. In an effort to speed things up, the company had assigned a man whose job was just to sharpen the saws and grind the axes, but it was all in vain. Nothing, I observed, can replace personal interest and private initiative as an incentive.

On the fourth day, the foreman handed out bulletins. At once the men cut them up into squares for rolling their cigarettes, without even bothering to read them. Since I was in the habit of reading anything that came into my hand, I glanced at mine, and realized at once the importance of the announcement. It was help straight from Heaven! In the bulletin, the factory director announced a premium for those who topped the norm by fifty percent. They would be proclaimed "Stakhanovites" and would receive the special prize of five quarts of whiskey! It seemed like the solution to my problem, for if my partner and I could achieve such a norm, I could spend Saturday at the main office collecting our "prize," and wouldn't have to work that day! But how could we manage it if we couldn't even seem to make the regular quota?

That night, I reviewed all I knew about "Stakhanovism." Alexei Stakhanov, a coal miner in the Don River basin, had tripled his quota one day. By planning his digging and using his tools exceptionally well, the next day he made five times his quota! He set such a record that he was presented to Stalin, received the highest decoration and was elected to the Supreme Soviet. His name became a legend, and a slogan for increasing production. As soon as the Russians occupied new territories, the second item in the propaganda campaign was explaining and building up "Stakhanovism." (The first item, of course, was building up the glory and greatness of Stalin.)

Actually, the Soviet bureaucrats killed the goose before it could lay the golden egg. As soon as the workers began to increase production in order to get prizes, the management decided that, if production could be increased when an inducement was offered, it could be done without special gifts. And so the quotas rose, and the entire impetus was lost. If someone did decide to raise his output, his co-workers were furious, for it meant that soon their production quotas would go up too, since such production had been proved possible.

I recalled that the first "Stakhanov" of the Lithuanian Soviet Republic was a bricklayer named Shaulitis who tripled his norm. My landlord in Raseinai, who was a bricklayer and the fastest in his trade, had been shocked — it was a blow to his pride. "It can't be done," he declared categorically, and decided to investigate. Sure enough, he discovered that five men had prepared the bricks and cement, and all Shaulitis had to do was to lay the bricks. "With that kind of help," the old man declared angrily, "I could do five norms too!"

Remembering this incident, I suddenly realized that here was the solution to my problem. With a prize of five bottles of whiskey, I could induce the other workers to turn over some of their cut lumber to me. They didn't make their own norms anyway, so why shouldn't they help me compete for the valuable prize which we would all share?

The next morning I carefully outlined my plan to Burak. "My friend, how would you like something to drink? I mean real whiskey, good whiskey! Of course it might not have that special taste that yours has, mixed with the horse manure, but it will be ninety-nine proof."

"What? Do you mean it?" cried the old man. "You mean the real stuff?" From the dark hole in the middle of his wild face a long, red tongue shot out, licking his lips greedily. He grabbed me by my jacket and shook me. I had never seen him so excited. "Where? How? Tell me, *golubchik*! Don't hold out on me my dear friend, I'll do anything you say!"

"Here, read for yourself," I said and showed him the bulletin.

"I can't read, I can just about sign my name, and not too well at that; read it for me, my pigeon, please." The old man sat down; just the thought of real whiskey made him nearly drunk.

I explained to him that if the two of us topped the norm and won the prize, Burak could have all the whiskey, since I didn't drink. But there was one condition: I, and only I, had to go to pick it up in town on Saturday. "It's a matter of honor to me," I explained, "that I can help fight the enemy at least this way."

The Chuvash agreed at once, but asked, "But how can we make it? We never even make the regular norm!"

"Well, we'll have to get some help from the others. Just leave it to me," I assured him. "Of course it will mean sharing with them and less whiskey for you, but there should be more than enough." Leaving him with a pat on the back, I walked off to our neighbors, the two men and two women who worked closest to us.

They liked the idea, especially the women. "Ah, good!" they said. "We'll bring home some whiskey." The men were thinking of their own personal pleasure. But then they began to worry about the difficulties in my plan. What about the foreman?

I outlined my idea to them. "You see, separately none of us makes the norm, so what difference does it make how much less of the norm we turn out? But if we get together and cooperate, we can win the prize! This is what you have to do: drop some of your lumber near us, and when the foreman leaves, carry it over to our pile. Of course the foreman will find out sooner or later, but it is to his advantage also, having made Stakhanovites out of greenhorns; besides, he wouldn't mind a drink himself. Now, is it a deal?" I finished with assurance in my voice; I was closing a big deal in a most capitalistic manner.

Everyone was thinking. The oldest one, after scratching his head awhile, finally said, "It's all well planned except for one thing. What a simple Westerner like you doesn't realize, but what we all know from experience, is that as soon as you show them that two men can top the norm, you'll wake up one morning and the norm will be raised."

It was true, they all agreed, so down went my plan. There was a deep sigh; someone had just knocked over a few quarts of good whiskey! I felt worst of all; here went my last plan to avoid Sabbath labor! I had to admit I was beaten, and got up to return to work. I approached the old Chuvash with a sad face and a broken heart. His grief was as great as mine. "Three more weeks before I can get a drink. Oh, three more whole weeks!" he mumbled to himself.

Three weeks! How could I have forgotten? I ran back to the four people. "Listen, comrades, you know we are not here forever, only for one month; actually, just about three weeks are left. They won't raise the norm immediately; it will take a few weeks and by then our time will be up. What do you think?"

I need not have asked. "That's it!" they shouted. "It's a deal! You're right! Why should we worry about the workers who come after us?"

The oldest one embraced me. "You're right! I heard that the Jews were the smartest people on earth, and you must be the smartest Jew!"

Not until Friday did the foreman realize what was happening. After making up the week's tally, he rushed up to me and Burak. "Hey, comrades, *chi,* you've done it! How did you do it? Think of all the whiskey that you're going to get tomorrow! Ahh!"

I shook his hand and assured him that we would not forget to tell the director that without his instructions and advice as a professional forester we could never have done it. "And by the way," I added, "you're entitled to a taste as well."

The next morning the foreman was all smiles. He ordered two more oxen to be hitched up in order to deliver the firewood of the Stakhanovites. He would go and personally report to the director, while the wood was being pulled through the factory gates. Since travel by oxen over these wretched roads was slow and laborious, he ordered the Chuvash to hurry the oxen along with his whip.

The foreman knocked at the director's door, and waited patiently for a reply. When he finally heard the word *"Zakhoditye —* Enter!" he opened the door and with great respect in his voice announced: "Comrade Director, I have with me the young fellow I told you about, the Stakhanovite. May we come in?" This was said in such a humble and subservient manner that I smiled to myself and wondered if a foreman in a capitalist country had to humiliate himself to such a degree.

The man at the table invited us in, and I was surprised to see that he was so stout; he looked like a typical bourgeois capitalist. Shouldn't he get ten years in prison just for sporting that big fat belly in such hard times? The director shook hands with both of us, and congratulated us on the "Stalin-like victory in the field of wood supply for the victorious Red Army. You are true Stakhanovite men!" He handed me a slip of paper stating the amount of whiskey to be received as the prize for the "great Stakhanov victory."

By now a young woman had come into the office, a reporter from the local "Red Star," the organ of the district Communist Party. She asked me a few questions about how I had come to achieve this great victory. I told her about my hatred of the Germans, knowing the military commandant would read the paper and might then reconsider my application for military service. While I was waiting for a call from the _Voyenkomat_, I told her, I had decided that my partner and I would do our utmost for the army, our slogan being: "Every batch of wood, another dead Fritz; every wagon of wood, a battalion of enemies dead."

At the window marked "Cashier" I joined the long line. When I got to the window, I learned that I would have to pay for the whiskey! The price would be deducted from my pay. Nothing was free; the prize was _permission_ to purchase the whiskey.

While waiting in line, I looked around. The people there were all officials, bureaucrats, members of the police. I was the only working man, a true proletarian, and they stared at me and my shabby, ragged clothing as if I didn't belong there, which was quite true. Here in this classless society, I was meeting the elite of the town, all getting liquor for their Sunday parties. This privilege was part of the special benefits they received for supporting the regime and keeping the working masses in line.

I observed that the women in the line were dressed in drab, mannish clothing. Was it because of shortages or was it Soviet policy? Later I learned that the concept of dressing up was considered bourgeois, and was thus unacceptable to Russians. Stalin was aiming not only to create a "classless society of social justice, with equality and no exploitation of the individual"; he also wanted to create a new type of person, one who rejected capitalist feelings and desires, a Soviet Person — _Sovietsky Chelovyek_. If any capitalist value stood in the way of this holy purpose — whether private initiative, the profit motive or family loyalty — it had to be rooted out. This had to be done even if it meant killing millions of farmers who had refused to join the collectives! A huge prison which contained two hundred million people had been created, but this did not seem to bother Stalin, or anyone else who was part of the Soviet regime.

While immersed in these thoughts, I noticed that no one was wearing glasses. I had thought that the peasants didn't wear glasses because they had little occasion to read, even those who could, and thus didn't need glasses; but here in town I had seen only one person wearing glasses, the old-fashioned kind. Had Stalin managed to create a Soviet superman with perfect eyesight? Or was there a shortage of glasses, in addition to all the other shortages in this country?

I stood in line, observing this special class of people, and I could tell who was higher in the Party echelon of the Soviet hierarchy, by the smiles and flattery they got from the others. Parasites! I fumed to myself; blind followers of the Party and Stalin, and all for a drink of whiskey! In this poor country, even the bribes were small and cheap, I concluded.

When I returned to the woods, my welcome was tumultuous. Coming from that disillusioning scene in town, I felt even closer to these poor people, the slaves of the system. The Chuvash, his arms wide open, embraced me and covered me and the whiskey bottles with kisses. I wasn't sure whether his kisses were meant for me, and landed by accident on the bottles, or the other way around. It didn't matter, but I still couldn't bear the close contact and stepped back. "Watch out, you'll break the bottles!" I told him.

I had to shake hands with everyone and then they insisted that I close my eyes for a surprise. I felt my shoes being removed, and old Burak said, "I noticed that your shoes are hungry; they always have their mouth open." They were the same shoes I had brought from Lithuania and they were falling apart, with gaping holes in the toes.

When I opened my eyes, I was wearing a pair of *laptee*, peasant sandals made of the inner bark of a tree. The saying goes: "He climbed the tree barefoot and came down wearing *laptee*." I took a few steps proudly, as if trying on new shoes in a store, realizing that it was their way of thanking me for the whiskey.

My next concern was how to prevent them from getting so drunk that they would not be able to get up on Sunday morning to work. My plan was to continue to win the prize every week, thus avoiding having to cut wood on the Sabbath. Without their hard work, the prize would be unattainable.

That night, I prayed with more feeling than usual, for I had once again felt the guiding hand of the Almighty. The escape from Raseinai, the march to Kaunas, the experience on the train with the Russian colonel and the trip across the border — there was surely a pattern to all this! Then the solution of my *kashrus* problem in Karobka, and now the inspiration which helped me to abstain legally from work on the Sabbath.... All this could have come from only one source: the Holy Lord of the Universe! But one question kept haunting me: why me? Was I more worthy than my little brothers? More than my beloved parents? And where were they now? What about all the other Jews under the Nazi yoke? Why had I been chosen? And for what?

All night I tossed and turned, awake among the drunken snores.

A few days later the local Party newspaper came out, proclaiming that

"All nationalities of the Soviet Union have risen to the call of the great leader, the father of all nations, the genius of victory, Marshal Stalin." Under these headlines was the story of how a member of the Chuvash _kolkhoz_, E. B. Buraksan, in response to the call of the great Comrade Stalin to supply the army with antifreeze, had doubled the norm of firewood for the local spirit factory! No mention was made of his partner, as if the two-man saw was being operated by the one man alone! I didn't mind not getting the credit, but I did learn from this episode how the Soviet press utilized every opportunity to consolidate the nationalities of the Union, and to demonstrate its anti-Semitism. From then on, whenever I saw a Jewish engineer or manager, an army captain, colonel or general, I knew that he would have risen higher in rank had he not been a Jew! There were one hundred and fifty Jewish generals in the Red Army at that time, but not one marshal.

There was one more interesting aspect to this affair. Since the sum total of wood delivered to the factory did not exceed that of the previous week, it should have surprised the director and caused him to wonder where the great Stakhanovite achievement lay! But he seemed perfectly satisfied to report to the Party "the great victory in the field of military wood supply." I couldn't help wondering if in fact the same thing were going on all over the country. Stalin, who seldom left the Kremlin, must have gotten many reports about great "Soviet achievements," about fulfillments of five-year plans, and no one ever bothered to verify the reports.

The following week, we repeated our "achievement." When I went to the office to collect the whiskey, I felt like an old hand. I looked down on the parasites who received whiskey for doing nothing, while my "brigade" actually had to work hard! As I left the building loaded down with the liquor, I noticed an old man wearing glasses. He was walking slowly under a heavy yoke, carrying two buckets of mash, careful not to lose a drop.

When he stopped to rest for a moment, a woman walked up to him, saying, "Good day, doctor. I've been looking for you; right here it hurts me terribly!" She pointed to her side.

At first I thought the man must be an old-fashioned male nurse, a _feldsher_, familiar all over eastern Europe. This was the kind of "doctor" who dispensed only two medicines: if the pain was below the waist, he recommended castor oil; if above the waist, _bankes_ — cupping, applying small heated glasses to the skin of the sick person to stimulate the flow of blood. But when I heard him telling the woman to come to the hospital clinic later for an examination, I realized that he was actually a physician. Now my curiosity was really aroused. Shabby clothes, eyeglasses, mash for his cow ... this didn't add up. In Poland, professional men were treated with respect, and remunerated handsomely.

So I walked up to the man and said, "Good day, Comrade Doctor; can you please tell me where I can have my eyes examined?"

The doctor put his buckets down and looked me over carefully, his eyes resting for a long time on the whiskey. "You'll have to go to Kuybishev, son; we don't have an eye doctor here. But you won't get any glasses anyway."

"But you wear glasses, doctor; where did you get them?" I asked.

Instead of replying, the doctor inquired, "*Chi*, you are surely not from here, son. Where do you come from?"

When I told him, the doctor said, "It's not your accent but your questions that told me you must be a foreigner. Well, if you must know, I bought these glasses years ago when I was a medical student at the University of Moscow. Of course the prescription needs to be changed now, but that's impossible. Now you tell me something, son: where did you get all that whiskey?" The old man's eyes shone as he looked at the bottles.

After explaining that I had been rewarded for superior achievement, and would be glad to treat the doctor to a nip, I felt it safe to ask, "Tell me, doctor, don't you think it's disgraceful for a physician to have to carry mash?"

The old man straightened up, threw back his shoulders and raised his voice like a general giving a command. "Comrade," he said, "you have been raised in a capitalistic society where it is considered disgraceful to work, and the working man is treated like a dog. But in our socialist society, as the great Comrade Stalin has said, labor is the pride of every man, and the working class is the glory of human society! I'm happy to be part of this society as a working man — whether in the laboratory, the hospital or carrying mash. Do you understand?"

He picked up the two buckets with difficulty, for it was obvious that they were much too heavy for his weak shoulders. He looked around, and before taking a step away he whispered in my ear, "A doctor and his old woman like milk just like anybody else, and a doctor's cow likes mash just like any other cow, so what can I do, son?"

I watched the old man walking off with tiny careful steps and I thought how symbolic this scene was. The Communist system had proposed the idea of raising the masses from poverty, but it turned out that they had managed to push everyone's standard down instead. They had intended to close the gap between rich and poor — but so far they had succeeded only in making everyone poor! They aimed to abolish money, but the Soviet citizen was more eager for money than any other I'd met. Abolish exploitation? The Russian was more exploited than any slave! No capitalist could ever suck the blood of the masses as did the Soviet government. What difference did it make to the working man whether an individual or a government enslaved him? Here was a practicing physician, a frail old man, carrying the mash for his cow, or he would have no milk. This was the result of twenty-five years of Communist rule!

I ran after him. "Here, doctor," I said, "you hold the whiskey and I'll carry the mash for you. And I'll see if I can convince one of the oxen drivers to drop off some more mash at your place."

The doctor thanked me with tears in his eyes. By now I had learned how to carry buckets of water without spilling a drop, but the doctor lived on a hill and I discovered that mash weighs ten times more than water. It was extremely difficult to climb up the hill and not spill a drop of the precious cargo. But how could I back out now? Besides, the doctor had told me that any time I needed medical treatment I should not go to the clinic, where there was always a long line of people, but should feel free to come directly to his house where I'd be a welcome guest. Suddenly it occurred to me that, with the approaching High Holidays, the doctor might prove very useful. I had to find a way of not working on *Rosh Hashanah* and *Yom Kippur*!

When my four weeks as a lumberjack came to an end, I returned to Karobka and was welcomed by the *babushka* and Anna and the children like one of the family. What a gift I'd brought them — a gallon of whiskey!

After taking off some for the teacher, and some for *Dedushka* Anton, Anna's father-in-law, I handed the rest to her, saying, "Here, Anna, put it away. When your husband returns from the war you'll celebrate, and you can tell him it was a gift from a friend of the family."

This was the wrong thing to say, for tears immediately appeared in the grandmother's eyes, the children dropped their heads and Anna herself began to sob aloud; she threw herself on the bed, crying uncontrollably.

Volka took a letter from the shelf and pointed to a line in it: "The enemy fire is unbearable. Who knows if I'll ever see you again after this terrible night is over?"

Lenka, the smallest one, put her hand on my arm and whispered in my ear, "Since then no letter has come." Zinka, the older girl, added, "That letter arrived right after you left...it's been four weeks now."

I felt terrible. Here I was safe in this quiet backwater while a husband and father was risking his life fighting. I could hear Anna sobbing, pleading with God to send him back alive. "Oh, Lord, send him back to us and let this terrible war be over already! Let him come back, even as a cripple, as long as he returns, for the sake of his little children!"

14

My TREASURED Hebrew calendar told me that *Rosh Hashanah* and *Yom Kippur* were fast approaching. What could I do to avoid working on these holy days? Where could I seclude myself to say the lengthy prayers in solitude, to come close to the *Ribbono shel Olam*?

Then another miracle happened! I heard that the old shepherd, who was in his late seventies, had given notice to the chairman that he couldn't continue to take out the herd any more. There was the answer to my problem! I approached the chairman at once. Before I had a chance to make my plea, however, he invited me to his house for supper in order to read a letter which had come for him and his wife.

It was from Lola, the youngest daughter of the old couple. While the old man was busy mashing up his leaves and cutting the newspaper into squares for tomorrow's cigarettes, the old woman pointed to a picture on the wall and said, "This is my Lolichka; she's no farm girl, you know. She is not a *kolkhoznitza*; she knows how to hold a pencil in her hand, and she can write even the biggest and longest address!"

Lola had a bright and pleasant face, and I told her mother that I could see she must be very proud of her. After the meal, I read the letter aloud to them. Then the chairman and I sat down on the bench outside in the evening air. I began to explain to him that since I had already gone through the various jobs a farmer needs to know, I would now like to try being a shepherd, especially since the old man was about to give up the herd.

The chairman began to laugh, but his laughter soon turned into a terrible fit of coughing caused by the acrid smoke of his homemade cigarettes. When he finally managed to stop coughing, he wiped his eyes with his sleeve, placed one hand fondly on my knee and the other on my shoulder and said, "You city boys think that a shepherd is an ignorant man, that he doesn't need to understand anything except chasing animals! Well, you couldn't be more wrong! It's the most responsible job on the farm; a shepherd has to know everything there is to know about animals — their nature, feeding habits, fattening them; he has to be an animal doctor. Chaim, you don't know what you're asking for! If you plow the fields, or sow them, the result won't be known until next year; but in herding, if you make a mistake, the same night you bring the cows back from pasture the women will know how much milk they're missing, or how much less fat there is in the milk, and they'll be ready to murder you! I'd hate to be in your shoes!"

Just then the old woman called to say the samovar was ready. The samovar is a Russian invention, a great kettle made of brass; it is filled with water, the metal tube inside is filled with glowing charcoal, and this heats the water until it boils. Russians are great tea drinkers, and will drink ten or fifteen cups a day. With real tea unobtainable now, the women colored the hot water with powdered tree bark, and for sugar they substituted dry sugar cane mixed with sweet potato. As the chairman noisily drank his "tea," he said, "Do you really want to be a shepherd? Hah! Forget it!"

I could see I was not making any impression on the old man. I would need the teacher's help, for only he could persuade the chairman. Thanking them for their hospitality, and telling them how much I looked forward to meeting their daughter, I said good night and hurried to the teacher's house.

I knocked on Goncharov's door, and when Yevgenia opened it, I saw that she was angry and upset. Instead of the usual sparkle in her eyes, they were red from crying. When I asked for her husband, she did not answer at once. Then she shouted, "I don't know where he is, and I don't care!"

I was astonished, for I had never seen her so furious. Realizing that this was one of those moments when it is best for strangers to stay away, I said good night and left.

As I passed the barn a low voice called my name. It was Goncharov.

"Nikolai Yefimovich, you scared the devil out of me," I said. "Why in the world are you hiding in the barn?"

"Believe it or not, Chaim," he sighed, "Yevgenia has kicked me out of the house." His face was drawn and tense in the moonlight. "We had a quarrel — a big one. Don't look so surprised; it happens, Chaim — women can be very excitable. Now she won't even speak to me. She's locked the door and refuses to let me in. We've had fights before, but nothing like this. This time I think she means business." He looked at me pleadingly. "Chaim, maybe you can talk some sense into her. Do you think you can help me?"

"I'll try — you're my best friend — but I can't guarantee results."

I went back to Goncharov's house, trying to figure out how I would handle this. I, who had never gone out with a girl, was about to become a marriage counselor! Somehow I'd have to get him back into his wife's good graces. Not only was he my friend, but I needed his help in getting the shepherd's job. I knew this couple quite well: he was an intellectual, and she liked to think she was one. She always tried to join our discussions and show off her knowledge and intelligence. Perhaps this was a key to the solution....

While she served me baked potatoes, I began to flatter her. "You know, Yevgenia, I've become so fond of your home and family, so accustomed to your wonderful library, to our discussions and to that superior intellect of yours, and, of course, to your beautiful children. What a shame that this has to come to an end...."

"Why should it?" she asked defensively. "You will always be welcome in this house. The library will still be here, and so will I and the children."

"Yevgenia Alexandrova," I went on, using her proper title as a sign of respect, "you are a *Comsomol* member, and I presume that you aspire to be a Party member one day. Surely you must kow that Marxism views marriage as an obsolete, capitalistic institution, another form of property ownership. Why should a dedicated Communist like you concern herself with this decadent and bourgeois institution?" I knew that her womanly pride had been wounded, but I wanted to appeal to her Communist soul. "Besides, you're lucky to have a husband at all, when all the young and even the old men are away at war, and many of them are dying. And Nikolai is not just any old husband — he's an exceptional man who could easily fit in among the intelligentsia of Moscow or Leningrad. So you had a fight! He admits he was wrong, and he says he's sorry. Where will you find another man like this? And what about the children?"

Yevgenia was silent. I thanked her for the meal, and as I rose to leave, she grudgingly said, "All right. Tell him he can come home. But he'd better watch his step!"

Goncharov, out in the barn, looked at me with eyes like a whipped dog's. "Well, what did she say?"

"You can go home," I announced proudly.

"Can it be true? Chaim, you are a genius! I'll never forget what you've done for me, never! But I'd still feel better if you came along with me . . . you never know with her."

With the help of Goncharov, I was appointed shepherd of the commune and began my training. I soon found out that there was a great deal more to tending a herd than just driving the animals to pasture and back, as the chairman had warned me and as the old shepherd kept reminding me. I'd always had a special fondness for old people and this Andrey Semyonovich won my heart immediately. Instead of *Dedushka*, I called him by a younger title, *Dyada* Andrusha — Uncle Andrey — which pleased him a lot.

"Son," the old man told me on my very first day with him, "you should understand that life comes from the forest. All the grains, seeds, all that grows, originated in the woods. I can spend a lifetime in the forest and never go hungry." The thin old man looked with warm and loving affection at the woods around him.

There was one thing in particular he must point out to me, the old man said. He took the herd deeper into the woods, where there was fresh green pasture. "Let them chew while we talk."

Dyada Andrusha turned to me with a serious look on his face. "Listen, Chaim. I had four sons. Two I lost in the First World War. The third fought with the White Army against the Bolsheviks. I lost him too. The fourth, the youngest, was a Red Army man and fell in the Kronstadt uprising, carrying a red flag. And my wife is buried right here." He took me by the hand and led me to where a grave was marked by a wooden cross.

"Why do I tell you all this? Because I am handing my herd over to you, and if you are still here when my time comes, I want to be buried here, right next to her. No fence should ever be put around our graves. Let the herd eat and fatten themselves on the grass; their manure will be our flowers. It will be our pleasure, because I found these animals much closer and warmer than any human beings." He bowed his head in silence, resting his hands on his cane.

This must be a daily ritual with him, I thought, noticing that the dog, who would never keep still, sat quietly as long as the old man stayed bowed down.

After a while he crossed himself, and straightening up, he limped off. "If you really want to be a shepherd, you'll have to love the animals as I do," he said.

The old man began to teach me about cows, calves and sheep. "Keep your eyes open," he would say, "for a dry nose and mouth. Always plan two days ahead where you will take them for grazing. Always start early in the morning on the rougher herbage, then move on to richer, sweeter, better grass. Then, when the sun is high, you take them to a shady place where they can lie down for a few hours and chew their cud; that's when they put on fat. But don't let them rest too early, because they're lazy; keep them moving. By noontime, the women will come to the edge of the forest to milk the cows, so keep them near the water. And remember, sheep don't drink fast-flowing water."

I marveled at the old man. He might be illiterate and ignorant, never having left his native village; haggard and bent in his patched-up rags, he looked like a scarecrow. But he knew nature, preferring the solitude of the forest to crowds of people. After a few more lessons, he was willing to entrust the herd to me.

"You still have a lot to learn," the shepherd advised me. "But Moscow wasn't built in one day! Let me warn you, though, about the main danger, wolves! They won't attack you if they aren't terribly hungry; and if you stand still and look a wolf straight in the eye, not running or showing fear, he won't touch you. Besides, the dog will fight them to the death. The sheep will indicate the first sign of wolves coming — they'll start racing madly in circles. Don't run after them, because you can't catch them anyway. Just help the dog fight, and make a fire; that's the best weapon against them! Above all, never say the word 'wolf' during the night and you won't see them during the day."

He invited me to visit him any time; he still had some homemade whiskey. He handed over the dog and staff with emotion and made it seem a ceremony, like a king abdicating and handing over the symbols of royalty to his successor. Patting the dog affectionately, he murmured, "Now listen, Vyeter, it's no use coming back to my house; you stay with Chaim, be faithful, and watch over him and the herd. You hear, Vyeter?"

The last thing the old man did was to give me a present. He took out a pair of _laptee_ from his bag, saying proudly, "I made them myself. If you ever have the time, I'd be happy to show you which tree bark is good for _laptee_ and how to make them."

Deeply moved, I shook his hand, thanking him. "We Jews," I said, "are taught by our religion to respect the old, because of their experience, because of all the good and the bad that have passed over them. I'm afraid you have had more bad than good, *Dyada* Andrusha."

Tears coursed down the old wrinkled face. A sheep came up to rub his head against his feet, then another one; a cow licked him all over with her long tongue.

"It seems they're saying good-bye too," I said. "They'll miss you."

"No," replied the old man, "they're not that smart; it's just a habit of theirs. Soon they'll do the same for you. It makes them feel better and safer, knowing that someone is watching over them. Just tickle them behind the ear when they come up to you, and they'll come every day."

I had to ask the old man one more thing. "Tell me, *Dyada*, do you really believe what you told me, that wolves will come if you mention them after sundown?"

The old man began to smile. "*Chi*, if people take something for granted, there must be some truth in it." He would not give a direct answer.

Then he told me that he had something to ask me. Could I speak Hebrew? When I said that I could, he looked around to make sure we were alone, and whispered, "They used to say that if a baby is left in the woods all by itself, with no human being ever talking to him, the baby will begin to speak Hebrew because that is the language of the angels. Is that really true?"

Astonished at this mystical subject which had found its way to an isolated village of the Volga region, I replied, "I do know Hebrew, but since I've never had the honor of speaking with angels, I wouldn't know for sure. But as you said — if people take something for granted, there must be some truth to it!"

The next day I was alone with the animals at the edge of the huge forest. As the herd settled down to chewing the tasty grass, I felt the solitude all around me. I began to understand why so many great men, spiritual giants, had been shepherds — Jacob, Moses, David and most of the prophets.

This was the ideal place for peace of mind, meditation, prayer and soul-searching. It seemed to me that every time I stood praying, with my eyes and heart directed to the Almighty, the trees joined me in prayer, swaying and whispering. Soon the birds joined in, and all Creation seemed to sing its praise of the Almighty.

At moments like this, I appealed to Heaven for the welfare of my family, my friends, my people. Feeling so near to God, the well of tears would open and not only did I pray, but I begged, demanded, beseeched _Ribbono shel Olam_ to save the captives in Nazi hands. My tears eased my soul and mind and afterwards I always felt better, calmer, reassured that I was not forsaken. And yet the worm of guilt gnawed ever deeper and deeper. My people were suffering so dreadfully under the Germans, and I was enjoying the beauty and solitude of the forest, the closeness to nature and to its Creator.

15

THE GERMANS were pushing the front closer to Moscow. In the southern sector they were approaching the Volga. The city of Rostov had already fallen, and with it the Don basin, the breadbasket of Russia. By cutting off the Volga, the enemy hoped to split the country in half and to attack Moscow from the rear, before the dreaded "General Winter" arrived.

The Russians fought with desperate determination, burning everything behind them as they retreated. Orders from above demanded that hundreds of thousands of acres of forest be cut down along the Volga to provide natural obstacles against the advancing German tanks.

In Karobka, three people were to be assigned at once to the military commandant of the Volga district. The chairman appointed two girls, but one man was also needed. He approached me. "Son, you have become a professional lumber man, a real Stakhanovite at the alcohol factory; I'm afraid you'll have to go."

I was heartbroken. In a few days the High Holidays would be here, and now all my plans were ruined! Instead of fasting and praying on *Yom Kippur*, I'd be cutting down trees! The smell of war was coming nearer, becoming reality as it drew closer and closer to my quiet haven. But who would dare refuse an order of this kind?

"*Dedushka*, I'm ready to go," I announced, "but I must have pants." I pointed to the rags which barely covered me. Oh, if Mama could only see me now, I often thought, she would wring her hands and cry over her poor, threadbare son!

An immediate search began in the village for a pair of pants, but with no luck; none could be found anywhere. Was it the great poverty? Or was it that they needed a shepherd so badly that he couldn't be replaced?

The day was almost over, and still no pants had been found. Before sundown, as I was bringing the herd back home, Summatov arrived. He was in charge of delivering the workers to the military commandant of the Volga district. The chairman was worried about not having his three people ready and tried to explain the reason for the delay, but Summatov assured him that it was all right. He had anticipated such a problem, remembering the time when he had to bring pants for me so that I could go to work at the alcohol factory. Therefore he had chosen an old Tatar from his own village to go with the girls.

I was relieved to get out of this assignment, and I wondered if Suleika had anything to do with it. She must have realized that the chairman would send me. Did she know that I was grazing the herd?

On *Rosh Hashanah*, I took the herd deep into the forest, so as not to be disturbed. The clearing rang with my broken-hearted prayers. I wanted to get closer to the "King Who sits in judgment"; with my face turned up to the sky, in a torrent of tears I cried out, "Remember us unto life, O King, Who delightest in life, and inscribe us in the book of life, for Your Own sake, O living God."

I knew most of the prayers by heart. The Psalms of David were especially appropriate for this day, with their comforting warmth, and their depth of feeling.

"The Lord is my light and my salvation, of whom shall I be afraid? The Lord is the fortress of my life, of whom shall I have dread? ... My father and my mother have forsaken me, but the Lord will take me up."

I pleaded for my family and for my people, for the world to be saved from the "dominion of arrogance and oppression," whether Nazis or Russians, whether in Europe or Asia. It seemed to me that I could see millions gathered before the great Throne of Judgment and I pleaded for mercy for them all. I missed the sound of the *shofar*, but the whistling of the wind in the treetops sounded like *"Tekiah! Shevarim! Teruah!"* bringing memories of past *Yamim Tovim*. Nine days later came *Yom Kippur*, the Day of Atonement; even the fish in the water, it is written, tremble in fear of that awesome day.

"All who enter into the world now pass before Thee, as a herd of sheep; as the shepherd musters his flock and passes them under his crook. On the first day of the year it is inscribed, and on the fast day of Atonement it is sealed and determined...who shall live and who shall die. And on the countries sentence is pronounced, which for the sword and which for peace, which to famine and which to plenty, and each creature is recorded for life or death...."

I wept as I recited these familiar words in the traditional chant. All the despair which filled my young heart, my loneliness for Mama and Papa and my brothers, my fear for their safety in German hands, all went into my plea to *Ha-Kadosh Baruch Hu*, the Holy One, blessed be He.

It was at that most exalted moment of prayer, intense meditation and closeness to God that a visitor arrived.

Immersed in my prayers and in thoughts of my suffering family and of *Klal Yisrael*, I heard nothing at first. Then the sudden whinny of a horse attracted my attention, and I saw the rider — Suleika. Quickly she jumped down from the horse, and faced me with a sullen expression in her eyes.

"Since you didn't come to see me," she said, "I came to see you." Then she flashed a quick smile and I could tell she wasn't really angry.

I could not be angry with her, either, yet I couldn't refrain from saying, "Well, of all days, you had to come today!"

"*Chi*, what's wrong with today? Anyway, what's the matter with you? Why are your eyes so red? Have you been crying alone here in the forest?"

I was not going to admit to crying. "Oh, it's nothing; I was looking up at the sky and something fell into my eyes; I've been rubbing them all day."

"No, I can tell you have been crying!" she insisted. "What's the matter with you today? Is today a special day for you?"

I tried to get rid of her without making her angry, but she kept bombarding me with questions. "I noticed that you were standing in front of that tree. Were you praying? Must you cry when you pray? To whom do you pray anyway, and do you really believe in God? How can an educated fellow like you believe in all that nonsense?"

"Tell me, Suleika — do you see the sun? Do you feel its warmth?" I began. "This is vital for all living things, and our world is placed just far enough from the sun to keep us warm; just enough and not too much. Suppose we were to move a few degrees closer to it or away from it. What would happen? We'd be roasted or frozen! Right?"

She nodded her head in approval. With the pleasure of a teacher who has succeeded in getting through to his pupil, I asked, "Do you think that all this came about by pure accident? That there's no Creator, no guiding Spirit?"

She placed her hand over her eyes to look at the sun, as if seeing it for the first time. "Then what about Darwin and evolution?" she suddenly asked with a smile, proving that she was not entirely ignorant.

I was sorry about the whole discussion; I should have ignored her, even risking her anger. On *Yom Kippur*, instead of dedicating the time to prayer, I was involved in a discussion on Darwin, and with whom? A Tatar farm girl! I felt ashamed and guilty before my family and before God.

Still, I felt I should answer her. "Evolution is not a fact; it is merely a theory, and it doesn't necessarily contradict believing in God." I started to elaborate on this subject.

She listened attentively and with concentration. When I finished there was complete silence.

I was trying to think of some way to send her home without hurting her feelings, and my guilty conscience was pressing me: here I am wasting precious moments of this solemn day, when my parents and brothers might not have the chance to pray for even one minute in German captivity!

With a start I realized she was talking to me. "Sometimes I *do* feel an urge for religion, but we young people have never had religious feelings like the older generation; and most of the old people are gone now. I was right," she continued, "today must be a special day for you, and I'm sorry I disturbed you. I'll go back now."

I wanted to make her feel better. "No, you're really not disturbing me. Still, you'd better go — the milkers are coming soon. Why should we give those gossips something to talk about?"

Jumping onto her horse, she told me that her father would manage to get me some winter clothes before the terrible cold set in. She soon disappeared in the thickness of the forest, and just in time; moments later, the chatter and laughter of the women milkers rang out close by.

Suleika's last words worried me a little. The winter clothes from her father — perhaps they were intended to be a dowry? Those things were precious, and many a young man might marry for less.

After the herd was watered and milked, I moved the cows deeper into the forest, to new pastures, hoping not to be disturbed until sundown. I tried to recapture the mood of *Yom Kippur*, the fervor and purity of heartfelt prayer; but it was gone. No matter how much I tried to immerse myself in the poignant words of the *Yom Kippur* service, I could not recapture the exalted feeling of the morning. Darkness fell, and I drove the cows back to their stable. The long day was over and despite all my prayers and tears, I felt far removed from the spiritual closeness I had found earlier in the forest; I had spoiled and wasted the holy day.

My "oasis within an oasis," as I called the peaceful forest, did not last long. I knew that the work of a shepherd was limited to the summer; and the merciless winter, when the animals were kept in the barns, was approaching rapidly. Cloistered in the vast forest, I utilized every possible moment for meditation and prayer, enjoying the seclusion and silence. I hoped that this time would never end, or that at least it would last until the first snows covered the grass — unless I should be drafted in the meantime.

Suddenly new directives arrived from Moscow, destroying my dream world and bringing me back to reality.

The Soviet peasant's own little "farm" was limited to a small lot behind his house. This was regarded as his private property, while the huge arable lands were government or *kolkhoz* property. The farmer tended his small lot with love and great dedication. His attitude towards the collective land was one of indifference.

A similar situation was found in relationship to livestock. A farmer was permitted to own one single cow, and no more! On this one cow he had to pay taxes, and the tax was to be paid in natural products! The farmer would watch over his precious cow more than over his wife, for the cow was his main source of livelihood; but the collective herd, which contained a few dozen cows, was neglected; it belonged to everyone, which meant no one. The small barn next to the peasant's house which housed his own cow and a few chickens was kept in good order. The collective barn, however, was a different story; the piles of mud and filth reached up to the cows' knees. Often there was no roof, or if there was one it leaked, and the cracked walls were wide open to the elements.

The farmer was permitted to keep a calf until it was four weeks old. After that the law said that he had to sell it to the government, for a standard price set in Moscow for the entire country. In order to avoid this, the peasant would usually take his calf to be slaughtered after the third week at the market in the nearest town, where it would bring a hundred times the government price.

The food shortage, and especially the meat shortage, was felt all over the country, particularly in the big cities whose inhabitants were on the verge of starvation. Meat was priceless and unobtainable. Factory workers were told, "The food goes to farmers and soldiers"; farmers were told, "The food goes for the factory and the army"; and so everyone lived on meager rations for a "higher" purpose: the dream of collective farming and communization. New regulations were enacted, permitting the farmer to keep his calf for six months; this was a minor concession aimed at increasing the meat supply to the official "black" market.

Unaware of the new regulations, I was astonished to discover that my herd had suddenly and mysteriously increased. I didn't count them every day, but I began to notice a number of new young animals. These proved to be especially lively and hard to manage, running and jumping excitedly, unused to "herd society." Where did all the new calves come from? No one had said a word to me. It was as if they'd all been born yesterday! Every day a few more appeared, until the number in my care almost doubled. It became impossible for me to run after them all day; and so, although I hated to give up my solitude, I had to ask for help.

The chairman was already aware of the problem, and called for volunteers. I protested that I should be allowed to choose my own helper, and I picked Anna, my landlady and the chairman's daughter-in-law. *Dedushka* Anton liked my choice, as herding would be much easier for her than working in the fields. I was glad to have his consent, since she was the only woman there whom I had never heard cursing or using vulgar language.

I did not want to have her near during my prayers, so I tried to interest her in a book, or to send her to the far end of the wide-ranging herd. One day at lunch, she suddenly asked, "Tell me, Chaim, have you been baptized?"

The black bread and garlic stuck in my throat. What had got into her? Had she noticed me praying, with my *tefillin* on my arms and forehead?

Astonished, I replied, "Anna, you know I'm Jewish and that we don't believe in your saviour, so naturally I haven't been baptized."

She seemed nervous, and said, "I don't mean that, exactly; I just don't know the right word for it. What I mean is, do you Jews have any ceremony or special prayer for a newborn baby?"

"What difference does it make? Besides, since when are children in the Soviet Union baptized?" I asked, puzzled.

With a wink of her eye she whispered, "Ah, but they are! There's an old farmer here who used to be a priest. He comes around every now and then and baptizes all the babies secretly." I was amazed, and very curious, but she refused to divulge more about that forbidden subject.

Anna continued: "You know that my mother is an old-fashioned believer; you've seen her praying. When you first came, she said that no man who wasn't baptized could live in her house. That's why she was very reserved around you in the beginning. But then she began having vivid dreams; angels appeared to her and told her that you are close to God. That made her change her mind about you, but she still can't understand how it is possible!"

"Well," I replied, "we Jews do have a ceremony and prayer at the birth of a baby, but it is definitely not a baptism!"

Anna was overjoyed. "That's all I mean," she exclaimed, "as long as you have God's blessing. Oh, I'm so happy! I must tell my mother and mother-in-law! You see, we were talking about you the other day...my sister-in-law Lola is a *krasavitza* — a real beauty — and just about your age. She's a secretary in Kuybishev, and she's coming home soon for a few days. But her mother and mine were worried, thinking that you're an infidel. Maybe now you'll stay here and become a member of the family."

My heart sank. So now Anna, too, is a matchmaker!

I said, "Look here, I can't tie myself to anyone; I might be drafted any day. Although I'd consider it a great honor to belong to your family and to the chairman's family, I'd rather that you look for a match some place else."

"But you don't understand!" she cried out. "Men are scarce, and she'll be an old maid soon. Anything is better than remaining an old maid! She's twenty-one already, and who knows if she'll ever find a husband!"

That evening I consulted Goncharov, the teacher. I asked him how I could get out of this without antagonizing anyone. Goncharov laughed his head off, and assured me I had nothing to worry about. The girl was trying to become a member of the "city intelligentsia" and wouldn't be pushed around by her parents.

"She'd never marry a Jewish shepherd boy from a backward village. Why, she'd be disgraced in front of her educated friends!" Thus Goncharov reassured me, and I tried to stop worrying.

Time and time again Anna brought up the subject. I tried to put her off politely. "After all, the girl has something to say about it," I said. "And she might not want a non-Christian."

"Don't be silly," Anna replied. "She couldn't care less! She's a *Comsomol* girl."

"But the family wouldn't completely approve of me," I argued. "After all, even if I've had God's blessing, I don't believe in your religion."

Anna thought about this, and then asked, "All right then, when is *your* redeemer coming?"

I was astonished. "Where did you learn about these things?" I asked. "I thought religion is the opiate of the masses, and is considered poison in the Soviet Union."

Instead of replying to my question, she said, "It's so disappointing; such troubled times and here our Messiah has already come and gone! When is yours coming? Maybe things will improve then."

I had to agree about the disappointment; I pointed out that this alone is enough to convince the Jews that the real Messiah has not yet come. Finally I ended the conversation with the old expression, "If the Messiah has come, why are things so bad? And if things are so bad, why doesn't he come?"

"Yes, it's true," Anna said. "All the killing, every twenty years a war, Christian nations fighting each other, and now Hitler!"

In due time Lola arrived. She was just as Goncharov had described her — bright, with big-town manners and a sharp, independent mind. The first time we met she asked me, "Where did you learn Russian?"

"Right here in the village," I answered.

"With no teachers? All by yourself? Amazing! Is Russian that easy to learn? And you a simple shepherd, spending all your time with animals."

"It wasn't hard for me; in fact, I even think in Russian now."

"What do you mean, 'think in Russian'?" she asked. The phrase sounded suspicious to her.

I replied, "At first I thought in my mother tongue, and translated into Russian. But after a while I found myself even thinking in the new language; that's what I consider fluency."

"I know what you mean. I wish I was at that stage with my French," she said. "Do you know French?"

"No, I never studied it. But why did you decide to take up French? Is there a chance for you to go abroad?"

"The Party and Stalin are encouraging the study of foreign languages. Someday the Red Army will liberate all those countries and we, the vanguard of the Party, must be fluent in all languages, in order to be able to serve well these oppressed peoples, and to fulfill our duty to the Party and our beloved Stalin!" She sounded like a cracked record.

Finally, Lola returned to her important position in the big city. The old folks and Anna remained my close friends, but they no longer had hopes of a match! I was relieved; and it seemed that being a shepherd had many unexpected advantages.

16

THE DAYS were getting shorter and shorter, and the birds, my singing partners, left for warmer climes. My herd, too, began to prepare for the cold; the cattle's coats grew thicker, and the sheep became woolier. Only I remained in my summer rags. My skin shriveled from the cold, but unfortunately produced neither hair nor wool; man is born helpless, and must adapt himself to his circumstances. And so — I froze.

With the thin sunlight departing earlier and earlier each day, I gained more time to read the newspaper before my audience of old men; I enjoyed sitting around the warm stove in the stables, talking and listening to the village folk.

One evening I noticed a loss of interest in my listeners. Usually, they hung upon my every word, mouths open. But now they paid little attention to my explanations, in spite of the importance of the subject, the "second front" promised by the Americans and the British. Occasionally a man would raise his eyes and exchange a look with his neighbor in silence; then both would drop their heads with a deep sigh. Finally I put down the paper; and to my surprise no one grabbed it to make cigarettes. There must be something serious brewing; I was sure of that, but what was it?

I asked questions, but no one would volunteer an answer. Had the Germans broken through towards Moscow? Had they crossed the Volga? Why were the villagers keeping secrets from me? Was I still not trustworthy, still suspected of being an enemy agent?

I rushed to the chairman's house to ask *Dedushka* Anton, but his wife would only say, "He's in the office with the Tatar, preparing for the meeting."

I took off for the teacher's cottage, for he certainly would not keep anything from me. His wife met me at the door; I didn't dare ask *her* about what was brewing in the village. I merely asked to see her husband and she replied that he too was getting ready for the meeting, and was in conference with Summatov.

Astonished at the unusual preparations for the meeting, I realized that there must be something extraordinary on the agenda. But since when was the teacher involved in a meeting? I had hardly ever seen him there. The matter was clarified by Yevgenia, who was eager to display her knowledge.

"This meeting is different! You know who is going to be there? Comrade Tomashova! That means something very important. Come along and you'll see for yourself!"

Yevgenia explained that Tomashova was the chairman of the propaganda branch of the Communist Party's district committee. The pride in her voice suggested that she was referring to a close friend of the great Stalin himself.

I hurried along to the meeting. The two rooms of the office were filled with people sitting packed together on the floor. I settled in a corner near the door of the third room. There, the woman who lived in the house had her bedroom, and I noticed that the icon over her bed had been removed for the occasion; apparently God and a Party chief cannot dwell under the same roof, and the woman felt much safer by removing God.

Everyone was whispering, waiting for the meeting to begin. I caught a word here and there, and the sum of their conversation was that something big was going to be decided tonight. Summatov, as chairman of the council of villages and a Party member, had complete authority to tell the peasants of the entire district what was good for them and how to respond to the call of the Party and of the great Stalin. But now he had found it necessary to summon a *nachalstvo* — a director and high Party official. This could only mean trouble for the downtrodden villagers.

Tomashova arrived shortly, and climbed out of a light carriage which was pulled by a young horse. She was a plump woman, dressed in clean, unpatched garments, which in itself called for respect. There was authority in her every move, and I noticed the flattering greetings she received, and the smiles on all the faces as she was welcomed. But underneath all the smiles there was anxiety; it was obvious from the expression in everyone's eyes, in the secret, sullen glances they shot at her.

At the table sat *Dedushka* Anton; next to him, Summatov, and to his right the Party delegate. Her head turned from side to side, and her piercing brown eyes darted here and there. She looked like an informer, and I could understand why everyone feared her. Her hands, fat and full, had clean nails; one could tell she was not a farm woman. A medallion hanging from her thick neck displayed Stalin's face on a red star, framed in gold.

In stark contrast were the peasants, sitting packed together on the cold floor, ragged, filthy, with gnarled, earth-stained hands. Their sweating bodies gave off a strong odor which, mixed with the heavy smoke of the crude homemade cigarettes, made the rooms almost unbearable.

The chairman finally opened the meeting, presenting Comrade Toma-shova. She began with the usual propaganda, bringing greetings from the victorious Red Army which, "under the leadership of the military genius Stalin, has been crushing the aggressive fascists, the enemies of all man-kind!" The people listened to this old stuff with apathy, cracking sunflower seeds and spitting the hulls on the floor, waiting for the main part of her talk. What did she want? What did she have in store for them?

Finally she came to the point. "I bring the call of the great Stalin," she cried with fervor, "the call of the victorious Red Army, the call of embattled Leningrad! Four million of our brethren are fighting off the cursed Ger-mans and their rotten allies, the Finns! The enemy is proclaiming to the whole world that Leningrad will have to give in or starve! The enemy is telling the world that not a cat or dog or rat is still alive in Leningrad, that the starving population has eaten them all, and that the army is eating frozen cabbage from the fields.

"But we will show these enemies of our glorious Soviet Union that we will never give up Leningrad! We, the Russian people, shall supply food to our heroic defenders! So I ask you, the people of Karobka, to send out at once all of your grain! All of it!"

A heavy silence settled over the room. The cracking and spitting of seeds stopped; the smoke poured out with greater volume from the open mouths. Now everything was lost! The peasants had paid off all the taxes in grain, they had shipped out all the additional tax levies for the war effort. They had hoped that the little that was left would be divided among them, a bit of food for the winter as a reward for all their hard labor. In fact, this would be the second year in a row that the peasants wouldn't get paid. Because of the poor harvest the previous year, the payments due for all the work they had done had been postponed until this year. The government had to collect its taxes, regardless of good or bad weather. And now for the second year they were being denied payment; their last crumb of bread would be taken from their mouths!

Comrade Tomashova looked over the mass of huddled bodies, their heads hanging down in silent despair.

Summatov tried to relieve the strain by announcing that "whatever the *kolkhoz* owed its members would be paid from the next harvest." He added, "Of course, after all taxes are paid to our great Soviet collective effort."

Not a word came from the crowd. The stony silence continued and filled the room. To speak up and object wouldn't do any good, for the grain would still be shipped out and the courageous one would be shipped out as well, to disappear, perhaps forever.

Summatov made the motion: "Answering the call of the beloved Stalin and of the courageous people of Leningrad, the workers of Karobka agree to send out at once all the grain available, and all that will be collected and threshed from this last harvest." His voice had lost its usual cheerful ring; it was hoarse and cracked.

Tomashova put the final seal of authority on it by asking stridently, "Is there anyone here who opposes the resolution of Comrade Summatov?"

Not a word, not a whisper.

"In that case," her voice rang out, "Comrade Chairman, you may pronounce the resolution passed unanimously."

People near the door began to stand up, ready to leave, when suddenly a voice called out and all heads turned to see Anna Mikhailovna, my landlady.

"Comrade Chairman," she began with a trembling voice, "of course we shall send our food to Leningrad at once. I shall be glad to give my last crumb for the army, for our husbands. And I have a brother and his family in Leningrad as well! But in order to work we must eat, and so I propose that the collective retain some food for the use of public kitchens."

While the Party delegate fixed her piercing eyes on Anna, everyone applauded and called out their agreement with her. Then Anna silenced the crowd, addressing herself to the Stalin medallion which gleamed from the fat neck of the Party delegate.

"Comrade Tomashova, you may report to our beloved leader Stalin that we will give anything, including our lives, to crush the cursed enemy!"

How I had underestimated Anna! Not only had she dared to speak out in order to save some food for the people, but she had been clever enough to take out an "insurance policy" for herself, sending off that message to Stalin! But Tomashova wouldn't give in so easily.

"You people have your own private land; you can still collect food in the forest; you can hunt! But the people of Leningrad can only hunt for Fritzes and Finns, and they can't eat those rotten fascists!" She smirked at her own grim joke.

Now the Karobka chairman, *Dedushka* Anton, who had been sitting quietly all the while, stood up for his daughter-in-law and for his people.

"That's exactly what's going to happen, Comrade Tomashova! The people will take off to the forest to pick mushrooms, and how can I stop them if they're hungry? Who will do the work then? Part of our harvest is eaten up by the rats, and part by the elements, all because we don't have enough working hands. Therefore, I think that Anna Mikhailovna is right; let's retain some of the yellow barley which can be cooked right in the fields, with a few drops of vegetable oil, and the people will be able to do a better job." He too made sure to obtain his "insurance policy," adding, "And don't forget to tell the great Stalin that I am a lieutenant in the reserves. Even though I'm not a young man, I'm nevertheless ready to join my sons who are in the Red Army, and we shall gladly give our lives for the beloved Stalin and Mother Russia! I'm ready to join the battle on a moment's notice! But we must take care of all these women whose husbands and sons are away fighting the enemy; they must be fed in order for them to dedicate their time to working and producing, instead of searching the forest for food!"

Tomashova finally gave in, but with a compromise: only those who worked in the fields would be fed by the collective; those who worked in the village close to home would have to eat their own food. After that day, yellow barley, with a sprinkling of oil, was cooked in the field for all the workers.

On the way home I asked Anna about her brother in Leningrad, and why his name was never mentioned in the house. She told me the story that Goncharov had told me long before, how her brother hadn't known how to sign his name until the age of thirty, and how the Soviet regime had sent him to school until he became an engineer. Then he had married a physician in Leningrad, and though as a Party member he was supposed to be proud of his peasant background, he was actually ashamed of his family and never even wrote home.

At home _Babushka_ took over from Anna, telling me of her disappointment in her son. "That's how they are, the younger generation," she said with a sigh. "They don't want to remember the days we were starving! I remember the time my old man came home empty-handed one evening after wandering around all over Sammarra, trying to earn a kopek." She wiped a tear and continued. "He said to the hungry children — do you remember, Anna? — 'I can give you meat; here's my leg, mother, cut it off and feed them! But I can't give you bread, children!'" She began to cry softly.

"Then the Americans arrived. They opened field kitchens; they fed the children first and then the rest of us. But now the youngsters call the Americans 'damned capulists.'" Shaking her head, she added, "They don't even remember their own mother; so why should they remember the American capulists who fed them, and saved them from starvation?"

She pulled me to the window. "There, you see," she said with emotion, pointing to some fields in the distance, "those are our fields. My husband hated the city after we almost starved there, so we came to this farm. But we had no luck; after we came, they started the _kolkhoz_ business....I keep telling my children and grandchildren where their land is located, so they will know in case a change comes... and I'll be dead by then." She said the last words accompanied by a gesture of her hands that seemed to say: it's hopeless, it's lost, all is lost....

The fierce Russian winter arrived with all its cruelty and harshness. Poland, too, has hard winters with cold winds, snow and ice; but at home winter arrived gradually, like a peaceful lamb which would become at times like a lion. In Russia, the elements tell you right from the beginning that _Dedushka Moroz_ means business. No wonder the Russians depended so much on their "Grandpa Frost" to stop the enemy.

Bitter cold winds are the introduction; they blow ferociously, and no matter how much clothing you put on, or how well you cover your head, they find their way in and penetrate, filling your very bones with cold and sadness, making you lonely and helpless.

Listening to the frozen forest trembling, and to the many trees which crack and fall, unable to withstand the fierce wind, you get the feeling that the Creator, in His anger, has decided to turn the world upside down. So you hide in the sheltering walls of the house, listening to the howling outside. Your eyes are useless in the terrifying darkness of the winter night; they can see nothing but fearful visions. It's your ears that serve you most, and so, waiting for the worst, you finally fall asleep.

In the morning a new world is born, all white, with not a speck of color. The storm last night was not a sign of the Almighty's destructive anger, but the throes of birth. Then, as you look more closely at the familiar houses and trees, you recognize the same old worn-out world, which has merely been covered with a new coat of paint by the artful brush of Grandpa Frost.

The farmers stopped sending the herd out to the pasture. My new jobs varied from day to day. I was supposed to report every morning for a new assignment, but how could I? I was still in my *laptee*, my thin clothes nothing but rags, with gaping holes between the patches.

Then *Dedushka* Anton arrived with a pack of old clothes. There was a *koofika* — a thick, quilted outfit, and new *valenky* — knee-high boots made of pressed wool. Rubber boots were unnecessary, for the snow was hard and dry; one could sleep on the snow and not get wet. The *babushka* presented me with a sweater she had knitted herself, and Anna gave me socks and gloves from homemade wool. It all came at the right time, for the thermometer hit thirty degrees below zero, and the snow reached the window sills after a few days of steady snowfall.

Life almost came to a standstill, except for the feeding of the livestock. The days were growing short, and the nights endlessly long. With no electricity, and not even kerosene for the lamp (for I was no longer a tractorist), and no radio, I was restless and lonely. I felt isolated and forsaken.

Then new orders arrived. With the enemy pushing on to Moscow, Stalin had ordered that all males from the age of fifteen to sixty-five, who for some reason were not in uniform, were to be given guerilla training. In Karobka, five people came under this category, among them the teacher and, to my great surprise, I, myself!

Including me was a sign of trust, I felt, for otherwise they wouldn't train me to be a guerilla, a partisan. Who knows, I thought, eventually they might even draft me into the Russian army; the Polish embassy, to my great sorrow, hadn't even bothered replying to my letters!

The guerilla training center for our district was in the Tatar village. Twice a week we'd ride there on a sled. A wounded Tatar, a sergeant in the Red Army who was just out of the hospital, was the instructor. After a hard day's work, three to four hours of crawling in the deep snow practicing guerilla tactics and snow camouflage taxed my strength to the utmost. Still, we found it not unbearable and often joked on the way home.

Goncharov, who was in charge of driving the sled, let the horse run free; on the smooth sheet of snow, the animal could be given free rein to find his way home, particularly at night. The horse seemed to feel the hard road which was buried in the snow under its hooves, or perhaps it followed the smell of smoke coming from chimneys that were miles away. Goncharov used the long ride home to joke and talk about the affairs of the village and to give me advice.

"You really should marry Suleika," he said. "Summatov can do a lot for you!"

I answered that I couldn't think of getting married now and, besides, I'd be in the army soon. But Goncharov never stopped teasing me, enjoying the role of matchmaker.

"You saved my skin that time," he'd say with a wink, "so now I'll help you become a lucky married man like me!"

Dedushka Anton, the chairman, invited me to go hunting one day. The very idea was repulsive to me: one might be justified in killing for food, but surely not for sport! I refused, and didn't hesitate to state my reasons. The old man didn't seem angry or insulted. Instead he asked me, "Now let me understand, you _do_ wear the _valenky_ — these cozy woollen boots — even though they come from a lamb, don't you?"

"There's quite a difference between killing for sport and killing for food or clothing. The first is a crime, while the other is essential and permissible," I answered hotly.

"And who told you that we do it for sport?" he asked as he gazed into the distant forest. "Have you noticed the shoes I wear when I go to a meeting in the city?" (He was always barefoot in the village.) "Have you seen my old woman's coat? Where did you think they came from? You can't buy shoes for money, and certainly not a woman's coat! It all came from the coupons we receive in trade for the animal hides. Now do you understand?"

He explained to me that an agent from the _soyuzpushnina_ — the government fur trust — comes to the village every month and collects all the hides, paying for them not with money, for nothing can be bought with money, but with coupons. The coupons are later redeemed for clothing and shoes at low prices.

The government fur trust was interested in fox skins, and especially in the rich sable, who was endowed in winter with a beautiful long-haired hide and a great, bushy tail. Shooting was not practical, for a bullet would ruin the hide: thus trapping was the preferred method. In comparison to other animals, the fox is considered clever; still, these people had "outfoxed" him by learning his weakness. After leaving his cave in search of food, the fox returns to his lair, finding his way back by following his previous footprints. It is this habit which cost many foxes their lives. The farmers would copy his footprints in wood, and although the fox was clever enough not to touch a trap, he was not intelligent enough to realize that the footprints he was following were not his own, and did not lead to his lair.

A day or two later, the hunter would return for his prey, hoping to find a dead fox, or one still fighting for his life and freedom. Then the hide was removed and dried in its full beauty. When I asked the old man what was done if the animal were still alive, he drew his hand across his throat and said, "Krrrr. . . ." He must have noticed the look on my face, for he placed his heavy hand on my shoulder and said kindly, "How do you expect to be a soldier, my boy? Suppose you have to stick your bayonet into the enemy's belly, hah?"

I agreed to go with him the next morning, not as a hunter but as an observer.

After nightfall, there was usually nothing to do; I couldn't read, for there was no kerosene for the lamp, so I would lie down and listen to the cry of the wind, which would carry me back home, or to any place of my imaginings, until I finally fell asleep. This night I didn't listen to the wind, for my conscience was bothering me. Why had I agreed to go hunting, to help murder those poor animals? Didn't that prove that I had descended to the level of an ignorant peasant?

I pondered the old man's question all night: Would I be able to kill a German in hand-to-hand combat? Would I even have the nerve to shoot at a distant target? Would my conscience leave me at ease if, instead of a knife, I used a bullet to kill the enemy? Isn't *his* mother waiting for his return, just as mine waits for me?

Finally reason took over. The Germans had started this slaughter, and there was no room for sentiment; any pity or weakening before the enemy was morally wrong! To kill a German was self-defense. In the words of the Talmud: "If one comes to kill you, get ahead and kill him first."

I couldn't fall asleep, thinking of the poor foxes who leave the cave in search of food for their kits, but will never return because hunters trapped them. The wind howling outside carried me away to my home, where the Germans were trapping and killing human beings, my people, in exactly the same way.

I thought of my family. How were they faring in this cold winter? Did Mama have a warm coat? All her clothes had been burned when Lomza was bombed. How grand she had looked in her Russian sable coat! How expensive it was! The Russians had charged five hundred _zloty_; there, one could buy a hundred pairs of shoes for that money. And here the peasant received two pairs of shoes! What exploitation of the poor! No capitalist would dare pay five or ten rubles and then sell the product for five hundred! Anton had to produce eight or ten hides to get one coat, while in Poland, for the price of one sable he could have gotten twenty coats!

The next morning we set out for the forest. Anton explained to me that the first thing a hunter must remember is not to lose his way, especially in the winter, when the whole landscape looks the same and can be confusing. Secondly, he must remember where he places the traps, for they might easily disappear overnight under additional snowfall. The old man used a knife to mark the trees so that we would find our way home; double notches on trees meant a trap had been laid there.

Suddenly he stopped, pointing to traces on the snow. "Here's one!" he exclaimed. The footprints began at the trunk of a large tree, leading to nowhere. He explained that the prints were fresh, and that their size indicated a large animal, while the depth revealed a heavy fox. I was standing at a distance, for the old man had advised me not to go too near. He didn't want so many human footprints, for the fox might become suspicious.

I wanted to know why he didn't remove the snow and simply take the kits from the cave. He laughed. "Because the fox is too smart for that. Do you know that the fox builds a dozen tunnels to and from her cave? You dig up one entrance, and they all run out in a dozen different directions!"

After placing all five traps, we sat down on a fallen tree trunk to rest and eat. Crawling around in the deep snow was hard on the old man; he was breathing heavily. I felt sorry for him; hunting and trapping was hard work, and then there was the killing and skinning, just to get a coat and a pair of shoes!

While we chewed the dry bread I spoke to him. "*Dedushka*, we have been good friends, right?"

"Right. I'd say very good friends."

"Will you promise not to tell anyone what I'm going to tell you?"

The old man reached under his fur hat and began to scratch his head out of habit. "I promise," he said.

I got to the point at once. "You say you might get as much as two pairs of shoes for that big fox? What do you think the fur trust will get for that hide?"

"Well," he began, and again scratched the back of his head, "I once asked the agent, and he said they might get as much as a hundred rubles after they work it out in a tannery."

"*Chi, Dedushka*, I have news for you," I said softly. "They sell it in foreign countries for big money. For instance, in Poland they sell it for five hundred *zloty*! In other words, for one sable they can get a hundred pairs of shoes."

The icicles hanging from his nostrils began to quiver, and his flat nose grew wider. Suddenly the nostrils shrank back to normal; he was controlling his temper.

He looked around to make sure nobody was near, and finally he burst out in a Russian lexicon of curses: "Those rotten low-down swine!" he shouted. "Here we are crawling around in snow up to our necks, and the last time they came, I practically had to get down on my hands and knees and beg to get a lousy coat for my wife — a plain cotton rag with a cotton lining! And those lazy slobs get all the money!"

He paused to catch his breath and then continued in a rush of words. "Look at our poor women; we raise our own cotton and wool, and they have to spin it by hand on the spinning wheel, and then make their own clothes. Last year my old woman suffered from cramps in both hands; the doctor called it rheumatism. Now, she needed a coat badly and couldn't use her hands to spin the wool for one, so I had to get two extra foxes to buy her the coat. And now you tell me that all the while, those selfish beasts, bloodthirsty dogs.... Wait and see how I fix them!"

On the way home he shot two wild pigs, which roamed the forest in large numbers. "This is for food," he stated apologetically. "I know you Jews don't eat pig, so I'll drag them home myself. You just carry my shotgun and shovel."

He was as good as his word. The fur supply of the entire village dropped drastically, and soon the local agent went to town and returned with a Party representative. A special meeting was called and the Party delegate came right to the point.

"Comrades," he said, "I bring you greetings from the victorious Red Army which, under the direct leadership of the greatest military genius the world has ever known, Comrade Stalin, will give the final blow to the German murderers, the fascist dogs! But to fight a war we need tanks, planes and ammunition; we have plenty, but we need even more. Therefore, our Soviet government buys your hides and sells them to the decadent capitalist countries for their spoiled women, in return for military goods."

He stopped and looked around, then continued. "The Party has heard that the fur supply in your village has declined. Why? Stalin doesn't need the hides for himself, you know! You have seen his pictures and you know that he wears the same working clothes as we all do, and so do all the women comrades in Moscow. These furs are for the bourgeois suckers, who pay for them with tanks and ammunition. Now, who can let down his own son in the war? And let me just remind you that the forest and all that's in it — the wood, the hay, the pastures — are all government property. If we were to cancel your permits and put up guards around the forest, and impose stiff fines for trespassers, where would you get firewood to bake your bread and warm your homes? How would you feed your livestock?

"I know you pay a yearly tax for using the forest, but we can raise that tax five thousand times! Now, please remember — we need those hides badly! They are essential for the war effort! However, the Party of Lenin and Stalin is always concerned with the welfare of the workers and farmers. Therefore we have requested, and the fur trust has agreed, to double the coupons for each hide."

I was sitting in a corner listening and watching the faces of the peasants. No one moved a muscle, smiled, or nodded his head, for everyone feared to show any disagreement with what the Party delegate was saying. He was the strong, merciless arm of the great Stalin. How skillfully the speaker combined flattery and threats to make his point, enforcing the will of the Party; how easily things were done with that magic, dreadful name, Stalin!

The next morning, the chairman called me aside and whispered, "Thanks to you, my friend, we'll be getting at least double coupons now! Those swindlers! Before the Revolution, you know, all these lands and forests belonged to Count Voronov. We were sharecroppers, and while he lived it up in Paris, we worked this land, and the forest was free for all. Who would have thought that one day we'd have to pay a tax to use the pastures or to collect firewood? And to be called trespassers! Count Voronov would never have dared, but our government of the workers and peasants takes away everything we produce. Is it not bad enough that we're always hungry, that we have to pay a tax for using the fields and forest? In winter we must hunt for them too, and get almost nothing in return...."

Because of the shortage of working hands, most of the harvest remained in the fields, bundled but uncollected, exposed to the elements and the field rats. Perhaps the lack of workers was only an excuse, for I was told that the same happened even before the war, when there were plenty of men around. The excuse then was that the old farm machinery broke down. But the truth was that no one really cared!

The combine was stuck, immovable in the deep snow. The crop had to be brought to the machine. The women climbed into the big sled every morning and it was my job to drive them out to the fields. There they removed the heavy snow from the bundles and loaded them onto my sled; I brought the frozen bundles of wheat or barley to the machine.

I took my time, filled with pity for the horses — their labored breathing, their bodies steaming from struggling in the snow, and their noses bleeding from the terrible cold. My slow pace was also appreciated by the women, who used the interval of the two-way trip to warm themselves around the fire, while the yellow barley was being cooked for our meal.

Unloading the sled in front of the machine was hard work. The sweat on my forehead froze the moment I stopped moving, and my overheated body cooled off so fast that I felt the frost permeate my bones. I looked forward to returning and warming myself in front of the fire with the women. Sometimes they just sat there, hands and feet close to the fire, without getting up to load the sled. I would make believe I didn't notice, and after a while, they would slowly begin to load again, while I attended to the fire.

One day they jumped up as soon as they saw me, and began to work with unusual speed. What had brought on this unusual enthusiasm? I saw Chairman Anton approaching on a sled, but since they didn't hesitate to loaf in his presence, I presumed it must be the woman who was with him who was the cause of this sudden flurry of activity.

The sled stopped in front of the fire, and the chairman beckoned to everyone, calling, "Come here, comrades, rest a while and warm up!"

Everyone seemed to know the young woman on the sled. She was heavy-set and well-dressed, and they all greeted her with smiles. "Greetings, comrades!" she shouted; Anton lost no time in getting to the point.

"Comrades, you all know Comrade Voronkina, who represents the Party and the government. She has come today on a special mission, so please give her your full attention."

The Party representative cleared her throat, but before she began to speak she wrapped her heavy sheep's coat more tightly around herself, and joined the rest of the women around the fire, thus demonstrating that she was sharing in their labor, working in the fields when it was twenty-five degrees below zero! She, too, was one of them!

Then her mouth began steaming. "My dear comrades! I come here not only on the order of the district Party secretary, but by the order of the great Stalin himself. As busy as he is with leading our Red Army to victory, he has taken the time to send us, the activists, the vanguard of the Bolshevik Party, the message that we must go directly to the people and appeal for money. You all realize that the fight for the Fatherland is costing a fortune; but who would refuse to help a husband, son, brother or father in his struggle to win this war for our beloved Socialist Fatherland? For our great Mother Russia! But still, the great Stalin said: 'We don't want to take the people's hard-earned money.' You all know how Stalin has at heart the good and the welfare of the working class! And so he decided that we shouldn't ask for money, but rather for a loan; and as soon as the war is over, the government will pay back every bit with interest. Stalin personally guarantees the 'victory loan'! Your chairman will appoint a person to go around with me to visit your homes and pick up the shares of the 'victory loan.' I'm sure you won't disappoint Comrade Stalin, our great leader, and that each of you will give as much as he possibly can. Remember: Stalin himself will be personally informed of every worker who makes a loan, its amount, and of who is unwilling to contribute his share in the struggle for victory over the fascist dogs!"

I watched their faces, but there was not a movement or a sound. The last words were a clear warning to those who might refuse to contribute.

Anton broke the heavy silence by saying, "Here is a young man who knows all the people, and he can be helpful in explaining the need for the victory loan." The chairman's heavy hand landed on my back.

The delegate stretched out her plump hand, saying, "Greetings, comrade; it is a pleasure to meet you, but how is it you are not in the army?"

I welcomed the opportunity to bring my case to the attention of a Party official, and at the same time let all these soldiers' wives hear that I was not a draft dodger.

"I wish I could answer that, comrade," I replied. "I have written to the draft commandant of the district many times, to War Commissar Marshal Timoshenko, and even to Stalin himself, but with no luck! It's certainly not right that I hang around here when all the men are off fighting, but it seems the army doesn't want Westerners."

The old man motioned to the women to return to work. They moved off quickly, without uttering a sound. Anton offered to take over my horse and sled and carry on with the work, so I could place myself at the disposal of the Party delegate and the collection of the victory loan.

Foreigners were rare in these parts, and Comrade Voronkina enjoyed this opportunity for conversation with a Westerner, as we rode along on the sled, between a gray, empty sky and the vast white earth.

I answered all her questions carefully, phrasing my answers so that I said nothing which seemed to disagree with the writings of Lenin and Stalin, for that was considered Trotskyism, which was far more dangerous than being a German spy!

Her questions seemed never-ending, and I was afraid I might slip, so I changed the subject and asked her a question: "Comrade Voronkina, can you explain the purpose of this loan," adding apologetically, "since I'm about to assist you in its success?"

She turned to me in surprise, her sharp eyes proclaiming authority and demanding respect. "How else do you expect Stalin to finance the war?" she said.

I was not satisfied with this reply; being ignorant about economics and the financial operation of governments, I had expected a lecture on the subject.

"I hope you don't misunderstand me, Comrade Voronkina. I'm not criticizing, only trying to learn. You see, in a capitalist country, where raw materials and factories are in private hands, and the government has to buy all its needs, from spoons to planes and tanks, it is necessary to float a loan in order to raise money. But under the Soviet system everything belongs to the state — the factories, the raw materials, and the finished product — and labor is paid for by food, which again is collected free from the _kolkhoz_ or _soukhoz_. So what is the purpose of the loan?"

She replied smoothly, without searching for words. "We are moving ahead to Communism, to a life of 'to each according to his need, from each according to his ability,' to the ultimate goal of abolishing money altogether. But now, we are only on the _road_ to socialism, and money as a medium of reward and distribution of the wealth must still be recognized. Temporarily, of course."

I could tell at once that I was getting the stock answer; she was "reading" from a textbook of the Party school. The horse was slowing down, his nose bleeding from the cold. We were on the way to the old shepherd, my predecessor. She had insisted that I take her there first. She must have heard that he had some money saved up.

"Let him contribute something to society besides herding sheep," she said. "After all, is not saving a bourgeois habit? Not trusting in the future is a capitalist approach. In a socialist society, no one has to worry about tomorrow. Let the government, the Party and Stalin take care of it!"

There was nothing more to ask. I felt much safer keeping quiet, for with Party people, one always walked on thin ice, never knowing when one might slip and "fall in."

After a while, she said, "I can tell by your silence that the matter is clear to you. Well, why don't you ask me some more questions? I like to discuss things with Westerners."

So I did ask, "In that case, why doesn't the government print more money?" And for safety I added, "Of course, if Stalin ordered a victory loan, I'm sure it's for the good of the country and the winning of the war, but we ordinary people are merely trying to understand the reason. Wouldn't it be more practical to print more money, and use talented people like you in some capacity other than going around collecting for a loan?"

For a long time, she didn't answer. Finally she came up with something.

"What do you mean, print more money? That is the capitalist way of robbing the working class. In our country, the interest and welfare of the people come before everything else." She sat back, satisfied with her answer.

I took a five-ruble note out of my pocket and said, "Comrade Voronkina, I've noticed the following inscription on single or five-ruble notes: 'The Government of the USSR.' Now perhaps you have a *chervontz* on you?" (All notes from ten rubles and up were called *chervontzes*.) She unbuttoned her heavy sheepskin coat, then three thick sweaters, and finally reached a pocket, pulling out a twenty-ruble note.

"Read the inscription, please," I said, pointing to the top of the bank note.

"The Government Bank of the USSR," she dutifully read. Then she looked more carefully at both notes. "Funny that I never noticed that before. Here it says the Government, and there the Government Bank. Why is that?" She looked at me, as though I must know the answer.

I felt on safe ground, for there was nothing political involved, so I stated my personal explanation: "Money is based on gold; according to the amount of gold a country possesses, its government prints bank notes. The Soviet gold is placed in the government bank, which prints only *chervontzes*, nothing less than ten rubles. And therefore these *chervontzes* are accepted outside the Soviet Union. But since no nation can operate on large bank notes only, singles and coins are also needed. So the government of the USSR prints all kinds of notes and coins, all less than ten rubles. They are not covered by gold, and therefore are not accepted outside the Russian borders. And so now we arrive again at the original question." I noted the puzzled look on her face. "What is the loan for? Can't the government print more rubles?"

She looked at me and said to herself, "I've never thought about it before. I wonder why."

I knew why she'd never thought of it: the Party delegates develop one-track minds; the Party line can never be questioned. They are taught what to think, not how to think; how else can their minds be controlled? She finally came up with something, but not being quite sure of herself, she put it in the form of a question.

"Perhaps the Party wants to curb the buying power of the people?" She smiled, satisfied with herself. Repeating her theory once more, she asked, "Am I right?"

I agreed with her partially. "You might be right; but in the villages you can't buy anything anyhow. Of course it's because of the war, since all goes for the front, and the farmers don't even get cards for clothing or anything else. They make their own clothes, and nothing can be bought; so how can you curb buying power which in reality doesn't exist?"

By then we had reached the old man's house. The shepherd greeted us at the door, inviting his guests inside. We could hardly breathe; the windows had not been opened since the first snow, and the two rooms served as a barn for his cow and chickens as well as kitchen and bedroom. I introduced the guest, standing in the doorway in order to get some fresh air, but the old man insisted that we come in and close the door.

"It's cold, my dear Chaim! And how are you? Why don't you come and visit me more often?"

He was talking to me, completely ignoring the Party delegate, while she held her woollen shawl against her nostrils to filter the thick air of the room. I wanted to get out as quickly as possible; even the bitter cold was preferable to the air inside.

"*Dedushka*, I'll visit you tomorrow and we'll talk. Right now *Barishnya* Voronkina is here for an important purpose."

This was Miss Veronkina's cue and she began at once. She had heard, she told him, that he had lost two sons fighting the White enemies of the Revolution (I had concealed the fact that he had also lost two sons on the opposite side) and that he had been a peasant all his life, and a respected member of the *kolkhoz*. Therefore, she felt sure he would help out the soldiers at the front now, by subscribing to the victory loan.

Without a moment's hesitation, he agreed. "Mark me down, daughter, for five hundred rubles!"

Voronkina turned to me in amazement. "That's what I call a true patriot, answering Stalin's call," she remarked with admiration. "Well, how much do you intend to give me right now? The whole amount, *Dedushka*?" she asked with eagerness and affection.

The old man suddenly opened his toothless mouth, and burst out in a loud laugh, while his eyes turned to the four corners of the dark, poverty-stricken shack.

"*Dedushka*, this is not a laughing matter! You are signing up for five hundred rubles and you have to give me something now — any amount will do, but right now!"

Still laughing, the old man placed his hand on my shoulder, and said in all seriousness, "*Chi*, I know the Soviet law better than you! For each hundred rubles one owes the government, he goes to prison for one month if he doesn't pay up. I sincerely want to help fight the rotten Germans for attacking Mother Russia, but I'm too old and have no money. So I'll sign up for five hundred and go to prison for five months. How is that for help?"

I looked at the delegate. Her face was flaming red. Was it because of the biting cold, or was it the fury of a Party official provoked to rage by a sign of opposition?

Holding her nose and leaning towards the old man, she began to shout, "*Grashdanin* (citizen, the title given to a person unworthy of being called comrade), you are an old fool! Our sons are bleeding on the battlefield and you are joking and laughing. *Tfuy!*" She spat in the old man's face, screaming, "I'll have you thrown in prison for anti-war propaganda and counter-revolutionary activities!"

She opened the door wide and said to me, "Let's go, comrade. You mustn't associate with this enemy of the people."

Fresh air filled the cabin, for she kept the door wide open to spite the "dangerous enemy of the Revolution," and I breathed deeply. I wanted to say something, but the shepherd saved me the trouble.

A loud, "Ha! Ha!" burst from his mouth again. "At my age, lady, you can't scare me with anything! Go right ahead and send me to jail, or even *k styenke* — to the wall (to be shot)! I have given the Red Army two sons, and what have you and the other Party members given? Ha! Ha! Ha!"

She slammed the door, and ran to the sled without looking back. The sound of the old shepherd's "Ha! Ha!" seemed to follow us all the way. Since it was time for lunch, we started off immediately, and neither of us spoke. When the village houses began to appear in the distance, she mumbled:

"If he were only ten or twenty years younger, I'd have taught him a lesson! Now he'll only get twenty years in prison, that old dog!" I was afraid to say anything, so I kept my mouth shut.

Finally we reached the chairman's house, where she was invited for lunch. She whispered to me, "You know something? I was sure the purpose of the loan was to cut buying power, but now I think it may be something else entirely. There is a shortage of paper — most of the paper mills are near Leningrad, and apparently they are not operating; and so, being unable to print new rubles, perhaps we have to pull in the old bank notes."

This gave me an opening. "Do you think it is right to send an old man to prison for twenty years over a few pieces of paper? He will surely die there!"

She managed a smile on her frozen face. "I personally think not, but a revolutionary can't be soft, even with an old man. The vanguard of the working masses must be tough towards parasites and enemies of the people! But I am willing to forget the whole thing if you promise to shut the old man up, and not let anyone hear about his dreadful joke."

I promised, for the sake of his life, and mine.

PART TWO

17

THE SNOW, packed hard and solid after the long winter, began to soften with the approach of spring. One morning I took out my well-worn Hebrew calendar and calculated how soon *Pesach* would be here. I had to plan carefully: how would I manage to observe this great holiday? What would I eat for the week of the holiday when bread was forbidden? *Matzah* was unavailable, so I would have to subsist on potatoes and vegetables. I was sure that Anna would help me as much as she could.

One day, as we were sitting around the fire eating our barley mush, Chairman Anton arrived. Although it was not unusual for him to check on us, we could see that this was not a routine visit. His horse had been galloping much faster than usual and he appeared to be in a great hurry. He held a sheet of paper in his hand as he approached us and each of the women feared that he was bringing tragic news of her son or husband.

But he came straight to me, hugged me affectionately, and without uttering a word, handed me the paper. I read it aloud. "You are ordered to report to the *Voyenkomat* at 9 A.M., two days after receipt of this notice. The enterprise where you are employed must provide you with transportation and a three-day supply of food. Failure to comply with this order is considered desertion in time of war."

The women began to sniffle and wipe their eyes. To them it was a familiar notice, the same one that had taken their husbands and sons from them. It revived bitter memories and tears.

With mixed feelings, I left the field with Anton to prepare for the trip. As happy as I was to be finally accepted by the army, I regretted that it had happened now, just a few days before *Pesach*. It would have been so much easier to observe the holiday here in the village. Who knew what difficulties I would encounter in the army?

In compliance with the official order, the chairman began to arrange a three-day supply of food for me. Anna and her mother began to bake *piroshki*; another woman boiled eggs; a third prepared dry kasha. The chairman's wife made a good supply of *sukhary*, slices of black bread which are dried in the oven. They last for a long time and don't spoil. (The Soviet army itself issued *sukhary* for emergency rations, because of their durability and light weight.) *Sukhary* brought high prices on the black market, and that might prove useful for me too.

The day I left the village, I was presented with a sack full of these traditional peasant foods, which was worth a small fortune in any Russian city and represented a real sacrifice on the part of these poor peasants. However, unlike other men from the village who had gone off to war, I had no wailing procession walking behind me. Anna, her mother and the children said their good-byes to me at home, asking me to write and telling me I'd always be welcome. My two best friends, the chairman and the teacher, prepared the horse and wagon and personally accompanied me to the *Voyenkomat*.

There was a feeling of loss when this interlude came to an end — this temporary, not unhappy period among the poorest and least educated, but the kindest and friendliest, Russians I had ever known. It was like leaving home again, and I was heartbroken. Old *Dedushka* Anton bade me farewell, Russian style — a bear hug and a kiss on both cheeks. He invited me to come back any time, "regardless of physical condition."

At the *Voyenkomat* there were over thirty men, most of them in their fifties or older. All had gotten drunk, in order to numb the pain of leaving a wife and children and the safety of home. After a medical examination, we were ordered to line up. I was taken aback to see one man without a single tooth in his mouth, and another who was a cripple, one leg being much shorter than the other.

The bad situation of the Russian army was obvious — now they were scraping the bottom of the human barrel.

When we finally managed to line up — which was not easy for drunken men — the military commandant appeared at the front stairs. He looked over the group of drunken discards, and grimaced with disdain. Then he saw me and came over to shake my hand. I was tempted to tell him that I was grateful that he finally trusted me enough to let me go to war, but he immediately began his formal address.

First he recited the standard praise of "the great and glorious Stalin," and then he came to the point. "You are drafted into the *trud-battalions* — the labor brigades. You will be taken to Kuybishev, and then to Syzran, into the oil fields. Your work is important; our planes and tanks cannot run on water. Remember — although you are not in the regular army, nevertheless the discipline must be just the same. Disobedience will not be tolerated, and desertion is punishable by death!"

Now things became clear to me. I was still not trustworthy! The ban against Westerners was still in force. I was not really in the army, but in a labor corps. I felt betrayed and frustrated. Revenge against the Germans was my dream, not work in the oil fields!

To make sure that there would be no desertions, all our civilian documents were taken from us. All our new military documents were given to the sergeant in charge of our group. Everyone in the Soviet Union must carry a passport, even in peacetime, and is subject to being checked by police at any time, in any place. In wartime, a person without a document can be summarily charged with desertion or spying, and shot. Thus all of us were obliged to stay close to the group and to the sergeant in charge. Desertion would be tantamount to suicide!

We boarded the sleds and rode all through the night, each of us carefully safeguarding his precious sack of food.

At dawn we arrived in the port city of Kuybishev. As the heavy fog came up from the Volga River, a raucous din of whistles from factories, trains and boats cut through the frosty air. The town was waking up. People were being called to another day of hard work for the defense of the Socialist Fatherland. They streamed out of the tall, ancient buildings which had been built in old Sammarra, the original name of the city. The rundown state of the old buildings was depressing, and I judged that they hadn't been painted since the Revolution. The workers were mostly women, poorly clad and half-asleep, and hunger was etched on their faces. Some of the men on our sled were eating, biting into large slices of farm bread, and the passersby stopped to stare at us enviously.

The traffic was very light; there was an occasional streetcar or taxi. The horses were tired, and since the streets were cleared of snow, the sergeant ordered us to get out and walk behind the sleds. He warned us not to stray.

"Remember, you have no personal documents, so you had better stick with the group."

While we were tramping along behind the sleds, I noticed the tricolor of France waving from a building on a side street. Soon I saw the Union Jack, and then some other flags. These couldn't be embassies, I thought, for they're usually located where the seat of the government is. The Russians had been priding themselves on Stalin's personal courage, how he and the government had remained in Moscow in the face of the German attack. Perhaps these are consulates, I thought. We passed a building with a flag and a plaque: Embassy of Iran. My pulse quickened in excitement.

Feigning ignorance, I asked the sergeant, "Say, comrade, what are all these flags?"

"Don't you know?" he replied. "These are the foreign embassies. They all moved here from Moscow, the cowards! When the Fritzes began to push against Moscow, they all got scared and asked Stalin permission to move out. What does Stalin say? He says, 'You can go ahead and move to Kuybishev, but I'm staying here, right here in Moscow with my people! And I can assure you the Germans will never take Moscow; I'll see to that personally.' So here they are, the capitalist dogs. But our Stalin is in Moscow!"

Suddenly it occurred to me that the Polish embassy must be here too. But where? And how could I find out? If only I had known, I could have gone to my embassy a dozen times before I was drafted! I had a fervent desire to visit the embassy before being shipped to the oil fields of Syzran. I had to find out if a Polish army really did exist, and why it was never mentioned in the newspaper reports from the front, and why my letters were never answered.

Finally we arrived at the railroad station. Outside there was a crowd of people — refugees, soldiers, crippled veterans, women carrying babies, all milling around in front of the station, since no one was permitted inside unless he had a travel permit and a ticket for the next train.

The sergeant ordered us to settle ourselves and wait in a corner while he went inside to see the military commandant of the station to arrange transportation. He reminded us again that if anyone left the group he would face charges of desertion and be shot!

Despite this, an insistent voice within me was saying: There is little time left; you still have your Polish passport hidden under your belt. Instinctively, I reached for it and felt it, my treasure, my citizenship, that one thin page with my photograph and the embassy seal. But where was the Polish embassy located?

An opposing inner voice warned me to be cautious: You can't ask where a foreign embassy is; this would invite immediate arrest. You know how sensitive the Russians are about foreigners, especially now in time of war! You'll be arrested and charged with spying! And if you do find out where it is and try to go there, suppose you are stopped on the way and asked for documents? Then what? Desertion means a bullet in the head!

I don't know how long I sat arguing silently with myself. I saw a streetcar in the distance approaching and the voice within me demanded a decision: You'll never forgive yourself, missing a chance like this! Perhaps there is a Polish army!

Impulse overruled reason. I asked someone where the bathroom was, and left. As soon as I was lost in the crowd, I jumped aboard the streetcar. My heart was pounding as I stared out through the windows, searching for foreign flags. I figured that all embassies must be located in one vicinity, to facilitate the Soviet authorities' control of them. When we reached the area where I'd first seen the foreign flags, I jumped off.

My hunch was correct. After walking some blocks, I was thrilled to see the red and white Polish flag at number 32, Lev Tolstoy Street. The entrance of the building carried a plaque: *Ambasada Rzeczpospolita Polska* — Embassy of the Republic of Poland. My heart beat faster and faster; it was almost as though I were back home. Suddenly I stopped in my tracks. There was a Soviet policeman guarding the building. Suppose he stopped me and asked for identification papers? The risk was too great! I walked around the block several times, for I needed time to think. Here I saw another Polish flag, and a plaque: Polish Embassy — Military Attaché. There was no policeman here. Without hesitation I opened the door and walked in.

At the desk sat a civilian and a Polish army major. I approached them and announced with pride, "Gentlemen, I'm a Polish citizen and would like to enlist in the Polish army." I presented my one-page Polish passport.

Both of them studied me and my document very carefully, and then looked at each other. After a moment the major said, "You'll have to report to the embassy around the corner. This is the military attaché's office, not a recruiting office."

I hadn't expected such a cold reception; still, I tried to interpret the major's attitude as a matter of procedure and bureaucracy, and asked in a humble tone, "Sir, may I go through this corridor to the embassy?"

"No," came the icy answer. "You must go around the outside of the building."

I took a deep breath. "But sir, I would like to avoid the Soviet policeman at the front door."

The major pulled himself up and stood at attention. As though I had questioned his word, he snapped, "A Pole should have no fear of a Soviet policeman, unless you are a criminal of some sort." Then he asked sharply, "How will you be able to face the enemy if you are afraid of a policeman?" He opened the door wide, pointed to the street and barked, "This way, please!"

Outside, I stood in shock for a moment. The cold air brought me back to reality; I knew that this was no place for me to linger. I began to walk, raging inside. Look who's talking about facing the enemy! That Pole, and all the others like him, gave up Poland without firing a shot. Here I'm volunteering to go to the front, and what happens? This Pole spits in my face! They're all cowards, but they guard their honor like heroes!"

By now I had walked around the block, still fulminating, three times. I knew that this was courting danger, for surely the policeman would begin to notice me. I waited for the moment he turned his back to resume his beat, and with a prayer on my lips I jumped to the door of the embassy, opened it, and closed it behind me.

Inside at last! My hand still on the doorknob behind me, I murmured a quick prayer of thanks and then looked around the waiting room; there was a young man sitting on a bench whose eyes were red and puffy as though he'd been crying. On the open door to the next room a sign read: Information. I entered the room and approached the clerk sitting at the desk.

"Sir, I'm a Polish citizen and would like to join the army. In fact, I've written to our embassy in Moscow many times, but I've never received a reply. I didn't know until today that you were in Kuybishev."

I placed my document in front of him. He checked it thoroughly, asked my name, age and birthplace. Then came the final question: "Profession?"

"Rabbinical student," I replied.

A cold look came over his face. He said, "You will have to go to Chkalov; that is the nearest Polish army camp. We cannot help you here."

Then he busied himself with his papers, ignoring me completely. After a few moments, without even looking in my direction, he said curtly, "Good day, sir!"

I knew about the city of Chkalov from my reading in Karobka. It was on the Kazakhstan border, part of the boundary between European and Asiatic Russia.

Puzzled and resentful, I raised my voice a little and said, "Sir, from here to Chkalov is two or three days' travel by train. How can I get there without a travel permit? And without a travel permit how can I get train tickets?"

Without looking up, he said, "That is your problem. You are the one who is volunteering, and to do so you must go to the army camp at Chkalov. This is an embassy, not a draft board. Good day!"

"Sir," I continued boldly, "I cannot accept your advice. I would like to see the consul or, if possible, the ambassador himself."

The man jumped up, finally faced me, and with flashing eyes screamed, "You will not see anyone, and that's final!"

Cowards when it comes to fighting the Germans, servile to the Russians, how arrogant and brutal the Poles could be to a helpless Jew!

"I demand my rights!" I shouted back. "And I refuse to leave this building until I see the consul or the ambassador!"

"And I say you will leave at once or I'll call the police and have you arrested!" the Pole shot back.

I knew I was defeated. Facing a desertion charge, I could take no chances with the police. With my head down, I walked out of his office thinking, I will have to serve in a Russian labor battalion; there's no choice. But is that a way to fight the Nazis? But what will I tell the sergeant? By now they must have searched the bathrooms in the railroad station. For all I know, they might even have boarded the train and be on the way to Syzran. I'm in real trouble now. I'm a deserter in time of war!

In the front room, as I hurried past the red-eyed man on the bench, he caught at my coat. I looked at him, and, pointing to the bench, he indicated that I should sit down next to him. I sat down.

"That's how they are, the Poles," he whispered in Yiddish. "When it came to fighting, they let the whole country fall apart within a few days; but as soon as they're back in power, they yell and scream at you and throw manure in your face. In a way the Germans are right, calling the Polish pigs."

I felt a sudden elation as I realized that he was a fellow Jew, who had apparently been hurt, just as I was. "Who are you and what are you doing here?" I whispered back.

He looked me over from head to toe. Then he said, "By your rags, I can tell you're a real _kolkhoznik_. How long have you been here in the Soviet Union?"

"Since the outbreak of the war," I replied.

"Then it's about time you realize that the less I know about you, and you about me, the better off we both are. Now listen! You sit here, and I'll open the outside door to make him think that you left. If one of the big shots comes in, I'll signal you and you walk right up to him and plead your case. Understand?"

He opened the door and slammed it shut, then tiptoed back. When he sat down he whispered, "You might be lucky and meet the ambassador himself, who is a decent man. There's even a Jew on the staff here."

"A Jew? In the Polish foreign service?" I was astonished. "Must be a convert to Catholicism," I said with certainty.

Before he had a chance to reply, the door opened and a plump, bald man came in. My new friend pinched me, and I jumped up and hurried over to him.

"Sir, I am a Polish citizen. Here is my passport," I blurted out. I unfolded the wrinkled paper, wondering if this was the ambassador in person. He listened politely as I continued. "And I would like to volunteer for the Polish army. I've written to the embassy many times but never received an answer." He examined the wrinkled paper with my photograph on it. I was surprised not to see any hatred on his face.

"Well, why don't you go to the information desk?" he said, returning the document to me.

"Sir, I must see the consul or the ambassador! I have risked my life to come here. I even had to sneak in so the policeman outside would not see me. When I saw our flag I felt like crying, and I thought, now I'm back home, in my own country! But that clerk at the information desk made me feel that I was not on Polish soil at all, but rather in a Gestapo office!"

The man's face darkened. He turned around and shouted to the man at the information desk, "Take this gentleman upstairs to Dr. Seidenman and report to my office at once!" He shook hands with me, and said good-bye with a friendly smile.

All the way upstairs, the information clerk maintained a sullen silence.

At the top, he pointed to a door, turned around and left. I read the sign on the door: Jewish Desk and Foreign Correspondence — Dr. Seidenman. Now it became clear to me what a Jew was doing in the Polish foreign service; he was a linguist, and was also in charge of the "Jewish desk."

In response to my knock I heard someone call, "Enter." At the desk sat a handsome man in his forties with a friendly, smiling face. I presented my passport and told him my story; and to prove that I was a rabbinical student I reached into my precious bag of food and pulled out my little book of Psalms and my *tefillin*.

With a smile, he said, "You don't have to prove anything. I already know you are a rabbinical student. It says so right here on this list."

He pointed to my name on a sheet of paper, and then he explained, "The embassy received a letter from the Union of Orthodox Rabbis of America in New York City, asking us to help the rabbis and yeshiva students in Poland and Lithuania. Enclosed was a list of names, and here is yours."

From Dr. Seidenman, I learned that everyone at my yeshiva — students, faculty and their families — had been shipped out of Raseinai just a few days before the Germans attacked Russia. Dr. Seidenman went on to tell me that now they were all prisoners in a Siberian camp 300 kilometers from the Arctic Circle. He had been sending them packages, and he corresponded regularly with Rabbi Naftali Leibovitz, the dean. I asked him to inform the rabbi of my safety and to tell him that I was volunteering for our army.

Dr. Seidenman told me that, since I was volunteering, I would need a letter of recommendation from the embassy. I waited while he arranged one for me. Thanking him, I remarked, "You know, Dr. Seidenman, it seems ironic that in time of war a young man in perfect health, who is eager to fight for his country, should need a letter of recommendation."

He didn't answer, but sighed and mumbled something quietly to himself. It sounded as if he'd said, "You'll need it, all right."

"What's that you said?" I asked.

"Never mind," he replied, and I didn't press the question.

I thanked him again for all he had done for me; we shook hands warmly, and I walked down the stairs in triumph.

As I passed his room I threw a smug glance at the information clerk, and then I sat down next to my friend on the bench and happily showed him my new document. "Come on," I said, "cheer up. Why don't you join the army with me?"

"They don't want me for a soldier," he replied. "They've assigned me to a 'higher obligation.'" He sounded bitter and sarcastic. He sighed, and his eyes filled with tears again. "They are making me a diplomatic guinea pig, that's all!"

I couldn't leave him like that, and decided I had to hear his story; perhaps I might even be able to help him. After all, I now knew Dr. Seidenman; also, I had a bag full of food, and food could buy anything in Russia.

He began to tell me his tragic story. His parents and family had left Poland for Palestine just before the war, but the Polish authorities had not permitted him to go with his parents because he was too close to draft age. How he had ended up here in Kuybishev he didn't say, but his parents had already sent him an entry certificate for Palestine. The Polish embassy had given him a passport, and had secured a British entry visa, as well as transit visas through Iran and Iraq. But they had not gotten him the important Russian exit permit; this, he was told, he would have to get from the Soviet Foreign Commissariat himself. When he asked the Polish embassy why they didn't secure the exit visa for him, just as they had all the other visas, he never got a clear answer. However, from overhearing things in the embassy he had learned that, when the Prime Minister of the Polish government-in-exile in London renewed diplomatic relations with the USSR, the Polish-Soviet border question was not mentioned, on the advice of Churchill. It was to be settled after the war.

It seemed that the Poles were using this Jew to test the Soviets' intentions about the border. He came from the city of Lutsk, which was now part of the USSR. If the Russians recognized the pre-1939 borders, he would be granted an exit visa as a Polish citizen and be permitted to join his family in Palestine. But if the Russians persisted in claiming eastern Poland, then he would be considered a Soviet citizen, who would not be allowed to emigrate to a capitalist country while Russia was fighting a war!

"And so instead of going to my mother in Tel Aviv, I might be shipped into the arms of the Siberian bear!" he wept. His whole future, and indeed his life, depended upon international diplomacy and politics.

Suddenly my heart sank as I realized that I was in exactly the same position! My home town, Lomza, had also been incorporated into the

USSR. I, too, had just become an international guinea pig! If I encountered the Russian authorities they might very well claim me as their citizen — and how could a Soviet citizen be volunteering for a "foreign" army? And, moreover, after deserting from the Soviet army! Suddenly all my admiration for Dr. Seidenman evaporated, and I saw his "help" as part of a cold-blooded plan to use innocent young Jews like me to test Russian intentions.

In a moment, I was running up the stairs, two at a time. I gave a quick knock on Dr. Seidenman's door, and without waiting for a reply I burst in. He was talking on the telephone and I had to wait. Many thoughts raced through my mind. One moment I loved him; the next I hated him. Was he tightening a noose around my neck for the sake of his own career? I knew only one thing: I would not leave the Polish embassy until an officer came to take me directly to the army camp.

When Dr. Seidenman finally ended his conversation, I burst out, "Sir, I'm not leaving the embassy premises! I'll sleep here in a corner overnight. I can't take any chances."

Dr. Seidenman gave me his friendly smile. "I have nothing against that; as a matter of fact, I meant to ask you where you were spending the night. If you can be comfortable on a bench all night, it's all right with me."

My anger and distrust left me and I was confused. It seemed he was, after all, concerned with my welfare.

When I went downstairs, the young man was no longer there. I was sorry he had gone, for in all the confusion I had forgotten to tell him that according to my Hebrew calendar tonight was *Pesach*.

Night fell soon; it was completely dark and I was alone. Upstairs, the embassy staff was celebrating *Wielkanoc* — Easter. Men and women were laughing and singing Polish songs. I could hear the clink of glasses. Their celebration didn't bother me. Nothing could interfere with my celebration of *Pesach*, meager though it was, and my prayer of thanks. Nothing but a Divine miracle had carried me through this day!

Sitting on the bench, I became lost in memories of former *Pesach* nights. The festive table, the lovely shining faces of Mama and my little brothers, Papa sitting at the head of the table like a king, myself at his right, and a guest or two at his left. Mama always sat at the other end of the table, the Jewish cook at her right, and then the children according to their ages. Little Shimon, the youngest, always asked the Four Questions, and Papa's voice would ring out as he began to chant from the *Haggadah*, "Slaves we were to Pharaoh in Egypt. But the Lord our God rescued us with His mighty hand...."

How happily we all sang, "It is God's promise that has stood by our fathers and by us. For not only one man has tried to destroy us, but in every generation there are those who try to do so. Yet the Holy One, Blessed be He, always rescues us from their hands...."

And how our voices would ring out: "In every generation a person must consider himself as though he personally came out of Egypt!"

We always filled one huge goblet of wine for Eliyahu *Ha-Navi*. Yes, I thought, it was he who took me across the border, in the guise of a Russian colonel; he was *Dedushka* Anton, Goncharov the teacher; and today the red-eyed young man on the bench and Dr. Seidenman.

I thought of the *afikoman*, the *matzah* which we ate at the end of the *Pesach* meal. Papa would purposely find an excuse to leave the room so that the children could hide it and then gleefully demand presents for its return. These memories came back to me with such force and clarity that the longing and loneliness opened a fountain of tears within me. But my aching soul wept silently and I made not the slightest sound. My body was in Kuybishev, but my heart and soul were far away across the bloody battlefields, back home with my beloved parents, my brothers, my friends...that the home no longer existed, that my family were not all alive, made no difference to my reverie. I didn't respond when someone touched my shoulder.

"Come on, young fellow, have some wine, let's celebrate. I've been upstairs, but I haven't forgotten that it's *Pesach*." It was Dr. Seidenman, with a bottle of wine in one hand and a glass in the other.

"Thank you, Dr. Seidenman, but you know I can't drink wine that is not kosher for *Pesach*."

"But this bottle is; a friend sent it to me from London. You can drink it, young rabbi."

I accepted the wine with thanks, remarking that I was not a rabbi — not yet, that is.

"Oh, yes you are," he insisted, smiling. "As far as the embassy is concerned you are a rabbi. And don't forget to tell the commission in the army camp as well that you are a rabbi. Remember that!" He returned to the staff party upstairs.

Now I had wine for my *Seder*, and from my sack I took a hard-boiled egg and cold potatoes. Of course there was no *matzah*. I celebrated my

Seder in the dark, and now my thoughts were of the present, not of the past. Were my family having a *Seder* under the Nazis? Were they all alive? Were they thinking of me? Finally the wine took effect, and I fell asleep on the bench.

The next morning twenty men gathered in front of the military atta-ché's office. A young lieutenant, only recently arrived from London, was in command. He was dressed in a British uniform but had a patch marked "Poland" on his left shoulder. He asked if anyone had served in the army before, and about fifteen men raised their hands. Next, he asked if anyone had been a non-commissioned officer. One big, clumsy-looking man stepped forward and claimed to have been a corporal; he was made the lieutenant's assistant. The corporal immediately took command, and his first act of authority was to shout at me, "You, Jew, carry my sack!"

I burned with resentment, but I told myself: That's the army, and you asked for it. Besides that, I thought there might in fact be some advantage in having to carry his sack as well as my own. Between both sacks I would be able to hide my face, in case the Russians were still looking for me. We boarded a streetcar and went to the same railroad station from which I had deserted the Russian army only yesterday. Today I was here as a Polish soldier!

At the station, we waited in a corner near the military commandant's office, and our lieutenant, taking the corporal along as his interpreter, went inside to arrange transportation. I found a place in the middle of the group, trying to conceal my face between the two bags, fearful that someone might recognize me as a deserter. I knew that if that happened the Polish embassy would not attempt to help me. They wouldn't dare claim citizen-ship for me in the face of Russian charges of desertion. They wouldn't start an international incident over one little Jew. I could imagine the response of the embassy: "Let him get shot! There are too many Jews anyhow!" For this reason I didn't dare reveal my secret to anyone.

After a short time, which seemed to me like hours, the two came out of the commandant's office. The lieutenant was furious, shouting and curs-ing. We soon found out why; the Soviet authorities, taking precautions against typhus and other epidemics, had ordered that every train pas-senger must take a bath in the public bathhouse and have his clothes deloused in a special heat chamber. Afterwards, one's travel permit would be stamped by the bathhouse superintendent and would be valid for three days. After three days, another bath would be required.

The Polish officer had tried to convince the military commandant that these regulations did not apply to foreigners like himself, who had just arrived from London where lice were practically unknown. Moreover, he had argued, he wouldn't consider risking damage to his new British uniform by putting it in the heat chamber. In fact, all the men would have benefited from a bath and a delousing, for they were scratching constantly, their hair and clothing thoroughly infested with lice! Nevertheless, they vigorously joined their lieutenant in his opposition, and added that it would be an insult to their Polish honor if they were required to take a bath like any ordinary Russian.

Personally, it didn't matter to me one way or the other, for I had taken a hot steam bath just before leaving Karobka. At this moment my only concern was to get on a train quickly, for every minute more here increased my risk. Being familiar with the Soviet railway system, I was sure that if we missed this train we would have to wait a day or two for the next one. It was obvious to me that our lieutenant knew nothing about the system and may even have assumed that it operated like the British railway system.

Then the Russian commandant, a captain, came out of his office. In a very polite and respectful voice, he tried to explain to our lieutenant that lice do not respect the immunity of foreigners. And furthermore, he said, there was nothing he could do about it: a regulation is a regulation, regardless of citizenship.

All of us, except the lieutenant, were amazed at the Russian captain's politeness, which was very uncharacteristic of a Soviet official. We thought he must simply be showing respect for a foreign uniform, and it made us all proud.

The Russian captain pointed to the little park nearby and said, "There, right behind that park, is the bathhouse. If the major will please take his men there immediately, there will be enough time to bathe and to catch the next train. If you miss the next train, you will have to wait at least another eighteen hours."

Suddenly it dawned on us why the Russian captain was treating our lieutenant with such deference: the Russian had mistaken the rank indicated by the lieutenant's uniform, thinking he was a major. Our lieutenant's insignia consisted of one large star; to the Russians this was the insignia of a major, while to the Poles the size of the star was insignificant, as the important thing was the number of stars.

At that moment the clumsy corporal blurted out in broken Russian, "But Comrade Captain, you are mistaken. He is a lieutenant, not a major."

The commandant flushed and became as red as a beet. He began to scream shrilly at our lieutenant, "In what army did you learn to disobey the orders of a higher officer?" He was shouting so loudly that he began to attract the attention of all the bystanders. "And remove your hands from your pockets when I'm talking to you, lieutenant! You will listen to me this time: as commandant of this station I am ordering you to take your men to the bathhouse now. You will report back to me in one hour, or I'll see to it that you never leave this station!" He wheeled around and marched back to his office.

The lieutenant's first reaction was bewilderment. He couldn't fathom what had made the commandant's attitude towards him change so suddenly. He was humiliated and had obviously lost face before his men; now his pride wouldn't let him give in. But I could not afford any foolish pride or stubbornness; with every passing moment here, I was risking my life!

I boldly stepped up to the lieutenant and said, "Sir, may I handle this? I can promise you that I'll see to it that you will not have to take a bath."

The corporal was furious. He jumped at me, shouting, "Get back to the ranks! Ha, ha! Look who is going to handle the case! What a joke! You just keep your Jew-nose out of this! That's an order!"

There was too much at stake for me to give up so easily. Ignoring the corporal, I addressed the lieutenant again. "Sir, if that corporal had kept his mouth shut, we would have had a chance, but as soon as he blurted out to the Russian that you're not a major — and it's only because he thought you were one that he was being so polite — it became a matter of principle with the commandant to exercise his authority. Won't you please let me handle this? I promise you that you, personally, will not have to take a bath."

All the while, the corporal was yelling at me, "Go back to your place, I said!"

"Shut up, idiot!" the lieutenant snapped at the corporal. "This man is right. I was wondering what made the commandant's behavior change so suddenly. It was because of you, you stupid idiot!" He turned to me. "I must get to a telephone and call the embassy, before anything else."

"But lieutenant," I persisted desperately, "you mustn't think you are in London; this is Russia, and the only telephone around here is in the commandant's office. Besides, how would it look for an officer to create an international crisis over a bath and a delousing?"

Apparently my argument struck the right note, for the lieutenant asked, "Well, what do you propose to do?"

"Sir, you take the men to the park, out of the commandant's sight, and I'll go into the bathhouse; when I come out, I'll have the travel order stamped for all of us."

How I was going to do it I didn't know at that moment, but I knew that the sack of food which I was carrying could accomplish what money could not. Of course, under normal circumstances I wouldn't have bread with me during *Pesach*, but this was for *pikuach nefesh*.

Entering the bathhouse, I saw a woman sitting at the cashier's window, and a little boy playing nearby. I began a conversation with the boy, and asked him if he was hungry. I knew that he was, for all children were on a ration of only 200 grams of bread a day. And I knew his mother was hungry too, for she was certainly in the category of "light worker," with a bread ration of only 400 grams.

The boy nodded, and replied, "*Konyechno* — Certainly!" To make sure that his mother would know how good I was being to her son, I sent him to her for a bread knife.

"I don't trust a knife to a child," she said with a smile, bringing it herself. As I sliced off a piece of my farm bread, I could see how hungry she was, and I offered her some too.

Overjoyed, she chewed it blissfully and said, "My, this farm bread tastes like cake, not like our mud bread; but why are you being so generous, comrade? Don't you know what this bread is worth on the market?"

I told her that I loved children, and that I was on my way to the army, where food is plentiful; and anyway, who needs money when one goes to war? She had to hurry back to the cashier window, but she managed to send the child after his grandmother, who turned out to be the manager of the bathhouse. She too thanked me for the bread I had given to her grandson, and gratefully accepted a slice for herself. Then I got to the point. "*Tyotya* — Auntie — I'm in a hurry. If we miss the next train we'll have to wait two more days, and by then I'll surely be out of bread. Would you mind stamping these papers? If I wait until all the men are out of the bath, we'll surely miss our train."

"Certainly, my boy," she agreed, and quickly stamped all the papers.

Back in the park, the lieutenant was amazed and delighted. He wanted to know how I had done it, and I assured him that I'd soon tell him everything; right now it was most important to report to the commandant, so that we wouldn't miss the train.

He asked me to go along with him as a translator, throwing a disparaging glance at the corporal.

To go along with him into the commandant's office was all I needed; it would be like stepping right into the lion's den! The commandant most likely had a description of me as a deserter. I politely refused, explaining to the officer that one does not change horses in midstream; besides, I didn't even know how to salute properly, while the corporal, after all, was an experienced, well-trained soldier. "A person is entitled to one mistake," I said magnanimously, trying to win the corporal's good will, dreading the thought that I'd be under his command for who knows how long. The corporal appreciated my move; he winked at me and smiled.

While the two of them were gone, the men discussed the lieutenant's accent. I had also noticed his limited vocabulary, and his Polish grammar was as bad as that of the corporal, who was an uneducated farm boy.

On the train, the lieutenant asked me to sit next to him. "I want to talk to you," he said. This aroused the jealousy of all the men and in particular that of the corporal. As we settled down, he turned to me with a smile and said, "Tell me now, how did you do it?"

This handsome and congenial young man was so pleased with me that I dared to ask a question of my own.

"First of all, can you tell me where you are really from?"

The corporal interrupted, "What a stupid question! Where do you think he's from, Turkey?"

The officer pointedly ignored the corporal and asked me, "What makes you think I'm not from Poland?"

I explained that we had all noticed his unfamiliar accent, which didn't seem to fit any area of Poland. "Besides," I added, "it seems to me that the Slavic psychology is alien to you."

The locomotive started gasping and hissing, and the train jerked a few times and began to move. Our conversation was suspended as we turned to watch the change of scenery. First we passed large warehouses and factories, then dreary slums filled with poverty which was galling even by Soviet standards, and finally wide-open spaces, steppes, as far as the eye could see — empty, silent, with no sign of man.

The lieutenant turned from the window and said, "Yes, you are right;

I'm not from Poland, but I am a Pole. I was born in Poland, and when I was an infant my parents emigrated to France — you know, with the mass emigration to the French coal mines. I was raised in French schools, but we spoke Polish at home. After the fall of France, I managed to get to England and there I joined the Polish army. As far as Slavic psychology goes, it is indeed strange to me; I just couldn't bring myself to go into those dirty baths! I think that's where the epidemics start, in fact, right in those bathhouses. And by the way, I hope you'll see to it that I don't have to go into one of them when we have to change trains again; we've got two more trains to take before we reach our destination."

He paused for a moment, and then remembered. "Now let's have the story. How did you do it? Bribery? It will be interesting to tell this story some day."

Before I began, I looked around to make sure that the compartment was occupied only by our men.

"You used the wrong word, sir," I began, "when you called it bribery. In Poland or in France one sometimes bribes an official, but not here! In Poland there were thieves, but not here! Yet everyone steals!" I lowered my voice. "Everyone except Stalin steals, but you don't call it theft, or you'll be talking about two hundred million thieves. There are no bribes here; the entire system operates on the principle of one hand washing the other. It's the rule of self-preservation and no man can exist here without stealing. It's because of the terrible shortages of everything. If a man wants shoes for his children, he steals where he works and trades it with the man who works in the shoe factory. Both are stealing, yet both are decent people and you can't call them thieves!"

The men around us were all nodding their heads in agreement. Then I explained what had happened in the bathhouse, and how the hungry child and the two women had enjoyed the bread and how one had called it cake. The lieutenant didn't understand.

"But did you have bread or cake?" he asked, confused, and all the men burst out laughing.

The corporal took over and tried to explain to the officer. "You see, sir, here in the Soviet Union every worker has a production quota, a norm, even the police. If a policeman doesn't make his monthly quota of arrests, he is considered negligent and won't be promoted. So imagine, sir, the manager of a bakery, who also has his production quota. He is allotted 100 kilograms of flour and must deliver, let's say, 125 kilograms of bread. Now suppose the oven got overheated and he was only able to deliver 123 kilograms? He wouldn't make his norm! And so to make sure, what does he do? When the bread is baking in the oven he pours in a bucket of cold water; this fills the oven with steam and makes heavy, soggy bread — so heavy that he's made 150 kilograms instead of his norm of 125! He delivers his norm, and has 25 extra kilograms to sell on the black market! His relatives are the channels; lots of families get by that way, and the public gets bread which is as heavy as mud!"

"And no one complains?" the lieutenant asked, astonished.

"No, sir, no one," replied the corporal, "because the bakery manager makes sure that white bread is always available for government officials. And that is why good farm bread tastes like cake to city people!"

Finishing his speech, the corporal demanded a taste of my farm bread for himself and the lieutenant. I couldn't refuse them, for they were in command, "but not for the rest of the men," I said, "since we may need it for some more — ah — bribes." I winked at the lieutenant, and he agreed with me.

The train pulled into the station at Kinel, some forty kilometers from Kuybishev, for a brief stop. Here we saw a surprising sight — the dispatcher on the platform was a pretty young girl. After the Revolution, the Bolsheviks had "emancipated" the Russian women, and they filled even the most physically demanding jobs, particularly during the war. This was especially noticeable on the railroads, but it was the first time that any of us had seen a woman wearing a red dispatcher's cap, signal flags in hand, receiving and sending off trains.

When the lieutenant spotted her, he was amazed and delighted. He called out in French, *"Bonjour, chérie! Comment ça va?* — Hello there, honey! How are you today?"

To his surprise, she called back, *"Très bien, mon soldat!* — Just fine, soldier!"

He jumped down from the train, hurried over to her and an excited French conversation ensued, with much eye-rolling and waving of arms. Then he called back to the men on the train, and announced, to my dismay, that we would be staying here for the night. He wanted to get better acquainted with this charming French-speaking Russian.

I jumped down and pleaded with him, reminding him that all our food, papers and equipment were already on this train. I called out to the dispatcher and begged her to give the signal for departure. I tried to convince her that, as a Russian patriot, she surely couldn't let twenty soldiers be detained from their military destination! We were, after all, defending the Fatherland. If we missed this train, we might have to wait two or three days for the next one.

She was convinced by my desperate pleas and waved her flags, signaling the train to leave the station. I grabbed the lieutenant and raced after our train, which was beginning to pick up speed. Fortunately he was slight, and I was strong, toughened from months of woodchopping and heavy farm labor. I managed to push him onto the last car and jump in after him.

As soon as he could catch his breath, the lieutenant glared at me, enraged and humiliated. "Insubordination!" he shrieked. "Just wait and see what you'll get from me when we get to the camp! Stinking Jew!" He ordered me into the troop compartment, and I sat down right next to the surly corporal.

"Well, well, Jew-boy! So you think you can push our lieutenant around, do you?" the corporal sneered, picking up his cue immediately.

"Those filthy Jews will ruin anything," grumbled one of the soldiers.

"Yes, everybody knows how they ruined Poland, the cursed kikes," said another.

"It's the Jews who started the war, and because of them we're sitting here, instead of being back home where we belong...."

I dreaded the thought that these men would be my comrades-in-arms. It was a relief when the sun set; they began to prepare themselves for sleep, for there were no lights in the compartments. I went into the corridor, looking for a window or a private corner. My heart heavy, I was filled with loneliness and pain. Although I had succeeded in getting us on our way, I had lost the friendship of the lieutenant. Moreover, I would spend this second night of *Pesach* surrounded by men who detested me, far away from fellow Jews or anything familiar to me.

How far away last night's *Seder* seemed now! I found some privacy in a corner near a window and engaged my mind and my heart in the holiday prayers and the *Seder* ceremony. When I returned to my companions they were snoring, but I lay awake a long time, listening to the sound of the wheels on the rails. Tonight they chanted, "*Avadim hayinu, avadim hayinu* — Slaves were we, slaves were we...."

The train passed into Asiatic Russia and we were in Kazakhstan, the second largest Soviet republic. A kaleidoscope of Asian nationalities began to appear. It was their faces rather than their clothing that told us which nation of the USSR they came from; Soviet shabbiness was common to all. There were Kazakhs, with their Mongolian features, Uzbeks — typical Turks, Georgians, who looked like Spaniards, Armenians, who looked typically Mediterranean and almost like Italians, and the Koreans, who looked quite Japanese.

We transferred to another train in Alma-Ata, the capital of Kazakhstan, and again in Tashkent, the capital of Uzbekistan. Other nationalities now appeared: the Turkmens, the Tadzhiks, the Azerbaijanis, the Kirghizis. We finally reached our destination. It was at the foot of the Himalayan Mountains, at the triangle where China, India, Afghanistan and Persia meet the Soviet border. After eight days and nights of travel, it was a relief to step down in the station of a small oriental town called Guzar.

THE HEADQUARTERS of the Polish army were located in a former prison, an old brick prison structure in the center of the small town. It consisted of four buildings in the form of a square; all windows faced onto an inner court. The camp itself was spread out over the vast sands which lay at the foot of the snow-covered Himalayas. Tents had been set up to protect the men from the merciless sun.

The first step in the processing was to have the entire body shaved, as a precaution against lice-borne epidemics. Afterwards, each man got a bucket of cold water for a bath and was assigned to a numbered tent. I was relieved to be separated from my traveling companions, and was pleasantly surprised to find that there was a large number of Jews in the camp.

An astonishing number of officers was present; for every ten soldiers, there seemed to be an equal amount of sergeants, lieutenants, majors and colonels. All these officers were well along in years, and I assumed that the Soviet prisoners-of-war camps in Siberia had aged them. But someone told me another theory: the younger officers, the cream of the Polish army, had been sent to the front to fight the Germans, and had either been killed or fallen into German hands. Those who had fallen into Russian hands were these elderly officers. There was also reason to believe that, with the organization of this "new army," all the officers had promoted themselves and raised their rank overnight; since there were no records to prove or disprove their rank, they were taken at their word.

I entered the tent to which I had been assigned and greeted the men sitting on the earthen floor with the traditional Polish army greeting: "*Czolem chlopcy* — Greetings, boys," but didn't get a single response. My initial enthusiasm began to cool when I noticed that not only did the men ignore me, they did not speak to each other either. Each seemed immersed in his own thoughts.

Something in the atmosphere was all wrong. Considering the fact that we were all volunteers, finally getting a chance to fight the Germans, why was there such a heavy silence? Why was there such bitterness on their faces? If they were afraid of war, why did they volunteer? No one had made them do it!

Looking around more carefully, I came to the conclusion that most of them looked Jewish; could it be that they were worried about Polish anti-Semitism in the army? Perhaps, I reasoned, they were still suffering the effects of their imprisonment in the Siberian camps.

My thoughts were interrupted by the sudden entrance of a very tall, robust, blond soldier. His face was dark with anger as he called out to the group, "I'm out too! The dirty rats!"

He tore off his uniform, flinging each piece to the ground and stepping on it, grinding it hard under the heels of his boots, as if trying to kill a living thing. When he had finished cursing the army, the war, the Germans and the Polish idiots in London — all in perfect Polish — he flung himself down on the ground next to me. He sat, resting his head on his knees, while his fingers began to dig in the sand nervously, as if he were trying to dig a grave with his bare hands.

I was astonished and puzzled at the man's behavior, and amazed at the silence and indifference of the others. I touched his arm and whispered, "What happened?"

He didn't reply, and didn't even bother to look at me. I still had a few leftovers in my food bag; I figured that a piece of *sukhary* would get his attention, and it did. As he began to chew the dry, hard bread, I asked, "What did you mean when you said, 'I'm out too'? Out of what?"

He looked at me as if I were an idiot. "Out of the army!" he shouted, beginning to get excited again. "I was good enough in 1939, good enough to defend Warsaw and get wounded. I was good enough to retreat to the Bug River and fall into Russian hands with the entire army. I was good enough for a Siberian prison camp; I was good enough for three months in this 'new army'; but suddenly I'm not good enough anymore! They don't want me! They falsified a paper stating that I have a contagious disease. These rotten Polacks!"

I couldn't understand and couldn't, or didn't want to, believe him. "Are you telling me that even though you're a veteran, and have served three months in this new army too, they have suddenly decided to kick you out?"

I could see he had no patience for me and my stupid questions. He bit off another piece of the hard bread and mumbled, "Yeah."

I couldn't stop myself and kept asking questions. "But when you entered this new army they must have given you a medical checkup. Didn't they detect your disease then?"

The man jumped up as if bitten by a snake and glared at me angrily. "Don't be a fool!" he shouted. "Can't you see I'm perfectly healthy? Otherwise, how could I have survived since the German attack on Poland? It's just a rotten excuse. I'm being kicked out because...they found out about me!" He stretched himself out full length on the sand and stared up vacantly.

Something forced me to continue prying. "What do you mean? What did they find out about you? What are you telling me? I don't understand...."

The soldier sat up and looked straight into my eyes. "How long have you been here, fellow?" he asked. "Ah, you just arrived this morning! Then there's something you should know. They kick out all the Jews! They don't want us with them on their way to Iran, Palestine and England — that's where this army is heading. So they ordered a second physical checkup for everyone, a guise to detect Jews! Now do you understand?"

I fell back on the sand, utterly crushed. All the questions which had puzzled me were cleared up at once: why the army was stationed on the Iran-Afghanistan border, so far away from the front; why there had been no answer to the letters I had sent repeatedly to the embassy; and the strange attitude towards me at the embassy and the military attaché's office.

Dr. Seidenman must have known all this; maybe that's why he went to such pains to furnish me with a letter of recommendation from the general. And when I had told him that I found it strange that I would need a recommendation, he had mumbled, "You'll need it, all right!" That was why he had instructed me to state my profession as rabbi! It all added up! Now I understood — they needed a few Jews for propaganda purposes, for free-world consumption. My connection with the Union of Orthodox Rabbis in the USA would serve this purpose very well.

Too bad, I thought, that Dr. Seidenman had warned me not to open the letter; I would have liked to read it. I touched it in my pocket a couple of times, making sure the valuable document was still there. It might be my ticket to redemption. This document might get me into this new army and give me my only chance of getting out of the Soviet Union. And where would this army take me? To Palestine! To Jerusalem! At home, I mused, they'll never believe that I was able to go to those holy places! But my optimistic reverie was disturbed by the anger and disappointment of the other soldier.

"Isn't there anything we can do about this Polish anti-Semitic policy?" I asked the men in my corner. They all looked at me with apathy, not bothering to reply. Only the blond soldier, finishing the last crumbs of bread, tried to explain.

"You can't fight an army from within," he said. "That's a crime punishable by death even in peacetime, and certainly now, in wartime. And outside of the army, to whom can we complain? To the Russians? They consider this army a gang of fascists and cowards who deserted the battlefield for a vacation in Persia and Palestine, who are secret enemies of the Soviet Union anyway. Can we complain to our Polish government-in-exile in London? Why, they might be the ones who ordered these anti-Jewish measures! And if General Anders is doing it on his own, by the time a letter of complaint could reach London — if it would even pass the Soviet military censorship — and by the time the Polish government there would take action, this army will be across the border!"

From the men I learned that this method of detecting Jews was not a Polish invention; the Germans were practicing that trick all over occupied Europe. Once rejected, one received a document in Polish and Russian, officially stating the reason for rejection; usually it read "typhus" or "cholera." Then the reject would receive some food and a train ticket back to where he came from. One of the men remarked that since I came from Kuybishev, I'd probably be sent back there, and if so, then it was my duty to go to the embassy and file a protest. I didn't have the heart to tell him that I was in this army for sure, carrying in my pocket a letter of recommendation from the general himself.

A sergeant appeared and called my name, and I was taken to a building in the center of the camp. An armed guard patrolled outside. Inside there were men filling out forms, getting undressed and, one by one, going through a door marked "Doctors' Commission." I filled out the detailed form and to the question "vocation" I printed in big letters "RABBI." Then I waited in line to get undressed and be examined. An officer collected all the forms. Noticing the large "RABBI" on mine, he called me out of the line and ordered me to enter the room marked "Military Commission."

In my most polite manner I said, "But sir, don't I have to undress first for the medical examination?"

With an irritated look, the officer glanced once more at my form, and replied, "It's all right, you'll undress later; we haven't much time." He opened the door and almost pushed me into the office of the military commission. So, I thought, simply by claiming to be a rabbi my Jewishness is established.

Sitting behind the table were three officers: a full colonel presided, flanked by a lieutenant colonel and a major. Hanging on the wall above them was a white eagle — the Polish national emblem — and a crucifix. The colonel examined my filled-out form. I was about to take my letter of recommendation out of my pocket when the major barked, "Stand at attention before a military commission!" I snapped to attention. Then, apparently to make sure that I was the right person, the presiding officer asked me my name, birthplace and birth date, and also my profession. He signed a paper and handed it to me. I gave it a quick glance, and recognized it as the same document the young soldier in my tent had shown me, printed in Polish and Russian, filled in with my name, the date, and of course the word "typhus."

My temper flared — the humiliation of three and a half million Jews in Poland seemed to be personified in my single person. And these clumsy, cowardly, professional militarists who had fled without firing a shot were denying my rights as a Polish citizen, and my dignity as a human being!

"Sir, as a civilian, may I ask a question?"

The chairman must have noticed the suppressed anger in my voice. He answered, "You may, but please lower your voice."

I'm not sure if I lowered my voice, or raised it even more, but I began with resolution: "I have risked my life to come here. I have been hoping and waiting for so long for the chance of fighting the enemy, and under your command, under our own flag. Instead, I have been rejected, against every principle of our constitution, in disregard of my rights as a citizen and a native son of Poland. As if that weren't enough, I've been humiliated and branded falsely as having typhus. I was not checked by a physician; I wasn't even told to undress. Is it in accordance with your conscience as Polish officers to sign a document which states that a perfectly healthy man has typhus? Isn't that perjury?"

The major, his face flushed with anger, jumped up from his seat. He

banged on the table with his fist and shouted, *"Psia krew! Milcz!"* —
popular Polish expressions, meaning "Dog's blood!" and "Shut up!"
respectively.

I didn't pay any attention to him, for I had the letter in my hand.
Presenting it to the chairman, I announced, "I happen to have a letter of
recommendation from the general himself, the military attaché in
Kuybishev."

The chairman took the letter. After all three officers had read it, he
asked me to return the fraudulent rejection certificate. Then he called in a
lieutenant and whispered some instructions to him.

He took me to a guarded tent. Before he left me, he warned me not to
leave the tent, and also not to try to escape. "The guards have orders to
shoot without warning!"

"What does this mean? Am I under arrest?" I asked anxiously.

"No," came the reply. "You are simply not accepted and also not
rejected; therefore, you are to be kept isolated from both groups. You'll be
supplied with food, and you should understand that the warning about
escape is merely a formality, for there is nowhere to run to, except the
desert or the mountains. In either one you'll die from thirst or hunger, if the
Russian border guards don't shoot you first!"

Before he left he reminded the guard that it was against regulations to
talk with me. "That means absolutely no conversation whatsoever; is that
understood?" he barked to the saluting soldier.

I went into the tent. It was completely empty. Besides providing relief
from the baking sun, the tent suited my mood. I wanted privacy; loneliness
had become precious, and here I could think and pray. I went to the far end
of the tent, away from the guard, and settled down.

Towards evening the guard brought me a plate of food: rice, bread and
two American sausages. The sausages weren't kosher, so I offered to
trade them with the guard in exchange for his portion of bread. Although
he was under strict orders not to speak to me, he couldn't resist the
sausages and we struck up a conversation. He asked me if I smoked.
When I said that I didn't, he almost jumped for joy. He told me that I was
entitled to two American cigarettes a day, and he pleaded with me to hold
them for him in exchange for his bread.

The extra sausages and the promise of cigarettes loosened his tongue
and, in time, the tongues of all the guards. Instead of keeping me in
isolation and silence, they talked to me constantly, and each had a different

explanation of the policy of expulsion of the Jews from this army.

According to one, it was the British who were demanding the removal of all Jews: something was brewing in Palestine, and the Jews there were arming themselves. England was determined to weaken the Jews of Palestine and feared, rightly, that as soon as this army would arrive there, all its Jewish soldiers would desert and join the Jewish underground. The Poles, eager to comply with the British demand, were nevertheless concerned about American public opinion. To be accused of anti-Semitism by the American press, while ostensibly fighting Hitler, was to be avoided. Therefore, a small number of Jews were kept in the army. (One of them was Menachem Begin, who went from Guzar to Palestine with this army, deserted, joined the _Irgun_, and chased the British out!)

Most of the Jews retained in the army were medical men, mechanics and truck drivers. A great part of the evacuation would be by truck, and there weren't many Poles who were experienced and skilled in these fields. I was angry at myself for not having registered as a tractorist! Why hadn't Dr. Seidenman told me about that? Now it was too late for me to change my official vocation from rabbi to tractor driver.

Finally I was given my rejection papers plus a ticket and a travel permit to Kuybishev. Our group of rejects was escorted to the railroad station in Guzar by a guard. We passed army headquarters; I asked permission to visit the Jewish army chaplain, and my request was granted.

The chaplain was a middle-aged man with the rank of captain. I told him my story, and asked for his intervention. He pointed to his several gray hairs among the black. "Believe me, I know what's going on," he said. "It makes me sick, but what can I do? Nothing! Absolutely nothing! In the army one must obey orders, and one of the orders is not to intervene. They have left no avenue open for appeal."

Helplessly, we shook hands. I could see his pain and humiliation; he was an officer, and was essentially under house arrest!

I told the chaplain, "While you were in the Siberian POW camp, I was in Lithuania, and there I read something which you'll never see in a Polish paper. How perfectly Churchill described the Poles: 'A beast of prey — glorious in revolt and ruin; squalid and shameful in triumph.' How right he is!" We shook hands in silence, and he led me to the door. Before parting, I added, "Only the Polish government would issue such false documents, and only Polish generals would sign them, knowing it was perjury!"

I alone had to wait for a Tashkent train, in order to connect with the trans-Siberian train bound for Moscow, which stopped in Kuybishev. While waiting, I could observe the bitterness on the part of the rejected men. I was also deeply hurt, but my pain was still less than theirs. Some of them had served in the Polish army since 1939, spent time in Siberian camps as Polish prisoners-of-war, and then volunteered for this army. And now they had been kicked out! In every one of Poland's wars, Jewish officers and men had fought gallantly. The graves of Jewish soldiers, and the Jewish disabled war veterans, and the many decorations awarded to Jewish soldiers testified to that. And now, when the Jews had a vital interest in fighting the Nazis, the Poles had rejected them! No wonder these men shouted to the Polish soldiers, their comrades-in-arms of yesterday: "We'll be back in Poland before you!"

A gaunt Jewish veteran sneered: "The Germans kicked you out of Poland and the Russians won't let you back in!" There was no reply from the Polish officers. Smugly, arrogantly, they stood in silence, ignoring their former comrades.

While I was waiting in Tashkent for the train back to Kuybishev, I had an impulse to return to Guzar and to register under an assumed name as a truck driver or a tractorist, but I was afraid they would recognize me. In the meantime my traveler's bread card would lose its validity, and without a card I might starve. Besides, I felt it my duty to report to Dr. Seidenman about what was going on, although I had a feeling that he knew all about it already.

I arrived in Kuybishev late at night, famished, for I had "cashed" in my last bread coupon two days before. No one was permitted to remain in the station, so I followed the crowd to the town square outside. There I searched for a spot where I could lie down and spend the rest of the night, for the embassy would not open until nine or ten in the morning.

I noticed that all the soldiers were walking purposefully towards a street on the right side of the station. It dawned on me that I, too, was still a soldier; my phony document attested to that; and I must be very weak, having had such a terrible "case of typhus" that I was discharged from the army. So I followed the tide of transient soldiers, many of them wounded and crippled, to a place where military personnel were apparently supplied with food and a place to sleep. I felt relieved that my papers would finally be put to a test. If I were given the same treatment as any other soldier, it would prove their validity.

The crowd of soldiers moved slowly through the dark street and then stopped at a large building, a former school. I noticed a sign posted on one of the two doors: "for commissioned officers only." No army in the world, it seemed to me, was more rigid in separating its soldiers and officers. The official explanation for this segregation was, of course, to "strengthen discipline"; but I was convinced that the true objective was to prevent uprisings. Furthermore, it would never do for the soldiers to see how well the officers were fed!

The line of men seemed interminable before the little window where cards were handed out for bread and a bed. The cripples leaning on their crutches cursed constantly, using every obscene word in the Russian vocabulary. I felt sorry for them: here were the wounded heroes of Mother Russia, waiting in line for food like beggars.

Finally I reached the small window. The officer asked, _"Kuda?_ — Where to?" I explained that I was on my way to Karobka, a village in the Kuybishev district; but I had to wait a day or two for my ride home. In the meantime, I needed food and shelter.

He read my paper once more; he gave me a ticket for bread and two meals a day, and a number for a bed. Then he said, "You can only stay here for two nights — no more. You understand, we need the bed and food for our own men; after all, you are from a foreign army."

I wasn't sure if I got the card because of my document's validity, or because of simple pity on his part. Anyhow, I gladly swallowed my lump of mud-bread and washed it down with a plate of watery soup. Then I stretched out on the hard, filthy straw sack which was my bed. I placed my treasure — the bag containing my _Tanach_ and my _tefillin_ — under my head, so that no one could steal it from me.

In the morning I hurried to the embassy. While waiting for the street-car, I noticed a line of people in front of a kiosk buying the latest _Pravda_. I joined the line to learn the news from the front. Suddenly my eyes stopped scanning the newspapers and books in the kiosk, and focused on some Jewish letters. Jewish books! How I longed to read some Yiddish writing; but I had only ten rubles left, and if I spent it on books, what would I live on? And how would I get back to Karobka?

When I came face to face with the salesgirl, I thought I recognized by her eyes that she was Jewish; Jewish eyes were especially full of sorrow in those days. Hesitating for a moment, I pointed to a paperback edition of Ilya Ehrenburg's _The Fall of Paris_ in Russian, and asked, "How much is that?"

The young woman smiled and said, "Oh, the great Ehrenburg — only 75 kopecks."

I wanted to linger there, so I asked, "Is it good? Have you read it?"

"I used to be a librarian in Kiev; I make a point of reading all the books that I sell," she said.

Somehow, I was now certain that she was Jewish, so I asked, "Do you have any Jewish books for sale? It's been so long since I've read anything in Yiddish."

Her face saddened as she picked up two books. "We do sometimes have Jewish books, but right now there are only these two — four rubles for both." I hesitated, for my ten rubles were all the money I had in the whole world. Then she said, loudly enough for everyone in line to hear, "Please, comrade, don't hold up the line. Do you want them or not?"

It was a hard decision to make, but the magic of Jewish print was irresistible. "I'll take both the Jewish books, but not Ehrenburg's. I only have ten rubles left, " I said, placing my last bank note on the small counter.

She took the ten rubles, gave me six rubles change, and said, "Here is Ehrenburg's book, free. Please accept my gift and read it very carefully. You'll find it worth your while."

I thanked her and stepped aside, and immediately began to leaf through the Yiddish books. One was *Questions in Leninism* by Joseph V. Stalin, and the other was *A Short History of the Communist Party Bolsheviks*, by the Party Propaganda Department. I was terribly disappointed. For this rubbish I had spent my precious rubles! I turned around, intending to return them, but then I realized the danger in returning a book written by Stalin. But what had she meant when she said, "Read Ehrenburg's book carefully"? What was so special about it? I leafed through it and discovered my ten-ruble note — a gift from a kind woman's heart.

As I placed the books into my sack, I paused for a moment. Somehow, it didn't seem right to be putting Stalin's ravings together with the holy Bible. I placed my only shirt between them, to separate the holy from the impure, the truth from falsehood! I placed the *Tanach* and the *tefillin* on top of the books.

I went directly to the embassy; this time I had no trouble finding it. I opened the door and walked in, unmindful of the sharp glance from the Soviet policeman. I didn't even bother to acknowledge the arrogant clerk at the information desk. Like an old visitor who knows his way around, I bounded up the stairs to Dr. Seidenman's office and opened the door, ready to pour out my news with all the bitterness inside of me.

Dr. Seidenman raised his eyes, took one look at me and said, "You too?" I realized then that he already knew, and had indeed known all along. Uninvited, I sat down across from Dr. Seidenman. He had turned very pale, and sat biting his lips in anger; he was talking to himself, murmuring, "So — even the general's letter didn't help! The dogs!"

I felt sorry for him, working in an office among enemies, Jew-haters. I couldn't be angry at him any more, but I still told him all the details, adding that I would have been accepted if I'd registered as a chauffeur instead of a rabbi. I asked him why he didn't raise a storm in London.

He replied that as a member of the embassy staff he could not discuss the reasons for his actions with me. "Your case is not lost yet," he told me, "for I might still be able to get you back into the army. But it will take a few weeks and some intervention. In the meantime, where will you stay, and what will you live on?"

I replied that I planned to go back "home" to Karobka. Given the confusion and inefficiency of Soviet bureaucracy, I reasoned that my discharge paper should be adequate protection against the charges of desertion for at least a few weeks, until I could go back to the army at Guzar. But he didn't share my confidence in this little scrap of paper.

"I consider it my duty to furnish you with a real document, a Polish passport." He spoke with closed eyes. The wrinkles on his forehead attested to the fact that he was making a difficult decision. "Only a very small number of these passports are issued; they are only for VIPs, but I shall get you one," he declared.

I thanked him for his effort, but then a new realization struck me. If the Poles don't want me in their army, why should they give me a passport? Why should they care if I'm arrested and charged with desertion from the Russian army? What do they care if I'm shot? One Jew less! The passports were only for VIPs, and who was I?

A guinea pig.

"Just a minute, Dr. Seidenman. I'm not so sure I want a passport," I said. "I don't want to be caught between the Polish and Soviet governments — a curse on both of them!"

I could see the struggle going on within Dr. Seidenman: his sympathy for me on the one hand, and on the other, his official duties. "Now listen to me," he said. "I can fully understand your point of view, but I can't agree with you. If a mother spits in the face of her son, he still remains her son!

You are a son of Poland, and General Anders' army does not represent Poland. If it is necessary that you become a test case, you must not avoid your duty. Besides, you don't have to present your passport to anyone if you don't want to, but it will be much safer for you to have it with you in case you are charged with desertion. You have nothing to lose, only to gain! Now, do you have a photograph?" he asked.

"No, sir," I replied. "But you might use the one on my old passport."

"Good!" he said with a smile. "You are also entitled to some clothes that were sent to the embassy by the American Jewish Joint Distribution Committee. What you're wearing is pitiful, but it will take at least three days to get the passport and the clothes. Where will you stay in the meantime?" I told him about the school near the railroad station where the army men were staying, and that I would try to persuade them to let me stay an extra day or two.

When I stepped outside, I noticed that the policeman had stopped patrolling back and forth; instead, he was standing stiffly near the door. I had taken only a few steps when two well-dressed men approached me. I assumed that they were foreign diplomats coming to visit the embassy, for I had never seen anyone in Russia dressed in a pressed suit, tie and hat. In fact, I had never seen anyone wearing a hat or a tie in all my travels in Russia. As they came face to face with me one of them asked in perfect Russian, "*Vy kto* — Who are you?" Before I had a chance to reply, the other one said, "*Pashli za mnoy* — Follow me."

I realized that they were not diplomats, but agents of the Secret Service. Instantly I stepped backwards and grabbed for the embassy door handle, for there I would be safe: the sanctuary of an embassy is recognized by international law. But then the policeman at the door grabbed me and pushed me away from the door so violently that I fell and rolled into the street.

At that moment a car came to a stop next to me; the two agents lifted me up and threw me into the car, which sped off immediately. They searched me for arms and took my precious bag away, but did not utter a word during the entire drive.

I asked naively, "Who are you? Where are you taking me? What have I done?"

Not a word came from them. Finally the car came to a stop next to a barred gate. The armed guards surrounding it wore blue caps with red bands. Then I knew that I was entering the lion's den, the dreadful Security

Service building. In comparison with that, the regular NKVD were angels!

The agents took me into a large room, where two civilians awaited me. I was told to sit down on a chair in the corner, and my bag was placed on the desk of the one who seemed to be in charge. They began to converse briefly in foreign languages — first in French, then in Italian, and then, I thought, in Spanish. All the while the man in charge stared intently at me. I realized that the switching of languages was because they suspected that I was a spy and therefore might understand some foreign languages; thus he observed me closely in order to detect a change of expression on my face when I understood what they were talking about.

How could I possibly prove that I was not a spy? In any other country, the task of proving me guilty would rest on them, but not here, not in Russia. I knew what these agents were capable of; they could make a man confess that he had bombed the moon! When they found the _Tanach_ and _tefillin_ in my bag, they would have evidence of my religious beliefs — a crime in itself. And my discharge papers from the unfriendly Polish army...and the typhus, which any doctor could detect as false, and my eating and sleeping with the military! I felt that the case against me was already wrapped up!

Then I began to reason: why haven't they searched my bag yet? What are they waiting for? If I'm a suspected spy, why aren't they looking for secret papers, maps, or codes in my bag? What did they want? Perhaps I should try my luck and ask for the bag, claiming that my bread is in there, and I'm hungry.

"Comrade," I addressed the one who seemed to be in charge, "may I ask for my bag? I have some bread in it, and I'm starving."

He placed his hand on the bag and poked it all around. Luckily the bread was on top; when he felt it he did not search any further. He picked up the bag and tossed it to me.

I took out some bread, began to eat, and an idea occurred to me. I removed Stalin's book and began to read while chewing my bread. All four men stared at me. One of them jumped up and grabbed the book out of my hands, shouting, "Aha! What kind of counter-revolutionary material is this?"

The other, puzzled by the Jewish letters, said, "Anti-Soviet propaganda, eh?" Then all four gazed at the open book. Upside down, the Yiddish letters looked even stranger.

I swallowed the piece of bread, taking my time. Then I said, "What did you call this book? Counter-revolutionary? Why don't you turn over the cover and see for yourselves?"

Their faces turned white when the chief took the book in his hands and read the first page, which was in Russian, as if reciting on stage, "*Voprosy Leninisma*, by Yosiph Visaryonovich Stalin. This is the greatest book ever published on the face of the earth! Go on, young man, continue to read it!" With a broad smile he handed the book back to me.

But I didn't stop there. I pulled out *The Party History*, and *The Fall of Paris* by Ilya Ehrenburg. Then I asked, "Would you like to see some more of my anti-Soviet propaganda?" and I had my hand on the little Bible inside the bag.

"Not necessary," the chief said, and I was sure I had won half the battle — they wouldn't search my bag any further!

The entire incident of these books struck me as odd: noticing them in the kiosk, buying them — and come to think of it, I had almost returned them — and having my money returned, all of it, all of it was Providence! My courage renewed, I walked up to the chief and asked, "Comrade, why are you keeping me here? What am I charged with?"

He looked at me, raised his eyebrows, and replied, "Well, young man, do you think you can fool us by covering up your activities with Stalin's books?"

"Pardon me, but I'm not trying to cover up anything! I'm a *kolkhoznik*, and I have to return to my village; the tractor is waiting for me there. Why don't you check with the chairman of Karobka? It's only seventy kilometers from here. I don't understand why you're holding me here for nothing."

His eyes pierced through me. I must have played my role well, for he said, "You must wait for the colonel. We'll see if you are really as innocent as you act. In the meantime, we'll check with Karobka." I knew he was lying, for there was no telephone in Karobka, and he'd probably never even heard of the little village.

The atmosphere improved. They offered me cigarettes and talked to me in a friendlier way. I wasn't sure if the change in attitude was the result of their error concerning Stalin's book, which I might report to the colonel, or perhaps was their way of softening me up. I continued to give the impression that I was an ignorant country boy, who was greatly impressed by the wisdom of glorious Stalin. The teacher of Karobka had warned me that any sign of intellect or political knowledge could be suspected as

Trotskyism, which was far more dangerous than being a spy!

Gradually, I regained my self-confidence. I wasn't afraid any more; I said my prayers softly, and stretched out on the bench. At midnight, the colonel finally arrived, and I was taken to his office. He was a stout little man, with a large stomach and fat neck. In a friendly tone, he invited me to sit down. He offered me a cigarette which I politely declined. While the colonel settled comfortably into his chair, I decided to take the offensive.

"Comrade Colonel," I began without waiting for him to start the interrogation, "if I may ask, why are they holding me here? Back home the tractor is waiting for me. In today's _Pravda_ I read Comrade Stalin's call to all farmers to increase production for the sake of our fighting men. How can I contribute my share if I'm wasting my time here?"

He leaned back, and focused his penetrating eyes on me. A chill went through me, to my very bones. Would my approach work, or was I being foolhardy? Had I antagonized the great man?

"So I heard." He finally broke the silence — a silence which seemed to me an eternity. "You are a tractorist. How do you like Soviet life? You were born and raised in a capitalist country, in fascist Poland; what do you think of life on a collective?"

I was an old hand at this line, and played the game to the hilt. "Comrade Colonel, when I first arrived in the Soviet Union I was sent at once to a _kolkhoz_. To tell you the truth, I did have my doubts about collectivism, but I thought: if millions of farmers all over this great land are happy and satisfied, there must be something to it! The very first week I was sent to a tractor school. Imagine, being able to learn a trade! And what a trade! A tractorist!" I said it with pride. "I had no worries about eating, I had a home, clothing, comrades, everything I needed. What else does a working man want?"

His next question came as no surprise. "But don't you think it's better for each farmer to have his own plot of land?"

"Of course not!" I lied vehemently, surprised at my skill in the game; any mistake might mean torture, confession, Siberia, or death. "You city people, perhaps, cannot realize what a tractor, a thresher, and all the other farm machinery mean to the farmer; how can one small farmer even dream of owning a tractor? You can have no idea of the wisdom, the practicality behind collective farming; the happiness, the relief for the poor farmer! The man who thought it all up was surely a genius! I honestly don't know which one it was, Lenin or Stalin. It's one of them, anyway. That's why I bought these books, to learn a little more."

One by one I took out the books, placing them on his desk. He glanced at them with satisfaction and said, "The great Stalin! *There* is a genius for you!" He motioned to me to return the books to my bag and said, "So you came back from the army after this terrible illness, and now you are returning to Karobka. All right. Then can you tell me what you were doing in the Polish embassy?"

"Oh, is that why I was arrested? Ha, ha, ha!" I laughed. "I'll tell the colonel the truth. I read in the papers that Stalin gave the Polish embassy 500 million rubles for Polish refugees. Now, for whom did Stalin intend that money? For those fascists? For those lazy dogs? No! It was meant for people like me, for working people! Stalin is the friend of the working man, the father of the laboring class! He wouldn't give a single ruble for the lousy capitalists, I'm sure! So I figured, since I'm here in town, why shouldn't I try to get a little of Stalin's good-heartedness? Not that I need the money, for I have everything I need in my *kolkhoz*, but just for the satisfaction of relieving those capitalist rats of some Soviet money."

The colonel sat there, expressionless, and I couldn't tell if my bluff had worked or not. Then he leaned forward as if to whisper a secret into my ear, and said very slowly, emphasizing each word, "Tell me, comrade, didn't you receive some documents, or a passport in the embassy?"

So that's it, I thought. That's what he's after! I looked him straight in the eye. "A passport? What do I need a passport for? I can live in Karobka, my village, for the next hundred years and no one will ever ask me for a passport. You know how it is in a village — everybody knows everybody else."

The colonel wrote something down, then turned to me. "Where are you staying here in town?"

"In the Army Center, near the train station; see, here's my ticket for the meal I missed because of your men."

Again silence filled the room; he stared at me as if trying to read my mind. The silence must have lasted a long time, and I had time to review everything that had been said. I had spoken freely, so that he would think that I was a jabbering fool, a dumb farmer, but would it work? Or would it backfire? These men were experienced interrogators; perhaps the passport business was merely a ruse and he'd get to the real point in his own good time. Had I convinced him at least that a talkative country boy like me would never do for a spy?

He must have weighed in his mind all possible accusations and charges against me. Finally he spoke up. "Listen, tractorist — Kuybishev for you is _NZP — Nye zakonnoye prozhivanye_ — an unlawful residence. You are not allowed to stay here in town; make sure to get out first thing in the morning. Is that clear?"

I felt safer now, so I pressed my luck. "Comrade Colonel, suppose the embassy tells me to come back the next day? You know how these capitalist bureaucrats are when it comes to dealing with a working man. Can you please give me permission to stay another day?"

The colonel rose and got ready to leave. "Now listen to me! I'm warning you; you're playing with fire. Kuybishev is _NZP_ for you and no one can change that, not even me!"

I was free! Unbelievable! The streetcar took me back to the Army Center. I was exhausted, physically and emotionally. Still, I could hardly wait until the morning so that I could tell Dr. Seidenman that I had been in the dreaded lion's den and had emerged alive!

Early in the morning I was at the embassy. The same policeman was on duty. I jauntily asked him for the time — he had no watch, and I opened the door with a feeling of triumph. They knew about the arrest, for the embassy kept a man on watch constantly; apparently, the two "allies" — Poland and Russia — kept an eye on each other. I told Dr. Seidenman and another official all that had happened.

My arrest resulted in getting the passport procedure speeded up. Then I was sent to the embassy basement for clothing and footwear. Boxes of clothing sent by American Jews were stacked to the ceiling, but here again anti-Semitism was at work. I was not offered the brand new shoes, or the excellent English shirts. Instead, the man in charge, without asking my size, tossed me a suit from America — it still bore the name Epstein on the cleaner's tag — a pair of old shoes, one military blanket, and four small cakes of American soap. These clothes, though used, and the soap, were worth a fortune on the Russian black market. Dr. Seidenman had also obtained five hundred rubles for me from the embassy relief fund, and presented them to me, together with my new passport!

This was a long piece of white paper printed in Polish, French and Russian. In the space marked "occupation," the word _rabbin_ — rabbi — was written in Polish and French, but in the Russian version the space was empty. At the bottom was a request in Russian, to all Soviet authorities "to render help and assistance in case of need to this citizen of the Republic of

Poland." This document with the attached photograph and the embassy seal certified my Polish citizenship, while the other document, signed by the military in Guzar, certified me as an ex-soldier rejected from military duty because of typhus!

As we parted, Dr. Seidenman wished me well. "I hope you'll be a Polish soldier yet!" were his last words to me — prophetic words, but it was to be in a Polish army of which he had never heard, an army not visualized by all the politicians and generals of the unfortunate Republic of Poland!

When I arrived back in Karobka I was welcomed with varying emotions: surprise, happiness, shock, and jealousy at my quick return. "He sure did win the war fast," the stableman remarked sarcastically.

I could hear them talking behind my back, and cross-eyed Nikolai sniggered: "A Jew can always find a way out; but not our men — they're too dumb!"

I showed everyone my document which officially declared in Russian and Polish: "Discharged from the army for reasons of health. *TYPHUS.*" All were impressed, especially with the Latin letters of the Polish language. The older people looked longest at the Polish eagle at the top of the document. Some even wiped away a tear; to them, the eagle brought back memories of the days of the Czar, when the Russian imperial emblem was a double-headed eagle looking to the east and to the west.

I had to invent a series of lies, since one lie required another. I went into great detail about the "terrible typhus epidemic" in the warm climates of Asia Minor. It was all news to them, and they had no reason to doubt me. They were completely isolated, and no one had read a newspaper to them since I had left.

Anna and her mother welcomed me warmly, while the children danced around me, bursting with happiness. Nevertheless I sensed a change in Anna and her mother. There seemed to be a coldness and aloofness in their manner, which I hadn't expected. At first I attributed it to sorrow and jealousy; Anna's husband hadn't written in months, and here I was, back from the army. Then I thought that perhaps they were afraid of my presence in the house because of my "contagious disease"! I assured them that the doctors had checked and double-checked before they would permit me to travel after such an illness, and only after being fully satisfied with my condition did they allow me to go home.

"I'm cured," I assured them, "but I'm just too weak for military service.

As soon as I get my strength back, I shall be called back to duty."

I inquired about the health of Chairman Anton, Anna's father-in-law and my good friend. She said he was seriously ill, but she wouldn't let me go to see him until I'd eaten. While her mother was preparing the food, Anna disappeared. I had finished eating when she returned, and she asked me to wait so that we might go together to visit her father-in-law.

All the way there she told me how difficult it was for a woman to feed her family without a man around the house; how a house needs food reserves, so the children will be assured of a meal the following day.

"But Anna," I said, "I thought the whole idea of collective farming is to obtain security and peace of mind."

She stopped for a moment and asked, "Where did you hear that nonsense, that horse manure?"

"I read it just yesterday, in Stalin's book," I answered, surprised by her vehemence.

"And you believe that?" she asked angrily. "Why, they couldn't care less if we all starved to death! Look at us — all we produce they take away! Everything is taxed. If we didn't steal, we'd die of starvation!" She lowered her voice to a whisper. "Those rats won't even send a death notice to the family if a soldier is killed. How can it be that not even one man from this village, from this entire area, has been killed? I hope it's true, please God! Yet half of our men haven't written for months! And do you know that not one woman has been notified of a man missing in action? You know why? Because a widow is entitled to a government pension for the children, and she's also supposed to be relieved of some taxes, and no Party official would dare to drive a widow to work like an animal... so they simply don't inform us! And without an official notice of death, you are not a widow — you are a dog like all the rest. Every fat city slicker scorns us because we're just dumb farmers. But it's we who give them food, and we stay hungry ourselves."

I was taken aback by Anna's impassioned outburst. She had never talked like this before, making it clear that she lived and struggled for only one purpose — to secure food for her children, to keep them alive, and to be both father and mother to them. "I owe it to my husband," she whispered through her tears. I tried to encourage her not to abandon hope for her husband's return. By now we were in front of the chairman's house, at the other end of the village.

The *babushka* was outside milking the cow.

"Let me help you, Mother," Anna volunteered, but the old woman refused.

"No, not now. Better go inside and see the old man." Then she turned to me. "Welcome home, Chaim! It's good to see you back! Go inside and tell him some stories from the big wide world. That's the best medicine for him; there's nothing like a good story!"

The house was dark. The chairman was lying on a wooden bed covered with a straw mattress. His face was even yellower than usual, and his chin bones seemed sharper.

"Come closer, my dear friend," he spoke softly. "If you've managed to overcome typhus, you have nothing to fear from me. It's just old age — a time which we all claim to look forward to, yet we dread it when it comes."

He took my hand in his cold palm and held it. "I like to hold on to youth," he said with a sigh.

I asked him whether he had seen a doctor. "No, no. A patient has to go to the city to see a doctor; a doctor won't come to a poor patient in a distant village."

The *babushka* came in, carrying two wooden cups of warm milk straight from the cow, and a potato pie. Then the two women went out to the garden. The old man, still holding my hand, listened to my stories with great interest. When I had finished the last drop of milk in the cup, he said, "Chaim, do you know why Anna came along with you here?"

I was a little surprised at the question. "She came to visit you. Isn't that the reason?" I replied.

He shook his head. "My friend, she came here with a purpose," he began slowly. "She has already visited me three times today. She came with you now about a matter of life and death." He paused for a moment. "First, you must give me your word — take an oath that not a word of what I'm about to tell you will slip through your lips!"

"I never take oaths," I replied, "but I promise you that I'll keep it a secret."

He sighed a few times; then he began to talk. "You know us well enough to judge for yourself that we're not the worst people in the world, right? But the fact is that we all have to steal. Not that we are common thieves — we have to steal in order to survive. All of us must steal, except Stalin. He doesn't have to steal, since it all belongs to him."

There was nothing in his words that I didn't already know. He motioned to me with his bony hand to come closer. I bent down, realizing that he was building up to the real story.

"Anna works like a dog to support herself and the children and her old mother, but they are still hungry. Her husband — my son — is in the war and can't help her. That's why I put you with them in the first place. And you were very good to them. You brought all your earnings to them instead of to the market — but when you left she lost her main source of support. Now, Anna and the storekeeper worked out a solution: between the two of them, they divided your earnings, which continued to come. They took for themselves what was yours."

He was still holding my hand tightly, and his hands were trembling. "They reasoned that they were stealing from the government, and not from you personally," he said, "because on the day you were drafted, all that was coming to you — your share in the collective — automatically became the property of the government. Stalin was to inherit whatever belonged to you. Of course, we never expected to see you back again. So Anna and her friend embezzled a little: they stole from the government what belongs to you. And now that you've come back, they're scared to death."

He stopped talking; he was exhausted. I said, "But _Dedushka_, how could they collect without my signature?" He didn't reply. "You mean they forged it?" I asked, astonished.

"No, my dear friend, they didn't need to forge your name. You had already signed plenty of papers. You see, every time you received food 'on account,' you signed your name, but you made a mistake; you signed on the bottom line of the paper. Anna noticed it, and so did her friend, the woman in charge of the store. They are clever, and they worried about the future. All they had to do was to fill in the empty forms which already had your signature on the bottom."

I began to laugh. The resourcefulness, the cleverness of these women! How practical they were! Bitter reality had taught them many cunning ways of stealing from Stalin!

Anton didn't let go of my hand. "So, my son, what are you going to do? Are you going to press charges against her? Will I, the chairman, have to arrest my own daughter-in-law?"

"Is that what's bothering Anna?" I asked. "I'll tell you what I'll do.

Tomorrow, first thing in the morning, I'll go to the store, and sign another paper on the bottom line! Come to think of it, I'd better sign a whole stack of papers, because I'll only be here for a few weeks. As soon as I recuperate from the typhus, I'll be called back into the army. Will that give you peace of mind?"

He laughed and coughed at the same time, and patted me on the back. "I told her all the time that you'd never give her any trouble! But the poor woman and her friend have been scared to death since you returned." He closed his eyes, mumbling to himself, "Thank you, son, thank you."

Peace replaced anxiety on the old wrinkled face. Here was a man with no demands, no desires, ready to leave it all without a struggle, except for one wish: to see his sons return safely from the war. I freed my hand from his grip. He was fast asleep.

19

I WAS HAPPY to see my old friends in Karobka, but I was anxious and impatient. I knew that if I failed to get back to Guzar before the Polish army pulled out of Russia, I would not only miss my chance to get out of the Soviet Union, but I would lose my only chance to fight the Germans. And there was still no news from Dr. Seidenman! He had assured me that I would be hearing from him soon; but how long was "soon"? With every passing day, my chances were diminishing.

Finally it occurred to me that I could "alter" the document in my possession. The paper stated that I had been released from the army because of typhus, but that shouldn't disqualify a man forever! Suppose I was cured! Suppose I was ordered by the military commandant to report back to my unit in Guzar! This would give me permission to travel. True, I would be missing a bread card, since the bread rations were issued by the local military commandant, whose name I was planning to forge. But somehow, some way, I would get a food supply from the village.

The only problem was where to get hold of a rubber stamp, to make my handwritten ratification appear official. I searched the entire village, but I couldn't find any rubber with which to make a stamp. I tried wood, but the words came out blurred, and the hammer and sickle looked very crude.

One day, when we were loading a shipment of grain for a government granary, I noticed the seal on the delivery bill. It read, "Military Delivery, Karobka-Booyan Region." My heart leapt; if I could get hold of this seal, I could delete the word "Delivery," and all of the word "Karobka" except for the capital letter K, which could stand for "Kommandant." It would then read: "Military K----- Booyan Region," with the national emblem perfectly located in the center! I knew that it was quite common for some letters of a rubber stamp not to come out clearly, especially when it was used hurriedly; and besides, who would bother to scrutinize a simple document which assigns a man to return to his army unit?

The difficult part would be obtaining the stamp, which was kept in a locked drawer in the secretary's office. The more I thought about the stamp, the more I liked the idea. I was very excited, for this seemed to hold my only hope for getting back to Guzar. I began to hang around the secretary's office, on the lookout for the coveted rubber stamp!

I made inquiries about Suleika, Summatov's daughter, thinking that perhaps she might be willing to get me a seal from her father's office; but I was told that she had volunteered for the army not long after I was drafted.

In the meantime, the routine of village life went on as usual. There were no real signs of war; not even an occasional plane cut through the clear sky. The season was changing, the warm spring sun melting the snow, exposing the bundles of grain left from last year's harvest. Much of it had rotted in the fields, but whatever remained still had to be collected and brought to the threshing machine to make room in the fields for the spring plowing.

Working in the fields, my mind was constantly preoccupied with getting to Guzar, my door to the free world. Jerusalem was beckoning, and that little seal was the only missing link! Over and over again I made elaborate plans for obtaining that stamp; one plan was more far-fetched than another, and I soon discarded each one in favor of a new one, equally ridiculous.

When my wagon was loaded, I drove it to the threshing machine, and dragged down the heavy bundles; unloading the wagons was entirely my job. I worked with great vigor and speed, eager to get back to the village, and the possibility of getting hold of that stamp!

Every day after work I went to the office with all kinds of pretexts, looking for an opportunity to use the stamp, but there was always someone in the office, and the all-important seal remained beyond my reach.

One day Ivan Antonovich, Anna's brother-in-law, came to visit his sick father. Ivan had been unusually lucky when he was drafted; being somewhat educated and older, he was not sent to the front, but was put in charge of a supply depot. "We ship supplies west, all the way to the front line, and as far east as Chkalov," he told me proudly. The name Chkalov rang a bell; I remembered the clerk in the Polish embassy mentioning the Polish army camp in Chkalov. Ivan told me that he was thinking of taking his wife and daughter with him. "If I'm shipped out to the front, she can always go back home," he said.

Immediately I said, "And I volunteer to go with you, to bring the horse and wagon back to Karobka!"

He was happy and I was happy. He was a good man to have for a friend; for he might take me all the way to Chkalov, in the event that I couldn't get the seal and make my own way to Guzar!

We arrived somewhere in the woods, where the army stockpiled supplies. Since I was a friend of the sergeant, I was admitted without a pass. All the soldiers there were very friendly, and invited me to take a trip with them to Chkalov for some sight-seeing. I had to decline because I had promised to return the horse and wagon to Karobka. I decided that if I couldn't obtain the rubber stamp within a week, I would return to this outpost and try to ride to Chkalov with them.

Four days later I arrived back in Karobka. The news from the front was bad, and getting worse. The Germans were advancing on Moscow, the Crimea had been lost and the enemy was pushing towards the Volga. Orders arrived requiring every village to send four people with shovels to dig trenches along the Volga River — great holes the exact size of the enemy tanks. If one of the huge monsters were to cross the river, it would fall in and wouldn't be able to get out. Also, thousands of acres of forests all along the eastern bank of the river were to be cut down to a certain height. A tank would thus get stuck on a tree stump and would be immobilized, the tracks spinning in the air uselessly. I was fortunate, for if I had not gone on that trip with Ivan, and had stayed in Karobka, I would have been the first one to be assigned, and all my plans would have been ruined.

The next day Natasha, the secretary of the collective, sent her little brother to tell me to come to her house immediately.

Natasha was terribly excited. Her words came out in a rush and I didn't know what she was talking about. She begged me, "Chaim, please, please, say you'll do it for me!"

"Do what?" I asked. "What are you so excited about? What's the matter?"

"Oh, it's because of that old fool, the delivery man! He left at noon with a delivery for the army but didn't take any papers. I'm responsible — it's all my fault!"

My heart began to pound as I realized the significance of her words. "And the receiving station won't accept the wheat without papers?"

"Don't be silly, Chaim! I guess you're still not a *Sovietsky Chelovyek*. In our country we take anything and accept anything — but without the documents, Karobka won't get the credit for it! Without the papers, our tax will stay on the books as unpaid! And I'll be held responsible! So take the papers, have the chairman sign them, grab a horse and chase after the wheat wagons as fast as you can!"

I took the forms and asked, "What about the seal?"

"Oh, my goodness, I almost forgot it! I've been so worried about my sick baby that I can't keep my mind on my job. I'm all mixed up. Let's go to the office, and I'll put the seal on it."

"There's no need for you to go, Natasha; give me the key and I'll do it. You know how the old man signs his name illegibly; let him sign first, and then I'll stamp it with the seal."

"You're right," she said. "Oh, Chaim, you're too good! Here's the key."

Little did she know how good I really was! An eye for an eye, I thought to myself; if the Polish high command can issue fraudulent documents, so can I. In my own handwriting, I wrote on the bottom of the Guzar document, "To return to army unit at Guzar at once!" I dated it and signed it with a flourish: "Captain Y. U. Smirnov, Military Commandant." The seal was perfect; or rather, perfectly "imperfect." Around the national emblem it read, "Military K_____ --- Booyan Region."

"So you are drafted again," was the general reaction when I let the villagers know that I was leaving Karobka once more. Old *Dedushka* Anton, Anna and her mother, and Goncharov the teacher all sincerely wished me a quick return. This time I was not entitled to the three-day food supply ordinarily given a draftee, for I had no instructions from the military commandant. But privately Anna and her mother baked bread for me, and of course I signed a few more receiving forms so Anna could collect on my documents. Better Anna than Stalin, I told myself.

Leaving Karobka, I hitchhiked along the roads with traveling farmers, sometimes by truck, sometimes by wagon. Most of the way I went by foot, until I reached my destination, the post of Sergeant Ivan Antonovich Raskin, *Dedushka* Anton's son. Naturally I couldn't tell him the whole truth — that I couldn't board a train since I had neither a travel permit nor a train ticket. (Ordinarily, a draftee received his travel orders and a ticket from the military commandant, and I lacked both.) So I told the sergeant that I had lost my travel orders, and that I was afraid to request another travel permit. I might be fined for losing military documents, and I hoped that he'd help me get on the trans-Siberian train in Chkalov.

"I'd hate to be branded a deserter," I pleaded with Ivan. My forged document and the bottle of homemade whiskey which I had brought with me convinced him that not only would he be acting as a good friend by assisting me, but he'd also be performing his military duty by helping a draftee to reach his destination. The fiery liquid in the bottle also warmed the hearts of the few men under his command; any friend of the sergeant was a friend of theirs.

They put me on the first army supply transport to Chkalov, which they had to guard until it would reach its destination. I enjoyed the trip, eating, sleeping and joking with the guards.

Arriving in Chkalov, I asked the soldiers to take me through the station, since I wanted to see the town and the market before boarding the train to Tashkent. Actually, what I had in mind was to find the Polish army camp. This time I would register as a driver and tractorist. The black market was near the railroad station, and as I walked through the market, squeezing through the crowds of people, I saw an old man in a Polish army coat. He was selling British military coats and uniforms at exorbitant prices, bragging that his merchandise came directly from England, and was made of the finest English wool.

I waited till the man was alone and then approached him. "*Pan z Polski?* — Is the gentleman from Poland?"

He replied in Polish, but with a slight Lithuanian accent, that he was from Vilnius. I knew at once that he was a Lithuanian, for no Pole would ever use the name "Vilnius." Too much hate, bitterness and blood divided these two peoples over that city, and its name — Vilna for the Poles, Vilnius for the Lithuanians — said all. I greeted him in Lithuanian, and the old man began to smile and shook my hand warmly. It must have been a long time since he had spoken to anyone in his native tongue. I explained that I had once lived in Raseinai, where I had learned to speak a little Lithuanian. Then I came to the point.

I asked, "*Ponas, kur Lenkijos Armjos?* — Sir, where is the Polish army located?" The old man jumped up from his bundle of old and new clothes.

"*Lenkijos? Kurvas vajkas?* — The Poles? Those Polish good-for-nothings?" he asked in derision. "They're gone! Why do you think I'm selling these uniforms?" Then he told me that the Polish army had just picked up and left. He had been dealing with the Polish officers, who were selling anything they could steal from the military supplies. These British uniforms had been purchased from them, just before they left for Persia.

I wondered if my last chance, the army camp at Guzar, was about to vanish too. Or perhaps Guzar, being the largest and the closest base to the border, would be evacuated last.

"How long ago did they leave here?" I asked the old man.

"Two weeks ago, the bums," he spat, returning to his seat on the bundles of uniforms. I didn't waste any time; I quickly found my soldier friends, who were roaming around the market, and asked them to take me back across the tracks. Before evening fell, I was on an express train to the east.

The military or industrial importance of a Soviet city could be judged by the number of controls one encountered when approaching it. If only one soldier or policeman demanded to see documents before the train pulled into the station, the city was of no great importance. In such cases I merely locked myself in the lavatory; if someone knocked on the door, insisting on seeing my documents, I would push my draft document through the slightly opened door, and it always proved to be satisfactory. However, if that was not possible, I had to resort to a more hazardous procedure: I would sneak past the policeman, to the other half of the car, the half he had already checked! As for ticket control inspections, this was easy: I would hide between cars, and then sneak into the cars already checked.

Now, as the conductor announced the next town, "Kzyl-Orda! Kzyl-Orda!" I looked out the window and realized that here was trouble — real trouble! Armed guards boarded the train as it was pulling into the station. Two armed guards entered each car, guarding every door of every car! A captain in a blue police uniform started checking everyone's papers! In great anxiety, I locked myself in the lavatory. Soon I heard him asking for all kinds of documents — travel permits, military identification. Apparently they were searching not only for deserters and saboteurs, but also for speculators, the black marketeers who operated by transporting their merchandise on trains, using fictitious travel permits.

Soon came the dreaded knock on the lavatory door. The captain called, "You, in there! Present your documents! Don't you know that you are not allowed to use the lavatory while the train is standing in the station?"

I opened the door a crack and handed him my forged Guzar paper. But it didn't work this time! "*Chto za chapukha!* — What rubbish!" the captain yelled. "Take this one away!" Immediately the door was forced open by a brawny sergeant.

I didn't give up. "Comrade Captain, are you trying to make a deserter out of me? Can't you see I'm returning to my unit?" The officer gave me a withering look. Without a word, he put my paper into his pocket and motioned to the guard. "Get him off the train," he said to the sergeant behind me and, with a shove from a rifle, I was pushed down to the station platform.

At the police station my interrogation began. Waving the forged document in my face, the captain bellowed, "Who are you trying to bluff? The Poles, those cowards, have pulled out of Guzar already! They weren't willing to fight like Stalin wanted them to; they just wanted to be fed and to wander around doing nothing. And you? Why are you so eager to serve the _Pans_? Maybe you're a _Pan_ yourself?!"

I could see the writing on the wall. The word _Pan_ means "Sir" in Polish; the many prosperous Polish landowners in the Ukraine and in Byelorussia had usually been addressed as _Pan_. After the Revolution, the word became synonymous with big landowners, rich capitalists and exploiters of the working class. In other words, in the Soviet vocabulary the word evolved into a derogatory and dangerous title: it came to symbolize an archenemy of the Soviet system.

"Comrade Captain," I pleaded, "I'm not a _Pan_; I'm an ordinary working man! I'm only trying to return to my outfit by order of the military commandant. How was I supposed to know that they've moved out? I was ill, and now I've been traveling for almost a week."

The officer lost his patience and began to bellow, "But you were ready to serve those Polish fascists, right? Then you're nothing but a fascist yourself! Those rotten Polish cowards, taking off across the border so they won't have to face the enemy!"

Now I realized that I was too late for Guzar. I had missed my last chance to get out of this vast prison called the Soviet Union! The shock drained me of all my energy. Indifferent to what the captain might do to me, I sat down on the ground, for my legs refused to hold me up.

He grabbed my shoulders and yanked me back up on my feet, screaming, "Who gave you permission to sit down? And maybe you're really a Fritz, and not a _Pan_?! You look like one! Are you a spy? Is that why you're trying to flee the country with those lousy Polacks?"

This last accusation jerked me out of my numb shock. If they were convinced I was a spy, I might be sent away to Siberia, or even be shot! Quickly I pulled out my Polish passport, printed in three languages, and presented it to the officer. "Here, Comrade Captain, this proves that I'm a Jew, not a German spy. And being a Polish citizen, I was only doing my duty, reporting to the Polish army!"

He looked over the document very carefully. Finally he mumbled, "Well, this has saved your neck." Placing the passport on his desk, he took a pencil and began to figure. "From Kuybishev to Kzyl-Orda is 35 rubles fare. Traveling without a ticket, the fine is multiplied to 35 times ten. Also, you have no travel permit, another 500 rubles fine. There you are, soldier! Just pay the 850 rubles and you can go free."

He said it calmly, while tearing my army discharge into small pieces. I could only close my eyes in pain. Not only was he tearing up my last hope of leaving Russia; he might also decide to destroy my passport, my only proof of Polish citizenship!

I begged him to give me back my passport, but he was enjoying his power and was adamant, "Only after you pay the fine — 850 rubles! Remember, I'm doing you a big favor; if I take you to the prosecutor you'll end up in prison!"

I emptied my pockets and showed him what I had — the few hundred rubles that Dr. Seidenman had given me. I said I'd gladly give them all to him if he'd only give me back my passport.

"And I don't need a receipt," I said, slowly and meaningfully.

He ignored my hint, however, and demanded the full amount. "Go out and find the money. In the meantime, I'll keep your passport!" was his final decision.

I rushed out to the market, which was located right in front of the railroad station. I had no time to lose: my only document — my passport, my only proof of citizenship — was in the hands of a greedy police officer, who might tear it up if he didn't get his bribe quickly!

I still had two bars of soap that I had received at the embassy. I approached the first woman with a European face that I saw, and whispered, "*Amerikanskoye milo?* — American soap?" There were no wrappings around the bars of soap and there was no English letter impressed into them, but the woman took one smell and knew that I had spoken the truth; not since before the Revolution had there been delicate, fragrant soap like this in the Soviet Union. I did not let her hold the soap; I couldn't trust her.

She eyed the soap yearningly and asked immediately, "_Skolko?_ — How much?"

Not knowing the market value here, I could only guess, so I replied, "_Tisyacha_ — A thousand." Without a word she took out 800 rubles and shoved them into my hand, pleading, "That's all I have with me; take it, take it please."

I realized immediately that I could have asked for a lot more. She noticed my hesitation, and added a loaf of bread to the bargain. I had no time for haggling, so I accepted the offer, and in a few minutes I was back in the captain's office. Fortunately, he was alone. I placed 500 rubles on the table and said, "Please, comrade, I need some money to live on until I find a job. And I don't need a receipt." Without raising his eyes from the money he said softly, "One more hundred and you may go. Remember, I'm doing you a favor!"

I put down 100 rubles and he silently handed me my passport.

I walked back to the market, keeping my hand on the passport in my pocket. I took a seat on one of the benches, and while chewing the fresh bread I reflected on my situation. As for Guzar, there was no point in trying to go there any more. To go back to Karobka was definitely out of the question; first, I had no traveling permit, and second, even the friendly villagers in Karobka might get suspicious about me coming back twice from the army! I had to face the fact that, for the time being, I was stuck here in Asiatic Russia, in Kazakhstan, in Kzyl-Orda!

To THE SOUTH of the trans-Siber-
ian railroad lies the Central Asian desert, and the dry plains of Kazakhstan.
Until the Soviet Revolution, the Kazakhs and their neighbors were nomads, living in tents, grazing their sheep wherever they could find grass, in
this place where water is so scarce. These five million nomads roamed the
vast desert which borders western China, living as they had a thousand
years before.

Until the Revolution, they were illiterate; they had a language but no
alphabet. Only their *mullahs* — Moslem priests — were literate, since they
had to know Arabic letters for reading the Koran. After the Bolshevik
Revolution, the population of Kazakhstan grew to over nine million, due to
the influx of Russians and other nationalities. They moved mainly into the
capital city of Verny, which was renamed Alma-Ata. All over the region the
Soviets opened schools and colleges, using the Arabic alphabet. Alma-Ata
became a cultural center, with a Soviet university. Then, more measures were
taken to speed up the Sovietization of these Moslem lands.

In Uzbekistan, the capital was moved from the historic city of Samar-
kand to Tashkent, where the population was more Russian and European.
Then, instead of the Arabic alphabet, which had linked these Moslem-
Asian peoples to their co-religionists, the Turks, Afghanistanis and Per-
sians, the official alphabet became Latin. In 1928, Turkey, too, adopted the
Latin alphabet, which undercut the Soviet plan to destroy cultural and
religious connections between these Moslem peoples. Stalin ordered the
"Second Language Revolution" and the official alphabet in all these repub-
lics was changed once again, this time to Russian-Cyrillic!

The awkwardness and absurdity of the change to the Cyrillic alphabet is obvious, for the letter V is one of the most used letters in the Russian language, and the Kazakhs can't even pronounce it! In their tongue, a V is pronounced as a P, thus changing Molotov to Molotop, and Voroshilov to Poroshilop. Their letter B sounds something like a P, leading to even more confusion. But Stalin, claiming to be "an old student of the origin of languages," had decreed it to be; and who would dare disobey?

In the early thirties, when the Soviets and Japanese battled on the Amur River over Manchuria, the Russians inherited a large population of Koreans. They showed open hostility towards their Russian conquerors, favoring their kinsmen, the Japanese. The Soviets then proceeded to transfer the entire population — overnight — to Kazakhstan. Thus, more than two million Koreans were dumped into the Kazakhstani desert.

This move defied all logic, and was contrary to the national and racial feelings of the two peoples involved. Korean Shintoists in the midst of Kazakh Moslems! Moreover, Arabic, the natural alphabet for the Moslems, was forbidden, while Japanese letters were permitted for the Koreans. The main Korean diet consisted of rice, hog and dog meat; to the Kazakh Moslems, the flesh of these animals was abhorrent.

And so the Kazakhs refused to live together with the Koreans, whom they considered unclean infidels. The government was forced to build separate villages and schools for the two hostile peoples. While the Kazakhs, as part of their traditional hospitality, never locked a door, the Koreans, dumped into a strange country with wide-open doors, did not hesitate to steal. And the Kazakhs, practicing desert law, had no compunctions about killing a thief right on the spot without bothering about a court of law.

Soon the desert sands began to grow crimson with the blood of Koreans and Kazakhs. A regime whose national anthem calls for blood, a country whose flag is red, is not shocked by the flow of foreign blood in a white, empty desert.

I had plenty of time to recall what I had read about Kazakhstan in the history books I had borrowed from Goncharov, as I sat on a park bench near the railroad station, taking stock of my situation and trying to plan my next move. I silently begged for the Almighty's guidance. I had no idea of what to do or where to go; He would have to show me the way!

An elderly Russian woman sat down next to me. We began talking, and I learned that almost every night the police searched this park for army deserters. I reflected upon my dangerous predicament; I had no legal

Soviet document to present, and so I could easily be accused of desertion. And if I showed them my Polish passport, it might make matters worse: a foreigner without any acceptable Soviet document might even be arrested as a spy!

I asked the old woman if I might spend the night in her house. "I'll pay you in bread or money," I said.

She stared at me suspiciously, and then got up and walked away in a hurry. Now what? Looking around, I saw a familiar landmark. In every Soviet city and park stand statues of Lenin and Stalin, presumably proclaiming the glories of Communism. I gazed at the marble figure of Lenin, leaning forward, with his index finger outstretched, pointing the way to the happy road to Communism. Next to him, seated on a marble bench and looking up devotedly at his leader, was the young Stalin. I noticed that Stalin was always portrayed youthfully, as though he could not age, and would live forever. The monument was surrounded by bushes and flowers, and fenced in with a chain for protection.

A story I had heard about Trotsky came to mind. Once, when the Czar's police were hunting for him in my hometown, Lomza, turning the city upside down in their frantic search, he found a safe hideout — in the attic of the governor's residence! I thought that perhaps I could learn from Trotsky and spend the night under that marble bench, the one that Stalin was sitting on. Surely no policeman would think of searching there!

Suddenly it was dark. In Kazakhstan there was no prolonged dusk or twilight; darkness fell suddenly, and within a few minutes it was black night.

People began to leave the park. I circled the monument again and again, waiting for the right moment to make my move. Finally the time came. I leaped over the chain and the flower beds and crouched down under the bench of the great Stalin.

Huddled under the bench, I thought: Lenin and Stalin, what do you see here in front of you all day? The market — the black market! Where capitalism thrives, and Communist law is broken! And where do all these black-market goods come from? They're stolen! According to Engels, by abolishing private ownership, the cause of stealing will disappear! What do you say to that? I asked the young marble Stalin.

I thought of home. Would they ever believe that I had slept in such a spot? I said my evening prayers and, thinking of my family, I drifted off to sleep.

I woke up early the next morning and hurried to the Labor Placement

Bureau, for only at a place of employment would I receive a bread card; and without a bread card, I could starve to death. I decided to register as a combine operator rather than a tractor man, because of the Sabbath. Driving a tractor offered no possibility of avoiding work on the Sabbath; however, on a combine-thresher, I could prepare the machine on Friday, and perhaps get someone else to start the engine the next day.

I was the first in line. The Kazakh official asked for my documents. I told him my name and said, "I don't have any documents."

His eyebrows raised, he addressed me in broken Russian: "Citizen, we don't hire men without documents. I should really report you to the police." His slanted eyes looked me over and sized me up to see if I was good for a bribe.

I breathed a little easier. If he really intended to call the police, he wouldn't have told me in advance. I was about to offer him some money, but then I thought of trying to bribe him without money. I explained that the police captain had become angry and had torn up my document. "You know how those Russians are when they get mad," I whispered.

At this, the official's lips parted and a broad smile spread across his face. He asked, "Aren't you _Ooroos_ yourself? Aren't you a Russian?"

I explained that I was Jewish, a refugee from Poland. "You can check by calling the police captain. Besides, I thought you needed combine men badly. Perhaps you could make an exception this time?"

The Kazakh reached over and slowly picked up the telephone, slyly watching every reaction on my part. Then he replaced the receiver and told me in his bad Russian, "I see you not afraid police, and we can use combine men. Last year's harvest still in fields."

He handed me a travel permit, a bread card, and a ticket to Djusali, a railroad station in the desert between Kzyl-Orda and the Aral Sea. He instructed me to report to the labor office in the town of Karmakhchi, one-quarter of a mile from the station in Djusali. I was overjoyed!

When I arrived there, after a bone-rattling ride, I could see a tall chimney right across the tracks, and an armed guard at the gate; evidently it was a military factory. I walked to Karmakhchi, which consisted of small groups of mud houses, scattered all over the sand. The wide, hot stretches of sand between the clusters of houses were supposed to be streets. The houses were grouped four or six together, facing each other and forming a small courtyard; each group appeared to be a small fortress. In front of each house was a small, crude fireplace — a few mud-bricks in the shape of an H placed on the ground, just enough to accommodate two pots. These were the kitchens! The only brick house in town was a two-story building, which housed the police station and the jail.

At the edge of the town, facing the emptiness of the blazing white desert, was the market. Produce, camel meat, dog meat, rice, tobacco, and the most delicious-looking cantaloupes and watermelons were on sale there. There was not a tree or a blade of grass in the whole town!

In the markets back home in Poland, there had been an overflow of merchandise and produce, and the sellers and peddlars had shouted and yelled, trying to entice the customers, always praising the quality of their wares and proclaiming their low prices. The supply was usually greater than the demand.

In Soviet markets the opposite was true. The demand was many times greater than the supply, and the seller had no need to advertise his wares, neither their quality nor their price. The customer would surely find him! Consequently, to a Westerner, used to the usual raucous, lively atmosphere of a market, a Soviet market seems as silent as a library! Everyone is quiet, buying and selling in low voices.

A keen observer can soon discern which is the legal and which is the black market. In the legal part where the *kolkhoznik*s sell their produce, there is usually a little talking and haggling; but in the "black" part, where factory-made goods are sold, there are only whispers. This market in Karmakhchi was astonishing, however; there was absolute quiet! Only the occasional bray of a donkey or camel, or the barking of a dog, disturbed the silence. The farmers were dressed in long white shirts which reached below the knees, and baggy white pajama-like pants. The women wore loose white smocks which reached the ground. All of them sat with their legs folded under them, selling their products without uttering a word. The terrible heat was so oppressive and exhausting that they didn't even bother to swat the flies away from the produce and meat. Walking through this hushed market, it seemed to me that either the entire market was legal or all of it was "black." In any event, I decided it was a dangerous place for a conspicuous man with a European face and no documents. I concluded that I'd better go and report to the labor office immediately, for the sooner I was "legalized," the sooner I could work, and eat.

Walking back to town, I spotted a tall lean man, a European, with a long gray beard. I was happy to see a Russian, someone I could talk to, and hurried towards him, intending to ask where the labor office was located. Suddenly two teenage boys jumped the man from behind, and tried to grab his bag. In the melee, the man was knocked down and the boys began pulling his beard and throwing sand in his eyes.

Seeing me approach, they grew frightened and ran away. They shouted curses back at us, but I recognized only one word: "*Ooroos* — Russian!" They quickly disappeared into the labyrinth of clay huts.

I assisted the old man to his feet and helped him brush the sand off his clothes. He thanked me profusely. When he got his breath back, I asked him, "Were those boys Kazakhs or Koreans?"

"What? You mean you can't tell the difference?" He was incredulous.

"No," I replied. "I've just arrived here."

"Welcome to the desert, young man," the old man said, shaking my hand. He studied me and then said, "My name is Lazer Kantor. I'm from Minsk." He was a Jew!

"You really fooled me!" I cried out with joy. "I was sure you were a Russian; in the Kuybishev district, most of the old Russians have long beards."

Still grasping my hand tightly, he raised his face towards the burning sun and, with eyes closed, spoke to Heaven. "Forgive me, Creator of the Universe," he whispered, "for standing here and talking while there's a *mitzvah* to be done. Abraham, our father, would have run and fetched this traveler a good meal by now." He was referring to the story of Abraham waiting in his tent, in the noonday sun, for travelers to pass by so that he could welcome them with hospitality and feed them.

"Let's go," he said, as he took my arm. "You must be hungry."

This was indeed a surprise; not only had I found a fellow Jew, but he wanted to feed me as well! In the starving Soviet Union, hospitality had died; people didn't invite others to share their food any more, not even close relatives. There was a Russian joke: "Come on over for tea, but bring your own sugar." The people were so hungry that they had absolutely nothing to share — and here was a man inviting me to his home to eat!

"No, please, grandfather," I resisted. "Thank you for your hospitality, but I only want to know where the placement office is located."

"But you saved me from those young thugs. I feel obliged to you; you can't refuse me!" he insisted.

"Thank you — I'll have some water, but I won't take your food. You don't owe me anything."

The old man began to laugh. "That shows how much you know about this place! Here water is scarcer than food! True, there is no bread here, but there are plenty of honeydews, cantaloupes and watermelons, and lots of good rice!"

As we walked to his house I asked, "Tell me, grandfather, why did those boys attack you? Is it because you're a Jew?"

He replied, "The Kazakhs don't know about anti-Semitism, but the Koreans do, somehow; Nazi propaganda transmitted from Germany to Japan and Korea reaches them in their own native tongue. But just being an *Ooroos* is good enough reason for either a Kazakh or a Korean to attack me. This time they were after the gold, though, and that's why they tried to grab my bag."

I was speechless. I had heard the USA called the *Goldene Medina* — the Golden Land, because there was gold in the streets. But here in the Soviet Union? Where everything belongs to the state, including human beings? Would they permit people to own gold? I said, "*Reb* Lazer, I know that Kazakhstan is the rice basket of the Soviet Union; but gold? Do you mean real, precious gold?"

"Precious indeed!" laughed the old man. "Would you like to smell it?"

"Since when does gold have a smell?" I asked, utterly confused.

He opened his sack a tiny bit; I bent my head down and the odor of stables overpowered me. I burst out laughing, and *Reb* Lazer Kantor joined me. "It's only horse and donkey manure," he said. "But we call it 'gold' because here it is as precious as gold!"

As we continued walking to his house, *Reb* Lazer explained that in this area there was no material for fuel, except straw, and it takes two large bundles of straw to make enough of a fire for simply boiling water. Furthermore, the straw burns so quickly that someone has to constantly feed more straw to the fire. However, dried manure burns slowly, for a long time, and so for this reason the natives kept donkeys for their manure, drying it in the hot sun. The refugees, not owning any animals, were forced to collect fresh manure in the streets, not even letting it dry out in the sun, for fear that someone else would grab it.

We stopped for a rest in the burning heat. I turned to the old man and said, "If they would only let people do business here! Trains full of melons could be shipped to Siberia and to the Volga region, and in exchange, back would come enough firewood for everyone. Oh, what a little private initiative could do for this country!"

Reb Lazer turned his head aside and closed his eyes. His beard began trembling. He placed his hand on my shoulder and said, "Son, never, never let me hear you say such words again! What you have just described is what our government calls 'speculation,' a capital offense in our Soviet society." He took my arm and we continued walking. As though quoting from a book, he added, "Comrade Stalin teaches us that personal initiative within the collective and for the collective is Bolshevik initiative and should be encouraged. However, personal initiative for private gain is nothing but speculation! Speculators are leeches on the wounds of the national organism, parasites which infest the entire national body."

I was terribly disappointed and frightened. I thought that I had developed a built-in warning system to judge a person's loyalty to the Soviet regime, and his trustworthiness. But now it seemed I had made a dreadful mistake. _Reb_ Lazer must belong to the Party, or he wouldn't be so fluent in quoting Stalin. Or was he being sarcastic? I tried to read his face, but the sun was too bright. Anyway, I'd have to be more careful from now on.

We entered a small courtyard, which had half a dozen mud houses clustered around it. There were no proper doors, only openings in the front walls. Near each doorway a few clay bricks served as a stove. Mr. Kantor's wife, standing in the doorway, greeted us warmly, and stepped outside into her outdoor kitchen. She invited me inside, and I curiously looked around their one-room house. There were two bundles of straw on the cement floor — the beds. In one corner was a bucket full of sandy water; in another corner an old fruit crate and two small boxes served as a table and chairs. This constituted all their furniture. Suddenly my eyes lit up as I spotted a _tallis_ and _tefillin_. No Party man would dare to be caught with these, I thought. He certainly must be one of us — one of those who cling to our faith in spite of all obstacles.

While the woman blew up the flame in her stove, I stepped into a corner and, facing the east wall, I put on my own _tefillin_ for my morning prayers. Mrs. Kantor called, "Lazer, Lazer, come quick!" In a moment, the two of them were standing in the doorway looking at me, tears streaming down their faces.

"You must stay with us," Mrs. Kantor insisted. "It's not every day we find a young man with _tefillin!_"

Then she began to apologize about the humble state of their house. "In Minsk we had a nice home, but here we are refugees; the natives here have never seen furniture, so we don't have any. In Rome one lives like the Romans, no?"

With a newspaper — a "refugee tablecloth," she called it — she covered the crate which served as a table. In comparison to their poverty, I was a rich man. After all, I had bread and a few hundred rubles. In addition, I knew that I'd soon have a job and receive a food card. The old man noticed my hesitation about accepting some of their meager food supply. "Don't worry," he assured me. "We are not destitute, thanks to our children." One son was a major in the air force, another a captain in the artillery, and their daughter was a physician in the navy. They hadn't heard from her since the fall of Sevastopol, he said. Before the children had enlisted, each one had signed away a percentage of his pay to be automatically sent to the parents; this way, they were army dependents, able to purchase small amounts of food.

In the ensuing conversation I learned that there was only one factory in town, the one near the railroad station. It was a military enterprise, so foreigners were not accepted for work there. Mr. Kantor then gave me directions to the labor office, and I immediately set out in the blazing heat.

When I got there, the Kazakh official asked me what my occupation was. When I proudly said, "Combine operator," he opened the door to the next room and called out, "Ai, Akhmatop, I think I have found what you are looking for!"

A heavyset man appeared in the doorway. Apparently he was already Russianized, for unlike the other Kazakhs, he wore a Russian-style shirt, dark pants, and a wide black belt. All male Kazakhs wore the native skullcaps, but this one displayed an uncovered head with a shiny brown skull.

He introduced himself, "I'm Akhmatop, the chairman of *Kolkhoz* Kuzar-Pash. We can certainly use a man like you." He spoke a fluent but ungrammatical Russian, with a heavy Kazakhi accent.

How glad they were to see me! The *kolkhoz* must have really been in great need of a combine operator, for the office cut much of the red tape, and Akhmatov personally escorted me to the police station to register. After that, he took me to the inn where Kuzar-Pash people arrived when they came to town. There we found a caravan of camels forming, and Akhmatov told me that with this caravan I would be traveling to my new home. He said that I should ride the camel next to his, "so we can talk while riding."

The big, ungainly animals made strange noises; I found their appearance very strange as well. A round drum of a belly sits upon four thin legs;

sticking out at one end is a tiny tail, and from the other end, a long, curved neck with a funny face. At the top there runs a long, bony spine with two humps in the middle. The nearest I had ever been to a camel before was in the zoo, back home in Poland. Now I'd have to ride one! I had the same feeling — eagerness mixed with fear — as when I was first introduced to horseback riding.

Remembering _Dedushka_ Anton's first lesson, that one should introduce oneself to a horse, patting him on the face, I tried it hesitantly and carefully on the camel. Fortunately, Akhmatov stopped me.

"Never do that!" he called out just in time. "Camels can bite!" He told me that camels don't like strangers, and particularly those who don't speak the native tongue.

Akhmatov gave me my first lesson, accompanied by the laughter of the surrounding Kazakhs. "When you pull down on the rope," he explained, "the camel lies down on his knees. When you finish loading, you climb on top and pull the rope upwards. He then gets to his feet and begins to walk. There's no need for patting or talking."

Following his instructions, I pulled the rope downward, climbed up on the camel, and settled myself between the two humps, on a double carpet supplied by the chairman for my comfort.

The caravan began to move. I had the usual worries on my mind: what would I do about kosher food and work on the Sabbath? Still, it was exciting to be doing something straight out of Biblical times: riding in a camel caravan across the vast desert. I had forgotten to ask how far it was to the village. As if reading my mind, the chairman turned around and said, "We'll have plenty of time to talk. It's 14 kilometers from here to our village."

I soon discovered that riding a camel was a little like being on a boat, or a seesaw. There was so much rocking back and forth that it was easy to become nauseous. The wide open spaces, the flat, endless sand, the melancholy songs of the camel drivers, and the huge red ball of sun at the edge of the horizon lulled me into a fantastic dream-like state. But I was soon awakened by Akhmatov's voice. He had slowed his camel so that he could talk to me.

Akhmatov had a thirst for information about the outside world, being cut off completely from any news beyond the Soviet borders. Most Soviet people utilized any chance of being with a Westerner to pump him for information about the world outside. Exercising caution, they would begin with some innocent little questions; then they'd ask for information about every detail of life in the free world. Most of the time, for safety's sake, they'd criticize the capitalist system, and praise their own Soviet way of life.

I was an old hand at answering such questions, always replying in a neutral way. By criticizing the regime, or showing a slight preference for capitalism over Communism, I might expose myself to most dangerous accusations — and possibly arrest and Siberia.

But Akhmatov asked only a few questions about Western capitalist life; most of his inquiries were centered around the Moslem countries. While I was fairly knowledgeable about the former, I was completely ignorant about the latter. The little I knew about the Moslem world was only in reference to the Arabs of Palestine. Akhmatov was afraid of speaking too frankly to me, especially since he was a Party man. He talked a lot, praising Stalin and the Party for what they had done for his people, forcing them to change from a nomadic life to the happiness of collectivism, opening schools, colleges and factories, and forbidding polygamy!

Time and again the chairman praised the wisdom and greatness of Stalin; and he recounted the difficulties of educating the people towards collectivization. I wanted to flatter him a little, so I said, "I admire your courage, for you had a much harder task than the Party men in Russia! There, the Party had only to convince the masses of the advantages of collectivism. But your people here in Kazakhstan had to be convinced to change their traditions and habits completely, to leave the nomadic life and settle down, to give up private ownership, to give up their extra wives! Imagine accomplishing all this with an illiterate and uncultured people!"

I had overdone it, for my last words injured his pride. I detected a tone of anger. "What do you mean, uncultured people? We have our culture and our customs! We have our social rules and our desert laws. We have no need to lock our doors, for strangers are always welcome to share our food, and thieves get killed on the spot. And what is wrong with having a few wives? Did not your forebears have more than one?"

I could not answer that, so I kept quiet.

The chairman taught me the standard greeting in Kazakhi, used day or night: *Assallam Aleikum.* It was easy for me to remember, since the Arabic sounded almost like the Hebrew *Shalom Aleichem.*

"And when someone greets you," he went on, "you reverse the order of the words and reply, '*Aleikum Assallam.*'"

He warned me never to enter a house or _kibitki_ — tent — when visiting someone. "Stay outside. If the man is at home he'll invite you in, and then you may enter. If he is not at home, the wife or daughter will come outside to talk to you, but will never invite you in! Don't ever go inside alone with a married woman, because by desert law the husband or any member of the family has the right to kill you, to save the honor of the family!"

It was late at night when we arrived in the village. Akhmatov invited me to his _kibitki_ and explained, "We do have houses, but we live in them only in winter time. All summer we prefer to live in the _kibitki_." I thought of Goncharov, the schoolteacher in Karobka: how right he was when he had said that evolution is needed to change people's habits! These people had houses, but they still put up tents next door to live in.

Akhmatov's tent was impressive. A small kerosene lamp illuminated the inside. The wall facing the entrance was covered with oriental rugs. In one corner there were some suitcases; apparently these contained the family's clothing. While the entrance and part of the tent floor were bare sand, the rest of the ground was covered with more rugs. The entire family was stretched out on them, sleeping. Akhmatov pointed to a spot on the ground, and told me to lie down and go to sleep. How odd it seemed, to be going to sleep in this tent, with a family of strangers! Nevertheless, the camel ride had been exhausting, I felt stiff and sore all over, and it was wonderful to lie down. I immediately fell into a deep sleep.

When I awoke, the tent was empty. Everyone was outside and busily at work.

In front of each tent, the women of the family ground grain in a primitive stone hand-mill. The women mixed the flour with some water, flattened the dough in a frying pan, and placed it on the primitive clay stove. In no time at all the "bread" was ready to eat; the Kazakhs called it _lepyoshki_, but to me it looked just like _matzah_. While the Jews today eat _matzah_ only on _Pesach_, I mused, the Kazakhs eat it every day of the year! In fact they didn't know any other bread but this, the Biblical "poor bread."

I decided to wash up. At the tent's entrance I had noticed an antique copper pitcher with a narrow gooseneck. I assumed it was for washing one's hands and face, but no sooner had I begun to wash than Akhmatov's mother suddenly appeared and started to scream. In a moment Akhmatov's wife rushed in and she too began to shout at me; then she grabbed the pitcher from me, and sent a child to fetch Akhmatov. I didn't know what was going on, and couldn't ask, since none of them understood Russian.

There were no towels, so I stepped outside, and instantly the hot sun dried my hands and face. Soon Akhmatov arrived on his donkey, and after silencing the screaming women, he turned to me. "I should have told you," he said. "Water is very scarce here; we never wash anything but the tips of our fingers and our nostrils, to get the desert dust out."

"You mean you never take a bath?" I asked, aghast.

He smiled and pointed proudly at his mother, all wrinkled skin and bones, and said, "You see my mother? She is 90 years old and has never had a bath in her life!" Now I began to understand why the Kazakhs scratched themselves even more than the Russians. And I began to wonder how I'd ever be able to exist here.

The chairman told me that I was not expected to start working the very first day. "Rest and get to know the people; you'll stay with me, and you'll eat with me." Turning to the excited children he spoke in Kazakhi, then translated his words into Russian for my benefit. "Children, this is Comrade Chaim. Show him around and let him get acquainted with our village."

I learned that in the offices in the cities of Kazakhstan, Russian was spoken; but in the rural areas Russian, the language of the conquerors, was deliberately avoided. Even teenagers who had been studying Russian at school for years pretended that they couldn't understand me. The chairman had to order his oldest son to speak to me in Russian, and he did so while showing me around the village.

Everywhere there was poverty. Outside the entrance to every tent was a set of flour-grinding stones, and the kitchen — the clay brick stove in the shape of an H. I learned to bow to every adult and to say "*Assallam Aleikum.*" Some invited me into their tents and offered me a drink of precious water from their copper pitchers. Apparently a drink of water was the most one could offer a stranger. In the entire village, there was only one well, and not even a real well; it was only a shallow hole in the ground. All day, the hole was dry; during the night it filled up with yellow, sandy water. At daybreak, the women came and dipped their buckets in, bringing them home a third full of sand.

Inside the tents, there were no tables, chairs or beds. The Kazakhs ate, slept and welcomed guests all on the same rug. In one corner, they all kept some suitcases to store their few belongings.

I was amazed, considering all the Soviet propaganda about free education, schools and colleges, at how little things had changed for these people; they were still living as they had lived for centuries.

When I returned to Akhmatov's tent, his wife was preparing the evening meal, surrounded by bawling, squabbling children. I could see a pot full of mutton boiling in milk, while in the other pot there was plain dry rice. The fire was kept up by frequent sprinkling with dung. I tried to think of excuses for refusing to eat the meat. I would manage with the rice, even though the sight of the greasy, filthy pot spoiled my appetite for that as well.

After sundown Akhmatov returned home. He washed — rather rinsed — the tips of his fingers and his nostrils, and then settled himself on the ground with his legs crossed under him, ready for his meal. In an effort to copy him, I also tried to fold my legs, but I found that I couldn't maintain that position comfortably for long. They all laughed, especially the children, who proudly showed me all kinds of tricks, crossing and twisting their legs into bizarre positions.

The women ate outside, while my host, his son and I ate inside. First, dried cantaloupe was served. I had seen it hanging in the sun, cut in long slices like bananas; it had a wonderful taste, fresh or dried. Then came *lepyoshki*, the flat, thin bread. I ate this too, grateful for the familiar taste. Next, a bowl of rice was placed in the middle of the carpet. I was accustomed to eating from one bowl with other people — Karobka had taught me that. But here there was a difference: the Russians had used spoons, but the Kazakhs ate with their fingers! My host dipped four fingers of his right hand skillfully into the side of the rice bowl, cupped them into the shape of a spoon and delivered a batch of steaming rice to his open mouth. His son immediately followed suit. When I realized that spoons were not used at all by these people, I decided to skip that course.

I claimed that I was already full, that coming from Russia, where food was so scarce, my appetite had diminished; I wanted to avoid insulting the hospitality of my host. After Akhmatov and his son cleaned out the rice bowl, his wife put some steaming mutton into the bowl; again the skillful fingers went into action, and again I abstained. After the meal was over, I thanked the host and his wife, and suggested politely that I'd like to find separate quarters for myself so as not to impose on them. The chairman offered me an empty house. He also told me that I could go to any garden, private or collective, and take all the fruit that I wanted.

I asked, "Why should a person be so generous in these difficult times, and let me take whatever I want from his garden?"

He explained that if this village were near a railroad station or a city, the people certainly wouldn't be so generous, for they would try to sell all their produce at the market. But because this village was out in the desert, 14 kilometers from nowhere, the fruit would only rot on the vine if people here didn't eat it.

Akhmatov also told me that in the back of the house assigned to me I would find a long narrow field of cucumbers. "You may eat as much as your heart desires; we don't eat cucumbers."

"But why do you grow something you don't eat?" I asked.

"The *Ooroos* like them, so the government makes us raise them," he said with a sneer.

Before I left, we were served tea in tiny clay cups; then one of the little boys took me to my new home.

Like all the houses in the village, it was a one-room mud house, with an open doorway in the front wall; there was a window opening, but no glass windows; and the floor was the desert sand. Since the Kazakhs themselves didn't sleep on beds, I didn't expect a bed, but here there were no rugs either; there was only sand!

Well, at least I'll have fresh air, I thought, and if it should become cold, I can cover myself with my army blanket.

I bedded down for what was the first of many dreadful nights. After dark, the mosquitoes came out in full force, and these mosquitoes were surely the most vicious and insatiable in the world! I tossed and turned on the sandy floor, but they were everywhere, stinging fiercely, and even managing to get under my army blanket.

The next morning, scratching the reddened, itching welts and worrying about malaria, I went to work. The chairman was already waiting for me, together with another Kazakh, whom he presented as my helper. Toli-payev bowed to me a few times, greeting me, his new boss, with the traditional *Assallam Aleikum*. He was a man in his fifties, who spoke a little Russian; he had been an assistant to many tractor men, but apparently he could not manage a tractor by himself.

I was about to complain to the chairman about the mosquitoes, but he quickly rode off on his donkey, in a hurry to organize the day's work. I mentioned my ordeal of the previous night to my helper, and he responded at once by inviting me to stay with him. "*Kushatch tozhe* — Also to eat," he added to his friendly invitation. I thanked him but politely refused, explaining that I preferred to live by myself, if I could only learn how to keep the mosquitoes away. He then asked my permission to leave and go to his tent;

he said he had something that might help me.

While he was gone I looked over the machine; it had been a while since I'd handled a combine and I was looking forward to it. The machine appeared to be workable, but it had been neglected for a long time and needed cleaning, greasing and oiling. I figured I could have it working in two or three days.

My helper returned, carrying a pan full of donkey manure. He presented it to me happily and told me to take it home with me, and to set fire to it before going to sleep. It would smoke all night, he said, and the smoke would keep the mosquitoes away.

Then his son appeared, leading a donkey loaded with two sacks. "One for you, and one for me," Tolipayev said, with a twinkle in his eye, patting the heavy sacks.

At first I thought it was flour, but when I read the label on the sack I was puzzled. It was chemical fertilizer, sent to the *kolkhoz* by the government of the Kazakh SSR to enrich and improve the soil.

I said, "But Tolipayev, what is this for? I'm not going to plant a garden; why do I need fertilizer?"

He whispered something to his son, who turned towards my hut, leading the donkey with the two sacks. Then he explained, "Manure doesn't always burn so well; sometimes the fire almost goes out. When that happens, this is what you do: take some of the powder from that sack and sprinkle it on the fire. You'll see — this brings the fire back up right away. My son will drop one bag off at your hut right now."

In my day's wandering about the village, I had indeed noticed that when the little smouldering manure fire in front of every tent was about to go out, the villagers would fan it back to life by sprinkling some powder on it, thus saving a precious match. I learned later that hundreds of tons of this chemical fertilizer had been sent to the Kazakhi villages by the government, for improving the soil, but the ingenious Kazakhs had found a more important use for it! Obviously no one had reported it to Moscow, not even the local Party members. Was this another way of taking revenge on the despised *Ooroos*?

I soon discovered that the precious manure was indeed a matter of life and death, and was considered more important than water. One can use the same water twice, or even three or four times, for washing; but manure burnt once turns to ashes, and that's the end of it. I had to get hold of manure somehow in order to bake my bread, cook my rice, and most of all, to fend off the vicious mosquitoes at night! From conversation with my assistant, I learned that the Kazakhs would gladly give you fruit, bread, even water, but would not part with the precious manure! That night, I used my manure very sparingly, and added more fertilizer to the fire. The heavy smoke did keep the mosquitoes away, but when I breathed it in it almost choked me. As soon as the fire died down, the mosquitoes let me know immediately, and I quickly got up to pour more fertilizer on the fire pan.

How dependent a human being is, I thought to myself. Our lives hinge on all kinds of things: food, water, air, money, medicine; but here in Kazakhstan, my life depended on donkey manure!

I resigned myself to living on fruit and cucumbers; I had abandoned any hope of baking bread or cooking rice since I didn't have enough manure. But I couldn't forgo sleep. I had to get enough sleep in order to be able to work on the combine under the blazing desert sun. And without manure, I would be unable to sleep; worse yet, I feared, I might even contract malaria from the mosquitoes.

The first day on my job, I noticed the slow movements of my Asian co-workers. It wasn't just the usual apathy and indifference so common in the Soviet Union; I realized that it was also the intense heat which made everyone slow and lethargic. The fierce sun had its influence even on strict Soviet discipline, for here the government permitted the workers to take an afternoon nap every day.

It was the first time I had ever seen all work come to a complete stop, from noon until three — and it was all sanctioned by the Party! During the afternoon siesta, I didn't sleep; instead, I went hunting for manure, for I felt my life depended on it. At the edge of the village, I came across an old Kazakh sitting in front of his tent, slicing cantaloupes and discarding the peels, throwing them to his donkey. These peeled slices were then hung in the sun and thus preserved for the winter.

The man's appearance was striking; his body was thin and straight, his head shaved clean. He had a silvery beard, combed and trimmed to a sharp point. His deep Mongolian eyes were bright and piercing. There was a donkey tethered to the tent post, and I decided that this man, and his donkey, would be my friends.

I bowed ceremoniously, greeting him with the traditional "*Assallam Aleikum.*" He returned the bow, but almost imperceptibly. I might have attributed his slight bow to his old age, but the cold look he gave me indicated hostility. He remained silent; he did not respond with "*Aleikum Assallam.*"

I would have disregarded his attitude, realizing that in his eyes I was a Russian, a non-Asian, and he had every right to dislike me. But my need for that essential manure drew me to him like a magnet. I was obsessed; I had to get some, no matter what!

I introduced myself to the old man, emphasizing the fact that I was not an *Ooroos*. "I'm a Jew, from Poland. A refugee." I repeated the statement twice, making sure that he would understand. His attitude changed at once; his face softened, he smiled and asked me to sit down, and offered me slices of fresh cantaloupe. I accepted his offer and took a seat next to his donkey, which was gobbling up the melon rinds hungrily.

The Kazakh introduced himself: "Samarkidze is my name," he said in broken Russian, but with dignity.

This was the first of many meetings between me and Samarkidze. Once he knew that I was a foreigner and not a Russian, the old man began to ask me for news of the outside world, especially Turkey, Persia and China. At first he claimed that he could not really speak Russian, but could only understand it. However, he soon dropped his pretense and began to converse with me in Russian, which he spoke quite well.

"In my youth I visited all those countries — Turkey, Persia, China," he told me. Being in his eighties now, I reasoned, he must have been around fifty when the Revolution "liberated" his country. When I asked him about this, he smiled sadly and shook his head.

"See the desert?" he cried, stretching out his arms in a wide circle, pointing to the vast sea of sand around us. "It wasn't white then — it was yellow and brown and our beautiful flocks covered it all." He told me that he had once been a rich man, driving flocks of sheep to the neighboring countries. Spring lambs and yearlings, old sheep and ewes, the various flocks had kept the people prosperous and proud. Then came the Revolution.

"The *Ooroos* were starving to death in their cities," he spat with contempt, "and Marshal Budyonny came and took all our sheep away from us, and shipped them off to the hungry *Ooroos* country."

His eyes still blazed as he told me this, although twenty-odd years had passed since then. He was referring to the Soviet Marshal Budyonny and his Cossacks, who had enforced Soviet rule in all these Moslem lands. They had suppressed any signs of nationalism with such violence and bloodshed that to this day the picture of the hated Marshal Budyonny never appeared in public, even though he was a high Party official.

I gave the old man my full interest and sympathy, and asked if I might visit him again soon; I liked to hear his stories. And so I became a daily visitor to Samarkidze's tent.

By the time the daily siesta was over, my belly would be full of canta-loupe, and my pockets full of manure. I became a thief, stealing not money, diamonds or gold, or even food, but donkey manure! I thought that perhaps I should ask the old man for the manure as a gift, or offer to buy it from him. But I had to reject the idea, for he might have been willing to sell or give it to me once or twice, but certainly not every day! Besides, I was sure that his wife, who came out of the tent every once in a while to check on him, would not allow him to part with the precious fuel.

To pacify my conscience, I told myself that the manure I was stealing was a deserved reward for my time, and for the pleasure I was giving the old man by telling him my stories and listening to his.

My fund of stories didn't last too long, however, and I soon became only a listener. He liked to tell me all about his younger days; he told me many stories, all in great detail, augmented by a little oriental exaggeration. His supply of tales was endless.

"Have you ever heard about the Koreans and the 'War of the Dogs'?" he asked me, combing his long gray beard to the ends, and clearly hoping that I hadn't.

"War of the Dogs? What's that?" I asked.

"Well," he began, "you know that we Kazakhs use many shepherd dogs for our flocks of sheep. For us, dogs are as vital as air is for breathing, and as the sky is for carrying the sun."

The Kazakhs had greatly resented the dumping of Koreans into their midst, he continued, and the Koreans themselves hated it, but neither of the two peoples would dare resist Moscow — until the Kazakhs began to lose dogs. These proud and generous nomads, who had never locked a door, had begun to notice some losses, but didn't know how to explain them. Then they discovered that their new neighbors, the Koreans, were fond of dog meat. Some dogs managed to escape from their Korean captors, and then made their way home totally blind — their eyes had been removed! And why? There was an ancient belief among the Koreans that, when old age comes and the skin shrinks, their already narrow eyes would become narrower and narrower until total blindness would set in. There was only one "remedy" for avoiding such a fate — eating a dog's eyes! The eyes had to be eaten while the person was still young, in order to preserve his own eyes, and, moreover, the eyes had to come from a live dog!

When some of the unfortunate dogs escaped and came home blinded, the Kazakhs' wild desert spirit responded. Inflamed with rage, they avenged themselves on the Koreans and thus began the War of the Dogs. Much blood was shed by both sides, until the Russians put an end to the dispute by confiscating all weapons.

On another hot afternoon, he decided to tell me about the time he was stabbed. "See these?" He pulled up his shirt and pointed to deep scars on his chest. "I'll tell you how I got them. One day I went to the city, and I noticed a Korean lying on the ground fast asleep, his face to the sun. I felt sorry for him, and figured that he didn't realize that our Kazakhstan sun would burn his face terribly. So I found a newspaper and covered his face with it, trying to shade him from the burning sun. And what do you think happened next?" He bent towards me, eyebrows raised.

"What happened?" I asked, like a schoolboy during a lesson.

He patted the scar on his chest and said, "How was I to know the Koreans' queer beliefs? They think that the soul leaves the body when a man sleeps, and therefore when a sleeping man's face is covered, his soul won't be able to find him, and he'll surely die. Another Korean passed by when I was covering the man's face; he jumped me with a knife from behind, screaming, 'What are you trying to do? Murder him just because he's a Korean?!' Before I had a chance to say anything, his knife landed between my ribs."

By now I had won his confidence, and he dared to whisper dangerous words into my ear. "*Nikolai jakhsi, Stalin djamman* — Czar Nikolai was good, Stalin is bad!" He didn't dare say these risky words in Russian; he whispered to me in Kazakhi, which I was beginning to understand quite well. He always referred to the "good old days under the Czar" when he had many flocks of sheep, and many tents — one for each wife and her children — and life was good.

The days and weeks passed uneventfully. Every day I operated the combine. There were plenty of cucumbers and fruit, as well as rice. Manure was supplied by the old man's donkey. I began to suspect that he knew what I was doing, but he closed his eyes to it. My assistant kept me supplied with the fire-enhancing chemical stolen from the government's fertilizer program!

The problem of how to avoid working on the Sabbath was solved perfectly, to my great satisfaction. Since my helper, too, had a problem with his Moslem day of rest, which was Friday, Tolipayev and I soon had a deal going. It came about on the very first day we worked together. I had carefully begun to question him about the rest day observed here.

"The normal rest day is Sunday," he told me, sounding like Soviet propaganda. "But at the call of our great leader Comrade Stalin, the people of Kazakhstan, like all the other nationalities in the Soviet Family of Nations, voluntarily gave up their day of rest in order to increase production and to win the war."

I had my doubts about this. No one had a personal interest in any job, particularly on the collective farms, and especially under the burning sun of Kazakhstan. In fact, I had to run my combine at half-speed and half-capacity, because of the laziness of the female crew, who were supposed to feed last year's harvest into the giant mouth of my combine. In addition, there was the terrible desert dust, which filled the lungs, nose and mouth with tiny dry grains of sand. The lack of water made the work twice as difficult. How then could I be expected to believe that they voluntarily gave up their day of rest?

Even though I didn't believe Tolipayev, I didn't question his statement. I dropped a hint that I wouldn't mind him taking off one day, that I could manage the machine myself. He could hardly believe what he had heard; with a whoop of joy he swept me up in his arms and began to sing! He would like to have his day off on Friday, he said; and to show his appreciation, he offered to give me a haircut and a shave!

I told him that his offer was very kind, but wasn't enough: I would rather have him cover for me on Saturdays, so that I could be free. He accepted the agreement happily, and continued to insist on a haircut and shave as well. I turned to my helper and thanked him for his generous offer. "But I don't need a haircut or a shave," I said. My faint blond beard was hardly noticeable. I didn't realize the significance of the haircut and shave until Friday came.

While Friday was officially a working day, in fact almost everyone stretched out the afternoon siesta to include the entire day. Most of the men gave and received haircuts in front of their tents. Each man was a barber, shaving the head of his neighbor with a razor blade, but without a drop of water! All heads were scraped to the scalp, thus eradicating thousands of lice.

The Kazakhs did not shave off their whiskers, though. Instead, they plucked each hair out separately, one by one, just like plucking feathers from a chicken. With each pluck, the victim grimaced in pain. This process was very time-consuming, and made me reflect on the fact that the Asian is richer than the European in one respect: he has plenty of time! After the face was plucked clean, a piece of mutton fat was rubbed on it to soothe the pain.

One day my helper invited me to a celebration that evening after work; he wouldn't tell me what the occasion was. It couldn't be a wedding, I reasoned, for there were scarcely any men of marriageable age around. It couldn't be for the birth of a baby, for surely I would have heard about it. No one would give me a hint, though, and I was eager to take part in their happy gathering, whatever the occasion was.

At siesta time, a sheep was brought to Tolipayev. My helper washed his feet, the tips of his fingers, and his nostrils, and then he covered his head. I realized I was about to witness a ritual. One of the men handed him a knife, and the other men stepped aside. Tolipayev forced the sheep to the ground, and, mumbling words I didn't understand, swiftly cut the sheep's throat. Again he washed his hands, and then the knife; he dried his hands and the knife on the sheep's fleece; then he handed over the knife and the slain sheep to the other men. A neighbor, watching the slaughtering ceremony, whispered to me that these were preparations for tonight's party.

After work, towards evening, we assembled in front of the tent where the party was being given. From inside, I heard a young boy's cries, and I realized that this must be a circumcision feast. The Moslems circumcise their sons at the age of thirteen, in remembrance of their Biblical forefather, Ishmael. ("And Ishmael, his son, was thirteen years old when he was circumcised.") Apparently the villagers continued to practice their ancient rite, and kept their secret well-hidden from the authorities.

Outside the tent, the women were all huddled over the clay ovens, busily cooking. The whole slaughtered sheep was simmering in a huge kettle, which was half-filled with milk. A second kettle contained rice and mutton fat, while a third kettle was full of corn boiling in grease. Near the fires, I noticed two empty fertilizer bags. I smiled to myself as I noted the Soviet government's "contribution" to the celebration. While the chemical fertilizer was definitely not enriching the soil, there was no doubt that it was enriching the cooking fires at this celebration of an ancient religious rite.

At sundown, the men sat in a circle on a thick oriental rug inside the tent. I sat near the entrance, in case I'd decide to leave early. My good friend Samarkidze was given the honor of washing first. A young man poured a few drops of water onto Samarkidze's feet, then onto his hands. The pitcher was then passed around the circle from man to man, and they all "washed" the same way, wiping their hands on their clothes afterwards.

The old man prostrated himself and mumbled a prayer, followed by the others. Then a goatskin container made the rounds, each man taking a few swallows. When the goatskin reached me, the host poured some of the liquid into the cup which I always carried with me. It looked like milk, but had a pungent, alcoholic smell, like whiskey. I asked my host what it was, and he replied, "Ah, this is *kissmiss*. Good, isn't it?"

I asked him what it was made of and he explained that it was mare's milk which was stored in a goatskin and fermented for over six months. This was their way of circumventing the Moslem prohibition against alcohol, for they were drinking milk and not whiskey.

Next, the guests all ate the rich rice, corn and mutton. They dug in with their hands and ate with great appetite. Fortunately it was dark, and no one could see what I did with the small portions of food that I took politely. I buried them surreptitiously in the sand behind me. I knew that this was a dangerous solution, for insulting the hospitality of a Kazakh could result in a dagger through my heart.

The days and weeks passed. My diet of cucumbers, fruit and rice began to grow monotonous. There were no books, radio broadcasts or newspapers in Russian, and I was bored and disgruntled. I decided to look for a way out of this desert *kolkhoz*. Worse yet, old Samarkidze was often ill and my visits became less frequent. Finally my fuel supply was depleted altogether. I tried to buy some manure, offering the little money that I still had, but no one would sell, since money meant nothing to them; there was nothing to buy with it. I offered them the rice that I would receive in the future, on the account of my work days, but they laughed in my face, for they knew from experience that after taxes hardly anything would be left for the membership of the collective, including me. I did have one thing left that I could barter with: the English-wool army blanket that I had received in the Polish embassy. But a blanket in Kazakhstan was worth a fortune, and no donkey could supply enough manure to pay for it! And who here could appreciate the value of an English-wool blanket? Besides, what would I use for cover at night?

And so I became a beggar. I began with my helper Tolipayev, who responded by bringing me some manure, but let me know that it was the first and last time, since he had to steal it from his family. I ended with the chairman, who responded in an "I-told-you-so" tone, saying, "Well, you weren't willing to live with me or with any other Kazakh; you had to live by yourself! If our food isn't good enough for your European stomach, it's just too bad! We give you free fruits, and you get plenty of flour and rice on your account. There is nothing in our rules stating that we must supply you with manure as well."

I concluded that I'd have to steal it. I would become a thief!

For my first raid I chose the garden of a Kazakh who lived near the place where my combine stood. The spot where his donkey was tied faced the back of my domain, the combine. Often during work I would entrust the machine to my helper while I visited the man's garden, picking watermelons and cantaloupes, treating my helper and the women workers to the fruit. Still, I had never dared touch the precious manure.

One night I sneaked back to my combine. There I waited for hours, peering and listening intently. Finally, when I thought everyone was asleep, I made my move. Slowly, stealthily, I crawled up to the donkey. I swiftly scooped up the "loot" and deposited it in my sack; since I couldn't see a thing, I scooped up some castor beans as well. When my sack was full, I began to creep away, dragging the heavy sack after me. Suddenly I realized that I was making tracks in the sand which would lead straight to my hut, so I turned around and dragged the sack in the opposite direction, crawling slowly towards the desert. Gradually, inch by inch, I reached the end of the village and beginning of the desert. There I stood up, slung the heavy sack over my shoulder, and hurried home, reaching my hut safely.

"There is no witness so terrible, no accuser so powerful, as the conscience which dwells within us," said an ancient philosopher. How true! I couldn't face that man; every time he glanced at me I was sure that he knew. I even stopped visiting his garden to pick watermelons, and though we all missed the fresh fruit, I couldn't bring myself to go in. Then, as my dung supply became depleted again, I looked for some other places. I was quite successful, and self-confidence began to replace fear. I decided to visit my neighbor again, for after all, I told myself, he was the closest and probably the safest.

I knew the "desert law": a thief was killed on the spot! And so I waited patiently next to the combine, making sure that all were asleep in the surrounding tents. I was an experienced thief by now, crawling on my belly like a snake, silently filling the sack, faking the tracks to the desert. Then, making a circle, I'd take off for home. But this time something happened!

As I was making the familiar U-turn from the edge of the desert, a terrible scream broke the silence of the night: "*Karapchook! Karapchook!* — A thief! A thief!" I was terrified. I had no doubt that I would be killed on the spot if caught! Luckily, the tracks that I had made leading to the desert paid off now, for the pursuers followed them, chasing the invisible thief into the desert. Soon barking dogs joined in the chase, and many more hoarse voices broke the stillness of the desert night.

"*Karapchook!*"

"*Karapchook!*"

I tried to run faster, but the sack was too heavy. I was approaching my hut when suddenly I heard the posse change direction; they were coming nearer and nearer, voices shouting and dogs barking wildly. I was almost paralyzed with fear — if I abandoned the sack, they would immediately recognize it as mine, but if I held on to it they'd catch up with me. I turned back, running towards the posse; I reached the combine first and hid underneath it, panting as I quickly buried my sack in the mound of rice.

Although it was a cool night, I was trembling and perspiring profusely. I hated myself for my failure, for my clumsiness and inefficiency as a thief. I was risking my life, and over what? A sack of donkey manure! The posse passed by my hiding place, and I heard them cursing the Koreans. I lay there under the combine for hours, until I was sure that they had given up and gone home.

My very survival now depended on a supply of donkey manure. I must find some way to get out of Kuzar-Pash, I decided; I couldn't continue this way any longer.

MY CHANCE to leave Kuzar-Pash
came sooner than I expected. One afternoon while I was at work on the
combine, Akhmatov's son came running to tell me that his father wanted
to see me right away. I stopped immediately and hurried to Akhmatov's
tent. I found him sitting on the ground, his feet tucked under him, his shirt
off but his pants on — and his wife was pouring water from the gooseneck
pitcher over his back and shoulders. Akhmatov was taking a bath!

Apologizing for the waste of water, he explained, "I have to go to a
Party meeting today. As a rule, before I meet with high officials my wife
washes my back; I can never reach there to do the job right."

Getting to the point, he said, "Tell me now, what have you done?"

I was completely mystified by his question. "What do you mean?" I
replied. "The combine is working beautifully. If you mean that it's running
below capacity, you should know that it's not my fault; your people are a
little slow."

"I mean, why are you being called to the police?" he said.

"What?" I cried. "This is news to me!"

He showed me a paper addressed to me which ordered me to "report
to the police station of Karmakhchi as soon as possible." "I'm sorry," he
said, "but there are no caravans going this week, so you'll have to walk to
the city."

I argued. "Since this is an official order, I think it's your duty to supply
me with transportation."

"We have no extra camels and no donkeys," he answered, "but since I
have to meet with the Korean officials in the neighboring village, you can
ride as far as there with me. From there you can go on foot to the city."

The Korean village turned out to be quite different from the Kazakh village. Inside their spotless little houses, the entire floor was raised on a bed of bricks; in the winter, a fire was built beneath the bricks, which became warm and heated the entire house — a forerunner of our radiant heating, and very cozy and comfortable. This raised floor was called a *kang*; the Koreans slept and ate on the *kang*, cool in summer and warm in winter. It was a far cry from the sandy carpeted floors of their Kazakhi neighbors.

Akhmatov told me he would see if anyone from the Korean village was planning to go to the city, in which case I could get a ride with them. But after conferring with the Koreans, he told me that no one was going today, and I'd have to go alone, on foot. "Go in that direction," he told me, pointing into the empty desert. "Don't turn right or left, just follow the sun west, and you'll get to the city. From there you can get to the Karmakhchi station easily."

The desert had no roads, nor any marks which were visible to me. I'd have to follow Akhmatov's instructions and continue to follow the sun, hoping to reach my destination. Supplied with two of my homemade *lepyoshki* and a bottle of water, I began my lonely journey. The sun was high; the heat was soon unbearable. To walk in shoes was impossible; my shoes, full of holes, quickly filled with sand. To remove them was intolerable, for the sand was burning hot.

A caravan of laden camels and villagers riding donkeys did come out of the Korean village after all, going in my direction, but no one would offer me a lift. At first I thought that perhaps this was the desert law — every man for himself, or something like that. But since when did Koreans have a "desert law"?

Later I encountered two young Koreans driving three camels. I told myself that surely they would not refuse me a ride. They stopped and asked me about myself, and when I told them that I was from Poland, one of them replied in perfect Russian, "The Poles have all left the Soviet Union. You are not a Pole, but a Jew!" Their eyes were full of hatred, and they refused me the ride.

While their refusal hurt me, their hate astonished me. For hours, as I walked along in the hot sand, my mind was absorbed by this question: how does hate travel? And what evil magic enables it to move so fast? These simple people had probably never seen a Jew before; in all Korea there is probably not a single Jew. In all Japan there might be a few hundred Jews;

and Japan, which has been occupying Korea for years, is an ally of Nazi Germany. Thus this hatred must be transported from Europe across the continent to Japan, and from there it gets to Korea. But what was strange was that these Soviet Koreans had been cut off from their homeland for years! There was absolutely no contact between the Koreans in Kazakhstan and their original homeland, not even postal service. How then could this hatred be transmitted from a people to their kinsmen over oceans and continents, and arrive intact?

I finally arrived in town and went straight to Lazer Kantor. He told me that the Polish community in Karmakhchi was in great distress; these Polish citizens suffered for every unfriendly remark about the Soviet Union which was made by the Polish government-in-exile in London. Hostility towards the Poles was intensified now as a result of some stupid remarks made by Polish government officials. Without any consideration for the fate of millions of Polish citizens under Soviet domination, they permitted diplomatic relations to deteriorate.

A few days earlier, Kantor explained, before I had been ordered to report to the police station, two Polish citizens had been called to the station. There, a major in the NKVD asked them to accept Soviet citizenship. The two men, both single, hesitated; the major told them to go home and think it over. The Polish community was also nervous about something that had occurred at the trial of a Polish-Jewish boy, two weeks before. One night, the young fellow, sitting in a restaurant with friends, had been overheard to say:

"What do people in the Soviet Union need a mouth for? Not for eating, for there is nothing to eat. Not for speaking, for we're not permitted to speak. Not for breathing, for we can breathe through our noses!"

He was arrested the same night. Two days later he was standing trial, accused of anti-war propaganda, counter-revolutionary activities, and aiding the enemy. His sentence was mild, considering the accusations: ten years in a Siberian prison camp.

In itself, the trial would not have been considered significant, for such trials were an old story in the Soviet Union. But the prosecutor's speech had been strange and ominous. Speaking of the defendant, the prosecutor had said, "This man eats Soviet bread, works in a Soviet factory, drinks Soviet water and breathes Soviet air; but he never once considered denying his fascist citizenship and asking for the honor of becoming a Soviet citizen."

At that time no one had paid much attention to these words; but now, two weeks later, they served as a warning. After several days, the two young Poles were again summoned to the police station, and again they were asked if they would like to accept Soviet citizenship. They must have declined the offer, for, in any event, they never returned from the police station. This was enough to terrify the rest of the Poles, most of whom had families and young children. One by one, all the Polish citizens were summoned to the station and "offered the opportunity to accept Soviet citizenship"; one by one they accepted. Actually, most of these people had no valid documents to prove their Polish citizenship; some of them had Polish marriage licenses, or a receipt for Polish taxes paid. The police had to take their word for it, for no one at the police station could read Polish. Many had no documents at all, and their only "proof" was the ungrammatical Russian that they spoke with a terrible Polish accent.

But there was one man who was in possession of a valid Polish passport, complete with a photograph and the official seal of the Polish embassy: me! Not that Poland deserved my loyalty, I thought to myself. I was certainly not willing to risk my freedom for the dubious privilege of Polish citizenship which wasn't worth the paper it was printed on. It was the alternative that bothered me — I was not at all eager to accept Soviet citizenship!

I got to the police station in Karmakhchi and stood in line with the other Poles, waiting to be "converted" from Pole to Russian. These Poles swore and complained, and cursed the Polish government in London. Naturally not a single word of criticism against the Russians was heard. There was one old man who had served with the Polish Prime Minister, General Sikorski, in Poland's War of Independence in 1918. This old man cursed fluently in soldierly language, regretting that he hadn't "shot that louse Sikorski then, when I had the chance!" There was no Polish chauvinism here; for the sake of their wives and children, they all readily accepted the honor of becoming Soviet citizens.

Since I didn't know any of these people, I stood by myself, not joining their talk, and wondering what to do. Should I present my passport? Perhaps it might save me from "forced conversion." Or should I keep my mouth shut about the passport? It was a valuable document, and might be very useful in the future.

While all the officers on the police force were Russians, the patrolmen themselves were Kazakhs. One of them called out the Polish names one by one, in his strange Kazakhi accent, until mine came up. He took me into a large office. A major in a blue uniform, which was the same as that worn by my interrogator when I was arrested in front of the Polish embassy in Kuybishev, was seated behind a desk. On the walls were pictures of Lenin, Stalin and the Asian Communist leader Ordzenikidze.

"Please be seated," the major said politely. "Do you smoke?" He offered me a cigarette.

"No, thank you, Comrade Major. I don't smoke."

"So — you work in Kuzar-Pash?" he began, and without waiting for my confirmation he continued. "I'm sure you realize that working on a Soviet collective farm, operating a Soviet combine, eating Soviet bread, drinking Soviet water, and breathing Soviet air practically make you a Soviet citizen. All we need is the paper formality."

I couldn't argue with such logic, and I was resigned to the inevitable, so I merely nodded my head.

"I presume that you concur with my point of view, and that you consider yourself a proud Soviet citizen. In that case, I must inform you that Soviet law does not permit dual citizenship. It is considered insulting to Soviet citizenship to share one's loyalty with any other citizenship, especially that of fascist Poland."

I was still confident that he didn't know anything about my Polish passport. No one did, except the police captain in Kzyl-Orda, whom I had bribed to give me back the document, and he would certainly not have reported it. So I nodded and said, "I understand."

The major suddenly raised his voice. "If you understand, comrade, then why don't you turn in your Polish passport?!"

His words, his tone and the furious look on his face drove a cold chill through my bones. Somehow he had found out about my passport! Was it the police captain at the station in Kzyl-Orda who had reported me, or was the NKVD digging up my past? I'd heard people say that the NKVD has the memory of an elephant; perhaps they had even dug up my desertion from the Soviet army!

The major grew impatient. "Do I understand by your silence that you refuse to accept Soviet citizenship?"

How could I buy a little more time? I finally spoke up. "Comrade Major, I certainly do not reject Soviet citizenship; I merely want to point out that what seems logical is not always the law, and what is the law is not always logical. By accepting Soviet citizenship, a person automatically rejects his former citizenship — correct? Correct, according to Soviet law; but Polish law prescribes a different procedure for changing citizenship. I must write to the president of the Polish republic, whose present residence is in London, and ask to be relieved of my Polish citizenship. Since the Soviet government recognizes the Polish government in London, I don't see how else it can be done."

The major leaned back in his chair, his eyes shifting back and forth. I figured that he would not dare to make a decision on his own on a matter which might involve international relations. He would have to contact the Soviet Commissariat for Foreign Affairs, and this could take months! His silence encouraged me; the legal hang-up which I had just created would buy me some time. It was well-known that Soviet orders are often reversed, sometimes within a few days. In the meantime, they wouldn't be able to force Soviet citizenship on me, and eventually they might stop the whole campaign of forced citizenship. There might even be a chance that the major would consent to my writing to London. And perhaps, I hoped wildly, knowledge of this case might create an uproar there, and possibly result in ending these "conversions."

I handed my passport to the major, like a diplomat presenting his credentials. He studied it carefully, checking and double-checking the photograph, the seal and the signature. I saw that he could not read the foreign languages; he read only the Russian text. If he had understood French or Polish, he surely would have noticed my profession: rabbi. Every clergyman is branded as an enemy of the Soviet regime; I could imagine the consequences of a Polish-Jewish clergyman refusing to accept Soviet citizenship by invoking a non-existent law!

After the major finished studying my passport, he scribbled something on a sheet of paper. Then he called in a policeman from the other office, and asked him to occupy his desk for a few minutes. I was sure he would call his superior; my document, and especially the new law which I had created on the spot, had thrown him into confusion, and he was going to ask for instructions about how to proceed further.

The man who came in to take his place at the desk was in regular police uniform, with the rank of lieutenant. His chest was decorated with medals and orders; two stars on blue velvet showed me that he had been wounded twice. He limped, dragging his left foot. He was of average height, had soft brown eyes and such a gentle, friendly face that I wondered how it was that he wore the uniform of the dreaded Soviet police.

He took the major's seat, and his eyes fell on my passport. He read the Russian column, but then, to my horror, he began to read the French column too! First he read the Russian text, then he repeated the French text to himself, a little hesitantly, but steadily. The Russian aristocracy under the Czar, as well as the intelligentsia, had spoken more French than Russian. I knew that such a person could not possibly be in the Soviet police; therefore I concluded that he must be one of the specially-trained NKVD men! It was just my misfortune that he had to wind up in Karmakhchi!

He reached the line which stated in French: "Occupation: RABBIN." He repeated the line twice, as though to make sure he had read it correctly. Then he raised his head and said with a smile, "So you are a rabbi?"

A cold shiver passed through me. I knew his smile must be a disguise for his hatred. My secret was out! In a few minutes the major would return with the news that the wonderful law I had just invented did not exist; and then the lieutenant would tell him that I'm a clergyman! I was finished, done for! I did not reply to the lieutenant's question, for I had lost the power of speech.

In a few minutes the major returned, but the lieutenant did not say a word to him about my being a rabbi; he merely asked permission to leave, and returned to his room.

The major's face was serious. Suddenly he raised his heavy hand and pounded on the table so fiercely that everything on it flew into the air. Jabbing his finger into my face he shouted, "You will not write to London yourself! You will not write to anyone! Do you hear me?! That is an order! If you write anything to anybody I will have you put away for good in a place that will make you forget that London even exists!"

Then he calmed down, and in a lower voice he told me that my case would go to Moscow for clarification, and in the meantime it was forbidden for me to leave the district. I was to report to the police station here in Karmakhchi every three days. I pointed out that it took me a whole day to get there, and another day to go back, which meant that the combine would stay idle for at least two days out of every three; the major changed it to every two weeks. He handed me a yellow document — the police would record each of my bi-weekly visits. He filed away my Polish passport; my case was undecided until further notice.

I didn't ask him about the current status of my citizenship. Was I a Soviet citizen now, or was I still a Polish citizen? It didn't matter....

Leaving his office, I came face to face with the lieutenant who knew my secret. My heart sank; but to my astonishment he smiled, opened the door for me and wished me good-bye. A miracle? Or a trick? What kind of a policeman was he if he did not immediately report my status as rabbi to his superiors?

When I returned to town, I told Mr. Kantor about the miracle — how the lieutenant had not betrayed me. He too was astonished and said, "But do you know who he is? He's not just a lieutenant; he's the police commandant!" Then he quoted an expression from the Talmud: "*Gam zo l'tovah* — This, too, is for the best!" He pointed out that it was to everyone's advantage that I would be coming into town to report to the police. "The High Holidays are coming and we need someone to conduct the services!"

"What?" I was surprised and excited. "Can you really organize a '*shul*' here? Openly? Is it legal?"

"No, of course it's not legal; certainly it can't be done openly. But just let me worry about the details. The main thing is that we have a *sefer* Torah, and, thanks to you, a cantor!"

A *minyan*, a quorum of at least ten men, is required for conducting services. Since no one would be permitted to take time off from his job to attend services, Lazer Kantor and his friends set up a plan: ten men would start the services, and every two hours, five men would get themselves excused from their jobs under various pretenses, replacing five other worshippers. The problem was where to hold the services. Since all houses were built facing a common courtyard, it would be impossible to conceal from the neighbors the fact that something unusual was going on. The sight of people congregating, singing and coming and going, would be highly suspicious and the police would surely be informed. However, there was one isolated house, and the location was ideal; it was at the edge of the Moslem cemetery. But Selim, the cemetery keeper, absolutely refused to rent it out; he hated Jews!

Nonetheless, Mr. Kantor persisted; he told the cemetery keeper that his wife was very sick and the doctor had ordered privacy and tranquillity. Therefore he was only asking to use the house for one month; he asked the keeper to not even visit the house, since she needed complete rest and must not be disturbed. Selim was adamant, but Lazer Kantor used some arm-twisting and a bit of blackmail. The deal was finally made after Mr. Kantor handed over a substantial sum of money to the keeper.

A primitive alarm system was rigged up. During services, a woman would be stationed outside. If the police appeared, she was to pull a string which would ring the bell, and all the worshippers would quickly disperse into the graveyard.

"You see, all we needed," said Mr. Kantor, "was a *chazan* who knew the prayers by heart. We don't have prayer books; there are only two in the whole town. And the younger people don't understand Hebrew anyway; you'll have to translate for them. So you see, that's why I said that everything is for the best. Without this police order for you to report every two weeks, you'd be stuck in Kuzar-Pash, and we'd be deprived of a cantor!"

He was happy, and some of his happiness rubbed off on me. We both repeated the Talmudic saying, "*Gam zo l'tovah!*"

I went to the inn where the Kuzar-Pash villagers always stayed when they came to town. There I found a camel caravan assembling to return to the village. There were only four men in charge of a dozen camels, so the leader assigned me one to ride on. The camel was old and skinny, and I bounced along between the sharp humps. It occurred to me that the leader may have purposely assigned this bony old camel to me. With no rugs or saddle for comfort, the camel's every move caused me excruciating pain. Soon my skin became inflamed and irritated, and each jog was torture.

After we had traveled some miles into the desert, I decided that I couldn't bear the pain any more and must change camels. I called to the caravan leader again and again to ask him to stop, but he and the three men with him were engrossed in singing their melancholy oriental songs, and ignored my calls.

Since the caravan was moving slowly, I decided to try to change camels while they were moving. I gingerly climbed off my camel; on the ground my legs felt much better, so I walked for a while to get some exercise. I reached up to touch each camel, patting them and feeling for some fat on the bones. Suddenly all the camels broke into a run; they were not loaded and, feeling they were nearing home, they sped along the sands, quick as the wind. The Kazakhs had not noticed that I was walking... or perhaps they had. In any event, the caravan left me behind. I called, I screamed, but all in vain; either they didn't hear me or they pretended they didn't. Suddenly I was alone in the desert.

I could have made my way back to the city, but it was miles away, and who knew when another caravan would be leaving for Kuzar-Pash? In the meantime, the combine would stay idle, and this would strain my relations with Chairman Akhmatov; with the High Holidays approaching I needed his good will. I decided to follow my nose and walk in a straight line to Kuzar-Pash, the way I had come.

The tranquillity of the desert night has a peculiar effect. I said my evening prayers with deep feeling...I was alone with God in the vast desert. From a distance, I heard a queer wailing sound; I knew these were the cries of hyenas, but the sound made me think of babies crying, outside, left all alone with no one to care for them. My thoughts drifted to memories of my little brothers. How were they? Did they think about me as much as I thought about them? What was happening to them under the Germans? Did they know where I was at all? How could I send them a message that I was alive?

I walked and walked, trying to keep to a straight line in the pathless desert, turning neither right nor left. The darkness became thick and dense, and I wondered if the plague of darkness that befell Egypt was like this. According to the Bible, it was such a compressed darkness that it could be felt! It seemed to close in on me, and I was short of breath; I prayed for a breeze to move the air, but in vain.

I felt thirsty and parched, completely dried out. Knowing that there were no villages until Kuzar-Pash made it worse; I would have given half my life for a drink of water. Perhaps if I called or sang I'd attract some human beings: a lone shepherd, perhaps, or a camel caravan. So I began to cry out loudly, shouting into the vast emptiness. It seemed to me that my voice carried for miles, but there was no reply. Finally fear began to overtake me, fear of the unknown. The boundless desert, the night, the loneliness... Like sand slowing down machinery, the dreadful solitude seemed to slow down my spirits. I needed company.

But I had God! I was not alone! I began to recite some psalms which I knew by heart. I let my voice ring out: "They wandered about in the wilderness, in the desert path; they could not find an inhabited city. Hungry and thirsty, their soul within them fainted. Then they cried unto the Lord when they were in distress; out of their afflictions He delivered them. And He led them forth on the right way, that they might go to an inhabited city."

Suddenly I saw a moving object to my right. First, the silhouette of one camel, then others — a whole caravan of camels! My prayers had been answered! I ran in the direction of the caravan, shouting loudly, "*Assallam*

Aleikum," but no answer came. Perhaps they were sleeping? The Kazakhs often did that — they went to sleep astride their camels, for the animals knew their way home.

Running as quickly as I could, I should have been getting closer to the ghostly caravan, but somehow it seemed to be getting farther and farther away, and then it disappeared.

How far had I run in this direction? Without a compass, I feared that I might wander aimlessly, never reaching a human settlement! And then the outline of a house appeared. I was overjoyed! I ran towards it, but suddenly it was gone. Then other houses appeared in the opposite direction. I ran towards them too, but they all faded as quickly as they had appeared. Did the desert have the power to create visions according to my wishful thinking? Delusions, hallucinations!

Then the faint outlines of more houses appeared, and tents; there were tents and houses everywhere, to the right and to the left. A whole village! I ran in all directions, even though I realized that it was a mirage — yet, suppose one of the houses or tents was real? Could I afford to miss a chance? I lost all sense of direction; I knew it, and it increased my fears....I was alone in the endless desert, lost, utterly lost....

In the distance, two small lights suddenly appeared. I regained my courage, and ran towards them, trying to reach them as quickly as possible, before they went out. Then it seemed to me that the two greenish lights were moving — but softly, quietly! The moving object came closer and closer to me; could it be the headlights of a truck? But why no noise? And is the distance from one headlight to the other that small? Is the radiator that narrow? Or is it the distance that makes it look so queer? And if it's not a truck, then what can it be? An animal! A wild beast!

Yes! The old Kazakh in Kuzar-Pash had told me stories about wild beasts attacking his flocks at night. The beasts lost their way in the desert, the old man explained, descending from the mountains in search of prey. Those fierce lights must be the eyes of such a wild beast: they shine in the dark, and they are close to each other....

I ran away furiously, too frightened to look back. What kind of beast is it? A tiger, a mountain lion, some beast I'd never heard of? Run, run... faster, faster — don't look back! It must be a tiger — I read once that their eyes shine in the dark....But what difference did it really make? Run, run!

I felt my strength waning. Gulping my tears, I began to pray: "My God, my God, why have You forsaken me? In You did our fathers trust! Unto

You they cried and were delivered...."

I was utterly exhausted. I tripped over a small bush and fell flat upon the sand. My legs wouldn't serve me any longer; they just refused to get up and run again! Looking up at the black sky, I whispered, "Father in Heaven, if I must die, don't let it be here, in a desert, without even a grave! Why couldn't I die at home, among my dear ones? Oh God, help me! Save me!"

I whispered "*Shema Yisrael* — Hear, O Israel"...and these words calmed me. I stopped resisting, and prepared myself for death. There was nothing I could do to change the situation. "The Lord is my shepherd.... Yea, though I walk through the valley of the shadow of death, I will fear no evil, for You are with me!"

My mind and body were drained, utterly exhausted — and I slept....

Standing before me was Papa, all in white. His shining, deep-set eyes seemed to look through me. He stretched out his right hand over my head, as though he were blessing me. I wasn't alone anymore — Papa was with me!

"Oh, Papa! Talk to me! Tell me, how is Mama? And Lazer, and Shimon? Oh, how I want to be back home with you all, to be all together again! I didn't want to leave — you and Mama made me go, and I couldn't disobey you. I remember Mama's words: 'Go, my son, go!' I never ate *treif* food, Papa, and I never failed to pray, or to wear my *tefillin*. I kept Shabbos, no matter how difficult. But Papa, my strength is diminishing and I'm getting weaker. Save me, Papa! Save me!"

Papa did not reply; he only caressed my cheek. Tears shone in his eyes. Were they tears of sorrow or of joy, of pain or happiness? One of his tears fell onto my face, and then another. Then, without having uttered a word, Papa disappeared, and I woke up. Papa's teardrops were still on my cheek. I sat up and looked around me; the red sun in the east foretold a new, hot day.

Were they really Papa's tears? Or was it dew? But there is no dew here in the dry desert!

But why had Papa been silent? Not a word, no advice, no message. Nothing! Nothing at all! Perhaps — Papa is dead? Dead? God forbid! Bite your tongue, you fool! But can a living person appear in a dream? Oh, what a foolish question! Of course Papa is alive; he's too young to die! But why the white robe? Because he is...? Did his soul fly across the continent to save his son in a night of terror, to protect me, to save me from the beast? What about the beast? Perhaps he too was part of the strange dream?

But if Papa is dead, then how is Mama? I thought. And the children! Who will take care of them? Oh, how I want to be back home! I'll never forgive myself for leaving! I should have disobeyed Mama when she said, "Go, my son, go!" — and yet....

The barking of dogs and the morning crow of roosters roused me from my reverie. Somewhere nearby there must be a village. Still wondering and worrying about Papa, I walked in the direction of the sounds, and after walking a kilometer, I saw a village of tents. On the outskirts of the village I met a small man leading a donkey. He was approaching the village from the same part of the desert that I had come from, and his donkey was laden with two dead sheep. He was chewing _lepyoshka_, eating his breakfast while he walked. I was hungry enough to beg him for a piece of his bread, which he gladly shared with me. When I asked him directions he pointed southeast into the desert. "That is the way to Kuzar-Pash," he told me. "About 13 kilometers from here." I asked him about the dead sheep, and he told me that he was the village shepherd, and he was bringing the carcasses to the chairman's office to prove that they had been killed by a beast; otherwise he might be accused of stealing, and selling part of his flock!

The bread fell out of my mouth. "A beast?" I asked. "What kind of beast?"

He pointed to his rifle. "I don't know what kind, but I hit him, all right! It was probably some kind of big cat, because the flock went into a stampede. It was dark when he attacked, but I could see his shining eyes. I know I hit him, because in the morning I traced his blood into the desert!"

So there really had been a beast last night! That part was real! Perhaps it followed me after it had been shot? Bleeding and weak, it may not have had the strength to chase me. These carcasses were my _kapparah_! I stepped closer and patted the dead sheep, filled with the terrible thought that I could have been in their stead!

The shepherd must have noticed my dehydrated state, for he offered me a drink — "Only three swallows, now" — from his leather bottle. Then slowly, like a sleep-walker, I turned and followed the sun to Kuzar-Pash.

Every two weeks, when I went to register at the Karmakhchi police station, I managed to avoid the lieutenant who could read French and knew my secret. I would stand for hours outside the police station, waiting until he came out of the building and limped off with his leg dragging; only then would I go in.

After registering, I would visit Lazer Kantor; I was constantly asking him if he could think of places where I could find a job. The conditions in the village had become unbearable for me; I was sick of cucumbers and rice, and of having to find new ways to steal manure. "I'll have to run away, if I can't find a job soon," I told him. "I can't stand it much longer!"

"Calm down, son," Mr. Kantor used to tell me. "Don't do anything foolish; believe me, they're experts at catching deserters here!" He explained to me that many Kazakhs had chosen to flee to the desert rather than report for the draft. Most Kazakhs had never even heard of Germany, and suddenly they were expected to go into battle against the Germans. They were naturally not eager to face an enemy they'd never heard of, to die without knowing why! Worse yet, while they were being drafted and forced to go to war, the Koreans were not drafted at all; they remained free to carry on and roam the countryside, free to steal from the Kazakhs as much as they could.

I had noticed that there were many young Korean men around, and Mr. Kantor explained why they weren't being drafted. In normal times, he told me, before the war, Koreans were drafted just as all other citizens were. Then the war broke out, and many Soviet army units fell into German hands. The Germans, mistaking the Koreans for their Japanese allies, shipped the Korean prisoners to Japan. There the Soviet-Koreans engaged in anti-Soviet propaganda, and sent broadcasts aimed at the Koreans within the Soviet Union. Stalin at once classified all Koreans as "traitors and enemies of the Soviet Union." No matter what the Koreans did to try to prove their loyalty, it didn't help. All Koreans were now removed from the armed services, and were barred from jobs in military factories, railroads, army supplies, and...from bakery shops! Even Korean Party members were not trusted any longer.

So now, they were filling up the cities, unemployed, bitter and depressed. They drifted into drinking and crime. There were reports of children disappearing, and the Koreans were even suspected of cannibalism! People refused to buy meat unless a piece of the hide was left on it, in order to identify it. Was it horse meat or camel or donkey meat? Or perhaps dog, cat or...?

All this had a terribly demoralizing effect on the Kazakhs, who were being sent to war to sacrifice their lives for Stalin and the Soviet Fatherland. Therefore, many Kazakhs of army age simply disappeared into the desert. Occasionally the authorities would surround and isolate whole villages, making it impossible for the families of the draft evaders to carry food to their men hiding in the desert caves. Some of these deserters died of starvation; others returned hungry and thirsty, begging for mercy, and some crossed the border into China. As for me, I couldn't just run away, for the police were always on the alert; if I were caught, that would be the end.

"If you run away now, what will we do for our High Holiday services? Please don't fail us," Mr. Kantor pleaded with me. All the arrangements for the secret *shul* were completed; he had rented the house from the cemetery keeper, and all the Jews in town were trying to arrange ways to be at the services. This was not easy; they had to avoid arousing any suspicion from their co-workers and supervisors. "Just don't let us down, Chaim. With the Almighty's help we'll have a *minyan!*" he ended with a deep sigh.

Since my required appearances at the police station had to do with "national security," Akhmatov was obliged to provide me with transportation. However, I deliberately refrained from asking him to furnish it, because my plan was to report irregularly and not *exactly* every two weeks: *Yom Kippur* falls nine days after *Rosh Hashanah*, and therefore, if I had already established a slightly irregular schedule, I could report on *Rosh Hashanah*, manage to "miss" a returning caravan and stay in town for the second day of the holiday, and report again eight days later, on *Yom Kippur*. If I were to follow my instructions and report precisely after two weeks, I would miss all three of the Holy Days. I therefore began to establish my irregular pattern, and any day that I saw a caravan preparing to go to town, as long as it was within a two-week period, I'd go along with them. And so, on the first day of *Rosh Hashanah* I reported early to the police at the Karmakhchi station, and then to God and His faithful clandestine congregation!

I had arrived on *Erev Rosh Hashanah*, just before sundown. Mrs. Kantor took me to the secret *shul*, telling me that her husband and another man were already there, "making all the necessary preparations."

"Is there so much to prepare?" I asked.

"Plenty," she replied, glancing behind her all the way to make sure no one was following us. She explained that they were expecting a full house at the evening services, but that probably only half of the people would attend in the morning. During the day people were supposed to be working, and if they all took the day off, the officials would certainly become suspicious. The plan was for certain men to sneak away from their jobs at different hours, thus insuring a *minyan* throughout the services.

It was already dark when we arrived at the Moslem cemetery. A number of shadows emerged from behind the old tombstones. Mrs. Kantor greeted them with the traditional "Good *Yom Tov*" and "Happy New Year," and the voices replied, "And the same to you!"

Sitting in front of the isolated house was the "guard," an elderly woman, closely observing every moving shadow. She was holding the end of a rope, ready to ring the bell and sound the alarm in case any uninvited stranger should appear. Inside, the house was illuminated by homemade candles. Mr. Kantor and his helper were still busy with last minute arrangements. A large rug had been hung on one wall, and a Torah scroll was leaning against it. The homemade candles flickered and sputtered, sending sparks of light in all directions, creating fleeting shadows throughout the room. Another rug, separating the men from the women, had been strategically placed so that both were equally close to a door and a window — emergency exits — in case the *shul* was discovered.

As the worshipers arrived and began to fill up the house, Lazer Kantor and his helper told us all what to do if we should hear the alarm bell. The congregants were middle-aged or old — there wasn't a single child present! When I asked Mr. Kantor about this, he explained that for reasons of safety he had ordered, "No children!" Some of those present were wearing uniforms of officers or enlisted men. There were some on crutches, some with a leg missing, some with an empty sleeve pinned to their side. Their chests were loaded with medals, and the insignia of nearly all branches of the armed services were represented.

The time had come to start the services. Mr. Kantor introduced me to the congregation, and he repeated the emergency evacuation instructions. He also requested the worshipers not to raise their voices — "neither in prayer nor in weeping, and that goes for the *chazan* too," he emphasized. He himself would stand near the women and read aloud because there weren't enough prayer books. "The men can repeat the prayers after the cantor," he said, assuring them that the cantor knew most of the prayers by heart.

The evening services passed without incident. Occasionally, carried away by the prayers, I raised my voice without realizing it; then Lazer

Kantor would remind me of our circumstances. The members of the congregation were overcome with emotion, praying and crying with hearts full of pain. Faraway husbands, sons, and brothers were fighting a bloody battle against the Germans. Many had lost their children, many their parents. For some of these people it was the first time in years that they were able to attend a _Rosh Hashanah_ service. And if they raised their voices in weeping, there was a guard to silence them, reminding them of the danger of being discovered.

In my heart, I was back with my family, suffering together with them, praying together with them. "Remember us unto life, O King, Who delightest in life, and inscribe us in the Book of Life, for Your own sake, O living God!" I prayed fervently, engrossed in every word. "Then shall the just also see and be glad, and the upright shall exult, and the pious triumphantly rejoice, while iniquity shall close her mouth, and all wickedness shall be wholly consumed by smoke, when You make the dominion of arrogance pass away from the earth!"

The second day, too, went well. People came and went, maintaining a _minyan_ at all times. Everyone was happy at having been able to outsmart the police.

"Let's hope _Yom Kippur_ will be the same," was the expression on everyone's lips. Elation and new hope sprang in their tired souls; their faces reflected the glory of the Heavenly Kingdom.

This was my first experience in the capacity of _chazan_. I wasn't certain of all the melodies; often, I filled in with sighs or tears. Later that afternoon, a few women came to me, bringing food for the holiday. What I couldn't eat they packed up, and I took it with me to Kuzar-Pash.

I had been absent from work for two days now, and the police registration accounted for only one. Fortunately, I found that a caravan was preparing to leave, and the man in charge assured me that no caravan had set out for Kuzar-Pash the day before, which was an excellent excuse for not being back on time. I picked a fat, well-padded camel for the ride back; there would be no more skinny camels for me — I had learned my lesson!

As _Yom Kippur_, the Day of Atonement, approached, I knew that I'd run into trouble telling the chairman that I had to return to the city and report to the police only eight days after my last trip. I racked my brains. Maybe...maybe this might do it...Our work was behind schedule. Because of the workers' laziness and the afternoon siesta, our combine worked at only half its capacity.

I suggested to Akhmatov, "Why not try to work during the night instead of the day?" I pointed out that by sleeping during the heat of the day and working in the coolness of the night, we could increase our productivity. There weren't enough people to work two shifts, day and night, but one night shift would be ideal. I managed to convince my helpers that night work would be better for us all; the dust, instead of choking them and irritating their lungs, would be carried away by the night wind. Besides, this would give them the whole day for themselves. Behind my plan was the hope that by working part of the night, and getting some sleep while my helper operated the combine, I could use the day for walking to town, and arrive there before sundown — in time to chant *Kol Nidrei* for the congregation. Akhmatov agreed, and we began working nights instead of days.

The morning before *Yom Kippur*, I set out at the crack of dawn. I took along a bottle of water and three *lepyoshki* which I had baked myself the day before. I would eat one during the journey, one just before sundown, when the *Yom Kippur* fast begins, and the third was to be saved for after the fast.

It was a tormenting journey. For one thing, I was sleepy; during the night I hadn't slept much because of the noisy machine. The sand grew so hot that I could have fried an egg on it. I removed my shoes for a while, but I soon had to put them back on, for my feet were burning in the hot sand. Much sooner than I expected, my water bottle was emptied. I had eaten one piece of bread; the other two I didn't dare to touch. My mouth was dry, and my head was beginning to spin. How far did I have to go yet? There are no signposts in the desert.

I began to fear that I had stopped to rest too often. Judging by my diminishing strength, and from the fact that the sun had already passed to the western side of the horizon, I tried to convince myself that the town was not far ahead. The thought of being late for the services drove me on. But my feet hurt me so much that I could hardly move them. I had to stop and rest, again and again.

The sun was about to set. I had to get some water before sundown; I wouldn't be able to drink until the next night. By now my body was dehydrated, every cell in it crying for water. Suddenly I noticed passersby and I was certain that the city must be quite close; I began to munch on my second bread. It was hard to swallow; I had to force it down my parched throat. I begged for water from every passerby, but no one responded. Finally one took pity on me and gave me half a watermelon. The fruit refreshed me a little, but my blistered feet wouldn't carry me any further.

My heart was crying. So close to a Jewish community, and services on _Yom Kippur_, and I felt I could not walk another step! Then I thought of Lazer Kantor's words: "Remember, Chaim, we are depending on you. After all the risks we took to organize the services, please don't fail us!" I tried to think about man's latent powers, the hidden reserves of strength which awaken only in time of danger. I remembered my escape from the beast that dreadful night. Where were my reserves now? I talked to myself as if body and soul were two separate entities — but to no avail.

An old Korean on a donkey passed by. No Korean ever helped a despised _Ooroos_, and any European face was anathema to them, so I expected no help from him. But suddenly he stopped, and turned around. Without saying a word he handed me his water bottle, then helped me up on his donkey. I held on to him tightly, and thanked him, first in Russian, then in Kazakhi, for I didn't know a word of Korean. He was as mute as his donkey! Soon we arrived in town. He gently pushed me off the donkey, and without saying a word, he kept on riding! I was amazed at his strange behavior. Was he really mute? Or was he Eliyahu _Ha-Navi_...?

The rays of the setting sun were reflected on the metal roof of the police station of Karmakhchi. Afterwards, when I appeared in the doorway of Kantor's house, he exuded relief. "Chaim! Thank God! I was afraid something had happened and you wouldn't make it!" he cried. I put my head in his bucket of water and drank and drank. Mrs. Kantor served me rice. I had to gulp it down quickly, for the sun's rays were almost gone. The fast of _Yom Kippur_ began....

Instead of candles, a kerosene lamp was burning in the synagogue. Its flame created flickering shadows, like human souls coming to participate in this holy night of _Kol Nidrei_.

A woman arrived, carrying a baby in her arms. I was surprised, for I knew that Kantor had forbidden the people to bring children with them. The woman unwrapped the baby, and it was — a Torah scroll! Everyone kissed the scroll with emotion and tears. _Reb_ Lazer placed it in front of the kerosene lamp. Then he turned to me and said, "Remember, if the alarm bell rings, forget about me, yourself, or anything else. Just grab the _sefer_ Torah and run! Run so fast that their unclean hands will not have a chance to touch this holy scroll!"

We were about to begin _Kol Nidrei_. There were two _talleisim_, prayer shawls, and Mr. Kantor and I were putting them on when the outside door opened. Two older women came in, and behind them a tall, well-dressed young woman. A wave of whispers passed through the crowd. Many of the worshippers covered their faces and began to move towards the exits.

Old Mrs. Kantor turned to one of the women and asked, "For God's sake, why did you have to bring *her* here?!"

The commotion was increasing. I asked Lazer Kantor, "What's wrong? Who is she?"

He whispered, "The girl is secretary to the district prosecutor and, of course, a *Comsomol*. No one trusts her; her mother shouldn't have brought her here. Who knows what will happen now?"

People began to leave. Immediately the girl's mother stepped up to the table where the Torah scroll was standing. She turned and faced the congregation.

"My dear brothers and sisters," she said, tears choking her words, "you all know that my husband was a Party man, and was killed delivering arms to the battlefront. My daughter is a member of the *Comsomol*, and has never seen the inside of a *shul*.

"On *Rosh Hashanah*, I attended the services here and kept it a secret from her. But a mother can't hide everything from her only child, and when she heard something about coming here on *Yom Kippur*, she begged me to bring her. First I refused, but I saw that she only wanted to pray for her dead father; how could I refuse? On the contrary, I was happy! Still, I was worried about her being a *Comsomol*, so to make sure, I swore to her, and I repeat my oath before you all, and before our holy Torah: if anything goes wrong, and my daughter is to blame, I'll commit suicide! But believe me, I know my child and she can be trusted!"

The woman's voice faltered, and all that could be heard were her muffled sobs, which were soon drowned out by the weeping of the others in the congregation.

The commotion subsided. People who were about to leave the room stayed. The woman took her place next to her daughter. When it grew quiet, I said, "I'm sure nothing will go wrong; we trust your daughter, just as you do. Why shouldn't we believe that the Jewish spark has been kindled in her soul? By coming here tonight, she, like all of us, is risking her life and proclaiming belief in the God of Israel!"

I began the *Kol Nidrei* prayer in a hoarse, low voice. The ancient melody sounded strange here, but the mood, the environment, were right; the weeping was heartbreaking.

"From this *Yom Kippur* until the next *Yom Kippur*, may it come to us in happiness!" I chanted.

Mr. Kantor occasionally had to remind the congregation of the reality outside. "Please, lower your voices. Try to cry only within yourselves," he begged them. But who can control waves of emotion? Indeed, here were not only waves, but an entire sea! Bitterness and pain, held in for so long, were finally finding expression, and could not be stopped.

"Oh Lord," I translated into Russian for the benefit of those who did not understand Hebrew, "Renew our days as of old!"....

"Oh cast us not off in time of old age; forsake us not when our strength faileth!"

Finally we came to the last prayer of the evening. With deep emotion the prayer rose up: "Our Father, our King! Have compassion upon us and upon our children and infants!"

"Do this for the sake of those who were slain for Thy Holy Name; who were slaughtered for Thy Unity! Do it for the sake of those who went through fire and water for the sanctification of Thy name!"

I cried bitterly; I was pleading for my family's safety. Completely unaware of my surroundings, I wept: "Because of this holy scroll which You gave us we have been murdered, robbed and tortured in every generation!" I stretched out my hand to touch the *sefer* Torah, but it wasn't there! Something had gone wrong!

I slowly opened my eyes. Through a veil of tears I saw the blue uniform of a policeman. He was the lieutenant who had read the French words on my Polish passport, who knew that I was a rabbi! He stood there in stern silence with his police cap in hand.

Old Lazer Kantor approached the lieutenant and said, "Take me. I'm guilty! This young man is completely innocent. I made him come here."

The officer replied with a thin smile, "No, old man, what can I do with you? That young man is the one I'm after!" He then turned to me and said, "Let's go. You're under arrest!"

Kantor followed behind us, pleading with the officer. "Please, lieutenant, take me; I'll confess easily, I'll sign, I'll admit anything you ask — just let him go!"

The lieutenant ignored Kantor, and he cried out to me, "Don't worry, my son, we will not rest, even if I have to go to Stalin himself....It was all my fault. May God be with you!"

I too was crying. "Don't torture yourself, Grandfather; it wasn't your fault. You only did what a Jew should do. It seems it has to be this way. Tell the people that I don't know any of their names, so they have nothing to worry about! May they all be sealed for a good year of life, happiness and peace." The old man stopped following us.

As the lieutenant and I went on to the police station, he remarked, "I could have arrested the old man, but what do I want with him? I'd rather have some interesting conversation with a rabbi."

I was frightened to death. I could already imagine the trial: a foreigner, a spy, confession beyond the wildest imagination, and then — twenty years in Siberia! I thought of the popular Russian expression: "May God give us health, Stalin will give us years!"

So, I fulminated, that girl *was* an informer after all! I had been wrong to trust her. But how did she do it? Maybe she walked out during the prayers, and no one noticed? And why did the lieutenant come alone? Where was the rest of his raiding party? They never run out of policemen here!

I was considering escape, but the pistol strapped to the lieutenant's belt convinced me to forget that idea. Soon he stopped for a rest; evidently the pain in his lame leg was bothering him. He took a seat on a large boulder, inviting me to sit next to him on the sand. "This will give me a chance to rest, and to find out a few things," he said.

I thought, this is it! It's not enough that he got me; he wants the names of all the other worshipers, too.

The lieutenant continued. "I'm interested in learning a little about religion. Since you're a rabbi, I'm sure you can explain a few things to me."

He was even more dangerous than I thought! I'll have to watch my every word, my every move, I told myself. I said nothing.

He must have noticed an ironic smile on my face, for he said, "You don't believe me, do you? Do you remember when I read the French on your passport? I didn't tell the major that you are a rabbi, you know; and I used to wait for you to come register, but somehow you always arrived when I wasn't in. If I had told the major about you being a clergyman, you can be sure you wouldn't be here any longer."

"Comrade Lieutenant," I pleaded with him, "don't I have enough trouble? You want to charge me with spreading religious propaganda? But to whom? To a police officer? You really must think I'm an idiot. Why don't you leave me alone?"

"But you are wrong," he replied. "I'm not an NKVD man; I'm an army officer, and I really am interested in the subject of religion. Who else can tell me about it if not a rabbi?"

"Lieutenant, do you actually expect me to believe that? I've seen you in the station. You're the police commandant, and you want me to believe that you're not an NKVD man! If you aren't, then why not let me go free? That might prove something."

"I'd be glad to let you go free, but then I'd be in trouble myself. The charge against you is extremely serious, but what I'll do is charge you with drunkenness instead, claim that you had too much *kissmiss*; and tomorrow you'll go free!"

Although I was relieved, I was still skeptical. A Soviet police commandant suddenly developing an interest in religion? He must be putting on an act, trying to get me to supply him with names and information. "Lieutenant, why do you suddenly have such an interest in religion? Besides, wouldn't you rather look for a Christian clergyman?"

"For years I've been hoping to find a clergyman to talk to, any clergyman; but you are the first one I've come across in all this time...."

Neither one of us said anything more. We got up and continued walking towards the police station. We went into his office, and he filled out a form charging me with drunkenness. He let me read it and then he said, "Now do you believe me?"

His manners and his gentle way of talking impressed me, but seeing Stalin's picture on the wall, I withdrew. My suspicions grew stronger again. Just a clever, deceptive cop, I thought. These are the very men who keep two hundred million people in line, and I — like an idiot — almost believed him!

"Look, Comrade Commandant," I exclaimed, upset and excited by the contradictory feelings I had about him. "It's against the law to propagandize religion. It doesn't make any difference if you're an army man or a policeman — I'd have to be crazy to talk about religion in a police station, right under the pictures of Lenin and Stalin!"

He calmed me down. "Shhh, not so loud! I might get into trouble myself! Listen, if I wanted a confession — any kind of confession — we have the means to get it from you. So why should I talk to you like a gentleman?"

I tried to think. On the one hand, he was right: they could force any confession they wanted out of me; they did have the means to do it. Many great heroes — old, hardened professional revolutionaries — had been forced to confess everything under the sun; there was no need for the lieutenant to handle me with kid gloves. But wait a minute — he must be faking. No question about it, tomorrow he'll undoubtedly charge me with propagandizing religion, illegal assembly, and maybe even spying or aiding the enemy.

"Who told you?" I asked him. "Was it that *Comsomol* informer?"

"There was no informer," he replied. "Look!" He pointed to the two small stars decorating his chest. "I'm an army man, a tank commander. I was wounded twice; the second time my leg was damaged badly, and I was recuperating in the Kzyl-Orda hospital. Because of the draft, the local police forces in Kazakhstan are undermanned, especially with the troubles from the Koreans. So some army officers like myself have been assigned to help the local police forces. As soon as my leg heals, I'll be going back to the front.

"The doctor ordered daily exercise, and tonight, while I was taking my usual walk, I happened to pass by the Moslem cemetery. Suddenly I noticed shadowy figures through a window, and I heard sounds like crying. I thought there must be something going on. I figured that since I was alone and had no help, I could manage at least to scare off the trouble-makers, or even arrest one. So I walked right in with my gun in hand only to find you inside, praying."

At once it all became clear: if he were telling the truth, then the girl was completely innocent. The old woman standing guard had acted according to instructions; when she saw the policeman approaching she had pulled the rope and sounded the alarm. Everyone had cleared out as planned; only Mr. Kantor and I did not hear the alarm, so we were caught. Then perhaps he was not lying?

I couldn't think straight; nothing made sense anymore. One moment I did believe him, the next I didn't. And what about his strange thirst for religion? Why was he playing cat-and-mouse with me? Why doesn't he come straight out and give me the third degree, and make me sign a confession?

"Tell me, lieutenant, why the sudden urge to learn about religion? I'd be an idiot to get involved in a thing like that. Do you want to learn about religion from an idiot?"

The lieutenant himself was deliberating, obviously making a serious decision. He had a problem, too; he had to decide whether or not he could trust me! After all, we were strangers to each other; if not enemies, certainly not friends. We were both going through a crisis — could the other man be trusted?

Finally the policeman broke the silence. "I hope you believe me; I _do_ trust you. Perhaps we'll postpone further conversation until tomorrow. I think you are tired, and so am I."

I was exhausted. My feet were sore and blistered from the long march in the desert and my throat was dry. Still, I knew I would not be able to sleep that night unless I cleared up the mystery of this man.

"Comrade Commandant, I'm ready to listen to you, even if it takes all night. I won't be able to sleep anyhow."

The lieutenant pulled his chair closer to mine, so that the guard in the other room wouldn't overhear us. First he told me his name — Mikhail Antonovich Krulev — and that he came from the Ukraine. He never knew his parents; they died very young, and he was raised by a distant relative, a priest. When the Revolution broke out, this priest joined the Bolsheviks and became a hardened atheist. He came to despise religion and everything connected with it. "And so you see," the lieutenant said, "I was raised in a home where religion was not only ridiculed, but actually hated."

He offered me a cigarette, which I declined. He lighted one for himself. I said, "I know what you mean; that often happens. Converts can become extremists or fanatics."

The officer continued his story. As a young man, he had entered the University of Kharkov, where he studied law. He became engaged to his professor's daughter, who was also a law student. Suddenly the purges descended; hundreds of Russians were arrested, most of them without charge. The professor, who was Jewish, was dangerously outspoken; he couldn't tolerate injustice. He taught that truth could only be crystallized when arguments and counter-arguments were presented. He particularly liked certain quotations:

"Justice without force is powerless; force without justice is tyrannical."

"Deciding a case without hearing the other side cannot be considered just."

"These may seem like simple statements," the lieutenant said. "From a great man like my professor one might have expected deeper thoughts and more significant ideas. But soon we learned that those statements were acts of heroism; for he, too, disappeared overnight. My Sonia didn't rest, trying to free her father. I used to beg her, for her own good: be still, wait and see; but she wouldn't listen. She went to Moscow with the idea of saving her father — and she too disappeared!"

The lieutenant's head dropped; he seemed on the verge of tears. After that, he continued, he switched his studies from law to mechanical engineering. Eventually he married a girl who was raised with him at the former priest's house. "She had wanted to marry me all along, even when I was courting Sonia. My wife hates Jews — maybe because Sonia was Jewish. I love justice; I suppose this is because of my law professor. I always want to hear both sides of a story. My 'uncle', the ex-priest, claims that religion is all nonsense, that it was invented by the rich to tranquilize the poor. On the other hand, there are millions of people who think otherwise; and I would like to decide for myself.

"When I read your passport and discovered that you are a rabbi, I knew that you were the right man for me. Then there was a new problem: could I trust you? Suppose you let it out that I was interested in religion? I'd be locked up in an asylum, or sent off to Siberia! But when I found you praying tonight, I said to myself, 'There's a man I can trust!' But I have to keep you under arrest overnight for my own protection. Now then, is there anything you want? Something to eat? To drink?"

Could I believe him? He sounded so convincing. It made sense, but was it real or only a trap? The lieutenant interrupted my thoughts: "Well? It's getting late and I have to lock you up now. Do you want anything?"

I asked only to be isolated from the other prisoners, so that I could have privacy for thinking and praying. Also, I asked that no food or water be brought to my cell. "We Jews are supposed to fast on the Day of Atonement from sundown until the stars appear the next night. I have walked a long distance from my village to town; I'm hungry and terribly thirsty. If there was water in my room I might not be able to resist the temptation."

My small cell had one high window. I reached up, pulled myself up by the iron bars, and tried to look outside. The whole town seemed like a cemetery, and all the small clay houses like tombstones. The cell was dark, except for the moonlight shining in between the iron bars. It was empty except for the mat of straw on the cement floor.

I lay down on the straw, but I couldn't close my eyes. Lieutenant Mikhail Krulev was on my mind. His story must be true! What reason would he have to make all this up? Why should he bother me? He seemed a sensitive person, a noble soul, and the fact that he wore that uniform was beside the point. What was important was that he could not stand Soviet injustice. And then another thing — there are usually no empty cells in a Soviet prison. But I had noticed many other empty cells with open doors, while passing through the long corridor on the way to mine. Why? It could only be because the commandant was a man of justice.

Then a new question arose. If the lieutenant let me go free tomorrow, wouldn't the prosecutor's secretary wonder what was going on? I still wasn't sure how trustworthy she was. I'd have to protect Lieutenant Krulev from the prosecutor's eye. Perhaps I'd tell her in private that the lieutenant hadn't seen anything in our _shul;_ that I had played drunk, and he had arrested me for that.

And another question: how would I explain religion to the lieutenant? The words of a holiday prayer came to mind: "And shine forth in the splendor and excellence of Your might upon all inhabitants of the world, that whatsoever has been made may know that You have made it, and whatsoever has been created may understand that You have created it, and whatsoever has breath in its nostrils may say: The Lord God of Israel is King, and His dominion ruleth over all."

What new life, what new meaning had been given to these words! If I had been chosen to be a tool in delivering God's message to a person who was searching for it, how could I refuse?

After my release I was told that the worshipers suspected that the prosecutor's secretary had something to do with the raid. Even her mother was convinced that her daughter was implicated. On the way home she cried, "Look what you've done! You have killed your own mother! I will kill myself!"

In vain the daughter swore, again and again, "But Mother, I had nothing to do with it! How could I have gone to the police? You know that I was right beside you the whole time!"

All her tears and pleading did not convince her mother, who insisted she would take her own life; all through the night the daughter and her aunt took turns standing guard over her. Finally morning arrived and, leaving the aunt to watch over her mother, the girl went to the police station. Using her credentials, she asked the officer on duty to take her to the prisoner. It was highly irregular, but she took the risk in order to talk to me before the arrival of the commandant or his staff.

The officer in charge agreed to let her see me, and said: "That young fellow? He must be a real spy or counter-revolutionary; the commandant ordered him kept in isolation, with no food or water."

The girl was stunned. So they've already started the rough treatment, she thought, and fearing for the safety of the other Jews, she told the officer that she had forgotten some documents and she'd be back later. She rushed to Mr. Kantor's house so he could alert everyone to escape.

Lazer Kantor was standing in a corner, wrapped in his *tallis*, praying. A knock on the door interrupted his words. The Kantors knew what the sudden knock on a door meant; they were expecting it. They opened the door with resignation, and saw not the police, but Lena, the prosecutor's secretary.

"Oh, it's you," spat the old woman and tried to close the door in the girl's face. But Lena was determined, and forced her way in.

The old man, seeing her, grumbled, "What do you want now? Haven't you done enough? Get out! I don't want to see your face!"

Lena said, "I know what you think, but I swear by all that's holy that I had nothing to do with it! Please listen —"

The old man interrupted her. "Don't make me laugh! Since when do people like you swear by all that's holy?"

In a subdued voice Lena replied, "Since last night! If you won't believe me, then I'll swear by my mother's life! But I didn't come for that; there are more important things to tell you. First, you must warn the other Jews to leave town immediately. Whoever can, should flee!"

The old man refrained from telling her that most of the Jewish men had in fact already left town, and were at the railroad station in the next town, awaiting the signal: whether to return home, or to disperse all over the area. Only the wounded veterans hadn't fled, because they couldn't; they'd have to depend upon their medals and army records to protect them.

Lena continued, "We have to collect money for a lawyer, maybe from Tashkent, Alma-Ata or even Moscow. Chaim is locked up in isolation, without food or water! I'll do whatever I can for him, but I mustn't leave my mother. Please, Mr. Kantor, you are the only one who can convince my mother not to commit suicide. Please, please try to convince her — I swear I'm not guilty!"

The old man was stubborn. "How can I convince your mother about something of which I myself am not convinced?"

The girl turned to Mrs. Kantor, took the old woman's hands and pleaded, "Grandmother, you are a woman; you can feel my heart! My father is dead, and now I'm about to lose my mother! Please help me!"

Mrs. Kantor believed in the girl's innocence. She promised to go and talk to the mother at once. Lena thanked her profusely and dashed out.

In the silence of prison, it was easy to get lost in a world of unreality. I had so wanted to dream of my family and my home last night. They say one frequently dreams at night of what he thinks about by day. I was constantly thinking about home, but no dreams came to carry me closer to my beloved family.

My mind wandered over battlefields and borders, back to my home. How had they spent the holidays under the Germans? Were they permitted to congregate for services? What services? I almost forgot — today was *Yom Kippur*!

I was deep in my prayers. Loneliness and solitude are the perfect conditions for meditation. The turn of keys in the door brought me back to reality. Standing in the doorway, straight and silent, was Lena, the prosecutor's secretary. She motioned to the guard and he closed the door behind her. She seems to be familiar with this place, I thought.

She read my thoughts and said, "My duties bring me here quite often, so the guards know me already. Tell me about last night. Do you accuse me too?" She broke into tears before she finished the sentence.

I felt sorry for her. Moreover, I felt ashamed of myself, for I had completely forgotten about her and her mother's vow to commit suicide.

"Please, please stop crying," I urged her. "Did anything happen to your mother?"

"No, but she's still threatening to kill herself! My aunt is keeping guard over her now."

"Well," I said, "you can tell your mother that I know that you are absolutely innocent."

Her sobs increased. "You know?" she asked. "Then you are the only one who believes me. Not even my own mother believes me! How do you know?"

"Well, I'll tell you what happened," I said, planning my story so that the lieutenant's interest in religion would be concealed from her. She might not be an informer, but she could unintentionally make a slip in front of the prosecutor. "The lieutenant happened to be walking by the cemetery when we were holding services. He heard the cries of a woman, and thought she was being assaulted. When he discovered only Mr. Kantor and me, he was confused; so I began to play drunk and make silly noises. He arrested me for drunkenness. I'll probably be released as soon as they open the office. You can tell Lazer Kantor to call the people together; we'll continue with our services today."

At nine o'clock sharp, a Kazakh policeman escorted me to the commandant's office. The commandant shouted at me and warned me that if it ever happened again, I would be severely punished. After the policeman left the room, the commandant smiled at me and we picked up our conversation where we had left off. I told him that the subject of religion would require many, many sessions, and since I had to return to the village, we could meet only once in two weeks, when I came to report at the police station.

"As you know, Commandant, by law I'm the 'property' of Akhmatov, the chairman of the collective Kuzar-Pash. I can't switch jobs without his consent, and he certainly won't let me go unless I get drafted or get a job in a defense enterprise. The only military factory in town won't hire me because I'm considered a foreigner. Perhaps you could help me? If I worked in town, we could meet frequently."

The commandant smiled and said, "But you're not a foreigner anymore. Your foreign passport has been taken away from you! I shall see what I can do. Stop in and see me later in the day."

It was afternoon when we finally managed to congregate for the *Yom Kippur* services. Because of the late hour, the prayers were said quickly. First there was the memorial service for the dead. This time, everybody, including the women, suppressed their crying within, so that no sound could be heard outside. However, when we reached the most moving part of the service, many people could not restrain themselves any longer, and the words broke forth: "On the first day of the year it is inscribed, and on the Day of Atonement the decree is sealed, how many shall pass away and how many shall be born; who shall live and who shall die; who at the measure of man's days and who before it; who shall perish by fire and who by water, who by sword and who by wild beast, who by hunger and who by thirst...."

And each of us thought of our dear ones: where were they now? And were they still among the living? And if not, where and how...? At least, dear God, in a Jewish grave, we pleaded....

TRUE TO HIS WORD, Lieutenant Krulev got me a job in the military factory. How happy I was to leave Kuzar-Pash! This was luxury in comparison. There was a restaurant, where I got one meal a day on my ration card. There was a dormitory for bachelor employees, and a small library. A person could live and work there without leaving the premises. Special passes were issued to all workers; the passes were renewed every two weeks and armed guards manned the entrance constantly. The factory worked night and day; two shifts, twelve hours each, seven days a week. Once in two weeks, everything stopped for the changing of the shifts.

The factory produced mortars for the infantry, and I was assigned to the foundry. There, forms were made from a special kind of sand and then were baked in an oven. When they were ready, molten metal was poured into them. The liquid metal was carried from the furnaces to the forms in large buckets. After the metal cooled, the forms were broken, and the sand reused.

All the hard labor was done by Kazakh men. The foreman was a Russian woman, a Party member, who was on excellent terms with the management. The head of the foundry department was a metallurgical engineer, Stepan Ilyanovich Kuzenkov. A tall man in his late fifties, he was always serious; no one ever saw him smile. Although the foundry was primitive, the next shop — the mechanical department — was highly advanced. It contained modern machinery from the USA, Sweden and Germany.

The foreman gave me the assignment of "in-between-man," carrying heavy loads between the two shops. It was hard, back-breaking labor. From the foundry, the mortars emerged rough, raw, and sandy. If the sand and dirt were allowed to get into the mechanical shop, they would ruin all the delicate machinery there. It was on these machines that the mortars were threaded and fitted with detonators to trigger the explosion. It was my job to clean the raw material, and then deliver it to the mechanical shop. At the furnaces, I loaded a wheelbarrow with raw mortars and took them to a special room which contained a six-cornered drum. After loading twenty-five mortars into the drum, I switched on an electric motor which, by driving a belt, made the drum revolve. The mortars, tumbling about inside the drum, cleansed and polished one another during this process. The time allowed each load was thirty minutes. It was terribly dusty and noisy inside that room, so I spent much of my waiting time hanging around the furnaces, or in the mechanical shop, observing the teenagers who handled the giant machines so expertly.

What intrigued me most, however, was the mystery of the furnaces. The sight of melting metal was a marvel to behold. Is that what it looks like in hell? I wondered. I pressed my eye to the little glass hole, watching for hours, while the hard metal, in a succession of stages, was transformed into a liquid. Some of the metal yielded easily, but some held out, rock-like and steadfast, until a new wave of oxygen was blown in. Then the red, flowery metal turned into a yellow-white creamy liquid. The world of metallurgy was new to me and I was fascinated.

My "partner" — the man who worked my job on the second shift — was a friendly seventy-year-old Russian. On my first day, he showed me around and gave me some advice. In appreciation, I always left a load or two of raw mortars piled up alongside our drum at the end of my shift, thus saving him the work of loading and pushing the wheelbarrow from the furnace to the drum.

One day he looked at my shoes, which were falling apart, and said, "Leave them with me and I'll fix them for you."

"But Grandfather, how can you fix my shoes when there's no leather to be had?" I asked.

"Leave it to me, young man. One hand washes the other, you know...."

I knew that stolen goods were traded for other stolen necessities. But what can one steal in a mortar factory? Who would want a stolen mortar?

How would he get leather to repair shoes?

I gave him my shoes. It was hard working barefoot; often, I'd step on a piece of hot metal or on a sharp splinter of steel. It was quite a relief, and also a surprise, to get my mended shoes back. I examined my "new" thick soles and realized at once what the old man had done. The drum belt!

"Grandfather, what have you done? How can we run the drum if the belt has been cut up?!"

"Don't you worry, son," he smiled, putting his arm around my shoulder. "I simply ordered another belt. This one was all worn out! The supply man needs his shoes fixed too; he'll see to it that we get a new one! There was a Kazakh in your job before you came, and he never helped me a bit; at my age every little bit of help counts, and it means a lot to me when you save me a couple of loads. I'm happy to have fixed your shoes for you. And remember: in our country, if you can't steal, you can't exist!"

The head of the foundry, Stepan Kuzenkov, noticed me hanging around the furnaces and trying to figure out how everything worked. When he saw how interested I was, he explained the entire operation to me in language that a layman could understand.

"You see, inside the furnaces, there's a war going on; some metals are stronger and some are weaker. They struggle and wrestle, reacting in a variety of ways under high temperatures."

Kuzenkov often invited me to his office upstairs. Like most Russians, he was hungry for news from the world outside the USSR. I had plenty of time on my hands, and we had many interesting discussions. Somehow this Russian knew a lot more than the official newspapers printed. As far as the Party line was concerned, he was definitely a skeptic. We became very friendly. Our friendship increased still further as a result of our mutual need for food — and I had rice!

I had brought a bag of rice with me from the village when I left; it had been paid to me "on account" for my work there. The restaurant on the factory grounds served only one meal a day. After presenting a coupon, one received a two-course meal: soup and kasha. It was never enough. Meat was served once a week, but, of course, it wasn't kosher and I wouldn't eat it, so the rice which I had brought from Kuzar-Pash came in very handy.

Cooking was no problem, for I had my own "stove" at work: after the liquefied metal had been poured into the forms, I simply placed my pot on top of one. By the time the metal cooled off, my rice was cooked and ready to eat. I was the envy of the entire shop; many hungry eyes watched me when I ate my daily rice, but I couldn't offer any of it, for there wasn't enough to feed the entire shop. But there was one man I could not refuse — the head of the shop, Engineer Kuzenkov.

Our "rice relationship" began when he happened to pass by me one day while I was eating my rice. He bent over me and said, "It tastes good, eh?"

I replied that it would taste much better if I had some salt, and maybe a bit of oil. "It's only unsalted rice and water, nothing else," I told him.

"Come to my office!" he ordered.

He took his seat at the desk, and I sat across from him holding my pot of rice. First, we talked about the slowness of the Americans and the British in their opening of the second front. There was a feeling all over the country that the Allies were purposely stalling.

Then, his eyes on my pot, he suddenly asked, "How is it that your rice is so nice and white? The little bit of rice we get on our ration cards is always yellow!"

I replied that probably the pure, well-cleaned and polished rice is shipped to Moscow, while the local people receive the lower quality; also, I thought, the local rice is probably mixed with *pshonka* — a yellow cereal. He let loose with a few Russian curses, while his eyes gazed longingly at my pot of steaming rice.

I said, "Comrade Kuzenkov, I would gladly offer you some of my rice, but I've already eaten from it."

He laughed and replied, "So what?" and suddenly he had a spoon in his hand and was digging into my rice with happy abandon.

"Ah, wonderful!" he said. "If you can get some of this white rice for me, I'll get you some salt and even a little fat."

I told him that the only fat I could use was vegetable oil, and that I would get him some rice — but only if I could take two days off from work. I felt a little foolish, since I hadn't been working there for long and I was already asking for time off! I explained that there was still some rice coming to me for my labor in Kuzar-Pash; but since I couldn't expect them to send it to me, I'd have to go there personally to get it.

Usually the members of a collective had to wait until the end of the year, and only after all taxes were paid and delivered in produce could they collect their share. However, one could sometimes get an advance, on account. If I could bribe the chairman, he might give me a larger-than-usual advance. And perhaps, while I was in Kuzar-Pash, I could buy some more rice from the peasants for Kuzenkov.

The next day, Engineer Kuzenkov brought me salt and a small bottle of vegetable oil; and again he shared my meal in a matter-of-fact fashion. He said that he would arrange for me to go to the village next week, and that he would give me a pair of gloves, knitted by his wife, as a bribe for the Kazakh chairman.

It was obvious that the monthly food supply that he received from the government ration cards was insufficient to feed his family. His salary was not large enough to buy food on the black market, and in a metallurgical shop there was nothing edible to steal! It was during those meals we shared together that I won his confidence. He even dared to mention the dangerous name "Trotsky" in our conversation — a name absolutely unmentionable in the Soviet Union!

Now again, I had to face the old problem of working on Shabbos, and I dreaded the thought. Until this point I had managed to avoid it, using all kinds of excuses, but now I was facing a blank wall. What could I do? I began to regret ever leaving the village. I should have thought about Shabbos before...but it was too late now!

Finally an idea occurred to me, which could possibly solve my problem. Our routine was to put 25 mortars at a time into the tumbler machine. If I could put in more than that amount, and still leave enough room for the mortars to tumble around, perhaps....

The next day I tested it. I tried 50. It worked! I tried 100 and then 125, and it worked again! There was one problem, though, with 125 — the mortars did not come out quite smooth enough, and the surface of the metal was grayish-white. So I tried increasing the running time from 30 to 45 minutes, and succeeded! The mortars came out smooth and shiny, according to specifications.

On Friday I doubled my normal output of mortars, and concealed the excess mortars in a corner of the tumbling machine room, which was always so full of dust from the machinery that no one ever went inside.

The old man arrived to begin his shift. When I showed him the heap of clean mortars ready to be delivered to the mechanical shop, he rubbed his eyes. "What happened?" he asked. "Didn't you deliver anything to the shop? The forelady will hang you!"

I explained to him that I did deliver the normal amount, but that I had not been feeling well, and I wanted to take it easy the next day. "So here is a whole day's quota, and I hope you'll match it with the same number, so I'll have it ready for delivery tomorrow."

The old man put his arm around my shoulders, and, with tears in his eyes, said, "Listen — I'm talking to you as I would to my own son, and I lost two of them in the battle for Moscow. Tell me, for how long have you been in the Soviet Union?"

"Since the German attack," I replied.

"Well, I've been here all my life," he said. "I've gone through hot and cold, and I want you to let me give you some advice: don't try to double or triple the norm! Never, you hear?! Never! You might become a hero for a while, even get your name in the paper, a Stakhanovite — for a week. But the next week, the management will say, 'Well, now, if it's possible for one man to increase the norm, why not increase the norm for everyone?' So for the same money and the same hours, you'll have to work three times faster, and produce three times as much! It would kill me! So I beg of you, don't do this to me! Have mercy on an old man! I've lived all my life among Jews and I know that you're a kind-hearted people. So please, let's be friends; we'll hide those mortars, and tell me you'll never do it again!"

I assured the old man that it was not my intention to become a celebrity, a Stakhanovite. "The last thing I'd ever do is to hurt you, Grandfather. It's just that I would like to take it easy tomorrow. Like you once told me, 'one hand washes the other.' Let's cooperate — I'll give you a day's supply, and you return one to me," I said.

"Look, my son, I'm too old to be fooled. I've lived all my life among Jews. You can tell me the truth! Why does it have to be tomorrow? Because it's Shabbos?" He pronounced the word "Shabbos" just like a Jew; it made me laugh. He laughed too. "If that's the case," he said, "I'll be glad to help you!"

I had no choice, and confessed that he had guessed right; I promised that I would show my appreciation by bringing him rice from Kuzar-Pash.

During the next week, Kuzenkov informed me that I could take two days off. He handed me the promised pair of gloves for bribing Akhmatov to give me a larger amount of rice. Mrs. Kuzenkov did not know me, and when I knocked on their door early one morning, she was taken aback and ran to call her husband: "Quick, there's a loaded camel outside, and some European wants to come in."

They were amazed when the Kazakh and I began to unload cantaloupes, watermelons, cucumbers, two legs of lamb and one *pood* of rice — a Russian measure equal to sixteen kilograms, or almost thirty-five pounds of rice! On the black market, one kilogram of rice cost 80 rubles, while in the big industrial cities of the Ural and Siberia, the price might be as high as 300 rubles! The Kuzenkov family, though living in the "rice basket" of the Soviet Union, could not afford to buy on the black market. They existed on the meager rations issued to them every month. How happy and grateful they were to buy a few kilos from me at half the usual price! Mrs. Kuzenkov beamed and said, "You Jews always know how to get a bargain!"

I entrusted her with my rice as well, for I didn't want to take it into the dormitory; I was afraid that my roommates would steal it. Of course, I couldn't be sure that Mrs. Kuzenkov would be any more honest, since hunger can turn anyone into a thief.

I was astonished at the nice home and furniture the Kuzenkovs had. I knew that the European managers of the factory were all refugees, evacuated hurriedly before the advancing Germans, and that most of them had brought almost nothing with them. Yet here was a home furnished fully in the European style. I stared at myself in the large mirror again and again; it was the first time I had seen myself in a mirror since I had left Lithuania. I couldn't believe my eyes and was shocked at what I saw! I looked rough, tough, like a hardened Russian laborer. I was sure that, if she were to see me now, Mama wouldn't recognize me!

Kuzenkov explained to me that they were not a refugee family, but had been transferred to Kazakhstan right after the Bolshevik Revolution. He did not elaborate, but I understood what this meant. Stalin's reign of terror had sent millions off to Siberia; some of the "better risks" were shipped here, into the Asian republics, filling these lands with Russians and at the same time punishing those who had shown little enthusiasm for the Communist regime. Kuzenkov's opinions, which he surely wouldn't have dared express to anyone but me, and the fact that he had been transferred, supported my suspicion that he was anti-Soviet.

I also gave some rice to my partner for his fine cooperation in my efforts to avoid working on Shabbos. One day he warned me, "Chaim, I've noticed something that I want to talk to you about; you are too friendly with the engineer. For your own sake, stay away from the big shots! You're spending too much time in his office, and no good can come from it!"

"Why?" I asked him. "What's wrong with being friends with a big shot?"

He replied, "My dear boy, I'm much older than you and have a lot more experience in life; so for your own good, listen to me. If you want to stay on here, keep away from the management! Before the Revolution, you know, we would address a person as *gospodin* — sir. Since the Revolution, we have all become comrades, address one another as *tovarishch*; but believe me, one could be closer with a *gospodin* than with a *tovarishch*, because the management and all the big shots are scared! They're afraid of me, and of you; they're afraid of everybody! And if you get too close, they're afraid that you might find out their secrets. And when you know too much of their business, you become dangerous to them. The minute they suspect that you know too much, they'll find a way to get rid of you; you'll see!"

Every Friday we prepared a day's worth of mortars in advance, and thus I was able to avoid working on Shabbos. Often, I wanted to increase production for the sake of helping the war effort, but the old man always made me change my mind. "Remember, you'll kill me!"

Considering all the engineers, managers and foremen, I wondered why none of them had thought of such a simple way of increasing output. And this had been going on for years! How many more deficiencies were there? How many more machines were operating at only half capacity, and wasting precious electricity?

Now that I was making my quota in such a short time, I had to be careful not to be noticed by the forelady, so I spent much time in Kuzenkov's office, reading his books. Unfortunately his library contained mostly trade books on metals and metallurgy, which I barely understood. Sometimes I wandered through the factory talking to the workers, or watched the metal melt in the furnace. The forelady didn't like it, but she never reprimanded me; apparently she was aware of my friendship with Kuzenkov, her immediate superior.

Thus I could always find time to accompany Lieutenant Krulev on the long daily walks which he took because of his injured leg. During these walks we became very close. "Call me Misha," he told me. We discussed everything under the sun, but primarily he was interested in religion. I was surprised to discover that this subject, which was so plain and clear to me, was quite difficult to explain to one who was completely ignorant.

Faith cannot be bought in the market, or even inherited. Faith has to grow like a tree; from a tiny seed, planted by parents, it takes root and grows upward. The deeper its roots, the more resistant it becomes to any storm. Disappointment and disillusionment hardly exist to a man of faith. And this highly educated man, who had been brainwashed in regard to religion, seemed to have an open mind on the subject.

I did not feel capable of giving lectures on faith. Things which I had taken for granted were not so simple anymore, and suddenly questions began to spring up in my own mind. I cautioned Misha that I was not really qualified to lecture him on such an important subject. There would be many questions that I wouldn't be able to answer; nevertheless, I'd try to tell him what I had learned, and what I believed:

"Even in ancient times, people knew that there was One Supreme power. But this concept was too high, too abstract for them, so they worshipped the sun, the moon, the forces of nature, even idols of clay, as representatives of the One Creator; they would sacrifice their goods, animals — even their own children! — to propitiate these gods, to avert evil, and to assure themselves of good fortune.

"Then came Abraham, the first Jew. Alone, he stood up against the entire known world, and proclaimed the belief in One God! A world immersed in idol-worship was shaken to its roots. Abraham spoke about a God Who cannot be seen or felt or touched. 'For no man can see Me and live.' Not only can He not be seen by the human eye, but He cannot be perceived by the human brain, or in the human imagination. 'He is not a body. He is free from all accidents of matter. He has not any form whatsoever,' states Maimonides.

"God is _One_, without beginning, without end. He created the universe from nothing — 'Existence out of non-existence.' In the beginning, God alone existed, nothing else. Even time itself is among the things He created, and He alone is eternal. All things are finite, but He is infinite. He is the Creator of all that exists; and since nature was created by Him, He has the power to annul the laws of nature, which is what people call miracles, though the tiniest detail of creation is in fact a miracle, and we humans take it for granted.

"Therefore Abraham proclaimed: 'I have lifted my hand unto the Lord, the most high God, the Creator of Heaven and earth.'"

Day after day we discussed various aspects of religion. It was fortunate that I had my little Bible, from which I could quote and read to him. When we came upon the story of Abraham preparing to sacrifice his son Isaac, Misha was shocked. "I thought you said Abraham was way ahead of his time. And what kind of a god demands a human sacrifice?!"

"In those days," I replied, "it was common practice to sacrifice children. They tried to placate their idols with the fruits of their fields, or with sheep or cattle; they would even sacrifice their own offspring! And here again, Abraham broke the chains, revolutionizing the attitude to human life! The people of Abraham's generation suspected him of talking a lot, but could he match the strength of his faith to that of the idol-worshiper who was willing to sacrifice his own son? So God tested Abraham. How deep, how strong were his convictions? Abraham proved himself; he was prepared to sacrifice his beloved son! And how deep-rooted were the convictions of the father and also the son, for Isaac, a man of 37, volunteered to be sacrificed!

"And He said, 'Lay not thy hand upon the lad, nor do any harm unto him.' It is a lesson for all times, for today's generation as well, that there is nothing in the world for which it is worth destroying a human life! No king, no leader, no party, no ideology has the right to take a human life, not even for the sake of God Himself! Only the One who gives life can take it!

"It is apparent that the human race still cannot accept this law. The world has become a slaughterhouse; men, women, and children are still butchered in the name of this or that religion or ideology! Christianity, Islam, Hitler, all killing, killing, killing for the sake of their beliefs!"

Misha opened the newspaper he carried with him. As usual, Stalin's picture appeared on the front page. He glanced at the picture, then at me, and smiled. I did not have to elaborate; I knew he understood....

Religion was not the only subject we discussed on our daily walks. Once I asked him why he always wore all his medals, and he told me this story: since Asia Minor has such a warm climate, most military hospitals and convalescent homes are located there. Because of the small pensions these disabled veterans received, they were forced to boost their income by selling on the black market; the Soviet police were involved in frequent skirmishes with these military heroes. The police, accustomed to unquestioning obedience, encountered violent resistance to their efforts to eradicate the black market.

In many big cities — Tashkent, Samarkand, Alma-Ata — rioting broke out. The police, trying to arrest the disabled black marketeers, were attacked by waves of crippled veterans. With their crutches and canes they broke the bones of many policemen; they used abusive language to the police, language unheard of in the Soviet Union:

"You yellow rats were hiding while we were fighting!"

"Cowards, hiding behind the police uniform!"

"Why don't you go and fight the Germans instead of us, you pigs?!"

The news about these riots reached Moscow, and the Kremlin sent a delegate of the Central Committee to get the situation under control. He was a senior officer in the army, with the rank of general; his name was Nikita Sergeyevich Khrushchev!

After surveying the situation, Khrushchev issued orders to the police to leave the disabled veterans alone, and not to interfere with their black-market activities. He also instructed all policemen to decorate their uniforms with every medal in their possession. As for non-veteran black marketeers, however, the rules were strictly enforced; they were arrested.

"As a result," Misha explained, "many of the civilian black marketeers now sell their items through the invalids, who are immune from arrest, and of course they receive a commission!"

"Wait a moment, Misha," I said. "If I understand you correctly, why, that's capitalism! There's the middleman, who gets a commission — a speculator! And the price is set according to the supply and demand — capitalism! And you say that all this is approved by a delegate of the Central Committee?"

"And that's not all," he replied. "Now many army deserters are pretending to be disabled veterans! Uniforms, medals, crutches — all these things are obtainable for a price!"

As the weeks went by, I wondered whether our discussions had any effect on Misha. Did I have any influence on him at all? And if so, would that be reflected in his behavior? The answer came soon and unexpectedly.

One day, on the way to the library, which was located outside the factory grounds, I was stopped by a young woman. "Pardon me, comrade. May I have a word with you?"

I knew the regulations: never discuss anything with strangers. There was a slogan on every wall: "Beat the enemy with SILENCE."

She certainly didn't look like a spy, but could she be a secret agent, testing me? One couldn't be careful enough... and working in the military factory, I had to be doubly vigilant.

"What can I do for you?" I asked her politely.

"You can help my mother and me! It's a matter of life and death!" She appeared to be in great distress.

"Then you'd better tell me who you are, who sent you to me, and what you think I can do for you."

"My name is Ida Tashman. Lazer Kantor sent me; he thought you might be able to help me. It's about my mother. Listen — she receives packages from America, from her brother who lives in Philadelphia. Some of the things we use ourselves — mother, me, and my three children. The rest she sells on the black market. She's 74, and the invalids who usually operate the black market don't bother her. In the last package my uncle sent, there was some toothpaste, which is unobtainable here, and worth a fortune. Mama has only one tooth left, so she gave me the toothpaste; but we need bread and rice more than toothpaste, so I told her to take it to the market. A woman bought it for 200 rubles, and five minutes later, she returned with a policeman! He arrested Mama, and she's in jail right now. The woman who did it is the police commandant's wife — maybe you can do something to get Mama out of jail?!"

"Citizen Tashman," I said, carefully using the standard address, "I'm sure the police will not be harsh on a woman of that age. Why don't you go to the police yourself and demand her release?"

Turning aside, she wiped her eyes. "I'm a schoolteacher. It's my duty to raise good Soviet citizens. Do you realize what it will do to me and my three children, having their grandmother in jail, arrested as a speculator? My husband is away fighting the Germans. I'd give my life for my mother, but who'll raise my children?" Tears were shining on her cheeks. "Please, I beg of you! My mother is a sick old woman. One more night in prison could be the end of her.... Her five sons, her daughter, and her son-in-law are all fighting the enemy! Please tell that to the commandant!"

The price of 200 rubles for the toothpaste was ridiculously low. The old woman must have known that she was dealing with the commandant's wife, and had given away the toothpaste for almost nothing. And that witch had turned around and had her arrested!

But how could I approach Misha against his own wife? And how would he respond if I were to use our friendship to protect a black marketeer?

At the usual time I reached our meeting place, and I decided to talk to Misha about justice and charity. Eventually I would bring up the matter of the old woman.

We were happy to see each other again. Within a few minutes I was able to bring up the subject. "You once studied law, Misha. It might interest you to know that the Hebrew word for justice is the same as the word for charity: _tzedakah_. In Hebrew, charity and justice go hand in hand. Of course, in a socialist society there is no room for charity. A janitor receives barely enough to exist, while a writer or composer in Moscow is entitled to a villa, maid, chauffeur and limousine. Does the wealthy man give to charity? No. Are there any charitable organizations in the entire Soviet Union? No. Charity is considered an insult in a socialist society. The Marxist slogan 'He who doesn't work doesn't eat' is the Communist view. But in the Jewish faith, charity is all-important! In Jewish justice, the rich man is obliged to be charitable to the poor man. Judaism does not condemn prosperity; rather it considers it a blessing, provided it is acquired honestly and justly. Wealth is considered as being entrusted to man to do good, to share with the poor — to do justice!"

Eventually I came to the point, the plight of that old woman. Sarcastically I said, "Today I heard about the charity and justice of your office."

Misha looked at me, his eyes registering surprise. "Do you know that old woman?" he asked.

"No, but I heard the story. I thought I'd ask you about it."

We were both silent, but I could feel his tension. Finally he said, "I have to go now; I'll see you tomorrow." When we parted he quoted, "'Happy families are all alike. The unhappy families are unhappy each in its own way.' Tolstoy wrote that, and he knew!"

On the way back, I thought about Misha's situation: he loved his children, his family, even his wife — but she was jealous and spiteful. Tolstoy's words were ringing in my ears. How true, how perfectly said! If they are happy, they are alike — it's the unhappy ones that are different from each other!

The very next evening, when my shift came to an end and I was leaving the factory, Ida Tashman was again waiting in front of the gate. This time she was all smiles. "Comrade, I can't thank you enough! Mama asked me to invite you for dinner Friday night. Please do us the honor and come!"

How quickly Misha had acted, even risking the displeasure of his wife!

"Tell me about your mother. What actually happened? How did she get out so soon?" I asked.

"So you really don't know? Come now, don't be so modest!" she said. "After I left you, I went home to put the children to sleep. They cried for *Bobbe*, and I cried along with them. I promised them that their grandmother would return from 'her trip to the city' the next day. Then I cried some more, and began to prepare my lessons. Soon I heard noise outside. The police commandant himself brought mother home! He said that it wasn't safe for her to walk alone at night. Then he handed me a bag. He refused to come in, and apologized for all the trouble. When he left, I almost fainted when I saw what was in the bag: the toothpaste, the 200 rubles, a large loaf of bread and some rice! What kind of magic did you use on that man? Anyway, you must come to dinner with us on Friday night; mother insists!"

"I'll come to see your mother," I said, "but don't bother to cook for me; I won't eat."

"Oh, I understand; you're afraid we're not kosher, is that it? But my mother keeps kosher, absolutely kosher, and besides that we don't eat meat at all. So can we expect you Friday night for a dairy meal?"

I went to their home the following Friday night. It was a shabby little house, but how good it was to be among Jews again! The old grandmother looked like my own grandmother, with the traces of the years etched on her face, and gnarled, hard-working hands.

She welcomed me at the door. "Come in, my son." In my ears rang Mama's last words: "Go, my son, go!" I held back my tears.

The three children, with shining faces, looked up at me and proudly exclaimed, "Thank you, Uncle!" and I thought of my own little brothers....

The wooden crate which served as a table was covered with old newspaper. In the center, a lonely candle burned, sending its beam over the room. The old woman noticed my amazement, and explained:

"A long time ago, my dear brother in Philadelphia sent me a box of Shabbos candles. I use only one at a time; they are so precious! I haven't seen my brother in 40 years, but he never forgets me! May the Almighty One bless him and his family!"

I went to a corner and recited the Friday evening prayers. The three children hovered around me; it was quite obvious that they had never seen a man praying. The magic of the candle, the shining eyes of the children, the traditional melody we sang welcoming the Shabbos Queen — the special holiness of this time was felt in every corner of the little house. What a heavenly feeling it was, this spiritual enjoyment of the Sabbath!

I recited the *Kiddush*, then chanted some Shabbos songs. The grand-mother wiped away her tears. "Eat some more, my dear — I haven't enjoyed a Shabbos like this for many, many years!"

The teacher, too, was moved. "Our heritage is alien to our children," she told me. "To them Jews are like gypsies — no land of their own, no history, no language, no culture."

"If you are aware of all this, why don't you teach them?" I asked. "Why don't you try to instill a Jewish pride in them that will serve them as a shield?"

A sad smile appeared on her face, and she shook her head. "That's easier said than done. It's too dangerous; if a child lets one word slip, we're in great trouble! And by the time they're grown up, it's already too late! Maybe now you can understand why so many of our youngsters are ashamed of being Jews. And you'll see; it'll just get worse and worse...."

The candle flickered, and went out; the room was enveloped in dark-ness. In the dying glow of the oven, I told the children about our past, about Jerusalem, our holy city; I told them about our kings: Saul, and David and Solomon. They fell asleep in the sweet trance of a glorious past. And I, with the three little children clinging to me, wandered off to my own dream world in the not-so-distant past. I was back home with my brothers, with the candles glowing on the Shabbos table, and Mama's hands raised in blessing....

I went to the market to buy a watermelon, and met Mrs. Epin, the mother of the prosecutor's secretary. After exchanging greetings, she said, "Chaim, I've been looking for you. Lena said to tell you that she must talk to you; it's very important. Come over tonight for tea." All the way back to the dormitory, I thought about the events of the last few days; in this land of spies and informers, one never knows when he has been careless. What does the prosecutor's secretary want? What can it be that's so important? I couldn't wait till the day was over; it was not mere curiosity, but cold fear that made me restless.

Mrs. Epin and her sister received me pleasantly. Then both of them went into the kitchen to make the tea, leaving me alone with Lena. I got right to the point. "All right, Lena, tell me what this is all about."

"I want to warn you about trouble," she said, "but I have to be sure no one hears this, not even Mother!" She got up and looked into the kitchen to make sure that her mother and aunt were not within hearing range.

"Don't torture me!" I cried. "Tell me, tell me, what's the trouble?"

"What's been going on in your shop?" she asked abruptly.

"If you wanted some information, you didn't have to scare me like that," I said defensively. "You could have come up to the factory and asked."

"I'm not asking you in my official capacity! And don't get mad — this is a social call, and I can draw the line between duty and friendship. I'm only trying to help you, to protect you. You know very well that, in my position, I can't be seen with a foreigner in public. That's why I couldn't come to see you at the factory."

"Well, what about the foundry?" I asked again. "What is it that you want to know?"

"I'm risking my life in telling you this," she said. "Swear that you'll never reveal to anyone the source of this information."

"I promise," I assured her.

"Okay. Yesterday, we sent off a report to the Central Prosecuting Office about your foundry; it's apparently using the wrong kind of metal for the mortars! I don't know much about it, but this is considered a very serious matter. When our office forwards a case to Alma-Ata, it always means real trouble. Those armaments are for the army, and there's a war going on! If it turns out that there's sabotage, heads will roll! And you, being a Jew, surely can't remain silent about sabotage. That would be helping the enemy!"

A cold chill passed through me. "But Lena, I'm only a simple laborer. How could I possibly know whether the metal was right or wrong? I know as much about metallurgy as you do. I still don't see what all this has to do with me!"

In a serious tone she replied, "I know you have nothing to do with it, but you once told me that you like to hang around the furnaces a lot. You said that they fascinate you. Don't you see? You're a foreigner and a Jew. The director and the head engineer have pull, and they'll manage to clear themselves of the charge, but they'll have to find someone to blame it on. You can be sure they'll find a scapegoat — and you'll be the one!"

Now I realized the risk she was taking in telling me all this!

"What should I do, Lena? Should I try to leave?"

"No, that would point the finger at you," she said.

"Anyway," I said, "I have no passport, no documents and nowhere to go. Leaving is out of the question." While I was speaking, my thoughts ran frantically and uselessly in all directions.

"The first thing to do," Lena said, speaking emphatically, "is to stay away from the furnaces! Don't help them load the furnaces; better yet, switch shops altogether."

I didn't have a chance to thank her, for just then the two women returned with the tea, chattering to each other and to Lena, and serving the boiling "tea" in thick glasses.

I was too preoccupied for social conversation. Soon, I excused myself, and after thanking Lena, I went back to the factory.

All night my mind raced feverishly. What was going on? Was the metal really faulty? And if so, who was responsible? The director, or my friend, Kuzenkov? Or maybe both? It made a certain amount of sense; Kuzenkov had been shipped out of the Ukraine because the NKVD considered him undesirable and untrustworthy. Maybe they had been right about him! The more I thought about it, the more convinced I was that Kuzenkov was a traitor. He had even befriended me, as a cover-up in case of trouble! I grew so enraged at the thought that I had a notion to go to his house right then, in the middle of the night, and tell him off! Then I calmed down and began to think more rationally; I realized that I had accused him, convicted and condemned him without a trial! Why not hear his side of the story? And perhaps there was in fact no sabotage! Maybe the prosecutor was really trying to frame Kuzenkov!

In the morning, as soon as my partner had taken over, I went upstairs to Kuzenkov's office. There was a book on his desk, which contained information about ingredients and showed the tensile strengths of various metals. After looking through the book for a while, I began to ask questions, and Kuzenkov seemed happy to answer them.

"Because you are a layman," he said, "I'll give you rounded figures, to make it easier to understand. In our mortars we use soft metal to increase the enemy casualties. That is the main purpose of mortars, you know — to injure the enemy's infantry or to kill them. So the more chips of shrapnel we can drive from the mortar, the better. For instance, we calculate that if the explosion will break up the metal skirt into one hundred pieces of shrapnel, it will kill or put out of action ten enemy soldiers. If the metal is harder, instead of one hundred pieces we'll get only seventy chips; and instead of ten, only seven enemy soldiers will be hit."

Then I took a deep breath and asked him, "How can the army be sure that you're using the right metal? I mean, with the right degree of softness?"

"They check on us," Kuzenkov replied.

"They do? How?"

"It's done by that navy lieutenant; you've seen her around," he said. "Haven't you ever seen her come into the shop and take samples? She has her own laboratory, and she tests our production for quality. The army doesn't trust anyone!"

I began to think that the entire accusation was nothing but a frame-up. Kuzenkov would have to be insane to use the wrong metal, knowing that the army was checking almost every batch. The navy lieutenant, I'd been told, was a chemical engineer, and had the loneliest job in the district. Because of her peculiar position, being the one who checked on the quality of the armaments, she was not allowed to associate with anyone in the factories.

I was now convinced of Kuzenkov's innocence; if he had something to hide, he would certainly not be talking to me so openly.

I said, "Stepan Ilyanovich, please listen to me. I have something very serious to tell you. Yesterday when I was in the library, a Kazakh approached me and asked me all kinds of questions about our shop. At first I suspected that he was a spy, and I slipped a note to the librarian asking her to call the police. He noticed it, and immediately showed me his security card. He was from the prosecutor's office! Then he asked me about the metal we use, and I told him to ask you, since I don't know anything about such things. This made him angry and he told me he doesn't need my advice, and warned me to keep my mouth shut or I'd be in trouble."

Kuzenkov's face turned white, and he started to tremble. I thought he was going to faint. When he managed to reach the sofa, I gave him a glass of water, and helped him to lie down. I asked if I should call a doctor.

"No, no, don't do that," he said. "I'll be all right in a minute. You are a real friend! This will give me time to clear up the mess. That woman must have reported me! She might be a chemist, but she knows nothing about metals! It's true that we sometimes run out of soft metal, you see; we've been expecting a trainload of scrap metal, but it hasn't arrived yet. The thing is, if we stopped production, we'd never catch up! We hardly make the norm as it is. So I told the director to mix in some harder metal in the meantime. We'll get a few chips less, but still, that's better than nothing at all! But that witch! How could she do this to me!"

He asked me to leave; he had to prepare his defense. We agreed to keep the whole thing secret. He thanked me again for my friendship, shaking my hand. I was now convinced of his innocence; he had even done it with the approval of the director.

As I walked down the stairs, my partner passed by. He wiped the sweat off his seamed face and said, "I'd hate to lose you, my boy. In my old age, you're a blessing for me, but I see that you won't last long here. I've told you before; stay away from the big shots! If you don't, they'll get rid of you one day!"

The next morning an official announcement informed the public that due to the necessity of overhauling the power station, the factory would be closed until further notice. It was a terrible blow to the people, for working in a factory entitled them to 800 grams of daily bread; and working in the foundry, to 1000 grams. Now, while they were laid off, they'd get only 400 grams a day!

Each shop retained a few men for maintenance, and I was one of them. "That Jew is lucky," I heard one of the Russian workers say. What they didn't know was that Kuzenkov and the director had kept me on the job for their own protection. I ran into my partner outside, and whispered, "You see, friendship does pay off sometimes."

But he only shook his head sadly. "You're wrong," he insisted. "You'll see; there'll be plenty of trouble for you!"

The director, who had always kept himself aloof and was seldom seen speaking to a laborer, suddenly appeared in the foundry, accompanied by Kuzenkov. He walked up to me, asked my name, and shook my hand; then both men glanced at each other. The director gave me a faint smile and said good-bye.

There was nothing to do in the foundry shop, so I was assigned to the power house. The foreman there ordered me to climb down into the piston hole, and wash out the oil and grease. I asked him to provide me with some work clothes, which any worker would be entitled to, doing such dirty work. But he refused, on the grounds that I was not a permanent worker in the power house.

I pleaded with him, "Look, comrade, I only have this one pair of pants and one shirt; if I go down into that oil and grease, there'll be nothing left of them! Please, can't you give me some work clothes?"

"If you don't like this assignment," he said, "you can go back to your foundry!" I thought about complaining to the union, but I knew from experience that the unions in Russia were not meant for the workers. So I took his advice as an order, and returned to the foundry. The next day, to my great shock, I was summoned to court!

"For disobeying orders!" I read the summons to Kuzenkov, telling him exactly what had happened. I assured him that I had done exactly what the foreman told me; I had returned to the foundry, and found some work to do there.

"Don't worry," Kuzenkov assured me. "I'll take up your case with the director at once. That rat in the power house doesn't know who he's starting up with!"

Everybody knew the usual fines handed out to workers for *progul* — coming to work late. The first time, it was a quarter of the pay for six months; the second time, it was a quarter for twelve months; the third time, it was one year's imprisonment. If the fines were this stiff for just coming late, what did one get for disobeying orders? No one knew, and I had plenty to worry about.

The courtroom was full of people. The only one who spoke was the prosecutor, an elderly Russian. The defendants were hardly given a chance to speak for themselves. Nobody had a defense lawyer, and the Kazakh judge was handing out verdicts with the speed of sound: months, years, all kinds of fines. It almost seemed as if the verdicts had been prepared the day before, and my stomach twisted in knots of fear.

When the policeman called my name, I approached the judge's bench. The prosecutor asked me to repeat my name, and then he told the judge that he had received a message from the factory director that he was withdrawing the charges against me!

The judge let me off with a stern warning to obey orders. "Like the great Stalin said: 'We are all soldiers, and we must act as if the enemy is in front of us!'"

I hurried straight to the shop to thank Kuzenkov for his help, but was told that both he and the director were out of town on official business. I was thinking all this time how wrong my partner had been; my friendship with the big shots had indeed paid off! However, when I entered my dormitory I got a shock: there, waiting for me, was a notice from the military draft office! I was drafted into the Russian army again! The old man had been right — they were intent on getting rid of me fast!

I was instructed to be ready to leave in two days. Sadly, I said good-bye to all my friends. Misha was in Alma-Ata, on his regular visit to the hospital there, so I didn't even have a chance to say good-bye to him. However, I did leave a note for him with Lazer Kantor, thus introducing the two, and perhaps opening a contact for the local Jews with the commandant. I hoped that they would never be in need of his influence....

THE DJUSALI-KARMAKHCHI Military Draft Commandant ordered us to assemble in Kzyl-Orda. We were 25 men under the command of a Kazakh sergeant, and except for me, the entire group consisted of men over the age of 50, mostly Kazakhs. Three of the men were from Kuzar-Pash; they recognized me, and stayed close to me. This was the first time in their lives that they had been outside their village, and they were very nervous about being shipped off to the *Ooroos* country. The sergeant warned us about desertion, speaking in both Kazakhi and Russian. Anyone attempting it would face the firing squad, he told us; "*K styenke* — To the wall," he said, with a grin on his face.

We saw that the square in Kzyl-Orda was filled with other draftees. A major ordered everyone to line up in two columns. Soon I realized that, just like my first time in the Russian army, I was being drafted into a labor battalion and not a fighting unit. Standing behind the major were three civilians, the "buyers." They represented various war industries, and were entitled to pick a number of draftees out of the Kzyl-Orda district. One of them was a giant, tall and broad-shouldered, the palms of his hands as wide as a chair seat.

Pointing to the lineup, the major said to this huge man, "Go ahead; you are entitled to pick first."

The big man strode through the lineup; occasionally he stopped and asked someone a question or two, mainly the crippled veterans, many of whom still walked with canes. He asked them about their health and strength, and sometimes reached out and felt their muscles.

I thought, This is how a slave market must have looked!

A motion with his enormous index finger was a sign to the sergeant following him that this "merchandise" was accepted. Then the sergeant wrote the man's name on a paper. My friend from Kuzar-Pash was whispering to me, and the giant noticed this. He walked over to me and asked, "Do you speak Kazakhi?"

In order to look him in the eyes, I had to bend my neck way back. "Not really, comrade," I replied. "Only a few words."

With a motion of the finger, I was "bought." In the end, the giant "bought" about thirty of us, including my three Kazakh friends.

He assembled our group in a corner of the square, and addressed us: "I represent _Stroitelstvo 92_ — Construction Company Number 92. Our job is building and repairing railroads. At the moment, our next assignment is Stalingrad! The name itself ought to give you pride! Our great leader, Marshal Stalin himself, entrusted us with this very important job. Under the heavy blows of our glorious Red Army, under the personal command of the greatest military genius of the human race, Comrade Stalin, the German fascist beasts are finally being driven out of our great socialist land. But as they retreat, they are blowing up all the railroad lines. In fact, they have a huge locomotive which pulls two long hooks behind it and rips up all the rails and cross-ties. We must work swiftly to rebuild the lines, in order to supply ammunition to our victorious Red Army which is pursuing the running dogs. It is our job to speed the push to Berlin and to victory!"

He then explained that "92" was on the way to Stalingrad, and that our group would join the main body of 92 in Tashkent. He also warned us: "Desertion from 92 is considered desertion from the army, and is punishable by death!"

At Aralsk, on the northern tip of the Aral Sea, we joined up with the main body of 92. Most of the men and women, I learned, had been working for 92 for years; they lived a nomadic life, never more than six months in one place. The railroad car to which my Kazakh friends and I were assigned was already occupied by a group of men, who looked us over with curiosity, surprised at hearing me — a European — speaking the Kazakh language with my friends.

Aralsk was a port city and thus had a large fish industry. For dinner, everyone received one salted smoked fish. Our initial pleasure changed to dismay when we discovered that the fish were full of maggots. The water on our train was for drinking only, so the maggots could not be washed away. To a Jew, eating maggots is more sinful than eating pork. I thought that perhaps, if I kept the fish outside the train window, the hot sun would dry it and the wind would blow the maggots away. So, holding the fish tightly, I rested my hand outside the window, waiting for the train to move. An old Kazakh was walking around the station, carrying a bundle of dried cantaloupe for sale. As the train began to move, the old man noticed my fish; quickly he pointed to his bundle and to my fish — he wanted to trade! Before the train picked up speed we concluded the deal! For the next few days, while my companions ate fish with maggots, I blissfully chewed on the sugar-sweet dry cantaloupe! I was certain that, once again, I had met Eliyahu *Ha-Navi*!

For me, this fishy story had a happy ending; but I remembered reading that it was maggots in the food of the Czar's navy, on the warship Potyomkin, that had caused the revolt of the sailors which had in turn sparked the Revolution which eventually toppled the throne of the Czars in 1917. Today, though, these enslaved Soviet peoples were trained to suffer in silence, not daring to utter a word of protest against the regime, even while eating maggots.

That evening, one of the Kazakhs disappeared. A deserter! Everyone was frightened. We knew what would happen if he were caught.

Soon our speeding train crossed the border of the Kazakh Soviet Republic into Russia, and early one morning we arrived in Stalingrad.

The original name of the city had been Czaritzin. It is located on the western bank of the Volga, where the river empties into the Caspian Sea. With a population of 750,000, it was the largest city in the region. During the Revolution, there had been heavy fighting there between the "White Generals," who were faithful to the Czar, and the Red Army under Lenin and Trotsky. Stalin himself had played a minor role in those days, being an obscure political officer on the southern front. Trotsky and his Red Army had liberated the city from the White Army, but, subsequently, Stalin had chased Trotsky out of Russia, and taken credit for all the victories. He renamed the city Stalingrad.

Hitler's orders to the German army were clear: "Take Stalingrad at any cost!" Conquering this city would split Russia in half, and would have enabled the Germans to advance on Moscow from the rear.

On September 15, 1942, the German Sixth Army, under the command of Field Marshal Paulus, reached Stalingrad. There it was stopped by the Russians, who fought bitterly and gallantly, while new reserves were being organized. On November 19, 1942, the Russians began their counter-attack from the north and the south. Four days later, the two Russian armies met, and the pincers were closed on the entire German Sixth Army and its foreign volunteers, who included the Spanish Blue Division, Italians, Rumanians, Hungarians, Czechs, Slovaks and Poles. This legion was trapped between the Volga and the Don Rivers; Marshal Paulus wanted to break out of the ring by retreating, but Hitler ordered him to hold his ground at any price. Marshal Mannstein made a supreme effort to break through from the southwest, but failed.

On January 31, 1943, a major of the Russian infantry, charging ahead of his men, captured Field Marshal Paulus and his entire staff. What an appropriate quirk of fate: the major who captured the command bunker was Jewish! The Russian victory at Stalingrad marked the beginning of the end for Hitler's vaunted "Thousand Year Empire."

I had seen many scenes of destruction: my home town, Lomza; Minsk in flames; Smolensk bombed out. But nothing could be compared to what I saw in Stalingrad! In the entire city, not one single house was left standing. We were fortunate to have bunks to sleep on inside our boxcars. The civilians and military of Stalingrad slept in the streets, or in holes in the ground.

The civilian survivors told us contradicting versions of how the city came to be destroyed. Some said that the Germans had blown up the city, block by block. Others claimed that the Russians had finished the job, that after the Russians retreated, the Red Army had bombarded the city constantly with heavy artillery and _katyushas_ — rockets — from across the river, destroying block after block.

The bodies of Red Army men were buried with honors, in every square of the city. Each grave was marked with the dead man's name, and a red star. The German corpses were loaded on trucks and dumped into the Volga River. The Russians said, "We shall eat pure Aryan fish for the next hundred years." Hundreds of thousands of German prisoners of war were shipped out immediately to Siberian prison camps, or to the coal mines of Karaganda, while their allies — the Rumanians, Hungarians, Spanish and Italians — were kept in Stalingrad and used to remove the debris from the city streets.

Battalion 92 moved in with machinery and manpower. We were nearly two thousand men and women, divided into brigades under trained foremen and technicians.

First we rebuilt the primary tracks at the main station; then we went to work on the reserve lines. We were not used to the arduous task of carrying the heavy crossties and steel rails; when the day's work was done, we were exhausted! Still, we realized that we were much better off than the people of Stalingrad.

At night, lying on my bunk, I immersed myself in prayer. On this particular day I had heard terrible rumors, unbelievable rumors. Three different people had told me that whenever the Germans found a Jew, they would kill him! I just couldn't believe it; I had never seen a word about this before. Nothing had ever been mentioned in the Soviet press, and I had read the newspapers almost every day.

The Stalingrad natives told me that wherever the Germans took over, they forced all the Jews into one small area. Then they would round up and murder every man, woman and child!

"It can't be true! It's impossible! No human being can be so cruel!" I said, not wanting to believe it. But I had seen with my own eyes what the German soldiers had done to the Jews of my home town.

I decided to go and look for Jews the next day after work; I knew that Stalingrad had a large Jewish community because the rabbi of Lomza, Rabbi Aaron Baksht, had often spoken about his previous position in Czaritzin.

The next day, as soon as we were dismissed from work, I took off for the city. I had walked only two blocks from the station when suddenly I heard frightened cries: "*Ya Polski! Ya Polski! Nye yestem Nyemtzen!* — I'm Polish! I'm Polish! I'm not a German!" a man was screaming. He was surrounded by a circle of Red Army men and was apparently an escaped prisoner. He was trying to convince the Russians that he was not a German but a Pole, hoping for better treatment. I pushed my way through the crowd to the highest in rank, a major.

"Comrade Major," I said, "I speak Polish. Can I be of any help?"

"Yes, you certainly can," the major thanked me. "It looks like this Fritz escaped from a prisoner-of-war train. See what you can get out of him while we check through his bag."

The man was stretched out on the ground, crying. He was wearing a civilian raincoat over his German army uniform. His face was covered by his hands, and he looked bruised and beaten. I stooped down and began to question him. Suddenly, he uncovered his face. We looked at each other — and both of us recoiled in shock!

I was looking into the eyes of Karl Hoffmann, the Nazi son of our family friend, dear Mr. Hoffmann. This was the very one who had beaten me and knocked me down in front of the German Lutheran Church in Lomza almost three years ago!

"Karl," I gasped, "is it really you? What's happening back home? When did you last see my family? Are they still in Lomza?"

Instead of answering my questions, he began to kiss my dusty shoes. "Please, please, for my mother's sake, help me! Tell them I'm Polish. Have pity on me; be a real Jew!"

I saw that the Russians had almost finished checking through his bag, so I said softly, "Now listen, Karl: I'll help you, but tell me, quickly, what's going on at home? Quick!"

"Your family is fine," he said. "We put all the Jews in a ghetto, for their own protection. You know how the Poles and the Germans hate the Jews! They are safe and protected and I myself supplied them with food. Yes, yes, I personally delivered food to your mother! Chaim, help me! Save me!" And again he began crying and kissing my feet.

By this time, the Russians had finished searching through his things, and the major ordered one man to pull off Karl's boots. A photo of a girl fell out of the first boot, and on the back of the photograph was written: "To my dear captain." The Russians couldn't read German, but the major could decipher the Latin letters of "captain." "What! A German captain!" the major exclaimed. One shot rang out, and Karl Hoffmann was dead!

The Russians looked at each other, pleased. "That rat almost got away!" a captain remarked to the major.

The major then turned to me, his finger still on the trigger of the loaded gun. "And you! What were you talking about with him for so long? Couldn't you tell right away that he was a German officer? Maybe you're one of them too?! Let's see your papers!"

I was in shock. It had all happened so fast: the words about my family, the mention of a ghetto, and the shooting. It was not the first time I had ever seen a man killed in front of me, in cold blood, but that was not a sight one becomes accustomed to.

"Your papers!" the major was screaming, pushing the gun into my chest.

"_Chi_, Comrade Major, you won't believe me if I tell you! That pig was the assistant to the Nazi commandant in my home town and I recognized him from the first minute. I was trying to get some news about my family at home out of him."

"Let me see your documents!" the major demanded, pushing the gun deeper into my chest.

"*Chi*, I belong to the Railroad Construction Company 92. We're draftees, and never carry any documents. I'm stationed at the railroad station only two blocks away. Comrade Major, you can easily verify this if you'll only take me to my foreman."

The trigger-happy major remained unconvinced.

A captain finally came to my rescue. "Major, he does speak like a *Chi Sammarra*."

The major withdrew his gun from my chest; I had passed the first test.

Then he and the captain took me to 92 to verify my identity. On the way, I told them that I was from Poland, which had become Western Byelorussia in 1939. I had learned my Russian in the Kuybishev District, and that's why I talked like a *Chi Sammarra*.

"Then that makes you a *Zemlyak* — from the same county that I was born in. I come from Stary Booyan, in the Kuybishev District," the captain said.

At the railroad station, the foreman verified my identity, and the two officers let me go free.

Lying on my bunk that night, my mind worked feverishly, reconstructing every word Karl had said. Why hadn't he mentioned my father, who had been his father's close friend? Did Karl deliberately avoid mentioning him? He had talked about Mama and the family but not about Papa. That dream about my father the night I was chased by the beast — could it be significant? Ever since then I had been wondering, deep down in my heart, whether Papa was still alive. Oh, why hadn't I asked Karl about him too? And what about the ghetto? Why was it never mentioned in the Soviet press? Karl said the Jews had been put in a ghetto to protect them from the Poles and the Germans. But since when was a Nazi a protector of Jews?

At first I had felt disgust towards the major for killing Karl in cold blood. But not anymore; perhaps the major knew about the ghettos, and perhaps he knew that the Germans themselves killed without mercy. And yet, Karl's cries rang in my ears all night. His dead body was constantly before my eyes, and I couldn't sleep.

Perhaps I should go and bury him? No — because of the curfew I couldn't go out at night, and in the daytime it would be suicide to be caught paying such respect to a German officer. Still, I told myself, for the sake of his father's memory.... The next morning, I asked to be excused for a few minutes. I ran to the place, but his body was gone.

Every day after work, I searched the huge city for Jews, in basements, in ruins and in holes in the ground. I asked everyone I met if there were any Jews around. The answer was always the same: "No, no Jews."

While I was searching for Jews, my co-workers were busy searching for trophies. To them a "trophy" meant food, shoes or clothing left behind by the retreating Germans. Despite warnings about the danger of mines and grenades, purposely rigged up by the enemy, the people entered and searched every bunker and hole in the ground. The most prized booty was a pair of Italian shoes. Shoes and boots had been a problem in the Soviet Union for years, and a pair of good ones was considered a treasure; but Italian shoes were the greatest treasure of all. The Italian troops wore shoes covered with steel for mountain climbing, and the person who was lucky enough to find a pair of these was assured of footwear for many years. The other precious item was soap, which for years had been in short supply. Because of the innumerable boobytraps rigged up by the Germans, many a man lost his hands and feet, and even his life, for a piece of soap. Yet, despite the explosions, the search did not stop. The most fascinating trophy of all was a loaf of vacuum-sealed bread. We had never seen old bread so soft and fresh!

There were some comical incidents too. The Kazakhs found what they thought was marmalade, and they spread it thickly on their bread and ate it. It was only after many were hospitalized with stomach pains that it was discovered that the marmalade was really shoe polish!

In a couple of weeks we finished rebuilding the tracks in and around the main station, and most of Battalion 92 moved on to the western branch of the line. However, one brigade — mine — was assigned to the Stalingrad tractor factory.

When we arrived at the huge factory, we were astonished to find brigades of Russian women clearing the rubble and preparing for the rebuilding of the factory, only days after the enemy had left. Our job was to reconstruct the complicated railway line within the factory grounds.

Before the war, this factory produced tanks and artillery, in particular long-barreled artillery for the navy. The finished product was delivered by way of the Volga River directly to the Black and to the Baltic Seas. One could envision the tremendous heat that had destroyed these buildings, for many of the long-barreled cannons were twisted like corkscrews! The people told us how these buildings had changed hands time and again, how the Red Army battled the Germans for each floor. As the Germans occupied one floor, the Russians would counter-attack. There was bitter hand-to-hand fighting. Some buildings were occupied by the Russians and the Germans at the same time, each on different floors. Finally, Soviet marines blew up the entire building, killing friend and foe alike!

We began repairing the lines, beginning at the bank of the Volga River, and continuing into the various shops and buildings. The banks of the river were littered with mounds of German steel helmets which had been removed from the bodies before they were dumped into the water.

It was a hot day, and the southern sun was baking the city. I was terribly thirsty, so I stepped over to the river to drink. I removed my shoes and waded out a few feet, where the flowing river water would be cleaner than the water near the bank. When I bent over to drink, I suddenly saw a pair of hard blue eyes staring up at me! For a moment I thought they belonged to Karl Hoffmann, and I blacked out — I fainted and fell into the water!

When I woke up, I was lying on the sandy bank, and standing over me, smiling, was the giant Zakharov. "So!" he laughed. "You're scared of a dead German? What's going to happen when you have to face a live one?! You're lucky I passed by; you could have drowned!"

I thanked him for saving my life, and told him the whole story: that I thought the dead German was Karl, and what had happened only a few days ago. It was somehow a good feeling to tell it all. And he believed me! The fantastic story of Karl Hoffmann was nearly as strange to him as it was to me. He told me kindly to take the rest of the day off, which I gladly did. I hitchhiked back to the main station, happy to be back in our boxcar and my own bunk.

Again, I tried to analyze the few words which Karl had said to me before he was shot. I was almost certain that he had intentionally omitted mentioning Papa. And now, a new suspicion began to gnaw at my heart: could Karl have had something to do with Papa's...I didn't dare say the word....

24

A NEW ORDER arrived: Battalion 92 was to pack up and move on. Instead of 92, another railroad *Stroitelstvo* would follow the victorious army's advances and rebuild the rail lines. Although officially we were not told our next destination, there were rumors that it was Murmansk and Archangelsk; this made sense because most of the cargoes from the USA were coming through the port of Murmansk, and the railways there were inadequate for the transportation of these huge shipments.

Everyone began to collect and hoard supplies. It was known that in the northern part of the country, salt was unobtainable, and in Stalingrad tons of salt were wasting away near the banks of the Volga, left behind by the retreating Germans.

Then there was the problem of clothing. Murmansk and Archangelsk are located near the North Pole; most of the year it is winter there, and the cold is unbearable. Soap, too, was on the most-wanted list, and became so expensive that it could only be traded for a large amount of bread.

Labor Battalion 92 was comprised of two types of people. The core consisted of professional railroad-construction workers. They lived their lives on wheels, together with their families. With the war mobilization draining manpower, Battalion 92 was supplemented with freed prisoners, and with draftees who for one reason or another were barred from regular service in the army.

The 30 men who filled the two tiers of bunks in my boxcar contained eight or ten draftees from Kazakhstan. The rest were ex-prisoners, including murderers. They were not trusted to join the armed forces, since it was feared that they might defect to the enemy instead of fighting them. These men were assigned to our labor battalion straight from the prisons. The boxcar was controlled by a tightly-knit gang of Ukrainians, who were dominated by a tall, broad-shouldered man with cold green eyes, and a bush of graying black hair. His head was long and narrow — like a cucumber, I thought to myself. He was called only by his last name, Kovalenko.

Kovalenko had been serving a 25-year sentence in a Siberian prison camp for choking a man to death with his bare hands. During his eighteenth year in prison, he was released and assigned to 92. He was a bully who frequently bragged that he could twist off a man's head as easily as a chicken's. While we were stationed in Stalingrad, the Ukrainians were obnoxious, but restrained. They didn't dare step out of line, since the city was full of police and the dreadful experience of a Siberian prison camp was still in their bones. But after we pulled out of Stalingrad, and started on our way to Murmansk, they began to terrorize the men in our boxcar. The bully Kovalenko became the overlord of the crew.

I began to feel like a lamb among a pack of wolves. The six Ukrainians were constantly itching for a fight, their sharp knives always ready to be drawn and used. I tried to avoid them, dreading the moment when I might be forced into a clash with them. It could hardly be avoided, cooped up together as we were, day after day, in the same boxcar.

I would get up early in the morning, usually while it was still dark and everyone was sleeping. I washed my hands, dipping my cup into the bucket of drinking water; then, stretched out on my bunk, under cover of my blanket, I put on my *tefillin* and softly recited the morning prayers. Whether we were on the job and had to report for work early, or traveling and keeping late hours, I always managed to say my prayers undetected, unnoticed by anyone.

One morning, when it was still black outside, I awoke and was about to get up to wash my hands. I suddenly heard sounds of a struggle going on in the dark; I heard men gasping, cursing and moaning. Then, as a train was passing our boxcar, something was thrown out of the door. The rhythmic sound of the passing wheels on the tracks, which was usually "tra-tra-tra-tatata," was interrupted and changed briefly to "blump, blump, blump," but soon reverted to the regular "tratata." In the total darkness I could see neither what was going on nor who the people involved were, but all my senses told me that a murder had just been committed!

I lay frozen with fear. With my eyes shut tightly, I heard the men hastily returning to their bunks. For what seemed hours I lay there, pretending to be asleep. When daylight came, and I heard people moving around, I carefully opened my eyes, and was told that Salim, one of the Kazakhs, had deserted. Just the previous day Salim had been arguing with one of Kovalenko's gang about some spilled soup. Perhaps the other Kazakhs suspected foul play, but, if so, they were too timid to say anything.

Later, one of them whispered to me in Kazakhi, "In our country, Salim might have tried to desert. But in _Ooroos_ country? Certainly not! In Kazakhstan he would find friends, relatives, desert, plenty of room to hide, but here? Why wouldn't he have run away before we left Stalingrad if he wanted to desert? Closer to Kazakh country! Why would he not tell us, his Kazakh brothers? No, no, he did not run away; he did not desert!"

I kept silent, for I felt the imminent danger to my own life. Now I began to wonder if the Kazakh who had disappeared while we were still in Kazakhstan had really deserted. On the road, there is no way of checking up on anyone, and the gang was counting on that. A dead man found on the tracks is not proof of murder; most likely it would be considered suicide or an accident. Besides, with thousands of men dying on the battlefront, one more dead would not matter. And who would stop a battalion of rail builders speeding to fulfill a government assignment because of one dead body? I thought of telling Zakharov, the kind-hearted giant who had saved me from drowning, but he was in the train ahead of us. Finally I concluded that I must forget what I knew, and instead concentrate on finding some way to become a friend — a very close friend — of Kovalenko! Only under his protection could I expect to survive; otherwise, sooner or later, I too might end up under speeding train wheels.

As we neared our destination, the Arctic Circle, it reminded the leader and his gang of the Siberian prison camps they had left. The further we traveled, the wilder they seemed to grow.

One night someone stole the bread from under my straw pillow. I knew who took it, but dared not say anything. During our stay in Stalingrad, the "King" and his gang had worked in a different brigade, so there hadn't been too much opportunity to associate with them. They hadn't shown open hostility towards me, although they knew I was a Jew. Perhaps it was because they hated the Kazakhs even more. However, I was certain that sooner or later they would turn against me. I'd better have someone to protect me, or....

There was plenty of time on our hands; all day we did nothing but watch the passing scenery through the open door of our boxcar. I kept to myself on my bunk, thinking and dreaming, longing for the warmth of the southern sun; and all the while we were traveling farther and farther north! Why did we have to travel so far? There must be a reason! And perhaps this was it: the Russians always boasted that in a socialist society, unemployment does not exist. I realized that full employment was achieved here simply by keeping people on the road! There were at least fifteen hundred people in Battalion 92, and for the next two months we would do nothing but travel! And all over the country there were millions of people on the road, constantly being transferred from one area to another in this vast land. This was their method of eliminating unemployment!

The sound of the speeding wheels accompanied us constantly, and occasionally we heard music: the train's whistle. To a layman, all train whistles may sound alike, but to the members of Battalion 92, our train's whistle could be distinguished from all others. We could tell if our whistle had "caught cold," for its tune became sour and thick; we knew what each sound meant, what it signaled to the stationmaster.

And, of course, we talked. The discussions ranged over many subjects, and everyone had something to say. Finally Kovalenko made a crack at me. "Say, Chaim," he said, smiling with his cold green eyes, "have you ever been in the Jewish capital?"

I assumed that he was talking about Jerusalem, so I replied, "No."

"Well," he said, "I've been there a number of times. My uncle once owned a farm there."

I was amazed! Kovalenko in Jerusalem? To make sure, I repeated, "Your uncle owned a farm there?"

"Sure, two kilometers from Berditchev," he said. Then I realized that he was not talking about Jerusalem, the holy city, but about Berditchev in the Ukraine, famous because the renowned Chasidic Rabbi Levi Yitzchok had lived there. Because the city's population was almost entirely Jewish, the gentiles joked about it, calling it the "Jewish capital."

Kovalenko continued: "So I go to the market there, and an old Jewish woman is selling bagels. 'Hot bagels! Hot bagels! Smell them yourselves! Fresh from the oven!' I looked at the steam still rising from the bagels and my mouth began to water; so I picked out two bagels, and I said, 'These smell good; how much?'

"'Five *kopek*,' she says. So I give her five *kopek*; and then she says, 'Here — smell them! To *eat* is ten *kopek*!'"

Everybody laughed and I, too, joined in; considering the company and the characters, this was a relatively mild anti-Jewish joke. But I was worried; first a joke, then a nasty comment, then insults, fights and, eventually, physical violence. I too might end up under the speeding train wheels unless, somehow, I could win the friendship of Kovalenko!

Because of the priority given to military trains, our train often had to stop and wait before entering a station. Frequently we waited for hours, and sometimes for days, before we were permitted to pass through a station and proceed on our way. At these stops, when we received our "dinner" — raw potatoes or flour — the mob would spread out to find firewood for cooking. Anything that could burn was broken up and thrown to the flames. Lumber, precious crossties, fences built around the tracks for snow protection, all were used for firewood.

Most of the time the trainmen informed us when we were going to have a lengthy layover. Then we were able to go to the nearby forest to collect mushrooms, and if there happened to be a stream nearby, we bathed and washed the only clothes in our possession — the ones we were wearing!

During one of these lengthy stops, Kovalenko and his gang were sitting around the fire, roasting potatoes in the hot ashes, and telling tales. Timidly, I said, "Say, Comrade Kovalenko, do you know the history of potatoes?" The entire gang burst into raucous laughter.

"Listen to him! The history of potatoes, he says!"

Kovalenko ordered silence. "Tell us, Jew — what do you mean? Is a potato a king? A country? How could it have a history? What're you talking about anyway?" He placed his powerful fingers around the back of my neck.

I answered, "You see, Kovalenko, everything on earth has a history, except God, of course. Take yourself, for instance. I'm sure you could write a book about your life: the house you were born in, your village, your father and mother, your family, your whole past since the first day you can remember."

His strong squeeze on my neck relaxed, and I could breathe more easily. Razolnikov, Kovalenko's right-hand man, began to laugh. "Come on! What kind of dumb talk is that?"

"Shut up!" Kovalenko said, and gave his best friend such a shove that he almost toppled over. "Shut up!" Kovalenko shouted again. "This guy knows what he's talking about. He's right; I could talk all night about the troubles I've been through, about my poor old Pa and Ma and our farm, and everything!"

For a moment, it seemed that Kovalenko was moved; his thoughts were drifting from the cold, wild steppes to the warmth of childhood, home and family.

"So what about the history of potatoes?" one of the gang finally asked, uneasy about Kovalenko's sudden nostalgia.

Kovalenko, scratching his head, was still thinking. "And what about what you said before — 'except God'; what did you mean by that?"

I moved closer to the fire. "You see, everything has a beginning, a growth, and an end — in other words, a history — except God. Those who believe in Him know He is the Creator, and has no beginning, no change, no history. Understand?"

Seeing their blank stares, I realized that I was on the wrong track. For a moment there was silence. Then Kovalenko said, "Maybe I understand or maybe I don't. It makes sense, or maybe it doesn't. Anyhow, let's hear about potatoes. I'm sure we'll understand more about that!"

"Potatoes were once unknown in Europe," I began, addressing myself to Kovalenko. "Can you imagine the Ukraine without potatoes?"

Razolnikov interrupted again. "I don't believe Russia was ever without potatoes. All of us would die from hunger!"

"Shut up!" Kovalenko snapped at him. "I told you to stop interrupting! When other people are talking, you shut up!"

Kovalenko motioned to me to continue. I was delighted; perhaps with talk like this, I might find favor in his eyes.

"Potatoes came from America," I continued. "The Indians there were the first to raise potatoes, and then they were introduced to Europe. A Russian sea captain brought back a bag of potatoes as a gift for Queen Catherine the Great. She liked them so much that she ordered the peasants to raise the 'earth apples' — that's what they were called in those days. But they resisted, not wanting to waste their land and their sweat growing something unknown to them that was a delicacy for the queen. She ordered them to be shot!

"Later she was visiting the German Kaiser, Frederick the Great. At dinner they served the 'American delicacy', and she enjoyed them as much as she had before. The sea captain was interested in taking another trip to America, and convinced the Czaritza of the tremendous value the 'earth apples' would have in feeding an army. She ordered him to go and bring back a whole shipload. Again, the farmers resisted planting them, and again some of them were shot. Finally some of the farmers gave in, but there was a terrible misunderstanding: instead of picking the potato tuber which grows under the ground, they picked the little green balls which grow on top of the potato plant! When these were served to the queen, she became sick, and ordered the navy captain to be shot! The farmers got sick from eating these parts of the potatoes too, and refused to grow that 'poison' any more. Finally they discovered their mistake, but in the meantime the innocent sea captain and many poor peasants had been shot for nothing! That's how those Czars used to be, you know; to them, killing a person was like killing a fly!"

This story made a great impression, and they all proceeded to discuss it in detail. Kovalenko removed his fingers from my neck altogether, and placed his heavy arm around my shoulders, which I interpreted as a sign of friendship. He was so impressed by my story that he offered me a baked potato.

"I'm telling you, comrades," he said to his gang, "the Jews are the most educated people in Russia. My father used to say that all the time! Can you imagine Russia, the Ukraine, without potatoes?"

He picked a large potato out of the fire, blowing on it and tossing it from one hand to the other. Finally, when it had cooled off to a bearable temperature, he stood up and exclaimed, "I hereby eat a toast to the brave sea captain who gave us potatoes and who was shot by that horrible Czaritza Yekaterina!"

"Bravo! Bravo!" they all shouted. Then a flood of stories about the Czars poured forth. What degenerates and murderers they all had been! Peter the Great had strangled his son to death with his own hands; Alexander the First had killed his own father, Czar Pavel; Catherine the Great had killed her husband; on and on went the litany of betrayal and murder.

It was not hard to understand why Communism had conquered the masses. With all its evils, it must have seemed like paradise compared to the dreadful rule of the Czars, who held the power of life and death in their vast domain, and used it so freely!

The stories kept coming, one after the other. It seemed as if a spring had been tapped by my few words; the men poured out tales of their youth, their life in prison, their grievances, past and present. Kovalenko was happy. He gave me a slap on the back, a visible demonstration of comradeship. I turned towards him.

"Kovalenko," I said, "the people like you and respect you. There's nothing to do here; why not have evenings of stories and songs? Everybody's so lonely and bored. Somebody should start that, just like the farmers do on the collectives, and you're the man to do it!"

My words hit the target. "Yes, yes. I like the idea!" Kovalenko said. He took me aside and whispered, "We can't ask the Party secretary to arrange anything; she's too lazy and stuck-up. We'll have to do it ourselves. I picked up an accordion in Stalingrad. I haven't played in years, but if you can sing, I could accompany you. Can you sing? Do you know any Russian songs, especially the new ones?"

"Sure I can sing; remember, I used to work on a *kolkhoz*, and there's plenty of singing there!" I said.

Without losing any time, he authoritatively announced to all the gang: "Next time, I mean on the next long layover, bring your friends and we'll have lots of songs and stories. Remember, it was my idea!"

When we reached a station about half-way to Murmansk, we heard rumors that our destination had been changed. Instead of going to Murmansk, Battalion 92 was now destined for the Ural Mountains, the District of Sverdlovsk. Another railway battalion was being shipped to Murmansk. In our train, some people were of the opinion that we would have been better off in Murmansk, while others argued the opposite.

We were told that there would be a long layover. That evening, most of the people on the train gathered near our boxcar. Anticipation of the evening's activities made the crowd lively and happy. They rounded up crossties and laid them in a circle around our fire, furnishing seats for some, while others stood or sat on the ground.

Kovalenko played a tune on his accordion, and everybody settled down. They sang, and Kovalenko accompanied them, as best he could. The songs were all very old; without radios, and always on the move, these Russians were unfamiliar with the latest songs about the war against the Germans. Now my repertoire of war songs, which I had learned during my days in Karobka, really came in handy, and I was made the *zapyevala*!

Kovalenko praised me, and referred to me as "my good friend." His words were music to my ears! He was particularly delighted when I announced a song about a partisan from the Ukraine. "That's my home!"

he shouted. I sang:

> In the forest an old oak stands,
> And under the oak tree a partisan lies.
> Not moving, not breathing, as if asleep,
> His golden curls are tossed by the wind.

As was customary, I repeated the last two lines, and the crowd sang along with me. The sound reverberated through the darkness of the endless forest; and my voice was like a pinpoint in that vastness. I continued:

> And over him an old woman, his beloved mother,
> Wiping her tears, is talking to her son:
> 'I gave birth to you, I raised you tenderly,
> And now your grave will be here, in the woods!'

The words, the melody, touched their hearts and their eyes glistened with tears.

> Your father was a partisan all the years,
> And there, under Poltava, he lies.
> I'm a widow now, with five children to raise;
> And you were the best of all, Andrey, my son!

The people were moved. Kovalenko was beaming with pleasure. This may have been the first time in his life that his popularity did not stem from his brute physical strength. He was not only the chairman and director of this concert; he was its sole musician, thus sharing in the applause. And when the crowd demanded more, he ordered me to continue, asking for more new songs.

Throughout the evening the crowd grew, as more and more people came down to join the singing. Kovalenko was supremely happy. He announced that we would have another concert the next night, if we didn't move on; or, if we did, we'd have it at the next long layover. For at least another week, there wasn't an extended stop, but finally we had another long layover. Our train did not get clearance to enter the station, and we were forced to wait near a small river flowing down through a valley. Many people bathed during the day, despite the freezing temperatures, and some washed their clothes.

That night everybody gravitated to our car; they wanted to hear another concert. A fire was made on the river bank; people sprawled on the grass, and many old favorites were sung. Then it was my turn, and Kovalenko demanded a "good one." By now I understood that, under his rough exterior, he was soft and sentimental and that for him a "good one" meant words which touch the heart and bring out tears. I figured that he, too, must have had a mother once. And so I sang:

> I know that at the window my old mother,
> Remembering me, will begin to sigh.
> Do not grieve for me!
> Do not weep for me!
> I shall return home, your beloved son!
>
> The night is dark;
> The moon is covered;
> The wind is humming;
> I know that at the window the old one is crying!
>
> Do not grieve for me!
> Do not weep for me!
> I shall return home, your beloved son!

Many of the people were wiping away tears. The magic word "mother" had its effect. The tears and sighs, the wish to return home safely, made a tremendous impact. Their voices stormed the sky as they sang along with me, "I shall return home, your beloved son!"

Now I began another song, a favorite one in Karobka:

> It is a dark night —
> Only bullets whistling over the steppe,
> Only the wind humming in the wagons,
> Isolated stars glimmering softly.
>
> In the darkness of night, I know you aren't asleep;
> At the baby's cradle, you are wiping your tears.
>
> You are waiting, you cannot sleep,
> Like a tired soldier who can't doze off at war!
> The angry whirlwind;
> The dry snow, whipping around my head —
> If I could only fly back to you!

Suddenly I was shoved forward so hard that I fell straight into the hot ashes surrounding the burning fire. As I picked myself up I saw that Kovalenko, just as astonished as I was, had jumped up and grabbed the assailant, screaming, "What was that for? Are you crazy?"

I rushed to the water to cool off my burning hands. Razolnikov and the whole crowd were in an uproar.

"Why did you hit him?" they roared. Apparently the man had been unaware that Kovalenko was now my friend. By now, he was bleeding from his nose and mouth, and the gang was not finished with him yet.

He cried out, "The devil was singing out of that damned Jew! Watch out; he'll get you all!"

This brought the concert to an unexpected end. The incident had proven that I had gained Kovalenko's friendship and protection.

On THE LAST DAY of every month, bread cards were issued for the next month. A bread card consisted of one coupon for each day of the month. Every day, we joined the line in front of the "bread window," and gave the "bread girl" the coupon for that day; in return, she handed out the bread ration for one day. Often, we'd "cash in" the next day's coupon, thus eating up the next day's bread; almost everyone was a day ahead on his bread card. Therefore, on the last day of each month, most people received no bread at all, for they had all eaten that day's ration the day before! The bread girls favored Kovalenko and me, because of our singing. In violation of regulations, they accepted our bread coupons two days in advance. This privilege, however, was not without its price; the result was that the last two days of the month we were without bread.

Theoretically, a person could divide his bread into three small portions, to be eaten at three different times during the day. But the trouble was that all too often one of the portions of bread was stolen, and we quickly learned that the safest place for bread was in one's stomach.

One day, as we were standing in line waiting to be issued our new monthly bread cards, when Kovalenko's turn came the girl whispered to him, and did not give him a card. Kovalenko stepped back as if bitten by a snake; his face turned white and angry. When my turn came, the girl said to me sternly, "Your card is in the hands of the Party secretary, Comrade Raskova!"

"Yours, too?" Kovalenko exclaimed. We were puzzled: why would the Party secretary want our bread cards? And why only ours? We were sure that there was some mistake, and since we hadn't eaten bread for two days, we hurried straight to Raskova's boxcar. She occupied an entire boxcar: half was her office and the other half was her private room. Yevgenia Fiodorovna Raskova was the Party secretary for the entire 92nd Battalion. Every Party secretary is a miniature "Stalin" who rules his own little domain, and she exercised her authority to the fullest. She had the appropriate characteristics for it: she was arrogant, had a dominating look, and walked with the gait of an army man.

Kovalenko spoke first. "Comrade Raskova, there must be some mistake; we were denied our monthly bread cards."

"No, there is no mistake!" she barked. "The Party is the vanguard of the working people in all aspects of life! The Party of Lenin and Stalin is in charge of everything! And you two have organized secret meetings, without permission, without authority! The Party will judge you!"

"But Comrade Raskova, we didn't organize anything!" Kovalenko pleaded with the voice of a humble and hungry man. "Secret meetings? Why, there were hundreds of people there! How can you call them secret?"

"Save your talk!" she snapped. "The Party will decide on your case tomorrow night. Get out!"

We left, and it was more than hunger that disturbed us now; being accused of organizing secret meetings is a very dangerous charge, particularly for an ex-convict and for a foreigner.

Kovalenko was clearly frightened. "From now on," he said to me, "you do all the talking." The fact that this big bully could break down so quickly made me doubly worried. I tried to cheer him up.

"Why are you so jittery? Surely the Party won't believe such nonsense! So we'll be hungry for another day; so what? The bread will taste all the better when we get our rations for tomorrow."

"And I thought you Jews were supposed to be smart!" he said. "Don't you understand what's at stake? It's not the bread I'm worried about; it's our lives! We could get twenty years for this! I'm not going back to a Siberian prison camp; I'll kill her first — her and that rat, the one who pushed you into the fire! And then I'll run away or commit suicide!"

"Look, Kovalenko," I said. "Calm down. If I'm going to do all the talking, I've got to understand a few things first. First, why doesn't she hand us over to the local police?"

Looking around to be certain that no one was within hearing distance, he began lecturing me: "How do you think one becomes a Party secretary?

Believe me, one climbs to this position over many corpses. It's just like the secret police: the way to advance is by 'discovering' enemies of the people, enemies of the Party and of the state. The more arrests you make and the more confessions you get, the more notice is taken by your superiors. If no trouble exists, you create it, and then step over the dead bodies to a higher position. We're moving into new territory, you see: she wants to prove her alertness, and we will be the corpses! She's certain we can be made to confess to anything: secret organizations, sabotage, anything! But if she hands us over to the local police, and then the train moves on, will she get the credit? No!"

"But why the hurry? Why is she putting us on trial tomorrow night? Why not wait until we arrive at our destination?" I asked.

"That's what I don't know," he replied. Then he exclaimed, "Hey, what about escaping? If we go on trial tomorrow, and they don't decide themselves, they'll send the report to 'the Unholy Trinity' and we'll be sentenced to twenty years! I swear I won't go back to prison!"

"The Unholy Trinity" was the nickname for three high-ranking officers of the dreaded NKVD. Sitting in Moscow, they judged miscreants from all over the USSR. On the basis of reports sent to them, the *troyka* condemned the accused to ten years, twenty years, or even life imprisonment. There was no defense lawyer; the accused and the judges never saw each other; there might be thousands of miles between them. In due time, the accused was informed by the local prosecutor or by the police that, on the basis of his "confession," he had been condemned by the *troyka* to so-and-so many years in prison.

"No, running away is not the answer," I argued. "How long can we expect to survive in the forest? And suppose we're caught? We'll be charged with desertion and that means the death penalty! No, we must find another answer; we can always find time to run away if there's no alternative."

There was only one man I could turn to: the giant Zakharov, who was a loyal Party man. Fortunately, his boxcar was stationed next to ours; I knocked on his door and found him alone. I got right to the point. "Comrade Zakharov, you once saved my life. There's an old Jewish proverb: 'If one saves a human life, it is as if one has saved a whole world.' Please — you helped me before, and now there's another man in trouble; you can save two whole worlds! He says if he has to go to prison, he'll kill himself!"

"Prison?" he exclaimed. I told him what had happened, and about our bread cards, and the trial tomorrow.

"So, to make sure you won't run away, she is holding your bread cards, eh?" he asked, with anger in his voice. "You must be very hungry, then?"

"This is my third day without bread," I replied.

He took out a few slices of bread, some cheese and two slices of salami. "That's all I have," he said. "Go on, eat it!" My respect for him grew with every bite. I ate the cheese and part of the bread; I was embarrassed by my hunger.

"I'll take the salami to my friend Kovalenko; it'll go down well with the bread," I mumbled.

Zakharov smiled and said, "Is it because Jews don't eat meat and dairy food together? Go on, take the salami, but don't give it to your pal! He should have known better than to trespass on the Party's functions! Any meeting, for any business whatsoever, must be organized by the Party, and only by the Party! Anyway, who actually called the singing party together?"

"No one," I replied. "It was all spontaneous."

"But someone had to announce that there was going to be a party," he said. "People don't just assemble by accident — not a hundred people anyway — and someone had to be the chairman, or the announcer. So who was it? You?"

"It was Kovalenko, but the idea was mine. In all fairness, though, the people asked for it. They demanded it!" I said.

"Look, young man," Zakharov said, "forget about fairness! That's futile, in face of the trouble you're in. Now it's every man for himself! Kovalenko announced the concert; he called the people together, not you. Here's your chance to get out of this mess!"

"Comrade Zakharov, you're a member of the Party; since you'll be at the meeting, won't you help us?" I pleaded.

After thinking for a while, he said, "There *is* one bit of luck for you two; the decision will not depend on Raskova or the other Party members. Your fate will be decided by the secretary of the Sverdlovsk District. In fact, the reason for tomorrow night's meeting is really a welcome arranged by the Party secretary of the Ural District. He'll be the highest-ranking officer present at the meeting, and he'll decide about you two."

Although Zakharov had not said anything specific, indirectly he had answered a lot of my questions. Raskova wanted to show her new boss how alert and effective she was. How right Kovalenko had been; she would advance her position by stepping over our bodies!

Zakharov appeared to be deep in thought. Finally he spoke: "He is a Siberian, and you know we *Sibiryaks* are good-natured people. I don't think he'll be too harsh on you."

I thought: true, the Siberians are known to be kind, but if this one has reached the rank of Party secretary, he surely must be just as ruthless as any of them.

"Tell me, Comrade Zakharov, do you know anything about the man? What is he like?" I asked.

"The only thing I know about him is that he's supposed to have published a book of poetry. He was a colonel in the army and was wounded twice, so he was appointed Party secretary for the Sverdlovsk District."

"A Party secretary who's a poet!" I was astonished. "Then he must be silk on the inside, and iron on the outside! Don't you think the two are contradictory?"

Zakharov ignored my question, but he did promise to help us at the trial.

"You should be there, in case the Party secretary from Sverdlovsk wants to ask you some questions," he said. This was my only invitation to attend my own trial!

I shook his hand, thanking him for his help and for the life-saving food. He picked up the salami, which I had forgotten, and handed it to me. "You can eat it later, without cheese," he smiled.

"If you're a *Sibiryak*," I asked, "how do you know about Jews not eating meat and dairy food together?"

"Never mind. We'll talk about it some other time," Zakharov replied.

I had a sleepless night, lying in my bunk, planning what I would say at the trial if we were asked to testify. I would have liked to read the book of poems which the Party secretary had written. If he was a poet, he couldn't be all bad....

I thought about what Ibn Ezra, the Hebrew poet, had written: "It is impossible to learn the art of poetry second-hand. Poetic inspiration comes only from the depths of the soul." So if the Party secretary has a soul, then he must have compassion too!

All night I prepared what I would say, and what I shouldn't say, to the Party court. I decided that my best defense would be to reveal the truth about Raskova. In my mind I went over everything I had heard about her, searching for what would discredit her in the eyes of the Party. From time to time, Kovalenko sneaked over to my bunk to tell me the latest details of his escape plan. He would steal a rifle, he said, so we could keep alive in the forest by hunting. "But first I'll choke her to death, and that rotten informer as well!" he hissed.

"Instead of talking about shooting and killing," I said, "just tell me more details about her, especially things that I can use against her."

He shrugged. "What else can I tell you? She's mean, she doesn't care about anyone else, and she wants to be served her meals in bed: breakfast, lunch and supper!"

I considered accusing her of engaging in bourgeois and capitalistic habits, but I realized I had to have more serious arguments. In order to save our necks, I had to drag her down politically, if possible. At least she'd go down along with us!

It occurred to me that I had never heard the new national anthem sung by anyone in the 92nd Battalion. Part of her job was to promote patriotism, loyalty to the Soviet system, to the Party and to Stalin. Among other things, she was guilty of failing to sing, and failing to teach the new Soviet national anthem to the members of the railroad brigade.

Goncharov, the teacher in Karobka, had explained the story behind the new national anthem. He told me that Stalin, in order to show his gratitude to the United States and Great Britain for their assistance, dissolved the _Comintern_, the Communist International. To further prove his sincerity, Stalin ordered a contest for a new national anthem, since the "Internationale" was the anthem of the _Comintern_. From all over the USSR, poets and song-writers submitted their entries. The winner was to receive fabulous prizes, honor and prestige, including the Lenin Order, the highest in the USSR, and the Stalin Prize, a Soviet version of the Nobel Prize, and a fortune of money as well. Since everyone was aware that the final judge would be the dictator himself, most of the poems turned out to be eulogies to Stalin, songs of praise to the national idol.

However, one of the poets, Alexander Tvardovsky, gambled on a different angle, one which was another of Stalin's favorite themes: Russian chauvinism! Stalin was a Georgian, not a Russian; he even spoke Russian with a slight accent and therefore seldom spoke in public. He had learned Russian in his native Georgia, when he had studied for the priesthood in a seminary. But he never became a priest; instead he turned to Marxism and eventually became the dictator of the whole Russian empire, and a Russian chauvinist like no Russian czar had ever been!

Tvardovsky wrote a poem extolling Russian and Soviet patriotism, not forgetting to insert phrases lauding Lenin and Stalin. The musical genius Shostakovich composed the music for the poem; and thus was born the new Soviet national anthem.

However, the people — including the Party members — had sustained some bitter experiences when accepting changes too quickly. They learned that things which were legal and proper today might become illegal and most dangerous tomorrow. Thus, Party members were reluctant to disseminate the new song right away, and the average citizen was in no hurry to learn it. I felt certain that very few people in Battalion 92 knew it, and I planned to criticize Raskova for failing to publicize the new anthem. At the trial I would charge her with being lazy, unpatriotic and unfit for her job.

The following night, all Party members — the "elite" of Battalion 92 — assembled in a large building next to the railroad station. At the head of the table sat the stout Raskova, and next to her, the Party secretary of the Sverdlovsk District. Kovalenko and I sat on the floor in a foyer outside the open door. After all, we had not really been invited; we had come on our own, on the advice of Zakharov. Kovalenko was terrified; the bitter memories of 18 years in a Siberian prison were still fresh in his mind. This big man, a bully who had terrorized so many people, now sat on the floor wiping tears from his eyes like a child.

Raskova opened the meeting and presented the guest: "The secretary of the Sverdlovsk District Communist Party, Bolshevikov, Comrade Chernikin! Under his leadership, we shall put *Stroitelstvo* 92 into operation over the entire Ural and all its mines!" Everyone applauded vigorously. Chernikin made a little speech, describing the extent of the industrialization of the Ural. He didn't forget to emphasize that all these forward strides were due to the great leadership of Stalin.

"Instead of shipping the copper and the other minerals of the Urals to distant factories, the great Stalin taught us to bring the factories to the mines, to the source of our socialist wealth! On Stalin's instructions, we did it in Magnitogorsk; instead of sending the iron ore to the plants, we moved the plants to the mountains! We'll do the same in Sverdlovsk, Nizhniy-Tagil, Serov, and all over the Urals!" He informed the meeting of what he expected of Battalion 92. He described the plans for developing the copper mines and connecting them with the industrial centers. "That's where 92 fits into the picture, helping to build the Socialist Fatherland!" he exclaimed.

I looked at Raskova. Her face appeared pale. Perhaps she felt her power weakening; after all, she would no longer be dealing with only the personnel of 92, but with university graduates in cities full of people with higher education. Would she be able to cover up for all her inadequacies and lack of education? Kovalenko was right; she needed corpses, and quickly, to support her shaky throne.

Ah, but you've picked the wrong ones! I addressed her in my mind. If you try to step over us, we'll drag you down with us!

Party secretary Chernikin had finished his speech and everyone applauded. Raskova stood up again, cleared her throat, and announced, "Comrades! I have here a case of two men that I want to present to you for discussion. If we were not on the road, I would have handed them over to the NKVD; that's what I intend to do as soon as we arrive at our new destination. This case is another example of how alert one has to be; even things which look innocent on the surface can develop into dangerous, subversive undertakings!"

She looked around, in particular at Party secretary Chernikin, to check the impression she was making on her new boss, and continued. "The two men are Stepan Antonovich Kovalenko and Chaim Alterovich Shapiro. Kovalenko is a former _kulak_ — a big landowner, who refused to join the collective in the vicinity of Poltava. When the Party confiscated his land, he choked a Party official to death! Why he wasn't shot, I don't know. He served a sentence of 18 years. Then he was sent to us for re-education in the socialist spirit, to make a good citizen out of him.

"But instead of being grateful to the Party and the Soviet government which gave him a second chance to lead a decent, patriotic life, he got involved with a foreigner from fascist Poland. The Red Army saved this foreigner's life, but he, too, has failed to show appreciation! And what did these two renegades do? Comrades, listen!

"It was Lenin and the great Stalin who taught us that the Party, and only the Party, is the vanguard and forerunner of everything in life! Who is leading the heroic Red Army to victory? The greatest military genius, Marshal Stalin, and his Bolshevik Party! Who is leading our great Soviet people to achievements in all aspects of life? Stalin and the Party! Who is leading the captive nations to revolt against the capitalists? Stalin and the Party! Stalin has warned us: 'We, the people, must be strong, to back up the army at the front!'

"These two renegades organized secret meetings! Toasts were drunk to the czars! Under the cover of songs, they increased their activities, inciting the working people. And what songs did they sing? Silly, sentimental songs! Songs which make our people weaklings and cry-babies, lonely for home and mother! Subversive songs! That's how these two tried to instigate desertion! And when one man tried to stop them, they almost killed him!"

Kovalenko pulled my sleeve, and whispered, "Now we know for sure who started this. It was him, the one who pushed you, that we beat up. It's no use — we're finished! She's too powerful to break. Soon they'll demand a confession from us; you'll see. Let's run away now, while we still can!"

Party secretary Chernikin asked, "Are the two men present?"

Zakharov rose from his seat and said, "Yes, comrade, they are outside."

Chernikin turned to Raskova. "Then, before we discuss this very serious matter, we shall hear what the two have to say for themselves. Don't you agree?" She realized that this was not a question, but an order.

Raskova called on Kovalenko to speak first. He stammered and mumbled under his breath, and Zakharov explained that Kovalenko wanted the other fellow to speak for him. Raskova gave me a nod, but I ignored her completely. Facing the new Party boss, Chernikin, I spoke directly to him.

"First, my comrade, Kovalenko, and I would like to thank the secretary of the Communist Party District of Sverdlovsk and the Urals for insisting upon hearing both sides of the story. Under our great democratic constitution — Stalin's constitution — every man is entitled to justice. I come from Poland, which also has a constitution; but, like in all other capitalistic countries, it was designed to serve only the rich. Secretary Chernikin's invitation to us to present our case embodies the highest ideals of Stalin's constitution!

"We wish to declare that we did not call for any secret meetings. Can you call a gathering in a wide-open field, with hundreds of people present, a secret meeting? Russians like to tell stories; there are many books published by the Party, like, for instance, *Russkeye Narodneye Skazky* — Russian Folk Tales. That night I told the popular story of how potatoes were introduced into Russia, and also of how the czars had tortured and murdered people! This is no secret; Stalin, the greatest revolutionary of all time, was pursued by the Czar's _Okhrana_, before he ultimately became the great leader of the Soviet people!

"And my comrade Kovalenko here — he informed the people that the czars were half-German, and cruel, wicked tyrants! How can anyone consider this kind of talk as an anti-Soviet conspiracy? I do confess, however, to one crime: we got together without the supervision or approval of the Party. But no one really called the people together; it was all spontaneous. The workers are restless; they need cultural entertainment. A great poet has said that after bread, what a working man needs most is poetry — poetry and songs! Yes, we sang songs that night — sentimental songs, songs written for the people's army by great Soviet composers! If these songs make people weaklings, as Comrade Raskova claims, how is it that we were victorious against the Nazis at Stalingrad, Moscow and Leningrad?

"The problem in Battalion 92 is that we have a Party secretary who does not mix with the people, who is not one of the working class. She is aloof; she's not one of us. She likes to be served — imagine, she demands to be served breakfast in bed!

"Recently I mailed a letter to Marshal Stalin. I realize that Stalin is busy winning the war, and that he has no time to be bothered with my letter; but still, I hope he will read it. I addressed it to Comrade Stalin, Secretary General of the Communist Party, for this position, I feel, is the one that is closest to his heart. I hope he will read my letter. I asked him, 'How can it be that our secretary of _Stroitelstvo_ 92 does not care for the welfare of the people?' I asked him, 'Do you get served breakfast in bed every morning like our secretary does?' I also asked him, 'Isn't the new national anthem obligatory for the entire country? If so, then why is it that the people of Battalion 92 have never heard it?'"

My "letter to Stalin" was a bombshell! There was a heavy silence in the room; one could almost hear the heartbeats.

Chernikin interrupted me. "What? You say that the workers of Battalion 92 don't know the new national anthem?"

"I assume so, Comrade Chernikin, for I have never heard anyone in 92 singing it."

"Do you yourself know it?" he asked me.

"Certainly!" I replied.

"What is your opinion of the new anthem?" he asked me.

"Excellent! The music is powerful and the words are perfect. As you know, Comrade Chernikin, one defective verse can ruin a whole poem. And the difficulties in writing a national anthem are great: it has to concentrate into a limited number of words the glorious past, the great present, and the hopes for the future. The man who wrote the words to our new national anthem must be a genius, for it has all of this in it, and can also be understood by the average person."

Chernikin scratched his goatee and, looking straight at me, he said, "The fact that the people had no occasion to sing the new national anthem does not prove they don't know it. And I can hardly believe that you, a foreigner, know the anthem, but our own people don't!" Raising his voice he said, "Kovalenko, sing the new national anthem!"

I watched Kovalenko approach the table. He shook his head and muttered, "I don't know it. Never heard it; not in prison and not in 92."

Zakharov spoke up. He turned to me and said, "Let's see if you know it." I knew that he was on my side, and that if he told me to sing, he must have a good reason for it.

I inhaled deeply, and began to sing:

> A Union unshattered, of free Republics.
> Welded forever, Great Russia!
> Welcome the creation, by the will of the people.
> Of the only, the mighty, Soviet Union!
> Greetings, Fatherland, our glorious one!
> A friendship of peoples, a bulwark of hope!
> Under the banner of Lenin, the Party of Stalin,
> Let them lead us to victory now!

Some joined in and sang together with me, others merely mumbled along; but everyone stood at attention. I noticed that Raskova was singing along vigorously; beads of perspiration glistened on her forehead. My voice grew louder. I was singing for my life! When the song ended, Chernikin was the first to applaud; then everyone joined in. Raskova too joined in the applause, no doubt fearing that every clap was a nail in her casket.

Chernikin sat down, and so did all the others. Then he asked me if I had anything more to say.

I replied, "There is one more thing. I don't know when Comrade Stalin will reply to my letter, but I do hope that you, the Party members at 92, will respond to my plea. It is natural to be lonely, especially when one is far away from home. It is human to sing about home, mother and faraway soldiers. So let the Party take its rightful place in 92; let us gather to sing our patriotic Russian songs, and we will be happy to follow you!"

Chernikin nodded, and told us to wait outside.

The instant we reached the foyer, Kovalenko began hugging me — a real Russian bear hug. "You're wonderful, wonderful!" he exclaimed. "That sow is finished now; it's only a matter of time for her! I bet she's wishing she never started the whole thing! I guess she didn't realize who she was accusing....But why didn't you tell me that you wrote to Stalin?"

"So who wrote to Stalin?" I replied, smiling.

"You mean...don't tell me you were only bluffing! Getting them all excited — was it really all a bluff?"

"Sure I was bluffing! It worked, didn't it?"

"But suppose they ask you for Stalin's reply?"

"Oh, come on! There's a war going on! Thousands of letters get lost, and trains are bombed every day. Who'll ever know?"

He grabbed me around the waist, picked me up in the air like a child, and danced around in a circle. "Oh, how I wish I'd had you with me when they sentenced me to 25 years! With your golden tongue I might have gotten off free!"

Finally we sat down on the grass outside and waited for the verdict. I used the occasion to ask him if he had really killed a man with his bare hands.

He looked around to make sure that no one was near. Then he said, "Look, you're the first person I've ever confessed to, because we're really good friends. Believe me, I had a good reason for it, and anyway, they didn't have proof that it was me who killed him. They only guessed! If they'd been sure, they would have shot me then and there. They condemned me on guesswork, without evidence!"

"But you did kill him," I said cautiously. "So they weren't really guessing. Now don't get angry; I only asked you as a friend. You've served your time already, so you have nothing to fear."

Then Kovalenko told me how he and his parents and his two younger brothers had worked hard and saved their money for years. Finally they purchased a small piece of land from the big landowner for whom the entire family had been working as sharecroppers. Soon after they had achieved the life-long dream of owning their own land, the Revolution broke out. Then came the collectivization of all farms. Rather than surrender their livestock to the new collective, many farmers slaughtered all their animals. Kovalenko's father killed their only horse. That night, the father died — probably from a broken heart. Soon a Party official arrived and confiscated the little Kovalenko farm, turning it over to the collective. The next morning, Kovalenko's mother did not get up; she too had died, from disappointment and despair.

"And that's too much for any man," he said. "I was the oldest son. I learned that this Party official was supposed to go to Moscow for a special course. It was winter time, and I waited for him outside the railroad station. I grabbed him and choked him and buried his body in the snow. The same night it snowed heavily, and all traces were covered up. Naturally, everyone thought that he was attending his course in Moscow. It wasn't until the spring, after the snow melted, that his body was discovered. There wasn't much left of it; the rats and wolves had seen to that. But they knew how I hated that swine, and that I'd threatened to kill him, so they gave me 25 years! Now you know the truth! Do you blame me?"

I was saved from replying by the noise of approaching footsteps. In the darkness, we saw the giant figure of Zakharov. "Is that you, fellows?" he asked.

"Yes," we answered, jumping up nervously.

He handed each of us a bread card and said, "Here! You're lucky that Comrade Chernikin is a *Sibiryak*, and he liked your singing! But you've learned your lesson, and next time, please be careful and sing only with Party permission!"

He pulled me aside, and I could see the smile on his face in the moonlight. Then he bent over and whispered in my ear, "Next time you write to Stalin, I want to read the letter first, you little scoundrel!"

We thanked him for his help, and rushed off to the bread car. Although it was after closing time, the girls issued us bread for the next two days! With every bite of bread, the friendship between Kovalenko and me grew firmer and closer.

Our home on wheels was getting closer to the Ural Mountains. Two locomotives together were unable to pull our train uphill, so a third locomotive arrived to push from the rear. We were passing through a deep gulch, with high stone walls on both sides of the tracks. These walls were decorated: responding to the universal urge to sign one's work and achieve a bit of immortality, the prisoners who had built this road into the mountains of the Ural had carved their names as well. When the train stopped for a few minutes, we were able to read an amazing collection of names of all nationalities, including a great number of professional titles — doctors, lawyers, clergymen.... Millions of prisoners, Stalin's free labor, had built the roads, tunnels and canals of his huge empire. And these names engraved in stone were their only memorial.

The train pulled into a siding near a small station. It seemed that we would remain there for a while. On the opposite tracks an army hospital train pulled in, carrying severely wounded soldiers returning from the battlefront.

Raskova, still trying to save her position after the disastrous Party meeting, decided that Battalion 92 should entertain the men of the Red Army hospital train. She came to our car as if nothing had happened, and asked Kovalenko and me to sing and play for "our heroes"! Actually, the members of Battalion 92 had asked us the same thing, but we had declined, on the grounds that such things must be organized by the Party! Apparently the request was then submitted to Raskova, or perhaps it had been her idea from the beginning. In any case, she requested that we perform, and of course we agreed.

After she left, Kovalenko said, "What a woman! Spit in her face, and she pretends it's raining! The nerve of her!"

Before sundown the preparations for the concert were completed. Those soldiers who could walk came out and sat down on the railroad crossties, placed there by the men of 92. Those who couldn't walk were carried out; the remainder preferred to stay in their train and watch through the open windows.

Raskova opened the concert with a pep talk full of the familiar Party line, concluding with praise for the Red Army and glorifying "the military genius, Marshal Stalin." Then she apologized for the lack of instruments. Several soldiers called out that they had instruments, but lacked the hands and fingers to play them. Raskova ordered the first number, the air force song. I began the song, accompanied by Kovalenko's accordion playing, and the crowd joined in singing:

We were born to make a legend into reality,
To remove the distance, the vastness of space.
Stalin gave us the reason, Stalin gave us wings,
In every heart, a fiery race!

Still higher and higher and higher!
We'll rush the flight, equal to birds.
And in every propeller there is beating,
The breadth of our borders, and Stalin's words.

That was followed by the navy song, and then the songs of the other branches of the military.

The melodies echoed through the forest, mingling from time to time with train whistles. The wounded were cheered, forgetting their pain and their missing limbs for a while; Battalion 92 was happily fulfilling its patriotic duty.

Raskova ordered: "Storytelling time now." The invalids were invited to speak. Their stories were of sacrifice, heroism, and patriotism. One emaciated cripple told how he and a friend were fighting in the battle of Sevastopol, when the friend was wounded. Suddenly they found themselves encircled by Germans, so he played dead. The Germans gouged out the eyes of his wounded friend and left him to bleed to death. But the blinded soldier didn't give up his life so easily; as soon as the Germans had left, he called for help, and the friend who had pretended to be dead came to him.

The blind man strapped bundles of grenades around his body, and cried, "I'm dying anyway. Direct me to the road!" He crawled to the middle of the road and lay there. Soon German tanks appeared — an entire column. The leading tank did not stop for a moment but ran right over him. It was blown up, and blocked the passage of the column for a full day, thus giving the Red Army a chance to counter-attack, and additional days to evacuate Sevastopol! And this was only one story; how many had given limbs, and lives, for Mother Russia!

I WAS SITTING at the door of the rail-
road car, watching the lights of the hospital train disappear in the distance,
dwindling to pinpoints in the dusk. Near me, a young fellow was crawling
around on all fours, trying to find something on the ground. I said, "In the
dark you won't find anything. Why don't you wait for morning? You'll have
a better chance then."

In a heavily-accented Russian, he replied, "By morning we'll probably
be miles away. I must find it here and now!" The fellow was cursing softly —
in Polish!

I got down and approached him. "What are you looking for?" I asked in
Polish. He was delighted to find another Pole, and introduced himself as
Janek Majewski from Warsaw. Although we were total strangers, our
common language made us feel friendly immediately.

He told me that he had recently been released from prison and drafted
into Battalion 92. He had lost the medallion which he always wore around
his neck. "Don't think that I'm religious!" he said apologetically. "It's just
that my mother gave it to me." I invited him to visit me sometime, so that
we could talk about home.

Our train passed through Sverdlovsk; then we moved on to Nizhiny-
Tagil, the second largest city in the Urals. There, Battalion 92 established
its headquarters, across the street from a tank factory. The local people
told us that seventy combat-ready tanks were being produced every day.
From there, our labor battalion spread out into the copper mountains all
the way to Serov. It was my first time seeing these rough red stones. They
were extremely heavy, for this ore was loaded with copper. Battalion 92
cut through forest and mountains where it seemed that no men had ever
trodden to lay the tracks which would carry the vital ore to the smelter.

The thick forest had to be cut down before we could build the railway.

383

The Kazakhs among us were amazed; back in their barren deserts, they had never seen trees of this size.

Some of us — Kovalenko and his Ukrainians, Janek and I — were old hands at tree-cutting. They had learned to be woodcutters in prison, and I'd received my training in Karobka. Woodcutters, though, need food, and this was one item that the Urals did not provide. Most of the food was imported from the Volga region, and there was never enough. As heavy workers, we were entitled to special rations, but received only 800 grams of bread daily, and at noon, a slop-soup that we satirically called *ballanda* — dishwater. There were no farmers around with whom to barter, so we went hungry....

As the days and weeks went by, our brigades penetrated deeper and deeper into the *taiga*, the vast forest wilderness of spruce, pine and birch which lay between the primitive and poorly-mechanized copper mines.

Then one day we were moved out of our boxcar home, and into barracks. It was obvious that we would be spending the approaching winter there. Kovalenko, his gang and I succeeded in moving into the same barracks. I invited my new friend, Janek Majewski, to move in with us.

The first night in the new barracks, we stretched out on our straw sacks exhausted, and I fell asleep immediately. Only moments later, I was awakened by sounds of a struggle. Someone was getting a "going-over," but the victim was putting up quite a fight. I recognized Tomulov with a knife in his raised hand shouting, "You Polack thief, I'll cut your throat!" Immediately, I realized that the victim was Janek.

I cried out to Kovalenko, "Stop them! They're going to kill him!"

But Kovalenko, sitting on his bunk, only shrugged, laughed and said, "So what? So then he won't steal anymore!"

I leapt down from my bunk, and grabbed the wrist of the man with the knife. His eyes were full of murderous hatred.

"Tomulov! Stop! You'll have to kill me first!" I shouted.

"Then give me back the bread that he stole from me! You invited that stinking thief to our barracks! Two slices of bread he stole from under my pillow, the sneaking rat!"

I promised to get the bread back, and turned to Janek, who was bruised and bleeding. I took him outside to wash up. Not knowing of my special position with Kovalenko, Janek considered me a hero.

"How did you dare stand up to that guy with the knife? You saved my life! I'll never forget you!"

I explained to Janek that I might have gotten scratched at most, because Kovalenko was my friend, and Tomulov knew it. I warned him never again to steal bread because sooner or later he'd get killed; here, where everyone is starving, it is one thing to steal money, gold or diamonds, but to steal *food* means instant death. "This is the law of the jungle," I said, "and in our jungle, Kovalenko is judge and executioner!"

We started talking, and soon Janek had told me much about his past life. Back in Warsaw, he had been a member of a gang of pickpockets. Proudly he said, "I wasn't just an ordinary purse-snatcher. I attended a special school for pickpockets, and we graduates never got caught!" Janek told me that when the Germans invaded Poland, he and two older brothers fled to Bialystok, in the east. From there they went to Minsk, capital of the Byelorussian Soviet Republic. Everywhere they went, they practiced their "trade."

In Minsk they noticed that the government bank was guarded at night by one old man. They figured that there must be no thieves in Russia, if the government could leave a bank with practically no protection. So the three of them planned a heist. When they completed the job, they had more than twenty million rubles!

"I tell you, we had so much of that paper we couldn't even count it; we had to burn some of it!" For safety's sake, they held on to the money without spending any of it. It seemed strange to them that the police were not disturbed about the robbery. Finally they lost their patience and decided to spend it; one of them went out and bought new clothes and whiskey for all, and invited some friends for a party!

What they did not realize, Janek said, was that Russia is not Poland. In Russia everyone is a government employee, and it is known how much he earns. If someone's spending is not in proportion to his earnings, he's under suspicion.

It didn't take long until they were arrested. Janek's two brothers were shot, and Janek, being a minor, was sentenced to 20 years. After three years in prison, he was released and shipped straight to Battalion 92.

I asked him if he knew why he had been released, but he didn't have the slightest idea. I explained to him that General Sikorski, the Prime Minister of the Polish government-in-exile, had signed a treaty with the Soviet government, and Moscow had declared an amnesty for all Polish citizens. I realized that there must be thousands of Polish citizens all over Russia — in prisons, in labor camps, in Siberian outposts — who couldn't read

Russian, perhaps not even Polish. The Polish government in London had abandoned them to the Soviets.

The next day Janek asked me to start teaching him Russian. He had a good mind and caught on quickly, but soon I discovered that his thirst for knowledge was not really cultural.

Besides our daily bread ration, which we received by surrendering a bread coupon, we got one meal daily, consisting of a watery soup. At noon, we stood in line and a girl punched a hole into that day's date on our cards. Then she wrote on a slip of paper "1 — ONE."

Another girl accepted this paper and poured the soup into the bowl of the person presenting it. To avoid the long lines and to save time, it was permitted for one man to present a number of meal cards and get food for his companions. Thus, if his slip read "10 — TEN," he would receive ten portions of soup.

One day, as I was sitting under a tree drinking my soup, which consisted of grayish water with some pieces of potato floating in it, Janek appeared and called me to follow him into the forest. He was carrying a small bucket full of soup! We stopped under a tree, and he looked around to make sure that no one had followed us. Then he poured out most of the liquid, until a layer of potatoes at the bottom remained. Gleefully he said, "Let's eat! From now on we'll pour out the slop and eat the real stuff!"

I could hardly believe my eyes. "Janek, where did you get all that soup? Have you been stealing again? This is government soup, and you'll be charged with sabotage! You know what that means!"

"Don't worry," he said, grinning. "This soup is not 'hot'. Trust me; I know my way around!"

"Janek, I know the Russians better than you do. Nobody would risk his life to give you a bucket full of soup, enough for a dozen men!" The smell of the hot potatoes was tempting; I was hungry enough to eat it all, but I had to find out how he got the extra portions.

"Look, Chaim, I want to help you," he said. "I'm trying to pay you back for helping me, so why are you giving me such a rough time? Let's eat! We haven't got much time." I was starved, so I gave in; but I warned him to be careful — very careful!

The next day at mealtime I decided to follow him and see for myself how he did it. He walked up to the window, presented a card and the girl poured *eleven* portions of soup into his bucket! I counted — *eleven*! Suddenly I remembered: during their first few days with Battalion 92, the girls used to write only a digit for the number of portions — a 1, or a 2, or a 4. Then they discovered that some people added another digit, thus turning a "1" into a "10," or a "2" into a "20." Since then, they spelled out the number in addition to the digit, writing "1 — ONE," or "2 — TWO." So how could Janek have changed his meal ticket from "one" to "eleven"?

Then I realized why he'd asked me to teach him to write Russian! And I, the fool, thought he wanted to be literate, to read newspapers and books!

Again he invited me to share his pail of soup. I said, "Janek, why does the cook always give you eleven portions of soup? Why not ten, or a dozen?"

It turned out that besides being a professional pickpocket, my pal was also a talented forger, and could copy any handwriting. I tested him by writing in both Polish and Russian. He duplicated both exactly! Then I wrote my name in Hebrew, which I thought would be much more difficult for him. However, after a few tries, he amazed me with a perfect imitation!

What Janek had been doing to the meal ticket was this: the Russian word for one is _odeen_; the Russian word for eleven is _odeenadzat_. Thus Janek merely added the few letters _adzat_, and instead of one bowl of soup he received eleven!

"Listen, brother," Janek said. "You and I are in this together! You taught me to write Russian, and we eat together! This is the only way to stay alive; otherwise we'll never make it back to Poland!"

The next day I handed him my meal ticket, and he changed it expertly from one to eleven. We shared one potful right away, and with the other eleven portions of soup potatoes I ran all the way to the barracks, shoving the pail under my bunk, to save it for our evening meal. We continued to do this every day, even though it entailed great risk. Even my best friend, Kovalenko, didn't know our secret. It was becoming more difficult each day to run to the barracks undetected and hide our evening meal, for our work site was further and further away from the barracks, and we had to be back chopping trees right after lunch. Also, we were the only ones who even had an evening meal, so we had to hide from everybody!

One day, an elderly man from our barracks became ill, got permission to leave work and returned to the barracks in the middle of the day. That evening when we returned from work, we discovered that our hoard of potatoes had been eaten; the container was still there, under my bunk, but it was completely empty, licked clean! There was no question that the old man had done it.

We were afraid that he might blackmail us and demand food every day, but we decided to continue our routine as though nothing had happened. The next day during lunch, I brought the bucket and placed it under my bunk as usual, except that this time it contained only half of the usual amount. The old man was lying on his bunk, pretending to be asleep. In the evening we found the bucket empty again. After five days of the same routine, the old man died. No one suspected any foul play, and there was no doctor to ascertain the cause of his death. Somehow, I had the feeling that Janek had something to do with it, but I did not pursue the subject. Food had become an obsession, and without Janek's help I would starve. Still, I became wary of him, realizing that he was ruthless. Stealing was a way of life, and so common as to be accepted as normal, but murder...?!

The creeping hunger began to have a destructive effect on the workers. A crosstie which could at first be carried by one man now required three; a rail which in Stalingrad had been carried by two men, now required four; and when the signal came to let go of the rail and jump back, sometimes a man was too weak and too slow, and the heavy rail landed on his feet. Janek and I were the lucky ones, carefully cherishing our secret.

But one day our luck ran out. The meal-ticket girl suddenly started writing the tickets with colored pencils; for each day she used another color, but we owned only the one precious black pencil! Hunger began to overtake us and to destroy the friendship between Janek and me. He constantly complained. "I was the one taking all the risks before! I was feeding you all this time! Now it's about time you did something. Get hold of some colored pencils!"

"But Janek, here in the wilderness? Be reasonable; where can I get them? Do pencils grow on trees?"

"I don't care; just get them, or else!" His eyes were threatening, even more than his words.

One day when I was talking to Zakharov he mentioned that he was going into town. "Town?" I asked, surprised.

"Yes," he replied. "About 25 kilometers east of here, there is a small mining town."

This gave me an idea. I figured that if there was a town, there had to be a school in the town, and in a school one might find colored pencils. For two days Janek and I saved our bread rations in order to have enough to trade for the colored pencils. I was also planning to take along the blanket which I had received in the Polish embassy. Although it was threadbare by now, the fact that it was English wool made it valuable.

Sunday was market day. At dawn I left the barracks, with Janek fervently wishing me good luck. He had tears in his eyes.

The small marketplace was full of people, but there was very little farm produce on display. To my surprise, however, there was a lot of American food for sale. And then I saw an American! For the first time in my life, a real American! He was tall, fat, and dressed in leather clothes. He must have been some sort of a specialist, perhaps a mining engineer. There were many things about him that made me certain that he was an American: his self-assurance, his apparent satisfaction with life, and his smooth face unmarred by worry, combined with the confident way in which he walked!

My first impulse was to ask him if he could send off a letter for me to my cousins in Palestine and in Australia. Who knows, I thought. He might even have colored pencils! Then I noticed that no one was talking to him, although everyone's eyes followed him with envy. I soon discovered the reason: wherever he went, a man followed him like a shadow!

I gave up the idea of talking to him and set out for the school, a large wooden building nearby. I waited patiently outside, because any "black market" business had to be done in private. Finally a woman came out, carrying a pile of books. I asked her whether they taught art in the school; she replied that she herself was substituting for the regular art teacher, who was in the army. What unbelievable luck! I asked her if it was possible to get colored pencils somewhere.

"Why? Do you sketch?" She was immediately interested and friendly. "No? Then you must be an artist, but you have no paint and so you'll settle for colored pencils, right?" she asked. I was tempted to tell her that she had guessed right, but I realized that then she might start to ask me questions about art and painting, subjects about which I knew nothing. I told her that I needed them for a friend, and added that of course my friend did not expect to get the pencils for free.

"What do you have to offer?" she asked immediately. Knowing what the best commodity was in hungry Russia, I offered her bread. She said, "My mother works in a bakery shop." That meant that she had enough bread; her mother probably stole it and brought it home.

"How about this blanket?" I said. "Pure English wool! You can tell it's made in England, maybe even in America! You can make yourself a coat!"

She felt the blanket, and her eyes began to glow. Gripping the blanket tightly, she asked, "How much?"

"A set of pencils of all colors, and five kilograms of bread," I answered.

"Wait!" she said, and rushed back into the school building. In a few minutes a set of colored pencils was in my pocket. She ran to get the bread from her mother, and soon I was on my way back to the camp. I was happy, about the pencils and the bread, but unhappy and anxious about having given away my last blanket. I'd be terribly cold during the nights; I'd never find another blanket like that one.

I arrived "home" just before dusk. For a while we lived "comfortably" again. Janek continued to falsify tickets with our new colored pencils, and I continued to perform my duties: running back to the camp at noon and hiding the soup potatoes under my bunk. Eventually, however, this became impossible, for the distance to the camp was so great that I could no longer make it back and forth in an hour. We began to bury our can of soup in the forest, and dig it out before going home. How often I thought of the idyllic life I had left in Karobka — or so it seemed to me now, gobbling watery soup, afraid of being discovered and shot at any moment!

One sleepless night, I thought of a *midrash* that I had learned years ago, about a king who had banished his son to a peasant hut. After many years of separation, the king had yearned for his son, and sent a servant to offer the prince anything his heart desired. The banished prince had requested some straw to mend his leaky roof....

So low had I fallen — thinking only of food, devising stratagems to get a bit more slop soup — that it had been weeks since I had actively prayed to be reunited with my dear family, and pleaded for the ultimate redemption. I resolved to concentrate on every word of my secret prayers, to bear hunger and suffering gladly, if only my beloved parents and brothers would be spared.

Soon new worries arose. The men had discovered that there was a tiny village in the vicinity, and Janek began to disappear every night, arriving late for work in the morning. I had to cover up for him, giving the foreman all kinds of excuses.

I scolded Janek frequently: "Where have you been? Do you realize what you're doing to yourself!" He would only smile and wink. One morning when I reprimanded him, he replied, "Chaim, how long has it been since you had eggs? A glass of milk? Bread and butter?"

The mere thought of these foods made my mouth water. "Ages, Janek, ages! I can't even remember the taste anymore!"

"Well, in that little village, my friend, I can get all the bread, milk and butter I want," Janek said. "And besides, I'm doing business — selling and trading; that's my profession, not chopping down trees in a dark forest!"

"But Janek," I said, "you're so worn out that you can't continue like this. Sooner or later you won't have the strength to walk!"

Of course Janek paid no attention to my advice. He continued to sneak off to the village every night. Every morning he returned with two eggs: "One for you and one for the foreman," he said. The foreman was glad to accept the bribe through me, but insisted on more eggs. Janek gave me some tobacco for him, saying, "This should keep him from marking me late."

One day he brought the tobacco back wrapped up in a sheet of *Pravda*. I grabbed the newspaper and began to read, hungry for news. Suddenly I came across a new ray of hope! There, in prominent print, was a message from Stalin to General Berling, commander of the Polish "Kosciuszko Brigade," congratulating him for "the heroic battle and victory over the German beast, the enemy of all the Slavic nations"! Next to it was printed another message, also from Stalin. This one was addressed to Wanda Wasilewska and the Union of Polish Patriots, congratulating them on the victory of their military unit!

"Janek!" I shouted, pointing to the paper. "There's still a chance for us to get out of this hole and fight the Germans! Look! Do you know what this says? There's a new Polish military unit, the Kosciuszko Brigade. Maybe we can join!"

The Kosciuszko Brigade was the nucleus of the new Polish army which would fight to free Poland from the Germans; and the leaders of the Union of Polish Patriots would eventually become the government of Poland.

Janek and I decided to volunteer. But how? We were in a wilderness, nowhere near a recruiting agency for military service. Printed next to the message from Marshal Stalin to General Berling were congratulations from the Presidium of the Supreme Soviet of the USSR to the Union of Polish Patriots. The very fact that such a message was printed indicated that the Union enjoyed official endorsement, for nothing was printed by chance in the Soviet press.

And so we sent off letters, addressed to the "Union of Polish Patriots" in Moscow, hoping that the post office in Moscow would know where to locate it. We wrote that we were Polish citizens who wanted to volunteer for the Kosciuszko Brigade, and asked for instructions on how to proceed.

In the meantime, Janek continued to disappear at night and arrive late for work in the morning. The foreman, bribed by the eggs and tobacco that Janek gave him, allowed Janek to recover from his night's work by napping under a tree for half a day.

I pleaded with Janek: "How do you expect to be accepted into the Polish army in your run-down condition? You'll never pass a medical examination! Stop your trading and speculating; you know what'll happen if you're caught! Don't you want to see your mother again? Don't you want to fight the Germans?"

But all my pleading was in vain. Janek would reply, "I want to get back to Poland, and see my mother, more than anything else in the world; but I'm doing so well in business that I'll come home a rich man!"

As the days passed and there was no response from the Union in Moscow, we began to wonder if our letters had reached their destination. Maybe they didn't pass censorship because they were written in Polish? Maybe there was someone here who was interested in keeping us from joining? We decided to write to Stalin personally. No one would dare stop a letter addressed to Stalin!

"But I can't write Russian that well," Janek protested.

"I'll write the letter; you just sign it," I replied. This time we dropped our letters directly into the mail chute of a passing train.

One Sunday morning, we all marched off to work except Janek, who had failed to show up as usual. The foreman marked him "present," expecting him to arrive soon. However, hours passed and there was no trace of Janek.

The foreman was growing panicky, and complained to me, "Where is he? That little Polack will get me in trouble! It was you who got me into this! I should have reported him the first time he disappeared, but you talked me into covering up for him!"

At noon I offered to go to the village and look for him. "No!" screamed the foreman. "I have enough trouble with one. If you're out of my sight, I'll have you charged with desertion!"

Janek did not show up at all that day, or the next. I knew something must have happened to him, for he would not do anything to endanger himself, the foreman and me. And would he be so foolish as to take a risk, now that we were trying to enlist in the new Polish army? The foreman warned me: "If he doesn't show up today, I'll report him!"

How could I find out what happened to Janek? Zakharov! Perhaps he knew something! But did I dare to tell him the whole truth? Wouldn't I be endangering the foreman, for having covered up for Janek all this time?

True, I thought, Zakharov is a fair man, a good man, a _Sibiryak_. Still, he is a Party man and a high official of Battalion 92. Wouldn't it be his first duty to report a desertion?

I remembered, back in the yeshiva, one of my teachers had said, "When you ask someone for a favor, it's his obligation to grant you the favor. But at the same time, it's your duty to make it easy, and as convenient as possible, for the person to do you that favor!" By telling Zakharov the truth, I'd be taxing his loyalty.

I remembered the unfinished conversation with Zakharov — how did he know about the Jewish dietary laws? Where in Siberia did he learn that Jews do not eat meat and dairy food together? Could he be Jewish? No — a Jew would have known that, besides not eating meat and dairy food together, I wouldn't eat pork, or _treif_ salami! Yet Zakharov had offered it to me when I went to see him, the night before the trial.

I decided to visit Zakharov anyway; perhaps he knew something about the disappearance of Janek. The living quarters of management were some distance away from the workers, standard procedure in the "classless" Soviet system. I knocked on his door.

When he opened it, he greeted me and smiled. "I'm glad you came tonight," he said. "We can talk in private. My roommate has gone to Sverdlovsk on official business." He invited me to sit down, and placed a glass of tea on the table, along with some bread, cheese and a few slices of pork.

I said, "Actually, I came to continue a conversation we began a while ago. It's strange that you should know about Jews not eating dairy and meat together, but that you didn't know that we don't eat pork. You've probably never lived among Jews, right?"

"Right," he replied. "I hadn't known about pork. What do you say to this?" He placed some hot dogs on the table and said, "It all comes from America: the pork, the milk, the salami — everything!"

No doubt the Americans don't realize that their shipments of food never reach the starving masses, who must be satisfied with slop soup once a day, I thought bitterly. I was terribly hungry, for since Janek had disappeared, I hadn't had the extra portions of soup. So I wolfed down the bread and cheese, and drank the hot tea happily.

Zakharov tried to remember where he had heard about milk and meat. Finally he said, "I'll tell you, since I've never lived among Jews I must have heard it at home."

"And you never heard about Jews not eating pork?" I asked.

"Never," he replied.

"And did your parents eat pork?" I asked.

"Sure!" he said. Then he suddenly added, "I want to show you something. I don't know what it is, but maybe you do."

He opened his luggage case, a huge wooden box with metal straps around it. After digging around in it, he pulled out a silver medallion on a silver chain. I studied the medallion with growing excitement. On one side, the two tablets of the Ten Commandments were engraved in tiny Hebrew letters; encircling the tablets, and also engraved in Hebrew letters, was the sentence: "Hear O Israel, the Lord our God, the Lord is One." On the other side there was a bas-relief of two hands with the fingers held separated, in the position in which the *kohanim*, the priests, bless the congregation in the synagogue. In a circle around the hands the priestly blessing was engraved in Hebrew: "May God bless you and keep you."

I was amazed at the craftsmanship and the beauty of the unusual medallion, but even more was I perplexed about its owner! "This is amazing, Comrade Zakharov! Wherever did you get it?" I asked him.

"First, tell me what it is," he insisted. "Can you read it? What language is it?"

I explained to him that the words were Hebrew, and that they declare the Jewish belief in one God, one Supreme Being. Then I explained the Ten Commandments. Finally I asked him again, "Who gave this to you?" He did not reply, and his eyes shifted from the beautiful silver medallion to me, and back again.

"Look, Comrade Zakharov, I assume that since you're a Party member you must be an atheist; why then should this medallion fascinate you so? But if you'd rather not talk about it, we don't have to." I was in fact eager to switch the conversation to Janek, my real reason for coming to see him.

He finally spoke up. Holding the silver piece gingerly in his huge hand, he said in a soft voice, "No, no. I want to talk about it. It was given to me by my father. I'll tell you. My father was dreadfully wounded in a train collision. My mother and I didn't leave his bedside for days afterwards. Right before he died, he motioned to my mother and she took this medallion out of a drawer and handed it to him. He couldn't speak, but he pressed this medallion into my hand and looked at me with tears in his eyes. He held my hand and the medallion tightly between his palms until he took his last breath!"

Tears filled Zakharov's eyes; he wiped them away with his sleeve, and I felt a closeness to this huge man. He continued: "After the funeral, I asked my mother for an explanation, but she constantly evaded my questions. She promised me that after I got married she would explain it all to me, and told me to hold onto this medallion and to guard it like a treasure, 'just like your father did, and his father before him.' She died while I was away fighting the Germans in the First World War, and so the mystery was never cleared up. Maybe you can explain this puzzle to me."

We both sat in silence for a while, staring at the silver medallion. The kerosene lamp cast flickering shadows on the walls, enhancing the mysterious atmosphere. Zakharov's eyes met mine, questioning, seeking an answer.

"Tell me, Zakharov, do you remember if there was anything about your father or grandfather that was different from the other farmers?" I asked.

Zakharov replied, "I never knew my grandfather, but my father was like all the other farmers, no different."

"Did your father ever attend church?"

"He did, although not as often as the others. Mostly on holidays, or for weddings and funerals."

"Think, Zakharov; any hint might help. Did your father drink?"

"He did; but come to think of it, I never saw him really drunk like the other farmers. Oh, and another thing: he never lost his temper with my mother and with us boys; he never beat her the way all the other men in our village beat their wives. Strange — I haven't thought about him for years. Yes, I guess you could say that he was different...."

"Zakharov," I said, "what I'm about to tell you might come as a shock to you. Listen...."

"In the early 19th century the Czar ordered the army to draft Jewish boys to serve for 25 years! His aim was not so much to increase his army, but to convert the Jews. Thousands of little Jewish children were abducted by the army, shipped miles away from their homes and families and forcibly baptized into the Russian Church. These abducted children came to be known as *kantonisten*. After their 25 years of service were done, they were given a piece of land and thus they escaped serfdom."

Zakharov was looking at me with wide-eyed disbelief, as my words began to take on meaning for him. "Did this really happen?" he asked.

"Yes, it did. And it could be that your grandfather was one of those children, you know — one of those *kantonisten*," I continued. "Who knows? Maybe *his* father was a silversmith, and fearing that his son might be abducted and torn away from his family and his religion forever, he made the child this medallion — to remind him of his home and his faith.

His family could have been *kohanim*, whose religious duty it is to bless the congregation in the synagogue. The outspread fingers and the priestly blessing written here point to that."

I explained to Zakharov that a *kohen* was a descendant of Aaron, the first high priest. "Just like me; I'm a *kohen*, a direct descendant of Aaron," I told him.

"Does this mean that I'm a Jew?" he asked. "I'm the third generation to carry this medallion."

"No," I replied. "Jewish lineage is determined according to the mother. She was probably Russian, so don't get excited; you're a gentile with Jewish ancestry, perhaps."

"You know," Zakharov said, "a lot of things become clear to me now. When I think about it, I realize that my father in fact hated the Church. He only went there on holidays, for my mother's sake. And he never kissed the hand of the priest, the way all the others did!"

Gently he placed the silver medallion back into the wooden box. This unexpected episode had almost made me forget the purpose of my visit. Finally I said, "Before I go, Comrade Zakharov, I wonder if you could find out about Janek. He…"

"You mean Janek Majewski?" he interrupted me. "You certainly have a habit of picking the wrong friends! First it was Kovalenko, and now Majewski. Well, he's in jail, and you can be sure that he won't come out for another twenty years!"

His words cut into my heart like a knife. There goes Janek's chance to get home! I had feared that something like this would happen sooner or later. Zakharov told me that the manager of the oil depot had complained that some kerosene drums had been opened and pilfered. A trap was laid, and Janek was caught red-handed, with a wrench for opening the drums, and a rubber tube for siphoning the precious liquid into his container.

"Is there anything we can do for him?" I asked.

"Nothing! Absolutely nothing!" Zakharov replied heatedly. "He's out of our jurisdiction, out of our hands. The oil depot serves not only Battalion 92, but all the mines and railroads in this area. And even if we could, I wouldn't want to get involved with him. Are you looking for trouble? Didn't you have enough with your singing sessions?"

I returned to the barracks, sad and depressed. I had been close to Janek, but apparently not close enough to stop him from taking such foolish risks. We were both from Poland, both about the same age, and both aiming for the same goal: getting home! And now he was done for; he'd waste his young life in prison, and maybe never get back to his beloved Poland.

Neither the guards nor the soldiers could prevent Janek from stealing — and from being caught. I thought of the story of Rabbi Levi Yitzchok of Berditchev; the town was a well-known center for smuggling tobacco, silk, porcelain and all other goods which were highly taxed in czarist Russia. One _Erev Pesach_, _Reb_ Levi Yitzchok approached one of the peasants, and asked, "Do you have any tobacco? I'd like to buy some."

"I've got lots; you can buy as much as you want!"

He went to another smuggler and asked for silk.

"How many yards do you want to buy? I've got every color there is; just put your money down and its yours."

Then _Reb_ Levi Yitzchok went to a poor Jewish cobbler, and asked, "Do you have any _chametz_ — any leaven? I'll pay you any price!"

"God forbid, Rabbi! How could you even ask such a thing? I wouldn't have _chametz_ in my house for a million rubles!"

And _Reb_ Levi Yitzchok raised his eyes to Heaven, and said: "Lord of the Universe! Neither the Czar's soldiers nor the fear of death can prevent the peasants from smuggling and selling stolen goods. And here is a poor Jew who wouldn't have _chametz_ in his house on _Pesach_ for any price, because You commanded it! No soldiers, no threats — and Your people do Your will!"

Today, a new tyrant reigns with force and terror, and yet all the threats do not keep people from stealing.... Now my poor, foolish friend Janek is done for!

My thoughts turned to Zakharov. Statistically speaking, there should be hundreds of millions of Jews in the world today; however, there are only a few million. Like the trees in the forest that we had chopped down today, live branches and entire limbs had been cut off from the living tree of the Jewish people! There was no doubt in my mind that Zakharov, like thousands of others, was a descendant of one of those _kantonisten_. Now, with their talents and abilities, they were enriching the people and nation who had abducted their ancestors!

27

IT FINALLY ARRIVED! My draft notice came from Moscow, directly from the War Commissariat; addressed to me personally, it advised me to report to the *Voyenkomat* in the city of Serov. I showed the letter to the foreman, and told him that I would leave for Serov in the morning. I didn't care if the management of Battalion 92 liked it or not; they were powerless in the face of an official letter from Stalin's office.

The news about my draft spread like wildfire; I hadn't known how many Polish citizens were serving in Battalion 92. Though it was spread out over a huge territory, they all found out that I had written to Stalin and had been drafted. Most of them had never heard of the Union of Polish Patriots, nor of Wanda Wasilewska or the Kosciuszko Brigade.

On the train, traveling to Serov to appear before the draft commission, I kept thinking about Janek. If only he had been more careful, we would now have been traveling together and perhaps returning home to Poland together as well. No doubt he too had received a reply from Moscow, but he was "not available" to accept the letter! Poor Janek!

I passed the medical examination and was given an official notice to Battalion 92, exactly the same notice that was given to the Red Army inductees. It stated that I must be relieved of my present duties, given a three days' supply of food, and furnished with transportation to the Serov draft office, "for conscription into the Polish army." These words had a strange sound; suddenly it was no longer called the "Kosciuszko Brigade," but "the Polish army"! But the official Polish government was in London, with *its* own army! I dismissed it as being merely the expression of a provincial official, who probably didn't realize the political implications of the word "army" — or perhaps he couldn't spell "Kosciuszko"!

As I walked into the office of Battalion 92, a big surprise was in store for me. I learned that I was not just an ordinary draftee: my case was to be handled by the Director General of Battalion 92, Colonel Gerasimov himself. I suspected that this was because the Director General wanted to get some favorable publicity out of the fact that I was the first Pole in our battalion to enlist in the new Polish army. Perhaps he wanted to be photographed in his full glory; the railroad people suffered from an inferiority complex in regard to the army men.

Although the railroad workers had been doing an excellent job under extremely difficult circumstances, nevertheless the army men used to sneer at them and consider them slackers: "A nice little nest you've built for yourselves, and safe too." "You're hiding in the rear, while we're bleeding on the battlefront." In an effort to combat this, Stalin had ordered that military ranks be instituted in the railway system, according to one's position and years of service.

The colonel was a big, fat man; a regular capitalist, I thought to myself. To my great surprise, Zakharov, in the uniform of a railway captain, was seated at the next table. The colonel asked me why I had volunteered for the Polish army. I was taken aback by the question.

"Because I hate the Germans," I replied. "I am young and able, and I consider it my duty to fight the enemy."

For a few moments he studied my draft document. Then he picked up the phone and called the draft office in Serov.

"This is Colonel Gerasimov speaking," he shouted into the phone. "Listen to me, Lieutenant! Suppose Marshal Zhukov were to draft men out of Admiral Kuznetsov's navy; suppose Marshal Semenko were to draft his air force pilots out of Marshal Govorov's artillery. Do you realize what chaos would result? Yes? Why then do you draft my men?"

He listened for a while and then argued again, addressing the other party as "Lieutenant" and repeatedly emphasizing his rank of Colonel. "Don't you understand?" he asked in a loud voice. "That letter from Moscow has nothing to do with Comrade Stalin! Our great leader is busy conducting the war; one of his minor functionaries wrote that letter, not Comrade Stalin himself. Lieutenant, do you realize that one hundred and twenty-five volunteer letters were mailed today from my Polish workers to Marshal Stalin? And all because you accepted this one man! How do you expect me to build the railroads? I will not allow this! I'll go to Sverdlovsk, and, if necessary, to Moscow! I, Colonel Gerasimov, refuse to honor your draft notice. Is that clear!? Keep your hands off Battalion 92!" He slammed down the phone.

He called another office. Speaking now in a subdued manner, he explained his situation, and then said in a pleading voice, "And all this for whom? For the Polacks? We organized an army for them once, and as soon as things began to get hot, they pulled out to the Middle East. And now another army? This time they'll probably run to the Far East! How do you expect me to build railways for the future of our socialist economy?"

He listened for a while; then he put down the phone. And then, right before my eyes, he tore up my draft document! Turning to Zakharov, he said, "Would he make a good foreman? You need a replacement, don't you?"

Zakharov agreed and added, "He would be very good with the Kazakhs; he even speaks their language." I realized at once what was going on. A bribe was being offered to me; they assumed that making me a foreman, with a hike in food rations, and a salary, would persuade me to stay on and not try to enlist again.

I quickly spoke up, explaining that I did not want to be a foreman. First of all, I said, I only knew a few words in Kazakhi; secondly, I was not the type who could push men to work. I almost used the expression "slave driver," but caught myself in time.

"You wanted to be a soldier; now act like one," the colonel said. "I'm ordering you to be the foreman of the Seventh Brigade, and you refuse? Where is your discipline?"

As delicately as possible, I explained to the colonel that when I first arrived at Battalion 92, back in Stalingrad, one man used to carry a crosstie, and two men carried a steel rail. Now it took three men to carry a crosstie and eight men to carry a rail. People are so weak, I said, that when the foreman shouts "Drop the rail!" some of the men haven't got the strength to back away fast enough!

"A friend of mine, Kovalenko, is still limping, walking with a cane; he almost lost two toes!" I said. "People are so desperate for food that they have been poisoned by eating wild mushrooms they find in the forest. The Kazakhs are like walking shadows; men are ready to cut each other's throats for a little food! For these reasons, Comrade Colonel, I cannot accept the responsibility of being a foreman; please appoint someone else."

The Director General said that he hadn't known that the food situation was that bad; no one had told him. Then he added, "Besides, the Sverdlovsk District was not prepared for feeding Battalion 92. But in the next budget, we'll be given the same food priority as the tank factory in Nizhniy-Tagil. Tell the men that I shall feed them properly!" he announced loudly. Thus ended my hopes for being drafted, as far as the management of 92 was concerned. But not as far as I was concerned!

The hunger was more visible on the big sturdy men. This was one situation where the little fellow had a better chance to survive. It broke my heart to see my friend Kovalenko walking with a cane. His tall body was bent; he was a shadow of a man, having given up all hope. There was no escape from 92; where could they run? They'd only be charged with desertion, which was a capital offense! And the bread card was valid only in 92; anywhere else it was null and void! That's what kept the men imprisoned.

But I had somewhere to run to: the newly-organized Polish army....And the only obstacle was a bread card! I knew that no draft board in the Sverdlovsk District would accept me now, because of Colonel Gerasimov's veto. But outside this district, I reasoned, the long arm of Colonel Gerasimov would not reach. So, if I could only get out of the district and find my way to another draft office, I might be accepted. Who knows, I thought — maybe I'd even find myself with a Jewish battalion! To be among Jews again, and be fighting the Germans, was almost too much to hope for; I thought about it day and night.

The foreman began treating me better than the other men. I didn't know whether this was due to Gerasimov, or to my good friend Zakharov. Every time the foreman needed some papers delivered to the office, he chose me to be the messenger. Since the office was invariably a great distance from where we were working, usually several miles away, this relieved me for long periods from the heavy labor. Also, on these long hikes through the forest, I often found things to eat: nuts, roots, wild cherries. Some people claimed that eating the wild cherries would make one insane; I ate as many as I could pick, yet my mind remained sharp and keen.

One day I wandered deeper into the forest and came across thousands of mushrooms. I had heard of many cases of mushroom poisoning, and I wasn't sure about these. I picked a capful and when I got back I showed them to Kovalenko. He took one look at them, and asked, "Did you eat any of them?"

I shook my head. "No."

"It's a good thing you didn't, my friend; if you had, you'd be dead before tomorrow morning! These are poisonous toadstools, and just a couple would have finished you off!" He encouraged me to look around some more in that same vicinity. "If there are poisonous ones, there must also be good ones; look carefully, and you'll find them." He taught me how to recognize the difference. between poisonous and non-poisonous mushrooms.

The next day, searching the same area, I came across a shack with a locked door. Looking through the window, I saw a table, a bed, some cooking utensils and tools. Judging by the tools, I realized that a combination of forester and "walking rail man" must live here. The extreme cold occasionally causes steel rails to crack, so the railway system employs men whose job it is to walk along the tracks, hitting the rails with a hammer. From the sound, these men can detect a cracked rail, and thus prevent derailments. Then I noticed that the roof of the shack was covered with dried mushrooms, probably picked by the man who lived here. I figured that I didn't have to worry about whether they were poisonous or not, for surely the forester knew the difference. The mushrooms drying on the roof were so tempting that my hunger pains quickly overcame the pangs of conscience. I climbed up on the roof and began eating the raw mushrooms. Suddenly I heard a creaking sound. Perhaps the owner was inside? I lay quietly on the roof, chewing and swallowing half-dried mushrooms. Then I heard sounds in the forest. I looked into the distance and saw a man with a rifle approaching. I realized that this must be the forester returning from his daily track inspection. I quickly stashed some mushrooms in my bag, climbed down and began to run. The man noticed me; he fired two shots but missed. That night, Kovalenko and I cooked and ate the mushrooms. I became violently ill, and remained sick for the next three days. I've never eaten another mushroom since.

OUR WORK WAS progressing very rapidly. After we finished building a small railroad station with three siding tracks, we began laying track in two directions. Very often the foreman sent me with reports and messages to the engineer who was in charge of the work force on the other end of the fork.

As I passed the new little station one day, there was a freight train standing on a siding. The cars were loaded with something yellowish. Hungry for any kind of food, I climbed up and discovered that it was *makukha*, a compressed cake of pressed oil seeds used as fodder for cows. It was hard as a rock. Although there is no nutritional value in it for people, nevertheless keeping it in the mouth and gnawing on it gave one a feeling of eating. I filled up my pockets, and returned to the men of my battalion with samples of my discovery.

That night a group of us sneaked to the train. It was guarded by two soldiers, but we managed to slip by them and fill up our sacks. The next day my foreman handed me some reports and told me to take a train and deliver them to an official in Sosva, a large city in the Urals. Kovalenko advised me to take along my sack of *makukha*. "You can cash in on it at the market. Charge them five rubles for a small piece; for larger pieces, ten rubles," he said.

It was early on a Sunday morning when I arrived in Sosva. Within an hour I had my papers signed, and was free to go to the market. All over Russia, market day is on Sunday, and usually the market is very close to the railroad station. I installed myself in a corner, opened my bag of *makukha*, looked around at the people and waited for buyers.

I noticed a soldier nearby who was selling tobacco. I stared at him; there was something familiar about him. Somehow this soldier reminded me of my cousin Zalman. He was standing there in a shabby army uniform, skinny and pale, his face long and thin, with great protruding ears. Could it be? Was it really Zalman? I "closed shop" and walked past the soldier, back and forth, back and forth several times. He glanced at me but paid no attention; he continued staring into the distance. So it's not him, I decided; it was only a resemblance.

Then I realized that perhaps I, too, had changed beyond recognition. Maybe that's why he didn't know me! But is it possible that I had changed so much that even my own cousin, who had been my constant playmate and close friend, would not recognize me? But if this soldier was Zalman, a Westerner, why was he still in a Red Army uniform? Why hadn't they kicked him out? I would never have peace of mind unless I found out for sure.

I walked up to him and asked, "Comrade, are you from Poland? Lomza, perhaps?"

Our eyes met, and the years and miles between Lomza and the Urals disappeared. "Yes!" he said, and we fell into each others arms, kissing and crying without embarrassment. All of our longing for home, parents and families, all the emotions which had been suppressed for so long, now burst out.

"Zalman! Is it really you?"

"Chaim! I can't believe it!"

After we calmed down, we talked. We talked for hours, hardly moving our eyes from one another. Zalman had been drafted into the Red Army while I was still in Lithuania. His unit had fought and retreated constantly. In the defense of the city of Rostov, on the Don River, Zalman had single-handedly destroyed a German machine-gun crew, and was wounded; dozens of little steel fragments had entered his body.

"Even now," he said, "every two weeks I have to go to the army hospital where the doctors remove more little pieces of steel from me." It was because he was a wounded, crippled hero that the Red Army did not kick him out when they got rid of the other "Westerners."

We spent most of the time talking about home, and wishing it were possible for us to remain together somehow. In a bitter time like this, it would have been a great comfort to us to have each other. But he could not leave because of his hospital visits, and I could not join him because I was "owned" by Battalion 92. He worked in a factory, making parts for tanks. He was permitted to work in a military factory only because of his record of valor in the army: he had three medals, an "Order of the Red Banner," and a citation for bravery from Stalin. But for me, as a Westerner, employment in that factory was out of the question. I told Zalman about my hopes of joining the new Polish army.

He said, "I'm an invalid, so they certainly wouldn't accept me. But as for you, the truth is that I'd hate to see you go. Real war is not anything like the children's games we used to play at home. Do you remember how we played? On the other hand, I know how good it is to kill Germans! I gave it to them, Chaim, but they got me, too! I still tremble when I think about it. I already knew what they were doing to their prisoners of war, and in particular to the Jewish ones, so I decided never to be taken alive! I was mowing down those cursed Germans like hay in a field. Finally I was all alone, my unit almost wiped out. There was only me and the Germans. So I gave them some more; take this, I said, for our family, for Lomza, for our people, for everything! Well, they hit me too; my body is full of steel, but for every piece of steel I killed a German!"

Zalman was shocked when I told him about the strange incident with Karlik in Stalingrad. Then we talked about his sister who had been able to immigrate to Australia just before the war. "I have her address," he said, "but I'm afraid to write to her. That's all I need, to be called in to the NKVD to explain my contacts with a capitalist country! She doesn't even know if I'm alive or dead...."

We sat quietly, immersed in our thoughts and sorrows. Zalman suddenly exclaimed, "Oh, it's already late afternoon, and we haven't *davened Minchah* yet!"

"What?" I asked, astonished. "Even after two years of brainwashing in the Red Army you still pray?"

Zalman glanced at me with surprise, and said, "You know, that insulted me! Did you really think that I would exchange the faith of our fathers for the faith of Marx, Engels, Lenin, and Stalin?!"

"I'm sorry," I said. "I only meant that after all the atheistic and political indoctrinations during your time in the Red Army..."

Zalman smiled. "Let me tell you, cousin, they have nothing to offer in exchange for our faith; absolutely nothing! Have you any idea how much money and manpower these Russians spend on propaganda? And you know what? Even though the whole idea of Communism, their entire program, is aimed at distributing the wealth equally, God plays a trick on them! They are poorer than any other nation on earth! I'm not speaking about wartime; I'm talking about how it was before the war. Our poor Poland had a much higher standard of living than the Soviet Union; here only the big shots live well, just like the czars, whom they killed."

We found a shady tree behind the station, a peaceful corner. From my sack I pulled out my little Bible and my *tefillin*. He pressed the little book to his heart, kissed the *tefillin* and said, with tears in his eyes, "It's been so long since I've had a chance to put on *tefillin*." Trembling, he put them on and we prayed and cried like two lost children, alone in a wilderness without friends or family. We didn't dare speculate on what the Germans might have done with our loved ones, but deep down we were terribly frightened, and our feelings were expressed in our outpouring of prayers and tears.

Finally we had to end our visit; I had to return to my battalion. I gave him half of my *makukha*, and in return he bought me two cooked beets, a luxury indeed.

Zalman and I parted, heartbroken, promising to visit each other whenever possible, and to stay in touch by mail.

$\mathbf{D}$ELIVERING MESSAGES to the other brigades was a sinecure which I appreciated; not only did it release me from heavy labor occasionally, but it provided me with a way to avoid working on Shabbos. Being assigned this work on Shabbos was vital, for then it was a full-time job. Battalion 92 spread out for many, many miles, and on Saturdays we delivered all the messages from every work brigade, on foot, an all-day job which often stretched far into the night. The foreman acquired a horse and wanted to assign this weekly job to one of his cronies. I knew the foreman was just as hungry as the rest of us were, so I bribed him with my Saturday bread ration and got the assignment. I would take my time, and ride back slowly, waiting for three stars to appear in the sky, declaring that Shabbos was over. If I returned to the brigade any earlier, the foreman might decide to put me to work chopping wood or laying track — a *chillul* Shabbos to be avoided at any cost.

One Shabbos, as I was riding through the woods, shots rang out through the forest, and I heard bullets whistling past me. I figured that the shots had come from a nearby prison camp which I had noticed earlier; it was surrounded by barbed-wire fences and machine-gun posts. The guards must have thought that I was an escaping prisoner. I took off as fast as my horse could gallop, through a hail of machine-gun fire.

Shaking like a leaf, I went straight to my foreman, telling him what had happened. He laughed, and said, "As a matter of fact, I wanted to ask you to deliver this message to the office of the camp today!" He told me the password, and chuckling, he said, "Go to the front entrance, so they don't shoot you!"

I approached the prison entrance cautiously. From a distance I waved my pass to the guard. He checked it at the gate and explained where the office was, a quarter of a mile away. I rode my horse slowly: just being in a Soviet prison camp, even as a free man, gave me the shivers.

Suddenly, from behind a thick clump of bushes and low trees, I heard someone singing a *niggun*. I couldn't believe my ears. As I listened more carefully, I could make out the Hebrew words: "*El ginas egoz yo-o-radi-tee...*" I made a mental note of where the *niggun* was coming from and hurried on to the office.

After delivering my message, I galloped off toward the clump of bushes.

In a clearing surounded by dense brush, I caught a glimpse of a bearded man with a radiant face, sitting on the ground singing softly with his eyes closed. The words and the sweetness of the *niggun* drew me closer to him. When he heard me approaching, he stopped singing and opened his eyes, eyes which seemed to pierce straight through to my soul.

"*Gut Shabbos a Yid,*" I greeted him.

"*Nye ponyemayu,*" was his cautious reply: "I don't understand." Had I been mistaken? But his pure and holy look assured me that I had not: he was singing the melodies that traditionally accompanied the third Sabbath meal. I realized that he was frightened; he must have thought I was some sort of *nachalnik* — official.

"I'm a Jew, from Poland," I assured him. "I heard that beautiful *niggun* as I was riding past and I had to see who was singing it."

He looked at me, not moving a muscle. "I know all the officials and prisoners in this camp, and I've never seen you before," he said in Russian.

I explained to him that I was from the railroad brigade, and was a former yeshiva student. "Look, I have my *tefillin* here. I always carry them with me. Would a *nachalnik* take a chance and carry *tefillin*?"

"*Tefillin!* For fifteen years I haven't put on *tefillin*!" Tears rolled down his face. "Could you come to me tomorrow?" he pleaded, and mumbled to himself, "*Oy Gottenyu*, finally I have *tefillin* but it's Shabbos and I can't put them on!"

When he calmed down, he told me that he was Nachman Baranov, a Breslaver *chasid*. He'd been convicted of teaching Torah to Jewish children and sentenced to 20 years in prison. For 15 years he'd been in a prison camp in the Karelo-Finnish Republic; when the Nazis attacked Russia the camp had been moved to the Urals. The prison had previously been guarded by NKVD men, and he would never have dared to sing *zemiros* then. But the NKVD guards had now been replaced by disabled war veterans who were more humane. He feigned insanity and became the camp "idiot," which made it possible for him to avoid some _chillul_ Shabbos.

Reluctantly, I explained to him that I couldn't come the next day, for I had to work. He insisted that I give him detailed instructions as to how to get to my bunk. I begged him not to come, for he would surely be shot trying to leave the prison grounds.

Ignoring my plea, he changed the subject and said, "So — you liked my _niggun_, eh? Let's sing! This is from _Shir Ha-Shirim_." The sweetness of the _niggun_ stirred my soul; it gave me strength, the spiritual uplifting which I so desperately needed in my dire circumstances.

The next morning, as I was finishing my morning prayers under my blanket, I felt someone touch me. I was terrified; I'd been discovered wearing my _tefillin_! I ripped off the one strapped to my forehead and stuck my head out of the blanket. In the dim light of dawn I recognized the white beard. "_Reb_ Nachman! You escaped! You'll be shot!" I cried out. All the terror I had felt for myself seconds before became terror for his safety.

"Sha!" he whispered. "The guard is right outside. Let me have the _tefillin_ — hurry!" He climbed into my bunk. Standing guard alongside, I heard sobbing under the blanket. I put my hand on the blanket, groping for his mouth to quiet him. The cloth was soaked with his tears.

I heard someone outside and rushed to the door. A soldier was waiting there with a rifle and bayonet hanging from his shoulder. He was contentedly chewing on a piece of bread; _Reb_ Nachman had bribed the guard with his food ration.

Soon he was out of the bunk. "I'll see you tomorrow, at the same time." Again I begged him not to risk his life. Choking with tears, he whispered, "Listen, young man: for 15 years I haven't put on _tefillin_. Now that I have a chance, so what if I'll be hungry? You think this is the first time I've gone without food? They locked me up for seven days without food once because I wouldn't chop wood on Shabbos. _Baruch Hashem_, I'm still alive!"

I felt miserable: I hadn't a crumb to offer him. Even worse, when he came again tomorrow, I still wouldn't have any bread. It was the end of the month and I had used up my ration. The new cards wouldn't be issued until the first of the month. During the day, I borrowed some bread from Kovalenko and kept it for _Reb_ Nachman. He appeared again at dawn, with the same guard. Afterwards, I offered him the bread, but he refused to take it. I followed him outside, begging him to accept it. The guard hissed, "*Vozmee, durak* — Take it, idiot!" I realized the guard had his own eyes on the bread, so I stuffed it into *Reb* Nachman's mouth.

For the next three weeks, *Reb* Nachman never failed to appear, always overjoyed with the *mitzvah* of *tefillin*. Then my brigade was transferred to the Serov District; I never saw *Reb* Nachman again.

My mother, Chava ז״ל, *ca.* 1922.

My father, Avrohom Yeshaya
(Alter) ז״ל, as a Mirrer Yeshiva
student, *ca.* 1910-1912.

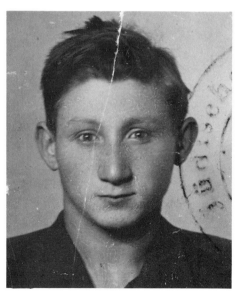

Me as a Kamenitz Yeshiva student.

I think I looked rather dashing in
my full dress uniform. The decoration signifies that I was wounded in
battle.

My headgear and fierce expression
should have been enough to send
the enemy fleeing.

A scene that greeted me throughout my winters in rural Russia.

Graduation from the tank officers' school in Ryazan.
The little one is General Pulturzycki and Misha is at the far right.

Cadets at the tank officers' school.

My T-34 tank and some of my platoon members.

Opening ceremony of a new bridge on the Vistula River. Osobka Morawski, the first Polish postwar socialist prime minister (in black coat, in the foreground), Marshal Rola Zymieski and General Spychalski (to his left), and Soviet Marshal Rokosowski (in rear).

An oriental (Kalmik) Soviet soldier in a German prisoner-of-war camp.

Countless Soviet soldiers surrendered to the Germans ...
the Germans starved them to death.

Dr. Isaac Stone with his friends in Nuremberg.

Hadassa Wenglinska,
later Mrs. Chaim Shapiro.

My cousin Zalman Szeniak ז״ל.

THE DAYS were getting shorter, and
winter was approaching. Ignoring the sunset, we worked on into the night,
for we had to lay our quota of rail mileage for the month. Strong floodlights
enabled us to continue to work after dark. I was working with a sledge-
hammer, pounding spikes into the crossties, which secure the rails in
place. Suddenly I couldn't see the spike! I looked again for the spike, but I
was unable to find the rail. Then I couldn't see my foot; I couldn't even see
Kovalenko, who was standing right beside me! The whole world grew
black before my eyes. Frightened, I screamed, "Kovalenko! I can't see! I'm
blind! I can't see a thing!"

Kovalenko laughed in my face. "You've got it, brother," he said.

"I've got what? Tell me!"

"Chicken blindness, that's what you've got! You'll see again as soon as
the sun comes up in the morning. I've heard that it's because there's not
enough fat and vitamins in our food; it makes people act like chickens at
night — as soon as the sun goes down they can't see a thing!"

Kovalenko led me back to the barracks. I couldn't sleep all night; I was
afraid to believe Kovalenko. After all, he was no doctor; perhaps I had
really become blind, totally blind! Overcome with terror, I lay on my bunk
and thought about all the things that I had hoped to do: to return home to
Papa, Mama and my little brothers; to see all my friends; all the books I had
hoped to read, and study; to see the destruction of Berlin; to visit Jerusalem, our holy city — and now it was all impossible! I was blind and helpless!
I was deeply depressed, terrified by opening my eyes wide but seeing only a
blank, black wall! Can a blind man cry? I found out that he can, for I cried a
river that night.

"My eyes are yearning for Your help and for Your righteous words...."
Over and over again I repeated the verse, waiting for the endless night to
be over.

Could the sun be out already? There were no roosters here to
announce the arrival of a new day. Hour after hour I stood at the window,
desperately waiting for the sun to appear. Several times I groped my way
outside, to get a better look at the horizon, but I saw nothing except the
same thick blackness.

In the cold morning air, I prayed as never before. "Oh, open my eyes,
so that I may behold wondrous things out of Your Torah" — the words of
the psalm poured from my lips with infinite yearning.

Suddenly there was light! I could see! I jumped up and down with joy. I
wanted to embrace the whole world and kiss everything that I saw!

"I can see! I can see!" I ran into the barracks and woke up Kovalenko.

"You woke me up just to tell me that?" he grumbled. "You fool! I told
you it was only chicken blindness. Chickens can see in the daytime!"

Because this was an ailment which could not be tested by a physician,
the management suspected that it was faked. But it became more wide-
spread; Kovalenko and another two men came down with it within the
next few days. Thereafter, as soon as the sun went down, we four "blind
men" groped our way back to the barracks, holding onto one another so as
not to get lost or fall.

"The only medicine for chicken blindness," said Kovalenko, "is vegetables. We must find some vegetables, any kind of vegetables!"

Because I was often the foreman's messenger during the day, Kovalenko instructed me to search the forest for vegetables. During one of my
hikes to the office I came upon a train. It was poking along very slowly, foot
by foot, because it was on brand new tracks, still untested. The train was
guarded by two armed soldiers. I struck up a conversation with them and
asked for a ride. The three of us sat on top of one of the cars and we
chatted. I learned that there was a food-storage depot only two miles from
our barracks. I was amazed to see that the soldiers had a sack full of
vegetables. When I told them about the chicken blindness, they gave me as
many carrots and onions as I could carry; I eagerly devoured a few. I
returned to the gang with my pockets full of carrots and onions, and
distributed the "medicine" to my pals.

We got permission from the foreman to leave our jobs two hours early
each day, so we could visit the food-storage depot. When we arrived there,

we found that it was guarded by only one soldier, a disabled veteran. We visited him every day, just before dark. Every day, one of us sneaked a sackful of the "green medicine" while the other three kept the guard's attention distracted. We wolfed down the raw vegetables on our way back, not caring about the taste; we only wanted to be able to see again!

Eventually, the guard began to suspect us. He refused to talk to us, and ordered us to stay away, or he'd shoot. Thereafter, we tried sneaking to the food depot, crawling on our hands and knees and hiding among the undergrowth, but his bullets began to fly in our direction! At first we thought the chances we were taking were worth it, but then one of us got hit, and the foreman put a stop to our nightly forays. By that time, however, we had stored away a good supply of vegetables and gradually our night vision returned. But never again would I take for granted the miracle of seeing, of waking each day to the light of the sun, of opening my _siddur_ and seeing the holy words, sharp and clear on the page....

31

A NEW TRANSPORT of men arrived fresh out of prison. They were mostly *bytoviki* — criminals, not political prisoners. However, among the few political prisoners, some were Poles. All these prisoners were supposed to have been released long before, according to the Polish-Soviet agreement, but they had apparently been forgotten by the Soviet prison authorities. There was something about these *bytoviki* that seemed very strange, however; many of them were fat, as though they'd been staying in a luxury hotel, not in a prison camp near the Arctic Circle.

During lunch hour, as I was sipping the slop soup, two of these men walked past me. One of them stopped abruptly, studied my face, and began to talk to me excitedly. It turned out that he had once studied in the yeshiva at Lomza, and recognized me. I was so surprised that I almost knocked over my bowl of soup. His name was Jonah Bromberg (who presently lives in New York), and he had known my father, who had been a frequent visitor at the yeshiva library and had attended many of the lectures. It was a bittersweet reunion; we talked about the good old days, and we talked about the present difficulties.

I said, "Bromberg, you must have had excellent food in that prison! Look how fat you are."

"Fat? Who's fat? Look at yourself — you're fat, too," he said. He explained to me that we were bloated, not fat, and he was much more swollen than I. The swelling was a result of chronic starvation and malnutrition; the thought of it frightened me.

"But how can one tell if one is swollen or just plain fat?" I asked, trying to be calm.

"It's easy," he replied. "Just press your finger into your flesh and then remove it fast; if you are really fat, the flesh will spring back, but if you're bloated, the flesh takes its time to get back to normal."

Bromberg's friend, apparently noticing my anxiety, patted me on the back and said, "Don't worry, you're still better off than I am." For a minute I didn't understand what he meant, but then he began to laugh, and I realized that he didn't have a single tooth in his mouth!

I asked, "How old are you? What happened to you?"

He was only nineteen years old! While in prison, he had suffered from a condition which results from malnutrition and vitamin deficiency. His gums had begun to bleed, and then the roots of his teeth began to rot; finally his teeth fell out, one by one.

As soon as they left, I pressed my finger into my thigh. I watched, horrified, while my flesh slowly — very, very slowly — returned to its previous state! Bromberg was right: I was bloated! I decided that I had to get out of there, and fast. I'd desert! I was willing to risk the firing squad, for the alternative was to starve to death in this wilderness.

From that moment on, my thoughts constantly revolved around escaping. I knew that here in the Sverdlovsk District, I had no chance of being accepted into the new Polish army, for Colonel Gerasimov had forbidden the induction of any men from Battalion 92. Also, if I deserted I'd have no documents with me. If I were caught, especially in the Sverdlovsk District, I could easily be traced to Battalion 92 and charged with desertion. However, I reasoned, if I were caught beyond the district — and the farther the better — it would be less likely that they could trace me to Battalion 92. In that event, I could plead to be taken to the nearest military commandant for immediate conscription into the army. What kind of a deserter would I be, if I were begging to be accepted into the army? And at the military commandant's office I would ask to be sent to the Polish army! Very simple! Just like that! I laughed to myself. There was, however, one basic problem: how could I escape from the Sverdlovsk District? It extended for hundreds of miles. And what about food, even for one day? Our bread cards were valid only here; outside, they were worthless!

One day, a Kazakh friend whispered a secret into my ear: "We Kazakh men want to write a letter of complaint to the Party back home!"

I laughed at him and his silly idea. "You're going to write _what?_" I shook my head, to point out the utter helplessness of our situation.

He told me that, in another brigade, a Kazakh had not been able to move fast enough because of weakness and near-starvation, and a train had struck him, severing both his legs. The Kazakhs had concluded that they had to write to the Party back home and tell them about the chronic starvation here, and warn that if help would not come soon, they'd all commit suicide. He asked me to write the letter, since they were all illiterate, and to send it to a relative of his who was a member of the Central Committee of the Kazakhstani Communist Party.

I refused, telling him that I didn't want to get involved in this kind of business. Besides, it wouldn't do them any good. However, in case they did decide to write, I advised him, "Don't drop the letter into the regular Battalion mailbox; drop it into the mailbox of a passing train."

Two weeks later, I was amazed to learn that a delegation from the Kazakh Republic had arrived to investigate the charges! First, they recommended that all Kazakhs were to be given a medical examination; the Kazakh officials had brought their own doctors with them — they didn't trust the Russian doctors!

My Kazakh friend, full of smiles, whispered in my ear, "You see? You don't know the Kazakhs! You said a letter would do no good, ah? The letter did all of us good!" He advised me that I, too, was entitled to this examination, for I, too, came from Kazakhstan! "You're a Kazakhi citizen, no? *Jakhsi* — Good!"

I was so happy that I almost kissed him, but my happiness was short-lived. Colonel Gerasimov was putting up a fight, for it was suddenly announced that the examination was only for Kazakhs over 50 years old! Since most of the Kazakhs were over 50, this satisfied the Kazakhi delegation. The only younger "Kazakhs" here were Europeans like me. We all envied the Kazakhs, who emerged from the examination with a traveling-pass back home, and a traveling bread card valid for 30 days anywhere in the Soviet Union.

I was standing in the bread line with a prayer in my heart, for I was already two days ahead on my card. I was now at the mercy of the girl. If she refused me, I'd have to wait until the next day. The pleading look on my face must have softened her heart; I walked out of the storage house happily with the daily ration of black bread in my hand — a priceless treasure! I chewed it slowly, crumb by crumb, so it would last longer.

Suddenly I noticed a man sitting on the ground, leaning against a wall; his mouth was hanging open and his head had fallen onto one shoulder. His large pleading eyes pierced me. I bent down and asked him what was the matter. He tried to answer, moving his lips, but no words came out. I realized that he must be dying of starvation. It was a daily occurrence around the camp: people just gave up, falling down and passing out from hunger. I took some crumbs of bread and placed them in his open mouth.

He swallowed, nodding his head in appreciation. It broke my heart to be giving away my precious bread, my very existence. Was it right to deny myself the bread, giving it to a stranger? Would he do the same for me? I chased away those thoughts. After all, I thought, this man is dying, and I'm still on my feet and working.

I put some more bread into his mouth. Noticing that he was having difficulty swallowing, I asked him if he'd like some water. He nodded his head. I brought water and placed the cup at his parched lips. After a few sips, I fed him some more bread. He touched my hand in appreciation, but he still couldn't talk. I didn't know what else to do for him. I couldn't just leave him there: what would he do at night, when it was cold and windy? I decided that the best thing would be to get him to the medical station, but he couldn't walk.

I asked two men passing by to give me a hand, and we carried him to the medical station. The nurse asked him for the name of his next of kin or any relations. The sick man, unable to talk, pointed to me. It couldn't make any difference now, I thought, so why should I deny it? I told her my name; I wished the man a speedy recovery and left the station.

A few minutes later I bumped into Kovalenko, and I told him what had happened. He became agitated. "And you're supposed to be so smart! Why, you're nothing but an idiot after all!" he berated me.

At first I thought he was criticizing me for giving away my bread. I resented this, and I told him that this was my business. "In my opinion," I said, "I did the right thing. I couldn't just leave a man dying while I had bread!"

"Would he offer you bread? Idiot!" Kovalenko yelled. "But I'm not talking about that," he said, lowering his voice. "I'm talking about the doctors and nurses; the first thing they'll do is to clean out his pockets and take the money, bread cards, anything valuable.

"And if he dies, they'll even remove his clothes and sell them on the black market!" Kovalenko paused for a moment, then continued. "_You_ are his relative! _You_ brought him in! So run to the station and claim his belongings!"

I realized that Kovalenko was right: I was not only inexperienced, but naive and stupid. Why hadn't I thought of it? Weak as I was, I ran with all my strength back to the medical station.

I opened the door and found the nurse going through his pockets! Red-faced, she said to me, "I was wondering where you went. I was just putting away his things for you." She handed me his document wallet and a small pocket knife. "He is sleeping now. The doctor is not in yet. Come tomorrow, if you'd like to visit him."

I said, "Is that all that you could find in his pockets?" I was suspicious because she had given me only the large document wallet which is carried in the jacket. She had failed to give me the small coin purse which was usually carried in the pants pocket.

The wrinkled face of the elderly nurse changed color, from red to white. In a furious voice, she said, "Are you accusing me of something?"

I placed my finger on my lips to quiet her down, and said, "Shhh! You shouldn't shout when a patient is sleeping. I was sure that my cousin always kept his money purse with him."

"This was all I found," she snapped. "Now, get out!"

I spent a sleepless night, for my conscience was troubled. The instinct of self-preservation was corrupting me; for within the sick man's document wallet was a bread card valid in any place in the USSR for the next 30 days! The sick man was 56 years old and was, like me, a European who had been drafted in Kazakhstan. Being over 50, he had been called before the Kazakh medical commission, and had been given a train ticket back to Kazakhstan and the precious 30-day bread card. Although the nurse had apparently stolen his money, God had sent the bread card to me.

I rationalized: the old man has no one anyhow. He's a refugee, just like me; otherwise he wouldn't have named me next of kin. So what difference does it make if he ever gets back to Kazakhstan or not? But a voice within me argued: still, he has a chance to *live* in the warm climate of Asia Minor, while here, in the cold Urals, he'll surely die! And how can I steal his last chance of life?

But he'll probably stay in the hospital a month, said the first voice. In the meantime, the bread card will lose its validity. You can use it right now! Didn't Mama tell you, "Go, my son, go!" So go now; it's your only chance! Otherwise you'll die in these forsaken Ural Mountains! And so the arguing, pro and con, continued within me, throughout the long night, until it was time to go to work.

Kovalenko didn't lose any time; first thing in the morning, he asked me for some bread. "You're a millionaire now! Let's eat!" he said.

I hadn't yet told Kovalenko about my plan to desert. I gave one coupon of my own bread card to him, with the understanding that it should last him for two days. In the meantime, I intended to go and visit the sick man; I had decided that, if he demanded his card back, I would return it to him unused. As soon as we finished work, Kovalenko and I walked over to the medical dispensary. I didn't like his coming there with me, but I knew nothing in the world would stop him from sharing the bread card. I was lucky that he had not stolen it during the night, or taken it from me by force.

In the dispensary, the same nurse told me that the old man had died during the night....

Kovalenko was in a cheerful mood, even though he criticized me for not asking for the old man's clothes. But my mind was far, far away.

I hardly heard Kovalenko's words; I was thinking about all that had transpired during the last few days. It was another miracle! That mysterious hand leading me to my goal — God had sent a food supply directly into my hands! It was more than a bread card, it was the push I needed to make this fateful and dangerous attempt at desertion. Mama! I called to her silently. I'm coming! I'm coming!

Kovalenko was eating the bread that I had given him. I took him outside and told him of my plan. "I hate to leave you, my friend! I wish we could run away together, but I have to join an army; I have to fight a war! Too bad they wouldn't accept you! Cover up for me as long as you can — the longer the better — so they won't start to search for me too soon. And here's a present for you: my bread card for the whole month, and my soup card as well! You know I could sell it, that it's worth a fortune, and I need some money for the road. Still, you're my best friend, and I want you to have it. Here, take it!"

Kovalenko stole a railroad man's cap and gave it to me. He said it would be useful, for it would mislead the guards at the various stations, making them think that I was a railroad man. There was a national holiday coming up within the week and usually the management celebrated by getting drunk; I figured that this would be the best time to start running.

The following day we were put to work unloading apples from Alma-Ata, liquors from Georgia and grapes from Uzbekistan. Our proletarian eyes popped out, just looking at all those crates; our proletarian mouths watered and stomachs growled just from smelling the aroma of all those delicious fruits. But in this classless Soviet society we were only allowed to unload them, but not taste them. We were watched constantly and were afraid to take even one grape.

The next night the management thoroughly celebrated the holiday. Many of the higher officials were drunk and insensible. It was the ideal time for deserting!

Waiting at the crossing for the train which would take me away, Kovalenko and I embraced and wept. Eventually a lumber train slowed down and I jumped onto one of the flatcars and lay down on the boards. I didn't know where the train was going and I didn't care, as long as it would take me out of the Sverdlovsk District. Lying there, I felt terribly exposed; there was nowhere to hide. I planned to jump off at the first stop, and try to board a passenger train, relying on my railroad cap to fool the police.

At daybreak, the train stopped at a water tower to fill up the locomotive. I climbed off and hid in the brush. After what seemed hours, a passenger train came along, slowing down before entering the station ahead. This gave me my chance to jump aboard. If anyone noticed me, he would assume that I was a railway worker. The nocturnal ride in the cold wind had chilled my bones, and the warm air in the overcrowded car was a soothing balm for my shivering body. From the passengers' conversation, I learned that the train was heading for Magnitogorsk. I figured that a rigid inspection of documents would take place at the station there, for this was one of the Soviet cities built especially for heavy industry, which now had become war industry. Along the way, the train stopped at a few stations, but the ticket and document inspections were quite perfunctory. I slipped through the inspections by simple, tested maneuvers: hiding in the restroom, crossing from one car to another. The main problem, however, was still ahead of me: how to avoid being arrested in Magnitogorsk. I didn't know whether this city was still within the Sverdlovsk District. Once out of the district, I'd be safe from the long arm of Colonel Gerasimov, Director General of Battalion 92.

The conductor finally announced that we were pulling into Magnitogorsk. I began to look around for an escape. To jump off while the train was still speeding meant suicide or injury. When it finally slowed down, the station platform appeared, crowded with armed police who jumped aboard each car for the document inspection. With my railway cap pulled low, I began to step down from the train, as if the inspection was not meant for me at all.

But one policeman thought otherwise. He stopped me at the last step. "Let's see your documents!" he said. I began fumbling around in my pockets for my non-existent documents. It was hopeless! From the corner of my eye, I noticed that a train on the other side of the platform was moving out. Without a moment's hesitation, I jumped off the last step of the train and dashed across the platform and onto the other train which was already picking up speed. I heard the policeman shouting "Stop!" He even fired a shot, but I was already "lost" aboard the other train!

This train was an express, speeding towards Chelyabinsk. What I hadn't realized was that not only Magnitogorsk but every city in this part of Russia was a center of heavy industry, full of great chimneys which belched black smoke constantly, and supplying the colossal Red Army with every type of modern arms! This meant that there were rigid controls everywhere. At Chelyabinsk I was trapped again; there, two policemen, not one, confronted me and demanded my documents. I began to search through my pockets, stalling for time, hoping for a train to move out, but it was no use; I was under arrest!

In the police station I tried to "explain" to the commandant: "I'm with _Stroitelstvo_ 33; they have my documents. We were on the way to Tashkent, but while I got off the train to drink some water, it moved away. Now I'm trying to catch up with 33." I figured that, with the poor state of communications in Russia, it would take them weeks to check on my story. In the meantime, I might persuade the commandant to deliver me to the draft office.

The commandant looked me over and said, "Tell me, who sent you to Chelyabinsk? What's your assignment? And who's your connection?"

At first I didn't grasp his query and I asked him to repeat it. "You heard me!" he shouted. "You know what I mean. Who's your connection?"

His questions rang a bell, for I had been asked exactly the same questions twice before. The first time was in Smolensk, when I entered the USSR; the second time was in Kzyl-Orda, Kazakhstan. Again I was under suspicion of being a spy! I had expected to be charged with desertion, but not espionage! I tried pretending that I didn't understand.

"What connection are you talking about, Comrade Commandant? The only connection that I have is with _Stroitelstvo_ 33, which is on the way to Tashkent."

The commandant became enraged. He pounded on the desk with his fist, then drew himself up in front of me, so close that I could smell his whiskey-laden breath. "I know you're a German spy; there's no use playing dumb. Just tell me what your assignment is in Chelyabinsk!"

"Comrade Commandant," I replied, "I'm a Jew. My name tells you that. How can you suspect me of spying for the Nazis, my worst enemy?"

Suddenly the commandant grabbed me around the neck with both hands and began to choke me. He screamed, "You are a German! You are not a Jew! Your hair is blond. You've got the look of a Fritz! Now speak up, you damn spy!" I wanted to speak up, but he was throttling my throat and not a sound could emerge. He must have realized that I was choking, for he let me go, still shouting, "Now tell me who your connections are, you rotten spy!"

How I wished I hadn't been born blond; in fact I wished I'd never been born at all! I repeated again, begging, "But I am a Jew! Please believe me! Bring a Jew here and let him test me! There are Jews in Chelyabinsk, I'm sure, so why not let me face one? Why should you even think of accusing me of spying for the Nazis?"

Nothing I said had any effect on him. Suddenly he pulled his pistol out of its holster, and pressed the barrel against my temple! The cold steel pressing against my head terrified me. If he was trigger-happy, it needed only one move of his finger on the trigger and I'd be dead! Then it occurred to me that if he was truly convinced that I was a spy, he wouldn't be satisfied unless he first pumped some information out of me, and one cannot pump a dead man. This realization brought a smile to my face. Suddenly, unexpectedly and inexplicably, I began to laugh aloud.

Apparently he interpreted this as a display of disdain, proving that he was right, that he had caught a "big fish," a real spy! He put his pistol back into the holster and said, "You *are* a spy, and I promise you that you'll talk! We have the means to make you!" He pressed a button, and ordered the entering policeman, "Lock him up!"

The cellar-jail was completely dark, without a single window. Only the long corridor was lit by a couple of dim light bulbs. The cells on both sides of the corridor were placed in such a manner that no cell faced another. The policeman pushed me into a cell and locked the door behind me.

I stood near the door for a while, trying to accustom my eyes to the darkness. Then, sliding my hands along the wall, I moved a few steps, hoping to find a bunk or a bed. Suddenly something moved in the cell. At first, I thought it must be a rat, but then I was able to discern the silhouette of a man, moving slowly towards the door. He opened a small, hinged panel in the door, and this enabled a bit of light from the corridor to penetrate into our cell. Then he moved back to a corner without uttering a word.

I looked around the cell. The ceiling was so low that I could almost touch it, and the walls were bare. Along one wall was a long bunk, constructed of wide boards; this was the "collective" bed. Standing in a corner was a ten-gallon can with a lid; this was the "indoor plumbing" — our collective toilet! My cellmate lay down on one side of the bunk, so I settled myself on the other side. It was obvious that he hadn't taken a bath in months.

Hour after hour we lay there. The darkness and the silence grew oppressive. I felt the need for prayer but under these circumstances it would be unseemly; how could I pray in a place like this? Tired, hungry and with a prayerful heart, I finally fell asleep.

Suddenly someone called my name; I jumped to the door. There was a policeman in the hall. He wrote a checkmark on a paper, and I assumed this was a sort of roll call. However, this happened three more times during the night. An awful lot of roll calls, I thought. It seemed to me that this cell was escape-proof, so why should they check so many times? And why should they check only me? The guard hadn't called anyone else's name but mine. I was perplexed.

In the morning, a bowl of slop soup was handed through the small opening in the door, but only for my cellmate. I began to fear that their tactic might be to weaken me physically by starving me, while weakening my nerves by waking me a number of times every night. Hungry, thirsty and exhausted, I would be more likely to confess. My cellmate took the soup and swallowed it with such speed that before the guard closed the window, my cellmate had returned the metal plate.

The appearance of this man — the stench of his body, and his animal-like eating — depressed me as much as my hunger and thirst. He had probably been a self-respecting man before he was placed in this hole, I thought. Does deprivation change a person to such a degree? Might I eventually become just like him? In the little bit of light that penetrated our cell where he was sitting, I could see that he had long, gray hair, and a bald spot in the center. Suddenly his fingers landed in the midst of his bush of wild, uncombed hair and he scratched his scalp violently. After a while, he raised his face to the ceiling, and the dim light revealed his features — he was perhaps 40, but in some ways he looked like a man of 70! What imprisonment can do to a man!

Can he talk? I wondered. Or have they silenced him forever? Trying to break the ice, I hesitantly said, "Good morning, citizen."

After a long, noisy yawn my cellmate replied, "And who told you it's morning, friend?"

"Didn't you just now eat breakfast?" I asked.

He laughed and shook his head. "Here, my friend, you never know. It might have been lunch. They mix you up so you'll never know: is it day or night? What day? What month? Confusion, absolute confusion!"

Now I began to try to estimate how long I had been there. The man was right, I thought. I'd only been here for about 24 hours and already I was losing my sense of time!

"Don't they ever take you out for a walk in the fresh air, in the sun?" I asked.

"Never, never," he replied. Then he asked me, "A tee za chto — And you, for what?" I was afraid to tell him that I was accused of being a spy, for the animosity towards the Germans was such that he might become hostile towards me.

"They haven't told me yet why I'm here," I replied. "And why are you here?"

He moved away and lay down on the bunk. After settling himself, he said, "It's a long story. You and I will be here for a long time, so let's not tell it all at once. What will we talk about a month from today? Three months? A year?"

His words made me shudder. Months? Years? Was it possible?

Mumbling to himself, he repeated, "Yes, comrade, months, years." We reverted to silence.

Some hours passed in absolute quiet. Then a guard brought some slop soup and a small piece of bread, but again there was nothing for me! I asked the guard for water, and he brought me some, but no food. Then came roll call. A policeman stepped up to each cell and called out the occupants' names. The prisoners replied "Present." After roll call, my cellmate said, "I saved some bread for you. Here, take it; incidentally, you passed your test."

I ate the bread gratefully and asked, "What test? What are you talking about?"

"Don't you know?" he said. He then explained to me that the reason they woke me up three times last night was to check my identity. "No one wakes up to a phony name; if the name you gave them wasn't your real name, you wouldn't have woken up every time they called it!"

Later he told me that his name was Ivan Rubarov, and that he was a chemist by profession. He was accused of sabotage when there was an explosion in his laboratory, and he had confessed, "just to get it over with!" He advised me to confess to whatever charges I was facing. I didn't pay much attention to what he said. But later he hinted again that, for my own good, I'd be better off confessing and making it easier for myself. The next time he received bread, he broke off half of his portion and gave it to me. I was deeply moved by his generosity; he, too, was hungry, yet he shared his meager portion of bread with me! Later we talked some more, and again he advised me to confess.

His repeated urgings that I confess, and his amazing generosity suddenly made me remember what Kovalenko had told me about his experiences in prison, where the NKVD had "planted" informers. That's it! My cellmate must be an informer! He was trying to win my confidence and to break my resistance! I played dumb, and didn't argue with him. I shared his bread and even his soup and waited fearfully for the forthcoming interrogation.

And then, unexpectedly, a ray of hope appeared in the form of a policeman who spoke with a "Jewish accent." He was making the usual roll call of all prisoners, and when he called out the name of my cellmate, Ivan Rubarov, it sounded like "Khubakhov," a sure sign that he was from the Byelorussian Republic, where there was a large Jewish population. This peculiar accent was the basis of many derisive wisecracks about the "Jewish accent."

Even before he called my name, I was at the small window in the door and, in Yiddish, I asked, "_Chaver, bist du a Yid_ — Comrade, are you a Jew?"

Without hesitation, the policeman replied in Yiddish, "_Avadde_ — Of course!"

Then, still speaking in Yiddish, I told him that his commanding officer was convinced that I was a German spy and that he refused to believe that I was a Jew because of my fair coloring. I begged him to do me a great favor and tell the commandant that I really was a Jew.

The policeman didn't promise anything, but I was confident that he would try to help me. After my conversation with the policeman, I noticed an instant change in my roommate's attitude. He suddenly stopped giving me advice.

Without a watch, and without knowing day from night, it was impossible to tell how long it took that Jewish policeman to take action — but he did!

It was some time later when the door was suddenly opened, and the same Jewish policeman called me out of the cell. He handcuffed my wrist to his own, and took me upstairs to the commandant.

425

"Well, young man," the commandant said to me, "you ought to kiss that man's hands!" He pointed to the policeman, who was standing at attention, still chained to me. "I was absolutely convinced that you were a spy; I was sure that only a trained, cold-blooded spy would laugh when a pistol was put to his temple." He took out his gun and, showing it to the policeman, he said, "This little trigger was between him and the grave. But I figured I'd better pump some information out of him first. He's a lucky Jew!"

He signaled to the policeman to remove the handcuffs. Turning back to me, he muttered, "All right then, I was wrong; you're not a spy, but you *are* a deserter!"

"Comrade Commandant," I said, "a deserter is a person who runs away from the army, away from the front. But I'm begging you to deliver me to the military commandant, so that I can join the army. How can I be called a deserter?"

He smiled, looked me over and said, "What I meant is that you are a deserter from a labor battalion." Then he ordered the policeman to take me to the *Voyenkomat*.

As we went outside, the policeman said, "You must be starving." I thanked him fervently for what he had done for me, and said that I had bread coupons of my own. But he insisted that I take his bread. We stopped at a bakery, and presenting his bread card, he bought a whole kilogram of bread and gave it all to me. "By the time you reach an army camp, you'll have eaten up your rations," he said. We conversed in Yiddish until we reached the draft office. How good it was to hear the *mama-loshen* again! Before the day was over I was accepted into the new Polish army.

IN CHELYABINSK I was told that
when I reached my destination — a small station near Moscow — a Polish
officer would be there to receive me. And, indeed, one was waiting for me
when I arrived. He said that we had to wait for another train which was due
to arrive soon with more recruits. Looking at the lieutenant, I could see the
reality of the calamity that had befallen Poland, for this officer personified
the wretchedness and misery that had overtaken my country. Back home,
when the Russian soldiers first entered Lomza, we had laughed at the
sloppy, miserable clothes they wore; we were accustomed to the Polish
officers who had always been dressed in perfectly fitting uniforms. In fact, it
was common knowledge that many Polish officers wore corsets to
enhance the tight fit of their tunics. "We lost the war because our officers
couldn't move fast enough on account of their corsets and tight uniforms"
was a bitter joke current after the defeat.

Now, here was a Polish officer dressed even more shabbily than the
Russians had ever been. His army coat was too big, and hung clumsily
from his shoulders, like that of a scarecrow. The four-cornered Polish
army cap was droopy; apparently the Russians wouldn't waste the wire
which was necessary to keep the caps stiff. The white eagle, the Polish
national emblem which decorated every army cap, was different too.
Traditionally, there was a crown and a cross upon the white eagle's head,
but now the eagle had lost his crown and cross, and he was bare-headed! In
addition, someone had turned the eagle's head and, instead of looking
westward, he now looked straight ahead.

Two more trains arrived, and our group increased. The lieutenant lined
us up in two columns. We were dressed in thin rags, and since the

temperature was below zero, we were eager to get into the new, warm uniforms, so we marched vigorously. The road led through a thick forest. It had been snow-plowed, and the piles of snow on both sides reached almost to our shoulders. After a few miles, we came to an army camp, with a guard at the gate. Our officer informed us, "This is the training camp of the Czechoslovakian army, under General Svoboda." After a few more kilometers we passed another army camp. This time we were told that it was the training camp of the "Tudor Vladimiresku," the Rumanian army.

The lieutenant explained that only a few months ago these men were volunteers in the German army, fighting the Russians. Now, having been captured by the Russians, they wanted to help them to conquer Germany!

Finally we arrived at the Polish army camp. When we entered, I thought that there had been some error, for it appeared as if we had entered a prisoner-of-war camp. It was full of men in German uniforms! It turned out that these Poles, too, were former German soldiers. While the Rumanians, Slovaks and Czechs had been fighting on the German side, in their own national units and in their own national uniforms, the Poles had been serving in regular German army units, in German uniforms.

Wanda Wasilewska and the commander-in-chief of the new Polish army, General Berling, went to the prisoner-of-war camps and urged the Poles to volunteer for the new Polish army. Again, these men switched loyalties; they now shouted "Long live Stalin!" as vigorously as they had screamed "Heil Hitler!"

We happened to arrive in time to listen to the grand lady, Wanda Wasilewska, in person! Addressing these former German soldiers, she thanked them "for volunteering to save the honor of Poland!" This, of course, was nonsense. These former German soldiers did not volunteer to save the honor of Poland. What they actually did was to exchange the miserable food of the prisoner-of-war camps and the hard work in the Soviet coal mines for good army food and warm clothes. A large number of them volunteered in the hope that somehow they might be able to cross back to the German lines; and, indeed, this happened many times. Some made it; others were shot by the Russians while crossing the lines of battle.

But Wanda Wasilewska boosted their morale by flattering them, by pretending that they were heroes. Speaking into a microphone in her delicate voice, she said:

"Soon, very soon, Germany will be defeated. A beaten Germany will surrender unconditionally, and the peoples of Europe will gather at the peace table. Who will speak for Poland? The Polish fascists in London? Will it be those leaders who shamed us by losing the war in a few days? Those cowardly generals and colonels who left our heroic soldiers fighting the Germans, while they themselves fled the borders to safety? It is common knowledge that the way to Warsaw is through Smolensk and Minsk. It is common sense that our place as Poles, and as Slavs, is to fight alongside our Slavic brethren, the great Russian people. It is common knowledge that Marshal Stalin wanted us Poles to fight along with the glorious Red Army. But what did those fascists do? They pulled out the Polish army from the Soviet Union to roam and to sail across the British Empire to safety! And so I ask, who will fight for Poland? How can we expect a seat at the victory table if we have barely fired a shot?" Despite the terrible cold, everyone stood motionless, spellbound by her oratory. Some of the things she said, I had never heard before. "The AK — the Polish underground, _Armja Krajowa_," she continued, "is paralyzed! It is not fighting! The AK is the best-armed underground army in Europe, but in comparison to the French maquis or the Yugoslav partisans, or even the Greek partisans, the AK is nothing! The AK cannot fool the world with false communiqués about heroic acts and great underground activities against the enemy. The world knows that the AK has a gentlemen's agreement with the occupying Germans and full cooperation in murdering the Jews. The AK is serving the Germans by not permitting the AL, _Armja Ludowa_ — the people's army — and the Soviet partisans to sabotage the railways and bridges leading to the German front in Russia! President Roosevelt has stopped the funds for the AK, because the US government has learned about the perfidy of the AK, and the cooperation between the AK and the Germans!"

She continued: "Our great poet Juliusz Slowacki has described our Poland as the 'Peacock and Parrot of Nations'. But, unfortunately, our beloved peacock has lost all its beautiful feathers! Our white eagle has been plucked by the vicious Germans! So who is left to save the honor of Poland? There is no one but us who can save, who can restore, the honor of Poland! Long live the friendship and brotherhood between the Polish and Russian peoples! Long live the best friend of Poland, glorious Marshal Stalin!"

The audience replied with wild applause, cheering, "_Niech zyje_ — Long live!"

"Bravo! Bravo!"

Wasilewska's speech brought back to me the words of the Pole in the German church back home in Lomza; it seemed like a hundred years ago. He had said, "I'm a faithful citizen to whoever feeds me." Yesterday the Poles had screamed "Long live the Germans!" Today, it was "Long live the Russians!"

After Wanda Wasilewska left, the camp divided itself into two groups. On one side were the former German soldiers, still in their German uniforms. The other group consisted of people like me, who had arrived from all corners of the huge Soviet Union. Although we were in rags and tatters, we still had our pride; we had not served the Germans! The two groups did not fraternize. We, the "Russian Poles," could not feel friendly towards any Pole who had served in the German army. As for me, I dreaded the thought of having to serve with these Nazis! Who knew how many Jews they had killed? And now they'd be my comrades-in-arms!

As we waited to be processed, some Polish officers appeared. A few of them went to the "German" side of the camp, but most of them came to our side. We soon learned the purpose of their visit. They were looking for volunteers for a newly established branch in the Polish army: candidates to be trained as political officers!

As far as armaments were concerned, the new army had no problem, for the huge Soviet arsenals were capable of supplying the most modern weapons. The problem was where to find experienced combat officers to train and lead this new army into battle. Polish officers were virtually impossible to locate, for most of them had gone with the army of General Anders when it left the Soviet Union. And even if any could be found, their help would have been insignificant; these Polish officers had been trained to fight an 18th century war, with horses and sabres. The new army being formed here was fully mechanized, and there wasn't a horse in sight!

The problem was solved by bringing in Soviet officers, some of whom were designated as "advisors." Some continued to wear their Soviet uniforms and Soviet ranks; others became more integrated into the army, wearing Polish uniforms and ranks. Some of the Soviet officers even "Polonized" their family names by adding "ski" to the end. Thus a Major Zavadov became Major Zavadovski. There were also many Soviet Poles among these officers; they usually had Polish names but, because they had been born and raised in the Soviet Union, they couldn't speak Polish.

The organizers of the new army realized that the civilian population in Poland would not be receptive to a Polish army which was led by Russian officers, or by Poles who spoke only Russian. Therefore, a number of officers' training schools were quickly established. It was a race against time: the German army was in retreat and in only a few months the Red Army might be in Poland. The Russians were hoping that this new Polish army would be the vanguard, liberating Poland. Then, after Poland was cleared of Germans, this new Polish army would win the confidence and support of the local population, to the disadvantage of the London Poles. Thus, it was essential that this new Polish army be led by Polish officers. The curriculum in the officers' training schools was greatly accelerated; courses which normally would take 18 months were condensed into three months. There were very few field exercises, no maneuvers and no simulated combat conditions; there was only classroom training. The cadets were told, "You'll get your field training on the battlefield!"

However, there was one branch of the army service which could not wait even a few months; this service needed officers at once, urgently! This was the political service, which furnished political officers to all army units. The new Polish army was copying the Soviet army's creation of _politruks_.

A _politruk_ was the Soviet substitute for a chaplain — but the religion was Communism. Every army unit had one, a clever creation of the founder of the Red Army, Trotsky. During the Bolshevik Revolution in 1917, most of the Czar's officers and generals had been murdered by the soldiers whom they had commanded. To train new cadres of officers would take time, particularly since all those who were trustworthy — the laborers, the peasants, the proletarians — were illiterate.

Trotsky bribed the surviving officers of the Czar's army by raising their ranks. However, because capitalists could not be trusted, Trotsky appointed a _politruk_, a guardian of the faith, who watched over the commander and over everything under his command. No order by any commanding officer was valid unless approved by the _politruk_. This created complications, because the _politruk_s were ignorant in military matters and many were illiterate. Still, the professional officer had to clear every order with his _politruk_.

Trotsky had intended this procedure to be only a temporary measure until new officers, who were trustworthy and literate, could be trained. However, Stalin overthrew Trotsky, and the _politruk_ became an established and permanent institution. From then on, the _politruk_'s job was to propagandize within the army, to educate every officer and soldier in the Party line, and to keep the Red Army loyal and faithful to the Party and to

Stalin! One of the duties of the *politruk* was to snoop around for any sign of opposition or even slight dissent within the armed forces. The political officer became the long arm of Stalin, helping to control the huge Red Army! Marshal Bulganin, Khrushchev and Brezhnev were all political officers, insuring the Red Army's loyalty both to Stalin and to the Bolshevik Party.

The new Polish army established the same system, disguised under a variety of titles. Each army unit had a *politruk* who was called a "political officer," or a "cultural officer" or "information officer." Their ranks ranged from lieutenant to colonel.

In this area, the ex-German soldiers were most useful. In addition to their stigma of being "boot-lickers," these particular Poles had been trained in a totalitarian army; they had been trained to obey, without any question, every order of their superiors. Thus they were ideally suited to become political officers.

Just as the Red Army, in its early years, did not trust the sons of capitalists to become combat officers, this new Polish army did not trust them either. The "Red Army of Workers and Peasants" was often led by illiterates, since it was their blind loyalty that was demanded, even at the risk of lowering the quality of the officer cadres. The government spent millions to enroll these men in officers' training schools, as long as they had the ability to learn. They would be the colonels, generals and marshals of the future. And to assure their loyalty, the government occasionally reminded them that if it had not been for the Party, then "You, Comrade General, would still be slopping hogs back on the farm!"

The former German soldiers were desperate to get into the officers' training schools. First, they reasoned, by staying in such a school as long as possible, they could postpone being sent to the battlefield; second, while they would never have become officers in the German army because of their "inferior" Slavic origins, here they could become commissioned officers. Third, they realized that this was probably the future army of Poland and that, by helping to liberate Poland, it might remain in power afterwards.

However, in their desire to get into the officers' schools, and their unfamiliarity with the thinking of Soviet officials, these German Poles made a mistake; they lied about the level of their education, declaring themselves all to be high-school graduates. In Poland, any high-school graduate was automatically assigned to an officers' training school, for there were few such men to be found. But the Soviet officers on the commission knew that in Poland, only rich men could afford to have their sons educated, and so they concluded that these German soldiers must surely be sons of capitalists, and thus were automatically disqualified; they couldn't be trusted to be officers with weapons!

However, they were ideal for the job of political officers. There, the essential thing was that they would happily speak and preach only the words which the regime put into their mouths. They would be faithful and extremely careful; one slip of the tongue and they might be shot!

However, most of these German Poles had one weakness: they did not know Russian! Some of them knew a few words which they had learned from little pocket-size dictionaries issued by the German army, but this was not enough. The command was searching for men fluent in both tongues.

As Poles who had been living in Russia, we were approached by officers seeking bilingual candidates for the political officers' school, to act as "middlemen" between the Russian and the Polish political officers.

Apparently I had the right qualifications. The captain spoke with me for a few minutes, switching from Polish to Russian, and urged me to sign up for the political officers' school. He said, "Within two weeks you'll be a captain, and within a year probably a colonel! All you have to do is to take this two-week political course."

I couldn't help but smile. "I used to think that an army was all orders. Here you are _asking_ me!"

He replied, "Of course we can order anyone to any branch of the service, but this is something special. We would like it to be on a volunteer basis, a result of deep ideological conviction."

I said, "I volunteered for the army in order to fight the Germans, not to talk politics."

"Well, don't you see that this, too, would be fighting the Germans? And why only Germans? Why not all fascists?" He then talked about the "fascist AK." "The AK doesn't fight! They just sit and wait! The only fighting being done in Poland is being done by the AL, the people's army. While our AL is blowing up bridges and trains, the fascist AK is cooperating with the Germans! Our AL accepts Jews in its ranks. The AK kills Jews, or hands them over to the Germans. Yes, it's true; the AK, on instructions from London, cooperates with the Germans in killing Jews! Now do you understand why we have to re-educate these men into hating all fascists, and not only the Germans?"

The captain was clever; he knew how to persuade me. His statement that the AK was helping the Germans kill Jews made a profound impression on me. At this time, I did not yet know about the vast tragedy that had befallen my people. I had heard rumors, unconfirmed whisperings, and because of the total silence on this subject in the Soviet press, I didn't know what to believe. I did suspect that there was trouble for the Jews under the German occupation, for I had seen it myself in Lomza, but never did I hear of — nor would I have believed — the brutal destruction of European Jewry!

The captain's words affected me. I replied, "Sir, may I think it over?" He agreed to wait overnight.

Before leaving, the captain said, "Call me 'Comrade', not 'Sir'." Who would ever have dreamed of addressing a Polish officer as "Comrade"? I thought: How ironic it would be if I were to become a political officer! We Jews have never sought converts to the faith of Abraham, Isaac, Jacob and Moses. Now I'm being asked to convert people to the faith of Marx, Engels, Lenin and Stalin!

It was easy to believe the captain's statement that the Poles were murdering Jews in cooperation with the Germans. I knew that all of them — the "rightist" AK or the "leftist" AL — would probably kill Jews most enthusiastically, since Jew-hatred was something that Poles absorbed from the cradle on.

I decided to refuse the captain's offer to make me a political officer. I had volunteered to fight the Germans, not to become a propaganda mouthpiece. But could I say no? This was an army, not a debating society. If they wanted me, they could order me! I spent a sleepless night, and I finally came up with a solution: to lie about my education. They surely would not order someone to make speeches and deliver lectures if he lacked the proper level of learning....

The next day I told the captain that I never got beyond elementary school — and it worked! The captain let me off the hook, but my low level of education classified me as a proletarian's son, eligible for combat officers' school.

A panel of three Soviet officers interviewed me. My knowledge of Russian impressed the chairman, and he pronounced me an "air cadet."

Another officer remarked, "But the card says he is a tractor man.

Wouldn't it be more natural for him to be a tank officer?"

The chairman agreed, and told me, "Well, you've just been moved from the air force to the armored division!"

Several hours later, a group of us boarded trucks, to be transported to the tank school. On the way, we watched Polish paratroopers jumping from planes. The Polish lieutenant, a former corporal, who was accompanying us, remarked, "In Poland we never had paratroopers; we never had a parachute school. You are now witnessing the first Polish parachute-jumping school!"

The trucks turned into a forest and we continued to travel. Finally, deep in the forest, we were ordered to climb off the truck. To our astonishment, all we could see were dense woods covered with deep snow; there was not a single building in sight!

We asked the lieutenant, "Where's the school? Where are the barracks? What about classrooms? Tanks?" The lieutenant only smiled. Following him, we hiked along a snow-plowed path. We began to see holes in the ground. Soon soldiers began popping out of these holes, greeting us. The lieutenant then explained that all the sleeping quarters and all the classes were in bunkers under the ground!

Apparently there weren't any bathing facilities, for we were ordered to undress and to wash ourselves with snow. The temperature was around zero. This was my first "bath" in this Polish army, and it was quite different from my first bath in the army of General Anders, under the hot sun of Guzar. While we were taking our snow bath, all our civilian clothes were burned in a big bonfire, in order to kill the lice and thus prevent the spread of disease. Then we were issued new army clothes.

Each of us was assigned to one of the underground bunkers. As I entered the hole, my eyes quickly had to adjust to the darkness. After a few moments, I became accustomed to it, and saw that I was in a small room with double bunks on all four sides, and a pot-bellied stove in the middle. There was no light except for two small windows in the ceiling, which had to be cleared of snow several times a day, to permit a little sunlight to enter. I chose the top bunk in the corner, in order to have more privacy for my daily prayers. The mattress was made of straw, as was the pillow. In my new uniform, I stretched out on my bunk, to warm up and rest my frozen body.

The fellow who occupied the bunk below me was pale and thin, all skin and bones. I wondered how he ever was accepted into the army. But as soon as he opened his mouth, I realized that this was not the first army he had served in; he had surely served the Nazis! In his German-accented Polish, he tried to engage me in friendly conversation, but I couldn't bring myself to speak to this former German soldier. I couldn't bare to look at his face, thinking that it was the face of a murderer who had probably killed many Jews.

I turned over on my bunk and faced the wall. But he was a talkative young fellow, about 20 years old, and he introduced himself as Ditlov. There was no one else in the bunker to talk to, and so he kept talking to me nonstop. I realized that sooner or later I'd be forced to associate with him, for after all, we'd be cooped up together until we graduated. Still, I couldn't help feeling repugnance towards this German; I could see blood on his hands, Jewish blood.

Finally he said, "Tell me, comrade, what have you got against me? Aren't you ever going to talk to me?"

I turned over, and looked at his pale, sharp-nosed face. "I'm a Jew and you were a German soldier! Isn't that a good enough reason not to talk to you? How many Jews did you kill?"

He sat down on his bunk without a word. After a long pause he said, "Would you believe that I never killed a Jew? In fact, I never even saw a Jew! You're the first Jew I've ever met."

I knew he must be lying. He had said that he was from Bytom, a town on the Polish-German border. In the yeshiva which I had attended, there had been a student from Bytom, so I knew that there must have been a Jewish community there. I said, "I happen to know that there was a Jewish community in Bytom."

"You are right, there *was* a Jewish community in Bytom, before I got there. When we moved in, all the Jews were gone. I really mean it; you're the first Jew I've ever seen!"

For several moments neither one of us said anything. Then I said, "Not exactly. You must have seen one Jew before — the one on the cross in your church!"

"For your information," he replied evenly, "I've never been in a church either."

This really shocked me; it left me speechless. He then went on to tell me that his father had been a leader of a Communist cell, and that the Gestapo had killed him. Afterwards, he and his mother moved to Bytom. When he reached the age of 17, his mother urged him to join the German army so he could cross into Russia. He had to lie about his name and age to be accepted. Right after basic training, he was sent to the Russian front. At the first opportunity, he crossed the line to the Russian side, and killed a German officer who tried to stop him. Once in Russian territory, he stated his real name and explained about his father, who was apparently known in Moscow. His story was verified by the *Comintern*. Now he hoped to serve the new Poland!

I was relieved of my anxieties after hearing his story; we shook hands and became friends. We talked about the fact that there were so many Polish-German soldiers. He said that some of them had been drafted into the German army, but most had volunteered. The Germans had given the Poles an opportunity to become "part Aryan." They issued a "Race Promulgation": any Pole who could prove that someone in his family had been a German, even if it was many generations back, was granted the honored status of *Volks-Deutsche* — not a full-fledged German, but a German of lesser purity, according to the amount of "pure Aryan blood" flowing through his veins. Everyone with the status of *Volks-Deutsche* was entitled to an increased monthly food ration: more bread, more meat and more sugar. Many Poles took advantage of this new ruling and dug up old family trees — some real, some fake — to prove that they had Aryan blood. Thus they resigned from being Poles, and proclaimed themselves *Volks-Deutsche*! Ditlov finished his story by angrily exclaiming, "For an extra piece of beef in their soup, those pigs switched from 'Heil Poland' to 'Heil Hitler' to 'Heil Stalin'! But then, these *Volks-Deutsche* had to pay a price for the extra food: Hitler drafted them into the German army!"

THE TANK OFFICERS' school was
still in the organizing stage. Inside these underground rooms, or as the
Russians called them, *zemlyanky* — earth caves — were blackboards,
charts, maps, tank manuals, pictures of fuel and oil systems, artillery
tables, armaments instructions and tactical books on tank warfare; everything except instructors! In the meantime we had regular army training:
marching, saluting and drills, the elements of discipline.

Soldiers traditionally detest kitchen duty, and in most armies it is
considered a punishment. However, this army was different; all the men
were hungry and undernourished, and kitchen duty was a reward! There
was always extra food around the kitchen and, to quote Napoleon, "An
army marches on its stomach."

Whenever the sergeant called for volunteers for the kitchen, all hands
went up; hardly anyone volunteered for any of the other duties. This
volunteer call was nothing but an empty ritual, for the sergeant had already
made up his list of assignments. I was overjoyed when my name finally
came up for the kitchen.

What luxury! I was surrounded by potatoes, rice, vegetables, cereals
and oil. There was also a large supply of American canned meat and hot
dogs.

The cook's main problem was finding enough firewood to fuel the two
giant kettles. The first assignment for any newcomer to the kitchen was to
chop wood. The boys were mostly city kids, who had never cut down a
tree in their lives; they didn't even know how to hold an ax properly. The
training in woodcutting which I had received in Karobka now proved
worthwhile. The cook, an old farmer, recognized my ability the moment I

raised the ax. He immediately appointed me to be in charge of the wood supply.

Because we were surrounded by forest, the boys hadn't been going far to find firewood. Indiscriminately, they had been chopping any branch or tree close to the kitchen, returning with wet, juicy wood which wouldn't burn. Even after a few days of drying, it produced a lot of smoke but no flame or heat. The cook cursed the soldiers and the wood, for he was never able to have the meals ready on time.

In the summer, it's easy to detect dry wood, but not in winter, when all is covered with snow. Every day I took my men for an expedition into the forest to collect firewood. I taught them whatever I knew of the art of woodchopping. The boys did not enjoy our forays in the deep snow, but the cook appreciated our efforts; he doubled and tripled our portions.

It was on one of these expeditions that we made a great discovery. The day was particularly cold. We were deep in the forest, searching for deadwood. The boys were cursing me for dragging them into the deep snow. Suddenly we saw a body hanging in a nearby tree, dangling from a parachute! The first thought that came to our minds was: a German! We were all unarmed except for our axes. Cautiously, we crept nearer, and then we recognized the Polish uniform. Quickly we cut the ropes and brought down the stiff and frozen soldier, who was still alive.

After regaining consciousness, the parachutist told us that he was one of many Polish men and women in training for partisan-guerilla warfare. In a special school they were taught the art of sabotage and of organizing civilian populations into resistance groups. After graduation as commissioned officers, they were dropped behind enemy lines to engage in their newly-learned trade. It was on one of these parachute-jumping exercises that he had been trapped in the tree. He couldn't release himself, and if it hadn't been for us, he would surely have frozen to death.

This Pole was a janitor's son from a small town. In 1939, when the Russians and the Germans each gobbled up parts of Poland, his town had been occupied by the Russians. The Soviets shipped out his entire family to Siberia, and there his parents had died. At the time, he was only a child and the Russians had placed him in an orphanage. He was certain that Stalin was the best friend Poland had ever had. I didn't dare ask why his family had been sent to Siberia in the first place; wasn't it Stalin who had sent the whole family away from their home? He hoped to return to Poland as an officer, and had dreams of perhaps becoming mayor of the town where his father had served as a janitor. He wanted to "teach a lesson or two to some of the people back home, those capitalists, those rotten fascists!"

The week went by, and the Sabbath was approaching. Oh, if I could only get some other duty, at least I wouldn't have to chop wood on Shabbos. I wanted solitude; I was longing for the Sabbath prayers. The best job for this would be guarding the residence of the commanding officer. According to my buddies, it was an old wooden mansion hidden deep in the forest. It must have been a retreat for some aristocrat in the days of the Czar. Now it was used as the residence and office of the commanding officer.

On Friday afternoon, when the sergeant called for volunteers to guard the residence, I raised my hand. The sergeant was surprised, and my comrades were shocked! I must have been the first one ever to volunteer for anything besides kitchen duty.

"I don't think you're ready for that post yet," the sergeant said. "You don't know how to 'present arms'." He was referring to the particular form of saluting which was supposed to create discipline and make soldiers of us. A regular salute was considered insufficient for a general or commanding officer. For them, a soldier had to perform a series of special motions with his rifle. In the last motion, the barrel was positioned exactly between his eyes, the left hand across his chest holding the barrel, and the right hand facing his navel, holding the rifle, his finger on the trigger.

The sergeant knew that I wasn't able to perform these motions perfectly. But I insisted that it was his duty to teach me and to give me time to practice. "How can I ever become an officer without being an expert on presenting arms?" I asked sarcastically.

The sergeant, however, was determined to keep me in the kitchen, for the cook had promised him that every day that I was assigned to the wood detail, he'd serve him an extra bowl of rice and meat! But I was determined too; I would do no woodchopping on the Sabbath if I could avoid it.

This sergeant spoke Polish with a Vilna accent. I often wondered whether Sergeant Kanauski was a Lithuanian Pole, or a Polish Lithuanian whose real name had been Kanauskas. Perhaps he had "Polonized" it to Kanauski in order to be accepted into the Polish army. Most likely he was a Lithuanian from Lithuania, for many Lithuanians spoke Polish. If so, he belonged in the Soviet army or in the Lithuanian division of the Red Army.

So what was he doing here? He probably wanted to get out of Russia, and he figured the best chance to do it was via the Polish army.

Although it was not my business, I made a mental note of my suspicion. Soon it turned out to be correct!

In ancient armies, officers would beat and whip undisciplined soldiers. Today, no officer is permitted to lay a hand on a soldier, so other ways of punishment were devised: peeling a thousand onions, or washing the floor with a toothbrush, or some collective punishment. By punishing the entire unit for the sin of one, the officer hoped that his peers would beat up the guilty one; there was no law against soldiers beating up each other! In extreme cases, the soldier was reported to the commanding officer and given a prison term.

In our army, where kitchen duty was a reward and there were no floors or toothbrushes, the sergeant used mostly collective punishment! Once he made us crawl on our bellies in the deep snow, with rifles in hand, for 30 minutes. This might have been good practice for infantry men, but not for us tank men. We figured he must have been a corporal in the infantry who had falsely declared himself a sergeant, since there were no documents to prove anything. And I suspected that he had been a corporal in the pre-war Lithuanian army! I heard him muttering to himself, "Rotten, cursed Poles."

For the sake of observing the Sabbath, I decided on a little blackmail. After all had left for their assignments, I approached him. "Sergeant, I'm a tractor man and I'm familiar with all the mechanical parts of a tank. I could help you a lot in the classroom. I know that you want to become a good tank officer, don't you? So how about a little cooperation?"

He barked at me, "Why is it that you don't want kitchen duty?" I couldn't answer that, for religion was unmentionable in that army. But he didn't wait for an answer.

"Then I order you to the latrine service! How is that, Jew?" he sneered.

That did it! I whispered back, in Lithuanian, "What are you doing here anyway, you Lithuanian phony?! You belong in the Soviet army, but you'd rather go to Poland than remain in the USSR, right?"

He turned white and was speechless for a moment. Then he shrieked at me in Polish, "_Bacznosc! Do roboty! Marsz!_ — Attention! To work! March!" Once at attention, one is not allowed to say a word. I grabbed the shovel and marched off to the toilets. On the way I prayed, "_Ribbono shel Olam_ — Master of the Universe — I tried my best, and even used blackmail, but nothing seems to work. Don't let me be forced to work on Shabbos!"

Then it occurred to me that this sergeant needed some time to let my blackmail sink in. He hadn't yet realized the potential danger he was in; what if I opened my mouth?

The latrines were large holes in the ground covered with two wooden boards. Once filled up, new holes were dug and the boards carried over. I almost cried when I found out that this was my job, together with two other soldiers. First we had to remove the snow, make a fire to thaw the ground, and then dig. And all this on the Sabbath!

Exactly ten minutes later, another soldier arrived to replace me. "The sergeant said you should report to him immediately," he said.

So finally it had sunk in! No one could have trained me to present arms as quickly and diligently as did that blackmailed sergeant!

After some practice, the sergeant finally gave his expert opinion: I was ready to present arms even to Stalin! He told me that normally guards were changed every four hours, but due to the extremely cold weather, the change of guards would take place every two hours. We changed posts with precise military discipline, and strictly according to regulations. After an exchange of passwords, the previous guard explained what my duties were on this particular post. Frozen and stiff, he was happy to hand over the post to me so that he could warm up in the guardhouse.

He reported to me hurriedly, "All is in order."

But the sergeant cut him short. "No, it's not! You didn't tell him about his duties to salute the commanding officer and any general by 'presenting arms'."

Suddenly I realized that I had never even seen the commanding officer; I had no idea what he looked like!

"There are always officers coming and going from that office, some in Polish uniforms, some in Russian. However, there's only one major in a Polish uniform; he limps a little, and that's the commanding officer!" said the sergeant.

It was one of those winter nights when the full moon in all its splendor reigns over the black, star-sprinkled sky. Along its path, the moon created long tree shadows in front of the lonely house. Isolated, and almost hidden by trees which reached way above its two floors, the wooden house stood silently in the forest. This was the private residence and office of the commanding officer.

According to my instructions, I had to constantly patrol on the open porches on all four sides of the house, as well as all around the house itself. If I had to stop for a rest, it had to be in the shadow, to avoid becoming a target for an intruder. I resolved to be an excellent soldier, to present arms perfectly to the commanding officer, executing all the required motions with precision. But what if I had to shoot an intruder? Would I have the nerve to kill? Would I be able to pull the trigger so easily?

There was no use denying it; I was scared! The house was totally dark. It was my first time on the post; I was alone in a deep dark forest and this seemed almost like a haunted house! I clutched my rifle tightly, even though I feared that I'd be unable to pull the trigger! The icy wind froze my face. The snow-covered trees trembled. I was afraid of the sound of my own steps, which were making the porch creak. Do steps in the snow sound the same as my steps on the snowy porch? I had to make sure, in order to tell the difference between my own steps and enemy steps in the snow. I stepped down onto the snow, rifle in hands, finger on the trigger, aiming at the whole world and nowhere!

"Please God, don't make me kill anyone!"

I kept moving all the time, marching back and forth. My rifle felt like a piece of ice even through my thick gloves.

Then I leaned against a tree and with greater-than-usual emotion I began to recite the Sabbath prayers: "Welcome the bride, the Sabbath queen." In a low voice, I sang, "Come, my friend, to meet the bride; let us welcome the presence of the Sabbath. Come, O Bride! Come, O Bride!"

I felt ridiculous. What a way to greet a bride, to welcome the peacefulness of the holy Sabbath, with a weapon in my hands!

A sudden noise disturbed my prayers, and I clutched my rifle tightly. The sergeant had cautioned me about wild animals which roamed the forest, and about tree branches which occasionally fell to the ground, making a sudden noise. I'd have to check on every sound, for it might be an intruder. I walked around the house very cautiously, holding my finger on the trigger, but there was no one there. I resumed my prayers.

I had just finished when the sound of a jeep cut through the cold air. At once, I took up a hidden position so I wouldn't be seen by a possible enemy. The jeep stopped in front of the house, and a Polish officer stepped out. Because of the distance, I couldn't see the officer's rank. Was he a major? Was he the commanding officer? In any case, regulations required that I must check him out. I shouted first in Polish and then in Russian,

"Stop! Who goes there?"

He stopped and said, "I am the commanding officer." He gave the password, "Volga," and I replied "Wisla," thus permitting him to continue walking.

I was determined to prove that all the training the sergeant had given me had not been in vain. I presented arms, executing perfectly all the motions required. The commanding officer passed by me, replying with a salute. He walked up the few steps and unlocked the door. Suddenly he turned around and said, "Guard, what is your name?"

I was just beginning to catch my breath, from the strain of standing at attention before the commanding officer. I turned around, still at attention, and faced him. He was on the porch in the shadow, while I was in full moonlight.

Before I had a chance to reply, he suddenly rushed down the steps, shouting, "Chaim, is that you? Chaim, my friend, my dear one, what are you doing here?"

Forgetting my duty as a guard, I cried, "Misha! What are *you* doing here?!" We embraced with great emotion, amazed at this miraculous meeting. Misha Krulev, the wounded tank officer, who had served temporarily as a police officer in Kazakhstan, was now in a Polish uniform, with a Polonized name, Krulevski!

The rifle in my hand brought me back to reality, reminding me of my duties. "I'm on duty and this is against regulations," I said, smiling.

"Regulations, my foot! I'm the commanding officer here and I can remove you from your post at any time! Come on, you're removed! Let's go inside; we have much to talk about. That's an order!"

He opened the door; the warmer air of the house hit our frozen faces. He lit the kerosene lamp, and we looked at each other once more. He said, "How do you think I'd feel with you standing out there freezing? From now on, all guards will stay inside the hall next to the porch."

He prepared some tea and we talked and talked. Finally I reminded him that the changing of guards would be taking place soon, and it would look awkward for the guard to be found inside, drinking tea with the commanding officer! "I don't want any special treatment. It's better that no one in my company should know about our friendship." He agreed, and I went outside to resume my post.

Soon the sergeant and my replacement arrived. While we were in the process of changing the post, Misha appeared on the porch. The sergeant called "_Baćznosc_ — Attention!" and dutifully reported that the changing of guards was being performed. Misha then informed the sergeant that from now on the sentry would stay in the hall, and only occasionally go outside and circle the house.

At the guard house, when the men heard about the new order, they all praised the commanding officer for his humane attitude towards the men. I didn't take part in their conversation, for I was still in shock; I sat in a corner, meditating upon this strange coincidence. There were thousands of tank officers, yet Misha had been chosen to command this Polish army tank officers' school. True, he was a mechanical engineer, an experienced tankman, a battle-wounded officer; and he also had some years of law school, all of which made him a logical choice to head the tank officers' school.

It also seemed logical that I, being a tractor man, should be assigned to this school. Still, there was enough room left to call it a miracle! For me, this was not a coincidence; there could have been a million other coincidences which would have sent Misha Krulev and me our separate ways. It was God's hand that had brought us together.

34

AFTER MANY DELAYS, classes finally began. At first, we learned only from charts, plans and pictures, and didn't see a real tank. To most of the men in the class, the charts of engines, and fuel and oil lines seemed almost incomprehensible. A few of us who had the advantage of having been tractor men were able to follow the lectures with ease. A few days later, a huge V-shaped 12-cylinder engine was installed in our underground classroom. It made a tremendous impression. When the instructor said that this engine had 550 horsepower, one of the boys exclaimed, "My father worked in the biggest flour mill in Poland, and the motor was only 200 horsepower!"

Those who had never driven anything in their lives, who were completely ignorant about mechanical power, found it very hard to learn from charts, without seeing and feeling a real tank. The instructors were disappointed in the progress being made. The former tractor men were given the task of helping the others to comprehend the complicated systems. In the yeshiva, we used to have a system called "third classes," that is, additional hours of study, late into the night, designed for slow but willing students. I proposed this to my buddies. They accepted the idea enthusiastically, but it was turned down by the political officer; evening hours were scheduled for political lectures, or reading.

One day, the clamor of approaching tanks rang through the forest and we rushed out to welcome them. Two shiny new tanks had arrived! We patted the ice-cold steel, impatient to climb inside.

Now we had tanks, and we had instructors, but there were still complaints. In the unheated underground bunkers we had to sit in our heavy winter coats. This made the men sleepy, which in turn made the instructors furious.

"Would you prefer the infantry?" they'd yell. "Would you rather chase after the tank like a dog, begging for a ride, or be riding inside, protected by its armor?" Slowly they evoked in us the pride of being tank men, "professionals," not just "simple infantry men."

Then a new order arrived: we were to pack up and move to Ryazan, a city 100 miles east of Moscow.

In Ryazan we all attended a huge military school for officer candidates, the Moscow Military College. Aside from training tank officers for the Polish army, the school's main function was to train infantry and artillery officers for the Red Army. Our Polish building was very close to the Russian building, yet we had no contact at all with the Soviet officer candidates.

The school was impressive. The dormitory was sunny and roomy, the walls and classrooms painted in clean light colors. To us, who had been living in miserable underground caves in an icy forest, this was like living in a palace!

Strict and total silence was the rule in the dining hall. We were at the mercy of the officer as to the time allowed for eating. If he was in a good mood, he allowed us 30 minutes, but more often, we had only 15 minutes for dinner. We marched into the dining hall and stood at attention in front of the tables, until the order was given to sit down. Then the race to consume our food began, for we never knew exactly when the officer would order us to stand up and march out.

During our first three days there, still hungry from the years of deprivation and near-starvation, we stuffed some of the extra food that we couldn't finish into our pockets. When there was meat on our plates, I saved it and later traded it with Ditlov for his bread. On the fourth day, after supper, we were marched into a room which contained a long table. We were ordered to line up along both sides of the table and to empty our pockets and place everything on the table. We were all embarrassed; out of our pockets came bread, cooked potatoes, even salt shakers! I was the only one who pulled out two American hot dogs!

We stood there in terrible silence, feeling humiliated and foolish. Then the captain spoke. "I am Captain Tamarov, your political officer. An army without discipline is like a herd of cattle. Discipline is meant not only for the benefit of the officers and the generals; on the contrary, Stalin teaches us that discipline in an army is mainly for the benefit of the soldier! You are future officers. If we cannot impress discipline upon you, how will you ever enforce discipline with the men you will be entrusted to lead? Look at yourselves! You, the future officers, are loading your pockets with food!"

He then looked over the food in front of each man, while we stood with our heads lowered in shame. His eyes fell on the two hot dogs on the table in front of me. "You!" he shouted. "What's the matter, don't you like the hot dogs?" I was petrified, and remained silent.

"Why are you standing there like an idiot? I'm asking you a question: why didn't you eat the hot dogs at the table?" he screamed and he moved closer to me.

Very apologetically, I explained that we were not given enough time to eat and were often hungry during classes. Then I found the courage to add, "This has a negative effect on our studies, for one cannot listen to lectures very well on an empty stomach."

He screamed at me, "And who appointed you to speak for the entire class? You can speak only for yourself!" Then he added, in a calmer tone, "But I like the spirit you've shown. It is good army spirit: all for one and one for all."

This was my first encounter with the *politruk* Tamarov. It was easy to detect by his facial characteristics that he was not a Russian, but a Mordvinian. I had been friendly with some Mordvinians in Karobka, and knew a few words in their language.

The next day, between classes, Tamarov approached me and asked, "Cadet, how is it that you are a Pole and also a *Chi Sammarra*?" He was referring to my Russian accent, an accent spoken only in the Kuybishev District. And of course, being a Mordvinian, he had recognized it immediately. I explained to him that I had learned Russian in the Kuybishev area, adding, "near Mordva." I'd even learned some Mordvinian words, I told him.

Tamarov gave me a sharp look, and his square brown face grew taut. He snapped, "I have never been in Mordva. I am a Russian. I speak only Russian. Is that clear?!"

"Yes, Comrade Captain!" I replied meekly.

Then he asked me, "Why don't you Poles know any marching songs?" As a political officer, one of his duties was to see to it that we sang inspiring marching songs. The Russians had beautiful ones, written for them by the best songwriters in Moscow. We Poles, however, since most of us were children before the war, did not know the Polish army songs, and the few that we did know were dull and slow, and contained a good deal about horses.

"Here we're supposed to be proud tank men; should we be singing about horses?" I asked.

Eventually, we Polish cadets began singing Russian songs, but we altered them slightly, replacing the Russian names with Polish. For example, in the "Tank Men's Song," we changed Marshal Voroshilov to General Berling, commander-in-chief of our Polish army! However, there was one Russian name we never dropped; we wouldn't dare replace the name of Stalin! We loved the "Tank Men's Song," which we sang on many long marches, spurred on by its invigorating tune:

> The armor is strong, and our tanks are fast.
> Our men are full of bravery!
> Standing in formation are Polish tank men.
> The Fatherland's faithful sons!

> Thundering with fire and in the sparkling glare of steel,
> Our tanks will embark upon a fierce march!
> When to battle Marshal Stalin will send us,
> And into battle General Berling will lead us!

Since tank men are actually artillery men on wheels, we loved the artillery song, easily translated into Polish:

> Artillery men! Stalin gave the order!
> Artillery men! The Fatherland is calling upon us!
> From a hundred thousand batteries,
> For the tears of our mothers!
> For our Fatherland!
> Fire upon the enemy!

As the days went on, we learned more and more about the mechanical aspects of a tank, as well as its armaments. We learned how to operate, disassemble and reassemble the machine guns and the cannon. We studied the maintenance of all moving parts, the engine, electrical system, radio, and of course the tactical operations of tank units in attack and in retreat.

At the same time, the political officer continued his lectures. His main themes were the unity of the Slavic nations in their stand against Nazi Germany, and General Stalin's great friendship with Poland.

The political officer was given an assistant, a former German soldier named Kruszynski, fresh out of the school for political officers. Naturally, he was eager to serve the "New Democratic Poland." I could imagine how well he had served the Germans, and how loudly he must have screamed "Heil Hitler!" by his obsequious manner and by the enthusiastic way he shouted "Long live Stalin!"

In Moscow, the Polish army published a bi-weekly paper called *Wolnosc*. For weeks, Captain Tamarov and his assistant had been asking everyone to write something for the paper, but no one responded. Most of the cadets could barely read and write, and besides, there was no time. I had never written anything, and my Polish vocabulary had dwindled. A language unused for a number of years becomes anemic and impoverished. Above all, I knew that Tamarov wanted "missionary" articles extolling the "new democracy" which we would bring to Poland. Both political officers persisted in asking, not ordering, us to write something for the paper.

One day Captain Tamarov approached me and said, "Colonel Krulevski told me that you can write; you must write something for *Wolnosc!*" This was how I learned that Misha Krulev had been promoted to the rank of colonel. I figured that if Misha had said that, he must have a good reason for asking me to write. I assured Captain Tamarov that I'd try my best.

I decided to call my article "Lessons in History." Writing an article in the Soviet Union was like walking on a tightrope. To come through unmolested by the political or security watchmen is the primary consideration. I didn't mind if the article would never be published, as long as the reason for its refusal would not place me in a dangerous spot. I didn't mind if the editor deleted everything I wrote; I didn't even mind if he put words that I hadn't said into my mouth; the important thing was to stay safe! Of course, it would be gratifying if some of my points were to come through, even if only partially.

Therefore, in the interest of self-preservation, I employed the standard trick of Russian writers; I quoted Lenin and Stalin liberally. No editor would dare to delete Stalin's words! By quoting these two, an overall favorable impression of one's article would be created, and yet some real thoughts could be smuggled in between the lines.

After much thought, I began writing: "In our school days, many of us considered history a dull subject. Yet, next to a thorough knowledge of the armaments entrusted to our hands, history is the most vital subject for us, the new soldiers of Poland! Stalin once said, 'History is a map!' In other words, just as an officer cannot lead his men without reference to a map, a nation cannot be led without reference to its history. Without a past, there cannot be a future! And today we, the men and officers of the Polish army, are writing the history of Poland. To quote Lenin, 'History is not written with pen and ink, by professors or historians, but by soldiers with their bayonets and blood!'

"Let us remember what Queen Jadwiga said in 1386, when she was being pressured to marry the Teutonic king, which would have meant that a German would be the king of Poland: 'A Pole and a German can never live in peace!' Instead she married the king of Lithuania, thus creating the Polish-Lithuanian Union.

"The leaders of pre-war Poland ignored Queen Jadwiga's warning about the Germans. They chose the grasping hand of Nazi Germany, rather than the helping hand of our Slavic brothers under the leadership of Marshal Stalin!"

The article continued: "What is a flag? Merely a piece of cloth. Yet, people are willing to die for it! As Lenin said, 'The Red flag of the Soviet Union is the symbol of the blood shed by the proletarians of the world.' For centuries Poles have been sacrificing their lives for their red and white national flag.

"And what is a national emblem? What does it represent? What does it tell us? To a Red Army man, the Soviet Red Star tells him of new and revolutionary ideas which emerged from bloodshed.

"In our days, what does the White Eagle emblem say to a Polish soldier? It says the same words of inspiration to us as it did to Stefan Czarniecki of old. When he was leading the Polish warriors against the occupying Swedes and Lithuanians, battling the enemy near Tykocin (Tiktin) on the Narew River, he suddenly came face to face with a white eagle, a rarity in that place. This strange bird spoke to Czarniecki's heart without uttering a word. It said, 'Go on to victory!' Do we soldiers of Poland need a better command than 'March on to victory'?

"And what is represented by a salute? After having been drilled for hours in the regulations and mechanics of a salute, it may seem silly to ask what a salute represents. But the question is not: what is the purpose of a salute? The question is: what does a salute mean? What is the deeper meaning behind it? And the answer is: it is an indication of a readiness to serve, a readiness to die for our cause! To the Red Army men, it means readiness to serve the Soviet Union, and readiness to obey and fulfill the orders of its great leader Marshal Stalin; to the American, it means service to the United States and its president; to the English, service to the king and the empire; to the French, their republic; and to the accursed Germans, it's 'Heil Hitler': to enslave, rob, and kill the conquered peoples.

"And what does our own Polish salute mean to us?" I went on to describe the differences between the two-fingered Polish salute and the various full-handed salutes of other nations. "In the days of General Dombrowski, when the Poles rose up against the hated Czars, it meant 'Faith and the Fatherland!' Later it came to mean 'Freedom and the Fatherland!' In our days, when the independence of Poland is assured by Marshal Stalin, our salute stands for 'Honor and the Fatherland!' For we are here to save the honor of Poland, fighting side by side with the victorious Red Army, under its glorious commander-in-chief, Marshal Stalin!"

When I finished writing the article, I handed it to Captain Tamarov. He asked me to translate it into Russian for him. After listening to it word for word, he patted me on the back. Several days later, a note arrived written on the stationery of the Union of Polish Patriots, thanking me for the article and asking for more; it was signed with a scrawled "W.W."! I was sure that this letter had been written by Wanda Wasilewska herself!

However, there was somebody who didn't like what I had written. One day Captain Tamarov sent for me; when I arrived I found that Lieutenant Kruszynski was there in his office as well. The captain asked me a strange question: "Do you consider it to be anti-Polish to salute with your full hand?"

It was quite clear to me at once that the former German soldier had opened Captain Tamarov's eyes to what he had understood "between the lines" of my article.

"Are you a Polish super-nationalist?" Captain Tamarov threw one question after another at me without waiting for answers.

When I tried to explain the meaning of my article, Lieutenant Kruszynski interrupted and accused me of chauvinism. (In Soviet vocabulary, "chauvinism" and "nationalism" were evil words; "internationalism" was a good word and, of course, "Russian nationalism" was even better!)

452

Although I was scared, I couldn't help being amused by the irony of the situation. Here I was, a Pole, being accused by another Pole of Polish chauvinism! And the funniest part of it was that I had to serve as a translator between my two accusers, for the lieutenant's Russian vocabulary was limited; I had to help him out with a word here and there, speaking against myself!

In the end, I was saved by the fact that I had quoted Lenin and Stalin, and that, moreover, Captain Tamarov himself had approved the article. I also showed them my note of thanks from the Union of Polish Patriots.

Nevertheless, Captain Tamarov "advised" me never again to write on political subjects. "Limit your writing to technical problems of the tank," he said. I never wrote again; my reputation had been damaged enough.

The officer of the day was Lieutenant Czarny, a former Polish army corporal who had earned his commission in the Kosciuszko Brigade. He sent for me and, when I reported to him in his office, he looked me over from head to toe. He then walked over to the rifle stand. After picking out the shiniest rifle, he turned around and tossed it to me. "Check for bullets," he ordered.

I reported that it was empty, and he said, "Good. No one, except you and me, should know that the rifle is empty. I'm sending you on a diplomatic mission!"

I thought: a diplomatic mission? Where to? London? Moscow? And with an empty rifle? It didn't make sense. Then he explained: today was graduation day for the Russian school. The cadets were becoming commissioned officers in the Red artillery and infantry. To celebrate the occasion, a party was going to be held in the evening; Polish officers were also invited.

Lieutenant Czarny explained that there might be some trouble; for the first time, whiskey would be served and the thirst for whiskey and entertainment was so great that some non-commissioned officers would undoubtedly try to get in. It would be my duty to stop them from entering. "No one below the rank of lieutenant is to cross the threshold!" he told me emphatically, and added, "This includes you too, for you are not an officer yet. So stay in the hall, and under no circumstances should you set foot inside. Is that clear?"

He told me that there would be a Soviet sentry on guard as well, who would also be "armed" with an empty rifle and with the same instructions. I was to cooperate with him fully. "This is more a diplomatic mission than regular guard duty," Lieutenant Czarny stressed. "There will be a lot of top Russian brass there; they'll be watching you perform your duty! Remember, you will be representing not only our school, but all of Poland! I'm trusting you to use the utmost tact and caution. You were chosen for this delicate job by the commanding officer himself, Colonel Krulevski.

"You might hear some jokes, wisecracks about Poland or about our army. Play deaf! Play dumb! Don't get into any discussions. Be polite, friendly, diplomatic. You'll be watched and judged, and with you the entire Polish army." He ended his instructions to me in a tone that would have been appropriate to my being appointed ambassador of Poland, at least!

I went to the huge building where the party was to take place. The front entrance was permanently off-limits to everyone except officers; all others were required to use the back door when entering or leaving. However, Lieutenant Czarny had told me to enter by the main entrance, since I was assigned to a post inside. As I opened the door, I noticed two large busts in the hall: one of Lenin and the other of Stalin. Directly in front of them, Russian soldiers were standing at attention. As I approached them, they dropped and crossed their bayonets, barring me from going any further. "*Tee kuda* — You, where to?" one of them asked. After I informed him of my assignment, he picked up a telephone, and in a moment a Russian officer appeared. He told me to follow him; he would take me to my post.

The entire corridor was covered with a deep red carpet. The walls were decorated with large paintings, and long, heavy draperies covered the windows. I had not imagined that in the land of the proletariat, in this "Red Army of Laborers and Peasants," so much luxury was enjoyed by the military! When I arrived at my post, my counterpart, the Russian sentry, was already there. We took up positions on both sides of the wide doorway that led to a large, elegant ballroom.

Inside, there was already a large number of new lieutenants. They were happy and gay and full of life, and obviously proud of the brand new stars on their shoulders. A band was playing both classical and popular music. There were some elderly officers as well, the "big brass." Most of them sported tomcat whiskers or well-tended handlebar moustaches.

The Russian guard and I had a lot to do. First, the saluting: a Russian or a Polish soldier never salutes if he is holding a rifle; he merely snaps his boots together and stands at attention with the rifle butt resting on the floor, until the officer has passed by. With so many officers coming and going, passing by directly in front of us, we were constantly snapping our feet and standing at attention. Then there were the constant arguments with the non-commissioned officers who tried to get in. Thirsty for a drink and eager for companionship, they tried all kinds of tricks and excuses to enter the ballroom. The Russian guard and I kept repeating, "Sorry, comrade, come back when you have a star on your shoulders."

Once, while we were busy turning away several aggressive sergeants, we failed to salute a Russian colonel who was passing by. He pointed to his epaulets which were covered with stars, and barked at us, "Where do you think these stars came from? Did a rooster drop them from the barn roof? Why didn't you salute?!" Of course, we weren't allowed to answer; we stood stiff as statues, staring straight ahead, while he abused us.

Next, I saw Captain Tamarov and his wife approaching. I gave him an especially enthusiastic salute; after all, he wasn't just any officer, he was my very own *politruk*! He stopped in front of me and asked, "Well, are you enjoying the party?"

I snapped once more to attention. By regulations I was not supposed to "report" to him; he was not the commanding officer, nor officer of the day, nor the commandant of the guard. Nevertheless, I did him the honor and gave him a full report of my duties, and how I was carrying them out. Then I added, "The party is lovely."

During my recitation, he had been standing at attention in front of me in a stiff, military posture. Now he winked at me and said in a very military manner, "Carry on, cadet. Do your duty!"

The hall was very crowded. The air was hot and the guests were perspiring, but they all seemed to be enjoying themselves. They danced old Russian tangos, and the band played sentimental tunes. Suddenly something went wrong. I saw Captain Tamarov bend over, looking for something on the floor. However, the crush of the dancing crowd made it impossible for him to find it. Red-faced and perspiring, Captain Tamarov retreated and stopped only a few feet away from me; his wife followed him, limping.

Suddenly I heard him speaking to me, and I turned to face him. He ordered me to go into the ballroom and find the heel that had broken off his wife's shoe. I was stunned, for there was hardly any worse sin in the army manual than for a guard to leave his post. And perhaps the second-worst offense was for any officer, no matter what his rank, to order a guard to leave his post.

As much as I would have liked to help the captain, I had to reply, "I'm sorry, Comrade Captain, but I'm on guard duty and am not allowed to leave my post."

"But I'm ordering you to leave it!" he shouted, thus calling the attention of everyone in the corridor to us. I realized that he wanted to show his wife, as well as the crowd gathering around us, that he was in a position of authority.

I tried to give him a face-saving excuse, and I said, loudly enough so that I could be heard over the sound of the music: "I have been given strict orders not to enter the ballroom."

I had underestimated the determination and stubborn pride of that Mordvinian, for instead of backing down and saving face, he began to scream at me. "But I have just changed your orders! Go into the ballroom; go at once!" He must have had too much whiskey, I realized, for surely he knew that the only person who could change a guard's orders is the officer who appointed him, or the commandant.

Nevertheless, I concluded that, for the sake of diplomacy and peace, I would overlook the regulations and follow his order. The situation was further complicated because he had shouted so loudly, and now everyone's eyes were upon us. In fact, my dilemma became a subject of conversation, and I heard a Russian officer saying, "Doesn't that idiot Polack know that he must obey an order given by any Soviet officer?"

The book of regulations was on my side, but diplomacy, and the requirement to obey the order of a Soviet captain, were on the other side. I was about to leave my post, thereby risking who-knew-what punishment, when suddenly I heard a deep voice call out, "Colonel Krulev! How good to see you. Or should I say Colonel Krulevski?"

I whirled around and there he was, approaching us — the commanding officer, my old friend Misha, with his wife! At once I prepared to present arms, the proper salute for a commanding officer. But the man with the deep voice, a Russian artillery colonel, continued talking to him, apparently explaining what was going on here.

Misha stepped right up to Captain Tamarov and me. As I began to present arms, he snapped, "What seems to be the trouble?" I was in a dilemma again: should I tell him that Captain Tamarov, his political officer, had ordered me to violate orders!? I finished presenting arms, Colonel Krulevski replied with a salute, and repeated his question once more: "What's the trouble here?"

How I wished he would ask Captain Tamarov the question, instead of me! Let him do the answering! But the query was addressed to me and it required a reply.

Many Russian officers were standing around us, curious about the outcome. I explained my duties and my orders; and to give Captain Tamarov a way out, I said, "Captain Tamarov didn't realize that I'm on duty; he must have thought that I was merely a doorman, and therefore he asked me to enter the ballroom to look for something."

"And you didn't go, because that would have been abandoning your post; is that correct?" said the commanding officer loudly. I detected pride in his voice. He glanced at the surrounding Russian officers.

"Yes, Comrade Colonel," I replied.

"Good for you, cadet!" he exclaimed. "That's the way to serve! Strictly by the book!"

Then he turned to Captain Tamarov and said, "And you, Captain — you thought he was a doorman, eh? Have you ever seen a doorman armed with a rifle? I suggest you read your army manual; you'll learn that not even Marshal Zhukov can order a guard to leave his post!"

Misha was violating a military rule himself, albeit an unwritten one: never criticize another officer in the presence of an enlisted man.

I realized that Captain Tamarov had been utterly humiliated and would not forget this reprimand in the presence of his fellow officers; I was sure he would seek vengeance somehow. But there was nothing I could do.

Then Misha said to me loudly, "Carry on the good work, cadet, and tell your immediate officer that I, Colonel Krulevski, want him to reward you with a day off from your duties!"

Misha took his wife into the hall, without any further attention to Captain Tamarov. Ignoring him completely added insult to injury, and a furious and red-faced Captain Tamarov hurried out of the building with his wife. I didn't see him again until a week later.

THE NEXT MORNING, I was praised in front of the entire class for sticking to my post, and serving strictly according to the manual, and was given a day off. This did not mean a pass to the city, for we Polish cadets were not allowed to socialize with Russian civilians; a day off meant staying in our quarters.

For a long time I had been thinking about writing a letter to my cousin in Jerusalem. She was the only relative to whom I could write, for all the rest of my family were in German-occupied areas. I had been suppressing my growing desire to write to her in Palestine because I dreaded the thought of inviting trouble.

I knew how suspicious the Soviets were of correspondence with any foreign land. When I had met my cousin Zalman in the Urals, he had given me the address of his sister in Melbourne, Australia; he told me that he didn't dare write to her, though, because to do so might cost him his job, or worse! Being a disabled war hero wouldn't save him from the consequences.

But now, as the day of graduation approached, I knew that I'd soon be a tank officer and be sent to the battlefield; and who knew what would happen to me there? I felt an irresistible need to notify someone — anyone — in my family that I was alive and in the army. And if I failed to return, God forbid, at least they could notify my parents about me, and tell them that I had died fighting against the Germans!

Before writing the letter, I thought about how I should mail it. Through military mail? This was out of the question; it would have to be by civilian mail. But where could I find a civilian who would be willing to mail a letter for me, and to a foreign country yet?!

Suddenly I thought of something: the public bathhouse! It was strange that a military school would not have its own bathhouse; perhaps it did, for the exclusive use of the Russian cadets, and we Poles were not allowed to mix with them even there. At any rate, every Friday the bathhouse of the city of Ryazan was closed to the Russian civilians so that the Polish cadets could use it.

But there were always Russian children hanging around the fence. First they came out of curiosity, to see the strange soldiers in strange uniforms. Then the children began to beg for soap. Since every soldier received a tiny piece of soap, we would give the leftover scraps to the children. I decided to ask one of the children to mail the letter for me, for the price of a whole piece of soap!

The next problem I faced was: in what language should I write? Soviet censorship was imposed on all correspondence, and to speed up the work of the censors, each letter had to be marked outside with the language in which it was written. I couldn't write in Russian, for my cousins in Jerusalem and Melbourne wouldn't be able to read it. I couldn't write in Polish, for that might be a clue that the sender was a Polish cadet, and they could easily trace it to me.

So I decided to write in Yiddish. I figured that in a city like Ryazan there had to be some Jews who could censor my letter. My gamble was that the letter would either reach its destination, or it would end up in the censor's waste basket because I had "forgotten" to write the return address. In either case I'd be out of danger.

Because I wanted to inform my cousin in Melbourne that her brother Zalman was alive and living in the Ural, I decided to write to her first. The next Friday, as soon as we entered the bathhouse and I got my piece of soap, I sneaked out to the fence. A little girl was standing well away from the other noisy children. I began a conversation with her, and asked her in a friendly way if she was a member of _Comsomol_. Fortunately she wasn't. Then I asked her to get me a ruble's worth of postage stamps. I gave her the money, and within minutes she returned with the stamps. Not knowing the amount of postage required for mailing a letter to Australia, I put all the stamps on the envelope. I promised her a whole piece of soap if she'd mail the letter for me. She was happy to comply, and went off to mail it, the soap tucked away in her pocket.

A couple of days later, a security officer lectured our class on the duty of an officer to keep an eye on the men under his command, and to make sure of their loyalty and trustworthiness. He said: "One thing you should watch closely is the mail. If a man receives a letter, and the sender's name is not the same as that of the receiver's, and the address of the sender is not the same as that of the immediate family of that soldier, you may assume that this return address is fictitious and the letter's content should be considered definitely suspicious."

The lecturer then continued, "And if there is no return address at all, the letter must be checked immediately! Although it is possible perhaps for a person to forget to write his name and return address, it is far more likely that they were left off deliberately! The letter might be telling your soldier to desert, to spy, to sabotage!" Then he said something that shattered me: "Even the civilian censors have instructions to destroy all letters which fail to show a return address!" I realized that I hadn't been so clever after all; mailing a letter without my name and address might not incriminate me, but it would never reach Australia!

So I decided to write another letter, this time to my cousin in Jerusalem. I wrote in Yiddish again; Hebrew was a forbidden language in the Soviet Union. I would take a risk by writing my name and military address on the envelope, but I would also fill my letter with praise of Stalin and the glorious Red Army. I was sure that my cousin would understand that I had put this in for my own safety.

I began my letter: "Dear cousin, I have the honor of serving under the Supreme Command of the greatest military genius of mankind, Marshal Stalin! I will soon become a tank officer in the Polish army of General Berling, and I will be privileged to fight the German beast, side by side with the glorious Red Army! Together with the heroic Red Army, I will liberate our home town and our family!" I was certain a letter like this would clear through the censors' check without creating any problems.

The same little girl mailed the letter for me. For the next few days I was worried, but when a week had passed and nothing had happened, I breathed more easily, thanking God that soon one of my cousins would know that I still existed. But how mistaken I was! It took them ten days, but they caught up with me!

All over the USSR, the greatest fear is of the nocturnal knock on the door. The NKVD, the dreaded secret police, usually apprehends its victims during the night. And so, when a Russian guard, armed with a rifle and bayonet, awakened me in the middle of the night, I knew the reason at once. The guard ordered me to get dressed in a hurry and to follow him.

When I asked him where he was taking me, he said, "To the commanding officer's office."

As we marched down the long corridors, I thought that perhaps they had even traced my first letter, to Australia, which meant that I would have gotten my poor cousin Zalman into terrible trouble. I had told his sister that he was alive and where he was. What a mess! Oh, Lord Almighty, help me; please help me now!

Inside the commanding officer's office, a major, wearing the blue uniform of the Soviet Counter Intelligence, was sitting at the desk. At his right sat Misha and at his left Captain Tamarov. With knees shaking, I reported to the commanding officer in the proper military manner; Colonel Krulevski ordered me to sit down.

The blue-uniformed major began. Waving a letter before my face, he barked, "Is this your letter?" I recognized it as the letter to Jerusalem.

"Yes, Comrade Major," I replied.

"Why did you send it by regular mail instead of army mail?"

"Because I thought that for a letter to a foreign country one needs stamps. So I mailed it by ordinary mail."

"How did you get stamps? And how did you get to a civilian mailbox?"

I told him the truth: that I had asked a child to mail it for me when we were at the bathhouse. I emphasized that I didn't think I was doing anything wrong by mailing it through ordinary civilian mail. "The fact is," I said, "I put my full name and military address on the envelope." I could see that Misha looked relieved.

The major pulled out some papers from his briefcase and handed one to Misha and to Captain Tamarov to read. Then the major glowered at me, and said, "Who are the people you were writing to?"

I replied truthfully; I told him that my parents were under the German occupation, and I couldn't write to them; that since graduation was near, I'd soon be going to the front to join in the great battle against the Germans, and therefore I wanted to let someone in my family know that I was still alive.

"Have you ever been in Palestine?" he snapped.

"No, Comrade Major."

"Are you a Zionist?"

"No, Comrade Major."

Apparently the major wasn't sure whether the other two officers knew what a Zionist was, so he explained to them. "Zionism is a chauvinistic movement among the Jews. Lenin and Stalin condemned Zionism; it was invented by the Jewish reactionaries, by the Jewish bourgeoisie, to misguide the Jewish workers into following some nationalistic dream. Zionism diverts the attention of the Jewish labor class from the international struggle of the proletariat. Recently Zionism has become an agent for the British imperialists, and it serves American espionage."

Then he turned back to me. "Are your relatives Zionists?"

"I don't know."

"They must be," he insisted. "Why else would they emigrate to Palestine?"

I replied, "I have only one cousin there. She was born and raised in Poland. She met a boy in Poland who was visiting from Palestine, and she married him. I suppose this was the reason that she went to live there."

"Do you suppose she has any contact with the fascist Polish army of General Anders?"

This question nearly floored me: I was astonished at how far their suspicions went. I hoped he didn't know that I had once gone to Guzar and had tried to join that army myself! I replied, "She is Jewish and so is her husband, and the Polish fascists don't like Jews. And I'm sure she wouldn't like them, either."

"Could she or her husband be serving the British in any capacity?"

"I wouldn't know."

Then he asked, "How many languages do you know?"

"Five."

"Is Hebrew one of them?"

"Yes."

"They speak Hebrew in Palestine, and English as well. Why didn't you write in either of these languages?"

"Because I don't know English, and I thought there wouldn't be a Hebrew censor in Ryazan; so I wrote in Yiddish, the language I always spoke with my cousin."

"If you are not a Zionist, why did you learn Hebrew?"

"I began to learn Hebrew when I was five years old!"

"Cadet, do you believe in God?" This question made me stiffen; I felt trapped. I stole a quick glance at Misha, hoping that he would help me out; but he remained silent. I had to answer this question.

"Comrade Major," I began, "when I was a child, almost every mother nurtured her children with religion. Some children got it by the teaspoon, some by the tablespoon; I got it by the bucket."

The next question proved that they had been investigating me. The major barked, "Why don't you eat meat?"

I answered, "Meat does not agree with me. My father was a vegetarian, and we never ate meat at home."

"So you are trying to be a vegetarian too?" he asked, and a faint smile appeared on his face. I was relieved to see him smile. I didn't reply, hoping he'd stop questioning me about religion.

At this point Misha interrupted and said, "Comrade Major, I have carefully read the Russian translation of this soldier's letter. In my opinion, there is absolutely nothing subversive about it. On the contrary; it reflects very well on the Soviet Union. Let me quote a few lines."

He picked up the paper that the major had handed to him, and read from it: "While England and America are stalling the opening of the second front, making up all kinds of excuses for failing to invade the continent, the Red Army, under the command of Marshal Stalin, is crushing the enemy. I shall be happy when the opportunity will be given to me to fight side by side with these heroic peoples of the Soviet Union. We shall liberate Poland soon; just think of it: I shall arrive home as an officer in a tank!"

Misha put the paper down and asked the major, "What is wrong with wanting to write to a relative? When this soldier lived in Poland, he wrote. Now he is here, and so he writes from here; so what?"

Captain Tamarov, who had been silent all the time, interjected, "Maybe that's why the Poles lost the war in three days — because of poor security!"

The colonel and the major both ignored Tamarov's remark. I was hoping that the grilling was over, but the major hadn't finished yet.

"Do you have any relatives in any other countries?"

This question stunned me! Could this mean that he also had my first letter, the one to Australia? Was he just waiting for me to say "no," so he could prove me a liar?

Although my mind was racing, I spoke slowly, watching to see if he'd pull my Australian letter out of his briefcase. "One of the dreadful things about capitalist countries is unemployment, something which doesn't exist in the Soviet Union. Poland was a capitalistic country and there was a lot of unemployment. Many young people left Poland; they went everywhere: to the USSR, to America, even as far as Australia."

At this point, Misha interrupted and said, "I fail to see any significance in all this. The hour is late. The only thing this soldier did wrong was that he didn't send the letter by regular army mail. I hope that he has acknowledged his mistake and that from now on he'll know better. I propose that the case be closed."

Apparently impressed by the commanding officer's opinion, the major began to pack up all his papers. He said to Misha, "I just hope your soldier won't write any more letters to foreign countries."

I was dismissed! I knew that I owed my freedom to Misha; I also knew that my record was damaged as far as political reliability was concerned.

General Pulturzycki was an elderly little man, in charge of training the Polish army. He always dressed in an elegant Polish uniform, but he spoke only Russian. When he occasionally said a few words in Polish, it was with a thick Russian accent. It was quite obvious to us all that he was a Russian general who, because of his Polish name, had been transferred to the Polish army. It seemed to me, however, that his face looked Jewish.

He was a strict disciplinarian, and we were constantly being drilled: "The tank is your mother, your father, your officer! Take good care of it, and it will take good care of you!" For that purpose, there were often inspection tours by higher officers.

An inspection by General Pulturzycki was a dreadful experience. For days everyone worked hard to be ready for him. Once, when he had passed a tank, his elegant uniform had become dirty. He assembled the entire battalion; pointing to his sleeve, he said, "If you walked past your mother and touched her arm, would your clothes get dirty?" All the crews and officers were punished.

The general always arrived in a jeep, followed by his adjutant, a captain, and together they began the inspection tour. Once my tank happened to be the closest to the side from which he arrived. I reported to him, in Polish, that my crew was ready for his inspection. He looked over the tank on the outside, and leaned over to inspect the interior. Suddenly he pointed to something with his baton. "*Eto chto* — What's that?" To my horror, I saw that he was pointing to the tips of the leather straps of my *tefillin* which were sticking out of their box! My heart stopped beating; in all the hurry, I had neglected to hide my *tefillin* completely!

If he ordered me to take them out, the consequences would be terrible. Besides, they would surely be confiscated, and where would I find another pair of *tefillin* in Soviet Russia? I was speechless for a moment. The general's face showed impatience, waiting for an answer.

Heaven must have been with me, for, still standing at attention, I replied, "These are leather straps that I picked up somewhere. I use them for electric insulation." He then shot a second glance at the straps, turned to his adjutant and his chauffeur and told them the inspection was over! All the crews were terribly disappointed; after all their work, he hadn't even checked their tanks.

I was absorbed in thought. A tank is full of clocks, instruments, gauges, artillery shells, ammunition and boxes of hand grenades; yet in all of this he had noticed two little straps! No Pole or Russian would have noticed them. He had to be a Jew! Moreover, he knew what they were; fifty years ago he must have been _bar mitzvah_!

From then on, I tried to avoid the main building where his office was located. I trembled at the thought of my _tefillin_ being confiscated...and I would surely be kicked out of the army.

The day before our graduation, I was told that Colonel Krulevski wanted to see me. I hastened to Misha's office, reporting as ordered. He smiled and said, "Relax. This is a social call. Suppose we forget military discipline for a while. You are Chaim and I'm Misha, just like in the old days in Kazakhstan. Remember?" He motioned for me to sit down, and lit a cigarette. He appeared to be rather nervous; he began to say something, and then stopped as though short of words. Finally he said, "Chaim, I don't know how to begin. I had great plans for you, and I failed. In fact, it is your fault as well as mine; we are both guilty. I underestimated Tamarov's determination to harm you."

Suddenly Misha changed the subject and began to talk about the school. "The school needs more tanks," he complained, "but it is very hard to get them. The front is burning up T-34's by the thousands, every day. The factories can't turn them out fast enough. And the reserve divisions and the Soviet tank schools have priority over us. The Poles, Czechs and Rumanians are the last on the list. I've been pressing Moscow to send more tanks to us, since I can't run a school with only the few jalopies we've got. Well, Moscow has finally agreed to give us six new T-34's, but we have got to go to the factory in Nizhniy-Tagil to get them. Someone has to go there and get those six tanks out of the factory bureaucrats, load them on the train, and make sure they get unloaded here in Ryazan. I thought you'd be the right man for the job." He stopped talking.

I failed to see the connection between a trip to Nizhniy-Tagil and my troubles with Captain Tamarov.

Finally Misha spelled it out: "Such an assignment requires an officer, of course. Well, Chaim...tomorrow every cadet in your class will graduate and become a commissioned officer; every cadet except you, that is. That wretch Tamarov vetoed your name!"

Misha couldn't meet my eyes; he gazed at the floor. I was in utter shock. Finally I found my voice, and I blurted out, "But why? What right does he have to block my commission?"

"Please understand, Chaim. In this Polish army, the political officer carries tremendous authority. This army is in the same position as the Red Army was at the beginning; it is still in its infancy, and the *politruk* carries almost as much authority as the commanding officer. I underestimated Tamarov's determination to take revenge. He vetoed your commission; he claimed that you are a Polish nationalist. You correspond with foreign countries, you're religious, you don't eat meat. He even suspects that you pray! He maintains that you cannot be trusted to command men and machines. He insists that you are not fit to bring democracy to the new Poland! And General Pulturzycki agreed with him in the end!"

I interrupted. "Did he also say that I abide by the army manual, refusing to leave my post even to search for his wife's lost heel?"

"Chaim, you'll never know how I stood up for you before General Pulturzycki! But no one can overrule a *politruk*, except Stalin! Tamarov practically forced the general to remove your name from the list. But don't worry. You'll be a sergeant, and you'll get your star in no time — by a battlefield promotion. Men win them every day, and I'll give you a special letter for your new commanding officer. You'll see; your promotion will come very soon."

All night I lay awake, accusing myself of stubbornness, stupidity, and everything else. Tamarov couldn't forget his humiliation at the party, and now he had his revenge. If I had retrieved the heel immediately, instead of quoting the army manual like an arrogant little know-it-all, I'd be a lieutenant tomorrow, like all my classmates. And I'd be going on that trip to Nizhniy-Tagil!

Nizhniy-Tagil? Why did the name seem to ring a bell?

Oh, my God! Another miracle! I suddenly remembered that the tank factory in Nizhny-Tagil was right across the street from the main office of Battalion 92, the very unit from which I had deserted! If I had gone to the tank factory — and no doubt I would have had to spend a few weeks there — someone would surely have recognized me! I would have been arrested and charged with desertion; a Polish lieutenant's uniform would not deter them. And who would I have turned to? The Polish embassy? It no longer existed, for the Soviet Union did not recognize the Polish government in London! And the Polish government in London did not recognize this Polish army!

They would have organized a "show trial," and in order to deter potential deserters, I would have been convicted of desertion and condemned to death, or, at best, to 25 years in a Siberian labor camp! I was overwhelmed by the realization that Tamarov had unknowingly saved me from a terrible fate. This was yet another miracle in the long list of miracles that I had experienced.

Graduation night came. One by one, the graduates ascended the stage. There, General Pulturzycki stood with a sword in his hand. Each graduate knelt before him, and he touched the sword to both shoulders, pronouncing: "I commission you first lieutenant of the armored service." After the ceremony, the general made a short patriotic speech in terribly crippled Polish, and all my classmates received stars.

In the corridor, the new officers were happily pinning on their shiny insignia. As I passed by, many expressed their regrets that I had not received a commission. Some felt that it must have been an administrative mistake. Several of them thanked me: "If it hadn't been for the help you gave us, we couldn't have made it."

One whispered, "Shapiro, if we weren't in the army, we'd all go on strike!"

I couldn't reply, for I was filled with disappointment and frustration, and tears choked me. I gave them a salute, and walked away. At that moment, nothing could make up for the humiliation that I felt, not even the miracle of my missing the trip to Nizhniy-Tagil.

All the new graduates were shipped out to various tank units, and I remained at the school. By this time the Red Army had pushed the Germans out of Russia. The battlefront was now in the vicinity of what was, in 1939, the Polish-Russian border.

I was ordered to report to the commanding officer's office. Misha handed me an envelope containing my travel papers. Normally, this was just routine procedure handled by some lesser officer, but Misha wanted to say good-bye to me personally. "In the envelope you'll find a special letter to your next commanding officer. I'm sure you'll become a lieutenant in no time!" He clasped my hand. "Good-bye, Chaim, and good luck!"

The parting was difficult for both of us. In the Soviet Union one could hardly trust anyone, including one's best friends; yet Misha and I had trusted each other since the fateful *Yom Kippur* night when we first met in Kazakhstan. Miraculously, we had met again at the tank school, and now we had to take leave of each other once more.

"Keep in touch whenever you can," he said. We parted with a smile and a vigorous Russian bear hug, but my heart was heavy — very heavy.

The speeding train was crowded with an artillery unit that was going to the battlefront. I was the only Pole on the train, and attracted special attention. From the Russians I learned that all the officers would remove their shiny gold or silver epaulets. This was a precaution of great importance. The German sharpshooters were able to pick them off like sitting ducks, since the gold and silver epaulets reflected the sunlight, thus making them easy targets for enemy snipers.

Outside the city of Oriol, the train was held on a siding, waiting for clearance to pass through the station. We were authorized to leave the train for one hour. There was a large military cemetery nearby, and many of us went to see it.

At the gate there was a huge Red Star; next to it, a sign read, "The Heroes of the Fatherland War." Inside there was a smaller sign: "The Heroes of the Lithuanian Division." A dreadful shock went through me — I too could have been buried right there! I had been about to join this Lithuanian division when I was rejected from General Anders' army in Guzar....As I moved closer, I could read the names on the stones; eight out of every ten graves bore Jewish names....

Imagining my own name on one of the stones brought the reality of war much closer. My eyes moist with tears, I recited *Kaddish*, the prayer for the dead. When I finished, I heard someone say "Amen!"

I turned around and there, to my great surprise, stood a tall Russian colonel. His chest was full of shining medals, including the two small stars on blue velvet that showed he had been twice wounded in battle.

I snapped to attention and saluted. He returned the salute with a smile and then said in perfect Yiddish, "I haven't heard *Kaddish* in years. *Shalom Aleichem a Yid* — Greetings to a Jew!" He stretched out his hand and introduced himself: "I'm Colonel Chaim Kryger."

I introduced myself and then, pointing to all the Jewish graves, I told him that I had volunteered for the same Lithuanian division.

The colonel showed me two hills in the distance and said, "You see those hills? That's where we fought the battle for Oriol. The Germans controlled the whole area from those hills. We got orders to take them at any cost. We took them all right, but the price was heavy! And you see that mountain? There, we lost 170 tanks in one day! That's when this Lithuanian division went into action; those boys fought like lions."

We talked about the war and about the Germans. Colonel Kryger remarked that he'd once had a high regard for the Germans, but not anymore. "You see, Sergeant," he said, "we found out that the Germans kill in cold blood; first, all Jewish prisoners of war, and then all non-Jewish Soviet officers. Finally, they starve all other Soviet prisoners of war to death.

"So now we're repaying the Germans! My men know that I don't want any German prisoners of war alive! That's one order they obey with enthusiasm. The Germans will never capture me alive, nor you either; just make sure not to fall into German hands!"

Then he added, "I'm a professional soldier. I have fought the Japanese, and I have fought the Finns, but I have never seen a greater coward than a disarmed German. You ought to see those German supermen when they're taken prisoner — like dogs, they lick your boots and kiss your hands, begging for their lives!"

I didn't want to talk about the Germans anymore. I said, "Don't you think we'd better get back to the train, before we're left behind?"

He replied, "Don't worry; they can't leave without me. I'm the commanding officer of the artillery unit."

As we passed Suma, the first enemy air attack on our train took place. Planes roared overhead, and bombs began dropping near our train. The train picked up speed, and when it pulled into a forest it stopped. We were ordered to get off and take cover.

Suddenly Russian planes appeared and engaged the German planes in combat. Meanwhile, the anti-aircraft guns, mounted on the flatcars of our train, began to fire at the Germans. From our hiding places among the dense trees we could see the air battle going on above. Two German planes were hit and the remaining planes fled. I thought of the German arrogance at the beginning of the war, how their bombs had destroyed defenseless cities, how they had strafed innocent women and children. How things had changed during the last few years!

The journey continued. We passed through devastated cities whose buildings were all skeletons. We passed through burned-out forests, whose black branches reached out to the sky like human hands. I thought to myself that they were crying to Heaven: "Look what man has done to us! Didn't we give shade and shelter to people, to birds and animals? And now all is flame and coal-black death!"

The cemetery and all those Jewish graves, the parched cities, the skeleton trees — all of this seemed to bring death closer and closer. I felt despair; I didn't want to die! I began to regret that I had volunteered. Why hadn't I stayed in the Urals?

Of course I had the normal instinct for self-preservation that everyone feels; no one wants to die. But there was something else too. I had tried to bury the dreadful thought before, but now I couldn't.

Was it possible that I was the sole surviving member of my family?

No, I told myself, it can't be! It's impossible; it's only an insane rumor; how could the Germans murder all the Jews? Maybe hundreds, even thousands, of Jewish families are suffering and homeless, but one would have to be insane to believe that the Germans are killing millions of defenseless men, women, and children!

Then the train stopped at Berditchev for a two-hour layover, and in this city which had been populated almost entirely by Jews — the Russian Jerusalem, the home of the famous Rabbi Levi Yitzchok — I wandered for two hours trying to find Jews. There weren't any. Ukrainians and Russians had taken up residence there.

My desperate and futile search for Jews came to an end. I *davened Minchah*, and it seemed as if Rabbi Levi Yitzchok and all the Jewish *neshamos* of Berditchev joined my supplications to Heaven.

At the railroad station, I met a Jewish pilot, a former resident of Berditchev. He told me that during the German occupation, the Germans with the enthusiastic help of the Ukrainian population, had massacred all the Jews.

Back on the train, I was still in shock from the pilot's story and what it meant for me. I realized that the Jew-hatred of the Poles was no less than the Jew-hatred of the Ukrainians, and that the Poles, too, must have helped the Germans murder the Jews! Was I really the sole survivor of my family?

The train sped along, getting closer and closer to the front lines. We passed cities with familiar names: Lutsk, Kovel, Brest-Litovsk. The German defense line was now at the Bug River. They were fighting fiercely, for they knew that, after the Bug, the next natural line of defense would be the Wisla (Vistula). And after the Wisla came Germany, and Berlin itself!

36

I SOON FOUND out that there are hardly any wounded tank men; the tank is either victorious in battle, or becomes a steel tomb for the crew inside. Even if the tank men did manage to escape from a burning tank, they would most likely face a barrage of machine-gun fire from the enemy tanks or infantry. It was somehow consoling to think that the Germans would never get me alive.

I was welcomed to the headquarters of the Third Infantry Division of the Polish army by a young captain. He invited me to eat, and we talked. He was Jewish and came from Brest-Litovsk (Brisk). Before the war, he had been a corporal in the Polish army; after the army disintegrated in 1939, he was drafted again, this time into the Red Army. He was promoted to the rank of lieutenant for his valor in the battle for Moscow, and then transferred to the new Polish army with the rank of captain. There he met his brother, who had been discharged from the Polish army of General Anders because he was Jewish.

"Can you imagine," the captain said, "an army issuing false documents?! Those bigots actually kicked my brother out, claiming that he had a contagious disease."

"Yes," I replied, "I can imagine it very well; I was in Guzar, too, and they issued the same phony document to me when they kicked me out!"

I realized that I had finally reached my goal: I was at the front. Because there were still Germans roaming the forest, the captain ordered two armed soldiers to escort me to the tank company. On the way there, we passed a Polish soldier sitting down and eating a hunk of bread and sausage; I looked again and saw what he was sitting on: a dead German. The sight made me sick.

I called out, "Hey, soldier! How can you enjoy your food, sitting on a dead man?"

"But this isn't any ordinary dead man," he answered, grinning. "This is a dead German! What's the matter, Sergeant, don't you like dead Germans?"

All the way to the tank company I couldn't get the sight of that soldier, sitting on the dead man and chewing his food, out of my mind. Does war make people act that way? Would I, too, become so hardened?

In the distance, artillery was firing. Finally we arrived at the tank headquarters, which consisted of a few officers in an underground bunker. A Lieutenant Kwiatkowski welcomed me at the bunker opening. He said that our commanding officer insisted on personally meeting every new man, but that right now he was out on inspection. He told me to wait outside; the air in the bunker was thick and hard to breathe. There was a small creek nearby, so I took off my boots and soaked my feet in the cool water. How good it felt!

I was astonished to see the guard smoking while on duty. He noticed my surprise and said, "Sergeant, you must be fresh out of school! Here at the front, you'll see that we do many things which are against the rules. We smoke; we hardly salute; when death is near, discipline is far."

During my short conversation with the guard, he told me that the commanding officer, Major Balabanov, was a Cossack from the Don River. I began to worry, for the Cossacks were known to be cruel and sadistic, and vicious Jew-haters. At home we used to hear stories about the Cossacks: how wild they were, how they were practically born in the saddle, and that when they joined the army, they took their own horses and weapons. We heard that the czars used to feed raw meat to Cossack soldiers, to make them even wilder. They were known as ferocious fighters and killers. It was said that during World War I the German soldiers panicked at the sight of Cossacks on their horses. And now I'd have to serve under a Cossack!

Soon an officer came galloping up on a horse. I was astonished: a horse in a tank company?

The guard whispered, "That's him, the commanding officer. He takes his horse with him wherever he goes."

Quickly I dried my feet and put on my boots. The commanding officer dismounted and entered the bunker. The guard took the reins and led the horse to the creek, and the thirsty horse started to guzzle the cold water. I noticed that the horse was wet, sweating from all that galloping. It was obvious to me that the guard was a city boy, or he would not have permitted an overheated, sweating horse to drink cold water.

I called out to the guard to stop the horse from drinking, but he ignored me. The horse continued to drink, and I yelled, "Take that horse away from the water! That's an order."

The guard said, "Why? The poor horse is thirsty."

Suddenly I heard a shout. "Guard! You heard the sergeant's order! Why are you standing there like an idiot?" It was the Cossack himself!

This was my introduction to my commanding officer. A few moments later, he and I were wiping the animal's sweat. He said, "I love horses, and I can see that you're a horse man, too."

I answered, "They say a man's best friend is the dog, but I think it's the horse!" He laughed, and I thought, Not bad for an introduction to a commanding officer.

Lieutenant Kwiatkowski reported my arrival to the major, without much formality. To me, just out of school, it sounded as if he were talking to the foreman on a collective farm: easy and familiar.

The commanding officer asked me, "How is it that you didn't get a commission in Ryazan?"

I didn't know what to say. To tell him that I was vetoed by the political officer might place me in a very bad position. Suppose this Cossack is a Party member, I thought. Instead of answering, I handed him the letter from Colonel Krulevski.

While he was reading it, I had a good chance to observe him more closely. His thick black curls were so matted and unkempt that I wondered if a comb had ever passed through them. He had a long face like a horse, a sharp nose, a thick moustache and beady black eyes under heavy eyebrows. I looked at him and thought about my ancestors' dread of the Cossacks, those fearless, merciless horsemen, born to kill and to get killed.

He looked up from the letter, smiling, and said, "Very well, soldier; report to Lieutenant Galivkov."

I snapped my boots together and replied, "Yes, Comrade Major!"

As I was about to leave, he said, "Sergeant, Colonel Krulevski mentions in his letter something about a 'personal war'. I fully understand that you, as a Jew, have your personal reason to hate the Germans. Now, I've noticed that you Jewish soldiers are too impatient, too eager to fight. But I can't permit recklessness; I can't afford to lose any tanks and men; both are irreplaceable! However, I give a free hand to all my men as far as German prisoners of war are concerned. To us tank men, prisoners of war are just a nuisance...."

Normally, each tank is commanded by a commissioned officer, because one tank has as much fire power as a platoon of infantry men. Only when officers are scarce is it permitted for a sergeant to be a tank commander. Apparently this was the case now, and perhaps my letter of introduction helped, for I was given command of a T-34 tank.

Every three or four tanks constituted a troop or a platoon under the command of a platoon leader who directed positions in battle and gave orders by way of radio, in a radius up to 25 kilometers. My immediate commander was Lieutenant Galivkov, a little Russian in a Polish uniform. He had a chest full of medals, including one for the battle of Stalingrad and another for the defense of Moscow. He liked to brag about his battle experiences, his tricks, tactics and victories. I became a good listener, and was eager to win his friendship. As we sat on the grass waiting for orders, I studied the medals on his chest, reading the inscriptions aloud.

"You know, Lieutenant Galivkov, I arrived in Stalingrad just a few weeks after you chased the Fritzes out," I said.

Galivkov puffed out a mouthful of smoke and said, "That figures. After *we* chased the Germans out, the Jews came in."

I felt like punching him in the nose. "What do you mean?" I said angrily. "Do you think there were no Jews fighting in Stalingrad? Why, it was a Jewish major who captured Marshal Paulus and his whole staff!" I was ready to deliver a whole lecture, but then my anger burned out as suddenly as it had flared. What difference would it really make? They believe what they want to believe, I told myself.

For the first couple of days we only sat around talking and playing cards. It was terribly disappointing; I was itching for battle.

Finally we went into action. Like heavy hail, the enemy's bullets splattered against my tank. I felt like kissing the steel which was protecting us, the four crew members. I felt terribly sorry for the poor infantrymen who were following behind our tanks; they had no protection whatsoever.

Inside the turret, looking through the periscope, I could clearly observe a beautiful sight: German soldiers fleeing wildly, leaving behind their wounded and dead, racing to get a ride on their own fleeing trucks; but their trucks wouldn't wait for them! Over the radio, Galivkov instructed me to cross the forest and to cut off the escaping Germans. We plunged through the forest until we reached the road. The Germans were caught in our crossfire. Not one of them escaped!

That night, the tanks stood mute and silent, their crews in deep, exhausted sleep. But I couldn't sleep; this was the first time in my life that I had fired on human beings; the first time I had ever killed!

Instead of feeling glory and satisfaction, I felt shame — I was ashamed for myself, ashamed for the entire human race. I had read and heard about war, and waited for this, but how terribly different it was in reality, seeing it with my own eyes!

How treacherous and deadly modern man is when he wages war, I thought. In contrast to the ancient warriors, modern man has refined warfare: he has invented bullets, tanks, bombs, so he can kill from a distance and avoid having to look his enemy in the eye when cutting his throat. He even fools himself: "*My* shot didn't kill anyone; it was someone else's!"

I wondered if everyone suffered from such thoughts after his first day of battle. Was I more sensitive than the others? Was it because of my Jewishness? Did the crew members hate the Germans more than I? But they had no greater reason to hate them than I had. That Pole who enjoyed his meal, sitting on a dead German, or my tank driver, a Kazakh from Asia Minor — they'd never even heard of Germans, until the day Germany attacked the Soviet Union. They didn't have more reason to hate the Germans than I had, and they had shot at them today too, but they were sleeping peacefully.

And the Germans! I observed them going into battle; our tanks were hidden in the forest and they didn't suspect our presence. Wearing unbuttoned shirts, their sleeves rolled up, and no helmets on their heads, they charged our Polish and Russian infantry. They ran right into the machine-gun fire. I had asked Galivkov, "Lieutenant, are these Germans crazy? Is their loyalty to their rotten Fuehrer that deep?"

The experienced Galivkov had burst out laughing. "No, no," he said. "They're just plain drunk! Plain whiskey-drunk! That's the only way their officers can make them get up and fight."

And what about our men, the Poles and the Russians, fighting against the drunken Germans? Was their hatred so deep and powerful that it could move them to attack, to kill the enemy, at the risk of their own lives?

"Enough!" a voice within me cautioned. "If you want to stay alive, stop being sentimental! Just think of what these same Germans did to Nosson and are doing to all the Jews, and you'll become properly hardened, like the rest of them."

But I still couldn't fall asleep. I heard small arms firing in the distance. That was apparently our infantry snooping around, trying to locate the enemy positions. The full moon was shining clearly and brightly. I got up from the moist grass and began to check and recheck every part of the tank, the tracks, the armaments, the motor.

My crew woke up and complained that I was disturbing their sleep. I apologized, but told them, "I might be naive with my fresh-from-school discipline, but remember: an immobile tank could be a death trap for us all — a fiery steel oven! Someday you'll thank me for being so fussy."

37

IT IS DIFFICULT to impose discipline on men who face death constantly. The members of a tank crew must live as equals rather than as officers and subordinates, since they spend hours together, dependent on each other, in one small steel box. The army rule, "One for all and all for one," is particularly true for them. The same steel walls of the tank which shield and protect the crew can be transformed into their coffin as well; thus, maintaining strict discipline can mean the difference between life and death.

Under the circumstances, my frequent insistence on carrying out the theory that I had learned in Ryazan made me look like a fool in the eyes of my crew. Once, before crossing a muddy field, I told my driver, "Try to cross the field on foot first; if you don't sink in, the tank won't either, for a person exerts more pressure per square inch than a tank does."

All three men burst out laughing. "It may all be nicely calculated in the book," the gunner said, "but in reality, we'll be up to our necks in mud!"

Our infantry division was eventually pinned down by the Germans in Wislowka, a small village near a railroad station. Since no enemy tanks had been reported, our commanding officer sent out two scout tanks, "to make the enemy move." Both of them were knocked out. It was not known whether they had been hit by anti-tank guns or bazookas, or by both. This knowledge was important, because the firing range of an anti-tank gun is much greater than that of a bazooka, which is effective only at close range.

Then the commanding officer sent out nine tanks, as a show of force: appearing to be about to crush the opposing forces with overwhelming fire power might cause them to run, thus avoiding further casualties to the tank unit. These preparations had to be made close enough to be clearly visible to the enemy, but not so close as to be within their range of fire. The theory was that if the enemy got cold feet and fled, this would achieve our objective without any casualties; on the other hand, if our demonstration of power did not work, then the alternative plan was to be carried out: engaging the enemy forces in battle and trying to destroy them.

Our tanks' show of force failed; the Germans didn't move.

Galivkov, who had just been promoted to the rank of captain, was in charge of executing the alternative plan. His voice came over our tank radio: "Don to Narew, Don to Narew." We had chosen for code names the names of two rivers which were near our respective home towns. "Proceed at top speed through the main street of the village. Don't stop or slow down. When they fire at you, we will see where they are hiding. Then we can knock them out, one by one. Stop on the other side of the village to engage the enemy in crossfire. Good luck. Repeat."

The faces of my crew turned white and tense and our bodies stiffened in anticipation of battle. In the distance I could see our two tanks still burning, emitting thick black smoke. We didn't know the fate of the two crews; had they managed to get out, or had their tanks turned into fiery ovens for them?

I noticed that the two tanks stood in a straight horizontal line, one directly in front of the other. This could only mean that both tanks had been hit simultaneously; otherwise, the moment one tank was knocked out, the other would have concentrated all its fire upon the enemy before being hit.

I urged the driver to get up to maximum speed, for we might be fired upon from both sides; the sides of a tank are its weak spots, because the armor is thinner and the fuel and oil tanks are located there. With the engine roaring at top speed, we rumbled into the village. I kept my eyes on the periscope, searching for any sign of an enemy fire-nest. Suddenly I noticed a pipe protruding from a window. In a flash I realized that these Polish peasants had no plumbing! At once I screamed to the driver, "Stop!" Then I noticed another pipe sticking out of a window on the opposite side of the street. Bazookas!!! I took aim, pressed the pedal, and our 132 mm. cannon destroyed first one house, and then the other!

Captain Galivkov's voice came over the radio, "Why did you stop? You disobeyed my order!"

I explained to him what I had seen and done, adding, "Now we're going through the village at full speed."

By this time, several of the straw roofs were blazing, and the wind was carrying the flames from house to house. The Germans began to flee, running into the nearby forest. Our Polish infantry gave chase.

This action brought me my first two medals: one Polish and one Russian. My tank crew also received medals. I pointed out to the crew that the driver's discipline had actually saved us all, for if he hadn't stopped instantly at my command, we would have been within the bazookas' firing range. To my crew, though, I became the lucky charm that had saved their lives!

Major Balabanov, presenting the medals, praised our crew, and then turned to me: "The good judgment, fast orientation, sharp observation, and quick decision-making that you displayed comprise the finest qualities of an officer." He declared that he was recommending me for a battlefield promotion.

I had no idea to what extent the Russian command kept a sharp eye on our Polish army, until the following incident. It was during a combined Russian and Polish attack on German positions. A frontal attack by tanks should last no longer than 30 minutes; if by then the enemy resistance has not been broken, the attacking tanks should turn back, for the superior strength of the enemy has been proven. Such situations require that air support and heavy artillery be brought in to weaken the enemy's resistance. In fact, the fate of a tank crew — life or death — is usually determined within the first 15 minutes.

This time it was taking much longer to dislodge the Germans than we had expected. As we watched helplessly, they knocked out three Soviet tanks ahead of us. This gave me the opportunity to spot the location of the German cannon; it was a tank entrenched underground, with only its cannon showing above ground, a common practice for tanks holding a defense line.

I picked up the enemy gun in the cross hairs of my gun sight, and touched the driver's back with my foot, a sign for him to stop. He made a sudden full stop. The tank lurched and for a second I lost my aim, but I quickly picked up the target again. I pressed the cannon pedal, and watched as thick black smoke rose from the enemy position. I whispered, "That's how all your enemies shall vanish, O God!"

Suddenly something hit us forcefully, and to our surprise the blow seemed to come from the rear. At once, the driver took off at full speed, zig-zagging in all directions to avoid being hit again. To our great relief, the tank performed normally, without any sign of having been damaged.

Later, when the battle was over, a Russian tank drove up to us and a colonel jumped off and approached me. Poking his finger into my face, he screamed, "How dare you stop in battle, you Polish idiot?! My driver ran into your tank and stalled!"

After a battle, everybody's nerves were at the breaking point; death had been imminent every moment. And here he was shoving his finger, and then his whole clenched fist, at me. He suddenly hit my driver in the face with his fist, and shouted to the approaching commanding officer, "That's the driver, the idiot!"

Major Balabanov stood up for us, telling the colonel, "My men have my permission to stop any time, anywhere, in order to take careful aim which will enable them to hit their target on the first shot."

The angry colonel, who outranked our major, was flushed with rage. But at that very moment, before he could speak again, a jeep pulled up next to us, and a Russian general stepped out. His face and clothing were covered with dust.

"Major Balabanov," the general said to our commanding officer, "I watched your Poles' performance just now and it was impressive indeed! I recommend that the 'Order of the Red Banner' be awarded the lieutenant who knocked out the buried enemy tank."

Balabanov replied, "Thank you, General Dobrinin. Incidentally, that tank commander is not a lieutenant; he's only a sergeant."

"Only a sergeant?" the general asked, surprised. "Well then, make him a lieutenant at once!" He shook my hand, and the hands of my crew, and drove off. Thus I received a battlefield commission; and how proud I was of the promotion and the medals! Misha had been right!

AT THE Wieprz River, the Germans fought bitterly. They were very much aware that after *this* river came the Vistula and Warsaw, and after Warsaw came Berlin! The enemy hastily constructed reinforced concrete fortifications on the western bank of the river, where their main force was concentrated. And in order to gain some extra time, some of their units remained on the eastern bank, to hold out as long as possible. The Polish army was assigned a dual task: first, to capture a small railroad station on the eastern side of the river, which would be essential for transporting the prefabricated bridges which our forces needed in order to cross the river; and second, to cross the river and liberate Lublin, one of the largest cities in Poland.

The rail line ran along the base of a hill where the Germans were well entrenched with plenty of artillery. From this hill, they were able to control the entire vicinity, including the railroad station.

Our commander told us, "The sooner we take the station, the faster we'll cross the river, and the fewer fortifications we'll face on the other side. Our artillery hasn't been able to dislodge the enemy from the hill. They've pinned down our infantry, and we can't get air strikes. So we'll take it with our tanks!"

During the last few days, Captain Galivkov's company had lost four tanks; my own platoon had lost two, and another had also lost two. The men were exhausted and their nerves were on edge. We were told that according to information received from the infantry, there were no enemy tanks.

Major Balabanov appointed Captain Galivkov to be in charge of this operation. I was appointed commander of troop B, which consisted of three tanks. A total of seven T-34's were assembled in the forest near the hill. Captain Galivkov and I walked up to the edge of the forest to observe the terrain; this was standard operating procedure for tank commanders before going into action.

Soon two Polish infantry officers appeared and told us, "There are lots of artillery and machine guns on the hill, but to the best of our knowledge, no enemy tanks." The hill was very steep and we wondered how the enemy had managed to drag artillery up there. The infantry officers explained that the other side of the hill was less steep. "Even trucks can drive up easily."

Battling an enemy on a steep hill was especially hazardous for tanks. There was a limit to how many degrees a tank could lean; at a certain point, the 35 tons could topple over. Enemy fire, even when it wasn't powerful enough to penetrate the tank's steel walls, could nevertheless be strong enough to tilt it to the point where it would tumble down the hill. An additional danger was the after-shock from the tank's own cannon fire, the backwards thrust upon the tank caused by the shell as it was fired from the cannon. An unfortunate combination of circumstances could upset a tilted tank, engulfing it in flames fed by its own fuel.

"Now here is the plan," Captain Galivkov explained. "My troop will move across that open field and start climbing up the hill. The enemy's attention will be focused on my four tanks. You'll take your troop around to the other side of the hill, under cover of the forest, and surprise the enemy from the rear."

All the tanks moved out. Before I lost sight of Galivkov and his troop, I saw them moving across the field at full speed, firing back at the Germans who were firing at them. Galivkov paid the price of open warfare, however, and lost one tank almost immediately. His remaining three began zig-zagging towards the hill, trying to avoid getting hit.

When I arrived at the other side of the hill, I noticed clouds of dust rising. For a moment I thought that because of our tanks, the enemy was fleeing on trucks and half-tracks. But when the dust settled, the outline of a German tank became visible. Then I made out two more, and then another two.

"Five enemy tanks approaching!" I radioed Galivkov at once.

Galivkov replied, "Engage enemy tanks. We'll get them in crossfire."

The essential task of a tank is to destroy enemy tanks, which, due to their firepower and mobility, can disorganize the infantry and throw them into panic. Therefore, whenever enemy tanks are sighted, all previous plans are cancelled until the foe's tanks are destroyed. Galivkov's tank began to ascend the hill, while his remaining two tanks halted at the foot of the hill, furnishing fire-cover. The German tanks, unaware of our presence in the forest, began firing on Galivkov and his troop. They were caught in our crossfire and within a few minutes we had knocked out three of the five German tanks, but they managed to hit two of Galivkov's troop.

When the dust was blown away by the wind, I suddenly discerned that one of the two remaining German tanks was a Pantera, the giant of the German tanks. And a T-34 is no match for a Pantera!

I reported the bad news at once to Galivkov, hoping that he'd make his way back down the hill. I told him that our three tanks would take on the Pantera and the other German tank, thus giving him a chance to come down.

Galivkov replied, "I'll concentrate on the Pantera from here." Since he was higher on the hill than the Pantera, he apparently felt that he'd be able to hit the monster from above.

Still enjoying the cover of the trees, my troop knocked out the fourth enemy tank. I could see some of the German crew bailing out, only to be cut down by our infantry.

Now the Pantera concentrated its fire on Galivkov on the hill. The monster tank was constantly changing positions, but suddenly I saw it make a full 360-degree turn! I was overjoyed, for it could only mean one thing: its track or driving wheel on one side was damaged, and it was thus practically immobilized.

I breathed a sigh of relief. Then I looked up, and I saw a terrible sight: Galivkov's tank was tumbling down the hill, enveloped in dust and black smoke!

Although functioning on only "one leg," the Pantera was still a dangerous opponent, for its turret, powerful cannon and the machine guns could still turn in all directions. Now, having finished Galivkov, it turned its fire on our little T-34.

We were still under cover of the trees and still mobile. I ordered my troop to concentrate their fire on the body of the Pantera while I aimed for its gun and turret. The Pantera's shells were landing all around us, so we moved a little deeper into the forest for better cover.

Suddenly there was a shattering blow. We were all still alive, but one track was damaged; we, too, were now immobilized! I reported this to the other two tanks, adding that we could continue to fire. Suddenly the inside of our tank filled with thick smoke. The fan inside our turret, whose purpose was to drive out the deadly fumes of our cannon shots and to bring in fresh air for the crew, was drawing smoke into the tank. It became hard to breathe, and we began coughing and choking.

I opened the turret. Outside, there was fire everywhere; the forest around us was burning. The driver tried to back the tank away from the flaming trees, but we were only able to move in a circle because of our damaged track.

The Germans, assuming that we were finished, stopped firing at my tank and began to concentrate their fire on the remaining two. Our immediate danger was from our own fuel tank, which might be ignited at any moment, blowing us up along with our remaining supply of ammunition!

"Abandon tank!" I ordered. The question, however, was how? To get out the way we got in, through the hatch on top, was impossible, for we'd be exposed to enemy fire, especially to the sharpshooters whose specialty was to cut down crews abandoning tanks. Besides, the tank was surrounded by the flames of the burning trees. There was a trapdoor at the bottom of the tank, installed for this kind of emergency. However, the clearance between the tank's floor and the ground was only 30 centimeters — about 12 inches. When the driver tried to open the trapdoor, the tree roots of the forest's floor made it impossible to open it fully.

Having no other choice, I decided that we should get out through the driver's window, rather than through the turret, to shorten the distance to the ground. One by one we began to bail out. While my three crew members were sliding down the hot steel, I glanced once more through the periscope. I could see the Pantera still firing at my other two tanks. I sent off one more plea to Heaven, "Spare my life, God! Spare us all! Keep the fuel tanks from blowing up for one more minute! And please, please give me a little wind to clear the smoke from my aiming device, so I can have one more shot at the Pantera!"

As my radio man tugged on my leg — the sign that they were all out and now it was my turn to get out — the view became clear. I brought the Pantera's turret into the cross hairs of my gun sight and pressed the pedal one last time. There wasn't time to find out whether I had hit or missed, for smoke obscured the visibility again.

Now I had to get out, and fast! As I slid down the hot steel to the ground, I felt something like a bee sting on my neck, but didn't pay any attention to it.

The four of us quickly crawled away from the tank, keeping low to the ground. When we reached the open field, we saw the German crew abandoning its Pantera, only to meet death from our infantry fire. Then a great shout arose: "Hurrah!" and our infantrymen stormed up the hill. Speeding ahead of the infantry were my two remaining tanks!

Now I felt a pain in the back of my neck, and warmth on my back. When I put my hand to the spot, it was full of blood! I felt a sudden weakness in my legs. Before blacking out I managed to whisper the traditional prayer at the approach of death: "*Shema Yisrael....*"

When I awoke, I was lying on a narrow cot. Where am I? I wondered. What happened? It felt so good to be on a bed, after so many nights of sleeping on the ground or on the ammunition boxes inside the tank. I realized that I was in a field hospital, in a large tent containing many wounded soldiers, both Poles and Russians.

So I'm wounded, I thought. I raised my hands: they were in place — two of them, both movable. I moved my feet with no difficulty. I passed my hands all over my torso, and everything seemed intact. Why then was I in a hospital?

Wanting to call a nurse, I tried to turn my head to the right, but it wouldn't move; then I tried to turn it to the left, and it wouldn't move. I tried to raise my head, and a terrible pain shot through my neck. I put my hands up and felt bandages all around my neck, making it rigid. I started calling for the nurse.

A young girl in white appeared. She took my pulse and smiled. "So you finally woke up, eh? You must be making up for a lot of sleepless nights; you've been sleeping for 48 hours!"

I wanted to ask her about my neck, which was now beginning to throb painfully, but she kept talking. "Don't worry, you're not hurt badly! Just luck, the doctor says; had the bullet gone in one millimeter deeper, you'd be dead or paralyzed for life. That's what the doctor said. You lost some blood, but you'll be as good as new in a few weeks."

When she finally stopped talking, all my questions had been answered. Then she said, "I'll bring you something to eat. You must be starving!" and she disappeared. The "bee sting" that I had felt while abandoning the tank was actually a ricocheting bullet; it had hit the tank first, and then my neck.

It had pierced the skin and flesh, but not deeply enough to cause real damage.

I got permission to walk around the hospital. A new group of wounded soldiers had been brought in and I watched the nurses bandaging them. The orderly collected their soiled uniforms and dumped them on a truck. Suddenly it hit me: where was *my* uniform? And my *tefillin*, *Tanach* and Hebrew calendar which were always in my pocket?

I rushed to the head orderly, asking him, "Where do they take all the uniforms?" He told me that two miles down the road a temporary laundry had been set up, where all the uniforms were deloused and washed. I asked him if I could go there with him on his truck.

"No! We have strict orders from the doctors: no one from the hospital can board this truck because all this laundry is contaminated."

I was heartbroken! My *tefillin*! All these years I had carried them with me, and now they were gone!

Outside the hospital I noticed a German three-wheel motorcycle parked near the door. Apparently it was a "trophy" belonging to some officer or doctor. I had never driven one, but I figured that if I could drive a tank, a truck and a tractor, I could certainly drive a motorcycle.

In the basket attached to the side there were some bottles of whiskey and an automatic rifle. Although I was still wearing hospital pajamas, I jumped into the driver's seat and took off. The chance of finding my *tefillin* outweighed all consequences!

In the middle of a field, I saw a column of thick smoke and steam ascending; this was the makeshift laundry. A big kettle was boiling, with heaps of uniforms piled up around it. Four old men in uniform were immersing the battlefield clothing in the boiling water.

I rushed up to them and told them that I had a hand grenade in my pocket and had come to warn them. They laughed at me. "Do you think we're that stupid? We go through all the pockets for that kind of thing!"

I saw that they had sorted the Polish uniforms into one pile and the Russian uniforms into another. I offered each one a bottle of whiskey if they could find my pants. "If you feel something big and round like a hand grenade — those are my pants!" I said.

They stopped everything and started searching; and I worked feverishly along with them. They had every batch of clothes marked with the day it had arrived, and since there were few uniforms, my Polish uniform was not too hard to find. And there, in the pocket, were my precious belongings!

Back at the hospital, a soldier was waiting for me: the driver of the motorcycle. Pointing to the motorcycle, he shouted, "You're in for it now! Do you know who that belongs to? To the colonel, the chief surgeon, Dr. Kravietz! Follow me!"

Dr. Kravietz?! I was overjoyed; it was a Jewish name!

Outside the huge tent, there was a small building which served as an operating theater. Next to it was a small stable, the office of Dr. Kravietz.

First, the doctor gave me a lecture on safety. "Do you know how our partisans got those motorcycles? They would string a thin wire across the road. Then the fleeing Germans would come along, riding at full speed, never noticing the wire. After they were caught, the partisans would kill the Fritzes and take their motorcycles and weapons.

Now, the anti-Soviet partisans have learned the trick and do the same to us! You, you stupid idiot, took off at full speed! You're lucky that you're still alive!"

Then he wanted to know where I went and why I had stolen the whiskey. I told him that I had pictures of my parents in my pocket, that my parents had probably been murdered by the Germans, and I had to get the pictures back.

"Let me see them!" he demanded.

I was in an awkward spot. I told him I would only show them to him in private, so he ordered the driver and the nurse out of the room.

I took out my precious _tefillin_, held them up to him, and said, "I've carried them with me all through the war. I haven't missed a day since my _bar mitzvah_. I had to get them back!"

His eyes filled with tears. He said, "I used to put them on too, until I was 18. My father was a tailor, a Lubavitcher _chasid_. I probably would have been a tailor too. But then came the Revolution, and I became a surgeon." He wiped his eyes. "You were due to go back to the front in a week, but I am ordering you to rest here for another two or three weeks. They'll have to win the war without you!"

WE DECORATED our tanks with slogans on huge banners, such as, "*Do Warszawy* — To Warsaw!" The heart of every Polish soldier was proud, for it was a Polish army which was going to liberate Warsaw, Poland's capital. True, the army was under Russian command, and the crews were of mixed nationalities, but still, there was a White Eagle decorating every tank!

However, the deeper we got into Poland, the greater were my fear and anxiety. Where were the Jews?

We liberated one city after another, but I couldn't find one Jew anywhere — not in Chelm, which had had a Jewish population of over twenty-five thousand; not in Lublin, where there had been fifty thousand Jews. The Germans, with the vigorous and enthusiastic help of the Poles, had made these and all other Polish cities *Judenrein* — Jew-free.

It was July 1944. Before the month was over, we had crossed the Vistula River. Slowly, our column of tanks rumbled over the bridge. When we came to within 12 kilometers of the capital, we were ordered to stop.

We didn't know why we had been told to stop our offensive against the Germans. Rumor had it that a huge army, well-prepared and rested, was to be concentrated for our final assault upon Warsaw and Berlin. The names of these two cities had a magic sound, a special meaning to these battle-scarred veterans; they signified the final victory over the German beast, and the end of the war!

The order came to dig in our tanks. This indicated that we were going to remain there for quite a long time. As the days went by, the tank crews were reshuffled. More Soviet officers and more Soviet tank men were assigned to our Polish tank units.

The entire front line became inactive and silent, though explosions could be heard coming from the direction of Warsaw. Every night we could see the sky glowing in the distance, from the flames raging in the city. Little did we know what was going on in the capital; it was only much later that we found out that we were witnessing the ill-fated AK uprising. Actually, this was the second uprising in Warsaw. The first had occurred a year before. The Jews of the Warsaw ghetto had revolted for forty-three days without any help from the outside. They were denied even a single gun, a single bullet by the well-armed Polish underground. Without any help, without the sympathy of the surrounding Christian population, the remaining Jews of the ghetto fought with homemade weapons, killing the well-fed, well-armed Germans and sacrificing their own lives — alone, alone to the end!

I lay on top of the tank, my face turned up to the bright stars. Why didn't these stars drop like shining bullets, all in unison, and destroy this cruel world? I was trying to understand the mystery of existence, of the way God was running His world, the strange and tragic path He had set forth for His chosen people, the Jews. Chosen for what? I asked myself in anguish and despair. Chosen to be murdered by the nations? To be a lamb among wolves?

From time to time, the tranquillity of the night was broken by explosions in the distance, followed by an intensified red glow suffusing the sky. Warsaw was burning!

I jumped off my tank and leaned against a tree to say the evening prayers. The panorama was impressive: hundreds of tanks buried in the earth, only their cannons protruding, thousands of artillery pieces scattered about like matchsticks. Surrounded by whispering trees, I said my prayers with such intensity that every word was a sigh from the depth of my heart.

Suddenly the radio man called to me: "Lieutenant! You are ordered to report to the colonel at once!"

I wondered what could be so important that it couldn't be relayed over the radio. I began to go over all the things I might have said to people to whom I had spoken during the past few days. Had I said or done something which would annoy the Soviets? Had my reputation as a Polish nationalist caught up with me from the Ryazan tank school?

I reported to the colonel, saluting snappily, but he did not return my salute; he merely said, "At ease, Lieutenant."

I was worried; why didn't he return my salute? It looked like trouble. Then I noticed that both his hands were occupied in hiding his lit cigarette. It was strictly forbidden to smoke at night, because a lit cigarette could serve as a beacon to the enemy, inviting enemy shells.

After inhaling a final puff, he ground out the cigarette. Then he placed his hand on my shoulder and said, "Comrade, we've been through a lot together. I hate to lose you, but orders are orders! I'm sorry, but you won't be going with us into Warsaw and Berlin!" He went on to tell me that the order had just come through: I would be sent to Chelm, where the Polish tank school from Ryazan was to be relocated.

With the liberation of more and more of the countryside, the new temporary Polish government had begun drafting Poles of military age into our army. Some of them were to become cadets in the tank officers' school. Most of them could not understand Russian, so the school needed tank officers who were fluent in both Polish and Russian. Apparently my good friend Misha, the commanding officer and head of the tank school, had requested my transfer.

The tank school was located just outside the city of Chelm in the Lublin District. When I introduced myself to a young Polish captain outside the commanding officer's office, he was glad to see me.

"For the last couple of weeks, Colonel Krulevski has been asking about you every day, wanting to know if you had arrived yet," the captain said. He directed me to the colonel's office. I knocked on his door lightly, and I heard Misha's voice: "Enter!"

I opened the door softly. He was sitting with his back to the door, leafing through a pile of papers. As I reported for duty in the proper military manner, he turned around. Strangely, he returned my salute with his left hand! He looked old and tired, and as he got up from his chair he leaned heavily on a cane in his left hand. It was only then that I noticed his right hand: it was hanging motionless.

Misha approached me and exclaimed, "My dear friend, am I glad to see you!" It broke my heart to see his crippled body, and I couldn't find words. For a moment we both stood there with tears in our eyes. Finally he spoke: "Cheer up, Chaim! You're all in one piece, right? And I see you got your lieutenant's star, and some medals as well."

I wanted so much to know what had happened to him. Had he gone into battle again? How was he wounded?

Misha said, "Let's go for a walk. My doctors tell me that if I don't walk a lot I might lose my leg completely." Before we left, he instructed the executive officer to arrange quarters for me.

As we walked, soldiers and officers saluted him. It was agonizing to watch him replying to each salute with a nod of his head; for with his left hand he held his cane, and his right hand was paralyzed.

Finally he began to talk. "One gets used to everything, my dear Chaim. When you hear my tragedy, you'll realize that _this_ is only a minor problem," he said, indicating his paralyzed arm. Then he told me how it had happened: He had been instructed to begin planning to move the tank school from Ryazan, in Russia, to somewhere in Poland. At that time there wasn't much to choose from, for only a small part of Poland had been liberated. He traveled to Poland, and after investigating a number of places, he decided upon Chelm, with its huge army barracks and classrooms.

He decided not to bring his wife and children to Chelm; he was sure they would suffer there because of the tremendous Polish hatred towards the Russians. The criminal activities of the Polish underground made it unsafe for a Soviet family to live in Poland. He decided to take his family back to their native village in the Ukraine. They traveled by train from Ryazan; then, by army truck, they began the final leg of their long trip home.

Misha was sitting in the cab next to the driver, and his wife and three children were sitting comfortably on the furniture in the truck. Then, as they were passing through a forest, they were attacked by a gang of the Ukrainian anti-Soviet underground. The driver was killed instantly. Misha jumped out of the cab with his gun in hand, but he was hit by a hail of bullets and lost consciousness.

Days later he awoke in a hospital. The doctors told him that his arm would be permanently paralyzed and that his leg was partially damaged. At first they wouldn't tell him anything about his family; later he found out that the Ukrainian gang had killed his wife and children in cold blood.

Misha's tragedy moved me to tears, and we both cried. I told him that I feared that I, too, had lost my entire family. From what I had heard, a Jew had no chance of surviving the war. The Poles, Germans, Ukrainians, Lithuanians, Latvians, almost all of Europe had one common dream, one common task — to exterminate the Jews. And it seemed they had succeeded. Misha and I wept for each other and for ourselves.

I became one little cog in one small gear of the huge machine that was training cadres of tank officers for the Polish army. Even though I wasn't sorry to be away from the battlefront, I wasn't at all happy about my assignment. By now I hated the Poles almost as much as I hated the Germans. I took out my anger and bitterness on the poor cadets, demanding strict discipline from them. In civilian life, no doubt they would have killed me for being so hard on them, and for being a Jew; but here I was in command — I was the authority.

In a dispatch of September 13, 1944, we heard that Marshal Stalin had congratulated General Zakharov, commander-in-chief of the second White Russian front, on the liberation of the city and fortress of Lomza, on the River Narew! My home town, Lomza, was finally free! Eagerly I awaited the restoration of the postal service. Although I knew well what the Poles and the Germans must have done to Lomza's Jews, still a little flicker of hope lingered in my heart. After all, I told myself, there were almost a hundred people in my close family circle, and over twelve thousand Jews in Lomza. Surely some of them must have survived!

As soon as postal service was restored to Lomza, I wrote three letters: one to my home, one to the city hall, and one to the military commandant of Lomza. Since my family had been well-known, I was sure that some of the city officials would know of their fate. I requested, as an officer, that they report my address to any member of my family or to any Jew in Lomza. Days passed, and no reply came....

I went to Misha. As the commanding officer, he'd be able to inquire directly about my family from the commandant in Lomza.

Ten days later, on one of our walks, Misha said, "Chaim, the military commandant in Lomza replied to my inquiry."

I stood still. I thought my heart had stopped beating. "Yes?" I asked steadily.

"He reported that there was not one living Jew to be found in the city of Lomza or in its vicinity."

I didn't say a word. I suppose I was prepared for it. But I couldn't believe it. I had to go, to search, to see for myself.

I asked Misha to give me a travel pass to Lomza. Perhaps I could find some hidden Jews. After all, I knew the city much better than any military commandant. "I must go to Lomza," I pleaded.

Misha promised to try to get me a pass. Although he was a colonel and my commander, he did not have the authority to issue such a pass because of the state of war which was still in effect. Two weeks passed, a month went by, and still no pass! I began pestering him: "Never before have I taxed your official duties! Never before have I asked you for a personal favor! But now I am begging you: You must get me a pass!"

He replied, "A war is still going on, Chaim, and you know that I have no authority to issue passes to anyone!"

I threatened to go AWOL, to be absent without official leave.

He said, "Chaim, we are at war not only with the Germans, but also with the AK, the fascist Polish underground. In Lomza, in the entire Bialystok region, the AK is very strong; they've assassinated the governor of Bialystok, and also the mayor of Lomza. They'll kill anyone in a Polish or Soviet uniform!

"We heard that there were a few Jews who had been hiding in the woods for three years, living in holes in the ground, managing somehow to survive. When our troops liberated Lomza, they came out of hiding, and then the AK murdered them all! I get reports on these matters, official reports, all the time. Do you want to be shot in the back by some rotten AK man? Now do you understand why I refuse to issue you a pass?"

For years, the AK had refrained from attacking the Germans; their motive was to maintain German pressure on the other enemy of Poland, Russia. For years, the AK held their fire and saved their arms for the day when the Russians and the Germans would both become exhausted; then the AK would liberate Poland from both enemies! Time had proven them wrong, and the AK did not liberate even one little Polish village. When they finally began their ill-fated uprising in Warsaw, the Germans liquidated them in three days.

After a number of Soviet officers had been shot in the back, the Russians took severe measures against the AK; they burned down villages suspected of harboring them, and AK men were shot on sight. Then the AK ceased to attack Russians, but took vengeance on anyone in a Polish uniform, or on any civilian who cooperated with the new authorities. This helped to increase Russian influence over the civilian Polish officials, since only under Russian protection could the Polish authorities find safety for themselves and their families.

Only in one area was the AK supremely successful: cooperating with the Germans, the AK exterminated Jews. After the Allies had liberated the concentration camps, many Jews returned to their homes, only to be murdered in cold blood by the AK. Their slogan was: "Any Jew that Hitler missed, we Poles will finish off ourselves!" Indeed, they succeeded in making Poland *Judenrein*. Jews in the concentration camps who were liberated soon learned that it was safer to remain in the camps than to go home.

I did not get my pass to go to Lomza.

On MAY 7, 1945, Germany surrendered. The war was over!

On a 24-hour pass, valid only for Warsaw, I visited the newly-organized
Jewish Committee. Pinned to the wall in the cluttered office were mimeo-
graphed sheets of paper containing thousands of names. Survivors were
searching for relatives, parents were looking for their children, children for
parents, brothers for sisters.

On one of these bulletins I found the following: "Any survivor of the city
of Lomza, please contact Yakob." It was signed with a familiar name, and
the address was in the city of Lodz. Lodz was too far for me to go, as my
pass was only good for Warsaw, but I wrote at once, identifying myself and
asking for news of my family, adding, "Please do not hide the truth from
me. I have resigned myself to the worst!"

For days I could hardly eat or sleep, just thinking and brooding and
talking to myself: Lomza without a single Jew!

At last the letter from Lodz arrived. I couldn't open it in public. I locked
myself inside one of the tanks: let no one see me crying, let no Christian see
the tears that I must shed over the calamity that has befallen my people!

Sitting in the driver's seat, under the small light, I read the letter.

"To my dear and only Chaim: I know who you are, and I knew your
family very well. Who in Lomza didn't? It is not easy for me to write the
whole truth, which is what you requested. I am writing this to you not with
ink, but with blood. Blood I still have, but not tears. They have all dried up; I
can't cry anymore.

"It's you and me, Chaim — just you and me.

"We are the only survivors of the twelve thousand Jews of Lomza!

495

Perhaps with the passage of time a few more survivors may be found.

"I'll try to be brief in this letter. In 1941, when the Germans occupied the city on the very first day of the war, they arrested one hundred prominent Jews; among them were your father, several of your uncles, and old Rabbi Cynowicz (whose son lives in Bombay, India). The next morning, they were all shot to death in the forest of Gatch, 13 kilometers from the city, and buried in one mass grave.

"Then every Jew was forced to live within the confines of the new ghetto. Violators were shot on sight. Our Christian neighbors eagerly cooperated with the German authorities, so that they could take over our homes and all our belongings.

"One freezing day in October 1942, everybody in the ghetto was driven on foot to the military barracks of the 71st Infantry Battalion in Zambrow, 27 kilometers from Lomza. Many died on the road, from cold, hunger or German bullets.

"In January 1943, we were all shipped to Auschwitz. It was there that I saw your mother and your two brothers for the last time. Your brother Lazer, who was tall and strong, was told to go to the line on the right — life! Your mother and your little brother Shimon were sent to the left.

"Lazer sneaked away from his line and joined your mother and brother. Clinging to one another, they were together on their last walk. Together, their souls went up to God....

"I think this is enough for the first letter. If you can stand more, write to me, or come and visit me. How did you end up in the army? Are there many Jews in the armed forces? How many Germans have you killed? Oh, how I envy you, killing Germans!"

Through my tears, I visualized Mama with her sweet, kind face, her gentle bearing, going arm in arm with her two sons on their last walk. I pictured Papa being shot like an animal in the forest. Oh God, I mumbled through my tears, why couldn't I have been with them? Why didn't I deserve to go to eternity with them? The pain in my heart would remain forever. My soul was engraved with the faces of my dear ones. How would I ever again be able to enjoy living? How could I go on?

Hunched there in the tank, I tried to share their agony in the gas chambers, the cremating furnaces of Auschwitz, muscle by muscle, bone by bone, limb after limb, the whole body yielding to the flames. The Children of Israel had sanctified His holy Name....

Thinking back, I realized that Karl Hoffmann, when I had encountered him in Stalingrad, must have known that Papa was dead. Perhaps he, personally, had ordered the massacre....And I recalled my dream in the Kazakhstan desert, when I was running from the beast. Papa had appeared, completely dressed in white. His tears had fallen onto my face. Yes, he must have been dead already then!

As time went on, I received additional letters from my *landsman* in Lodz.

He wrote: "Why didn't we fight? You must understand, dear Chaim, that the Germans were deceptive. No sane person could have imagined that Germany, the center of knowledge, education, science and culture, would become a ravaging beast.

"At first, the Germans took away our intelligentsia, and then our able-bodied men, to labor on German farms. At first, people received letters from their loved ones, assuring them that everything was fine, that they had more food than we had in the ghettos.

"Soon wives and children began to look forward to joining their husbands and fathers. Occasionally we'd hear a rumor that the Jews were being murdered in those camps, but who could believe such nonsense? One day, the Gestapo in Lomza took 50 men from the ghetto, saying that the men would return in a day or two. Several days passed and the men did not return. Then the Germans requested an additional 100 men. The ghetto committee demanded to know the whereabouts of the last 50 men, and refused to furnish additional men until the 50 men were returned.

"The Gestapo chief became enraged. 'I'll teach you dirty Jews a lesson,' he screamed at us. 'If I don't get 100 men within the hour, I'll shoot the entire ghetto leadership!'

"Not a single Jew was furnished to the Germans, my dear Chaim. You should have seen the courage of the ghetto committee; proudly, with their heads held high, they marched off to their execution!

"After that, the Germans started catching Jews at gunpoint in the streets and in their houses.

"And always, there was the excruciating hunger! Only someone who has been starved for months and years can understand what hunger does to people! I even witnessed cannibalism! Don't worry, it wasn't among Jews; we could never descend to that depth. It was among Russians, prisoners of war, whose camp was next to ours in Zambrow. There were thousands of Russians in that camp, and like us, they were slowly starving.

"One day, twenty guards — ten Germans and ten Ukrainians — led those thousands of Russians to an immense pit and there they were all mowed down with machine guns. We heard the shooting for hours.

"They had been officers, pilots, tank men, fighting men. Only a short time ago, they had all been brave soldiers in the Red Army. How was it possible that ten Germans and ten Ukrainians could kill thousands of fighting men with not a sign of resistance? The answer is: hunger! Hunger makes people turn into cannibals, and hunger makes people resigned to their fate, glad to get it over with, welcoming death as a relief....

"As for us, a Christian sea of hate surrounded us; the animosity of the Polish population, their enthusiastic cooperation with the Germans, made it virtually impossible for any Jew, even if he did manage to escape, to remain alive. If a Jew succeeded in hiding in the forest, the AK would find him and kill him. If he managed to avoid both the AK and the Germans, he faced the danger of being reported by the farmers from whom he had to beg or steal food. Packed into the trains which took them to Auschwitz, the Jews begged for a drop of water, and their Polish neighbors spat in their faces!

"Whenever someone reported that a Jew was hiding in the woods, the forest was encircled and combed, and he was found and shot on the spot. The patriotic informer was then awarded the shoes of the dead Jew, and one kilogram of sugar!

"Only in the eastern provinces near the Russian border, where the Russian partisans operated, did a Jew have any chance of being accepted into an underground group, and then only if he was in possession of a gun.

"Then too, you must consider the closeness of Jewish families. Would a Jew forsake his old parents, his wife, his children, and flee to the woods to save his own life? Unthinkable! Your brother Lazer, for instance, was young, strong, healthy. He was told to go to the right, while your mother and Shimon were ordered to the left. How could he watch them leaving without him? He chose to share the fate of his mother and brother.

"In your last letter you asked about the attitude of the Christian clergy. I will tell you about our experience in Lomza. A delegation of the Jewish community went to the office of the local Catholic bishop in Lomza, Lukomski — you remember him. They wanted to plead with him to stop, or at least to slow down, the shedding of Jewish blood by his faithful flock. His secretary hinted that in order to see the 'very busy' Bishop Lukomski, a nice gift to the church fund would be helpful. He clarified his remark as follows: 'It would be most appreciated if the gift would be in American dollars, or pure gold. Then, surely, your delegation would find grace in the eyes of the bishop.'

"The delegation went back to the ghetto and frantically took up a collection. Women donated their gold jewelry, including their wedding rings. The Jews pinned great hopes on the powerful influence of the bishop upon his flock.

"When the delegation returned to the office, their gift was accepted most graciously. Then the secretary explained that the bishop was very busy, and promised to set a date for the meeting.

"The meeting never took place, Chaim. Every time the Jewish delegation returned to the bishop's office, the holy man was unavailable."

In later letters my friend described some of the terrible details of life in Lomza's ghetto — the hunger, the cold, the suffering — and yet in spite of it all, the constant activities, the spirit of hope and faith.

The people had refused to die.

"When the Germans' real intentions finally became clear, there was one vital *mitzvah* that remained for the Jews: to stay alive! In addition to the normal instinct to survive, we also felt that it was our holy duty. We had to remain alive in order to be able to tell, to testify, to assure the continuity of our people. Suicide was rare. Life was miserable, useless, aimless, futile — but especially in a time like this, no Jew could desert his family, his people, by taking the easy way out and committing suicide."

I read the letters to Misha. He was moved to tears. Placing his good arm around my shoulder, he said, "I know how you feel, Chaim; I'm very familiar with that feeling. Alone like a stone...all you want is to see your loved ones. I would give half of my life just to see my children once more." We walked in silence, immersed in our pain, yearning and mourning for our loved ones.

41

POSTAL SERVICE to foreign coun-
tries was restored. The first letter I wrote was to my cousin in Australia. I
couldn't bear to tell her what I knew about the fate of our families, and the
Jews of our city. I wrote her only what I had written before: that her
brother Zalman was alive, and that I had met him in the Ural.

Hatred of the Poles, Germans, Lithuanians, Ukrainians — hatred of all
Christian Europe — was boiling within me. I realized that I could not build
my future in a cemetery; and all of Europe, especially Poland, was now one
immense Jewish cemetery. I began to think about deserting. I heard
rumors that many Jewish soldiers and officers had deserted and escaped
to the American zone in Germany. But they were lucky, for their units
were stationed near the German border. I was in Chelm, in eastern
Poland, almost on the Soviet border! How could I desert without being
apprehended?

Then two things happened which made me decide to desert as soon as
possible, despite the difficulties. First, the army began requiring all tank
officers and air force officers to sign up for seven years. Thus my hopes of
being discharged in the near future vanished. Then, I received a letter from
the Siberian city of Akmolinsk; it stated that my cousin Zalman had died
and was buried there. His roommate had found my letter among his
possessions. Why was Zalman transferred from the Ural to Akmolinsk,
and why hadn't he mentioned this in his letters to me? Had he been
arrested and sentenced? A wounded war hero?

His death was a terrible blow to me. Only the two of us were left in
Europe, out of our entire family. Now it was only one! I had hoped that we
would build a life together, but now he, too, was gone! I didn't know if I

could bring myself to inform his sister in Australia that he was dead; I had just written to her, telling her that he was alive.

I decided that I had to tell her the bitter truth. I wrote the letter with tears streaming down my face. On the way to the post office, two teenagers spat on my uniform and ran. Furious, I grabbed my pistol, ready to fire — but then I realized that they had insulted my uniform, and not me. I couldn't have cared less about the Poles' internal political squabbles. Let them kill one another, I told myself; just let me get out of this hateful uniform and away from this accursed land!

I began to visit the railway station whenever I could, observing the timetables of trains heading west, towards the German border. One day I asked a railway official about a train to Lodz.

"At 5 P.M., on the fifth track," he answered. He didn't know that I was an experienced railway man, who had built railroads in Russia. One glance at the tracks and I saw that the station had only three tracks: two active and one used for a siding. I guessed that it was because of my uniform that he was giving me the runaround; most likely he was an AK man.

I pulled out my pistol. When he saw it, he turned pale and began stammering incoherently. Mumbling an apology, he said that he was new around here and thought that there were five tracks. Then he began crying like a baby. "Please, sir," he begged, "for the sake of my small children, don't kill me."

"And how many Jewish children have you killed?" I said. My pain and my anger were uncontrollable.

He fell at my feet, crying, "None! None! Never have I hurt a Jew!"

I ordered him to stand up, and said, "You're lucky that I'm not one of your AKs, or you'd be dead right now. Now run!"

He ran frantically, but tripped on the platform. I saw him lying there, holding his hands over his face, paralyzed with fear. Yes, he was lucky that I was a Jew....

I continued to plead with Misha for a 30-day furlough. I wanted to go to Lomza; I had to go. I wanted to see once more the bombed-out site of our old home; to ask the Polish neighbors what they knew about the last days of my family; to visit that spot in the forest of Gatch where my father and the rest of the hundred men had been shot. I wanted to go to all of the concentration camps in Poland, especially Auschwitz; I wanted to look at the chimney through which my mother and my brothers had ascended to Heaven! In that holy place I wanted to recite _Kaddish_ over the ashes of the millions of Jews who had been murdered.

And then I would desert! I would forsake this accursed land which was soaked with Jewish blood! I vowed to leave Europe forever.

I didn't dare reveal my plans to Misha; I didn't want to tax his loyalty to the state. Yet I had a feeling that he could read my thoughts, that he suspected that I planned to desert. Surely he was aware that many Jewish officers and soldiers were fleeing across the German border to the American, British and French zones.

One day, Yakob, the friend who had supplied me with so much information about my family, sent me a note saying good-bye. He was leaving this rotten Poland. "The train from Poznan will take me directly to Frankfurt, and then to Berlin," he wrote in the last line.

All night I studied that last line. Why did he tell me this? What difference did it make how and where he'd cross the border? Was it meant as a hint for me?

I had never written to him of my eagerness to desert because I was afraid of censorship. And he, too, would never dare advise me to desert, for if his letter were opened, it would be terrible for him.

Although the war was over, the Polish regime still had a fight on its hands: an internal struggle with the AK. A state of war was still in effect and a deserter would be shot, with or without a trial.

Yet the more I thought about it, the more I realized that this was exactly what Yakob was trying to tell me. He probably mailed the letter minutes before his train pulled out, finally feeling safe enough to hint to me about a route of escape.

But if the road was clear for civilians, was it also safe for a man in uniform? No answer could be found between his lines. Probably he himself did not know. I'd have to find out myself, I concluded.

Misha's health began to fail. The doctors decided he needed a rest. He informed me one day that he was being replaced, and that he'd be going to the Crimea to recuperate. I felt that this was my last chance.

"Misha," I pleaded, "I must see the death camp where my mother and brothers perished. I'm entitled to that much after serving almost three years!" He nodded in agreement.

Two days later I received my furlough pass for 30 days. After handing the paper to me, Misha gave me a bear hug; his eyes were moist. He said, "Chaim, promise me you'll be careful. Those AKs can't stand to see a live Jew, particularly a Jewish officer."

The next day Misha climbed aboard a light plane flying to Kiev. Towards evening, I heard terrible news in the officers' mess hall: the plane had crashed and Misha, a general and the pilot had all been killed instantly. There was speculation about the plane having been sabotaged by the AK.

Two caskets, containing the bodies of my dear friend and of the general were brought back to the tank school. They were placed upon two tanks and received a formal military funeral. Tank cannons, aimed at the sky, were fired in their honor. I wept helplessly.

With my furlough papers in hand, I was all set to depart. Then something happened which changed my plans drastically.

An entire class of tank officer cadets — fifty men in all — had deserted _en masse_. It seemed that one of the instructors was an AK man. He took his class into the field for firearms practice, with live ammunition, and they failed to return.

Our new commanding officer was a Russian colonel who had fought in a tank from Stalingrad to Berlin. He took immediate action, dispatching tanks and infantry from a nearby garrison to search the area, including the forests, for miles around. All the deserters were apprehended, except the officer, the sergeant and eight cadets. The other forty gave themselves up without resistance.

The commanding officer imposed a curfew on all military personnel: all leaves and furloughs were suspended. All forty deserters were condemned to death by a military tribunal. Thirty-nine were shot by the firing squad, but one was spared by the president of Poland, Boleslaw Bierut; the cadet wasn't even eighteen. The telegram with the order to spare his life arrived minutes before the execution.

Day after day, my furlough was dwindling. The curfew was still in effect, for reprisals from the AK were expected. Now that Misha was dead, I feared that I wouldn't be able to obtain another furlough, and probably not even an extension of the one I had.

The AK reprisals did not materialize and the curfew was finally lifted. There were only six days remaining of my furlough. To visit Lomza and Auschwitz was now out of the question; there wasn't enough time. I had to look for another way to get out, to leave this country and never return.

The new commanding officer called a meeting. He read us the order from Marshal Rola Zymierski: "All officers are requested to sign up for five more years of service; tank and air force officers for seven years." It seemed that they were particularly interested in Polish officers like me, who had served at the birth of this army, and who had received their training in military schools in Russia.

Fortunately for me, I still had six days of furlough remaining. Processing the documents of all those officers would take time; therefore my reenlistment was postponed until my return.

I wanted so much to visit Lomza, my father's grave and Auschwitz. Perhaps I could still make it in six days. On the other hand, six days was not much, and transportation was undependable. It might take days to reach Lomza, and still more to reach Auschwitz.

In addition, I needed time to investigate the possibility of crossing the border. How was it done? Was it safe for a man in uniform? How could I explain my presence in Poznan, on the German border, when my papers called for a furlough in Lomza, on the Russian border?

Finally I came to the decision that my first duty was to escape. My parents and my brothers would forgive me for not visiting the sites of their deaths. In my ears rang Mama's last words to me: "Go, my son, go!" And this surely was the time to go....

At the station, instead of taking the train east to Bialystok and Lomza, I took a train west to Warsaw, from there to Lodz and then on to Poznan.

AT THE STATION in Poznan, I hung around a group of Soviet army personnel. Although I was wearing a Polish uniform, I hoped that the Polish MP's, seeing me standing with the Russians and speaking only Russian, would assume that I was one of the many Russian officers in the Polish army, and not bother me.

From the Russians' conversation I learned that their destination was Berlin, via Frankfurt am Oder. Without arousing their suspicion, I tried to find out how the crossing took place, but to no avail. None of them had ever crossed the border by train before. They had always gone by army truck.

My mind was working feverishly. Suppose there was a border-control inspection on the train? Suppose they asked me, "Why are you going to Germany, if your pass calls for Lomza?" I had no choice; there was no retreating at this point. I knew that if I didn't cross the border now, I would be tied up for another seven long years in this country which I'd come to loathe.

When the group of Soviet army men boarded the train, I joined them, grabbing a seat next to the lavatory. I figured that the same tricks which I had successfully used on Soviet trains in Kazakhstan might work here too; I could hide in the lavatory and move from one coach to another.

The Russians were drinking and laughing. In contrast to their gaiety, I was anxious and frightened. I gazed out the window, looking at the Polish countryside for the last time. To my mind came the words of the great Polish-Lithuanian poet, Adam Mickiewicz, on leaving his beloved land:

Lithuania, Fatherland of mine.
You are like health!
Only one who has lost you,
Knows how to appreciate you!

I, however, wanted to scream and shout to my native land: "Poland! You are accursed! Only those who leave you know how rotten you are! Your heart is made of stone, your hands are soaked with blood! Your people are bloodthirsty beasts. The cries of dying women and children never disturbed you. And when the trains to Auschwitz stopped at your stations, you refused to offer even a sip of water to the Jews who were dying of thirst. You are like Moab, who refused bread and water to the hungry and thirsty Children of Israel as they passed through their land. May God's curse be upon you and your land forever!"

Only one who had lived in Russia for some time could detect the subtle change in the Russians' behavior as we neared the West. Inside Russia, no one would have dared tell a joke about the Soviet regime, or Stalin. Now, as we approached the western border, they told jokes about Stalin, about Mother Russia, about the government and the army. They laughed heartily at even the feeblest remarks. It seemed that the breeze of freedom blowing from the West had an effect even on these faithful and patriotic Soviet citizens.

The conductor, a Pole, announced, "Prepare to get off!" I began to wonder: had we crossed the border already? Where was the border, anyway? Weren't there any visible signs? And how could there be no inspection? I ran after the conductor and asked him if we were approaching Frankfurt. "No," he said, "we're still in Poland; the bridge across the Oder River is bombed out. All passengers must cross the bridge on foot."

My face must have turned white, for when I returned to my seat, the Soviet officer next to me offered me a drink of whiskey. "You look pale, comrade," he said. "What's the matter with you?"

I was terribly frightened; I hadn't expected to have to pass through *two* border controls. What should I do now? Should I go back and try another way? But my furlough was running out. I looked out the window and I could see the Oder River, the new border between Poland and Germany; I saw the temporary wooden bridge swaying under the vehicles crossing it. On our side of the bridge was a booth painted red and white, the Polish national colors, and standing in front of it was a Polish officer. On the other side there was a red booth with a Soviet flag and a Soviet officer. I couldn't decide what to do. Could I take the risk and march across the bridge together with all the Russian military men?

Before the train came to a stop, a plan began to develop in my mind. I would take the chance of not being asked for documents, by getting lost among the crowd of Russians. But what about my Polish uniform? Among all the Russians, it would be spotted instantly! I'd try to fool the Polish officer by speaking Russian loudly, and maybe he'd assume that I was one of the many Russian officers who wore Polish uniforms; maybe he wouldn't stop me for documents, seeing me in the company of so many Russian officers....

But what about the Russian guard on the other side of the bridge? He'd surely wonder why a Polish officer was crossing the border. There were no Polish army units stationed on German soil; and so what if I could speak Russian? Lots of people could speak Russian! He might detect my slight accent, and stop me and ask for my papers.

My *Chi Sammarra* accent from Kuybishev had helped me before; let it come to my rescue just one more time!

There wasn't any more time to think, for the train had now come to a full stop. All passengers were ordered to get off and walk down the hill to the bridge and the border-control booth.

My legs were trembling; my heart was pounding furiously. I fully realized the risk I was taking: I would soon face freedom or a firing squad.

This was the third time I had deserted, but now I was more frightened than ever before. I couldn't bear to think of being arrested and charged with desertion after having almost reached the threshold of the free world!

The Russians were lively and noisy. I realized that I wouldn't be able to raise my voice above this noisy crowd, and so the Polish officer at the border probably wouldn't even hear me speaking Russian. And if he stopped me and asked to see my pass, I'd be done for!

Then, suddenly, I thought of singing! Yes, singing! I had been a *zapyevala* many times before — why not now? If that Polish border guard heard me singing, he'd be convinced that I was a Russian!

"Hey, comrades!" I called out, over all the noise. "We're getting close to Germany; how about a song?"

"*Pravilno! Pravilno!* — Right! Right!"

The major, the highest in rank, said, "Since you came up with the idea, you be the *zapyevala*."

I stepped into the center of the group and began to sing at the top of my lungs, with all my heart and soul! It was a song known to all; that's why I had chosen it. It was an old battle tune full of a soldier's certainty of victory and promise to return home soon.

We passed the Polish border checkpoint while I was in the middle of the stanza; all were silent, and my voice rang out loud and clear. The Polish officer at the booth clicked his heels and gave us the proper salute. When we returned the salute, I made sure to give him the Russian one, with my full hand. Then the entire crowd sang out the stanza twice. It had worked! Blessed be the Almighty!

But I knew that the most dangerous part — the Soviet border checkpoint on the other side — was still ahead. I continued singing.

Again the crowd responded, singing the refrain twice in their hoarse voices. I was about to begin another stanza, when suddenly the major barked, "*Smirno* — Attention!" An army jeep, driven by a chauffeur, with a Russian general sitting in the back, was approaching us.

The driver slowed down, and we saluted the general. When he stood up in the jeep to return our salute, a terrific shock passed through me. Could it be? Was I dreaming? Who was this man?

The general was the same Russian who, almost five years earlier, in 1941, had come to the railroad station in Kaunas, Lithuania, loaded with luggage. I had helped him carry his things aboard the train, thus avoiding the Lithuanian and Russian controls, and evading arrest. The whole incident had been strange and inexplicable, and I had thought of him all these years as Eliyahu *Ha-Navi*, disguised as a Soviet colonel, sent from Heaven to save me. Thanks to him, I had made it safely across the Soviet border.

Now he was a general, his hair was grayer and he was a little thinner. Our eyes met, and I wondered if he recognized me.

Immersed in my thoughts — wild, unbelievable thoughts — I hardly heard the general's order: "At ease, comrades. Go on with your singing."

An officer next to me brought me back to reality. He tugged at my sleeve and shouted into my ear, "*Zapyevala!* You heard the general's order; now go on with the song."

I continued.

Longing for an end to war, for home and family, the men sang out the last stanza again and again, as if praying: "Oh, how to live to that day!"

My voice was lost among all their voices, and it worried me; we had almost reached the Soviet control booth, and the officer at the booth wouldn't hear me singing. My plan had failed because of the absence of one more stanza!

The officer at the border control left his post and started walking towards us. It was obvious that he had only one thing in mind; he had noticed one man in a Polish uniform: me!

Suddenly the general's jeep sped by us, made a U-turn and stopped in front of the border-control officer, preventing him from approaching our marching group. The general engaged him in conversation, while we kept going. Moments later the crisis was over; we were on German soil, where a train was waiting for us.

I was too frightened to look back, but oh, how I wanted to see his face once more — Eliyahu _Ha-Navi_, disguised as a Russian general.

I BOARDED THE TRAIN with mixed feelings. What a twist of fate — my road to freedom was over this blood-soaked German soil!

We had a brief stopover in Frankfurt am Oder, the first German city on our route. It was bombed out, its streets littered with rubble and broken wood.

The artillery lieutenant who was sitting next to me told me that he needed a haircut and suggested that I accompany him to the barbershop across the street from the railroad station. We set out together.

I said, "Comrade Lieutenant, can you trust a German barber? He might just cut your throat."

The lieutenant smiled and said, "It's true that they hate us enough to do that, but you don't know the Germans; when they're beaten, they become the world's greatest boot-lickers! Watch this!"

The lieutenant dropped his cigarette butt into the dirty gutter. Instantly, a shabby man rushed to the spot, picked up the cigarette butt and put it into his pocket. Then, turning to the lieutenant, he removed his hat and bowed several times, muttering, "*Danke schoen! Danke schoen!* — Thank you very much!"

How true were Winston Churchill's words: "A German is either at your throat or at your feet; let them stay at your feet!"

Berlin! I arrived in the morning. The skeletal buildings reminded me of bombed-out Lomza and Stalingrad. The German air marshal Goering had proclaimed: "No enemy plane will ever reach our cities, or you may call me Meyers!" To his poisoned mind, the greatest insult would be to be called by a Jewish name. But their cities had been bombed and destroyed, thanks to the air forces of the Allies!

The streets of Berlin were patrolled by military police in jeeps, four in each jeep. Each MP represented one of the four occupation forces: the US, Britain, USSR and France. I was still in my Polish uniform, and the Soviet MPs on those jeeps worried me. If any Russian MP were to take a notion to check my papers — for Polish military personnel were seldom seen in Berlin — I'd be arrested, sent back to Poland, and charged with desertion! I walked aimlessly through the streets, hiding behind the skeletal walls every time I heard the roar of a passing jeep.

Suddenly I saw a young civilian who was wearing a Star of David in his lapel. I spoke to him in Yiddish. "You're Jewish! Am I happy to see you!" After a warm handshake, I told him my problem. "I need help; I've deserted from the Polish army."

He pulled me behind a crumbling wall, and took off his overcoat. "Here," he said, "let's switch coats. Your coat won't make problems for me since I have the honor of carrying a tattooed number on my arm from the concentration camp; it's obvious that I'm not a Polish officer! My civilian coat will protect you until we reach the Jewish refugee center."

As we were switching coats, he noticed the five medals on my chest. "Better get rid of them," he said. "They can get you in trouble."

Without hesitation I tore them off my uniform. As we passed the river, I dropped my medals into the water. "I'd gladly exchange all these medals for one Star of David," I said. "But why are you wearing one? Is it still obligatory?"

"No, no, it's not obligatory anymore," he replied. "Years ago the Church forced us to wear yellow stars in order to shame us. In our time, the Nazis ordered us to wear them, to separate us from the Aryans. But now we're wearing our Star of David voluntarily, with pride, to show them that there are still Jews alive! _Am Yisrael Chai_ — the Jewish people lives — in spite of them all!"

In the Jewish refugee office, I was given a card as a former inmate of Buchenwald. After a meal and a shower, some fellows that I met there took me to a place where Belgian soldiers were loading empty drums onto trucks. The Belgian army convoy was supposed to go to Hanover, in the British zone. I don't know if it was with the knowledge and agreement of these Belgians, but my friends helped me climb into one of those drums, right in the center of the truck.

Towards evening, the convoy took off, traveling for hours through the Soviet zone surrounding Berlin. After a bumpy ride through the night, which seemed endless, the convoy stopped. I heard Russian voices; apparently we had reached the Soviet-British checkpoint. The Russians checked every truck, even opening some of the drums.

Shivering from the cold and the terror of being discovered, I crouched in my drum, praying for help from Above. Fortunately, the inspectors didn't open my drum, and I arrived safely in Hanover. There, the Jewish Committee got me a travel permit and a train ticket to the American zone.

It was in Nuremberg that I met a lovely young Jewish girl named Hadassa, a refugee like me. She had kind blue eyes and a sweet and pleasant face. Like all survivors, she had her story. One night, the SS raided the Jewish homes of her native town, Sosnowiec, in southwestern Poland, and arrested all the Jewish girls. She was only sixteen when they broke into her home and took her away from her parents, four little brothers, and a baby sister. She was sent to the Sudetenland of Czechoslovakia, to a concentration camp in the city of Oberaltstadt. She was one of the youngest of the two thousand girls held there, the "baby" of the camp.

These girls were used as slave labor by the German firms Ettrich and Kluge, working in their huge spinning mills. Starvation, beatings, constant hard labor, illness — all these took their toll. The SS supervisors were women, and not quite as vicious as the men. On May 8, 1945 — after almost four years — the few survivors were liberated.

Hadassa learned that her entire family had been shipped to Auschwitz. She was the only one who remained alive.

Where does a penniless Jewish boy take out a penniless Jewish girl in post-war Nuremberg? To the Palace of Justice, of course. There the nations of the world were passing judgment on the Nazi leaders. The entire building was cordoned off by American military police. Entry was permitted only by special passes, and Isaac Stone, an American State Department officer, was my pass-supplier. He provided us with two passes daily, and we took full advantage of them.

And so the two of us sat there every day, glued to the little earphones, she listening to the proceedings in German and I in Russian. There, before our haunted eyes, were the archfiends, Goering, von Ribbentrop, Jodl, Streicher, and all the rest.

The murderers who had tried to destroy our people faced the two of us who had lofty dreams of rebuilding it.

There were many young couples like us. And since none of them had any surviving family, young people would get married quickly. The Displaced Persons Camp in Furth, run by the UNRRA (United Nations Relief and Rehabilitation Agency), would make one wedding for four or five couples at a time. It meant having a home again, having a family again — and a future!

And so we dreamt and planned, sitting in that courtroom, face to face with these modern Hamans; the one of old had not succeeded, but these had come close, so close to their goal!

One day, an American MP officer came over to me as I sat watching the proceedings. He whispered something in my ear, but I didn't understand a word; English was one language I didn't know. In those days I didn't know a thing about the CIA or the FBI, but when an American officer beckons with his finger, one must follow.

Before leaving I said to Hadassa, "Maybe he noticed me pushing the Russian button on the headset? Anyway, if I'm not back in two hours, get in touch with Isaac Stone."

Magic words! And who was Isaac Stone? A man of many titles: "Angel of Nuremberg," possessor of a doctorate from Cornell, officer in the US foreign service, assigned to the Nuremberg trials of the Nazi leaders. He knew a number of languages, including Russian and Yiddish, and he became a brother to every survivor. He demonstrated pure _mesiras nefesh_ — self-sacrifice — for the pitiful remnant of our nation.

Since no civilian mail was in operation yet in post-war Germany, he would take letters from survivors to mail to any country. Eventually hundreds of letters began to arrive in his name from all corners of the world. Then packages of clothing from relatives, societies and synagogues arrived for him to distribute to the camps. Officials were shocked — how could one man receive so much mail? He was ordered to report to the general.

By the time the general had finished talking with him, or perhaps by the time he had finished talking to the general, a special warehouse was set aside exclusively for his use. Also by order of the general, he was provided with an army truck and a driver, to be available at all times.

And that's how I met him. I wanted to send off letters to Australia,

Palestine, and America. When he heard that I came from Lomza, he asked if I had known his uncle, Draznin. I told him that he had been one of my father's friends and that his pew in the synagogue was next to ours. This formed a bond between us, and we became very close. Many times he would ask me to take a jeep full of clothing and deliver it to the DP camp. I knew that Dr. Stone would do everything in his power to help me with whatever it was that this American MP wanted me for.

The American officer showed me into a room where three serious-looking officials were sitting. How relieved I was when I saw that one of the three was none other than Isaac Stone! They asked me all kinds of questions about Russia, and Stone served as the translator.

During the interrogation, one of them, whom they called Dr. Mazeh, began to speak to me in Russian. I was surprised at his perfect Muscovite accent and I was sure that he must be a native, for no American could possibly speak such a beautiful Russian!

The final question was: is revolution possible today in the USSR?

I still remember my reply: "In a country of that size, you would need at least a thousand people to make a revolution. But you wouldn't even be able to find two! In Russia everyone dreads the midnight knock on the door.

"There's a joke about a man who is unable to fall asleep because of fear. He finally gets out of bed and goes over to the mirror. He looks at himself and says, 'One of us is an informer!'

"So how could anyone make a revolution there?"

Stone led me to the door. Before leaving I said to him, "You know, the name Mazeh rang a bell. I couldn't remember where I'd heard it before and then it finally came to me: the star witness in defense of the Talmud and the Jewish people at the Baylis blood libel trial was Rabbi Mazeh, the last offical Rabbi of Moscow under the Czar. Is this Dr. Mazeh related to him?"

Isaac put his arm around me and said, "Chaim, your memory is something! Dr. Mazeh is the rabbi's son! But he is totally Americanized, totally assimilated!"

I then told Stone that I had to hurry back because my bride-to-be was probably thinking that I was under arrest.

"What?! You didn't tell me! When are you going to be married?"

"As soon as I can find a decent suit and she can find a decent dress," I answered him.

"For heaven's sake, Chaim! With all the clothing that you delivered, why didn't you take something for yourself and your bride?" he exclaimed.

I said, "In Russia, one grabs and steals whatever one can. That's just part of Soviet life. Over there, I never took a shirt, or even a shoelace, that didn't belong to me, and I surely won't start stealing clothes now!"

A few days later, Stone presented me with a gray suit, and Hadassa with a blue-green dress, "to match her eyes," he told me, smiling. Stone even attended our wedding!

We were three young couples, all of us survivors of ghettos, concentration camps, or Siberia; we were married by an old *rav* from Kiev or Kharkov; I can't remember his name, and he surely wouldn't remember ours, for he performed hundreds of marriages in that postwar year. No couple had parents to lead them to the *chuppah*, or brothers and sisters to attend them....

44

THE VAAD HATZALA, the rescue arm of the American Union of Orthodox Rabbis, realized that rabbinical students were arriving from the concentration camps, from Siberia, and from the hideouts of the partisans. Therefore, they established yeshivas in various cities in Germany and France. One of them was established in a town near Nuremberg, Windsheim-bei-Nuremberg. I joined the yeshiva.

Finally, I returned to the books I had missed for so long, for five long terrible years! There I was reunited with some of my former colleagues and roommates, whom I hadn't seen since our days together in Lithuania. So few of them had come back!

How happy Hadassa and I were when we knew that we would become parents. We had lost our whole families and now a new Jewish soul was to be born. We did not want our baby to be born on the accursed soil of Germany. But where could we go? Palestine was closed to the Jews by the British. America had a long waiting list. Even after the Holocaust, it seemed that the world was still closed and locked against us. What about France?

I discussed the matter with Stone. The Vaad Hatzala had opened a yeshiva in France near Versailles, and we wanted to try to go there. Anywhere but Germany! Stone said he would write to the French High Commissioner on our behalf. We were sure it was a waste of time, but we felt that there was nothing to lose by trying.

How surprised and elated we were when, a few weeks later, a reply came from the headquarters of the French occupation forces in Baden-Baden. It was signed by "le Général d'Armée Koenig, Commandant-en-

Chef Français en Allemagne" — we'd be allowed to enter France for a period of three months!

The Joint Distribution Committee, the charitable arm of American Jewry, paid for our trip to Paris. The yeshiva was located in Château La Papienière in the village of Bailly, near Versailles. But it was far from a hospital, and Hadassa's time was approaching, so we received permission to live in Paris. The "Joint" rented an entire hotel on rue Emile Zola 10, for refugees like us, and we were given a room and meals free of charge. I would travel daily to Bailly by train.

Three months is a very short time for the slow-moving process of emigration, so I began to work on it frantically. My cousin in Australia sent us a landing permit, with a letter: "Dear Chaim, you are the only survivor of the entire family that I left in Europe. I would love for you and your wife to come to Melbourne, and we will help you as much as we can. But I must tell you that, out of the entire Jewish community of Australia, very few of the fifty thousand Jews here are orthodox like you!" That settled it. Australia was out.

I found a contact to _Bricha_, the secret underground that was smuggling Jews into Palestine. They agreed to take us, and we happily awaited their instructions about when we would leave. Then their agent informed me that I could go, for they needed my military experience, but not my wife! They would not take the responsibility for the safety and well-being of a pregnant woman at a time when they had to devote all their energy and attention to fighting the British and the Arabs. It was far too risky!

I said to him, "I don't understand your superiors. Believe me, I'm no less important to my wife than I am to the Jews of Palestine! Could they possibly think that I would leave behind a pregnant wife in a strange country, and go off to fight a war? Who would take care of her?"

I also showed him our Australian landing permit, but to no avail. "These are my orders," he told me.

I was in contact with Rabbi Y.M. Gordon, the former dean of the yeshiva in Lomza, and a dear friend of my father. He had also survived the war somehow, and had gotten to the US. He worked tirelessly in New York to get us an American visa.

On a Friday night, an ambulance took my wife to the hospital. On Shabbos afternoon, at five o'clock, our first son was born.

When I returned to the hotel, euphoric, I entered the lobby and couldn't understand what I saw: all the other refugees were standing there, smiling and cheering with tears in their eyes. They hugged me and kissed me, wishing me *Mazal Tov*, over and over.

I stood there, taken aback. How had they found out already? Who had told them? My wife had only just today given birth and I hadn't spoken to a soul.

"How did you hear?" I asked.

"It was announced over the French radio!" they said, smiling.

I couldn't believe my ears; could it be that General Charles De Gaulle had nothing more important to announce on Radio Paris than the news that Hadassa Shapiro had given birth to our firstborn son?!

Finally the mystery was solved and I discovered what the source of my confusion was. It seems that two historic events occurred simultaneously at five o'clock in the afternoon on November 29, 1947: our first son came into the world, and the General Assembly of the United Nations voted in favor of the establishment of a Jewish state in Palestine!

We finally made it to the blessed shores of America. The Almighty has blessed us with five children and fifteen grandchildren, and we have been privileged to see all our children follow the path of Torah Judaism. We hope and pray that our future generations will continue in this golden path, until the coming of the *Mashiach*!

NOT THE END!

Escape from Europe: a Chronicle of Miracles

by Chaim Shapiro

From *The Jewish Observer*, May 1973.
Reprinted by permission of the publisher.

"The Almighty has many messengers."

OF THE YESHIVOS that escaped Nazi destruction, some made it on a grand scale—namely to Japan. Some went to Siberia. Others were dispersed. Yeshivas Mir was saved by three people — one Jew and two non-Jews. Thinking back, one becomes amazed at the series of acts, minor and major, the speed of the operation, the efficiency of activities ...then the puzzle pieces fall into place, fitting with precision, as though the result of perfect planning. In recalling the details of the Escape of the Yeshivos, a series of miracles seems to emerge—*nissim gluyim.*

MIRACLE ONE: *Open Borders*

In 1918, when Poland and Lithuania became independent, a bitter dispute erupted between the two countries over the city of Vilna (*Vilnius* in Lithuanian). The Lithuanians claimed the city as their ancient capital, while the Poles also claimed the city. The League of Nations awarded the city to Lithuania. In 1920, the Polish army marched in and annexed the city to Poland. The Lithuanians then declared Kovno (*Kaunas* in their tongue) as the temporary capital, and a state of war lasted between the two countries until 1938.

In September 1939, Poland was divided between Hitler and Stalin, granting the eastern part of Poland, including Vilna, to the Soviets. They offered the Lithuanians the return of their ancient capital as part of a "mutual defense treaty," which permitted Soviet military bases inside Lithuania. The Lithuanian politicians were on the spot. No Lithuanian could resist regaining the ancient capital; on the other hand, they knew the implications of giving the Russian bear a foot in their country. Finally (on October 10, 1939), the Russians forced them to sign the treaty. And so the borders changed and were temporarily opened, and Vilna returned to Lithuania.

This miracle was utilized by all yeshivos. Most of the yeshivos in easten Poland faced a choice between physical destruction by the Germans and spiritual annihilation by the Russians. The Soviets, as sworn enemies of religion, would never permit the existence of yeshivos. Until then there was no escape: No one could leave the Soviet Union and there was no place to go. Suddenly the Soviet-Lithuanian border was opened and Vilna was transferred to Lithuania. All yeshivos plus thousands of refugees immediately flooded the city. The Lithuanian authorities ordered all yeshivos to move into Lithuania proper, to avoid overcrowding the city. Thus the Yeshiva of Mir moved to Kajdani, Kaminetz to Raseinai, Kletsk to Janovo, and so on. Then, just as quickly, the "safety hatch" closed, and the Soviet-Lithuanian border, like any other Soviet border, was sealed for good.

The Lithuanian haven was not meant to last. The Russian bear's paw gained entry — military bases plus a well-financed Commuist Party — and before long the bear would swallow the pigeon. So everyone concentrated on emigration — but where to? Palestine's doors were locked by the British, and only a handful of applicants received British entry certificates. The U.S. was shut tight, while American Jewry naively trusted their "friend" President Roosevelt. And Roosevelt's intimate Jewish friends lulled American Jewry while precious time ran out. Rumors were spread that President Roosevelt promised 5000 visas for rabbis and rabbinical students. We waited for them. And we waited. But they never arrived.

A person must have three items to travel: (a) a passport, without which one does not even exist legally; (b) an entry visa to the country of his ultimate destination; (c) and a transit visa, to pass through other countries en route to the ultimate goal. Most of the *Roshei Yeshivos* did have passports, for they had traveled on behalf of their yeshivos, but the students and the faculty had none. Since Poland was occupied by Germany, the only place one could get a Polish passport was at a Polish Embassy, and because of old enmities, there was no embassy in Lithuania.

Rabbi Avrohom Kalmanowitz זצ״ל, the "father" of the Mirrer Yeshiva, had been carrying the yeshiva on his shoulder since World War I. As a seasoned world traveler, he had no difficulty reaching America, from where he dispatched passports for his entire yeshiva. It had cost him a fortune, for the Polish embassies tripled the price of passports. And so the

Mirrer Yeshiva people were equipped with passports, but no visas, while the other yeshivos, not blessed with a president of Rabbi Kalmanowitz's calibre, remained without passports.

MIRACLE TWO: *Transit Through Russia*

No Jew could travel through Germany — only through Russia. If one had a visa to America, the route was through the USSR and Japan; if he was headed for Palestine, his itinerary was the USSR and Turkey or Iran. However, Poland was in a state of war with the USSR, so logically no Polish citizen would be permitted transit via the USSR. Yet to everyone's surprise, the Russians did permit Poles to cross their country, and the Soviet consul would stamp his transit visa on a Polish passport. (They had apparently recognized a grand opportunity to dispatch spies all over the world with the flood of refugees.) However, the Soviet consul feared that some "transit passengers" might get stranded inside the USSR, and he insisted on a visa from another country before he would stamp his transit visa.

A secret printing shop began to operate in Vilna, producing British entry certificates to Palestine. It was organized by the Jabotinsky's Zionist Revisionists (later known as the Irgun, presently constituting the Herut Party in Israel). They would supply false British certificates to their party members and to *chalutzim* [pioneers]. There was also another "visa factory" which would falsify any visa for a high price in American dollars, provided one had a passport.

MIRACLE THREE: *Japan comes to Kovno*

Most foreign countries maintained their diplomatic and consular offices to the three Baltic republics (Lithuania, Latvia, Estonia) in Riga, Latvia's capital. Travel to Latvia was prohibited, making it impossible to get to the Japanese consul. Suddenly Japan opened a consul in Kovno. Anyone who had a passport and an ultimate visa was issued transit through Japan without difficulty. When presented with a Japanese transit, the Soviet consul gladly gave his transit. Mir had passports, but no visas, and the rest of us did not even have passports! Then a number of changes took place in the little republic.

On June 14, 1940, the Soviet government accused the Lithuanian government of unfriendly acts against the Red Army bases. It demanded

521

the establishment of a new government "more friendly" to the USSR. The next day an ultimatum was issued to include Communists in the new government. While the government accepted the ultimatum, the Red Army began to take over the country. On June 17, President Smetonas escaped by plane to Germany, while Justas Paleckis, a Communist journalist, formed a new government. He immediately ordered new elections, fixed for a Communist majority. Then on July 21, Lithuania requested admission "to the happy family of Socialist Nations under the guidance of the father of all proletarians, Comrade Stalin." On August 3, the Supreme Soviet of the USSR accepted and approved the request, proclaiming Lithuania as the 16th Soviet Republic. (A similar fate befell the other two republics.)

MIRACLE FOUR: *Destination Curaçao*

Under Soviet rule again, we lost all hope for emigration, for no one leaves the "Socialist heaven." Yet, the Soviets still continued to issue visas—they were no longer "transit visas" but "exit visas." Apparently they had not sent out enough spies, or they simply wanted to get rid of an undesirable element.

A rumor spread that the consul of the Netherlands was issuing visas to Curaçao, a Dutch island in the West Indies. The entire Mirrer group, in possession of passports, received those "Curaçao visas." But when they came to get the Japanese transit "en route to Curaçao," they found the consulate closed — when Lithuania had become an integral part of the USSR, all diplomatic and consular activities were moved to Moscow. In fact Holland had issued the Curaçao visas hours before closing.

Several days later a Mirrer student chanced upon an Oriental. Correctly presuming him to be the Japanese consul, he asked him, as a special favor, for a transit visa through Japan on his way to Curaçao. The Japanese gentleman replied that he had been ordered to close the consulate and had already dismissed his secretary. The student then pleaded, volunteering to serve as his secretary, and to help in making out the necessary papers. He agreed, and two boys from Mir sat all day stamping visas for whoever presented a passport. (Some claimed later that many visas were stamped upside-down, but they were honored anyway.) The Soviets continued to issue exit visas. This put the printers of counterfeit visas into more feverish activity than ever, for they could reproduce any visa in Latin letters, but when it came to Japanese, they were at a loss.

The British became suspicious over an increase in entries to Palestine via Syria from Vilna, and they informed the Soviets. They became furious over the prospect of a visa factory operating under their very noses. Furthermore, they themselves had issued visas on fake documents. A search began, but the "Zionist Conspiracy" could not be found. Instead they arrested my roommate from the Yeshiva of Kaminetz, Yitzchak Gelbach (Lukover). Yitzchak had illicitly published a ten-year calendar, reasoning that since we were destined to live under a Bolshevik regime, we would need a long-range *luach* to know when the Jewish holidays would occur. He was sentenced to ten years in a Siberian prison camp. (He was freed after the war. A Breslaver *chassid*, he immediately ran to the *kever* [gravesite] of the Rebbe. He met the daughter of the only Jewish family there....He now lives in Jerusalem with children and grandchildren.)

Mir had passports to Curaçao with Japanese and Soviet visas, and was ready to leave.

When they came to the Intourist office for travel arrangements (the only permissible way to travel through Russia), they were told that first, the price had gone up; second, payment must be made in American dollars. Possessing one American dollar was illegal in the Soviet Union and one could earn ten years in prison for this crime. The Intourist officials "promised" not to prosecute for bringing dollars (a hollow assurance); or, they insisted, "have your relatives in America cable the $400 per person." And in those days $400 was a fortune. Mir was desperate!

One yeshiva fellow, who possessed a German passport with a "J" for "JUDE" on it (which meant second-class citizenship), mustered the audacity to complain to the German consul who was in the process of closing. The Nazi consul found it amusing to tease the Soviets on behalf of a Jew. He called up: "Don't you accept your own currency?" That Jew was the only one to travel for rubles; all the others were forced to pay in dollars.

Rabbi Kalmanowitz, with the help of the *Vaad Hatzala*, raised money for the travel expenses for three months. Thus between January and March 1941 the students and faculty were transferred in small groups via Trans-Siberian Railroad to Vladivostok, where they embarked by boat to Kobe-Ku, the port of Japan. Once in Japan, they waited and hoped for entry to the U.S. But in December 1941, Japan attacked Pearl Harbor and the U.S. declared war on Japan. To make matters worse, Poland had also declared war on Japan. Thus the Mirrer Yeshiva people, possessing Polish passports, became enemies of Japan overnight. Since Japan's only ally was Germany, they feared that the pathological hatred for the Jews would transfer from Berlin to Tokyo. Remarkably, the Japanese behaved correctly under the circumstances.

Rabbi Kalmanowitz had the delicate task of supplying money to the yeshiva in time of war. The anti-Japanese hysteria in America made sending funds to the enemy unthinkable, even for sustaining the yeshiva and other refugees. The need was imperative, for while the Japanese were correct and even cordial in their treatment of the Jews, they certainly would not feed them. Rabbi Kalmanowitz managed, with the silent approval of the U.S. government, to maintain the yeshiva in Japan, and then in Japanese-held Shanghai, by sending funds through Switzerland. After the war, in September of 1946, he finally welcomed the entire yeshiva in San Francisco.

MIRACLE FIVE: *A Ben-Torah in Stockholm; no Dutchman in Chita*

Those of us from the Yeshiva of Kaminetz (located then in Raseinai), like all other yeshiva students, had given up any hopes for emigration. The Soviets announced a deadline for accepting emigration applications. We could not even apply, for first one needed a passport and a visa, and we had neither. And even if we ever obtained passports, we could no longer get Curaçao or Japanese visas without traveling to Moscow — and who could travel to Moscow? How we envied Mir! And how bitter we were.

Then suddenly passports arrived from the Polish Embassy in Berne, Switzerland, mailed to us by an American Kaminetz student, with the help of the *Vaad Hatzala*. But we were still without visas, and the remaining days of registration were few. We then received letters from Stockholm, Sweden, granting us Curaçao visas. We later learned that they were sent by a *ben Torah*, a refugee from Germany, who on the verge of starvation spent his food money on Curaçao visas, issued by the Dutch Embassy in Stockholm. (He is well-known today as Rabbi Shlomo Wolbe, *Rosh Yeshiva* in Beer Yaakov, Israel.)

Now that we had "proof" of intention to emigrate, we all registered with the Soviet office, presenting all documents, including the three personal photographs required. To receive the Soviet exit visa, however, we first needed the Japanese transit. So we mailed our visas and passports to the Japanese embassy in Moscow requesting a transit. They all came back — refused.

We were dismayed. Some attributed the refusal to the form of the Curaçao visa—it was an independent letter rather than a stamp in our passports. Apparently the Japanese consul in Moscow consulted the Dutch consul, who explained the defect to him—all Curaçao "visas" were only "annotations" and not legally acceptable—and thus the rejection. We reasoned that we would have to find a Japanese consul who could not consult his Dutch counterpart. Someone discovered that in the city of Chita, in the Soviet Far East, there was a Japanese consul. We immediately mailed our passports and Stockholm-Curaçao visas to Chita, confident that no Dutchman would be there to "open his eyes." The consul was a gentleman indeed, immediately mailing back visas to everyone. Some people who received those Chita visas (thanks to Rabbi Wolbe) had relatives in America who paid Intourist for their transportation, and made it to Japan. Others, myself included, were victims of the slowness of the Soviet mail, and lack of money for Intourist. When we finally were about to receive the Soviet exit visa, they closed the office. We missed the deadline.

MIRACLE SIX: _Safe in Siberia_

Anyone who applies for emigration from the USSR is automatically an enemy of the Soviet regime, for only a fascist will leave the Communist heaven for the Capitalistic hell of the outside world. And such a person is treated accordingly: Siberia, for reeducation into Soviet reality. The dreadful prospect of Siberia was hanging over our heads like a nightmare. The long, cold nine months of winter, the taiga with an average temperature of twenty below zero, the hard labor, prison life—and what would become of _Shabbos?_ and _Kashrus?_ There was no way of escape, for the regime had the addresses and three photographs of each applicant. Little did we realize that this would be the biggest miracle of all. Only one week later, on a Saturday and Sunday, June 14 and 15, 1941, all visa applicants—_bnei Torah_ all—were rounded up, packed into boxcars and shipped off to Siberia. Then, the following Sunday morning (June 22) the German Army attacked the Soviet Union. The Nazi war machine pushed into Russia with full deliberate speed, all the way to Moscow. And with the same speed, only seven days ahead of the Nazi juggernaut, the boxcars with their precious cargo traveled to various prison camps in Siberia, to safety.

As anticipated, the conditions were oppressive and the climate unforgiving—especially for _bnei Torah_ who were not accustomed to physical labor, the [climate of the] taiga, and starvation. Yet eighty to ninety percent returned safely, saved from Auschwitz.

As I record my memories — whenever I chance across a first or second generation Mirrer *talmid* or a Siberian alumnus — I am reminded of the *z'chus* of Rabbi Kalmanowitz זצ"ל and (יבדל לחיים) Rabbi Wolbe (by grace of his Curaçao visas, hundreds escaped the Nazi onslaught, finding refuge in either Siberia or Japan), and the consuls of Japan and Holland in Kovno.

I have attempted to track down these two gentlemen. I have not succeeded in the case of the Japanese consul, but I have discovered that the Dutchman is Mr. J. Zwartendijk who lives now in retirement in Rotterdam. While serving as temporary consul in Kovno, he once asked permission from Her Majesty's Ambassador to Riga, Dr. I.P.J. de Decker, to issue a visa to Curaçao for a friend. When the Japanese and Soviet consul accepted his annotation, he then issued 1400 more, thus saving many Jewish lives. (One visa can cover an entire family of people.) He did this totally on his own, defying orders to close shop, wholly from humane considerations.

Mr. Zwartendijk will go down in our history as a noble saver of lives. May God bless him with long life, health and joy.

GLOSSARY

The following glossary provides a partial explanation of some of the Hebrew, Yiddish and German words and phrases used in this book. The spelling and explanations reflect the way the specific word is used herein.

AFIKOMAN: part of the middle MATZAH that is traditionally hidden by the children during the Passover SEDER and must be eaten at the close of the meal.

AM YISRAEL CHAI: "The people of Israel still live!"

AVADIM HAYINU: "We were slaves..."; part of the SEDER liturgy.

BA'AL MUSAR: one who scrupulously follows the teachings of the MUSAR movement.

BAR MITZVAH: a Jewish boy of 13, the age at which he assumes religious obligations.

BARUCH HASHEM: "Thank God!"

BITACHON: faith and trust in God.

BOBBE: grandmother.

CHAMETZ: leavened foods that are prohibited during Passover.

CHASID: a disciple of a REBBE.

CHAZAN: cantor.

CHEDER: (Y.) religious primary school for boys.

CHILLUL SHABBOS: desecration of the Sabbath.

CHUPPAH: the wedding canopy.

CHURBAN: destruction of the First and Second Temples.

DAVEN: (Y.) to pray.

ELIYAHU HA-NAVI: Elijah the Prophet.

ERETZ YISRAEL: the land of Israel.

EREV PESACH: the eve of Passover.

GAM ZO L'TOVAH: "This, too, is for the best."

GAON: a very learned man; a genius.

GUT SHABBOS A YID: (Y.) a traditional Sabbath greeting from one Jew to another.

GOLDENE MEDINA: (Y.) lit., the golden country; the United States.

HAGGADAH: the story of the Jews' redemption from Egypt, read on Passover during the SEDER.

HA-KADOSH BARUCH HU: The Holy One, Blessed Be He.

HASHEM: God.

HAVDALAH: blessing recited at the conclusion of Sabbaths and festivals.

IRGUN: paramilitary Zionist organization active prior to the founding of the State of Israel.

JUDENREIN: (G.) free of Jews.

KABBALAH: the mystical tradition in Judaism.

KADDISH: prayer recited by mourners.

KAPPARAH: atonement.

KASHRUS: Jewish dietary laws.

KLAL YISRAEL: the Jewish nation.

KOHEN, KOHANIM: member(s) of the priestly tribe.

KOL NIDREI: opening prayer of the YOM KIPPUR service.

KUGEL: (Y.) a crusty baked pudding made from noodles or potatoes.

MA'ARIV: the evening prayer service.

MAMALOSHEN: (Y.) lit., the mother tongue; Yiddish.

MASHGIACH: dean of students in a YESHIVA who acts as spiritual guide and adviser.

MATZAH: unleavened bread.

MAZAL TOV: "Congratulations!"

MESIRAS NEFESH: self-sacrifice.

MIDRASH: homiletic teaching of the Sages.

MINCHAH: the afternoon prayer service.

MINYAN: ten adult male Jews, the minimum for congregational prayer.

MITZVAH: Torah commandment.

MUSAR: Torah ethics and values.

NAZIR: an ascetic.

NIGGUN: a chasidic melody.

OY GOTTENYU: (Y.) "Oh God!"

PESACH: the festival of Passover.

PIKUACH NEFESH: a matter of life and death.

RAV: rabbi.

REB: (Y.) a respectful form of address.

REBBE, REBBEIM: (Y.) Torah teacher(s).

RIBBONO SHEL OLAM: Master of the Universe.

ROSH HASHANAH: the Jewish New Year.

SEDER: the order of the Passover eve ceremony recalling the exodus from Egypt and the liberation from bondage.